THE
Golden
Hands
COMPLETE
BOOK
OF
Dressmaking

RANDOM HOUSE
NEW YORK

Dress

THE
Golden Hands
COMPLETE
BOOK
OF
making

Library of Congress Cataloging in Publication Data
The Golden hands complete book of dressmaking.
Originally published under title: Golden hands
encyclopedia of dressmaking.
"The greater part of the material published in this
book was first published . . . in 'Golden hands.' "
1. Dressmaking.   I. Golden hands.
TT515.G59   1973   646.4'3'04   72-11419
ISBN 0-394-48548-3

Manufactured in the United States of America
First American Edition

CONTENTS

Generally speaking

Shirtmaking

Muslin~making

Blousemaking

Dressmaking

Pantsmaking

Know-how

CONTENTS *(Continued)*

Sewing for children

ACKNOWLEDGEMENTS

Photographers:

Malcolm Aird   John Carter   Chris Lewis   Tony Moussoulides
Peter Watkins   Clive Boursnell   Richard Dormer
Sandra Lousada   Peter Rand   Jim Williams   Camera Press
Trevor Lawrence   Philip Modica, Fotopartners
Michael Stuart

Text:

Elizabeth Baker   Alison Louw   Valerie Punchard

Our thanks are due to Vogue Pattern Service and The Butterick
Publishing Company for permission to reproduce photographs of
completed garments from their range of patterns.

Introduction

Here is a dressmaking book which can be used by readers on every level and adapted to the individual's specific needs. At last there is a book which assumes nothing of the reader: she may be an experienced dressmaker looking for a reference book on techniques and finishes, or one new to dressmaking whose greatest need is straightforward know-how. Certainly every woman who takes pride in making clothes with fit and flair – or who hopes to – will find many aspects of dressmaking clarified and potential problems eliminated.

Unlike so many books of its kind, this one lays the groundwork by presenting equipment and basic tools, and shows how to make your sewing machine work for you. A range of natural and synthetic fabrics, and their particular qualities and capabilities, is reviewed to give the dressmaker greater scope in using these to their best advantage.

One invaluable lesson to be learned by everyone who uses the Golden Hands Encyclopedia of Dressmaking is the importance of completing each step carefully and accurately. And the book's logical progression of techniques and garments makes it so much simpler. Before proceeding with the mechanics of sewing, you learn to chart your own measurements, and take into account any figure problems which will need special attention. These are really the fine points which result in attractive, well-fitting garments and defy the world of mass-produced fashion to match them.

An indispensable feature within the book is the Golden Hands Graph Pages, a set of basic graphs including a dress, skirt, blouse, pants and accessories. We give the instructions for making basic and well-fitting garments from these graphs; one can then adapt the pattern to make several other designs. However, the reader will gain as much satisfaction in applying methods and techniques learned from the book to her own use of commercial paper patterns; she need not feel limited to the selection of patterns offered within the Graph Pages.

The final chapters of the book deal with making clothes for children; these are easy to make, practical and, not the least important, attractive. They are a sure temptation for any reader who realizes the money-saving potential in sewing for children.

But the only way to satisfy your curiosity fully about the many aspects of this book is to glance through it. And then we dare you to go no further . . .

Chapter 1

The basic tools for successful sewing

Generally Speaking

Any sewing aid which is specially designed to make your work easier is a good idea. But now that the home dressmaking industry offers you so many gadgets, it's difficult to decide which are really necessary. Here is a list of basic aids that you will need for the simplest dressmaking, and which will help you to achieve more professional results.

Basic equipment

Sewing machine. The most important piece of equipment in the sewing room is, of course, the sewing machine. Whether it is a treasured family heirloom or a gleaming new model, it is very important that the machine stands on a firm base at a comfortable working height, and that a light shines directly on the needle when stitching.

Hand sewing needles. Size 8 for dressmaking. Size 9 for sewing fine fabrics such as silks or chiffons. Size 7 for heavier work such as sewing on buttons. Use either the medium length sharps or long millinery needles, whichever suits you best.

Pins. Steel dressmaking pins, at least 1 inch or $1\frac{3}{16}$ inch long, are the best. Nickel-plated pins may bend during use and could damage fine cloth. Glasshead pins are very sharp (made from needle rejects), but have limited use since the heads break easily.

Scissors. You'll need a good pair of sharp cutting shears, with handles that comfortably fit the hand (left-handed shears are available for those who need them), also a pair of small dressmaking scissors to use while making up your garments.

Tailor's chalk. At least two pieces are essential for marking, one white, one blue.

Tape measure. A good tape measure shouldn't stretch, so use one made of glass fiber.

Tracing wheel. This is used for marking pattern outlines on to fabric. Choose one made from steel with sharp points.

Dressmaker's tracing paper. A special type of carbon paper for use with a sharp-pointed tracing wheel. Use with care, if at all, as it can mark delicate fabrics. Tailor's chalk is preferable.

Thimble. A steel-lined thimble is best since it gives longer wear. It should fit the middle finger of your sewing hand.

Triangle. This is also known as a tailor's square and is used to obtain fabric grain lines in pattern making.

Yardstick. This is used for measuring hems and connecting points for straight seams. It should be firm and straight.

Steam iron. A medium-weight iron with heat controls is essential. Use cleaning fluid to keep the base of the iron clean.

Ironing board. This should stand firmly and have a smooth-fitting cover securely attached under the board. Covers made of heavily dressed cloth are not suitable, since the dressing can be transferred to the iron, particularly when wet.

Press cloth. A two foot square piece of finely woven cotton or lawn is essential for steam pressing. Thicker cloths hold too much moisture and may harm the fabric. A good press cloth should be free from imperfections such as holes, frayed edges and prominent grains, all of which can easily be transferred to the fabric being pressed. Also, it shouldn't contain any dressing because this will stick to the iron and mark the fabric.

Press board. This is necessary for pressing pleats and flat surfaces. You can make one quite simply from a square of cork or plywood about 30 inches by 20 inches. Pad it with a folded blanket and cover with sheeting.

Buying a new sewing machine?

A sewing machine is a big investment so if you're thinking of making a purchase, it is important to know the types which are available and what they will do.

There are many makes of sewing machines on the market, all differently priced, but today's machines fit into three main categories: straight-stitch, swing-needle (or zigzag) and swing-needle automatic. Here are some tips on what to expect from each type of machine.

Straight-stitch. This machine sews only with a straight stitch and most will sew in reverse as well as forward. Some attachments come with the machine and others can be obtained at extra cost. Ask about this when buying. Straight-stitch machines are in the lowest price bracket and prices vary according to quality.

Swing-needle. This machine does zigzag stitching in addition to straight stitching. The zigzag stitch is useful for finishing seams, hems, making lace insertions and buttonholes. Some swing-needle machines have an automatic buttonhole reverse and most come with a good range of attachments. These machines are in the medium price range.

Swing-needle automatic. This machine has all the facilities of the straight-stitch and swing-needle, but it can also do embroidery. Various effects can be achieved by inserting special discs into the machine or by engaging settings which are built into the mechanism. These are the most expensive machines to buy.

How to choose a machine

If you need a machine for light dressmaking only, any of the previously mentioned types, straight-stitch, swing-needle, or swing-needle automatic, will be suitable.

If you want a general-purpose machine to cope with all the household sewing and mending, be sure that the machine you choose will take heavy work.

If you need a machine for tailoring, it is advisable to choose from the straight-stitch and swing-needle ranges only. A fully automatic swing-needle machine has only a limited use for tailoring.

Testing

In most cases, it is possible to test a machine at home for a few days and this will give you a chance to see if it is really suitable for your needs. If you do have a machine on approval, first of all read the instruction manual carefully to see if there are any restrictions on how you can use the machine.

Here is your opportunity to try the machine on different types of cloth, especially those you are most likely to be working with later on. If you are testing the machine for heavier work, remember to stitch over double seams in a medium-thick cloth. See that the machine passes the work through evenly, that it does not hesitate in front of the seams or jump off when it has stitched through the thickest part.

It is important to test the speed of the machine. For instance, if you think you will be doing a lot of household sewing, particularly items like sheets, bedspreads, and curtains which have long, monotonous seams, then you will want a machine that can cope with this work quickly as well as correctly.

Do not be misled by a claim that a machine will 'break in'. Many machines are set at one speed only, but some of the newest and most expensive have a built-in gear to increase the stitching rate. You can adjust the speed slightly by regulating machine controls, but transmissions vary and some machines will operate faster than others. By learning to operate the controls, you will always be able to use a very fast machine at slow speeds, but if a machine stitches slowly, it is because the transmission is low-geared.

When you're testing, make sure that the pressure foot and tension are at the correct setting. Settings vary with different manufacturers, and these details will be pointed out in the manual. Also check that the stitch size is correct for the setting engaged, and that the thread number and needle size are correct too.

How to find the correct thread number and needle size
Many machines are tested, and set, to work best at a certain thread number. Therefore, find out from the manual which are the recommended numbers for that machine.

To help you, here is a chart setting out the comparisons between the American and Continental sizes.

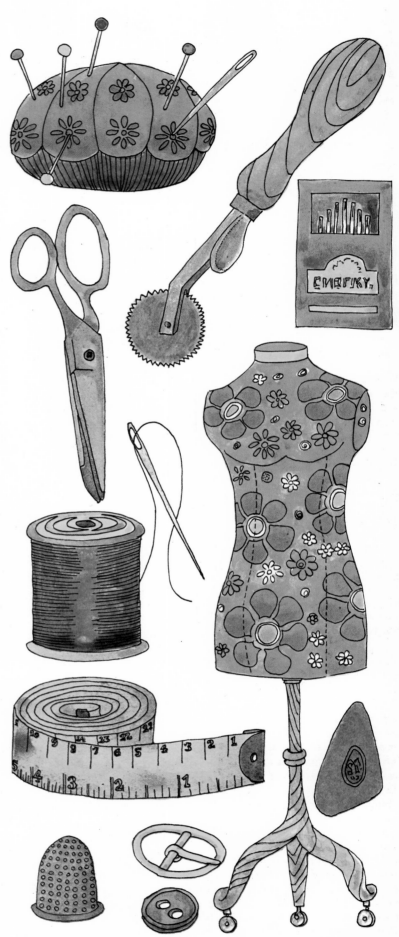

Thread number	Needle sizes	Continental needle sizes	Type of material
40	16	100	Heavy fabrics
50	14 } 12	90 } 80	Medium fabrics
60	10	70	Light-weight fabrics

Stitch size and tension
To obtain the correct stitch size and tension (the tightness balance between both threads) adjust the controls on the machine as shown below.

For the top thread feed control, adjust the dial on the front of the tension spring, which reads from 0-9. The higher the number, the tighter the thread feed.

To adjust the tension on the bobbin, loosen or tighten the tiny screw on top of the bobbin case which holds down a spring in the shape of a little steel clip.

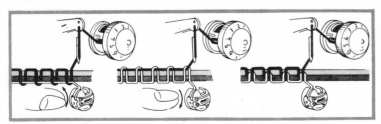

Different gauges of sewing thread, such as silk, cotton and mercerized cotton, can affect stitch size and the tension. So, before making a garment, always test the stitches on layers of the material you are preparing to sew.

Finally, having tested the performance of the machine before buying, satisfy yourself that it carries a good guarantee.

Chapter 2 What your sewing machine can do

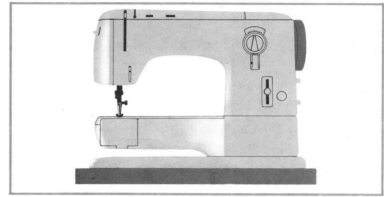

▲ *A free arm machine, useful for stitching narrow parts of a garment*

Sewing machines can produce exciting effects, in a few minutes, which would take hours of working by hand. Their potential was briefly described in the previous chapter, but there are many more things today's machines can do. This chapter sets out to help you find which type you want, and since buying a sewing machine is a critical business, it's important to assess your needs before making a choice.

Buying a sewing machine?

Before buying a sewing machine, you should ask yourself the following questions:

a. How much do you expect from your machine?
b. How much sewing do you do?
c. How much are you prepared to spend?

Choose a machine to suit your needs

When buying a sewing machine you should consider the various electric models on the market and choose the one with the facilities you are going to need.

A straight-stitch machine is only capable of straight machining, which means that all overcasting, finishing and buttonhole making has to be done by hand.

All that most people need for everyday dressmaking is a sewing machine with a good straight stitch and a reverse for ending off seams, a zigzag stitch with adjustable width, and an attachment for making neat buttonholes. A machine which does stretch stitching and basting is also an advantage.

However, the more a machine can do, the more expensive it is, and it is pointless to spend money on attachments you will never use. A swing-needle or zigzag machine saves a lot of time, and is therefore worth the extra cost. Apart from the usual straight stitch, swing-needle machines have a manual control knob for engaging a zigzag setting, and both the stitch length and width can be varied. With practice, all sorts of uses for this machine can be discovered, particularly overcasting and working buttonholes.

Read this chapter carefully, noting the points which apply to your particular dressmaking requirements, then set about finding a machine which answers your needs and is also in your price bracket.

Special attachments

Apart from the general-purpose foot on your machine, a zipper foot and a buttonhole foot are the most useful attachments.

The zipper foot. This is constructed to enable you to stitch right up to a zipper edge without the zipper teeth being under the presser foot. The zipper foot is usually provided with a new sewing machine as part of the purchase. When buying a zipper foot, make sure that it is for your particular make of machine.

The buttonhole foot and button plate. Some buttonhole feet are specially grooved so that the buttonhole can pass underneath.

▲ *Special foot for narrow braiding* ▲ *Special zipper foot in action*
▼ *Lace trim stitched with zigzag* ▼ *Programmed scalloping cuff trim*

▼ *Fine pin-tucking on a cuff* ▼ *Fine zigzag for frills*

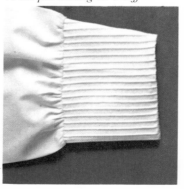

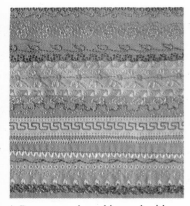

▲ *Programmed machine embroidery*

▲ *Machined tailor's tacks*

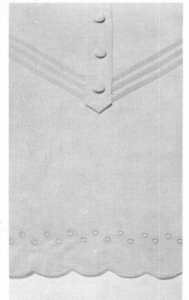

▲ *Pin tucks, eyelets and scalloping*

▲ *Shell edging on fine fabric*

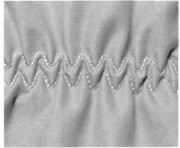

▲ *Serpentine stitched elastic*

It helps if the foot is made of plastic, as you can see the work through it. The button plate is for stitching on buttons, which may be helpful if you have a lot to attach, but hand-sewing is usually sufficient.

Other useful features

Hems. The rolled hem foot is ideal for edging scarves and for very fine rolled hems on chiffon. The foot does all the work for you by rolling and stitching in one operation. There is also a blind hemming or blind stitch foot for making hems on medium-weight fabrics. But, on the whole, hems should be worked by hand.

Darning. A darning foot and plate for darning household linen and clothes.

Gathering and shirring. Most machines have a special foot which will gather and shirr all fabrics.

Tailor's tacks. As you can see from the photograph, there are machines which make tailor's tacks like the hand-worked version.

Bias binding. The binder foot stitches on the bias binding and binds the raw edge in one operation.

Running stitch or 3-point zigzag. This stitch is ideal for stitching fabrics which fray easily, like linen or any loosely woven fabric, and is used on stretch terry cloth. It has the function of a neatening stitch. The serpentine stitch is similar to the 3-point zigzag and is used for stitching on elastic as shown here.

Sewing for decoration

Many machines today do some embroidery, and a quick look at the machine manual will tell you all you need to know about this.

Some have disks or cams which are inserted into the machine and contain the blueprint of the pattern, while others have a dialing system programmed into the machine.

As you can see in the photographs, there are other methods of decorating with a sewing machine. For instance, on the cuffs shown here, a narrow zigzag stitch is used to edge a fine fabric and to stitch on lace. Here are some other useful decorating effects:

Pin-tucking. A special grooved tucker foot used with twin needles was used for the example shown on this page. The spacing of the tucks can be easily varied.

Eyelet foot and plate. This is for making eyelets, as shown in the photograph.

Shell edging. A special programmed stitch was used for the shell edging in the example.

Free arm or flat bed machine

Having decided what you want your machine to do and the type you are going to buy, you then have to choose between a free arm and a flat bed machine. The difference between these two machines is slight. The free arm is usually a little more expensive and is available in a variety of models. It can be useful when you are stitching narrow parts of a garment, such as sleeves and cuffs, and particularly if you are going to flat-fell the seams, as these sections will fit around the arm of the machine. All free arm machines have a special plate which you can put around the arm to make a flat bed for supporting the work.

Sewing classes

Having bought a new sewing machine you will want to make full use of it. Many companies give free lessons on how to use their machines, and these lessons are worth attending.

Summing up

The chart on the left covers all the special features discussed in this chapter and will help you to see at a glance the type of sewing machine which will be the most useful for you.

Type of machine ▶	Straight stitch	Basic zigzag	Zigzag special	Zigzag deluxe
Straight stitch and reverse	✓	✓	✓	✓
Zigzag with adjustable width		✓	✓	✓
Basting	✓	✓	✓	✓
Adjustable stitch length	✓	✓	✓	✓
Zipper foot	✓	✓	✓	✓
Roller foot		✓	✓	✓
Buttonholes and button plate		✓	✓	✓
Rolled hem foot	✓	✓	✓	✓
Blind hemming			✓	✓
Darning		✓	✓	✓
Gathering	✓	✓	✓	✓
Shirring	✓	✓	✓	✓
Tailor's tacks			some	some
Bias binding		✓	✓	✓
Industrial overlocking				some
Running stitch or 3-point zigzag		some	some	some
Serpentine stitch			some	some
Pin tucking		some	✓	✓
Eyelet foot and plate			some	some
Shell edging			✓	✓

Chapter 3

Needles, threads and stitches

Generally Speaking

With the wide and ever increasing range of fabrics on the market, both in natural and man-made fibers, it is important to realize that now there is the right sewing thread for every type of fabric. Successful dressmaking depends on using the right thread because if both thread and fabric share the same characteristics, they can be laundered together, ironed at the same temperatures and will also shrink and stretch together.

Types of thread

The natural threads are silk and cotton. Cotton thread is mercerized or unmercerized. Mercerized cotton is specially treated to give it luster and greater strength. Silk thread is a multi-purpose thread and combines strength with elasticity.

Of synthetic threads, the most commonly used are those made from polyester fiber.

Thicknesses

Threads, whether natural or synthetic, are produced in various thicknesses; the higher the number the finer the thread. The most commonly used thickness is 50, but for finer fabrics 60 can be used. When machine stitching, it is important to remember that whatever you use on the spool you should also use on the bobbin.

Sewing synthetics

When sewing man-made fiber fabrics, and mixtures of natural and man-made fibers, a synthetic thread should be used.

Synthetic thread is usually stronger than natural thread and an interesting feature is its stretchability, which is particularly important when sewing fabrics with stretch, such as synthetic knits. With these fabrics a great deal of stress is put upon the seams during movement and activity, so if the thread can stretch with the fabric it minimizes the chance of broken stitching.

Cotton-wrapped polyester thread is also suitable for sewing fine leather which has a good deal of stretch in it.

Sewing cotton and linen

For these fabrics a mercerized cotton thread is used for most purposes. If you sew cotton or linen fabric with a synthetic thread, it will not be able to withstand the heat required for pressing and will melt.

Unmercerized cotton is used for basting; not having the polished surface of mercerized thread it does not slip out as easily.

Sewing wool and silk

Wool can be sewn with silk thread or a mercerized cotton. Always sew pure silk with a fine, lustrous pure silk thread.

Fabric	Fiber	Thread	Needle sizes Hand-sewing	Machine-stitching	Stitches per inch
Fine such as lawn, georgette, voile, chiffon, organdy, net, lace	synthetic and mixtures	synthetic extra fine	9–10	9 to 11	12 to 15
	cotton and linen	mercerized 50	9	9 to 11	12 to 16
	wool	mercerized 50 or silk	9	9 to 11	12 to 16
	silk	silk	9	9 to 11	12 to 14
Lightweight such as poplin, gingham, silk, cotton	synthetic and mixtures	synthetic	8–9	11 to 14	12 to 15
	cotton and linen	mercerized 50	8–9	11 to 14	12 to 15
	wool	mercerized 50 or silk	8–9	11 to 14	12 to 15
	silk	silk	8–9	11 to 14	12 to 15
Medium-weight such as gabardine, brocade, tweed, water-proofed fabrics	synthetic and mixtures	synthetic	8–9	11 to 14	10 to 12
	cotton	mercerized 50	7–8	11 to 14	12 to 15
	linen	mercerized 40	7–8	11 to 14	12 to 14
	wool	mercerized 50 or silk	7–8	11 to 14	12 to 14
	silk	silk	7–8	11 to 14	12 to 14
Heavy-weight such as coatings, canvas, heavy home furnishing fabrics	synthetic and mixtures	synthetic	6	16 to 18	10 to 12
	cotton	mercerized 40	7–8	14 to 16	10 to 12
	linen	mercerized 40	6–7	14 to 18	10 to 12
	wool	mercerized 40 or silk	7–8	14 to 16	10 to 12
	silk	silk	7–8	14 to 16	10 to 12
Some special fabrics					
velvet	synthetic and mixtures	synthetic	8–9	11 to 14	10 to 12
	cotton	mercerized 50	7–8	11 to 14	10 to 12
	silk	silk	7–8	11 to 14	10 to 12
fine leather and vinyl		synthetic		14 to 18	8 to 10

Threads for decorative stitching

For decorative stitching, such as saddle stitching, topstitching, channel seaming and some hand-worked buttonholes, buttonhole twist is used. This is a special, thick silk used to emphasize stitching and is not to be confused with button thread, which is an extra strong waxed thread used to sew buttons on men's clothing, overalls or shoes.

Having stated the importance of using the same thread on both the bobbin and the spool, buttonhole twist is an exception. It is used either on the bobbin or on the spool. Just remember four things about buttonhole twist.

1. If used on the spool, slacken the spool tension.
2. If used on the bobbin, slacken the bobbin tension.
3. If used on the bobbin, stitch from the wrong side of the garment to achieve the desired effect on the right side of the work.
4. A thicker needle and larger stitch length is required.

In most cases, a 40 mercerized cotton is a suitable companion thread to buttonhole twist but it is best to experiment first with your own machine to find the right combination.

Threads for sewing home furnishing and upholstery fabrics

Here a very strong durable thread is needed because it has to stand up to a great deal of stress and hard wear. A polyester and cotton fiber mixture is ideal for this work. In this thread the cotton is wrapped around the polyester fiber, otherwise the very strong polyester strands used would cut the fibers of the fabric. In appearance it is similar to button thread.

This thread is also used on canvas, thick leather and suede.

Other threads

There are other threads on the market, such as embroidery threads, invisible thread, and so on, but this chapter concentrates on those which are most used in dressmaking.

A word on color

Always choose a thread one or two shades darker than the fabric as this will work in lighter, becoming the same color as the fabric.

Needles

It is important to use the correct size needle for the particular thread and fabric. As a general rule, the lighter the fabric, the finer the needle should be. The chart here shows you at a glance the needle and thread sizes for various weights and types of fabric. There are also different types of needles. A ball point needle is specially made for knitted fabrics so that the needle will not cut the fibers of the fabric and cause it to run. There are spear point needles specially made for leather and suede.

Keep a range of hand-sewing and machine needles handy in various sizes and always remember to keep them sharp and straight —don't wait for your needle to break before changing it.

Tension and stitch length

Many sewing faults are traced back to old machine needles and the use of the wrong thread and tension. Therefore, once you have chosen the fabric, the appropriate thread and needles, and before you start stitching on the garment, test on a double scrap of the same fabric to find the correct tension. Also, be sure to test the stitch length to see if it has the right appearance, counting the stitches per inch as given in the chart. If you see the fabric puckering it may mean there are too many stitches to the inch, in which case you will need to make the stitches larger. Test until you are satisfied—it is well worthwhile.

Vogue Couturier Pattern reflects the result of perfect seaming ►

Chapter 4

Generally Speaking

How do you measure up?

The important point to aim for in dressmaking is to achieve a really perfect fit. So it is essential that you know exactly what your personal measurements are before you begin. All commercial paper patterns are made to standard sizes, but even if you are one of those rare people with perfect proportions, or you buy a pattern size which should fit your figure type, you may have to make slight adjustments to it. The chart set out on the facing page contains all the measurements you will need to use when working with paper patterns, plus instructions on where to take them. Before filling it in, enlist the help of a friend or a willing husband, and you'll soon have your personal measurement chart to keep by you for constant references whenever you're dressmaking.

Taking your measurements

Study the first two columns carefully before you start so that you will be familiar with all the measuring points, then take the measurements over a smooth-fitting dress, or slip. You will need to pin a length of $\frac{1}{2}$ inch tape or straight seam binding around your waist before you start. This helps you to obtain exact bodice length measurements. Make sure you do not measure tight but allow the tape to run closely over the body without dropping. Of course, you will be using your non-stretch inch tape! It's a good idea to take measurements more than once for complete accuracy and also to take them towards the end of the day, if you intend to make evening clothes, because body measurements can vary between morning and evening. You could even divide the 'Your Measurements' column into a.m. and p.m.!

Why your pattern is larger than you

When you measure through any paper pattern, you'll find that it is larger than your own measurements. This is because every pattern has tolerance, (or ease) built in, so that the garment cut from that pattern feels easy and comfortable to wear.

The standard allowance for ease is 2 inches for bust, 1 inch for waist and 2 inches for hip measurements, but these amounts vary according to the fit of a garment and the fabric used for making it up. Here are two simple examples. If you use a bulky fabric, the standard allowance for ease must be increased by at least 1 inch to 2 inches to allow the bulk of the fabric to settle around the figure. A loosely fitting style, on the other hand, will have extra ease built into it, and the extra amount required will already have been added to the standard ease in the pattern. If you measure through the Golden Hands blouse pattern, which is a semi-fitted style, you can check this for yourself. You'll be coming across the term tolerance, or ease, frequently in the following chapters, where you'll also discover its importance, particularly during the fitting stages of dressmaking.

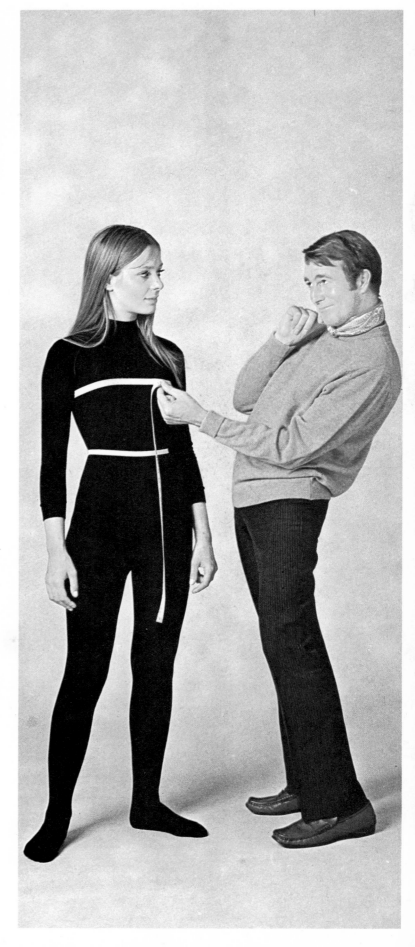

	Where to measure	Your measurements
1. **Bust**	Over fullest part of bust and around back	
2. **Waist**	Lay tape into natural waist curve	
3. **Hips**	Over highest part of seat and thickest part of thighs	
4. **Shoulder**	From neck to imaginary armhole seam	
5. **Shoulder across back**	From armhole seam to armhole seam	
6. **Center back length**	From nape of neck to waist	
7. **Center front length**	From base of neck to waist	
8. **Front length (i)**	From center shoulder to waist	
9. **Front length (ii)**	From center shoulder to highest point of bust	
10. **Width across front**	From armhole seam to armhole seam, half way between shoulder and bustline	
11. **Width across back (i)**	From armhole seam to armhole seam over shoulder blades	
12. **Width across back (ii)**	As 11, with arms extended forward	
13. **Armhole**	Over shoulder point, around underarm, back to shoulder, with arm against body	
14. **Side seam**	From armhole to waist line	
15. **Underarm sleeve seam**	From lowest point of armhole to wrist with arm extended outward 45°	
16. **Outside sleeve length**	From point half way between shoulder and underarm seam, over bent elbow, to wrist	
17. **Sleeve length to elbow**	From shoulder point to elbow	
18. **Neck (i)**	Around base	
19. **Neck (ii)**	Around neck	
20. **Forearm**	Around fullest part of arm muscle	
21. **Wrist**	Over wrist bone	
22. **Top arm**	Around fullest part	
23. **Center back full length**	From nape of neck into waist, to hem	
24. **High hip**	About 3in below waist line over hip bone	
25. **Skirt length**	From waist line over side hip to hem	
26. **Pants depth of crotch**	From center front waist line through crotch to center back waist line	
27. **Pants inside leg**	Stand with legs spread Measure from inside crotch to below ankle bone (Finished length depends on heel height worn.)	

Dressmaking terms

Basting. A continuous row of long, hand or machine, stitches to hold two or more layers of fabric together.

Ease. To hold in fullness without showing gathers or pleats.

Face. To finish raw edges with matching shapes.

Grain. Lengthwise, or warp threads running parallel to the selvage. Crosswise, or weft threads running across fabric from selvage to selvage.

Interfacing. Fabric between facing and garment to support an edge and hold a shape.

Interlining. Inner lining between lining and outer fabric for warmth or bulk.

Marking. Indicating pattern detail on fabric. Showing seam allowance for cutting. Showing fitting corrections.

Nap. Fibrous surface given to cloth in finishing.

Notch. Small 'V' cut in the seam allowance to eliminate bulk in outward-curving seams.

One-way fabrics. Fabrics where the surface interest runs in the same direction. This includes prints, nap or pile as well as warp-knitted fabrics.

Pile. Raised woven-in surface on velvets and fur fabrics.

Slash. To cut along a given line to open a dart or a fold.

Slip-baste. To baste a seam through a folded edge from the outside to match perfectly plaids or stripes for stitching.

Snip. A small cut made either at right angles or at a slant to the raw edge of a seam allowance to enable it to spread and follow a stitched curve.

Stay stitches. A line of stitches made by hand or machine within a seam allowance to prevent stretching.

Tailor's tacks. Tacking stitches made with double thread where every second stitch forms a loop. Can be made in one continuous row or over a few grains of the weave, to form a single tack. Used only to mark pattern detail through two layers of fabric.

Top-stitching. A line of machine stitches made on the outside of a garment parallel to an edge or seam.

Chapter 5

Coming to grips with your figure

Generally Speaking

Many people make their own clothes so that they can obtain a personal and distinctive look. One of the major advantages, however, is being able to achieve a perfect fit, which is so important for a really good-looking garment. So, before you start making your own clothes, it is essential that you identify your own personal figure type and are aware of any problems you may have. You can then select styles which flatter your figure, making the most of your good points and drawing attention away from your faults.

Most of us have figure problems. Sometimes it is merely a matter of bad posture which can be corrected with a little practice, but in fact very few people have such a perfect figure that they do not need to adapt designs or alter paper patterns in order to make them fit correctly.

If you work on the basis that almost any design can be adapted to any figure (except in extreme forms of fashion), all you have to do is recognize your own particular size and figure problem and take them into consideration when cutting out and fitting the garment. Naturally certain styles will be more flattering to one figure than to another.

In this chapter we have given suggestions with each of the three main figure types, to help you make the most suitable choice of style and fabric. With this knowledge, you can create a perfect picture whatever your figure problem, and feel really confident that your whole appearance is pleasing.

Which type are you?

There are three main figure types, which the chart on these pages illustrates: the figure with standard body measurements, the figure with a large bust and the figure with large hips. You'll be able to identify yourself with one of these whether you're tall or short, small or large or anywhere in between.

To find out which figure type you are, stand in front of a mirror, perfectly relaxed, just wearing your normal undergarments and compare yourself to the figures illustrated.

What is your problem?

Having decided which figure type you are, you may then find you have particular figure problems like narrow, very straight or sloping shoulders, a rounded back, high tummy or a neck that's set forward. Some figure problems need special attention, and affect your choice of style as well as requiring careful fitting, while others are only a matter of making minor alterations to your pattern and do not greatly affect the style of dress you should choose.

The two most common figure problems, which involve adaptation of style, are illustrated on the facing page, with suggestions for choosing suitable styles. All fitting problems will be dealt with in more detail in later chapters.

Standard body measurements

The figure of standard proportions has a bust two inches smaller than the hip measurement. So, whatever your size, if you have this proportion, standard sizes will fit you without much alteration.

The choice of your clothes will depend on your height and whether you are broad or slim. If you are slim, perfectly proportioned and of average height, you are lucky and can wear almost anything you like. If you are large, wear garments that fit to the body, with well-fitting shoulders, as unnecessary bulk increases the impression of size. Avoid horizontal stripes and gathered, full skirts. If you are short and plump, always aim to achieve an elongating effect in the way you dress. This does not depend on the length of a garment, but on the vertical design detail. If you wear a belt or separates, they should match.

If you are tall and thin, soft styles, blouses, pleated, gathered or flared skirts, wide belts, tweeds and fluffy fabrics are all good for you.

Large bust

If your bust measurement is more than your hip measurement, you are topheavy and yours is merely a fitting problem. Buy patterns to fit your bust and take them in by the necessary amount at the hips. The best designs for you are those which minimize the width across the top. You should avoid any bulk such as gathers and folds, shoulders should fit well and fabrics over the bust should be smooth. Scoop or 'V' necklines, which break up the area, are most effective on your figure type. If your hips are really slim, then you will look good in skirts made from tweeds and other heavily textured materials.

Figure Types

Figure Problems ▶

Large hips

The most feminine figure type is often referred to as pear-shaped. You are the girl with a good bust line and trim waist, but with larger than standard proportioned hips. To make your own clothes, buy patterns to fit your bust measurement and when you cut your garment, add to the width of the skirt pattern around the hips.

A-lines in skirts and dresses, and fitted bodices with full skirts are good for you. Remember that you will create an illusion of all-over smallness if you accentuate the smaller proportions of your top half and camouflage the fuller part of your body, especially if the outline of your garment flows into a little more width toward the hem. Straight skirts and dresses need very well-fitting blouses or bodices, perfectly plain and without too much ease. The soft blouse look is not the right style for you, unless you are really thin.

Rounded back, very sloping shoulders, a neck that is set forward and a high tummy

If this is your problem, your figure needs the very best support you can afford. Then it's a question of adapting the designs you choose.

As you appear narrow across the top and wide across the hips, triangular-shaped designs are ideal for you because they fit across your smallest points and skim over larger areas.

Never wear tuck-in blouses, but adapt them to short over-blouses, making sure that they are carefully proportioned to the length of your skirt.

Your neck is a very important point to watch because it will always appear short. Avoid high or large collars and aim for a neat, clear line. Adapt designs to a flat, fitting collar, a soft, narrow roll or even a plain, finished line around the base of your neck. If your neck is very thin, you can wear a close-fitting roll or mandarin collar if you like.

Bust larger than hips, flat tummy and very straight shoulders

If this is your problem, adapt the designs you choose. You will look best in fitted garments, without the bulk of gathers and folds. If you are broad or short, avoid waist seams and belts.

Always aim to minimize the width across the bustline, choosing soft, wide necklines on a straight, fitted dress. Keep trimming high above, or well below, the bustline. Draping should be used sparingly and be asymmetrical, leaving the bustline well-defined. A-line dresses (semi-fitted at waist and hips) will do nothing for you, since the line will be lost; but you can adapt this line to a fitted dress flared gently at the hem.

Make a point of choosing toning colors for your blouses and skirts and beware of shirt blouses, which can look very masculine on you.

Always choose a well-fitting shoulder line, with the armhole seam high on the shoulder to lessen the appearance of width. Avoid wide or short sleeves which will add to the width.

Fabric and design-how they go together

The first step toward making a dress for yourself is deciding on a style. Choose one in which you would like to see yourself, but study it carefully before buying the fabric.

Does the style suggest a soft line? Does it cling or does it drape? Does it have sculptured lines or geometric seaming? Does it suggest a tailored look or a more feminine outline? When choosing a fabric, always be guided by instinct and taste before taking anything else into consideration. Nothing is more frustrating than making a dress and finding the finished result is not as you imagined it would look. The reason for this, in many cases, is the wrong combination of fabric and style.

Use this guide to help you choose the right fabric for the style of dress you want to make.

Style	Clinging	Soft line	Draped
Detail	Soft and feminine, fitting closely to the body.	Unpressed pleats, gores or gentle flares.	Tight draping across the body, soft draping, cowl necks.
Fabric Suggestion	Plain knit jersey, lightweight silk or wool, crepe cut on the bias.	Soft or loosely woven fabrics, heavier crepe and jersey.	Lightweight crepe, chiffon, georgette and jersey.

Prints and patterns

First, consider the style you have chosen and decide whether a printed or patterned fabric would be more suitable.

For the best results the style should be simple, because too much seam detail will break up the fabric design. Details such as belts, tabs or collars can be given clarity and look most effective in a plain fabric to match one color in the design. If you long for a beautifully seamed garment, this will always look best made up in a plain material.

Secondly, it's a good idea to drape a length of fabric over yourself in front of a mirror before you buy it, to see if the color really suits you.

Your choice of printed and patterned materials will, of course, be influenced by current fashion trends, but here are some hints on how to look at prints and patterns and make the best choice.

1. Two-color prints

On a printed fabric, the prominence of the design is an important factor. If the fabric is printed in two colors only,

the design appears to be balanced. Two-color prints are suitable for all figure types.

2. Three-color prints

As soon as a third color is introduced, and this need only be a different shading of the two colors, the balance is broken and the design is immediately projected from the background. For instance, white daisies with navy centers on a navy background give the impression of overall interest. As soon as the center is picked out in yellow or any other color it is no longer just navy blue and white you see, but white daisies standing out from a dark background.

Three-color prints, or projected designs, can be worn by

most figures, but if you are of large or small proportions do look carefully at the size of the design. A large design is more suitable for the larger figure, and a small design is more suitable for the smaller figure.

3. Directional prints

Large multi-colored prints can be worn successfully by most figures, but again if you are large or small, you must carefully consider the direction of the design. If you study the print from a distance, you'll see that one or two strong colors stand out from the

background and form the direction of the design, which can be round, oblong, diagonal, crisscross, vertical or horizontal So, if you are large or short, the correct choice is the design which has continuous, lengthwise interest. This includes crisscross materials and diagonal prints.

4. Plaids, checks and stripes

When choosing plaids, checks and stripes, take into consideration your body movements when walking because brightly colored checks and plaids emphasize movement. Since body movement is relative to size, if you are large or short, be especially careful when looking at these fabrics. Large movements are emphasized by large checks and small movements drowned by them, so choose the smaller

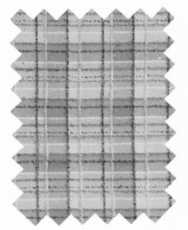

patterns in blending colors if you are short.

As a point of interest, the large figure can wear bold, brightly colored plaids and checks to great effect, if the garments chosen are of generously cut design, such as travel coats or long evening skirts.

If you come across patterns with overchecks and outlines in bright, contrasting colors, always look at them from a distance. If your impression is of a large check or widely-spaced stripe, do remember this will determine the effect of the finished garment no matter how small the basic pattern is. Choose these fabrics with care and if you are large or short, avoid them altogether.

Tailored, sculptured, geometric seaming

Design encloses body in a fitted, heavier garment, or holds a certain shape dictated by fashion.

Firm weaves such as worsted woolen, real or imitation linen, heavy cotton, double knits, certain man-made fiber fabrics, tweed and silk.

Chapter 6

Understand your dress form

Generally Speaking

Dress forms are an invaluable aid to the home dressmaker. At those times when you need to check an inaccessible area and there is no friend at hand, a dress form can come to the rescue. Dress forms can be bought in many sizes and shapes and most women with standard measurements can find a form which will suit their shape and which needs no alteration.

But if you do have a figure problem, your clothes will need even more adjusting and a form is of even greater value. Since you cannot buy a form incorporating the problem it will require certain adjustments. You can make these yourself very easily and quickly by padding, as this chapter will show.

Of course, when choosing a form you will have to make quite sure that no part of it is larger than any of your measurements—it is one thing to pad out the form but another to make it smaller.

What you will need

Have handy some tailor's wadding (a roll of cotton will do, provided it is not too soft), some old nylon stockings, a small upholstery needle, plenty of pins and one or two old nylon slips which you won't mind cutting up. The slips are for covering the form, so if you want to give it a more decorative look buy a length of pretty printed nylon jersey instead.

If you have the problem of sloping shoulders, you will also need a pair of ready made cotton shoulder pads.

With these items you can pad the form to suit your figure—whatever your requirements.

Padding the top half of the form

Using a bodice muslin. Make yourself a bodice muslin with all the ease pinned off as shown in Muslin-making chapter 23.

To find out which areas of the top half of the form need padding, pull the muslin over the form, then mark each area where the muslin does not fit properly with tailor's chalk. Remove the muslin.

Cutting the padding. Lay the wadding down flat, then cut out layers of wadding large enough to cover the whole of each marked-out area. The only area not covered this way is for sloping shoulders which are dealt with separately below.

If one layer of wadding is not sufficient to correct the shape, it will require building up with more layers.

Cut all the layers for one particular area to the same shape as the first, but reduce them in size so that you graduate the shape to follow the contours of the body (figure **1**).

Pin all wadding layers firmly in position (figure **2**).

At this stage the edges of the layers of wadding will form sharp ridges since they are the same thickness all the way through.

So pluck out the edges until each layer tapers into the shape desired.

Stitching the padding in place. Cut the nylon stockings into single layers large enough to cover each padded area.

Stretch and pin the nylon over the padding, then slip the muslin over the form again to check that it is padded correctly.

Remove the muslin and sew the nylon in place using a small upholstery needle (figure **3**). Sew to the form and avoid catching the wadding in the stitches as the thread will gather it up and distort it. You may find that you are unable to remove all the pins used for holding the wadding in place. This does not matter—the ones that remain can be left there for good, or they may eventually fall out.

Sloping shoulders. With this figure fault you will need to raise the shoulderline on each side of the neck, so use the cotton shoulder pads for this.

Slip the muslin over the form to check that the bustline of the form is in line with the bustline of the muslin.

You will find that the outer shoulder rests on the form while the inner shoulder rises above it. Pin off the excess fabric on the inner shoulder so that the shoulderline fits correctly on the form. Now the bustline of the muslin and the bustline of the form should coincide.

If the bustlines do not coincide, padding may make a difference of about 1 inch either up or down. But if the bust level varies by more than 1 inch you must disregard the bustline fitting on the form, fitting the bustline of your garments on yourself instead, and confine your fitting on the form to the shoulder, which you adjust as follows.

Cut out a small shape from the thick end of the shoulder pad so that it will fit into the neck over the shoulder seam of the form (figure **4**).

Pin the pad in position and check with the muslin that you have achieved enough lift. If not, cut out pieces of wadding to the shape of the pad but smaller, and pluck out the edges of each cut shape to flatten it. Lay these pieces under the pads to build up the inner shoulderline until the muslin fits correctly.

Cut sections from the nylon stockings to cover the pads and pin and sew in place as before.

Finishing the padded surface

If more than one area of your form is padded, it will now look slightly lumpy. To give the form the smooth appearance of a well-rounded figure, and also to give you a good and easy surface to work on, here is a quick method for making a new cover.

The cover for the form must be very close fitting, so use the muslin pattern to cut out the form cover.

Cut a bodice Back and Front from the nylon jersey, cutting both pieces on the fold and leaving seam allowances on all seamlines. The amount of seam allowance needed depends on the amount of stretch in the jersey, but this can be trimmed as necessary afterward.

Pin the Back and Front on the form. When you are satisfied that the fabric sits firmly around the form, and will not create folds when you run your hand over it, trim the seam allowance to about $\frac{1}{4}$ inch.

Overlap and pin the seam edges and hand sew them together (figure **5a**). Also hand sew the armhole, neck and waist edges firmly in place.

Padding the hipline

To complete the adjustments to the form you must, of course, also check that the hipline measurements are the same as your own. If you find that they need adjusting, work as follows.

▲**1.** *Wadding cut in graduating sizes* **2.** *Wadding pinned in place* **3.** *Covering the wadding* **4.** *Shoulder pads fitted for sloping shoulders* **5.** *Stages in covering the form; a. covering the bodice; b. covering the lower area; c. the padded form complete* **6.** *Skirt pattern adapted for form cover*

Using the basic skirt pattern from Skirtmaking chapter 10, make a skirt muslin, pinning off all the ease.

Slip the skirt over the form and use tailor's chalk to mark any areas that need padding.

Cut out layers of wadding and pad the hip area as you did for the top.

Since most adjustments to the hipline will take up fairly large areas, you may find that a nylon stocking is not wide enough to cover each padded area. So pin the wadding sections very securely in place and use the nylon jersey fabric to make a solid cover.

To cut a well-fitting cover, use the basic skirt pattern for your guide. But make the following adjustments to the pattern: Straighten the side seams (figure **6**), then fold away the ease by pinning a lengthwise fold down the middle of each pattern piece as shown.

Measure the length of the form from waist to lower edge, allow a little extra length for adjustment, and cut the pattern to this measurement.

Using the adjusted pattern, cut out the nylon jersey fabric, with Center Front and Center Back on the fold of the fabric, allowing seam allowances all around.

Pin the cover to the form. Overlap the side seams and hand sew them together. The hipline cover must finish at the waistline. Handsew the waistline of the bodice and hipline covers together, having overlapped them with raw edges open (figure **5b**).

At the waist edge trim the raw edge close to the stitches then pin and baste a $\frac{1}{2}$ inch tape around the waistline (figure **5c**).

Firmly handsew the lower edge of the cover to the form so that it cannot ride up.

Generally Speaking

Chapter 7

All about fabrics and fibers

Did you know that there are now pure wool tweeds and suedes that you can pop safely into a washing machine? Or that men's jackets can be baked like hot potatoes in the oven to set their shapes forever? Or that tweeds can now be knitted and that socks are being made with a permanently anti-odor finish? It would be difficult to imagine what dress departments, fabric stores, not to mention laundry bills, would be like without the enormous advances made over the last twenty years in the textile industry by fiber and yarn manufacturers, weavers and knitters, who are continually developing more and more fibers and fabrics.

It's worth making the effort to find out what a fabric is made of and how it is put together. You may also be missing out on some of the truly marvelous recent discoveries that are making fabrics more exciting, easier to care for—and sometimes cheaper.

To begin with, there are two basic points to get straight. First, it's important to know whether a fiber is man-made or natural, or a blend of both. In a world which is more and more labor-saving minded and price-conscious, man-mades do have some definite advantages. They are easy to care for and their production quality and cost can be closely controlled. But there are no man-made fibers which combine the best of the innate qualities of natural fibers. For example, many man-mades are non-absorbent which makes them inclined to be sticky and sweaty to wear, and they lack the thermal qualities which make the naturals warm in winter and cool in summer. Man-made fabrics also tend to create static electricity which attracts dirt.

In many cases the answer lies with blends which combine the best qualities of both natural and man-made fibers. (The increasingly popular cotton/polyester blends for shirts give the tough crease-resistance contributed by polyester combined with the cool comfort of cotton.)

The second point to get clear is what we all mean by names. If you think of satin, you probably imagine a fabric with a smooth, shiny surface. In fact the word satin not only describes the appearance, but is also the name of the basic weave which produces this finish. It could be all silk, all nylon, all acetate, or a blend. So the names in the Fabric Guide that begins on page 24 indicate the appearance of the weave or knit, but the fabrics can usually be made up in any fiber, or combination of fibers—though there are a few exceptions to this such as muslin, which is always cotton.

This question of weave and knit is becoming increasingly complicated. Most fabrics traditionally were woven, with a warp and weft thread. Now knitted fabrics, are becoming very popular, and this is a faster and sometimes less expensive method of production than weaving. Knitting machinery is getting so sophisticated that several different types of fabrics which used to be thought of exclusively as weaves—like twills, crepes and tweed-textures—can now also be found made in jersey fabrics.

However, most people still think of appearance in terms of cotton, linen, wool and silk. In the Guide, weaves and knits have been grouped together in categories most commonly associated with these natural fibers. One always thinks of tweeds as wool, but you would be surprised at how many are made of acrylics or acrylic/wool blends these days.

So when you go shopping, first know what kind of woven or knit appearance you want, and what qualities you expect of it—then ask your salesman to give you full details about the fiber mixture, and the finishes.

	MACHINE	HAND WASH
1	Very hot maximum wash (185°F) to boil	Hand hot (118°F) or boil
	Spin or wring	

White cotton and linen articles without special finishes.

	MACHINE	HAND WASH
2	Hot maximum wash (140F°)	Hand hot (118°F)
	Spin or wring	

Cotton, linen or rayon articles without special finishes where colors are fast at 140°F.

	MACHINE	HAND WASH
3	Hot medium wash (140°F)	Hand hot (118°F)
	Cold rinse. Short spin or drip dry	

White nylon.

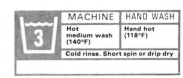

	MACHINE	HAND WASH
4	Hand hot medium wash (118°F)	Hand hot (118°F)
	Cold rinse. Short spin or drip dry	

Colored nylon: polyester; cotton and rayon articles with special finishes; acrylic/cotton mixtures.

	MACHINE	HAND WASH
5	Warm medium wash (104°F)	Warm (104°F)
	Spin or wring	

Cotton, linen or rayon articles where colors are fast at 104°F but not at 140°F.

	MACHINE	HAND WASH
6	Warm minimum wash (104°F)	Warm (104°F)
	Cold rinse. Short spin. Do not wring	

Acrylics; acetate and triacetate, including mixtures with wool; polyester/wool blends.

	MACHINE	HAND WASH
7	Warm minimum wash (104°F)	Warm (104°F) Do not rub
	Spin. Do not hand wring	

Wool, including blankets and wool mixtures with cotton or rayon. Silk.

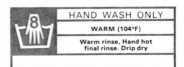

	HAND WASH ONLY
8	WARM (104°F)
	Warm rinse, Hand hot final rinse. Drip dry

Washable pleated garments containing acrylics, nylon, polyester or triacetate, glass fiber fabrics.

Processes and finishes

Crease resistance. Almost all fabrics have a tendency to crease and some, like pure linen, crease far more than others. To counteract this, the yarn or fabric is chemically treated to give it added springiness and resilience. Most crease-resist finishes radically alter the structure of the fiber throughout its life. Drip-dry and easy-care usually applies to garments like shirts and underwear and indicates that they should shed their creases if they are hung out to dry after washing. The question of whether or not to iron applies equally to non-iron, wash n' wear, as well as drip-dry and easy-care. Although you won't have to give your clothes the thorough going over a madras cotton shirt requires, they will look crisper and smarter if you do iron them lightly.
Trade marks: *Tebilized® Wrinkl-shed® Vitalized®*

Machine washability. What is so wonderful about machine washability, you may ask yourself as you sort through your load of dirty laundry. Practically everything—when you consider that the fabric in question is pure wool tweed and pure wool jersey and knitwear. The men behind the Woolmark guarantee have devised a process of treating wool yarn which prevents shrinkage. What to look for when buying clothes is Machine Washable or Washable, Shrink-Resistant on the label, followed by detailed washing instructions.

Pre-shrunk. Fabrics can stretch quite badly in manufacture. To correct this, and to prevent them from shrinking when washed at home, they are pre-shrunk as part of the finishing process. The pre-shrunk process often combines the same qualities as drip-dry and crease-resistant finishes.
Trade marks: *Sanforized® Tebilized®*

London shrunk. A famous finishing process applied to wool suitings which are moistened and then allowed to dry out naturally. This leaves them in the ideal condition for tailoring.
Trade marks: *Lanaset® Resloom®*

Permanent press. To pleat wool permanently, the fabric is chemically 'processed' and then fixed by steam pressing. More rigorous treatment can be given to man-made fibers and special blends. They are soaked with chemicals and then 'cured' by literally baking them at high temperatures in ovens! This process permanently sets pleats and creases and is particularly suitable for skirts and men's pants. The heat treatment is now being applied to entire garments which claim never to crease, wrinkle, stretch or lose their shape and are also fully machine washable. At the moment this heat treatment mostly applies to men's wear, especially pants.

Fashioned. Fully fashioned denotes that knitwear or stockings have been 'fashioned' into shape on the knitting machine. Semifashioned applies to knitted garments that are only partially fashioned.

Mothproofing. There are distinct differences between mothproof and mothproofed. The first denotes fabrics which are inherently mothproof: For example no moth has the right kind of digestion to cope with acrylics or polyesters. The second applies to wool fabrics, something moths are especially fond of, and indicates that a garment is treated against moths for life. If you suspect repeated washing or drycleaning has removed the proofing, you can always take the proper precautions to discourage moths.
Trade marks: *Boconize® Erustomoth®*

Flameproofing. By law, many items have to be treated for flame resistance. However, this can wash out if you use soap or a detergent containing soap. One of the best answers is to make those items which should be flameproof from special fabrics, or have the finished garment flameproofed. Always wash flameproofed fabrics according to the directions.
Trade marks: *Banflame® Fire Chief® Flamefoil® Pyroset®*

Rainproofing. When does a shower become a downpour? When you discover your raincoat is only water-repellent, and not, as you might have hoped when you bought it, waterproof, and you get very wet. The words "Water-repellent", "Rain resist" or "Showerproof" sewed onto a tab inside your raincoat can mean it has been treated with silicones to resist a certain amount of water. Waterproof means one hundred percent resistance to rain and that the article is made from a rubberized or plastic-covered fabric or treated with wax. N.B. This term can only be applied to garments which have reinforced seams!
Chemicals: *Scotchgard® Zepel®*
Trade marks: *Aridex® Cravenette® Impregnole® Neva-Wet® Rainfoe®*

Luster finishes. A few years ago, when crisp cotton with a shiny finish was in fashion, resins and starches were applied to it to give a luster. This gloss finish is now primarily applied to home furnishing fabrics in the form of glazed chintz.
Trade marks: *Everglaze® Vita Glaze®*

Special note

The trade names, processes and finishes mentioned in this particular chapter are by no means a complete summary of those which are available. Golden Hands has merely selected for each category samples of what can be obtained easily on the American market today.

Useful definitions of fabric and fiber terms

Bulking or high bulk. A process which fluffs out the fibers of the yarn to give extra softness, stretch and absorbency. It also gives a pleasant, deeper texture particularly in knitted fabrics made from acrylics or polyesters.

Count. The yarn count indicates the thickness or fineness of cotton, wool or linen yarns. The higher the count the finer the yarn.

Denier. The same as count, but is used for silk and man-made filament yarns. As in stockings, the lower the denier figure the finer the yarn.

Mercerized. Cotton yarns, specially treated under tension, to make them extra strong, colorful and lustrous.

Spun yarns. Made from fibers spun to various thicknesses—from the softly spun yarns used for nice Shetland sweaters (woolen spun) to the fine, tight, smooth yarn (worsted spun) used for fine worsted suitings.

Warp. The lengthwise threads in woven fabrics.

Weft. The crosswise threads in woven fabrics.

21

Natural fibers

	qualities	ways to wash
Cotton	*Cotton comes from the ripe, fluffy seedpod of the cotton plant.* Cotton is a cool, strong fiber, easy to wash, absorbent and therefore extremely pleasant to wear. Great advances have recently been made with easy-care finishes.	All cottons will be washable under Codes 1, 2 or 4, depending on their finish and color fastness.
Linen	*Linen is spun from the fibrous stalks of the flax plant.* Linen fabric is very tough, absorbent and cool to wear. Its strength actually increases in washing—thus its age-old use for sheets and household linen. Pure linen does crease, but new blends with man-made fibers and the development of crease-resistant finishes are making linen much more of an all-purpose fiber.	If washing is advised, Codes 1, 2 or 5 will apply. It is important to pay special attention to the instructions, because the treatment or finish given to linen fabrics may vary considerably.
Wool and animal fibers	*Wool fiber comes from the fleece of the sheep. Other animal fibers include the luxurious, and expensive, alpaca (alpaca goat or S. American llama); cashmere (very soft goat); vicuna (vicuna llama from S. America); mohair (crisp shiny fiber from the angora goat, used for men's lightweight suitings); and angora (angora rabbit).* Wool has inherent warmth and resilience. The most versatile of fibers, it can be spun and woven into both the lightest crepes or heaviest tweeds and is cool in summer, warm in winter.	Dry cleaning is recommended unless the article is stated as washable.
Silk	*Silk comes from the filament spun by the silkworm for its cocoon.* The most luxurious of fibers, silk has a lustrous, live quality and takes color to a deeper intensity than any other fiber.	Silk should be dry-cleaned unless stated as washable, when Code 7 is advised (warm water, do not rub, spin dry, do not wring).

What are man-made fibers?

Fiber family name	qualities	ways to wash
And Trade Names		
Acetate Acele, Celaperm, Chromspun, Estron	*Acetate is derived from cellulose, the raw materials of which are cotton linters or wood pulp.* Regarded as the most silk-like of the man-made fibers in wide use. Acetate drapes well, and is woven into satins, taffetas, brocades and surahs. It is extensively used for silk-like jersey, and linings.	100% acetate fabrics can be washed easily, in *warm* (not hot) water at Code 6. They should be washed frequently to avoid over-soiling, then ironed with a warm iron while still damp.
Acrylic Acrilan, Courtelle, Creslan, Orlon, Zefran	*Acrylic fibers are produced from acrylonitrile, a liquid derived from oil refining and coal carbonization processes.* Easy-care and crease-resistant, acrylic fibers most closely resemble wool and are very popular for knitwear and light, washable tweeds.	Acrylic fibers wash easily, under Codes 6 or 8, and dry quickly. A cold rinse should always be given before drying, to avoid creasing. Always iron *dry*—do not dampen for ironing.
Modacrylic Dynel, Verel	*Based on derivatives of oil refining and coal carbonization processes.* Modacrylic fibers are used for both garment and industrial fabrics. Strong, hard-wearing and flame-proof, they are very practical for children's clothing.	Washing at Code 6 is a simple matter, but only a cool iron should be used when the article is quite dry.
Elastomeric Glospun, Lycra, Numa, Vyrene	*These are stretch yarns with a high degree of elasticity, based on segmented polyurethane.* Elastomeric fibers are used in foundation garments, swimwear and stockings.	These fibers are always combined with others which dictate the washing intructions. Do not iron.
Nylon Antron, Blue C Nylon, Caprolan, Chemstrand Nylon, Dupont Nylon, Enkalon, Qiana	*Nylon's raw materials are benzene from coal, oxygen and nitrogen from the air and hydrogen from water.* Nylon is extremely strong and has inherent elasticity. It can be spun into fine silk-like fibers which make it ideal for stockings and lingerie. Its crease-resistance and quick-drying qualities have given nylon a large share of the men's shirt market.	Knitted as well as woven nylon fabrics shed creases and are easy to wash and quick to dry. White nylon should be laundered according to Code 3. Colored nylon at Code 4. It is often drip-dry and minimum or non-iron.
Polyester Avlin, Dacron, Encron, Fortrel, Kodel, Terylene, Trevira, Vycron	*Polyesters are made from ethylene glycol and terephthalic acid, derived from petroleum.* A very strong fiber, polyester is frequently found as a blend with wool or cotton. Used alone, polyester is often 'bulked' or 'crimped', and knitted to give a durable and practical fabric.	Woven or knitted into jersey fabrics, polyesters should be washed at Code 4, usually drip-dried and ironed only with a warm iron when necessary.
Triacetate Arnel	*Primary raw materials in the manufacture of triacetates are wood pulp and cotton linters.* Triacetates have a dry, crisp silky handle and slightly shiny finish. They have easy-care qualities and are crease-resistant.	Always washable, at Code 6 or Code 8 for permanently-pleated fabrics, triacetates are quick drying and require little or no ironing. Must not be dry-cleaned with trichlorethylene.
Viscose Rayon Avril, Bemberg, Coloray, Colorspun, Cupioni, Enka Rayon, Fortisan, Spunlo, Zantrel	*With a wood pulp base, viscose rayon is a cellulosic fiber and is probably the most widely used of all man-made fibers.* Rayon is the old 'art silk' rayon and is still used today for linings or 'brushed' as a cheap wool substitute. It is also used as a blend where its absorbency is balanced with a stronger but non-porous fiber.	100% viscose rayon fabrics may be washed at Codes 2, 4, 5 or 7, depending on the particular fiber content of the fabric, and individual instructions must be followed carefully. A medium-hot iron is usually suggested.

Knitted and stretch fabrics

Pronunciation of some words given in italics.

1 Jacquard knits. Patterned double knits with a design incorporating up to four separate colors.

2 Tricot. (*Tree-coe*) A fine single-knit jersey used for lingerie, as a backing for bonded fabrics and for very light blouses or summer dresses.

3 Stretch fabrics. The use of the new elastomeric yarns, e.g. Lycra, and bulked synthetic yarns means that many woven fabrics not normally expected to have stretch can now have this property added. Some degree of stretch can also be imparted by modified weaving techniques or special finishing treatments. Knitted fabrics have natural stretch properties, because of their loop structure. Stretch fabrics are used for bathing suits, ski pants, babies' rompers and so on.

Bonded and laminated

4 Almost all fabrics can be bonded, a process which literally sticks two fabrics back-to-back. Sometimes a very thin layer of foam is used as an adhesive; or thicker foam, combining adhesive and insulator, giving added bulk. Bonding is most commonly used for giving body to rather light unsubstantial fabrics.

5 Vinyls. Fabrics can be laminated with polyvinyl chloride (PVC)—a strong fine plastic waterproof film—for rainwear or upholstery. Vinyl coated fabrics can be bought by the yard and make practical tough play clothes for small children.

Wet-look

Ciré. (*See-ray*) Wet-look, shiny finish originally imparted by waxing the surface. Now mostly produced from PVC film (see above) or other plastic film coating, but also by heating the surface of the fabric, usually nylon, with hot rollers.

Non-woven

6 Felt. A dense, fibrous fabric made by interlocking fibers like wool under heat and pressure. Used in heavyweights for flooring, light for walls and fun clothes.

7 Interfacings. Non-woven interfacings for garment shaping, such as Pellon, can be cut in any direction and are available in several different weights often with a fusible backing.

Silky looks

1 Crêpe de chine. (*Crape-de-sheen*) A luxurious lightweight satiny crêpe.

2 Faille. (*Fie*) Soft fabric with light, flat horizontal rib.

Foulard. (*Foo-lar*) Light, soft twill-woven fabric, usually silk or rayon. Often used for scarves and men's ties.

3 Grosgrain. (*Grow-grain*) Fabric with pronounced fine horizontal rib.

Ottoman. Heavy fabric with pronounced horizontal ribs. Originally made with silk warp and wool weft.

4 Peau de soie. (*Poe-de-swah*) Very soft satiny dress silk with a lustrous sheen.

5 Satin. Basic weave which produces a smooth shiny finish. Fabric could be silk, all rayon, all nylon, all acetate, or a blend.

Sateen. Smooth shiny weave, often confused with satin, but sateen is woven on the weft, satin on the warp. Often cotton.

Sharkskin. A smooth, heavy, shiny-surfaced fabric with a stiff feeling.

6 Taffeta. A crisp handling, plain-woven fabric, sometimes very expensive. Cheaper quality ideal for linings.

7 Shantung. Plain-woven fabric, originally hand-loomed from silk, with imperfections in the yarn giving a rough slubbed effect.

Honan. A fine, crisp, smooth fabric, suitable for blouses and dresses and, in heavier weights, men's tropical suitings. Its name derives from a province in China.

Thai. (*Tie*) Comes from Thailand. A beautiful, rich-looking fabric, heavier in weight than Honan. Dyes brilliantly in jewel colors, plain, shot or plaid.

8 Tussah/wild silk. Natural fiber from the silkworm in its untreated form, with uneven texture and usually natural beige in color. The fabric is called tussore.

9 Surah. Twill-woven, lustrous fabric, with a soft feeling.

10 Silk. Hand-blocked pure silk. Silk is a fiber, not a fabric. "Pure silk" may only be used where there is no metallic or other weighting of any kind, except that which is an essential part of dyeing.

Silky looks (contd.)

Sheers

1 Chiffon. Sheer delicate fabric with a plain weave and a soft floating quality.

2 Net. A mesh fabric in various weights.

Tulle. Fine silk or nylon net with a six-sided mesh, used for veils or evening wear.

3 Organza. Lightweight, semi-sheer, plain-woven fabric of silk or nylon, with a very crisp finish.

4 Georgette. A fine crêpy fabric with a light but quite crisp feeling. Can be of wool, silk, or man-made fiber.

Brushed and pile

5 Brushed fabric. Material that has had the surface raised to provide extra warm feeling.

Chenille. (*Sh-neel*) Tufted fabric woven from a specially made tufted chenille yarn. Expensive, due to the elaborate method of producing the yarn.

6 Corduroy. Tough, cut pile fabric with a wide or narrow rib and a plain back.

7 Fur fabric. Woven or knitted deep pile fabric made to imitate fur or fleece.

Suede cloth. Woven or knitted fabric with a tight surface to resemble suede. The nap is close and on one side only.

8 Velvet. A plain or figured fabric, originally of silk, with a thick cut pile to give a smooth, rich luxurious finish. Velvet can now be crease-resistant, water-repellent and fully washable, and made of nylon and other fibers.

9 Velveteen. A cotton fabric with a short close weft pile, made to look like velvet. It has a plain-woven back.

Rich fabrics

10 Brocade. Richly figured Jacquard-weave fabric with a pronounced design on a satin background, often incorporating several colors.

Damask. A glossy Jacquard-woven fabric similar to brocade, but flatter. Traditionally associated with curtains and table-cloths.

11 Cloqué. (*Cloe-kay*) Multi-weave fabric made from yarns of different character which give a raised or "blistered" effect.

12 Matelassé. (*Mat-e-lassay*) A multi-weave fabric with a strong quilted look.

13 Moiré. (*Mwa-ray*) A heat and pressure finishing process which gives a watered or waved effect to fabrics.

14 Lamé. Silvered and gilded metallic threads which are incorporated into all types of fabric to give sparkle and glitter. Nowadays, many of these threads are washable.

Lacy fabrics

15 Eyelet embroidery (broderie anglaise). Embroidered fabric (traditionally cotton) with cut-out designs.

Chantilly lace. Well-spaced isolated floral motifs with clear net background constructed from a finer yarn. The main parts of the design are generally outlined with heavier thread.

16 Guipure. (*Ghi-pure*) Heavy open-work lace, usually cotton.

17 Leavers. A delicate lace made on the Leavers lace machine, similar to other well-known lace.

18 Ribbon lace. The patterns in the lace (e.g. flowers) are outlined in ribbon.

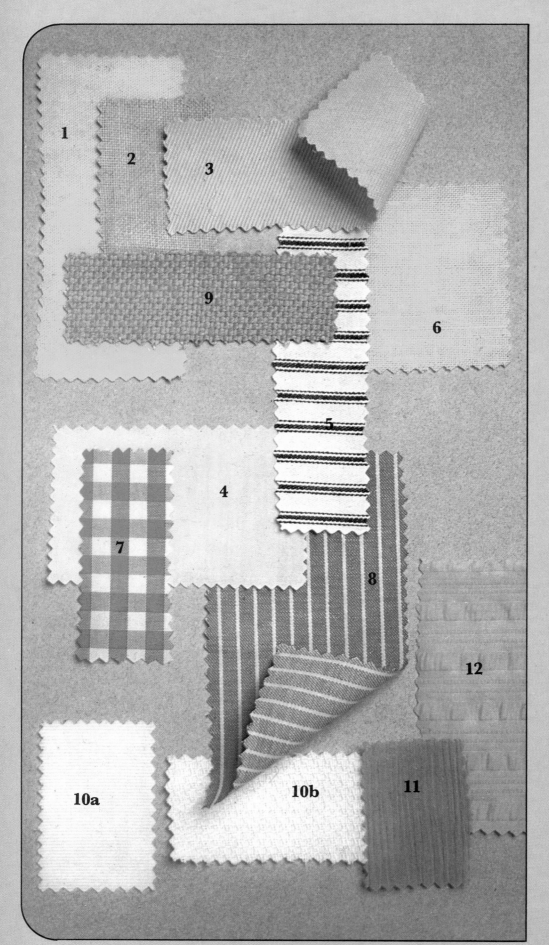

Cotton and linen looks

Firm weaves

1 Sailcloth. A very strong, firmly woven canvas. Originally used for sails, it is now available in various weights, plain or printed.

2 Canvas and **Duck.** Tightly-woven cotton or linens in various weights, in a plain or rib weave. Duck is slightly heavier than canvas.

Unbleached muslin. Plain-woven mid-weight cotton, which always has a matte finish.

3 Gabardine. A tightly-woven fabric with a marked diagonal twill weave.

4 Poplin. Plain-woven fabric with very fine horizontal ribs.

5 Ticking. A striped firm cotton originally used for mattresses.

6 Slub weave. A slub-woven fabric, typical of a "linen look" showing the characteristic slubs or unevenness of the natural flax yarns.

7 Gingham. Yarn-dyed plain weave cotton fabric in stripes, plaids and checks.

8 Denim. Very tough washable strongly twilled fabric, usually cotton, often with a slightly "faded" appearance.

Madras. Fine cotton shirting with a woven design in stripes, plaids and checks. Authentic Madras is from India and has a slightly mottled, slubbed effect.

9 Hopsack. A firm fabric with an even, double weave.

Textured

10 Piqué. (*Pee-kay*) Firm, woven fabric with horizontal rounded ribs or cords (10a). Types of piqué include "waffle" piqué with fine honeycomb weave (10b).

Crêpon. (*Cray-pon*) Fine shirting fabric, using crêped yarns for a tree-bark effect.

11 Plissé. (*Plee-say*) Knife pleats, patterns or "blistered" effects created by a weaving or chemical process. The word means "pleated" in French.

12 Seersucker. A fabric with an alternating crinkled stripe or design made by weaving with warp threads at varying tensions, or by treating fabrics like linen and cotton with caustic soda solution, causing the treated parts to contract.

Lightweight

13 Batiste. Soft, semi-sheer, lightweight fabric, originally of flax, now can be cotton or a variety of other fibers.

14 Organdy. Feather-weight plain-woven cotton with very crisp finish.

15 Lawn. A fine light fabric similar to handkerchief cotton and lovely for shirts and lingerie.

16 Lace. Hand or machine-made fabric consisting of a network of threads drawn into decorative patterns.

Muslin. Traditionally muslin was plain-woven open gauze, usually cotton. Now muslin refers to a cheap, heavier, often unbleached, general-purpose fabric.

17 Voile. A fine plain-woven open-textured fabric.

Shiny

18 Cotton satin. Satin-woven cotton, often treated for high-luster and crease-resistance, is found chiefly in good-quality printed home furnishing fabrics.

Napped and pile

Flannelette. Cotton flannel, with its slightly napped warm surface and solid feeling, is traditionally the material for "flannel" petticoats and nightdresses.

19 Terrycloth. A soft highly absorbent cotton toweling fabric with closely woven loops on one or both sides.

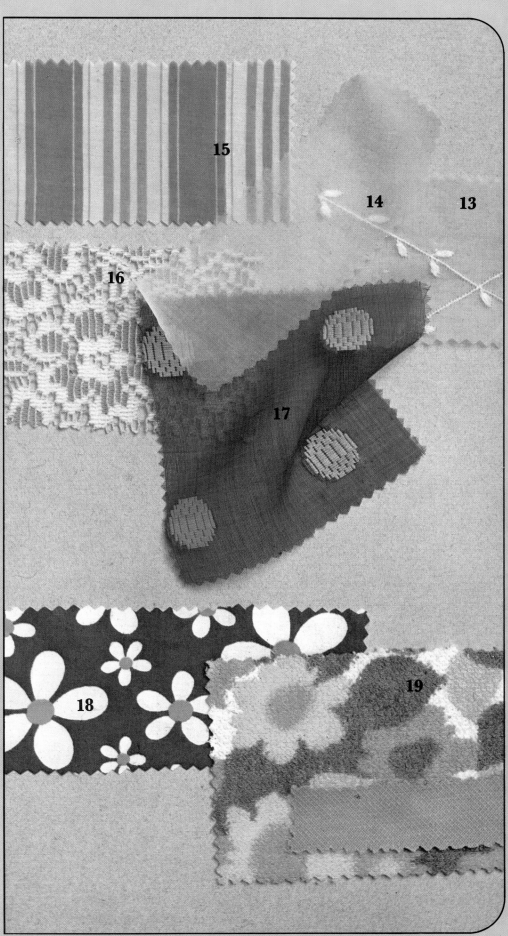

Woolen looks

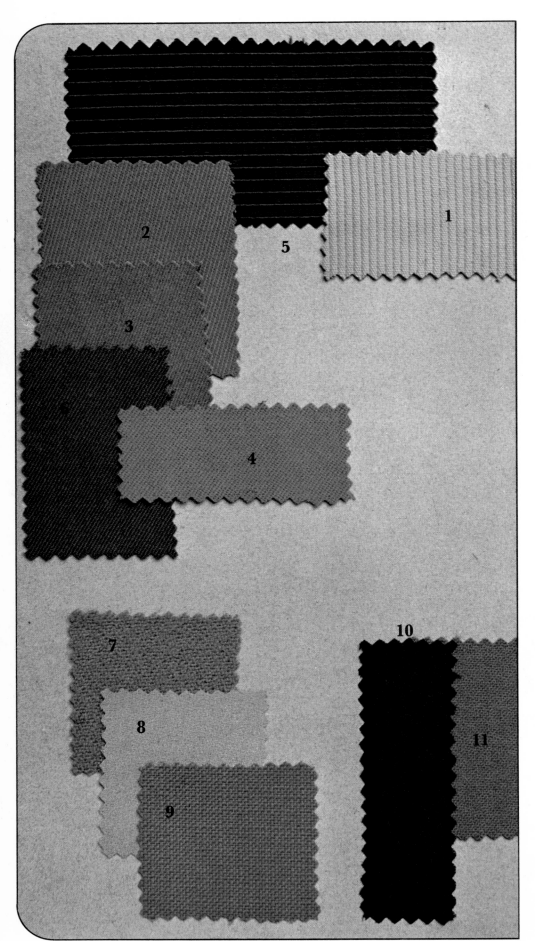

1 Bedford cord. A hard-wearing fabric with heavy rounded ribs or cords running in the warp direction.

Bengaline. A heavy smart fabric with fine crosswise rib, similar to faille. Sometimes made from wool (worsted), but can be from cotton, silk or other filament.

2 Twill. A fabric with a particular type of weave characterized by a diagonal rib called a "twill."

3 Cavalry twill. Twill with a pronounced double diagonal ribbed weave.

4 Gabardine. A tightly woven fabric with a marked diagonal twill weave.

5 Ottoman. Heavy fabric with pronounced horizontal ribs. Originally made with silk warp and wool weft.

6 Whipcord. A rugged, long-wearing fabric distinguished by a prominent upright slanted twill.

7 Bouclé. (*Boo-clay*) A fabric woven or knitted with looped or knotted yarn to give a curly look to the fabric surface.

8 Crêpe. (*Crape*) Fabric with a slightly crinkled or "puckered" surface, using highly twisted crêpe yarns or chemical treatment.

9 Hopsack. A firm fabric with an even weave.

10 Alpaca. Fine, very expensive fabric, which is plain- or twill-woven. It can be made either wholly or with a high proportion of the long hair of the alpaca goat.

11 Barathea. A closely woven fabric with "pebble" surface, of twilled hopsack weave used for tailored wear.

Covert cloth. Usually twill-woven, covert cloth has a softly mottled surface and a good solid feeling.

Serge. Heavy worsted fabric with a simple flat rib.

Napped

Angora. Fabric made from the hair of the angora rabbit giving a warm, soft wool with very fluffy surface.

12 Broadcloth. Wool broadcloth has a glossy, napped surface, and a twill weave. Usually dyed in dark colors.

13 Doeskin. Compactly woven wool with a smooth, short nap.

14 Flannel. Plain- or twill-woven traditionally all-wool fabric with a softly napped surface.

15 Velours. Warm fabric, usually of wool, with plain or satin weave and a short, thick pile in one direction.

16 Melton. A heavyweight wool coating with the shortest nap of any of the napped wools, and a "felted" appearance.

Mohair. Available in many weaves, colors and pattern. Long-haired mohair is a natural fiber from the angora goat, exceptionally warm to wear.

Lightweight

17 Challis. Soft and supple lightweight cloth, often delicately printed.

18 Georgette. A very fine, sheer, matte fabric, usually in a plain weave, made of a twisted yarn, not necessarily wool, to give a pebbly, crêpe effect.

19 Nun's veiling. Very fine plain-woven fabric, mainly used for babies' and children's wear. Can be of wool, silk or cotton.

Tweeds

20 Tweed. Roughly surfaced, traditionally woolen fabric, often with distinctive patterns (e.g. checks) obtained by weaving several colored yarns. Well-known types include Donegal tweeds from Ireland with a distinct slubbed surface texture, and Harris tweed, a tough, colorful pure wool fabric handwoven in the Outer Hebrides islands.
These are typical tweed patterns:

21 Herringbone

22 Shepherd

23 Glen plaid

24 Tattersall check

25 Houndstooth check

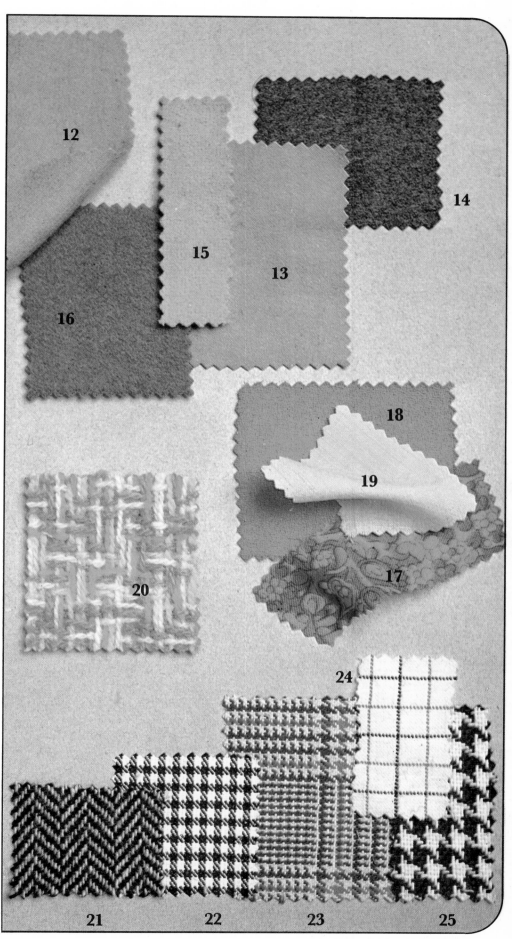

Chapter 8

Linings, interlinings and interfacings

In dressmaking, the correct choice of under fabrics—linings, interlinings and interfacings—is most important and makes all the difference to the finished result. The wrong choice can be disastrous. So, to help you avoid such disasters, this chapter sets out to explain the difference between these under fabrics, the function of each type, and what to use. Remember that you need an under fabric which can be washed or dry-cleaned successfully with the garment, so be sure to check this important point when buying.

Linings

A garment and its lining are made separately, and when the lining is not stitched into the seams it is replaceable.
Choosing the correct lining fabric can sometimes be confusing, but if you keep in mind what you expect the lining to do for the garment in question, it should help you to make the right decision.

Functions of a lining
There are several functions which a lining can perform, the general function being to make the inside of a garment neater. A lining also prevents a garment from coming into direct contact with the body and so helps it to wear longer.
Linings help garments to hang well by insuring that they slide over those areas where there is a tendency to cling. They add bulk to a garment and so help garments to keep their shape. Linings also help to prevent creasing and seating, but for greater protection against these a garment has to be mounted or interlined.

The difference between lining and interlining
Interlinings are mounted onto the fabric and made as one, whereas linings are constructed separately. And although the practice is widespread, the outside fabric should not be mounted onto the lining fabric.
Different fabrics are used for lining and mounting. Whereas there needs to be a perfect marriage between a top fabric and its interlining, this is not the case with a separately constructed lining, and it is rare for lining fabrics to be suitable for mounting.
In addition, mounting with an unsuitable fabric will often prevent you from working the outside fabric properly, such as in pressing when the outside fabric may require greater heat than the lining can stand. So if you want a mounted dress lined, you should line it in addition to mounting it.

Methods of attaching linings
Most linings are made separately from the garment and then attached to the neckline and armholes by hand (figure 1), or caught in with the facings by machine.
Couture touch. Couture dressmakers assemble a lining by hand

and sew in each section over the corresponding section of the garment (figure 2). This avoids creating any folds and creases which a separate and loose lining often makes. In addition, the lining is securely attached to the garment and friction is reduced to a minimum; therefore, the lining will last longer.
Strictly speaking this time-consuming task is a labor of love, but it is well worth the effort. While you may not want to go in for this sort of finish, it does help to explain one reason why couture garments are so expensive and last so long.

Types of linings
Here is a chart giving suitable lining and fabric combinations.

Linings		
Outside fabric	**correct lining**	**substitute lining**
Cotton: dress-weight cotton	pre-shrunk treated lawn	Japanese silk (washable)
suit-weight cotton	synthetic taffeta	
Linen	Japanese silk	imitation Japanese silk
Pure silk	pure silk according to weight	rayon or other synthetic taffetas
Wool	pure silk or rayon taffeta	
Man-made fiber fabrics	synthetic taffeta	

Interlinings or underlinings

The term interlining is often applied to that layer of fabric between the outside fabric and the lining which adds warmth to a garment. But interlinings in dressmaking are fabrics used for mounting. Used in this sense the terms interlining and underlining are synonymous and you will often find the term underlining used instead of interlining.

Functions of interlinings
Interlinings are used to help prevent creasing, stretching out of shape and seating, to give body to fabrics, and they are particularly important for a sculptured look. With interlinings, direct hand sewing to the outside fabric is avoided, thus giving that exclusive couture finish.
In addition, there are some fabrics which would not wear successfully if they were not mounted, such as a number of soft and loosely woven suitings and coatings, and the soft tweeds mentioned in Skirtmaking 19 for the bias skirt. Fabrics such as these are not just mounted, but are properly backed with the interlining sewn to the wrong side of the outside fabric permanently before the garment is made.

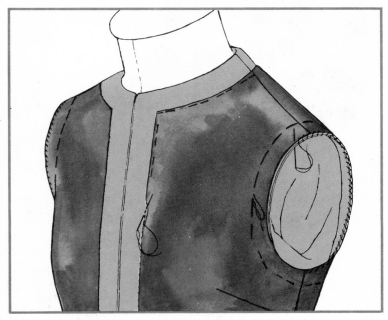

▲1. *Attaching a lining to the neckline and armholes by hand*

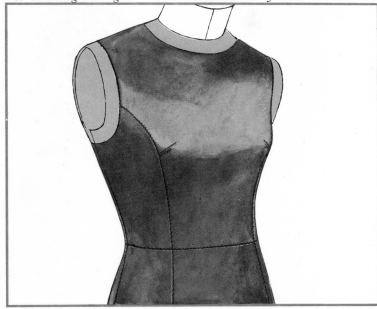

▲2. *Assembling a lining the couture way, section by section*
▼3. *Basting an interlining to the wrong side of the top fabric*

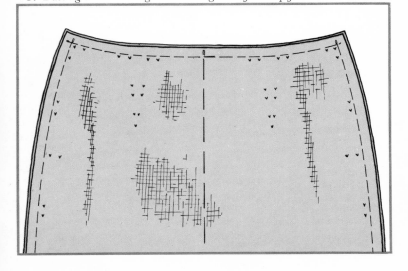

Applying interlinings

Interlinings are basted to the wrong side of the top fabric before stitching (figure **3**) and then top fabric and interlining are made as one.

To finish interlined seam allowances, overcast them by hand. Always avoid machine finishes as they tend to curl the two layers of fabric, thus creating a thick and hard seam edge which makes an impression through the fabric and often shows up noticeably on the outside.

To prevent interlinings from folding up inside hems, it is necessary to prick stitch fabric and interlining together just below the hemline before the hem is turned up (figure **4**). Also, when sewing the inner edge of hems and bias facings to a mounted garment, do not sew through to the outside fabric, but catch the interlining fabric only to give the outside a smooth finish.

Facings should be caught lightly to seam allowances only and not be sewn firmly in place, so work under the facing edge and hand sew loosely.

For the method of backing see Skirtmaking chapter 19.

Types of interlinings

The correct combination of outside fabric and interlining fabric is especially important and compromises can be disastrous.

Unfortunately, many of the interlining fabrics used by couture designers are not readily available, and usually they are very expensive. Most of them are made of pure silk and often cost more than the outside fabric, which is why interlined dresses are so very expensive.

However, here are a few interlining fabrics which are easily obtainable and reasonably priced.

Interlinings	
Outside fabric	**suitable interlining**
Silk, rayon, fine wool, cotton and linen	pure silk organza or a soft Japanese silk
Heavier dress and suit-weight wool	soft lawn or mull

▼4. *Left: overcasting interlined seams by hand. Right: prick stitching interlining and top fabric together just below the hemline*

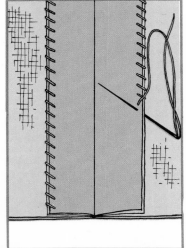
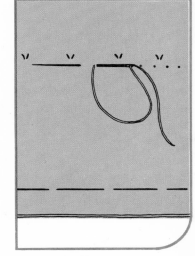

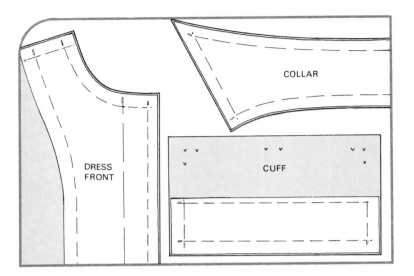

COLLAR

DRESS FRONT

CUFF

Interfacings

Areas such as collars, lapels, cuffs, belts and opening edges are interfaced to maintain their shape (see above). Interfacing strengthens, prevents stretching, and adds body and crispness without bulk.
The choice of interfacing is large and selecting the right one needs practice. The wrong choice of interfacing can mar the finished appearance of a garment, no matter how beautifully made it might be (figures **5**, **6** and **7**).

Dressmaker's and tailor's interfacings

To help you in your choice, you need to understand that there are differences between dressmaker's interfacings and tailor's interfacings—this will greatly reduce the list of possibilities and so make the choice easier.
Dressmaker's interfacings can be used for most fabric weights, but tailor's interfacings need the expertise of a tailor to combine and work them successfully.
Dressmaker's interfacings are those which you can stitch in with the seams, and tailor's interfacings are worked onto the wrong side of the outside fabric and stop at the seamlines.
Canvas is not too useful to the home dressmaker and is best left to the tailor as he knows how to work with it.

Functions of interfacings

The following chart gives you a guide to the type of interfacing which goes with a particular fabric. But remember that interfacings also come in different weights and degrees of stiffness and some, like soft pre-shrunk lawn, are not stiff at all. The difference between a very stiff collar and a soft one is in the interfacing, so the correct weight and stiffness to choose will be determined by the function it has to perform. You might even need more than one type of interfacing in a particular garment.
Some interfacings are designed for special jobs. A very stiff interfacing such as permanently stiffened cotton, for example, is used for belt making or to form a firm inside support for a full skirt.
In Blousemaking chapter 29 it is suggested that interfacing and top fabric should be bought at the same time, and a simple method of testing for the correct choice is given, which is worthwhile repeating. If you are striving for a soft effect, place an edge of the interfacing into the folded edge of the top fabric, and if the fabric rolls over the interfacing in a gentle, soft roll it is the right interfacing to use. If sharp points and a hard edge are formed, you have chosen the wrong interfacing.

Interfacing fine and see-through fabrics

A problem with fine fabrics can sometimes be the shadow caused by an interfacing. If a lawn interfacing is appropriate for the fabric you are using, it is available in different colors so you can choose a shade to match the fabric.
For see-through fabrics use pure silk organza which is so colorless that it can be used for most fabrics.

Types of interfacings

Apart from the many woven interfacings such as lawn and muslin, there are also the iron-on, woven interfacings and non-woven interfacings. It is useful to know something about these.
Iron-on interfacings. These must be used with the greatest care since not all fabrics will react favorably to them.
Unfortunately, once they are ironed on these interfacings do not always stay permanently in place, and sometimes work loose unless they are stitched to the fabric around the edges. Also, as they become detached they will decrease in stiffness and eventually you will have no more support than an ordinary mull or lawn would have given you. They do, however, save working long rows of basting when making the garment.
Do not use iron-on interfacings on large areas as they are not designed for this, and take particular care to find out if the one you buy can be washed and dry cleaned.
Non-woven interfacings. These usually carry the manufacturer's recommendation for use and combination with fabrics. There is little to add, since they are tested and designed for use with special fabrics. Be sure to ask for the right type and weight for the particular fabric you are using and for the function the interfacing has to perform.
Non-woven interfacings should not be used on large areas as they are not designed for this.

Interfacings	
Outside fabric	**correct interfacing**
Dress weight: cotton linen wool	pre-shrunk treated lawn iron-on or non-woven interfacing as recommended by the manufacturer
Suit-weight: cotton linen wool	treated cotton interfacing, such as bleached muslin iron-on or non-woven interfacing as recommended by the manufacturer
Man-made fiber fabrics	non-woven interfacing as recommended by the manufacturer for very light fabrics (lawn, voile, etc.) pure silk organza
Pure silk	fine lawn or pure silk organza
See-through fabrics	soft organdy or pure silk organza

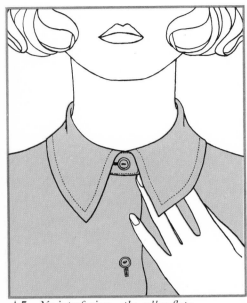

▲ **5.** *No interfacing—the collar flops*
▼ **6.** *Interfacing much too stiff—collar chokes*

Vogue pattern   interlined to perfection ▶
▼ **7.** *The right interfacing—the right look*

Chapter 9

Meet the basic stitches

Generally Speaking

Most sewing in the realm of dressmaking today can be done on your sewing machine—the more sophisticated the machine the greater the variety of stitches to choose from. However there are times when hand-sewing comes into its own, especially when it concerns finishing seams, hems and other fine detail. It is here, too, that you can give your clothes the couture, custom-made look sadly lacking in so many off-the-rack garments.

On these two pages you will find all the stitches you will need to do just that. Some of them will be shown again when they relate to a specific technique.

Back stitch
This is a very firm stitch and is worked by taking the needle and thread back one stitch on the side facing you, inserting the needle just in front of the preceding stitch. The resulting stitch at the back is twice the length of the top stitches.

Blanket stitch
This is a commonly used stitch for neatening seams on all sorts of woolen materials. It is worked from left to right over the raw edges. It is an alternative to the zigzag stitch of the sewing machine.

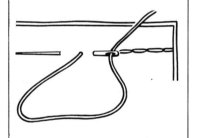

Blind stitch.
This is a more closely worked version of the invisible hem stitch.

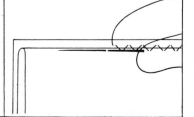

Even basting
This stitch is used for seams which will take quite a lot of strain during fitting. Use suitable length of stitch and thickness of thread to suit the material. An occasional backstitch will help where firm basting is essential.

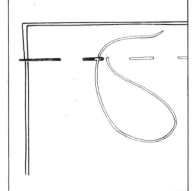

Felling stitch
Felling is a form of hemming one piece of fabric to another piece. The edge can be folded or left raw. While it is a very strong stitch, it has the added advantage of a neat look.

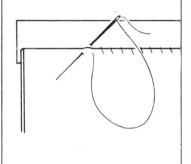

Herringbone stitch
This is the ideal stitch for turning up single hems when you are using non-frayable material and also for basting facings. Work from left to right of work, taking a small stitch in the hem and then a one-thread stitch in the fabric.

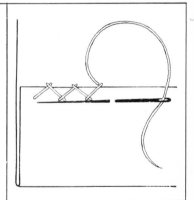

Invisible hem stitch
The rule to remember when turning a hem is to keep the stitches loose. If the thread is pulled tight, it will leave indented marks on the right side. Take up very little thread from the garments and a good deep thread from the hem. Leave a small loop every four or five stitches which will ease out during wear. Start and fasten off on the hem, never the garment.

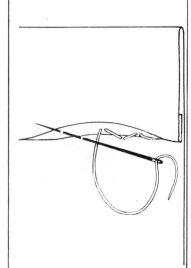

Overcast stitch

This is the usual way of neatening cut edges and, of course, stops them fraying. As you can see from the diagram, it is worked diagonally, with small evenly spaced stitches.

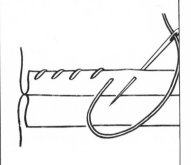

Prick stitch

This is a version of back stitch, worked over a single grain of fabric, forming a tiny surface stitch.

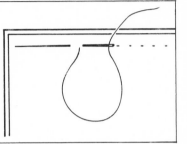

Running stitch

The most elementary of all sewing stitches, this is used when seaming and gathering. Weave needle in and out (as shown in the diagram) before pulling the needle through.

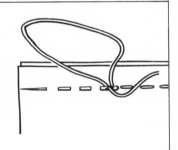

Slip stitch

This stitch gives an invisible finish and is worked in an almost straight line as opposed to the zigzag motion of a felling or hem stitch.

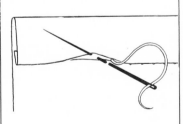

Whip stitch

This is a very fine oversewing stitch worked from right to left. It can be used to finish off the edge of very fine fabrics by turning under the edge $\frac{1}{8}$ inch and whipping to look like very fine cording.

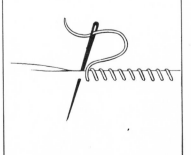

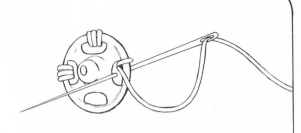

Ball section of snap

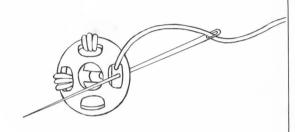

Socket section of snap

Sewing on snaps. Sew on the ball section of the snap first to the upper section of the opening. Press against the lower section of the opening leaving a tiny mark to show the position for the socket section. Oversew into one hole two or three times passing the needle **under the snap in the next hole** until each hole has been firmly stitched.

Ball section of snap goes on front part of opening, and socket section goes on back

Chapter 10

Theme and variations on a simple skirt

Every one of the elegant skirts shown here can be made from one single pattern, and you can even make that yourself. So instead of having to buy seven different patterns, you simply adapt this one to make the style of skirt you want. The basic skirt pattern is a simple flared style, but in later chapters you will discover how this pattern can be used to make all the variations sketched here. With the length of skirts and the moods of fashion constantly changing, you can be certain that this is one pattern which will go to any length to suit your needs.

What you wear with your skirt is important and demands careful thought, because an unsuitable combination can spoil the effect of any garment. Of course, there is an enormous variety of clothing to choose from for wearing with a skirt, but a collection of blouses provides the ideal answer and gives you the scope to choose the perfect partner for the length and style of skirt you wear.

The blouses sketched here are some variations on the basic blouse from the Golden Hands Graph Pages, and instructions for making all of them are given in later chapters.

If you make your own blouses and skirts, you can have fun choosing color schemes, and you'll be surprised how many different outfits you can make up if the colors are carefully chosen to match or complement each other and fit in with the rest of your wardrobe.

An introduction to drafting

Making your own pattern may sound like a formidable task, but if you work from a graph, you'll discover it is fun and very easy—in fact, drafting from a graph is the simplest form of pattern making. This chapter starts off with the simple flared skirt, and if you follow the step-by-step instructions carefully, you can't go wrong. Read on and you will see some of the advantages of making your own pattern. The graph is for a 36in hip, 26in waist and 23in length, but you will find the instructions give all the information you need for altering the size of the graph pattern to your own measurements, including full instructions which give the secrets of lengthening and shortening a flared skirt.

Although you will make the pattern to your own size, your individual proportions may not be standard, and you will need to make certain alterations to the pattern. So when you have cut out and basted the skirt, the following chapter describes fitting in detail and shows how to transfer any alterations to the skirt pattern. You will then have an individual pattern which takes all your personal skirt fitting problems into account.

You can use this corrected pattern to make the skirt variations illustrated here. And, because the pattern fits you perfectly, there should be very little fitting to do when you use it again for making up other variations of the basic style.

Theme: the flared skirt...

Straight

4-gore

6-gore

Knife-pleated

Dirndl

Bias-cut

...Variations

39

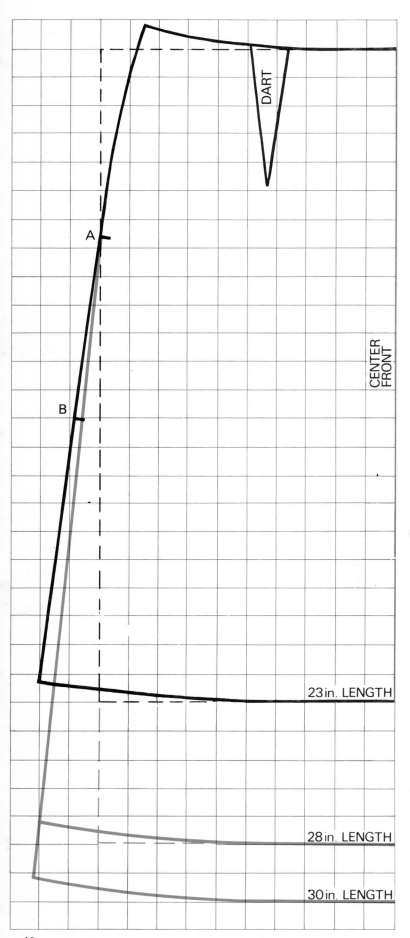

DART

CENTER FRONT

A

B

23in. LENGTH

28in. LENGTH

30in. LENGTH

Pattern making from a graph

To make the pattern, you will need the following equipment:
- ☐ Yardstick
- ☐ Tape measure
- ☐ Tailor's square, or a 45° set square from an art supply store will do just as well
- ☐ Soft pencil
- ☐ Large sheet of brown wrapping paper, with lengthwise grain lines

To make a pattern from a graph, just count the squares and translate them into inches. Each square represents one square inch. Here, we use a rectangle of dotted lines to make it easy to obtain the pattern shape, the position of the darts, and the curves. The size of the rectangle is based on the length of the skirt and the hip measurement. The pattern shown on the graph is for size 36in hips and 26in waist. Instructions on changing the size and length of the pattern are given at the end of this chapter, so read first and then take action.

N.B. You do not need to draw the grid squares onto the brown paper, just transfer the outline of the skirt.

How to copy the rectangle and obtain your pattern shape
First, fold the edge of the paper under 1in along the lengthwise grain lines, to give a strong working edge to the center front of your paper pattern. Starting with the black rectangle for the front, count the squares on the center front line of the graph. Measure down 1in from the top and mark in pencil. Then count down for the length of skirt required and mark. Count the squares along the horizontal dotted lines and measure the distance on the paper, making two more pencil marks opposite those on the folded front edge. Connect these points using a yardstick, making this the dotted vertical line, marking it as it appears on the graph.

At this stage, it is very important to double-check that the distances between the folded edge and the dotted vertical line are equal, top and bottom, or the pattern will become uneven.

To make the horizontal lines, lay the tailor's square on the folded edge and your first pencil marks, and draw dotted lines across to complete the rectangle.

Make the rectangle for the back skirt section in exactly the same way. These rectangles now give the guidelines to count from, to obtain the pattern outlines, the position of the darts and points A and B (the balance marks). The balance marks are important and have to meet when you stitch the skirt seams together.

For the waistband, mark out a strip 1¼in wide and 13in long, as shown on the graph. This is half your waist measurement. For the waistband to fit snugly, no ease is allowed.

How to alter the graph size
If the size on the graph is too small for you, it is quite easy to increase it. This is how to do it.

Make the patterns as before, but instead of making the fold along the center front edge of your paper 1in, increase the fold to 2in. Next, refer to your measurement chart in chapter 4 for your waist and hip measurements, remembering to add the necessary ease to your own measurements.

Then divide the difference between your measurements and those

◄ *Graph pattern of skirt front for size 36in hip, showing 23in length in black, and 28in and 30in lengths in red. Each square = 1 square inch*

on the graph by eight (this is because you are working on half sections of the pattern only). For example, to increase the pattern to a 40in hip and a 30in waist, you will have to add 4in to the graph pattern size—4in divided by eight means that you will have to add ½in to each center line and side seam. To add ½in to the center lines, unfold the edge of the paper by this amount. To add ½in to the side seams, measure outward from the given line and draw a new line. Make sure that the point where side seam and waist seam meet stays the same distance from the upper horizontal line of the rectangle.

You can reduce the size of the pattern using the same technique, but subtracting at the center lines and side seams instead of adding.

How to alter the graph length

The graph pattern shows a 23in length skirt in black and 28in and 30in lengths in red.

To increase the length to 28in or less the rectangle is increased to the desired length and the pattern made as before. This gives the same flare at the hem as in the shorter version.

For lengths over 28in the flare needs to be increased. To do this, first draw up a skirt 28in long as above. Then extend the line of flare by the required length as shown for the 30in length skirt. If you want to shorten the skirt, it is not necessary to alter the flare.

Cutting out the pattern

You are now ready to cut out the pattern. Before cutting out, be sure that you have marked the folded edges, center front and center back, and balance marks. Cut around all the shapes—cut into the darts, too. It is best to transfer this pattern onto stiff white paper (from an art supply store), since the original will be used later to obtain all the outlines for the other skirt styles you will make.

Fabric requirements

In the next chapter you will be cutting out your skirt. Here is how to calculate the amount of fabric you will need, depending on the width you have chosen.

54in width—for sizes 34½, 36 and 38in hips: your skirt length, measured over side hip, plus 8 inches for seam and hem allowances and waistband.

For 40, 42 and 44in hip: one-and-a-half times your skirt length, measured as above, plus 8 inches.

36in width—twice your skirt length, measured over side hip, plus 11in for seam and hem allowances and waistband.

Choosing your fabric

Having made the pattern and worked out the yardage requirements, it is time to choose your fabric and get everything ready for cutting out.

When choosing fabric, make sure it's easy to work with and practical to wear. When you buy, make sure you ask for skirt or suit weight cloth. Choose from any of the following:
☐ Firmly woven worsted woolens, cottons and linens
☐ Fine grain tweeds
☐ Firm man-made fabrics like acrylics
☐ Mixture fabrics such as wool or linen, which have been blended with nylon, acrylics or polyesters
   You will also need:
☐ Sewing thread
☐ Hooks and eyes
☐ 7in zipper
☐ 1yd stiff grosgrain ribbon or belting 1in wide

Graph pattern of skirt back for size 36in hip showing 23in length in black, and 28in and 30in lengths in red. Each square = 1 square inch ►

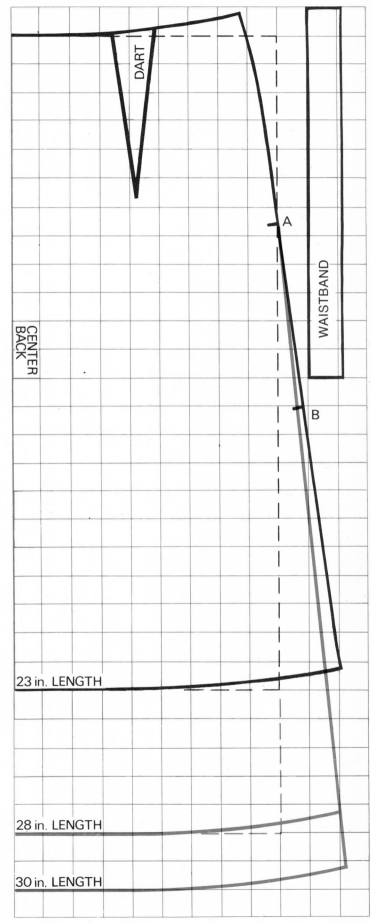

Chapter 11

Preparing to sew the skirt

Having bought your fabric and made the basic skirt pattern from the graph in the previous chapter, you are now ready for the important stages of cutting out the skirt.

Here is the equipment you will need:
☐ Basting thread
☐ Sewing scissors
☐ Tailor's chalk
☐ Pins and needles
☐ Firm table surface

Preparing the fabric

It is essential that the fabric is perfectly smooth before you begin to cut it out. If it has become creased through packing and folding, press the whole length carefully, using a table surface or press board rather than an ironing board. Leave the fabric folded lengthwise with right sides together, and steam the creases out on the wrong side of the fabric using a damp but not wet cloth. Press both sides of the folded length.

Set up your cutting area on a table large enough to take the full folded width and length of the fabric, and fold the fabric as shown in the following layouts and instructions. If you don't want to use a table top, a sheet of hardboard, 4ft wide by 4ft long, will provide you with an excellent cutting surface.

If the fabric is 54in wide, unfold it so that it lies flat on the table. Then, for a hipsize of under 40in, refold the fabric with wrong side out, so that the selvages (finished edges) meet at the center fold line (see layout far right). Smooth out the layers of material toward the new folds to make sure the fabric lies perfectly flat, then secure the selvages to the center crease with pins. For size 40in hip and over, simply fold over the selvages until the pattern width is accommodated (see layout near right).

With narrower fabrics, fold lengthwise, selvages together, smooth out and pin.

Laying out the pattern

Before laying out the pattern pieces, make sure you have marked all pattern details such as center front, center back, and the balance marks on the side seams.

Place the center front and center back lines of the skirt on the fold as shown in the appropriate layout.

Pin both pieces around the edges, making sure they lie flat and are firmly anchored through both layers of fabric.

N.B. Since the pattern is cut without seam or hem allowances, leave enough room around each piece for ¾in seams and a 2½in hem.

Marking the pattern detail on the fabric

Before cutting, transfer the shape of the paper pattern onto the fabric by marking around the edges with continuous tailor's tacks. Once you become more familiar with paper patterns and working on fabrics, you can mark pattern details after cutting.

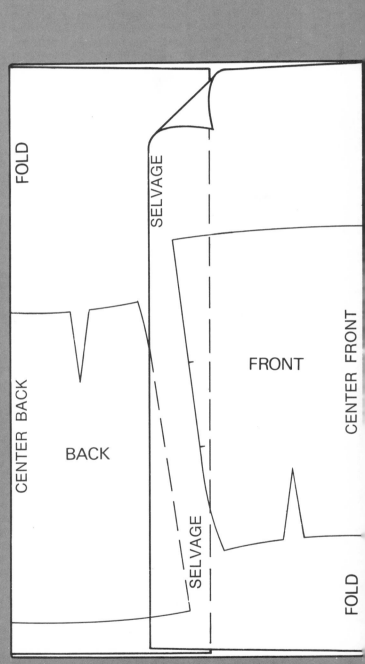

The layout for size 40in hip and over, on a 54in wide fabric

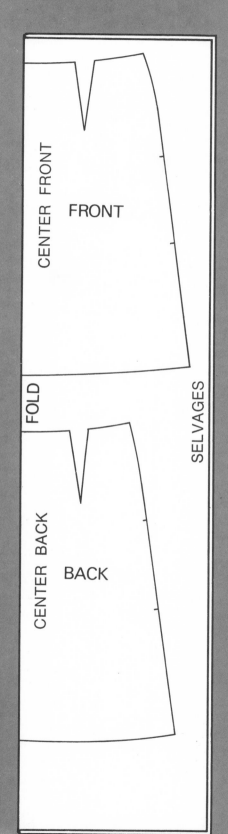

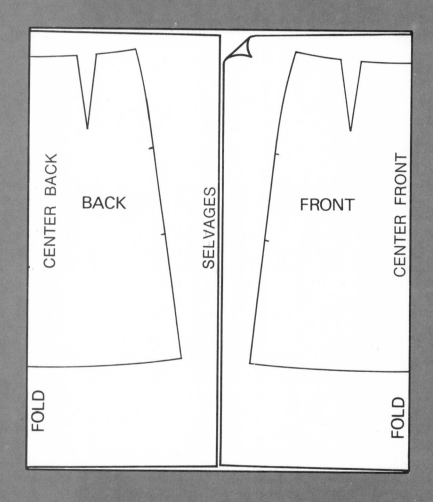

CENTER FRONT

FRONT

FOLD

SELVAGES

CENTER BACK

BACK

CENTER BACK

BACK

SELVAGES

FRONT

CENTER FRONT

FOLD

FOLD

FOLD

**The layout for sizes 34½,
36 and 38in hip,
on a 54in wide fabric**

**The layout for 36in wide
fabric**

Making continuous tailor's tacks

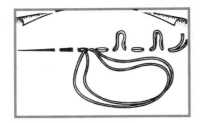

Thread the needle with basting thread, pulling it through so the ends meet and the thread is doubled. Make the stitches ½in long, leaving a loop about the size of your finger tip on every other stitch as shown.

Make tailor's tacks carefully around the pattern and into the darts. Work a single tailor's tack to mark the balance marks A and B, using a double thread, and make a back stitch leaving a loop.

N.B. Before cutting, you must add on the hem and seam allowances. Add 2½in for the hem and ¾in for the seams. You can mark these with pins or tailor's chalk. A chalk line is the best method, provided the edge of the chalk is kept sharp by scraping it with a knife, as a thick line can alter the width of your allowances.

Cutting

This is a magic word for even the most experienced dressmakers. It is the point of no return—check once again that all markings and allowances are correct and the fabric is perfectly flat.

Insert the scissors from the top edge of the fabric and cut along your pin or chalk lines with firm, short movements through both layers of fabric. (Do not cut into the darts.) As you cut, keep the paper pattern flat on the fabric and hold it firmly in position with your hand alongside the scissors. This prevents the fabric lifting, which would alter your seam allowance.

After cutting, set aside the remaining fabric which you will need later for making the waistband.

Remove the paper pattern pieces from the fabric.

Separating the layers

Separate the layers of fabric held together by the tailor's tacks by pulling them apart gently along the tacking lines. This will flatten the loops on the top fabric and give enough room to insert the scissors between the layers and cut through the tacks. Be careful when doing this not to cut the skirt fabric.

When you unfold the pieces, the seams and hemline will have a row of tailor's tacks to guide you when you make up the skirt.

Basting for fitting

To baste your skirt together, start with the darts, creasing them down the center, so that both rows of tailor's tacks meet evenly to form a sewing line. Pin. Working from the top edge of the skirt toward the points of the darts, baste them together with small stitches. Use single thread and make flat stitches. Secure ends well with a double backstitch.

Working on a flat surface, place the back and front pieces together with right sides facing and seams coinciding. Make sure the balance marks on the hipline on the back and front correspond and that both layers of fabric lie flat. Pin seams together.

Hold the pinned seams up, and if one side puckers and makes the seam swing out instead of hanging straight, unpin the seam and gently stroke out the fullness. Pin again.

Still working on a flat surface, baste the right side seam. On the left side seam measure 7in down from the waist seamline and leave open for the zipper. Baste the rest of the seam.

The expert touch

After basting the darts and seams, press the seams open with very light strokes, so they will lie reasonably flat for fitting. The importance of pressing as you go can't be stressed enough, because it really does make all the difference.

A complete guide to fitting comes in the next chapter.

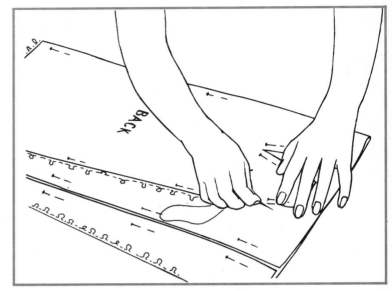

▲ *Marking the stitching line with tailor's tacks*

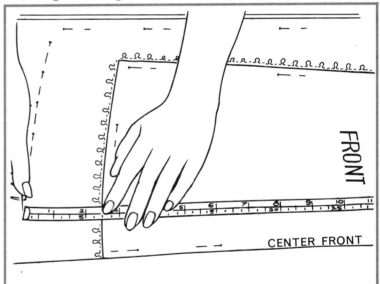

▲ *Marking the hem allowance with a line of pins*

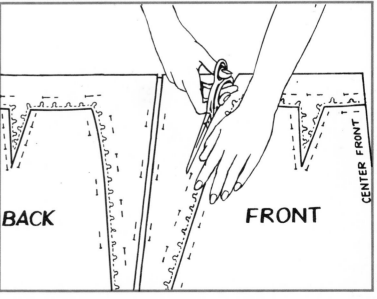

▲ *Cutting out the skirt after adding the seam allowance*

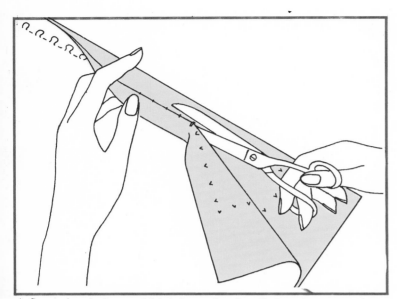

▲ Separating the layers of fabric by cutting the tailor's tacks

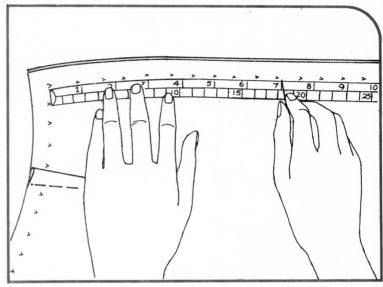

▲ Measuring the zipper opening   ▼ Two looks for the finished skirt

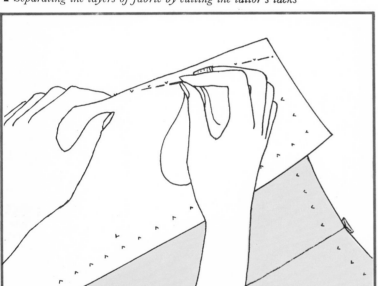

▲ Basting the darts with small stitches

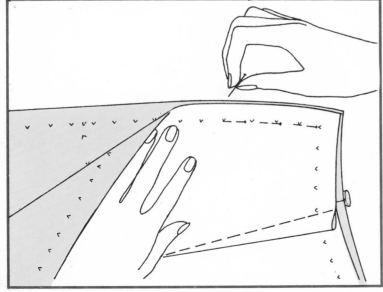

▲ Pinning the side seams before basting

45

Chapter 12

When it comes to fitting—persevere!

Your skirt is now ready for fitting. It is a good idea to find someone to help you with this, because although it is possible to fit clothes on yourself, it is not always very easy to do if you have a difficult fitting problem, or, for instance, if you need to pin and make adjustments to the back section.

Slip on your skirt and pin together the opening for the zipper in the seamline. Adjust the skirt around your waist, lay the belting along the waist seam marking, and pin it to the top of the skirt.

Your skirt should fit closely to the figure around the waist and hips and fall to a gentle flare at the hem—it should not fit tightly at any point. Now comes the moment to get things absolutely right. The guide here shows some of the common faults, and on the next two pages you will find out in detail the best way to correct them.

1. 'Pulling' lines across waist and hips
The skirt is too tight around the body.

2. The skirt pulls in below the seat
The skirt is just too tight over the seat.

Fitting guide

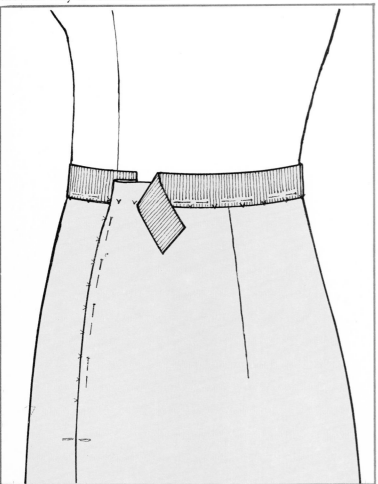

Undo the skirt and pin new side seams all the way down.

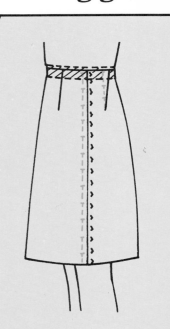

Pin new side seams on the back section.
Take any extra width at the waist into the back darts.

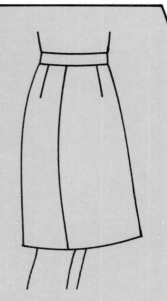

3. The skirt hangs loosely around the body

It is simply too big.

4. Creases below waistline at the front or back

At the back it's usually the combination of a long waist and a high seat.

At the front it's because your natural waistline tends to dip.

5. The skirt juts out at front or back hem

This means you have either a high stomach or a high seat.

6. Skirt juts out at front and back hem, and side seams hang inward

This usually means that your waist is large in proportion to your hips.

▲ *Faults and their causes ..... and how to correct them* ▼

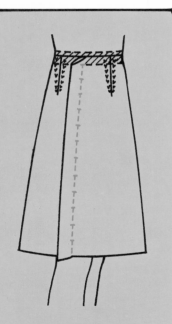

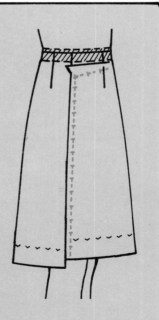

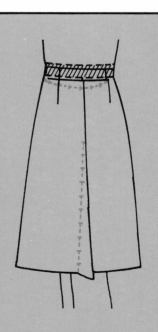

Pin away the fullness into the side seams. You may also have to let out the darts to allow the skirt to hang properly. If you do, take the extra material into the side seams.

The waistline requires re-shaping. Pin a crease across on the fabric below the waistband. Do not pull the excess up under the waistband as this will result in an incorrect waist fitting.

Pin a small crease toward the side seam on the section which juts out, enough to give you the correct hang.

Pin a crease below the waist-band and across the side seams so that the skirt hangs straight. Do, however, watch your hip-line as this may need to be taken in. If so, take in the amount on the side seam.

Tracing your alterations

Take your skirt off very carefully to avoid displacing the pins. Mark the alterations by tracing over the pins with long stitches in basting thread, taking care to catch in only one layer of material at a time. Trace the alterations on both sides, so that you do not lose all the markings when you take out the pins.

Remove the belting, marking any alteration you may have made to its length.

Marking and correcting after fitting

Now you are ready to correct and mark the skirt for stitching. The diagrams on the right show how to do this, taking each fitting in the same order as before.

Code:

small checks = the original line of tailor's tacks
red dashes = alteration lines
scissors = where to trim off surplus material

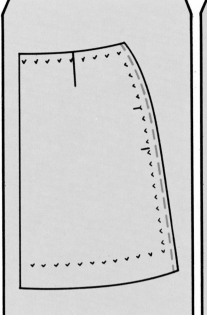
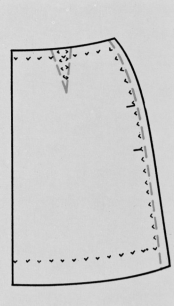

Fitting guide

Is one hip higher than the other?

If you have one hipbone higher than the other, first cover all the main faults mentioned in this chapter and then prepare the skirt for a final fitting.

You will then see how your high hipbone affects the general hang of the skirt. If it is not affected, you need only let out the seam slightly over the high hip in order to accommodate the higher curve.

If you find, however, that the hang of the skirt is affected, then you will need to adjust it on the opposite seam as well, by lifting into the waistband.

Transferring alterations to paper pattern

Once you have marked and corrected the skirt, it's a good idea to transfer the fitting corrections to the paper pattern right away, so that when this pattern is used again you can be sure of a really good fit.

To do this, measure all the alterations and draw them on the pattern in pencil. You can cut out the alterations to the waistline curve after first having made sure you have marked the pattern accurately.

If the skirt was taken in, mark the alterations to the side seams in pencil against the side seam on the pattern. Do not cut this off, since the same skirt made in another fabric may fit you.

Just make a note of it so that when you re-cut, you can baste the skirt inside the side seamline.

If you had to let out the side seams, extend the paper pattern by attaching a strip of paper down the full length and draw the alteration onto it.

1. Letting out side seams on both sections

Undo these seams all the way down and fold the pieces on center lines, as they were after cutting.

Measure the difference between the original side seams and the alteration marks on both the left and right sides of each piece of the skirt. On each piece, add the difference together, halve it, and measure this figure out from the original side seams, using pins or chalk. This is very important. When pinning the skirt, you might have taken up unequal amounts. The skirt would then be unbalanced if made up to the pin marks. Make a new line of tailor's tacks. Remove original markings.

N.B. When pinning seamlines, remember it's a good idea to lay the work flat on a table and bend down to look into the pin line at table level. You will be able to see if even one pin is out of line.

2. Letting out side seams on back section

Work as for (1.), but on the back section only.

Next, the darts.

You have already trace basted the extra amount to be taken into the darts. Now lay the back skirt section flat, right side up, and measure the distance between the trace basting at the top of each dart. Add these figures and divide into four. Turning the skirt section wrong side up, pin this amount off from the darts, starting at the waistline. Take up the fullness by running into the original stitching line at the point of the dart.

Make tailor's tacks over the pins to form a new stitching line.

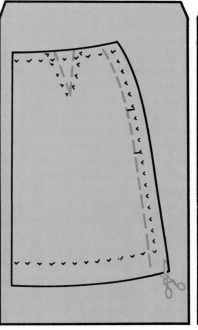
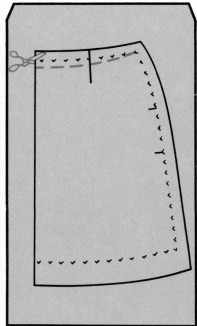
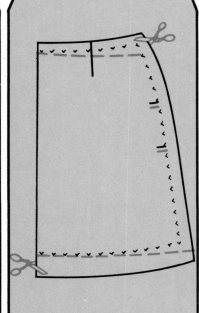
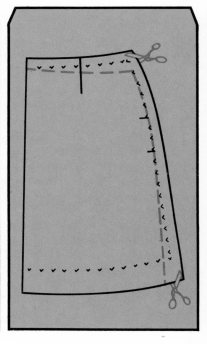

Take note ..... Take action

3. Taking in the side seams

Work as for (**1.**), but instead of measuring out from original side seams, measure in.

Let out the darts on the front and back sections in equal amounts. Pin off the surplus into the new side seams, starting at the waistline and tapering into the seam at hip level. Make tailor's tacks over this new line of pins. Mark the corrections with new lines of tailor's tacks and trim off surplus material, leaving correct seam allowance.

4. Re-shaping the skirt at the waistline

Turn the skirt inside out. Fold front and back sections on center lines. Pin the side seams together and pin along the waistline.

Measure along the depth of the crease between the trace basting and, starting with the full depth at center back or center front, pin a new waistline through the double layer, gradually curving up into original seamline so that the curve ends at the side seam.

Make a new line of tailor's tacks along the pin line and remove the original markings. Cut through tailor's tacks to separate layers and trim off any surplus material, leaving correct seam allowance.

5. Lifting a skirt that juts at the hem

Undo the side seams and to correct the jutting section displace the balance marks ½in upward. The depth of the crease you pinned when fitting may not be quite correct, since the skirt was basted together at the side seams and you may need a greater displacement than ½in. Try the skirt on again and check. Take care when you've reached the right amount of lift, as you may find it necessary to take in the side seam on the lifted section. Finally, level the waist and hemline. To do this, always level to the section which remains unaltered. In this way, if you lifted the front section, level this to the back section and vice-versa.

Make the new lines of tailor's tacks. Trim off surplus material, leaving correct seam allowance.

6. Lifting skirt at top of side seams

If it is necessary to take in the side seams, do this first. Undo side seams and lay skirt sections together, right sides facing. Measure the amount to be taken in. There will be more at the hem and less at the hip, with the line disappearing into the waist.

Use a yardstick to chalk out a straight line from hem to hips and then pin a gentle curve from waist to hips. Make a new line of tailor's tacks along pins for the side seams and trim off surplus material, leaving correct seam allowance. To re-shape waistline, pin and baste side seams together in new line, then fold skirt on center lines and pin side seam to side seam and darts to darts. Pin along waist seam.

Measure out depth of crease between trace basting and pin new line from side seam tapering into original waistline.

Make new lines of tailor's tacks. Trim off surplus material. Cut through tailor's tacks to separate layers.

Chapter 13

Give your skirt a neat finish

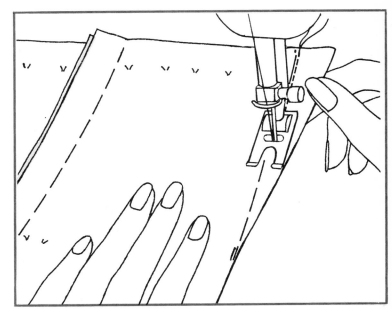

Having re-basted the seams and darts after alteration, and tried on your skirt again for a final check, you are now ready to stitch the darts and seams.

In this chapter you will find out how to put in the zipper properly, step-by-step, and how to stitch your darts for a really professional finish. Just to get you started, the illustration on the left shows you how your skirt should look when it is finished.

Stitching the darts

Seams and darts

Thread your machine with the same color as your skirt, and test the stitch length and tension on a double scrap of skirt material. It helps when stitching darts and seams to remember the shape of the human body. At no point where clothes cover us is there a sharp corner. Even the slimmest figures have gentle contours, so, when stitching the seams, always try to run the straight lines gradually into the curves. Switching direction suddenly will cause an unsightly pucker.

Stitch the darts and side seams, following the basting lines, and allow the dart ends to taper off smoothly. Start at the top of the side seams and stitch just outside the basting lines. If you stitch over the basting, it will be difficult to remove; also, as there is some 'give' in basting, your skirt might be too tight. Finish off the lines of stitching either by tying off the ends of thread, or by stitching backwards for about an inch to lock the threads.

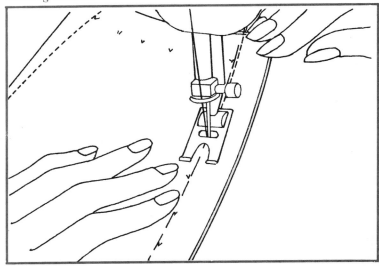

Stitching the side seams

Pressing hints

Pressing in dressmaking is quite different from ironing when it is just a question of smoothing out a surface. Pressing means fixing a certain shape which you have taken the trouble to fit and stitch. To retain this shape, use a lifting and pressing movement and adjust the pressure according to the weight and texture of the fabric. Some fabrics, such as woolens and linens, require a heavy pressure to stay in position—others, such as rayons, silks and man-made fibers need only light pressure.

If you use a damp cloth for steam pressing, do not keep the iron in the same place until the cloth is dry, but lift and press again repeatedly, until all the steam has gone. Even if you are working on fabric which does not need steam, it is a good precaution to use a dry cloth under the iron.

With some of the new man-made fiber fabrics, it is a good idea to ask for washing and pressing instructions when buying the fabric. As a general rule all fabrics made of man-made fibers should be pressed with a cool iron.

With mixtures of natural and man-made fibers, the seams may be difficult to press properly. In this case, use heat applicable to the base fabric, making sure at the same time that the fabric is protected by a cloth throughout the pressing.

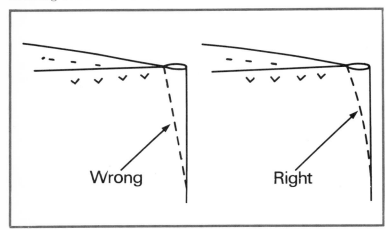

Wrong   Right

The wrong and right way to stitch a skirt dart

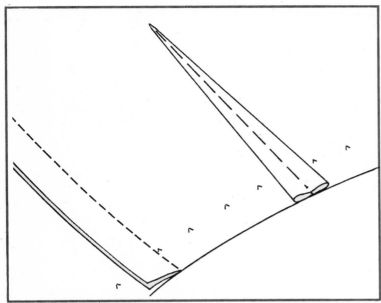

Dart basted flat ready for pressing

Pressing the darts and side seams

Some darts are turned to face the center of the garment and are pressed in that position—others are cut open to within 2in of the point and pressed open. But the darts on the flared skirt are pressed flat, with the center of the dart over the dart seam, which shows a neat flat finish from the outside.

Fold the dart centers to dart seams, pin and baste. Lay the pressing cloth (damp or dry, according to the fabric you are using) over the darts and press gently. Take out the basting and press again, to fix the shape.

Next, the side seams. Remove all basting other than the balance marks, lay the skirt over the ironing board and press the seams open, starting at the bottom. Do not press the side seams downward. The flare in the skirt means that the fabric is cut slightly on the cross toward the hem—and if you press into the seam starting from the top, you could stretch it.

When you have pressed the seam open and flat, you may find when you lift the edges that they have left impressions. Remove these by laying the damp cloth under the seam edges and, without touching the seam crease, press out the impressions.

Seam finishing

After the seams have been stitched and pressed, they must be finished off, to prevent fraying during wear.

There are various ways of doing this. If you are using a firmly woven fabric, use the zigzag stitch on your sewing machine to overcast the seams. Again run up the seam edges, not down, because, as with pressing, these edges could stretch if they are not stitched in the right direction. If you do not have a swing-needle machine, either overcast the raw edges by hand or just trim them neatly with pinking shears.

Putting in the zipper

First close the zipper opening with basting stitches and press open carefully, as for a seam. Take out all the basting and press again to remove any impressions made by the basting thread. As the seam is now open, take great care not to stretch the edges. Undo the zipper and, with the right side of the skirt facing you, lay the back seam edge of the skirt to the outer edge of the right-hand zipper teeth, and pin. When fitting a zipper, never stretch the seam over it, as this will cause it to wave. Also, the zipper and the seam should never be at equal tension; the zipper must always be held taut. If the opening turns out to be too short, undo the seam a little more to accommodate the zipper fully.

Pin across the seam to catch the zipper tape. After pinning, you should see the fabric rise a little over the tape between the pins. Baste the right-hand zipper tape securely into the back seam edge of the skirt with firm small stitches. Using the zipper foot on your machine, stitch the zipper in, about $\frac{1}{8}$in from the edge.

Close the zipper after stitching and lay the front seam edge to cover the teeth completely, far enough to meet the stitching line on the back seam edge. This will allow for recession when the zipper is stitched in, and yet still insure that the material covers it completely. Start pinning the front seam edge to the zipper from the bottom upwards, putting two or three pins across the seam edge and zipper tape. Then pin the top of the zipper to the seam, before pinning the rest. By doing this, you will easily be able to see how to distribute any fullness you might have had in the seam. If there is too much, ease this out toward the top. (It should never be more than $\frac{1}{4}$in.) Trim off after stitching, so that both top edges are level. Baste the zipper in firmly and machine stitch about $\frac{3}{8}$in from the seam edge. Then take out all the basting and press gently, wrong side up, using a cloth. This applies to metal zippers only. Nylon zippers need only the lightest touch when being pressed.

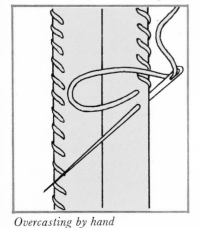

Overcasting by hand *Overcasting by machine*

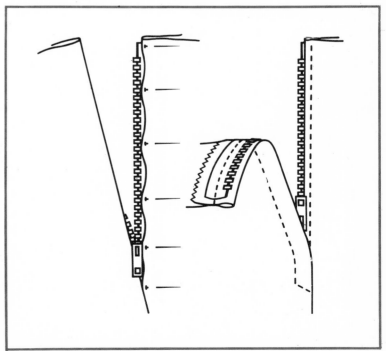

Skirt back seam edge pinned to the zipper *Zipper stitched in position*

Making skirt hangers

For looped hangers cut two 6in lengths of straight seam binding to match the skirt. Fold double to form loops. With loops pointing downward, pin the ends ½in over the waist seamline, on the inside of the skirt, just behind the zipper on the back and 1½in from the right side seam on the front. Baste into position.

For flat stitched hangers cut two strips of silk or lining 4in long and 1in wide. Fold lengthwise and machine stitch ⅜in from the fold. Pull them through with a small safety pin and press flat. These are attached after the waistband is finished (see paragraph on waistband fastening on opposite page).

Putting on the waistband

Cutting out the waistband

Use the fabric from the bottom of the skirt length and fold it in half, selvages together.

Lay the waistband pattern on the fold and pin, first making sure that the fabric is lying perfectly flat. If you find, as a result of the fitting, you need to add to the length, now is the time to do it. Mark the waistband with tailor's tacks and cut it out, adding the same seam allowance as on the skirt, that is ¾in. Cut the tailor's tacks to separate the layers.

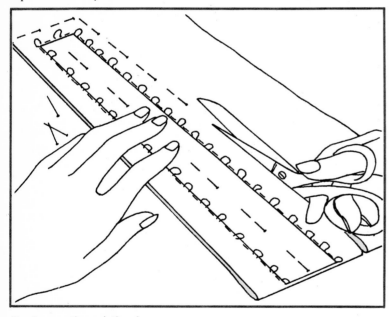

Cutting out the waistband

Stitching on the waistband

First measure the waist seam on the skirt and make a mark exactly halfway. This mark will be just in front of the right side seam, as all side seams in dressmaking are laid toward the back by 1in on either side. The length of the skirt waistline should be 1in more than the waistband. Mark the center of the waistband and pin into place on the skirt waist seam, matching center marks. Then lay the end of the waistband to the zipper opening in the seamline, back and front, making sure that the waistband is level with the seam edges at the opening.

The skirt waist seam is fuller than the closely fitting waistband because the skirt needs more ease immediately below the waistband to fit smoothly.

Distribute the fullness evenly between the center mark and both ends of the waistband, taking care not to make creases. Baste into position on the seamline. Remove all tailor's tacks. Stitch the waistband into place as close as possible to the basting line.

Mark the center of the belting, and lay it along the upper seam marks on the right side of the waistband. Baste firmly and stitch. The belting may be a little tighter than the fabric waistband. This happens through the natural spread of the fabric and will disappear when the stiffening has been turned under. Do not tighten the fabric waistband, as this could make the finished waistband buckle.

Remove all the basting, trim the waist seam on the skirt to ⅜in, as the double layer would be too thick, and press the seam into the waistband on the wrong side.

Turn under the seam edges on the front and back of the waistband even with the zipper opening.

Fold over the belting and pin.

Pin and baste the belting to the waist seam and sew by hand.

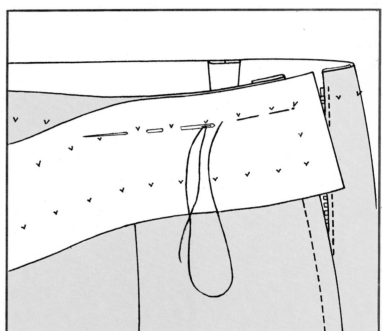

Basting the waistband into position

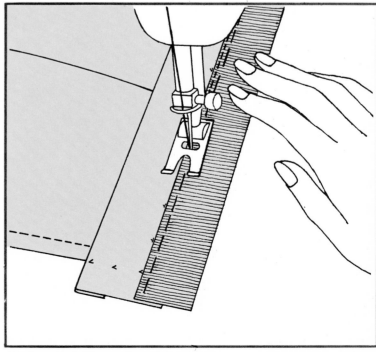

Stitching the belting to the waistband

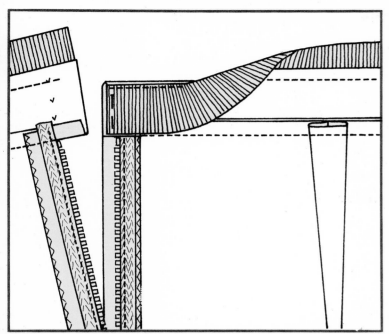
Folding over the belting and pinning

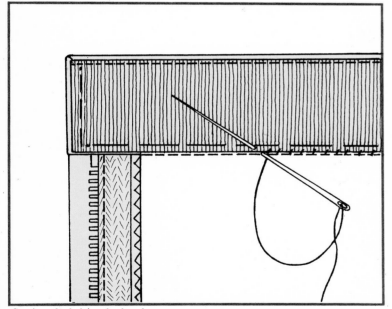
Sewing the belting by hand

Waistband fastening

Sew two hooks and eyes on the inside of the waistband, one at the top and the other just above the waist seam. Sew the eyes on the back edge, and hooks on the front. The loop of the eye should come over the edge $\frac{1}{16}$in. Hand sew over the sides of the loop and through each ring separately. Set the hooks back $\frac{3}{16}$in. Sew under the hook, over the double wire, and then through each ring separately. The hooks and eyes are sewn on in this way to prevent the skirt gaping when the give in the hand sewing makes them move toward each other slightly.

If you are using flat skirt hangers, now is the time to fit them lengthwise to the inside of the waistband. Do not loop them. Turn hangers under $\frac{1}{2}$in at each end, pin one on the back, just beyond the opening, and one on the front, beyond the halfway mark. To test their position, put the skirt on a clothes hanger. If the waistband droops, adjust the front skirt hanger until the waistband is level. Sew on securely by hand.

Turning up the hem

First pin up the hem along the line of tailor's tacks to check that the length is correct and that the hem is straight. If you have to level the hem or alter the length, ask someone to help you.

Before taking out the pins, trace along the crease of the corrected length with long basting stitches. Take out the old tailor's tacks. Before sewing the hem, make sure that the depth is even all around—measure this carefully and cut off any surplus.

Machine finish the edge with zigzag stitch, or overcast by hand, making sure you do not stretch the full sides.

Pin up the hem to the new line from the inside and baste about $\frac{1}{2}$in from fold edge. When pinning up a hem, always lay it on a table and insert pins toward the hem at right angles to it. This allows you to distribute any fullness evenly and prevents a twist on the finished hem.

Press the hem lightly with a cloth before sewing, remembering to press out the impressions left by the edge. Baste again about $\frac{1}{2}$in from the top edge, to hold the hem in place for hand sewing. Take the full depth of the hem into your hand and, without creasing it, turn under $\frac{1}{4}$in of the upper edge with your thumb. Sew invisibly behind the hem, taking up very little thread from the skirt and a good, deep thread from the hem.

Don't pull the stitches tight, as this will show through to the outside. Leave a little loop about every four or five stitches, which will ease itself into the other stitches. (This is a useful couture tip.) Always secure the ends of your stitches on the hem, never on the outside fabric.

Remove all the basting, and press the hem for the last time. Do not leave the skirt over an ironing board after pressing, as this would make little puckers on the outside of the hem. Lay it smoothly on a flat surface.

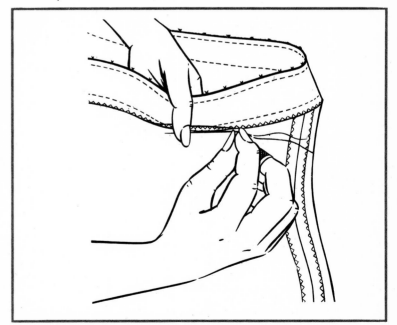
Hand sewing the skirt hem

Pressing for finishing

Pressing gives the final touch to any garment. Turn the skirt inside out and make sure you have removed all the basting stitches. Always use a cloth (damp or dry, depending on your fabric) and press the waistband firmly into place, still keeping the skirt flat. Then pull the skirt over the ironing board and press everywhere, except along the hem.

Chapter 14

Fine finishes

So far in Golden Hands only one method has been given for finishing the waist seam of a skirt, but there are many other ways of doing this. Each method is designed to do a specific job, so that once you know how to use the various finishes, you will be able to adapt them to your personal needs. Some fabrics dictate the way in which they must be finished, but the waistbands described here can be used successfully on all the fabrics suggested for skirts in Skirtmaking chapter 10, and are the most commonly used.

The waistband with enclosed stiffening

First, make a paper pattern for the waistband.

To work out how long to cut the waistband, measure your waist and add 2in for wrap.

The stiffening, which can be either belting or grosgrain ribbon, should be 1in wide, and the waistband must be twice as wide as the stiffening, plus $\frac{1}{4}$in. The $\frac{1}{4}$in is taken up when the waistband is turned over the top of the stiffening.

So, for a size 26in waist, the pattern will be 28in by 2$\frac{1}{4}$in.

Don't add ease to the waistband unless you like it loose.

Lay the pattern on single fabric. If you use a strip of fabric from the side of the skirt layout, check the grain lines. In many fabrics the fact that the grain on the waistband runs in a different direction from the skirt does not matter, but if the fabric you are using has a marked grain, it is a point to watch.

Pin the pattern onto the fabric and mark around it with long, flat basting stitches.

Add $\frac{3}{4}$in seam allowance all around and cut out.

How to mark out the fabric waistband

WRAP	BACK	FRONT

Basting and stitching

The wrap of a waistband always goes on the back of the skirt and tucks under the front fastening, to line up with the side seam. With the right side of the fabric facing you, mark off 2in from the left seamline and then mark the center between this point and the right seamline. With right sides facing, raw edges even, place the waistband to the skirt and pin, letting the wrap extend over the opening. Baste and sew in place.

Cut the belting or other stiffening exactly to the length of the waistband pattern, that is, with wrap but without seam allowance. Again, mark off 2in from the left and find the center of the rest. Pin and baste the belting over the seam allowance of waistband and skirt with the bottom edge of the stiffening just meeting stitching line. Stitch in position along edge of stiffening.

Fold seam allowance over the stiffening at each end, making the front edge even with the zipper opening, and baste. Fold waistband over the stiffening and turn under the seam allowance along the lower edge on the inside of the skirt. Pin and baste to skirt along the stitching line. Hand sew into position with firm stitches and slip stitch turned-in ends to close. Remove basting.

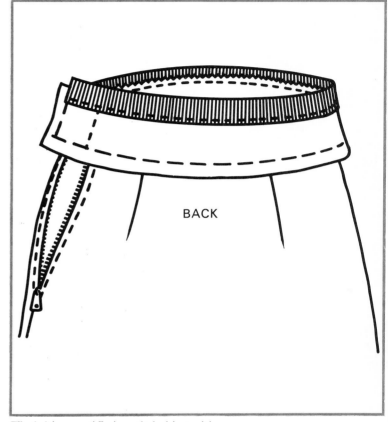

The belting or stiffening stitched in position

Attaching hooks and eyes

The hook and eye fastening for this type of waistband is slightly different from the one used for the flared skirt.

Using two hooks and one eye, first sew one of the hooks to the front edge of the waistband, about $\frac{1}{4}$in from the end, and make a bar by hand on the back of the waistband, even with the zipper opening, as shown on the opposite page.

When the zipper is closed, with the wrap tucked underneath, the waistband will fasten in line with the side seam.

How to make a bar

The bar sewn by hand goes across the center of the back of the waistband, in line with the hook, and is sewn from the top toward the bottom.

Thread a needle with strong machine twist to match the skirt, pull it double and make a knot at the end. Insert the needle from the back and return it into the fabric about $\frac{1}{2}$in farther down, placing the tip of your thumbnail under the thread as you pull it through to prevent it from becoming too tight. This tack makes the foundation of the bar.

Now return the needle to the top of the tack and repeat the stitch four times, being careful not to pull the thread tight at the back. Then, before you make the buttonhole stitch, work over the back threads and whip them firmly down to the fabric to prevent the bar from stretching.

Buttonhole stitch over the tacks, as shown in the photograph, keeping the tip of your thumbnail under the threads to avoid

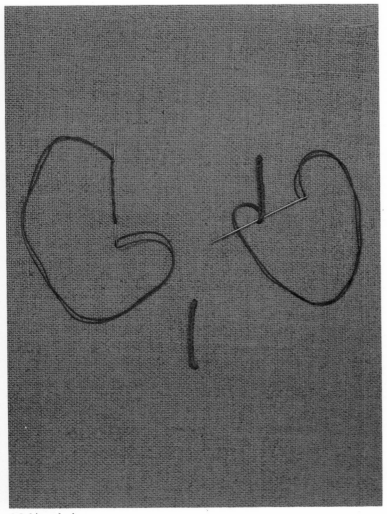

Making the bar

catching the fabric in the stitches. Make the stitches as close together as possible without overlapping them, and fasten them off at the back when you have completed the bar. If the knot at the back of your work is unsightly, cut it off now.

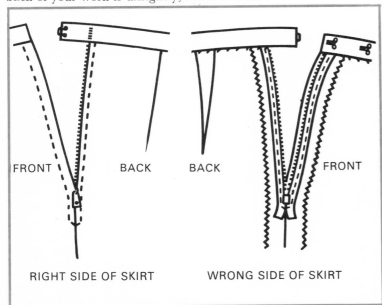

The finished waistband with correct setting for the hooks, eyes, and bar

Finishing the fastening

Sew the eye to the edge of the wrap, on top of the waistband and not underneath it, leaving the eye extending as shown.

To find the correct position for the second hook, close the zipper and the hook and bar, and place the second hook on the inside of the front waistband $\frac{1}{8}$in farther in from the eye.

When you sew the hooks, eye and bar into position, make sure that the stitch catches through to the stiffening for extra hold, but do not stitch through to the outside. It is important not to place the second hook 2in from the front edge of the waistband (the length of the wrap) because, depending on the thickness of the fabric, this measurement sometimes alters slightly and the fastening might stretch. The strain would then break the hand-made bar, which only holds the top of the waistband down.

Hangers for this waistband can be either one of the types described in Skirtmaking chapter 13.

The soft waistband

So far the two most popular methods of making a stiff waistband have been covered, but you may prefer one without stiffening which is soft and less constricting.

This type of waistband should not be deeper than 1in, because it would turn over at the top. And, for extra support, the waist seam allowance on the skirt must be the same as the width of the waistband, or else it will wrinkle. It will also wrinkle if it is too tight, so the soft waistband must fit around you less snugly than the stiff waistband.

Using the previously prepared pattern, add 1in ease and work exactly as before, leaving out the stiffening.

The hidden waistband

The waistbands made so far are visible and are fixed to the top of the skirt. This type of waistband is hidden, and the best materials to use are either belting or stiff grosgrain ribbon.

Since this waistband is not supported by fabric, it is advisable to use a wider belting than you have used for the others. The best width to work on is $1\frac{1}{2}$in.

This type of waistband must be curved and fit to the body.

To obtain the curve

Don't pleat the belting, since this only results in an unsightly kink in the waist seam, but use the following method:

Cut the belting to the length you require for your waist measurement plus 5in. Lay it flat on an ironing board and press over the belting with a hot iron and damp cloth. Before the steam

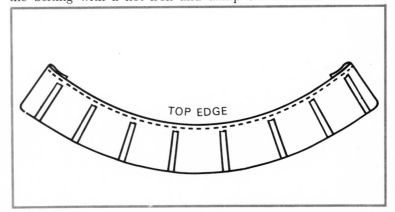

The belting, correctly curved, and ready to use

has dried remove the cloth and gently pull the lower edge of the belting into a curve. Dry off the dampness on the belting with a hot iron, fixing the shape and pressing in the fullness around the top edge. To prevent this edge from stretching when you attach it to the skirt, run a stay stitch through it on the sewing machine, feeding it into the machine from the front and letting it run out behind the needle, without pulling it.

Now measure the inner curve to the length that you need for your waist size. Add 1in at each end, and cut off the rest. Turn under each end $\frac{1}{2}$in, then fit the band to your waist. It should lie around your body closely but not tightly.

Basting and stitching to the skirt

Take out the marking for the original seam allowance of $\frac{3}{4}$in on the skirt waist seam, and mark a new line $\frac{3}{8}$in from the top edge. This is necessary because, as you turn the waistband under, it will take up some of the length. This would make your fitting incorrect. Following the sketch, lay the short, inner curve of the belting to the inside of the new waist seam line and stitch into position close to the edge of the belting.

Cut a length of straight seam binding in a matching color, $\frac{1}{2}$in shorter than the top edge of the belting, and lay it over the raw

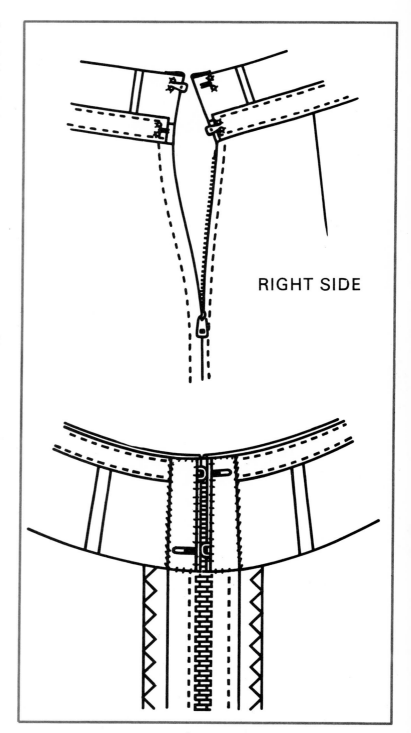

RIGHT SIDE

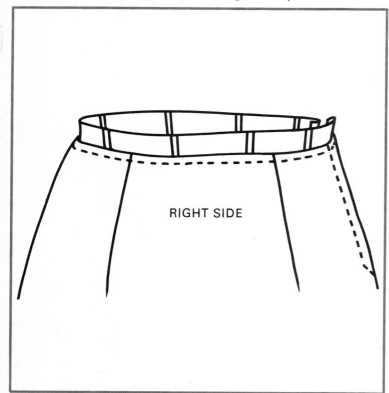

RIGHT SIDE

The curved belting stitched to the inside of the waist seam

waist edge on the right side of the skirt and the belting, leaving $\frac{1}{4}$in at each end uncovered.

The lower edge of the seam binding must cover the row of stitches. Baste and stitch into position along both edges of the seam binding.

Hooks and eyes

To fasten this waistband, use hooks and eyes on the edges of the waistband opening and place a hook to an eye and an eye to a hook. Since the waistband must not fit tightly into the waist, this method will insure that they cannot come undone. They must be sewn to what is now the outside of the waistband, which is later tucked in, otherwise the top hook could not be done up when the skirt is finished.

Above: the hook and eye setting for the hidden waistband with seam binding covering the raw edges
Below: hidden waistband fastening with finished edges, seen from inside

Now turn the belting and seam binding to the inside of the skirt and baste along the upper edge. To finish off the edges, cut two strips of seam binding $2\frac{1}{2}$in long. Turn under $\frac{1}{2}$in at each end and sew them over the edges of the waistband, covering the raw edges at the top, and passing them under the hook-bars as shown in the diagram. Slip stitch in place all around. If the skirt fabric is heavy, you may find it an advantage to machine stitch along the folded edge at the top of the skirt, to prevent the waistband from working up over the top. On normal skirt-weight fabric, though, it should be enough to attach the bottom edge of the belting in a few places, such as the seams and darts, with a light holding stitch.

Hangers

If you want to make skirt hangers for this waistband, use the flat type, as described in Skirtmaking chapter 13. Ideally, this waist finish should hang on a spring-loaded skirt hanger; otherwise the skirt may pull out of shape.

Zipper in a straight seam

Although the overlap type of zipper opening (the one used on the simple flared skirt) is the most commonly used in side seams on skirts, you may wish to put a zipper into the center back or center front seam of a skirt. In this case, the zipper will have to be stitched in so that the stitching lines are equal on both sides.

Prepare the opening by basting the seams together and pressing them carefully, as for the side seams.

Remove the basting. Open the zipper to the bottom, and lay it in the skirt opening so that the seam edges just cover the zipper teeth on both sides. Baste the zipper into position.

To make sure that the seams lie perfectly flat and don't push each other up, close the zipper before you machine stitch it in.

If the seams do push up, take the seam edges back a fraction until they lie flat, still keeping the zipper completely hidden. Start stitching about ⅜in from the seam edge on one side and stitch down until you are even with the zipper end. To make the miter at the end, turn the work and stitch toward the seam. Pivot the work on the needle and return on the other side in the same way.

This method of inserting a zipper is most successful when it's used on a straight seam. But for a curved seam, the overlap on one side is safer, since the equal distance of the stitching line on both sides —down into and then up into the grain, over the rigid tape of the zipper—would tend to drag the seam and make it twist.

Since skirt zippers are always of the heavier variety, it is not advisable to insert them by hand, except in very fine fabrics where you would use a dress-weight zipper. This is covered in a later chapter.

A word about the invisible zipper

To insert this type, you must have the right zipper foot for your sewing machine to enable you to put in the zipper properly. Carefully follow instructions to get the correct finish. Without the correct foot the result will not be satisfactory.

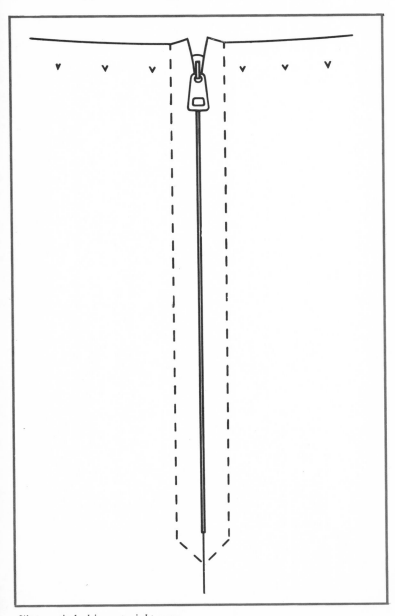

Zipper stitched in a straight seam

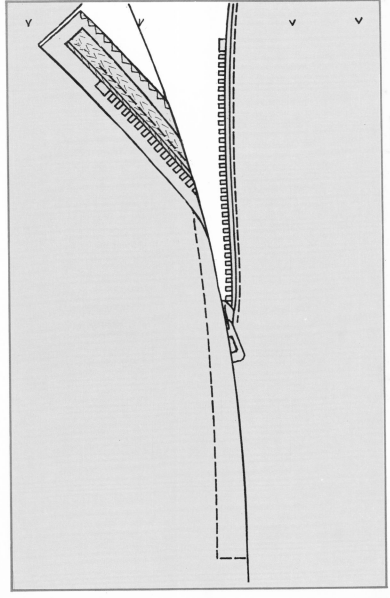

Zipper in a curved seam

Chapter 15

Focus on hems

Making a hem is not just a method of tidying up to complete a garment. The length of a skirt is often such a fashion point that the eye is immediately drawn to the hem. Stitches which show on the right side, or an uneven length, are instant give-aways, so that a perfect hemline is essential if your garment is to have a professional look. Each type of hem has a definite function and gives the final hold to the outline. Some garments need extra weight at the hem to make the skirt hang properly, so the depth of the hem has to be considered. Garments made from extra-fine fabric, such as chiffon or voile, need a finely rolled hem for a soft, light, wispy look. Special hems like these come in later chapters.

The basic dress and skirt are finished with a conventional hem which is correct for the firm fabric used. However, it is the fabric, along with the cut of the garment, which dictates the method to be used for finishing the hem, and there are many different techniques for doing this.

Important rules for finishing hems

Here are some basic rules which must be followed whenever you are making a hem.

The most important point is to pin it up in the right way, for this is where you either make or mar your hem.

Always pin at right angles to the hem, however wide or narrow it is; never slant the pins or place them parallel to the edge of the hem. This could cause a shift in the layers of fabric you are pinning together and result in a twist in the finished hem which will spoil the hang of the garment as well as look ugly.

Always work with the hem lying flat on a table so that the weight of the garment is supported. By working in this way you will be able to see that the folded edge of the hem is straight. Or, if you are working with a curved hem, you will be able to see that the fullness is evenly distributed and directed straight toward the raw edge. If the fullness is twisted or forced to one side, it will make a kink in the folded edge and the hem will end up with a series of points in it.

Always baste the hem about $\frac{1}{2}$in from the lower edge. Make stitches between $\frac{1}{2}$in and 1in long, depending on the fabric and the length which holds it in position best. Never pull the stitches tight.

Always give the hem a light pressing (steam press only if the fabric requires it) and shrink in any fullness around the raw edge. Be careful not to press too hard over the basting stitches, as they might leave impressions in the cloth which are difficult to remove. Always press with the hem lying flat on the ironing board, making sure that the garment is supported over the back of a chair so that it cannot drag away from the iron. Never pull the skirt over the ironing board, as it can pull out of shape when warm.

Always press the hem on the wrong side—it should never be necessary to press it on the right side.

▼ *The wrong way and the right way to pin up a hem. Always place pins at right angles to the hem, never horizontally as in the top picture*

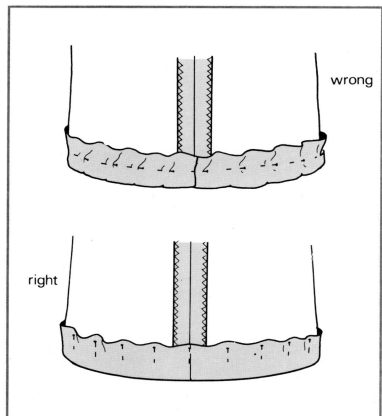

The flared hem

When you are faced with a hem which is curved and you have too much fullness to shrink, or you are using a fabric which will not shrink at all, make the hem as narrow as possible, sometimes as narrow as half the width of the normal hem allowance.

Then, using a small running stitch, gather in the fullness along the raw edge and draw it up to fit the skirt. Fasten off the stitches well so that the hem will not stretch again.

To finish off the raw edge on this type of hem, don't use the machine zigzag but overcast by hand. After a final pressing over the sewn edge, sew the hem in place using the invisible hemming method shown in Skirtmaking chapter 13, p.53.

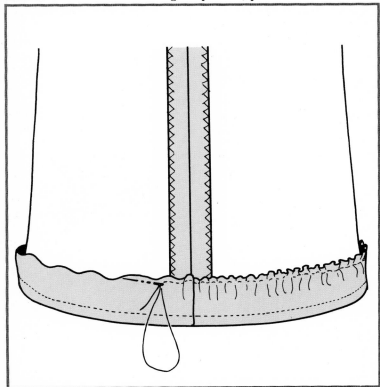

▲ *Gather the fullness on a flared hem with small running stitches*

The hem with a straight folded edge

When the hem is straight and you are using a lightweight fabric, simply turn under the raw edge $\frac{1}{2}$in and use a slip stitch to sew it to the skirt. This method applies mainly to fine cotton fabric or to special hems where extra weight is needed to help the shape of the skirt. It is a good precaution to press the folded edge first, though you must be very careful when doing this since it is possible to stretch a straight edge under heat and pressure.

The pleated skirt hem

When a hem has to endure a lot of hard pressing, as on pleated skirts, it is important to make the hem finish as flat as possible. You can never completely avoid leaving an impression with hard pressing, but by making the hem flat the marking will be less obvious. In this case, use a catch stitch. This means you do not need to overcast the raw edge except when the fabric frays a lot, and the hem will be as flat as you can make it.

The hem in thick fabrics

When you are working with a heavy tweed or other thick fabric, overcasting is not quite enough to finish off the raw edge of the hem — it should be bound. You can buy bias binding already cut and turned under which is ideal for this purpose, but make

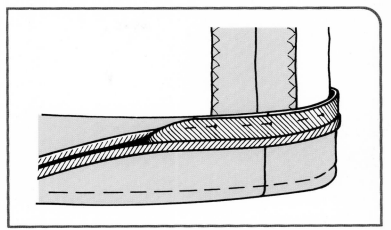

▲ *How to pin bias binding to the raw hem edge when using a thick fabric*

sure you buy rayon bias binding, as cotton bias binding is usually too stiff.

Prepare the hem in the usual way. Then take the bias binding, unfold one edge and pin and baste it to the outer edge of the hem, with the raw edges even. Stitch the binding to the hem, using a slightly longer machine stitch than you normally use for the seams. Fold the other edge of the bias binding over the hem edge and sew into position along the back of the hem with a running stitch. Press the bound edge before you begin sewing the hem to the skirt.

Although the stitches already covered are those most commonly used for hems, you often need a stronger stitch for heavy fabrics, because the friction between the two layers of fabric is greater. Therefore, to make the hem secure and also to allow for movement, use an invisible catch stitch and sew with a slightly stronger thread.

To do this, turn the hem edge back as for the hem on the flared skirt and work the catch stitch, catching the material from the garment and the hem each time.

In some fabrics you may find that the bound edge is too thick to turn back easily. Therefore, turn the whole of the hem under and catch stitch along the crease between the garment and the bound edge, as shown.

When you have finished and taken out all the basting threads, you will see how you can move the hem without it being loose or dropping out of line.

▼ *How to work catch stitch under a bound hem edge*

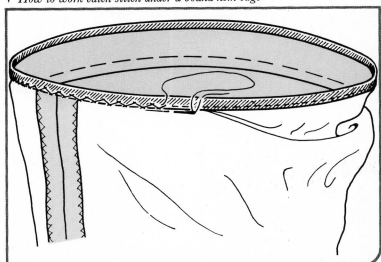

Chapter 16

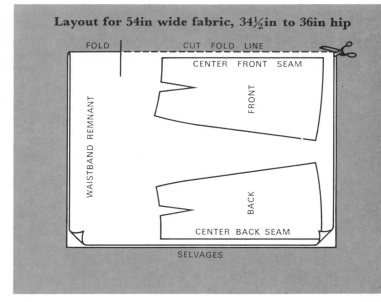

One pattern – many skirts

Knee-length, midi or long, gored or dirndl–which is right for you? Here you see how easy it is to experiment by altering the basic skirt pattern from Skirtmaking chapter 10. It is transformed into a four-gore skirt in a choice of lengths, and a dirndl. There is a pleated variation in the next chapter. Once you have mastered these styles, you can try adapting the pattern even more yourself.

The four-gore skirt

The stages for making this skirt are the same as for the simple flared skirt in Skirtmaking chapters 10-13, except that you allow for, and stitch, a center front and center back seam.

Fabric requirements

54in width—for sizes $34\frac{1}{2}$ to 42in hip, your skirt length plus 8 inches. For size 44in hip, allow $\frac{1}{4}$yd extra.

36in width—for all sizes ($34\frac{1}{2}$ to 44in hip), twice your skirt length plus 11 inches.

Remember to buy a 7in skirt zipper and matching thread; also, hooks and eyes, seam binding and belting or stiffening for the waistband.

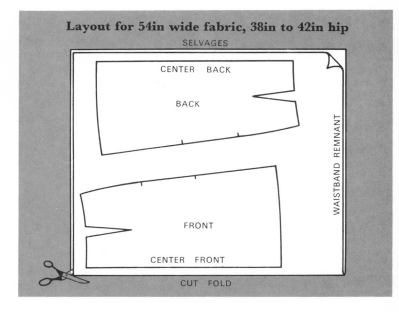

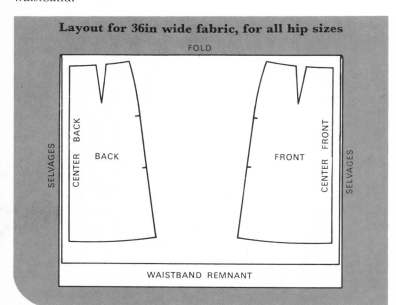

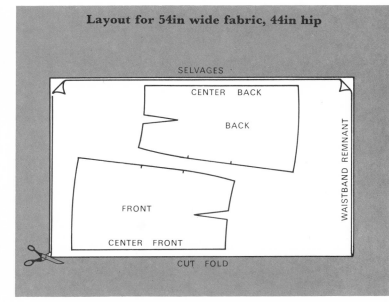

Layout and cutting

Using the basic flared skirt pattern from Skirtmaking chapter 10, select the correct layout for your size and fabric width (see diagrams opposite). Remember that the center front and center back seams should always be cut on the straight grain of the fabric.

Before you cut out the skirt, cut the fold to the length of the paper pattern. This will help you to remember to leave an allowance for the center front seam when you are cutting out the pattern pieces.

Making the skirt

Mark around the pattern with tailor's tacks. Add $\frac{3}{4}$in seam and $2\frac{1}{2}$in hem allowances all around. Then follow the basting, fitting, stitching and finishing instructions given for the simple flared skirt, with the addition of a center front and center back seam.

Topstitching

If you want to give the center front and center back seams added importance, topstitch them before you put on the waistband and sew up the hem. Using a slightly thicker machine twist to make the stitches stand out from the fabric, run a parallel row of stitching $\frac{3}{8}$in from the seam, on each side of it. You can also work topstitching by hand, using a $\frac{1}{4}$in running stitch.

Three different looks from the basic flared skirt pattern. Just adapt the length and choose a suitable fabric for any occasion ▶

The dirndl skirt

There isn't an easier skirt to make than the gathered dirndl. You can make it from a strip of fabric about 1¼ times your hip measurement or, if the fabric is fine enough, you can use more for greater fullness. But to take the guesswork out of making this skirt, use the pattern for the basic flared skirt given in Skirtmaking chapter 10 as a guide.

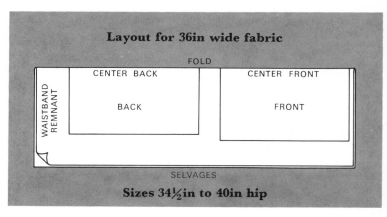

Fabric requirements
54in width—for all sizes (34½ to 44in hip), your skirt length plus 7 inches.
36in width—for all sizes (34½ to 44in hip), twice your skirt length plus 11 inches.
N.B. This style is only flattering to sizes over 38in hip if the waist is small and neat.
You will also need a 7in zipper, ½in wide straight seam binding and matching thread. Remember to buy hooks and eyes and belting or stiffening, if necessary, for the waistband.

How to prepare the pattern
Preparing the pattern is simple. To obtain the fullness required for the gathers, just lay the basic pattern on a sheet of paper and square it off as the diagram opposite shows.
Remove the basic pattern from the paper and mark the skirt sections, back and front.

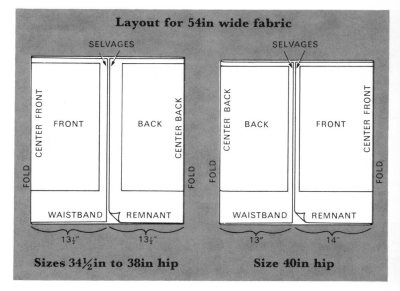

Layout and cutting
After selecting the correct layout for your size and fabric width, place the squared-off pattern pieces on the fold of the fabric as indicated in the diagrams on this page, mark around them and mark the center lines on the skirt.
Cut out the fabric, remembering to add ¾in seam allowances and 2½in hem allowances.

Making the skirt
Stitch the side seams and insert the zipper.
Make a row of stitches for gathering the waist on each side of the waist seam, ¼in apart, on the right side of your skirt. It is important to stitch on the right side of the fabric because you must always pull up gathers from the wrong side.
When stitching the gathering stitches, use the longest stitch setting on the sewing machine and slacken off the upper tension. This will make it easier for you to draw the threads of the lower stitches into gathers later.

The waist stay
Before you gather the waistline of the skirt, first prepare a stay tape or a waist guide.
Cut a length of ½in seam binding the length of your waist plus 1in for ease.
Mark this strip by measuring against the original basic pattern as follows. Starting with the left end of the tape, measure off the back section of the basic pattern from side seam to center (excluding the width of the darts). Mark this measurement on the tape with basting thread. This mark will be the center back. From this mark, measure off the same amount again to find the position of the opposite side seam.

Then, using the front section of the basic pattern and starting from the opposite end of the tape, measure and mark from side seam to the center front and from the center front to side seam as before.
When you have finished marking the tape, pin it to the side seam and center marks on the skirt.

Preparing the waist seam for the waistband
Pull up the gathers by picking up the thread ends of the two rows of machine stitches and gently ease the fullness into even gathers along the waistline between the pins.
Pin on the seam binding, placing the pins at right angles to the waistline, then baste and stitch the tape to the skirt (see diagram at top of opposite page).

Notes on stitching gathers
When you are stitching gathers to a straight piece of fabric, always make sure the gathers are uppermost. If you leave them out of sight, under the tape or other straight fabric, you'll find there is a tendency for them to get caught up into the seam.
As you are not able to hold them out of the way of the machine needle, the gathers are likely to tilt and bunch, and the finished result will be bulky and uneven.
If, sometimes, you cannot avoid leaving gathers out of sight or under the work, make a row of basting stitches on each side of the seamline, to prevent them from moving.
Now that you've prepared the waist seam, you are ready to stitch on the waistband.

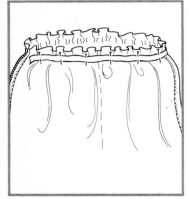 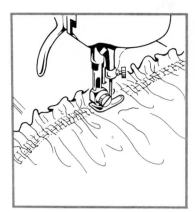

▲ *Waist stay pinned into position* ▲ *Stitching gathers over waist stay*
▼ *How to prepare the pattern for the dirndl by adapting the basic skirt*

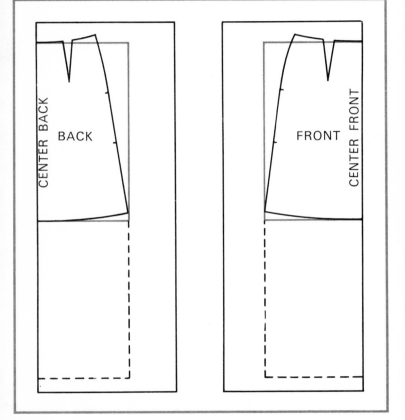

Versatile waistbands

You can use any of the waist finishes (except the invisible waistband) given in Skirtmaking chapters 13 and 14 for the dirndl skirt because the waistbands are attached by using center markings. This means that, regardless of the position of the seams in relation to the waistband, provided you always make the center marking on the skirt opposite the opening and match this to the center marking on the waistband, you can put the zipper where you like, in the side seam, the center back, or center front seam.

Evening dirndl

The dirndl is an ideal style to make up as a long evening skirt and preparing the pattern is, again, very simple. Measure the side length from waist to floor. When doing so, be sure to put on the shoes you will be wearing with the finished skirt, because a high heel can take up as much as 3 or 4 inches. Then, all you need to do is to add the extra length to the pattern by extending it from the hem, indicated by the dotted lines in the diagram above.

Chapter 17

Knife-pleated skirt

This smart knife-pleated skirt, which flatters any figure, is a variation of the basic skirt pattern.

Suitable fabrics

The fabric you use for a pleated skirt should be crease-resistant, but it should also be capable of taking a sharp crease under pressure and steam. Worsted woolens are particularly suitable; so are some acrylic fibers such as Orlon; polyester fibers such as Dacron and Trevira; linens, firmly woven wool tweeds and a number of mixed fiber fabrics.

Before buying any fabric, it's a good idea to ask if it will pleat well.

Fabric requirements

54in width—for all sizes (34½ to 44in hip), twice the skirt length plus 11 inches.

36in width—for all sizes (34½ to 44in hip), four times the skirt length plus 21 inches.

You will also need a 7in zipper and matching thread. Remember to buy hooks and eyes, seam binding and belting or other stiffening if you need them for the waistband.

Adapting the basic pattern

To begin, make a copy of the flared skirt pattern in Skirtmaking chapter 10 to use as the basic pattern, but do not cut out the darts—just mark them in pencil.

Using the yardstick, extend the balance marks on the front and back right across the pattern pieces, as illustrated. The extended balance marks become meeting marks for the

pleats to insure that they will lie flat and hang well when stitched and pressed.

To obtain the cutting line on the pattern, measure the distance from the center front and center back lines to the lowest point of the dart. Measure and mark off this distance all the way down to the hem, making a series of pencil marks parallel to the center back and center front.

Connect these marks with a yardstick, taking the line through the center of the darts right up to the waistline, and down to the hem.

Now mark the pattern sections on each side of the new cutting lines, as front, side front, back, and side back. This will help you to avoid putting the wrong pieces together when you lay out the pattern.

Cut out the pattern pieces along the cutting lines.

Knife-pleated skirt in Trevira ►
▼ *Front pattern, with cutting line*

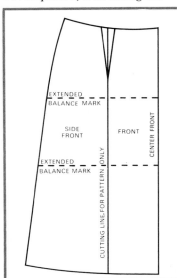

Layout for 54in wide fabric

Leave the fabric folded and lay it flat on the cutting table, allowing enough area to work on one complete section of the skirt at a time. Starting with the front section of the pattern, measure 2½in from the fold and pin a line parallel to the length of the pattern pieces. Lay the center front line of the pattern along the pin line and pin the pattern down onto the fabric.

Then, measure 5in from the cutting line of the front section and mark the distance in the same way to the length of the pattern piece with a pin line.

Lay the cutting line of the side front section of the pattern along this pin line, securing the section with one or two pins so that it cannot move. Using the yardstick, lay it along the line of extended balance marks and make sure they go straight across both front and side front pattern pieces.

Now lay out the back skirt sections in the same way.

Make whatever adjustments are necessary to insure that the pattern sections line up correctly, and then pin them down securely onto the fabric.

Layout for 36in wide fabric

Open up the fabric to the full width and length on the cutting table. Fold in half so that the raw edges meet as shown in the layout diagram.

A point to watch—if you have bought a fabric with a nap, or a one-way design (this means the surface interest on the fabric goes in one direction, up or down), you must cut the length in half across the width, turn one layer and lay it in such a way that the surface interest runs in the same direction.

Before cutting, make sure the right sides of the cloth are facing each other—many a fine fabric has been spoiled by laying it out carelessly. Otherwise you will find after cutting that you have two right sides or two left sides and cannot match them up to make a whole garment.

When you lay out the front and back pattern sections, you must allow an extra ¾in for a seam on the fabric before you measure out the center line pleats. This is because the center front and center back are now on a selvage and not a fold as in the 54in width. Having done this, you can proceed in exactly the same way as described for the 54in layout.

To prepare for cutting

Now it is time to cut out the darts along the pencil lines (do not cut the fabric). Make sure that you curve them into the cutting line at the ends—don't let them finish on a sharp corner as this will make the pleat seam poke out at the end of the dart.

Tailor's tack around all the pattern pieces, remembering the balance marks on the pleat lines as well as on the side seams.

Mark out a ¾in seam allowance along the side seams and a 2½in hem allowance.

When marking and cutting the seam allowance at the waist edge, more than the usual ¾in is needed. Therefore, do not follow the curve of the waistline, but take the normal seam allowance at the side seam and waistline point and then cut straight across to the center on both back and front. This gives you an extra ¾in seam allowance at the deepest point of the curve.

You will see when you have pleated the skirt that because of the curves of the side darts and waistline, extra seam allowance is needed to catch the right pleat at the front and left pleat at the back into the waistband.

Mark the normal waistline of the pattern on the fabric and leave the trimming of any excess seam allowance until after the skirt sections have been pleated.

After you have removed the pattern pieces, connect the balance marks with long lines of basting stitches.

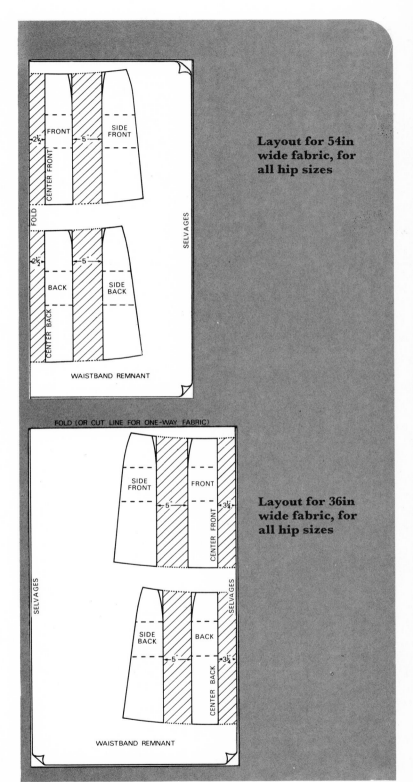

Layout for 54in wide fabric, for all hip sizes

Layout for 36in wide fabric, for all hip sizes

Pleating the skirt with soft pleats

Before you separate the layers of the skirt sections, you must first decide which way you are going to pleat the skirt.

One way is to lay the pleat lines together, baste them all the way down and then stitch them like a seam as far as the hipline, about 7in from the waist, and press the pleat to one side from the inside of the skirt. This sort of pleating will give the skirt a soft look. If you are going to do it this way, you'll have to mark a fold line between the pleat lines of the center front and side front sections, as shown in the illustration.

Pleating the skirt with tailored pleats

If you prefer a crisp, tailored look, lay the pleats from right to left on the outside of the skirt, matching the balance marks and basting them down securely along the edge.

Press them very lightly into position and topstitch about $\frac{1}{16}$in in from the edge, as far as the hipline.

Don't press the pleats in very sharply at this stage, but make up the skirt first.

When making the waistband, any of the methods in Dressmaking chapters 13 and 14 are suitable.

Special notes for finishing the pleated skirt

1. When you fit the skirt, do so with the pleats basted together. Turn back to the skirt fitting guide in Skirtmaking chapter 12. When you have corrected the faults, fit the skirt again with the basting removed and pleats loose. They should hang straight and closed—not jutting forward or pulling open. If you see the pleats spreading, fan-like, toward the side seams, you will need to lift the skirt and pleats into the waist, until the pleats hang straight. If you see one pleat hanging badly, then this will need to be pulled up from the inside.

2. Before you stitch on the waistband, make sure the pleats are caught flat and firmly into the seam, then trim seam allowance.

3. If you've cut the skirt with a center front seam, refer to the side seam in the child's pleated skirt in Skirtmaking chapter 21 for the hem finish. The easiest way to finish off the hem is to leave about two widths of the hem unstitched at the bottom of the seam in the pleat, turn up the hem, and then stitch through all layers to the bottom edge of the hem as shown below.

4. When turning up the hem, make hem at inner crease of the pleat about $\frac{1}{4}$in shorter, as below, to prevent pleats from showing.

5. Before you finally press in the pleats, make sure that you have removed all basting threads and tailor's tacks.

6. Sometimes pressing the thickness of pleats leaves impressions on the fabric which show on the right side. To remove these, carefully press under the pleats, on the wrong side.

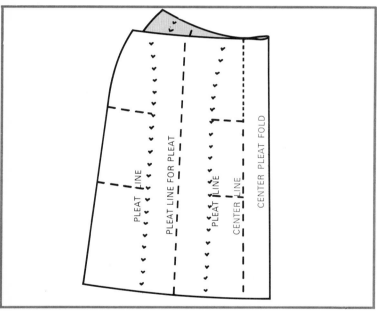

▲ *Pleating so that pleat lines meet on inside of skirt, making soft pleats*
▼ *Pleating from right to left on outside of skirt, making tailored pleats*

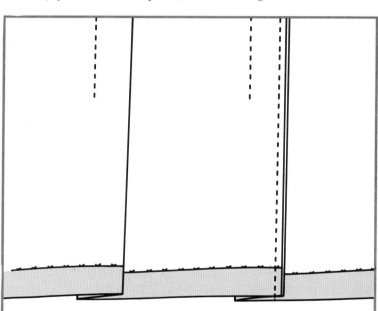

▲ *Hem finish for the seamed center pleat*
▼ *Finished hem for pleated skirt, showing raised inner points of pleats*

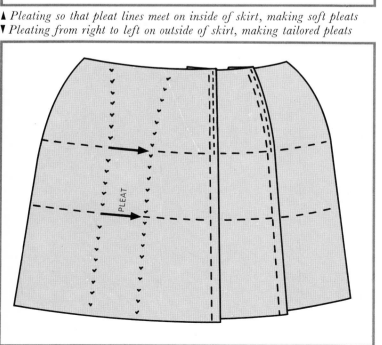

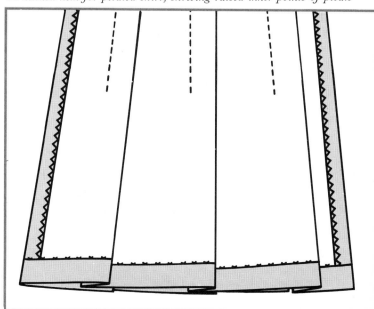

Chapter 18

The six-gore skirt

Variations of the basic patterns add versatility and personality to your wardrobe. Making the conversions increases your skill and knowledge of pattern making. In this chapter, the basic skirt pattern is converted to a six-gore, or paneled, version which can be made in three different styles. By adding a slight flare to the panel seams, the skirt takes on a young and lively swing—very flattering for a larger figure. Or, leave the panels straight, and make a beautifully tailored six-gore skirt. The third version with straight panels and a knife pleat on each side of the back panel provides ease of movement, making the skirt suitable for the golf course or the bowling alley. For all versions, use the pattern for the knife-pleated skirt in Skirtmaking chapter 17.

Six-gore with flared panels

Extending the pattern

Pin strips of paper 2 inches wide along the panel seam edges on all pattern pieces, as shown in diagram 1.
To make the flare, measure 1 inch out from the point where the hem and side seam meet. Using a yardstick, connect the hipline to this point to make the new panel seamline. Extend the hem to the new seamline.

Suitable fabrics

All the fabrics suggested for the basic skirt in Skirtmaking chapter 10 are suitable for the flared six-gore skirt.

Fabric requirements

These yardages are for a 23 inch skirt length.
54in wide fabric, without one way: $1\frac{3}{8}$ yards for hip sizes $34\frac{1}{2}$ to 38in; $1\frac{1}{2}$ yards for hip sizes 40 to 44in.
36in wide fabric, without one way: $1\frac{1}{4}$ yards for hip sizes $34\frac{1}{2}$ to 44in.
One way fabrics: Add about one extra skirt length to all the above yardages.
Extra length: If you want the skirt to be longer (or shorter), add (or subtract) twice the difference in length to (from) the above yardages on both 54in and 36in wide fabric.

Notions

☐ 7 inch skirt zipper
☐ Belt stiffening
☐ Matching thread

Cutting out

Choose the correct layout for your size and fabric width from page 69, and place the pattern pieces on the fabric as indicated. Add $\frac{3}{4}$ inch seam and $2\frac{1}{2}$ inch hem allowances and cut out the pattern pieces.

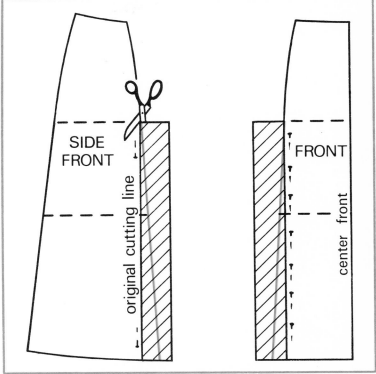

1. ▲ *Extending the panel seams to increase the flare*

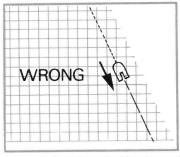

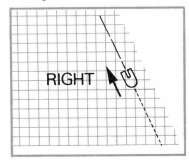

2. ▲ *Stitching into the bias (wrong), and* ▲ *stitching with the bias (right)*

Stitching the seams on the bias

Because the flare on the skirt has been increased, the seams now slant toward the bias. This is not a true bias as for the bias-cut skirt, since the seams do not run at a 45° angle to the straight of the grain (see diagram 2).
It is a good precaution to stitch such seams with the bias, i.e., from the hem upward. Stitching into the bias can make the top layer of fabric stretch, thereby gathering or dragging the under layer and making the seams hang badly.
Generally, seams should be stitched from the top of a garment downward, because there is often a little fullness in the fabric, caused by the finish or the weave, which cannot be detected until the two layers have been firmly joined by machine stitching. If the seams were stitched upward from the bottom, such fullness would be passed into the waistline, neck or armholes, seriously upsetting the fit of the garment.
Pressing out the fullness before stitching may seem the obvious answer, but not all fabrics benefit from being pressed first. If the weave is slightly uneven, the fabric can be distorted. Pressing before cutting should do no more than remove creases.

Fitting

Baste the side and panel seams. Try on the skirt and follow the fitting instructions for the basic skirt in Skirtmaking chapter 12.

Taking in at the waist. If you need to take in the waist, do not deepen the darts along the panels (i.e., the curved parts of the seams). Leave the panel seams as they are and make one small dart in each side front and side back piece, halfway between panel and side seams. If you take this fullness into the curve of the panel seams at the top, it can create the impression of a big stomach and high seat and the curve becomes too steep to form a good line.

Topstitching the panels

Topstitching the panels gives the seams a little extra support and emphasizes the flare at the hem. You will see from diagram 4 just how effective the topstitched panels look.

If you are topstitching the panel seams they must be prepared. Trim the seam allowances on the front and back panels to $\frac{1}{4}$ inch as shown, but do not trim the seam allowance on the side back and side front sections. Fold the untrimmed allowance over the trimmed one, and baste flat into position.

With the right side of the skirt uppermost, run a row of machine stitches on the panels only, about $\frac{1}{2}$ to $\frac{3}{4}$ inch from the seam. This will look best if you use a slightly heavier machine twist and a larger stitch setting.

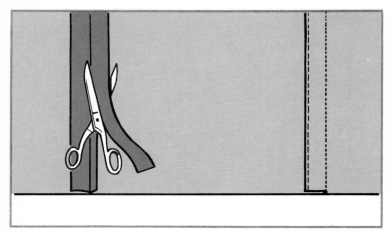

▲ **3.** *Trimming the panel seams*   ▼ **4.** *The topstitched panel seams*

Layout on 36in wide fabric without one way for all hip sizes ($34\frac{1}{2}$ to 44in)

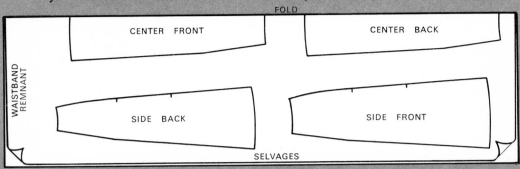

Layout on 54in wide fabric without one way for hip sizes $34\frac{1}{2}$ to 38in

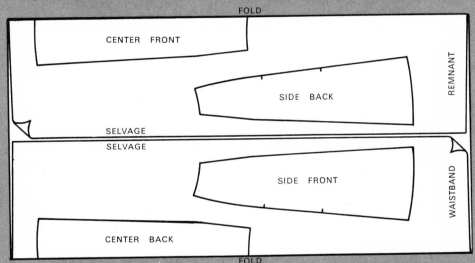

Layout on 54in wide fabric without one way for hip sizes 40 to 44in

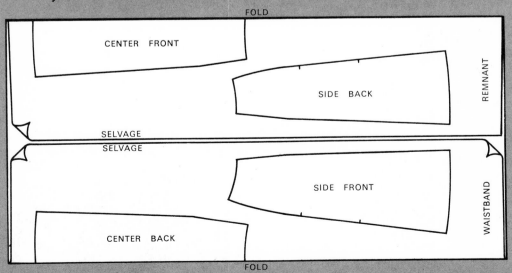

Chapter 19

The bias-cut skirt

You will have noticed that the use of the basic skirt pattern from Skirtmaking chapter 10 is wide and unlimited. In this chapter you will see what happens when you turn the pattern grain lines by 45 degrees and cut the skirt on the cross or bias of the fabric. If you prefer a little extra flare at the hem, this chapter will tell you how to add it. Fabrics for bias-cut skirts have to be chosen carefully—and you will find that plaids and checks will give you interesting effects.

Making the pattern for the bias-cut skirt

It is easier to use complete back and front pattern pieces when laying out the bias-cut skirt. Fold two pieces of paper in half, large enough to accommodate each basic pattern piece. Lay the back and front pieces on the paper with the center lines on the folded edges. Pin down the pattern pieces securely. Draw around the outlines and remove the pattern.

If you are going to add extra length to the pattern, do so now. Unless you want to increase the flare, cut out the new pattern. When it is unfolded, you will have a complete front and back section for the skirt.

Adding 4 inches to the basic flare

Extend the point at which the hem and side seam meet outward by 1 inch. Using a yardstick connect the hipline to this point and draw a line for the new side seam. Then extend the hemline to meet it. Cut out the pattern along the new lines and unfold it.

Marking the grain lines for the bias-cut skirt

To make sure that you place the pattern correctly on the fabric when cutting, mark the grain lines as follows:

With the pattern pieces still folded, place a set square along the fold as shown in the diagram. The diagonal opposite the right angle is the grain line. Draw it on the pattern, then unfold the pattern and extend the line.

The new grain line becomes the straight of grain and the old grain line, which is also the center line, goes through the bias of the fabric. This insures that the skirt is cut on the true bias.

Suitable fabrics for bias cutting

When choosing fabrics for garments cut on the bias, you need to be a little more selective.

First decide on the effect you want to achieve.

If you want the bias-cut skirt to play its true role with a soft, clinging and figure-hugging effect, choose a soft crêpe.

If you are cutting on the bias for the effect it has on a pattern such as a check or plaid, you will have to be very careful when choosing the design. Stripes can also be cut on the cross, but are difficult to match in the seams on a narrow flare such as this.

When choosing plaids or checks, it is essential that you find a regular check, that is, the check must be a perfect square. If it is

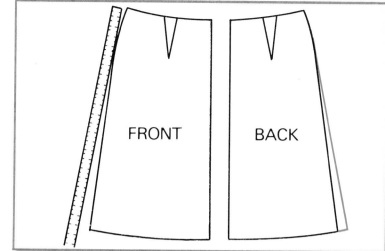

▲ *Increasing the basic flare on the skirt pattern*

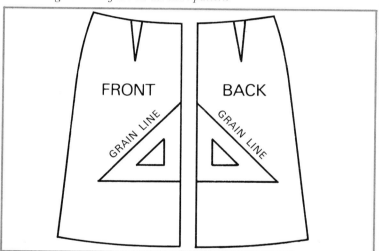

▲ *Finding the straight of grain on the pattern with a set square*
▼ *Folding the fabric to see if the check is perfectly square*

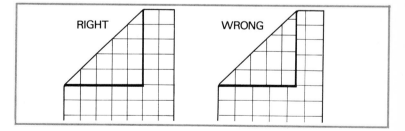

not, the skirt will look as though the diagonal is not true and will result in differing slants on each side of the seams.

It is often difficult to detect an irregular check when the difference in length of the sides is minute. If the weave is prominent enough, quickly count the number of threads in the warp and the weft that make up a square. If they are equal and the design still looks a little irregular, fold the fabric diagonally as shown in the diagram above so that one selvage meets the straight of the grain. All checks along the folded edge should have equal amounts of the squares showing.

The weight of the fabric is also important. There is always some drop in bias-cut fabrics, and a heavy fabric can result in a drop which distorts the pattern and looks very ugly.

Thus, when choosing slightly heavier fabrics, look closely at the weave. If it is firm, the strength of the weave will help the cloth to keep its shape.

Yardages

You will need more fabric when cutting a garment on the cross than on the straight of the grain.

Here are the yardages for sizes 24 and 26 inch waists:

For a 36 inch wide fabric you will need approximately 3 times the skirt length.

For a 54 inch wide fabric you will need approximately $2\frac{1}{4}$ times the skirt length.

Allow an extra $\frac{1}{8}$ yard for each size larger; that is, for a 28 inch waist allow $\frac{1}{8}$ yard extra, and for a 30 inch waist allow $\frac{1}{4}$ yard extra. In addition, if you have had to make the pattern wider to fit you, allow a further $\frac{1}{8}$ yard extra.

The above yardages do not allow for pattern matching, for which you must add one extra fabric pattern depth for each pattern piece. If the fabric has a pattern where one color runs down or across the pattern and does not form part of the definite check or plaid, allow an extra half skirt length.

For lining requirements, see Skirtmaking chapter 20.

Preparing the fabric for cutting

On a regular check or plaid the diagonal is obvious. But where the diagonal is not obvious, it is best to mark the direction of the bias on the fabric first.

Straighten and trim the raw edges on both ends of the fabric along the grain as shown in Skirtmaking chapter 21. Then unfold the fabric and lay it full width, face down, on a cutting table.

Take the top right-hand corner and fold it toward the lower left until the raw upper edge meets the left selvage. Pin edges together. The fold line is the true bias of the fabric. Use long basting stitches to mark it.

Next, unfold the fabric and, using the whole front skirt pattern, place it over the basting line (see diagrams 1 and 2). The center front line should coincide with or run parallel to the basted bias line. To allow for a drop in the fabric which could make the skirt slightly narrower, mark out $1\frac{1}{4}$ inch for seams in case you have to let them out. Chalk or pin the seam allowances and the usual hem allowance. Mark around the pattern using a flat basting stitch without loops, as the fabric is single.

Mark the bias at the other end of the fabric in the direction shown in diagrams 1 and 2, and lay out and mark up the back pattern. If you cut the skirt from fabric which has a prominent color running down or across it, fold the fabric from left to right when finding the bias for the back section, and use the alternative layout 3 as a guide.

Making the bias-cut skirt

The instructions are the same as for the basic skirt in Skirtmaking chapters 11-13, except that you will need a little more time, as the skirt has to hang. After you've basted the skirt together, and before fitting, it is important to let it hang for at least 24 hours. The drop in the fabric should be dealt with now, so that the fitting and the hem level will not be affected.

Hang it from three loops of tape, one pinned to each side and one in the center of the waist. Better still, if you have a dressmaker's dummy, slip the skirt over it and pin it to the dummy around the waist.

Fitting the bias-cut skirt

You will see that a skirt cut on the bias does not present the same fitting problems as one cut on the straight of the grain. The bias is more pliable and inclined to mold itself to the figure, so a lot of faults disappear in the soft hang of the fabric.

The skirt may appear tighter than the pattern size. If so, use the extra seam allowance to let it out.

The waist darts should be reduced to a minimum. Let them out as far as you can so they will be as short as your figure shape allows.

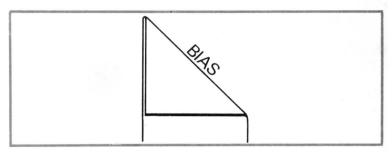

Finding the bias on the fabric

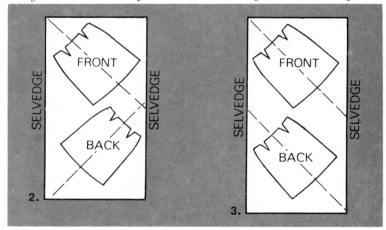

Skirt layouts: 1. For 54 inch wide fabric without one way. 2. For 36 inch wide fabric without one way. 3. For 36 inch wide fabric with one way.

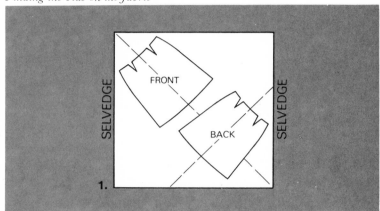

Take the surplus into the side seams or, if this causes strain, ease the fullness into the waistband.

This is a delicate fitting point and needs a little perseverance to get the right result. When you have achieved it, however, you will see that the effort was worthwhile. Trim seam allowances to $\frac{3}{4}$ in. Do not fit for length at this stage.

Stitching the seams in the bias-cut skirt

There are certain precautions which should be applied when you are stitching seams that run into a bias. These were covered in Skirtmaking chapter 18 and are of no concern here because they do not apply when stitching the seams in the bias-cut skirt.

For now, just observe the following points and all should be well:

1. Do not pull the bias-cut seams through the machine as you are stitching, but instead just guide the fabric through gently.

2. Slacken the tension on the presser foot so there is less likelihood of the fabric layers being pushed or dragged in opposite directions.

3. Before basting the seams, insert pins at right angles to the seamline to prevent the fabric layers from slipping. Then baste, using small but not tight stitches.

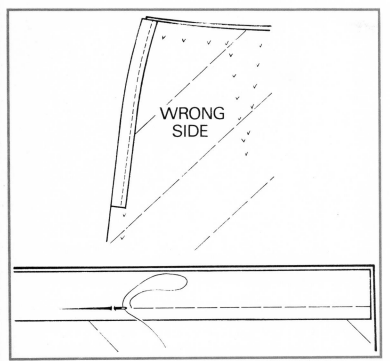

WRONG
SIDE

Above: inside of the zipper opening with lining strip basted in place
Center: detail of the lining strip along the zipper opening
Below: the mounting or interlining sewed in place with long stitches

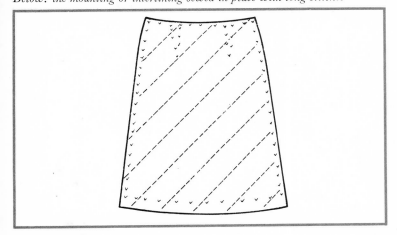

Pressing the stitched bias-cut seams

When pressing the seams, never use a pushing movement. Always press, lift and press, or else the seams may stretch and bulge.

Putting in the zipper

To prepare the opening for the zipper, run a basting stitch in double thread along the seamline of the opening, back and front, before basting the side seams together. This method may not give sufficient firmness to heavier fabrics, in which case use the following method: Cut two 1 inch wide strips of lining fabric on the straight of the grain, the length of the opening. Use one strip on each side of the opening, laying it along the edge of the $\frac{3}{4}$ inch seam allowance on the wrong side of the fabric, with $\frac{1}{4}$ inch projecting over the seamline. Make sure the work is lying flat while you prepare the opening so that the fabric does not pucker.

Sew on the strips with long running stitches just inside the seamline, catching only a thread or two from the top fabric. Stitch the side seam, catching down the bottom edge of the strips, and press. Baste the seam allowance under carefully and insert the zipper before removing any of the basting threads.

Stitching on the waistband

To make the waistband use one of the methods shown in Skirt-making chapters 13 and 14. Before you finally stitch it to the skirt, try on the skirt again with the waistband basted in place.

Never make a tight-fitting waistband for this type of skirt because the bias cut will cause the skirt to roll up over the waistband.

Lining the skirt

To help the skirt retain its shape during wear, it is advisable to make a smooth-fitting lining.

Cut it to the same pattern with the center back and center front on the straight grain of the fabric.

The lining should be an easy but perfect fit. Stitch the lining so that the seams and darts face toward the body when it is sewed into the skirt. If the seams and darts face the skirt, they will make impressions which show on the outside during wear. Skirts cut on the bias tend to show everything!

Mounting the fabric

In mounting, two pieces of fabric are stitched to one another and handled as one.

Mounting or interlining bias-cut fabrics is a very difficult task and requires a lot of dressmaking know-how.

If done incorrectly, it can have disastrous results. For example, the bias-cut fabric may drop in huge folds over the mounting. Thus, mounting should be avoided except in one instance.

Mounting or interlining becomes essential if you are making the skirt in one of the lightweight, high bulk tweeds which contain a high percentage of mohair or simulated mohair and where the weave is rather open. They are very cozy and warm and when cut on the cross they can be worn by many figure types without looking bear-like and clumsy.

Using the skirt pattern, cut an interlining from lawn or soft pre-shrunk cotton, cutting it on the bias as you did for the top fabric. Pin and baste the mounting to the inside of each skirt section, using very long basting stitches along the straight of the grain.

To support the fabric permanently, it is necessary to anchor the interlining or mounting to the fabric. Use matching thread and make rows of stitches along the straight grain of the fabric about 4 to 5 inches apart, as shown in the diagram. The stitches should be about 1 inch long on the mounting surface of the fabric, should only just catch the skirt fabric, and should not show on the outside of the garment at all. Do not pull them tight.

After mounting, make and fit the skirt as before.

This type of skirt also needs a lining. Here are two ways to do this:
1. Make a loose lining cut on the straight of the grain as before.
2. Make a lining from heavier taffeta which is cut on the cross and the same as the skirt. Stitch the darts so that they face the inside of the skirt and slip stitch the lining to the skirt over the hem. This leaves the inside of the skirt very neatly finished. When you have the skirt dry cleaned, remember to separate the lining from the hem; otherwise, the seams, which often fold to one side during cleaning, cannot be pressed properly.

Pressing bias-cut garments

Always press along the straight of the grain. Pressing into the bias can distort the fabric and result in very ugly bulges which no amount of shrinking and pressing will remove.

Place the garment over an ironing board and turn the work as you proceed, so that the straight of the grain is always before you.

Let the work cool down a little before moving it on. This is particularly important when there are raw edges, such as the hem edge, still unfinished. If the weight of the fabric is allowed to drag the work, you will find that the warmth from the iron will continue to do its work and make the hem edge look rather fluted.

Chapter 20

Many a lining between skirt and slip

Your skirt making know-how isn't complete without the inside story on skirt linings. Lined skirts not only hang better, resisting creasing and the tendency to sit out, but they wear better too. Instructions for two methods of attaching linings are given on the following pages.

After skirt linings, this chapter goes on to the more frivolous business of pretty half slips, which can be made by adapting the Golden Hands basic skirt patterns. You can make your half slips glamorous and feminine by using delicate fabrics—fine nylon lace, Dacron or eyelet embroidery—giving them a luxurious look with lots of lace trimming.

A half slip made of a firm fabric, such as taffeta, helps an unlined dress or skirt to hang better, but for a smooth outline keep lace trim flat, avoiding bulky trimming which would show on the outside of the garment.

Lining a skirt

Fabric requirements

Be selective when choosing lining fabric and remember that it must be firmly woven without being stiff. Here are some fabric suggestions with hints on how to choose them in relation to your skirt fabric.

For skirts made in firmly woven heavier fabrics:
    ribbed taffeta; heavy nylon taffeta; pure silk
    paper taffeta; cotton and rayon twills.
For skirts made in lightweight fabrics:
    Arnel taffetas, most soft rayon taffetas.

If you like the feeling of a satin lining, don't choose a crêpe satin because this will stretch and not keep the shape of the skirt well. It is important to remember that if you have chosen a washable fabric for the skirt, the lining should be washable too.

Work out the fabric requirements as for the skirt you are making, but add only 1 inch for the hem allowance and disregard the waistband allowance completely.

Making the lining

Cut the lining exactly as the skirt, except when making the knife-pleated skirt where the lining is cut as the basic skirt without the pleats.

Add only 1 inch for the hem allowance.

Stitch and finish the seams of the lining, leaving the opening on the right-hand side instead of the left. When you put the lining into the skirt, the seams must face each other so that the right side of the lining is against the body.

Turn up the hem of the lining 1 inch shorter than the skirt. You do not need to sew the hem by hand. Instead, turn the raw edge under $\frac{1}{2}$ inch, pin and baste. Turn the edge up again $1\frac{1}{2}$ inches and stitch. If the lining is cut for a flared skirt, make the hem narrow

enough to cope with the fullness.

Attaching the lining to the skirt

Here are two methods to attach linings, either of which can be used. Method 1 is to hand sew the lining into the skirt after it has been finished.

To do this, turn under the waist seam allowance on the lining. Pin the waist seam of the lining to the waist seam of the skirt, matching seams and darts. Use a firm slip stitch to sew it in place. Method 2 is to stitch the lining into the skirt so that it is permanently fixed.

Here the made-up lining is stitched to the skirt before stitching on the waistband. Lay the lining and skirt waist seams together wrong sides facing. Pin, baste and stitch and use as one fabric when you put on the waistband.

To deal with the zipper opening for both methods, turn the lining opening under and hand sew it around the zipper, catching it to the zipper tape along the machine-stitched line. Be sure to ease the lining opening around the zipper slightly, otherwise the zipper will pucker.

The lining in a full skirt, such as a dirndl, is often used to hold the shape of the skirt, especially around the hem. The easiest and the prettiest way to do this is to attach a frill to the hem of the lining—a very full skirt which needs a lot of support could take two or more frills. The frill width can vary from 6 inches upward, but keep in mind when deciding on the width to use that the narrower the frill, the crisper it is.

To make a frill, cut a strip of fabric $2\frac{1}{2}$ times the measurement around the hem of the lining. Join the ends of the strip to form a circle and hem along both raw edges by machine or hand. Make two rows of gathering stitches along one edge, then gather the fabric to fit the lining at the hem. Lay it around the lining with the lower edge of the frill even with the lining hem, and stitch.

If you make two frills, the second one should be deeper and set higher on the lining over the first frill, but both frill hems should be even with the lining hem.

You may like to add a finishing touch and trim the frill and lining hems with lace edging, especially if you make the lining for an evening dirndl. You'll see how to attach the lace to the hemlines in the illustrations on page 77.

Half slips

Fabric notes

The fabrics suggested for linings in this chapter are all suitable for half slips, but since you'll be wearing the half slip with more than one garment, make sure the fabric is washable.

The amount of fabric needed is the same as for the skirts. Check your slip length and decide if it really needs a hem; if not, deduct the hem allowance. And if you decide to trim the hem edge with lace, deduct the width of the lace from the length of the slip.

Ways to trim the fitted half slip

Inserting lace

Use lace insertion to trim seams such as panel seams on the six-gore slip (diagram 1 on page 77).

To obtain the pattern for the six-gore half slip, use the four pattern pieces for the knife-pleated skirt in Skirtmaking chapter 17, but do not allow for the pleats. Lay all the pattern pieces on double fabric with the center back and center front on the fold. Cut out, allowing a $\frac{3}{4}$ inch seam allowance around each pattern piece. Stitch the side and panel seams, then trim the panel seam allow-

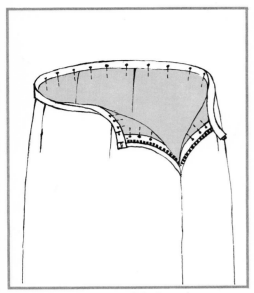

▲ *Attaching lining after finishing skirt*

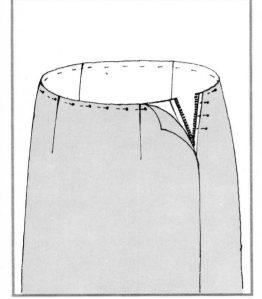

▲ *Attaching lining before finishing skirt*

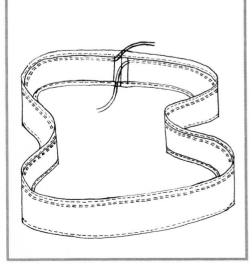

▲ *Gathered frill for a full skirt lining*
A pretty frilled half slip for a full skirt ▶

Dress: Vogue Pattern

ance to $\frac{1}{4}$ inch and press the seams open.

Using 1 inch lace insertion, lay it over each seam on the right side of the slip and pin and baste it in place. Engage a small zigzag setting on your machine and stitch along both sides of the rows of insertion, close to the edge. Then trim away the fabric and seams under the insertion, close to the stitching line, being careful not to cut into the lace. (See lower diagrams opposite.)

Another attractive way to use the lace insertion is to set in one or two rows above the hemline 1 to 2 inches apart (diagram 2), depending on the width of the insertion.

To insert lace into the hemline, measure out the distance from the lower edge of the hem first, and make a row of basting stitches for each row of insertion to guide you. Lay the lace along the basting line(s) and use the same method as before to stitch it on.

Lace edging

Use lace edging to trim the hem (see diagrams 1, 2 and 3). Manufacturers make matching lace edgings and insertions so it should not be too difficult to coordinate them. You will need $2\frac{1}{2}$ times the length of the hem edge.

Gather the lace (which often has a fine but very strong gathering thread woven into the edge) to fit the hem of the slip.

To prepare the hem edge, finish the raw edge with a zigzag stitch or overcast it, and lay the gathered lace edging over the edge on the right side. Either sew it in place by hand with running stitch or backstitch, or machine stitch it using a zigzag setting.

Flat lace edging

If you are making a straight and fitted half slip, a deep lace edging stitched on flat and not gathered can make an attractive finish (diagram 4). When cutting the lace you must allow 3 to 4 inches extra on the width around the hem edge because as you stitch on the lace, the stitches will work the lace into the fabric and tighten it up. Make sure you always pin and baste the lace before you stitch.

Prepare the hem edge as you did for the gathered lace edging and attach the flat lace to the finished edge. Or finish the hem in the usual way and stitch the flat lace over the fabric, with the lower edge of the lace even with the hem edge.

Attaching flat lace

An alternative way of attaching flat lace to a hem is with Paris stitch. This method is mainly for trimming household linen and therefore should be used only if you are working with a heavier fabric such as ribbed or heavy nylon taffeta and trimming the article with a coarser lace.

Turn up the raw hem edge to the depth of the hem allowance plus the depth of the lace. Baste the lace along the folded edge and hand sew it in place using Paris stitch, as shown opposite. Then carefully trim away the surplus fabric on the wrong side.

All-over lace slip with a fitted waist

If you want a really glamorous half slip, you can easily make one from all-over lace (diagram 5) using one of the Golden Hands basic skirt patterns.

You will need two fabrics for the lace slip:

The lace, which should be fairly fine and have a small design.
The backing, to give the lace strength in wear. This should be a fine nylon taffeta if you use nylon lace, or rayon or silk taffeta to back other laces.

Calculate the amount as for the skirt, but omit the hem allowance. You will also need a fine baby lace edging $\frac{5}{8}$ to $\frac{3}{4}$ inch wide for trimming the hem.

Cutting out the lace slip with fitted waist

If you intend to wear the half slip under fitted garments, it is essential to keep the waistline smooth, so choose a fitted skirt pattern for the half slip.

Using the back and front skirt patterns, cut out the lining adding a $\frac{3}{4}$ inch seam allowance but omitting the hem allowance. Remove the pattern and cut out the lace in the same way.

Stitching the lace slip with fitted waist

Place the lace over the taffeta and pin and baste the two fabrics together so that they won't slip when you work them as one.
Stitch the side seams and darts.

To finish the hem, first stitch carefully along the hem edge (which is trimmed to the length of the finished slip) to hold both fabrics together securely, then overcast or zigzag the raw edge. If the fabric is very fine, you can turn the edge under $\frac{1}{8}$ inch and whip it, as shown.

Finally, trim the hem with the lace edging.

Making the fitted waist

Fit the slip in exactly the same way as you fit the skirt.

To close the opening, use a lingerie zipper, obtainable at some stores. For the waistband, use the waistband pattern with the wrap end (see Skirtmaking chapter 14), but make it only half as wide as the skirt waistband and, of course, leave out the stiffening. Use a simple loop and button fastening at the ends of the waistband.

Make the loop by hand, like the bar in Skirtmaking chapter 14, large enough to take a button—a small flat button is best. With the zipper closed, line up a button to the loop and sew it on.

Lace slip with an elasticized waist

If you are using a fine fabric for the slip and don't plan to wear it under fitted garments, you can finish it with an elasticized waist seam. However, you must allow for this when you cut out the slip. Cut out the lining and lace as for the fitted half slip, but let the side seams run almost straight from the hipline to the waistline without changing the slant of the side seam.

Baste the lace to the lining and stitch the side seams as for the fitted slip, but don't stitch the darts or allow for a zipper opening. Turn under the whole waist seam allowance ($\frac{3}{4}$ inch) and baste it down close to the folded edge. Fold the raw edge under $\frac{1}{4}$ inch, pin and baste it to the slip and machine stitch close to the edge to make a casing about $\frac{1}{2}$ inch wide, leaving a small opening to insert the elastic. Using $\frac{1}{4}$ inch wide elastic, lay it around your waist and stretch it slightly. Add $\frac{1}{2}$ inch for overlapping the ends when you stitch them together and cut off the amount you require. This is the only way to calculate the amount of elastic you will need because the stretch varies with different manufacturers.

To thread the elastic through the casing, attach one end to a safety pin and insert it in the casing by gently pushing then pulling the fabric over the pin. Make sure that you leave some elastic protruding from the casing so that you can stitch the ends together. Lay one end of the elastic $\frac{1}{2}$ inch over the other end and sew the overlapped ends together securely by hand. Then let the elastic disappear into the casing and distribute the fullness evenly. Sew the opening.

Slip with a lace panel

Diagram 6 shows a half slip with a lace center panel. Use the pattern for the six-gore slip, under "inserting lace," and simply make the center panel in all-over fine lace with a backing.

1.

4.

2.

5.

3.

6.

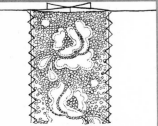

Lace insertion stitched over the seam on the right side

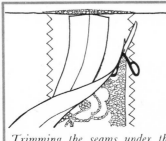

Trimming the seams under the insertion on the wrong side

Add the finishing touch to a slip with lace edging and matching insertion

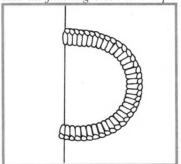

The hand-made loop for the button

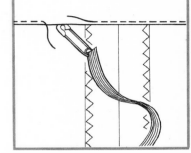

The elasticized waist seam casing

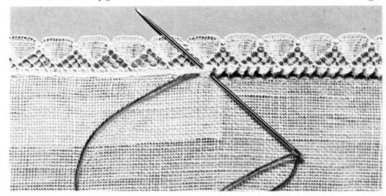

Sewing on lace, using Paris stitch, with the surplus fabric partly trimmed

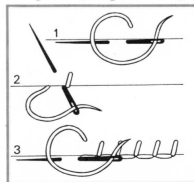

Paris stitch is used mainly for trimming household linen and is not suitable for fine fabrics or very fine lace.
Turn up the seam or hem allowance plus the depth of the lace on the edge to be trimmed. Baste the lace along the folded edge and hand sew it in place with Paris stitch. Trim away the surplus fabric.

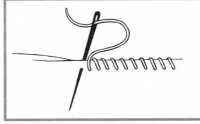

Whip stitch is a very fine overcasting stitch worked from right to left and can be used to finish off the edge of very fine fabrics. Turn under the edge $\frac{1}{8}$ inch and whip it to look like very fine cording.

Chapter 21

Basic pleating for skirts

Inside every small girl is a fashion expert in the making, and every mother ought to encourage her daughter to develop good dress sense. She may be tied to blue jeans and a T-shirt most of the time, which is all the more reason to encourage her to enjoy pretty clothes occasionally. The best way to learn is by sheer trial and error, which can be fun but expensive if you have to buy every item, especially considering how quickly children grow.

As no one wants a wardrobe full of expensive mistakes, dressmaking is the obvious answer. Here is a swinging pleated skirt any little girl will love to wear. Whether you add the shoulder straps or not will depend on the shape of her stomach. Later chapters include instructions for making more clothes for children, boys as well as girls.

A word about a little girl's fitting problems

Before you start making this skirt, it's a good idea to go over the basic shape of little girls and the skirt fitting problems that arise as a result of their shape at this age.

Generally, skirts will not stay up or they ride up and jut out so that the front looks shorter than the back. Pleated skirts look particularly clumsy because all the pleats tend to bunch together in front. Let's look at the reasons for the bad fitting.

If you observe the profile of a little girl's figure, you will notice that the curve of her spine through the waist toward the seat is concave and that her stomach is quite high and curves from the abdomen to the chest. This is typical of most very young figures. There is no waistline, and although there is a difference in the measurements around the body, the extra inches are taken up by the height of the seat and by the upper thighs.

The hip bones are not sufficiently developed to stop the waistband of a skirt from falling down, and the roundness of the stomach encourages the skirt to ride up if the waistband is tight. The only way to counteract this problem is to attach narrow straps to the waistband. These are worn over the shoulders and crossed at the back so that they don't slip down. For a child with narrow or sloping shoulders, it may be necessary to stitch a brace across the front of the straps to hold them in position.

Although the straps are strictly functional, they can become an attractive part of the skirt if made in the same fabric. They are versatile too, as sweaters and shirts can go under or over the straps. With the straps doing most of the work, the waistband can be made quite loose so that the skirt will hang better.

Although you might think an elasticized waistband is a good alternative to the straps, it pulls the waistband into the figure too tightly and only makes the problem worse. The reason for using an elastic waistband is to give easy expansion and not simply to hold up the skirt.

The pleated skirt made up in a woven synthetic fabric ▶

78

How to work out basic pleating

In basic pleating, the length of the pleat fold is the same as the pleat distance (or half the pleat depth). Therefore, you require three times as much fabric as the measurement you are fitting. This could be a waist or hip measurement, but in the case of a small child it is the waist measurement. Here's how to work it out.

Step	For example: making a skirt for a 23in waist measurement with the pleats 1in apart: 23in + 2in = 25in
1. Take the waist/hip measurement loosely and add the correct ease.	
2. Multiply by three. This gives you *the amount of fabric needed for pleating*.	$25 \times 3 = 75$in
3. Decide on the distance you want between the pleats and divide the waist/hip measurement plus ease by this figure. This gives you *the total number of pleats*.	$25\text{in} \div 1\text{in} = 25$ pleats
4. Deduct the waist/hip measurement plus ease from the amount of fabric needed. This gives you *the amount of fabric to be divided into pleat depths*.	$75\text{in} - 25\text{in} = 50$in
5. Divide by the number of pleats. This gives you *the depth for each pleat*.	$50\text{in} \div 25 = 2$in

How to work out pleating for the given width

In pleating a skirt from one width of fabric, the length of the fold is *not* equal to the pleat distance. Apply what you have learned about basic pleating, but remember, you are working on a given width of 54in. As you work it out this time, compare the two charts.

Use this column to work out the pleating yourself for a child's skirt in 54in width. Just fill in the spaces.

Step	For example: making a skirt for a 23in waist measurement with the pleats 1in apart: 23in + 2in = 25in	(your working)
1. Take the child's waist measurement loosely and add 2in for ease.		___in + 2in = ___in
2. You are working on a given width of 54in fabric. Deduct ½in seam allowance from each end.	$54\text{in} - 1\text{in} = 53$in	$54\text{in} - 1\text{in} = 53$in
3. Decide on the distance you want between the pleats (for small children 1in is best) and divide the waist measurement plus ease by this figure.	$25\text{in} \div 1\text{in} = 25$ pleats	(Pleat distance = ___in) ___in ÷ ___in = ___ pleats
4. Deduct the waist measurement plus ease from the amount of pleating fabric.	$53\text{in} - 25\text{in} = 28$in	$53\text{in} - \text{___in} = \text{___in}$
5. Divide by the number of pleats.	$28\text{in} \div 25 = 1\tfrac{1}{8}$in	___in ÷ ___ = ___in pleat depth

The all-around pleated skirt for 2- to 7-year-olds

This pleated skirt is made from just one width of 54in fabric and is therefore quite inexpensive to make. It's practical to make because it has a full round of pleats calculated in such a way that you can get it out of the shortest possible length of fabric. But before you can work out the pleating for it, it is necessary to know how to work out pleating in general.

Suitable fabrics

The fabric used for a pleated skirt should be crease-resistant, but able to take a sharp crease under pressure and steam.

Worsted wool, Dacron and a number of synthetic mixtures, linens and firmly-woven tweeds are good for pleating.

If you want a really hard-wearing, hard-washing and pleat-retaining fabric, you can't go wrong if you choose from the range of woven acrylic fibers (for example, Orlon and Acrilan). They can be machine-washed and still retain the sharp crease of the pleats, needing only the slightest touch with a warm iron to make the garment as good as new. What is more, you can pleat woven Orlon permanently yourself.

When you buy the fabric, always remember to ask if it pleats well and whether it needs washing or dry cleaning.

Fabric requirements

For 2- to 7-year-olds—54in width only, the skirt length plus 9in. Measure the strap length, and if this measurement is more than 27in, you will need an extra 3in of fabric.

If you wish to use a narrower fabric, you must allow the skirt length plus 3in for each extra width you cut to obtain the correct length for pleating.

You will also need two No.2 hooks and eyes, one snap fastener size 0 and thread to match the fabric.

Preparing the fabric before cutting

Before you start cutting the pleated skirt, it is essential that the fabric is perfectly square in the grain. To square the fabric to the grain, use the thread-drawing methods illustrated below, and cut the fabric along the line of the drawn thread.

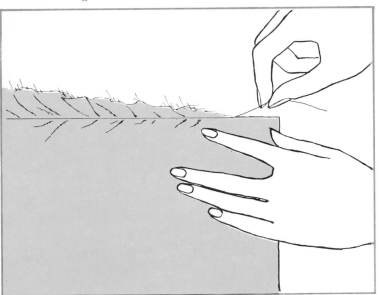

▲ *Finding the straight of the grain by drawing a thread out of the fabric*

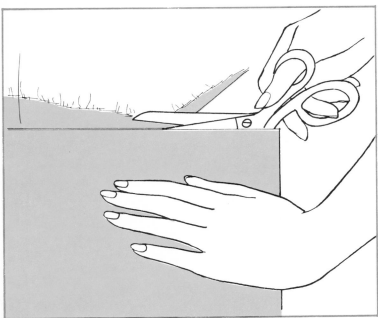

If you are using a weave where the thread cannot be drawn, or it is hard to see the direction of the grain, the easiest way to square the fabric is with a tailor's square or set square and yardstick.
Carefully place the selvage along the straight edge of your cutting table and smooth out the rest of the fabric over the table. Be careful not to force it in any way. Lay the tailor's square along the selvage near the raw edge, then lay the yardstick along the top line of the square and draw a chalk line right across the fabric.
To check that the fabric is perfectly straight, repeat the operation about 10in farther down and measure the distance between the two chalk lines. The measurement should be the same on the selvage and right across the fabric. Cut the fabric on the line nearest the raw edge and brush off the other chalk line. The fabric should now be perfectly square for cutting.

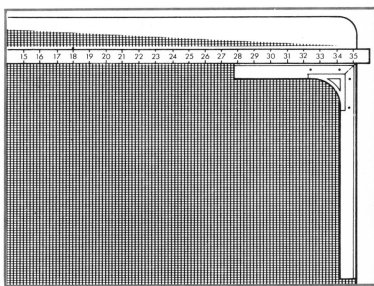

▲ *How to straighten the grain using a tailor's square and yardstick*

How to cut the skirt

Making a pleated skirt from one length of 54in width is so simple that you don't need a paper pattern.
Open out the fabric to the full width across the cutting table. Measure the length of the skirt along the selvage, allowing 2in for the hem and ¾in for the waist seam, then take this measurement right across the fabric, marking a straight line with pins or chalk. Cut along this line. Put the remaining fabric aside for the straps and waistband.
Finish the hem first, before you start pleating. Turn up 2in along the cut edge of the fabric and baste. A 2in hem is deep enough, since it is almost impossible to lengthen a pleated skirt after a lot of hard wear and washing, and moreover, you will be able to adjust the length sufficiently from the straps.
When you are sewing the hem, leave 3in at each end just basted—don't sew yet.
Press the hem and remove all basting stitches except those at the ends. Turn the fabric right side up and lay it flat on the cutting table with the hem toward you.

Starting the pleating

Have the pleating chart open in front of you with the measurements you need to use. Pleat from left to right, marking each pleat line with a line of pins.
Measure a ½in seam allowance on the left selvage and make a line of pins.
As the skirt opening will be on the inside of a pleat, it is necessary to start with a half pleat, which means halving the pleat depth. Do this and pin off this amount from the seam allowance pin line. Now make the whole pleats, starting with the pleat distance followed by the pleat depth.
Repeat until you have marked off the required number of pleats, less one (24 in the example), all the way across the fabric. The last pleat (25th in the example) is the top of the opening, so for this you need only measure out the pleat distance. Turn under the remaining fabric and selvage.
Having measured out the pleats, check to make very sure that you have made the right calculations for fabric width and body measurements.
Fold along each pleat distance line, bring the fold over to the right to fall on the pleat depth line and baste down securely.
Make sure the hemline and waistline remain straight.
Baste the end pleat fold under.

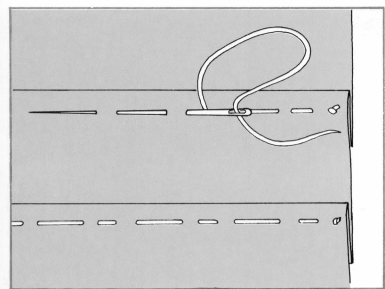

▲ *Basting the pleats down using a long and a short stitch*

N.B. When you're basting down lots of small pleats or any folded edge on springy fabric, use the basting stitches illustrated. Make a short stitch between each long stitch to give extra hold.

Pressing
Lay the pleated fabric, still flat and open, over a pressing board, making sure that the ends which extend beyond the board are supported. Press with a warm iron, using a damp cloth.
To secure the upper edge of the pleating, make a row of machine stitches just above the waist seam. Remove all basting stitches except those holding the end pleat, and press the pleats in again, more firmly, making sure you press each pleat in its original crease.

Stitching the side seam
To stitch the side seam of the skirt, lap the end pleat over the halved pleat depth you measured out from the left selvage and baste it in position.
Turn the skirt to the wrong side. Use the seam allowance pinned on the left selvage for the seamline guide, since you may have slightly more or less fabric in the pleat depth on the right selvage. Leave an opening 3in long at the top, unfold the hem and stitch the selvages all the way down.
Press the seam open for 4in, from the bottom edge, so that you can finish the hem.
Now snip the selvages toward the seam, just above the hem, and press both selvages together all the way up.
Overcast the snip with fine hand stitches to prevent fraying.

Finishing the opening
To finish the 3in opening, turn back the selvage seam allowance on the back of the skirt (the left end when you were pleating) to the length of the opening. Sew it down by hand using a catch stitch.
Snip the selvage on this side toward the seam so that it will lie flat. The front turning, or right end, remains just folded and does not need to be stitched back.

To prepare the waist seam
Make a mark opposite the left opening. Then make running stitches along the back waist seam, pull up the stitches and gather in one inch. This will give the skirt a little fullness around the seat to stop the pleats from spreading.
Gathering the fabric at the back of the skirt has caused the mark

opposite the opening to shift toward the back so, before attaching the waistband, you must make a new mark. Otherwise, the waistband will not go on evenly.
Measure out the distance halfway between each side of the opening and the mark opposite, and make two more marks.

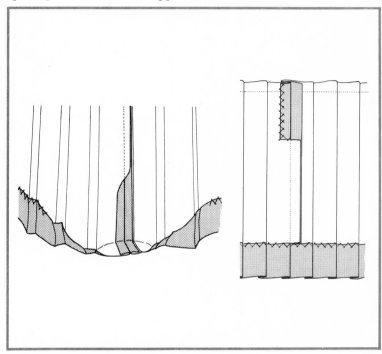

▲ *The side seam pressed open in the hem*   ▲ *Finished side seam and opening*

These are to indicate the center front and center back.
To obtain the correct length for the waistband, measure along the top edge of the skirt and cut a 3in wide strip of fabric the same length plus ½in seam allowance at each end. You will not need any extra wrap because it wraps in the depth of the pleat.

Fitting the skirt
Baste on the waistband and try the skirt on the child. Pin on two lengths of tape for the shoulder straps, crossing them at the back. Mark the lengths needed on the tape.
The skirt should hang almost free around the figure.
If you see that there is a pronounced drop at the back, try easing the skirt up into the waistband at the back. Be very careful, though, not to drag the fullness of the pleats from the sides of the skirt. If this happens, do not take the skirt up any farther.
Stitch on the waistband and finish with hooks and eyes for the fastening. Sew a snap fastener inside the fold of the opening so that it won't gape.

Attaching the straps
Measure the length of the straps from the tape used for the fitting and add 6in to the length. This makes room for adjustment for 2 to 3 years of growing.
Cut two 3in wide strips of fabric to this length. Fold them in half lengthwise and stitch them as for the soft belts (Know-How chapter 58), leaving one end open.
Turn in the raw end and hand sew firmly to the inside of the waistband about 2in on each side of the center front and center back marks on the skirt.
Now give the skirt a final pressing to seal in the pleats. Pay special attention to the pleat which goes through the hem in the side seam. The thickness of the seam inside the hem will need extra pressure to crease in the pleat.

Chapter 22

Fling yourself into kilt-making

The most famous of all pleated skirts is, of course, the Scottish kilt. An authentic kilt is very full and heavy and made from yards of fabric, but there are many ways this can be pared down and still resemble the original.

This chapter gives you a simple method for working out the pleating and calculating yardage for any size, and for skirt lengths up to 23 inches. But if you like the elegant look of the full length version shown here, you can make it from a commercial pattern and use Golden Hands pleating know-how to help you achieve perfect results.

Choosing your fabric

Although kilts are associated with Scottish tartans, they can be made in other fabrics, including plain cloths, provided that the fabric pleats well (see the suggestions for the child's pleated skirt and the knife-pleated skirt in Skirtmaking chapters 17 and 21).

The authentic fabric for kilts is a fine wool and because of the amount of fabric used it is best not to choose anything too heavy or bulky.

If you are choosing a man-made or mixture cloth for the adult kilt, make sure that it will respond to being pressed and molded as a natural fiber does. This is important if you want to make the best of the fitted lines on this pleated garment.

Points on pleating

The kilt is fully pleated, which means the length of the pleat fold is the same as the pleat distance (see Skirtmaking chapter 21).

Since it is a bulky garment to make and handle, it is a good idea to practice first on a child's kilt, then you can make one for yourself from the same working sequence.

Working out the pleating

This requires a little mathematics, but it is simple if you follow the step-by-step chart shown here. First, take note of the following points:

1. The kilt is fitted, so calculate the amount of fabric needed by the hip measurement, which is the largest part of the body it has to cover.

2. The width of the plain front panel is in proportion to the hip measurement and takes up about one quarter of the circumference. This can be varied, however, to suit your own taste. When dividing measurements for the panel, calculate to the nearest inch —it is so much easier.

3. Allow plenty of ease when you take the hip measurement, as the thickness of the layers of fabric will take it up. The chart shows you how much ease to add.

4. The calculations for the adult and the child's kilt are the same and are based on a 54 inch wide fabric.

Full length for glamour. Vogue Pattern made in Menzies tartan ▶

What to do	For example	For your own use
	Making a kilt for a 30in hip and 25in waist, with 8in panel and 1in pleats.	
1. Take the hip measurement and add 3in ease.	30in+3in=33in	....in+3in=....in
2. Deduct the width of the panel. This gives you the area to be pleated and also the number of pleats.	33in—8in=25in (25 pleats)	....in—....in=....in (....pleats)
3. Multiply by three. This gives you the fabric needed for pleating.	25in×3in=75in	....in×3in=....in
4. Add twice the panel width (the kilt has a double wrap-over).	(8in×2=16in) 75in+16in=91in	(....in×2=....in) ....in+....in=....in
5. Add the seam allowance ($\frac{1}{2}$in) for each pleated section to be joined together.	91in+1in=92in	....in+....in=....in
6. To finish the upper front panel add 5in.	92in+5in=97in	....in+5in=....in
7. To finish the under front panel add 1in.	97in+1in=98in	....in+1in=....in
	=the total width of the skirt.	

How much fabric to buy

The example in the chart gives a skirt width of 98 inches, which easily fits across two widths of 54 inch fabric, or twice the skirt length. But if the total width of the skirt exceeds 105 inches, an extra skirt length is needed for the additional pleats. There will, of course, be an extra seam which must be allowed for.

For the total yardage add $3\frac{1}{2}$ inches on each skirt length for the waist seam and hem allowance, and $2\frac{1}{2}$-3 inches for the waistband. If you are buying a check or tartan, make sure that the pattern can be matched across all sections and that you buy enough fabric to enable you to do this.

As explained, all the instructions for working out the fabric in this chapter are based on a 54 inch width. It is possible, however, to use narrower fabric, but there will be more seams in the pleating.

Royal Stewart tartan gives this girl's kilt an authentic Scottish air ►

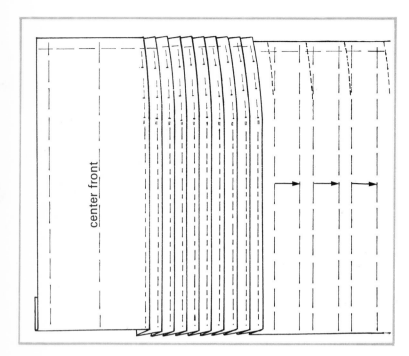

▲ *Above diagram shows basted pleats. Hem is turned before pleating*

Preparing to pleat

Study figure 1, which is the pleating diagram. You will notice that there is an inverted pleat at the inner edge of the upper front panel. This is an extra pleat not accounted for in the pleat number (allowance was made for it in the 5 inches added for finishing the upper front panel, when calculating yardage). The inverted pleat enables the panel to lie flat and hang well. The pleat sequence for the kilt remains the same for all sizes apart from the measurement for the panels and the number of pleats. The pleating diagram indicates a left-hand fastening. For right-hand fastening, simply reverse the reading of the diagram.

Making the kilt

Cutting. Prepare the fabric for cutting as for the child's pleated skirt in Skirtmaking chapter 21. Measure and mark the skirt lengths across the fabric, add hem and waist seam allowances and cut.

Making the hem. Make the hem before pleating, leaving 3 inches to each side of the seam(s) just basted. Press.

Pleating. With the fabric right side up and following figure 1, mark all the pleat lines, seamlines and edges with basting. Also mark the center front on both panels. Where the fabric is to be joined, finish with a half pleat depth and seam allowance and start the next section with a seam allowance followed by a half pleat depth.

Starting with the left panel, pleat from left to right pinning as for tailored pleats (see Skirtmaking chapter 17). Make the inverted pleat by folding the upper front panel edge to meet the fold of the last pleat.

You are now ready to baste the pleats. Since the skirt is fitted from the hipline into the waist, baste each pleat from hipline to hem only and leave the top pinned for tapering.

Stitching the seams. Join the skirt sections, making sure as you baste and stitch each seam that it forms the inside crease of the pleat. Finish the hem at the base of each seam. (See the side seam for the child's pleated skirt, Skirtmaking chapter 21).

Tapering the pleats

The chart here shows you a simple way of calculating how much to taper each pleat.

What to do	For example 25in waist, 30in hip	For your own use
1. Add 2in ease to the waist measurement.	$25\text{in} + 2\text{in} = 27\text{in}$	$\text{in} + 2\text{in} = \quad\text{in}$
2. Find the difference between this figure and the hip measurement plus ease (3in).	$33\text{in} - 27\text{in} = 6\text{in}$	$\text{in} - \ldots\text{in} = \quad\text{in}$
3. Divide the amount equally by the number of pleats (don't forget the inverted pleat!)	$6\text{in} \div 26$ pleats = about $\frac{1}{4}$in for tapering each pleat	$\text{in} \div \quad$ pleats = $\quad$ in

The dash lines indicated on figure 1 show you how to taper the pleats. Roll under the edge of each pleat and bring it to meet the distance line of the next pleat. Be sure that each pleat runs back into the original line at the hips.

The fitting

Baste the top of the pleats firmly into position and press the pleats all the way down.

Cut a waistband the full length of the waist edge and baste it to the kilt.

Try on the kilt, and wrap the panels so that the center front lines meet. There must be enough ease for the panels to stay fully wrapped and not pull away from each other.

Use the fitting hints for the knife-pleated skirt in Skirtmaking chapter 17 when you look at the pleats. You will find the skirt fitting guide in Skirtmaking chapter 12 useful, too.

Mark any faults and correct them, unless you find you need to cut a curve for the waist—this should be done after you have stitched the pleats.

Finishing the kilt

Stitching the pleats. Remove the waistband and topstitch each pleat close to the edge from the waist to the hipline. Press.

Curving the waist. If you need to cut a waist curve, do so now. With the panels wrapped in position, fold the kilt in the center front lines and pin it together along the waistline. Curve the waist following the instructions in Skirtmaking chapter 12. Baste the top of the pleats along the new seamline.

Fringing. To finish the upper front panel you can make your own fringe from the kilt material.

Cut a strip about 2 inches wide, a little longer than the length of the panel. Carefully lift out the threads from one edge until the fringe is about $\frac{3}{4}$ inch wide. Lay the fringed strip on the facing fold line of the upper panel as shown in figure 2 and stitch along this line. Trim, then hand-sew the inside raw edge to the facing.

Finishing the panels. Fold under the 3 inch facing on the upper front panel and the 1 inch turning on the edge of the under panel over the hem. Baste and hand-sew as shown in figure 3.

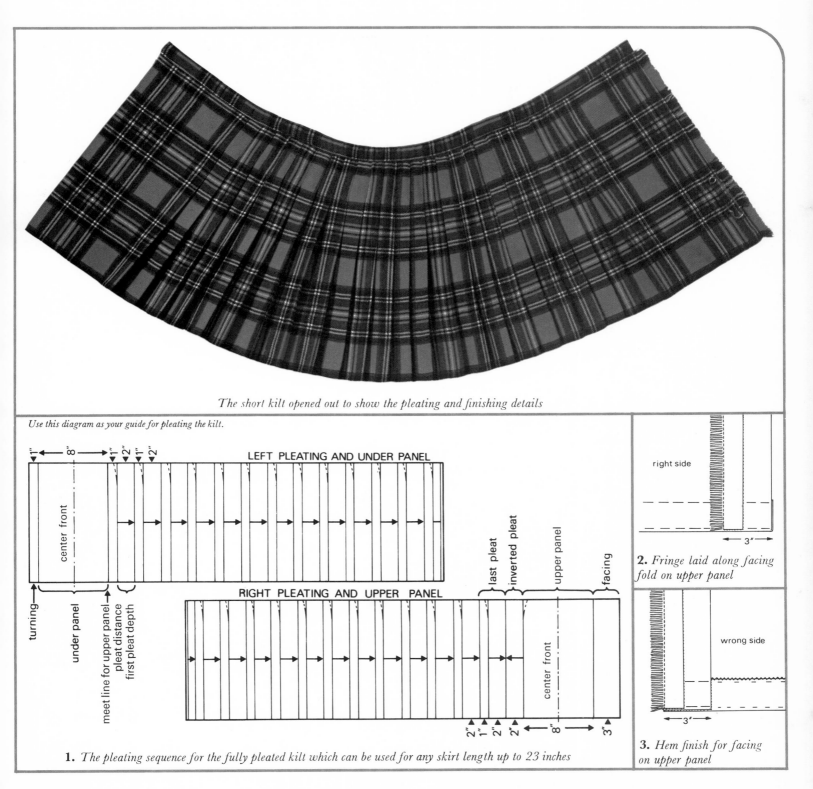

The short kilt opened out to show the pleating and finishing details

Use this diagram as your guide for pleating the kilt.

LEFT PLEATING AND UNDER PANEL

RIGHT PLEATING AND UPPER PANEL

2. *Fringe laid along facing fold on upper panel*

3. *Hem finish for facing on upper panel*

1. *The pleating sequence for the fully pleated kilt which can be used for any skirt length up to 23 inches*

Fastening the waistband. Before you attach the waistband, consider the way you want the kilt to fasten. You can fasten it with a hook and eye, but if you want to be traditional, make a tab and buckle fastening—for this you can use the instructions for the buckle belt with pointed end in Know-How chapter 58.

The tab should project about 5 inches from the end of the waistband and there are two methods of attaching it, depending on the type of waistband you are making.

Method 1. If you are making a waistband with an elasticized back, the tab must be attached before you finish the end of the waistband. Make the tab a fraction narrower than the waistband, insert the raw edge into the end of the waistband on the upper front panel, then stitch twice across the end to secure it.

Method 2. If you are making a plain waistband, cut the tab slightly longer than 5 inches and make both ends pointed. Lay one pointed end onto the end of the waistband and topstitch neatly, following the shape of the point.

For both methods, the buckle can be stitched straight onto the waistband in line with the tab, or you can make a belt end for it and then sew it securely to the waistband. Use strong hooks and eyes or a trouser hook and bar on the under panel to hold the wrap in position.

Chapter 23

Fitting with a muslin

This chapter introduces a new method for fitting—how to make the muslin, or toile, a mock-up version of the final garment. This method is used by couturiers and professional dressmakers to insure a perfect fit.

Once you have made your own personal blueprint you can put your scissors into expensive material without the nagging doubt at the back of your mind, "Will it fit?"

Make your basic pattern from the Blouse Graph Pattern on pages 98 and 99. There will undoubtedly be variations between it and your actual measurements so check back carefully with your figure chart on page 13.

The completed bodice muslin

A muslin saves endless fitting problems later on and you can use this same muslin when making up commercial paper patterns, to check where they need altering.

▼ The basic blouse pattern
This is used to make . . .

▼ . . . the bodice muslin
This is a mock garment, a fitted bodice in this case.
The alterations on the muslin are used to make . . .

▼ . . . The muslin pattern
This is a waist-length version of the basic pattern from which you cut . . .

▼ . . . the new pattern
This is your personalized adjusted and corrected pattern from which the blouse is cut.

Original pattern	
Bodice muslin	
Muslin pattern	
New pattern	
Original seam line	- - - - -
New seam line	- - - - -
Grain line	————

Making a bodice muslin

You may have a suitable plain remnant from which you can make your muslin. Or a used sheet with enough sound material left to make your mock-up blouse would do, bearing in mind that the material you use must be firm enough to stand sewing and fitting. Alternatively you will need 1¼yd 36in wide cotton or sheeting which you can purchase from fabric stores or large department stores. You will also need paper for patterns, a tailor's square or 45° set square, two pencils (one colored), a ruler.

 Making the muslin pattern

Measure your length from the neck to the waistline, back and front (see Generally Speaking chapter 4), and mark off these measurements on the Back and Front patterns.

Lay the Back and Front patterns together at the side-seam with the lower stitching line of the side bust dart meeting the balance mark on the Back. Draw a pencil line across both pattern pieces to connect the waistline marks. This will give you the pattern length required to make the muslin.

Lay these pattern pieces on a large sheet of paper. Draw around the edges and into the darts. Mark the waistline and balance marks. Then copy the penciled waist onto the muslin pattern.

Cut out and trim the muslin pattern at the waist.

 Cutting the bodice muslin

Fold the material or sheeting lengthwise. Place the Back section of the muslin pattern to the fold line and the Front section to the selvages.

Allow at least 1in seam allowance at all seam edges, except at the Center Front where it wraps over, and at least 2in at the waist.

Transfer all the pattern markings on to the fabric, then cut out and remove the pattern.

Open up the cut fabric pieces and draw in the grain lines of the fabric with colored pencil.

 Marking the grain lines on the muslin

To find the lengthwise grain, measure about 3½ inches in from the Center Back and the Center Front lines and draw a line parallel to each of these.

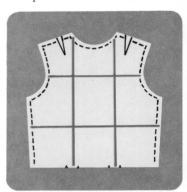

To find the crosswise grain on each piece, lay a tailor's square or 45° set square to the Center Back and Center Front and draw lines across the fabric halfway between the waistline and the side bust dart and halfway between shoulder and underarm seam.

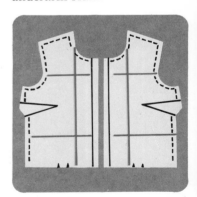

 Fitting the muslin

Pin and baste the shoulder and side seams and darts. Do not baste the pleats in the waistline; they will be pinned into darts when you fit the muslin.

Try on the bodice over a slip. Pin the fronts together down the Center Front line.

Always start fitting from the shoulders downwards, working towards the waist.

NECK AND ARMHOLES

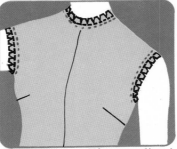

1. Problem The muslin is tight and pulls or is raised around the neck or armholes.
Correction If it's the neckline that is tight, snip into the seam allowance. Mark a new neckline on the muslin around the base of the neck and snip to this line until the garment sits without straining.
The correction is exactly the same for the armholes.

2. Problem Thin arms. The armhole is too large.
Correction Raise the underarm curve into seam allowance.

3. Problem Thin neck. The neckline is too large.
Correction Use the seam allowance on the muslin to mark the correct position for the neckline. If the neckline is still not the right size, you will have to baste strips of fabric around the neck on which to mark the new stitching line.

SHOULDERS

Color Key to fitting

The bodice muslin

Original seamline `- - - -`

New seamline `-- - --`

Problem color

Correction: color

Grain lines `———`

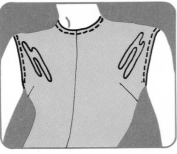

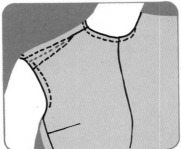

4. Problem Straight shoulders.
The fabric strains at the outer end of the shoulder seam.
Correction Undo the shoulder seam and let it out.

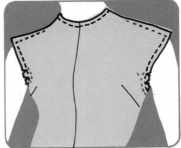

5. Problem Sloping shoulders.
The seam rises above the shoulder at the outer edge and there are often drag lines from the inner shoulders towards the underarm.
Correction Take the surplus material into the shoulder-seam. Snip the seam allowance around the underarm curve, lifting the material on the Front until you have a smooth fit. Do the same for the Back and watch the crosswise grain.

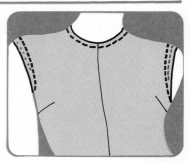

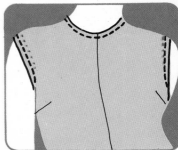

6. Problem Shoulders too wide or too narrow.
Correction To find the position for the armhole-seam, follow the crease of your underarm around the front on to the top of outer shoulder points. Continue working this line towards the back. When halfway down the back move your arm forwards very slightly and continue to work towards the crease of the underarm. This is to allow ease for movement.

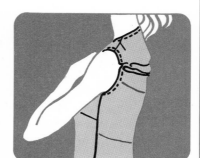

7. Problem Rounded back. This often accompanies round shoulders.

The horizontal grain lines tilt down toward the side seams.
Correction Undo the side seams. Lift the back side seams until the grain is straight, and pin. Use the balance marks as a guide to see that you get the same lift on each side. Rip the shoulder seam, then lift the fullness around the armhole into the shoulder seam by deepening the dart.

If the problem is very pronounced, undo the shoulder darts and take the depth of the darts and the surplus fabric into the neckline by making two darts on each side of the center back.

Repin the shoulder seams and mark a new armhole line to match up with the line on the front section, because the original line will have moved in on the shoulder. Re-mark the underarm line, which has also been displaced, but allow plenty of width across the back.

8. Problem Straight, very erect back.

The horizontal grain lines drop at the back toward the center.
Correction If the drop is between the neck and underarm, pin a fold right across the back section, starting at the center, until the grain runs straight. Any fullness below that point can be let down into the waist seam, but only as far as the straight of the grain will allow. If this isn't enough, you will have to pin another fold line, tapering off toward the side seams, below the armhole.

The bodice front should hang straight from the shoulders now, and is ready to be fitted into the waist.

Pin off the ease and fullness into the side seams, beginning at the underarm edge. The bodice muslin should now fit comfortably but not loosely over the bust.

The fullness below the bust should fall straight toward the waistline.

Pin off the side seam into the waist without causing the fullness under the bust to be pulled sideways.

Then, starting at the waist and using the pleat marks as your guide, pin this fullness into darts which should finish at the point of the bust.

Lengthen the pleat marks in the back section into darts also.

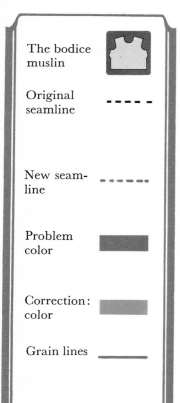

The bodice muslin	
Original seamline	– – –
New seamline	- - - - -
Problem color	
Correction color	
Grain lines	———

BUST AND WAISTLINE

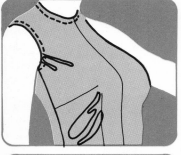 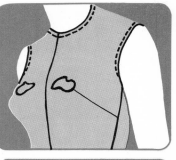  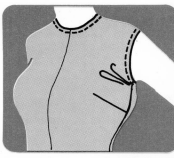

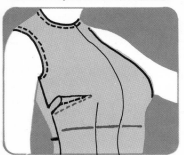 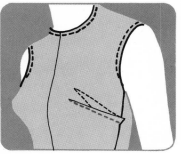 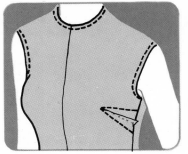 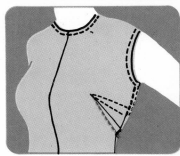

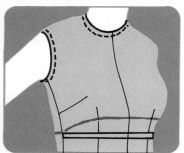
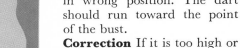

9. Problem Full bust.

Usually shown by drag lines from the bust toward the side seams at the waistline.

Correction Pin a tape in a straight line across the front of the muslin, starting and ending at the seamline on the lower grain line. Allow the grain line, but not the tape, to rise when the bust has taken it up. Mark the muslin along the edge of the tape, using a different colored pencil so that you cannot confuse this line with the grain line.

Remove the tape.

Undo the side seams and lift the fabric into the side bust dart on the lower stitching line only.

Check the crosswise grain line on the lower half of the muslin and don't pin any more into the side dart than will allow the grain line to run straight across the pattern.

The side seams will now be shorter, so pin a new line for the waist.

10. Problem Side bust darts in wrong position. The dart should run toward the point of the bust.

Correction If it is too high or too low, drop it or raise it.

11. Problem Shallow bust. The point of the side bust dart creates fullness over the bust and does not run out smoothly. You will notice that the lower grain line curves downward toward the center front.

Correction Undo the side seams and let out the side bust dart on the lower stitching line, allowing the fabric to drop into the waist until the grain line runs straight across the pattern.

Repin the side seams, taking in the surplus width from the front.

Your armhole may need re-shaping around the front.

12. Problem Underarm bulge.

Pulling under the armhole.

Correction Slant the side bust darts by making them a little lower at the side seams. Let out the side seams between the underarm dart and the armhole line.

89

Balancing the muslin corrections

Mark all pin and pencil lines with basting thread.

Remove the pins and rip the stitching.

Fold the back section on the center back line, matching all edges, and place the front sections together.

Compare the alterations on the

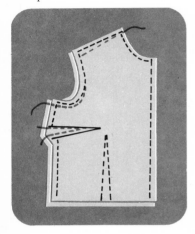

left and right side of each piece. Even out any differences, as for the skirts in Dressmaking 6, except where you have made alterations for uneven sides. Trace the new lines on both sides of the muslin.

Pin and baste together again for a final check.

Preparing the muslin

Rip the basting on the muslin. Cut off all seam allowances and cut out the area between the stitching lines of all darts. Cut the back section of the

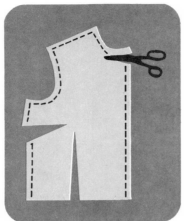

muslin along the center back line, unless you have made adjustments for uneven sides. (See notes on "Uneven sides," p.93.)

As the left and right bodice pieces are now the same, you need to work only with the half which corresponds to the pattern.

With the right sides of the muslin pattern and the corresponding muslin pieces uppermost, lay the muslin front section on the pattern front and the muslin back on the pattern back.

Having pinned away the ease into the side seams in the last chapter, you will see at once that the pattern is much wider than the muslin. Shirt blouses must have a 3 or 4in ease over the bust, and to make them blouse at the waist they are cut with very little shaping. Ignore the under bust dart on the muslin until later, when you will be shown how to alter the pattern to fit larger bust proportions.

Preparing the new pattern

Place the original basic back and front patterns onto a large sheet of paper and draw around

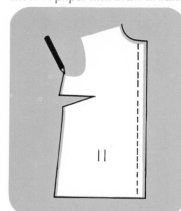

them. Draw into the darts and transfer all markings onto the new pattern. Allow enough room around each piece for corrections.

Making the new pattern

Original pattern	
Bodice muslin	
Muslin pattern	
New pattern	
Original seamline	- - - - -
New seamline	- - - - -
Grain line	————

NECK AND ARMHOLES

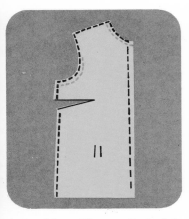

1. Problem The muslin is tight around the neck or armholes.
Altering pattern Mark the new neckline or armhole onto the new pattern.

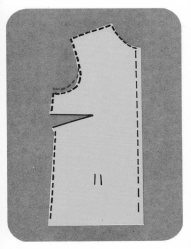

2. Problem Thin arms.
Altering pattern Mark the new underarm seam on the new pattern.

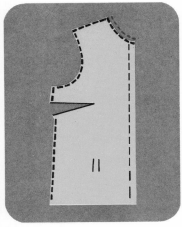

3. Problem Thin neck.
Altering pattern Mark the new neckline on the new pattern.

SHOULDERS

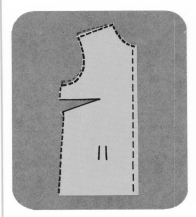

4. Problem Straight shoulders.
Altering pattern Mark the new shoulder line on the new pattern. If the armhole is now too large, it must be raised at the underarm.

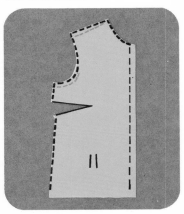

5. Problem Sloping shoulders.
Altering pattern Mark the new shoulder line onto the new pattern. If the armhole is now too small, it must be lowered at the underarm.

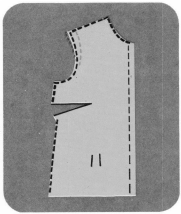

6. Problem Shoulders too wide or too narrow.
Altering pattern Mark the new armhole line over the shoulder onto the new pattern.

BACK

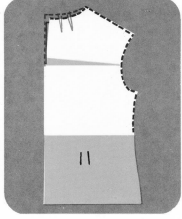

7. Problem Rounded back.
Altering pattern The back pattern section needs extra length between the base of the neck and the waist. If you have only deepened the shoulder dart, mark the new dart length on the muslin pattern and adjust the shoulder seam and armhole line.

If the problem is pronounced and you have pinned neckline darts, pin the center back of the muslin pattern to the center back of the new pattern.

Measure the distance from the neck to the highest point of the curve on your back and draw a straight line across the pinned muslin pattern at this point.

Unpin the top part of the muslin pattern and cut along the pencil line to within $\frac{1}{4}$in of the armhole.

Measure the extra depth of the darts you pinned on the muslin at the neck (that is, the depth of the new darts less the depth of the discarded shoulder dart), and open up the slash across the pattern by this amount.

The muslin pattern has now swung outward and away from the center back line, so use the center back line of the new pattern as your guide. Lay the muslin along this line and copy all the fitting alterations. Complete the neckline in a shallow curve as shown, connecting the shoulder line to the new center back. Adjust the shoulder seam as pinned.

Mark the two neck darts onto the new pattern, otherwise the neckline of the new pattern will be too large.

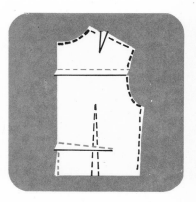

8. Problem Straight, erect back.
Altering pattern If there is too much length between the shoulder and armhole, pin a fold across the muslin pattern to the same depth as on muslin. If there is too much length between the armhole and waistline, mainly concentrated in the center of the back, pin a dart across the muslin pattern, about 4in above the waistline, beginning on the center back line and tapering toward the side seam, to the depth of the one pinned on the muslin. On the blouse, you need only correct the extra length between the shoulder and the armhole and adjust the armhole on the new pattern to preserve the original shape. For corrections below the armhole, lay muslin pattern on new pattern. Shorten the center back line by the depth of the pleat and let out the side seam by the amount the center back line is tipped forward.

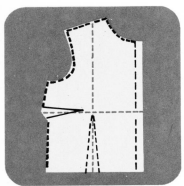

9. Problem Full bust.
Altering pattern All the corrections for a full bust are transferred from the muslin onto the muslin pattern. Using the muslin pattern as a guide, a corrected muslin pattern is drawn up, then this corrected muslin pattern is used to make the new pattern, using the basic pattern as a guide to allow for the ease required.

Transfer the markings for the darts and side seams from the fitted muslin onto the muslin pattern.

On the front muslin pattern, draw a straight line from the waist upward through the point under the bust dart and draw a horizontal line across the pattern through the point of the side bust dart.

Cut the pattern on the penciled horizontal line only.

Lay the front muslin pattern along the straight edge of a sheet of paper.

Move the bottom half of the muslin pattern away from the top half, the distance between the crosswise grain markings and the colored line drawn on the line of the tape. Pin both pattern pieces to the straight edge of the paper along the center front line. Cut the penciled vertical line to within $\frac{1}{4}$in of the shoulder line.

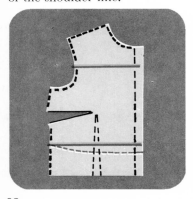

To find the distance by which the pattern should be spread, make the following small calculation:

Measure the depth of the under bust dart in the waistline and deduct $2\frac{1}{4}$in (the normal depth for an under bust dart).

Beginning with the lower side section, spread the pattern outward by this amount. Pin into position.

To obtain the extra depth required for the side bust dart, pivot the upper side sections of the pattern until the distance between the cutting lines on the side seam is the

amount by which you have lengthened the pattern, plus the extra depth of the side bust dart.

Find the pointed ends of the darts in the center of the pattern spread. Use the muslin to mark in the depth of the darts.

Lay the muslin over the pattern and check the dart position. If you had to raise or lower the darts, transfer the new position to the pattern.

Straighten the shoulder line before cutting out the new muslin pattern.

Remember that the upper and lower stitching lines of the side bust dart must be of equal length and that you will have to make an adjustment to the lower side seam.

Cut out the correct muslin pattern. To adjust the new pattern, lay the corrected muslin pattern along the center front line of the new pattern. The corrected muslin pattern will be smaller, because there is no ease in it. Use the corrected muslin pattern to adjust the new blouse pattern and add the ease onto the side seam, which must be $\frac{3}{4}$in

on both back and front. This must be measured from the top of the side seam on the pattern and taken all along the side seam. Mark in the alteration to the darts.

Check the size of the armhole. The ease in the blouse should continue over the bust. So when you lay the muslin pattern onto the new pattern, the lower armhole curve should be $\frac{1}{2}$in outside the armhole line of the muslin pattern and should taper into the armhole on the muslin pattern at the underarm, halfway along the armhole toward the shoulder. Always remember to measure the length of the side seams after adjustments and even them up, as the length should remain static. The extra length is added to the hemline of the new pattern.

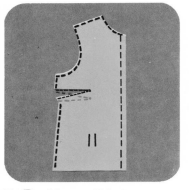

10. Problem Side bust darts in wrong position.
Altering pattern Using the muslin, draw in corrected dart positions on the new pattern.

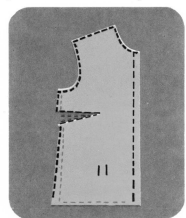

11. Problem Shallow bust.
Altering pattern Copy the new dart and side seam, allowing $\frac{3}{4}$in for ease, and adjust the length on the new pattern,

trimming off the extra length on the front hemline.
Reshape the underarm curve if necessary.

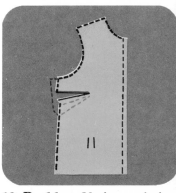

12. Problem Underarm bulge.
Altering pattern Correct the slant of the underarm dart on the muslin pattern.

To let out the top of the side seam on the pattern, fold the lowered dart in the stitching position.

You will see that the lower stitching line of the dart projects over the side seam. The amount by which it projects gives the extra width needed at the top of the side seam.

If you had to take more fabric into the dart, remember to adjust the lower edge of the pattern accordingly.

Transfer corrections onto the new pattern.

UNEVEN SIDES

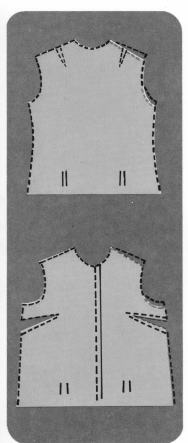

If you find after adjusting the muslin that you have pronounced differences, such as one sloping shoulder or one high shoulder, or one side of the bust larger than the other, make corrections as follows:

First compare and balance all the fitting alterations on the muslin, with the exception of the differences.

Draw up the other half of the new back and front pattern sections identical to the first half. Cut out the pattern pieces, leaving 1in seam allowances all around and 2in at the hem.

Join the back pattern sections along the center back line and pin the front pattern sections together along the center front line.

Correct the new pattern, making the adjustments on each side of the pattern as required. Trim the pattern along the new seamlines.

When cutting, you must unfold the fabric and use the complete back and the complete front sections of the pattern.

ALTERING THE SLEEVE PATTERNS

If you have made the armhole larger or smaller, you will of course have to alter the sleeve pattern by the same amount. Most sleeves need only minor adjustments and these can usually be done when fitting the cut-out sleeve. But here are four pattern adjustments which must be done before cutting, because they affect the shape of the sleeve cap as well as the fit of the sleeve.

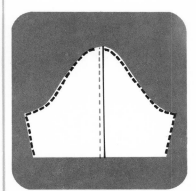

Thin upper arms

Pin a small vertical pleat about ½in deep (depending on the size of the armhole alteration) through the center of the sleeve pattern. Pin the pleated pattern onto a sheet of paper and pencil around it for the new pattern.

Large upper arms

Cut the pattern through the center from the hem to the top of the cap. Pin the pattern to a sheet of paper, spreading the pattern pieces apart by the required amount. Pencil around the spread-out pattern for a new sleeve pattern.

Heavy shoulders

Slash the pattern vertically from the shoulder to within ½ inch of the hem edge. Pin the pattern to a sheet of paper and spread it by the required amount, tapering it toward the hem. Pencil around the spread pattern pieces for a new sleeve pattern.

Straight shoulders and large upper arms

Work as for large upper arms, but also raise the cap of the sleeve by the same amount you let out of the shoulder seam if the underarm seam has not been raised.

Here are four pretty styles which can be made from the Golden Hands Blouse Graph. Instructions on the previous pages will ensure a perfect fit.

Chapter 24

About commercial paper patterns

Muslin-making

Commercial paper patterns are the greatest invention since the sewing machine as an aid to successful home dressmaking, and any sewing course would not be complete if it did not teach you how to use them properly. In using the specially designed patterns from the Golden Hands Graph Pages you have become familiar with pattern shapes, how to adjust them for fitting, and how to adapt them to other styles. Now is an appropriate moment to introduce commercial paper patterns into Golden Hands dressmaking and in using them, show you how you can apply all the knowledge you have gained so far. Many people think that paper patterns are hard to use and their instruction sheets difficult to follow. This chapter may help to dispel this belief.

Facts about commercial paper patterns
Today, commercial paper patterns are as nearly perfect as you can ever expect them to be and the home dressmaker now has the best of all worlds—a perfect combination of design and fabric as well as a better, more lasting finish, and clothes which are so much cheaper.

The drafting and grading of commercial paper patterns has reached such a high level that if you are a standard size you can make a dress without trying it on at all and yet achieve a reasonable fit.

As far as sizing is concerned, you may find that one particular commercial pattern fits you better than another but, apart from small differences in detail, they are all very similar, as the big pattern companies adhere strictly to an international sizing code.

There was a time when the name on a pattern catalogue was an indication of its fashion content, but this is no longer so. The pattern industry is a very competitive one and each company caters to a variety of tastes and requirements. Also, changes in fashion can now be translated quickly and effectively into paper pattern form, making each catalogue as exciting as a shop window.

The cost of patterns varies according to the design or the contents of the pack. Some cost slightly more because there are several variations in one pack, while with others it is the individual design which is expensive (as with Vogue Couturier patterns) and the cost of the pattern should be compared with the end result. You cannot expect to have an exclusive design for the price of a mass produced one—the cost is relative and you get what you pay for.

When selecting a design, decide on the purpose of the garment and choose accordingly. For casual outings choose a simple but good design and leave the special, more complicated, designs for those occasions when you want to look beautifully dressed. This way you will enjoy making and wearing your clothes.

Reading a commercial paper pattern
In the pattern envelope you will find sheets of tissue paper with shapes printed on them; these are the pattern pieces. Sometimes they are all printed on one sheet; if so, cut them out, leaving a margin around the outlines.

If you are not sure what all the lines and symbols mean, take a pattern from the Golden Hands Graph Pages and place it beside the commercial paper pattern. Compare and identify the markings. Here the basic blouse pattern and Vogue Pattern 1002 are used (figures **1** and **3**).

The lines. The outline of each pattern piece is a heavy solid line inside of which is another, lighter line. This inner line may be broken or continuous. These double lines are the seam and cutting lines, the space between them, usually $\frac{5}{8}$ inch, being the seam allowance with the inner, lighter line as the seamline. When there is only one line, it indicates that that line must be placed and cut on a fabric fold or no seam allowance is needed.

Hemlines are rarely given, but the hem allowance is written against the solid line at the bottom of the pattern.

Inside each pattern piece you will find a variety of lines—stitching lines, lengthening and shortening lines, darts and grain lines. The lines usually carry wording to say what they are, but if in doubt, find the key to them on the instruction sheet.

Although the major pattern companies are now producing printed patterns only, you might come across some patterns which have perforated markings instead of printed lines. If so, lay the pattern on a hard dark surface and read the key to the perforations. Then connect the relevant perforations with pencil lines so that you can see at a glance where the seams, darts and other lines are. Apart from the fact that these patterns are perforated instead of printed, they are cut to size exactly like the others, with seam allowances included.

Read the key to the perforations carefully and if you still find them confusing and want to make sure that you will not make any mistakes when cutting, mark the seam and dart lines with a red pencil—that is red for danger, do not cut!

Symbols. Looking at the printed pattern, you will see a number of symbols—large dots and tiny dots, diamonds, triangles and squares. These all have a meaning, some have to be matched to another symbol of the same shape either on another pattern piece or on another stitching line on the same piece, such as with darts. The diamonds along the seamlines or seam allowances are the balance marks, and by having them printed in groups they are also a code to the seam in question.

On perforated patterns you will find cut out "V" notches and perforated symbols in varying shapes and sizes. These have the same meaning as symbols on the printed patterns.

The symbols are very important, and using them as they are meant to be used will help you to avoid making time-wasting mistakes.

Personalizing commercial paper patterns
You will now find out just how valuable the bodice muslin is (see previous chapter).

If you have not made one already, you should do so now and then transfer all the fitting corrections to the Golden Hands basic blouse pattern. This will save you time and trouble later.

To correct the fit of the commercial paper pattern, lay it over the corrected Golden Hands pattern or muslin and see what adjustments are necessary.

If you have to make drastic alterations, such as those for a rounded back, pin the muslin under the pattern and make the adjustments using tissue paper or soft wrapping paper and transparent tape. Remember that the muslin has no seam allowance, so take this into account before cutting out the new shape.

Adjustments to length should also be made at this stage. Lengthen or shorten the pattern as shown in previous chapters. If the seams are shaped, always connect them carefully to avoid "stepping" when you cut out the fabric.

Fitting alterations to sleeves are covered later in this chapter.

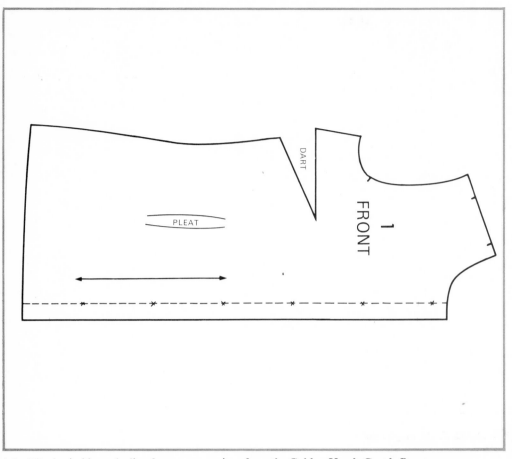

▲ **1.** *The basic blouse bodice front pattern piece from the Golden Hands Graph Pages*
▼ **3.** *Vogue Pattern 1002 showing the bodice front pattern piece*

▲ **2.** *The second skin bodice muslin without ease*
▼ **4.** *The Vogue Pattern dress muslin with ease*

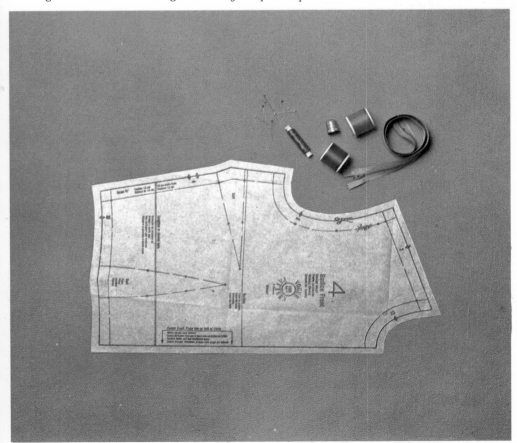

Use your personalized Vogue 1002 dress muslin for fitted styles from any commercial paper pattern

The muslin pattern can be used with front and back fastening bodices

The instruction sheet

Each commercial paper pattern comes with an instruction sheet. Use this to identify the pattern pieces needed for making the particular version you have chosen. The sheet also contains layouts for all sizes and fabric widths.

The actual instructions on the sheet are merely a guide to the assembling of the various sections and the finish of the garment. As you will have discovered from previous chapters, the Golden Hands step-by-step instructions always include preparing the garment for fitting. So, using the instruction sheet, first read "baste" where it says "stitch" as you prepare the garment to be fitted. Then read through the instructions again, step-by-step as you make the garment, and you will find that they really help the dressmaking to go easily and smoothly.

Making a dress from a commercial paper pattern

Vogue Pattern 1002 has been chosen to give you a full working example of how to use a commercial paper pattern. This pattern is a simple waisted dress which is "Vogue's guide to perfect fit of fitted garments."

It is being made up as a dress muslin which can be used later to adjust other patterns (figure **4**).

This dress muslin differs from the Golden Hands bodice muslin (figure **2**) which was made without ease to help you make the correct adjustments for figure faults. The dress muslin, however, not only incorporates the fitting corrections which you should have copied already, but also includes ease (or tolerance) so that you can make sure there is enough room for movement.

Do not throw the bodice muslin away when you have made the dress muslin because you will be shown later how to use the two together.

Cutting out

Make the dress muslin from unbleached muslin or soft cotton, buying the amount stated on the pattern envelope. Do not use old, heavily used fabric because the results will not be the same.

The pattern has seven pattern pieces. Position them on the fabric as shown on the pattern layouts.

Start pinning the pattern on the fabric. Here you will encounter your first snag. Patterns made from tissue paper do not have the same resistance to creasing as the sturdy Golden Hands patterns. Therefore, to avoid losing on your pattern size, fasten down the center of each pattern with two or three pins or, if it is laid along the fabric

fold, pin it at right angles to the fold at intervals of about 10 inches. Smooth the pattern out toward the seams.

To check how much the pattern decreases in size, make a chalk line along the pattern edge before pinning further, then pin it down all around and see how much the pattern has moved in. If it has moved by $\frac{1}{8}$ inch or more, you will need to cut outside the cutting line, otherwise at least $\frac{1}{2}$ inch will be lost from the size of the pattern.

When you position the pattern pieces, leave a small margin between them even though the seam allowances are already marked on the pattern. If the fabric has a tendency to fray, it is wise to cut a little more than the given seam allowance.

Cut out the pattern.

Marking the pattern detail

The seams cannot be marked with continuous tailor's tacks, like the Golden Hands patterns, because of the inclusion of the seam allowance, so make small slits through the pattern along the stitching lines, at about 5 inch intervals, and make single tailor's tacks through them. For the balance marks, make a tailor's tack at right angles to the seam line.

It is best to mark the symbols with different colored threads. But make a note of what each color represents on the symbol key to prevent confusion later.

One very important point to remember: Where darts are marked with solid lines only, always make a tailor's tack where the dart goes across the seamline. It is all too easy to take up a little more, or less, in the darts than specified and you will then find that the seams do not match.

Assembling the dress from the instruction sheet

With the fabric details clearly marked you are ready to start assembling the dress. Lay the instruction sheet before you as you work and following the text and diagrams, pin and baste the seams.

Stop when you get to the facing stage. Join the skirt to the bodice along the waist seam ready for fitting.

Since the waist seam is always a very delicate fitting point, even on the slimmest figure, it is essential that you fit it with waist belting. This does not have to be put into the finished garment, where it may be too stiff for your requirements, but it is the only safe way to check at the fitting stage that the finished waist seam will be in the right place.

Cut a strip of 1 inch wide belting ribbon to the length of your waist, plus 1 inch for fastening over and adjustment. Pin and baste it to the waist seam of the dress, easing in the tolerance of the waistline evenly. The seam should run along the center of the belting.

Leave a small piece unstitched at the back on each side of the opening so that you can fold the seam allowance along the opening and fasten the ends of the belting.

Fitting the waisted dress

After copying all the fitting adjustments made from the Golden Hands pattern onto the commercial paper pattern, only the new fitting problems associated with fitted dresses are left to be checked.

The ease or tolerance requirement is very important and varies according to the figure. Even if you are a standard size, there may not be enough ease included with a fitted dress, so it is a good idea for all figure types to fit and adjust the pattern. Fasten the back opening, and sit, stoop, then stretch your arms forward to make sure that the stress on the seams does not distort or split them.

If you want tight fitted sleeves, your arm movement is restricted at all times as your waist is by a fitted waist. To compensate a little for these restrictions, allow plenty of ease (no bulk though) over the bust and across the back. Set in the sleeves really high and make sure that the sleeve cap is not tight across the upper arm.

Another important point to watch when making a fitted dress: Always fit the dress after meals because body measurements change during the day. An evening dress fitted in the morning may become too tight and uncomfortable to wear at night. Victorian ladies used to stay in bed until after midday if they wanted to look slim at night!

Altering the sleeve pattern to fit

Thin arms (figure 5). Make a pleat along the center of the sleeve pattern as shown in the correcting of the short sleeve pattern in Muslin-making chapter 23, page 93.

Large arms (figure 6). Cut through the pattern as shown in the correcting of the

5. Altering the sleeve pattern for thin arms

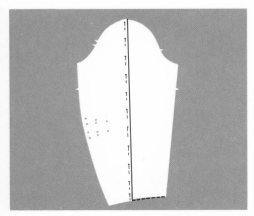

short sleeve pattern in Muslin-making chapter 23. Make a new pattern.

Muscular forearm and top arm (figure 7). Slash the pattern from hem to seamline at the crown of the sleeve cap. Spread the pattern sideways by the required amount as shown. This will form fullness between the crown and underarm which should be lapped and pinned to enable the pattern to lie flat. Make a new pattern adding the amount of the fullness pinned off to the crown of the sleeve cap.

Large upper arms (figure 8). Cut the pattern as shown; spread it outward by the required amount. Draw a new pattern.

Very straight arms (figure 9). If, at the fitting stage, you find there is a lot of fullness at the back of the sleeve cap and that the curve of the sleeve does not follow the arm, move the crown of the sleeve forward by moving the balance mark, which meets the shoulder seamline back by $\frac{1}{2}$ inch or more. If this only shifts the problem of fullness from one place to another, correct the sleeve cap by pinning off the required amount and then correct the pattern.

Slash into the sleeve seam on the pattern as shown, then pleat off the required amount across the sleeve cap and redraw the pattern.

Finishing the muslin

Finish the muslin, following the instructions. Mark in colored pencil on the muslin anything worth noting for further use. Keep the muslin in a safe place because it will help you time and again to check the fitting of other patterns.

Adjusting the pattern after fitting

Transfer the markings from the dress muslin to the pattern pieces where you have made adjustments to the fitting.

Using the pattern again

Although you can use a commercial paper pattern more than once, when you have to start ironing it to get the creases out, it is time to buy a new one. The creases can be ironed out, but it seems that the paper shrinks and retains the width taken up by the creases.

It is not a good idea, though, to copy the pattern pieces onto firmer paper because there is no stiff edge to work around and the result could be very inaccurate, especially on large areas.

If you have to copy a pattern piece after a severe alteration, use soft wrapping paper which can be bought in rolls. Remember to continue both the cutting and seam lines onto the new pattern, otherwise you will lose the seam allowances where you made the alterations.

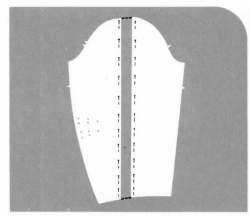

▲ 6. *Altering the sleeve pattern for large arms*
▼ 7. *Altering sleeve pattern for muscular arms*

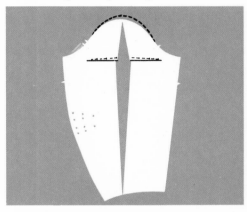

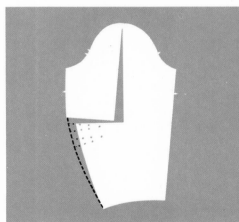

▲ 8. *Altering sleeve pattern for large upper arms*
▼ 9. *Altering sleeve pattern for straight arms*

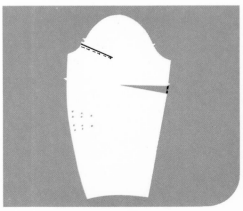

Basic Blouse Graph Pattern

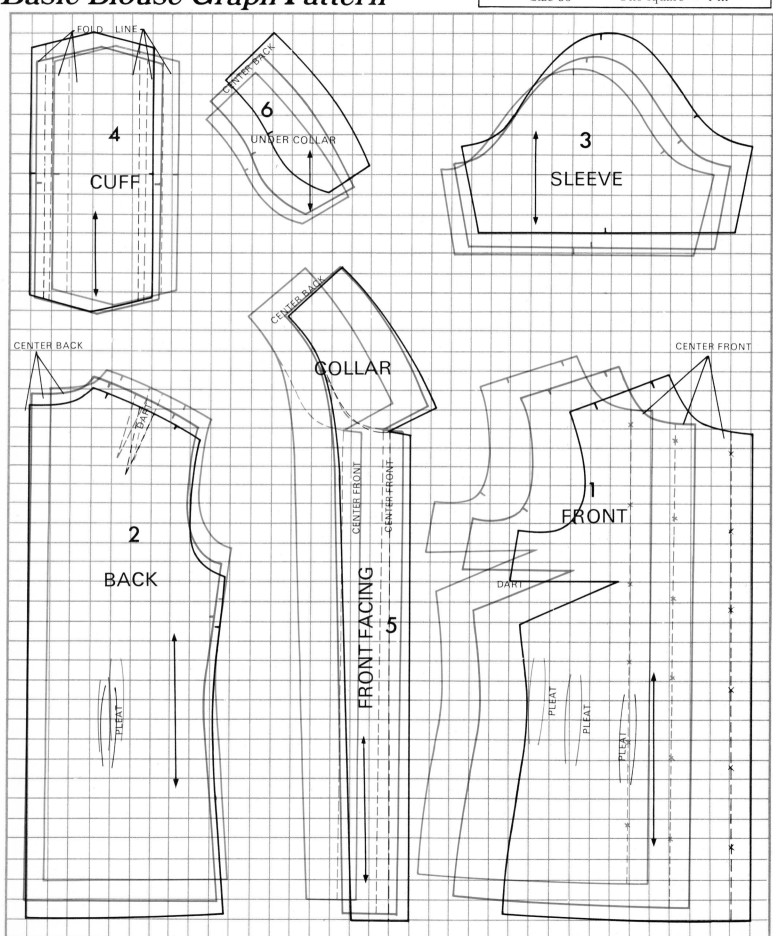

KEY

Size 32½
Size 34
Size 36

Straight of grain
One square = 1 in

4 CUFF

FOLD LINE

6 UNDER COLLAR

CENTER BACK

3 SLEEVE

COLLAR

CENTER BACK

CENTER FRONT

2 BACK

DART

PLEAT

5 FRONT FACING

CENTER FRONT

CENTER FRONT

1 FRONT

DART

PLEAT

PLEAT

PLEAT

The outlines given are the stitching lines.
Refer to page 139 for seam allowances
and check with the following chapters for
any variations.

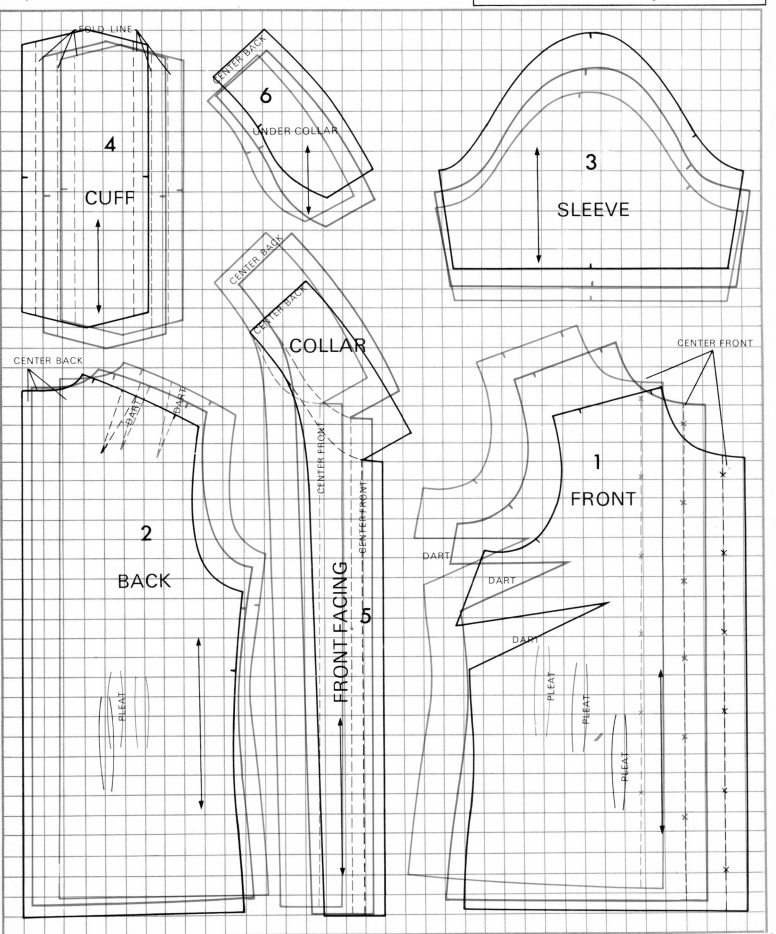

Chapter 25

The basic blouse

Here we give you instructions for making one of the most useful garments in every woman's wardrobe — the basic shirtneck, short-sleeved blouse. If you have already made the muslin, remember to transfer all your corrections before cutting out the blouse —you will be assured of success at a fraction of the cost of an off-the-rack model. Instructions for making a variety of other exciting blouses are given on the following pages.

Choosing the fabric

The choice of fabrics for making blouses is exciting, because there is such a variety of lightweight materials available— plain, patterned or textured.

Here is a list of the most suitable fabrics for the basic short-sleeved blouse and variation shown here. The fabric needs to be crisp enough to hold the tailored shape of this blouse, but many other fabrics, which are not suitable for the basic style, will be included later for the other versions you see here. The first list has been especially selected for the beginner:

Firmly woven cottons: poplin, men's shirting, Swiss cotton, lawn, denim, piqué.

Linens: embroidered or other fine blouse-weight linen.

You can add the following to your list if you have a little practical experience in handling finer fabrics:

Silks, pure and artificial: shantung, Honan and fine Thai silk.

Man-made fibers: woven Terylene and Courtelle or similar acrylic and polyester fibers; triacetate and rayon fabrics.

The yardage

The yardage needed for the basic green blouse with pointed cuffs is on the yardage chart which appears below. For the floral, roll-sleeved variation the yardages are the same except for the following sizes, which all need $\frac{1}{4}$ yard extra: sizes $32\frac{1}{2}$ and 34, 54in wide fabric, without one way; sizes 36 and 38, 36in wide fabric without one way, 54in wide fabric with and without one way; sizes 40 and 42, 36in wide fabric without one way, 54in wide fabric with and without one way.

When you are buying your fabric, remember that you will also need four buttons and matching thread.

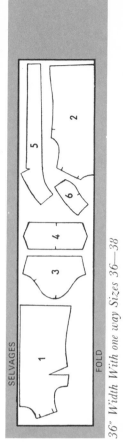

36" Width With one way Sizes 36—38

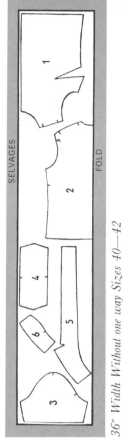

36" Width Without one way Sizes 40—42

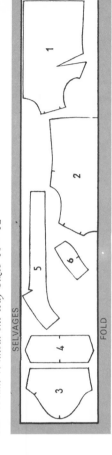

36" Width With one way Sizes 40—42

36" Width Without one way Sizes $32\frac{1}{2}$—34

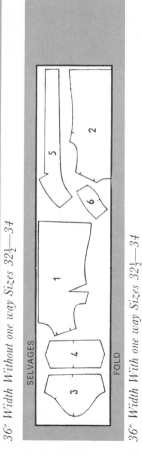

36" Width With one way Sizes $32\frac{1}{2}$—34

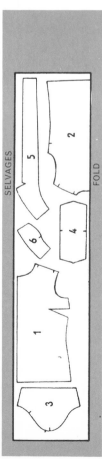

36" Width Without one way Sizes 36—38

Blouse yardages

Sizes				$32\frac{1}{2}$	34	36	38	40	42
36" Without one way	..			$2\frac{1}{2}$	$2\frac{1}{2}$	$2\frac{5}{8}$	$2\frac{5}{8}$	$2\frac{3}{4}$	$2\frac{3}{4}$
With one way	..			$2\frac{1}{2}$	$2\frac{1}{2}$	$2\frac{5}{8}$	$2\frac{5}{8}$	$2\frac{7}{8}$	$2\frac{7}{8}$
54" Without one way	..			$1\frac{1}{2}$	$1\frac{5}{8}$	$1\frac{7}{8}$	$1\frac{7}{8}$	$1\frac{7}{8}$	$1\frac{7}{8}$
With one way	..			$1\frac{3}{4}$	$1\frac{3}{4}$	2	2	2	2

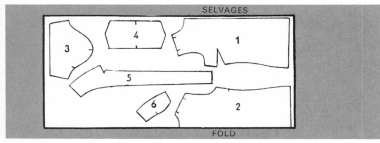

54" Width Without one way Sizes 32½—34

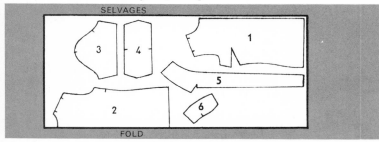

54" Width With one way Sizes 32½—36

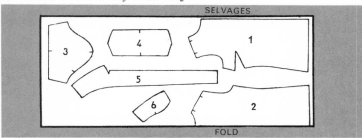

54" Width Without one way Sizes 36—38

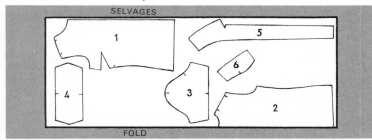

54" Width With one way Sizes 36—38

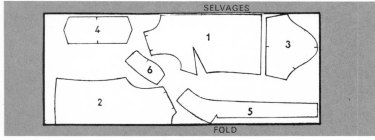

54" Width Without one way Sizes 40—42

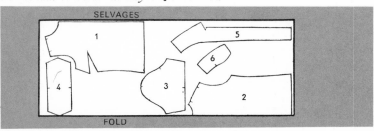

54" Width With one way Sizes 40—42

Two moods of the basic blouse, instructions are given here for both.

Altering the collar

The collar fitting will not be affected by the alterations to the pattern except where your neck is larger or smaller than the pattern size.

Depending on whether the neck line has been altered at the Back or Front, or both, cut out the collar pattern along the broken lines indicated on the sketch.

Place the cut pattern on to a sheet of paper.

To make the collar larger, spread the pieces by the required amount and pin them in place.

To make the collar smaller, overlap the sections by the required amount and pin them in place.

To make a new pattern, draw round the pinned pattern and cut out.

Front facing, under collar, cuff

Any alteration to the collar must be transferred to the under collar.

If the Centre Front length of the pattern has been altered, alter the length of the front facing.

Any alterations made to the sleeve hems will affect the cuffs, so alter the cuffs accordingly.

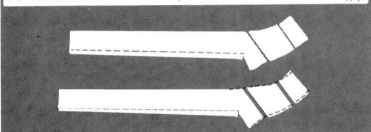

Before cutting—a word on seams

Shirt blouses are usually designed for hard wear and continual washing, and it is therefore wise to make them in materials which withstand both.

The seams must be strong to stand up to this treatment. So, for the blouses shown here, a flat-fell seam is used, where all the raw edges are stitched firmly in position.

Flat-fell seams are the traditional type of seaming for shirts.

Seam allowance

Up to now all Golden Hands patterns have used $\frac{3}{4}$in seam allowances. But to avoid double seam trimming on the shirt blouse, and to give you the correct seam allowance when you come to stitch the flat-fell seam, allow only $\frac{5}{8}$in for seams with this pattern.

Preparing the fabric for cutting

Green basic blouse with pointed cuffs. Straighten the fabric and fold it lengthwise, selvage to selvage. Use a large table for cutting out, which will accommodate as much of the fabric as possible and enable you to lay it out smoothly.

Select the correct layout from the Basic Blouse Graph pattern and follow it carefully.

Pin all the pattern pieces securely on the fabric, with the center back on the fold as indicated, and using any corrected new pattern pieces you have drawn up. If the fabric you are using marks easily, don't use too many pins.

Remember, no seam or hem allowances are given on the pattern, so mark these on the fabric around each piece. Allow $\frac{5}{8}$in allowance for both seams and hems.

Cut out the blouse pieces.

Floral, roll-up sleeve variation. Before cutting out this blouse you will have to alter the basic blouse sleeve pattern as shown in the diagram on this page. Place the pattern (or new sleeve pattern if you had to make one in the last chapter) on a sheet of paper about

twice the length of the pattern, and draw around it. Remove the pattern from the sheet of paper.

Straighten the slope of the underarm seam and extend it for 8in.

Mark the fold line 3in down from the old sleeve edge.

Cut out the pattern along the new lines as indicated.

The cutting instructions and layouts are the same as for the basic

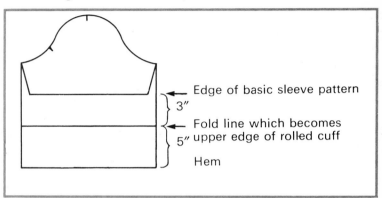

Adapting the basic sleeve pattern for the roll-up sleeve blouse variation

blouse, except that you will not need the cuff pattern and will substitute the sleeve pattern you have just made for the one in the layout. The yardages given on the preceding page will accommodate the extra length of the pattern.

Marking the pattern details onto the fabric

Use continuous tailor's tacks to transfer all markings from the pattern to the fabric.

If you are working with fine fabrics, use a fine thread to avoid damaging the cloth. Make the tailor's tacks with a single thread and small stitches $\frac{1}{4}$in long. These will not fall out as easily as long stitches.

To make the dash lines on the cuff and the center front line on the facing and blouse, remove the patterns, measure the distance from the edge of the pattern pieces, and mark the fabric with pins. Tailor's tack along the pin lines.

Marking the curved dash line on the collar is optional; it is simply the dividing line between facing and collar. However, if you disregard it, be careful when machine stitching that you stitch right into the point where the collar and center front meet.

Marking the buttonholes at this stage is optional. These can be left until you are ready to make them. If you do mark them, use a contrasting colored thread, so that you cannot confuse them with the center front markings.

Remove all pattern pieces from the fabric.

Pinning and basting

Separate the pieces of fabric by cutting the tailor's tacks as previously shown. Use small scissors on fine fabrics, as they are less likely to snag the material.

Pin and baste the blouse bodice together for fitting.

First baste the underarm darts, remembering to taper the darts to the curve of the body.

Pin the shoulder seams, disregarding the shoulder dart (unless you have fitted a shoulder dart to overcome the problem of a round back).

You will see when pinning that you have some ease along the back — this must be held in between the balance marks. Baste. If you find the material is too stiff to take the ease, pin and baste the shoulder dart indicated on the pattern before basting the shoulder seam.

Pin and baste the side seams.

Pin the pleats by bringing together the stitching lines.

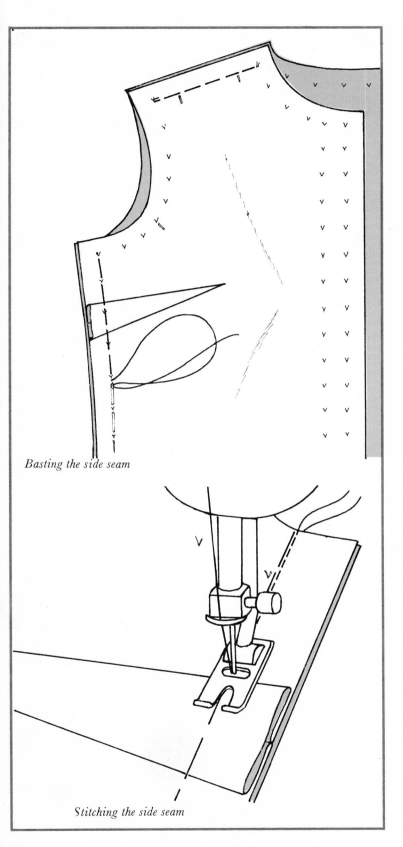

Basting the side seam

Stitching the side seam

Stitching

Rip the side seams and stitch the underarm darts. Fasten off the stitching securely at the ends.

Flatten by bringing the dart fold to meet the stitching line. Baste and press in position.

Baste the side seams again.

If you are using shoulder darts, stitch them and press toward the center of the back.

Stitch the side and shoulder seams.

Instructions for stitching a flat-fell seam are given on page 105

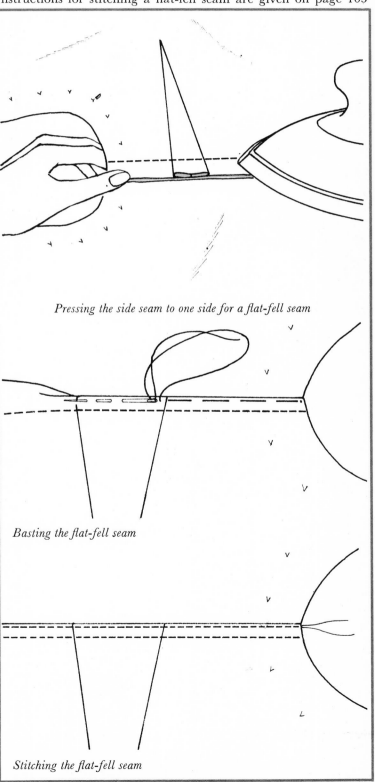

Pressing the side seam to one side for a flat-fell seam

Basting the flat-fell seam

Stitching the flat-fell seam

Fitting

Try on the basted blouse and pin the front sections together along the center front line.

Check the fitting and make any alterations necessary. If you prefer less fullness around the waist, make the pleats deeper.

Pin and baste again where the blouse needs altering, and try it on again to check that it now fits correctly.

Attaching the collar

Stitch the under collar pieces together at the center back. Press seam open.

Working with the under collar uppermost, pin it to the neck edge of the blouse, right sides facing. Match the center backs, and make sure the front edge of the under collar falls on the center front of the blouse.

Baste in place. It is important to baste the collar down with small stitches because of the adverse pulling of the fabric along the neckline.

Stitch along the seamline and remove the basting. Fasten off the threads securely at each end.

Snip the collar seam allowance where it meets the shoulder seam of the blouse to within a fraction of the stitching line.

Press the back neck and collar seams into the collar.

Snip into the seam allowance of the front neck edge of the blouse only. To enable you to stitch on the collar and facing in one movement, cut into the seam allowance of the neck edge at the center front to within one or two grains of the stitches. Press seam open.

Be careful not to stretch the seam when pressing, and turn it carefully on a sleeve board to avoid making creases on the collar. By pressing the seam in this way you lessen the chance of ridges showing through the facing and collar.

Stitch the collar and facing pieces together at the center back seam. Press seam open.

With right sides facing, pin and baste to the blouse, working with the under collar and blouse front uppermost. Make sure that the markings on both collar and under collar match perfectly. Stitch around the outer edge of the collar and down the fronts.

Having snipped the neck edge at the center front, you can stitch into the corner of the notch on the top collar and facing by turning the seam allowance of the wrap on the neck edge out of the way of the needle before you stitch it to the facing.

You will notice that the top collar is slightly fuller than the under collar. This is to allow for the roll when it is turned out.

Carefully snip into the corner as shown, and cut across the points of the collar to take away the surplus fabric.

Turn the collar and facings to the inside and carefully baste around the stitched edges. Press the edges gently.

Turn in the seam allowance along the inside edge of the facings as far as the shoulder seam. Pin and baste.

Finish the edges by machine stitching close to the fold edge.

Turn under the seam allowance on the collar along the back neck seam, pin and baste so that it lies just on the previous stitching line. Hand sew it down.

Press the collar from underneath.

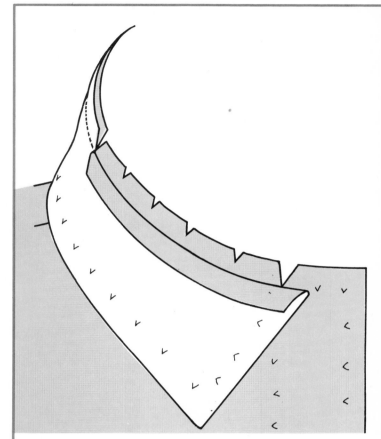

Snipping the neck seam allowance

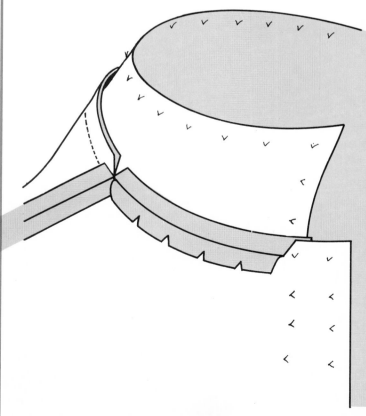

The pressed neck seam allowance in position

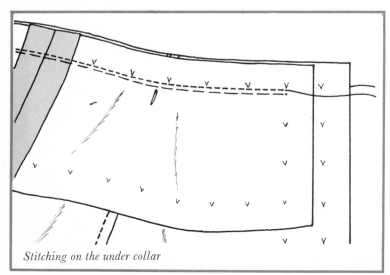

Stitching on the under collar

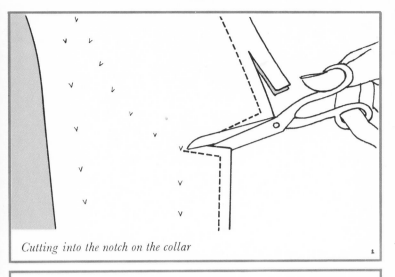

Cutting into the notch on the collar

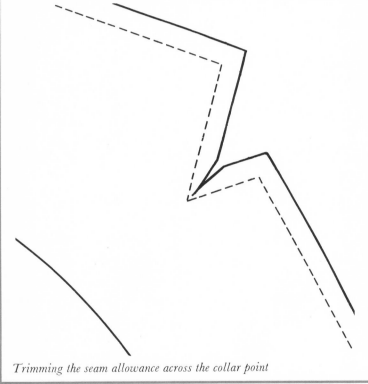

Trimming the seam allowance across the collar point

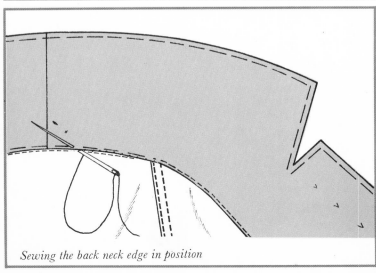

Sewing the back neck edge in position

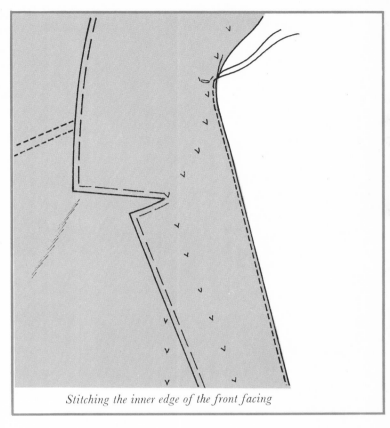

Stitching the inner edge of the front facing

Stitching the flat-fell seam

Trim the seam allowance on the back section to $\frac{3}{16}$in (this edge goes inside the fell), leaving the front allowance at $\frac{5}{8}$in.

Press the seam toward the back of the blouse, the wider seam allowance covering the trimmed edge.

Turn under the edge of the upper seam allowance so that it is even with the trimmed seam.

Pin and baste over the trimmed seam edge.

Stitch the seam down, close to the edge.

This seam can be worked on the inside or outside of a garment.

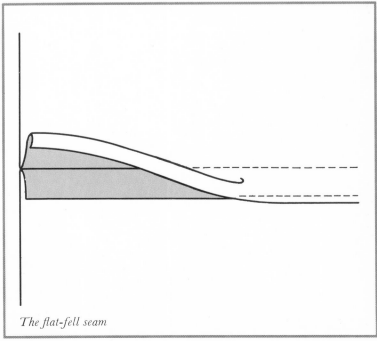

The flat-fell seam

Chapter 26

Finishing the blouses

The character of a blouse is determined by the fabric used to make it and the style of the collar and sleeves. The basic blouse and variations are very casual-looking garments, but you will soon see how to change the effect by using the different sleeves and neck finishes described in later chapters. In this chapter we show you how to stitch the sleeves and add the finishing touches. The instructions for both blouses are the same, except where otherwise stated.

Making the sleeves
Pin, baste and stitch the sleeve seams.
Prepare these seams for flat-fell seaming and stitch them as you did on the bodice in Blousemaking chapter 24.
Make two rows of running stitches or machine gathering stitches around the cap of each sleeve, one on each side of the seamline. Carefully draw up the ease, which is approximately 1½in, on each side of the balance mark at the top of the sleeve and fasten off the gathering threads over a pin.
Try to shrink in the fullness by pressing. Place a pressing ham (available in some notions departments) at the end of a sleeve board, lay the cap of the sleeve over it so that the sleeve hangs down, and gently press the fullness into the fabric. You may need to use a little steam here, but make sure that the fabric does not mark.
Remove the pressing ham, pull the sleeve over the sleeve board and press the rest of it.

Setting in the sleeves
When pinning, basting and stitching the sleeves into the armholes, always work from the sleeve and not from the bodice.
Pin in the sleeves, matching the side seams to the sleeve seams and the balance marks on the sleeve caps to the shoulder seams. Any fullness on the sleeves should be evenly distributed without any folds or creases.
If the fabric is too stiff to take all the fullness, ease it out by deepening the seam allowance around the sleeve cap only and not on the underarm section.
Baste in the sleeves and stitch. Remove all basting thread, press the seams toward the blouse and trim the seams for flat-fell seaming. When you have completed the flat-fell seams, press carefully over the end of a sleeve board.

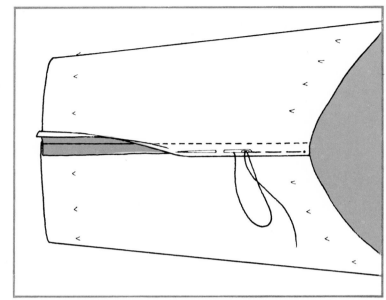

▲ **1.** *Basting the flat-fell seam on underarm seam*
▼ **2.** *Making two rows of stitches on the sleeve cap*

▼ **3.** *Drawing in the ease on the sleeve cap*

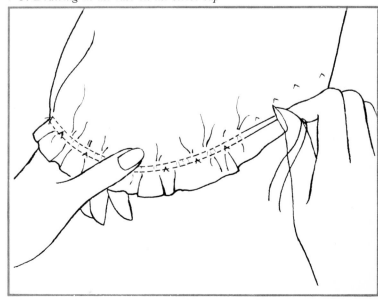

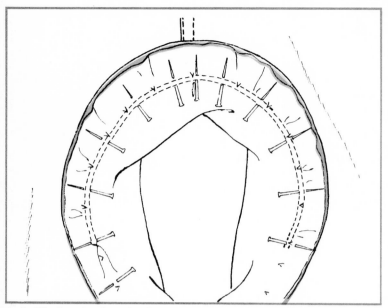

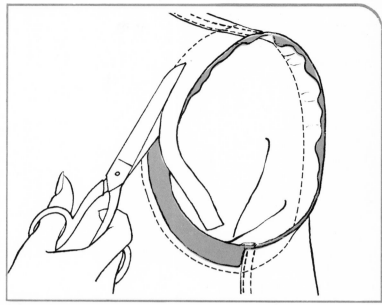

▲ **4.** *Pinning the sleeve in place*
▼ **5.** *Basting the sleeve in place.*

▲ **7.** *Trimming the armhole seam allowance*
▼ **8.** *Basting the flat-fell seam around the armhole*

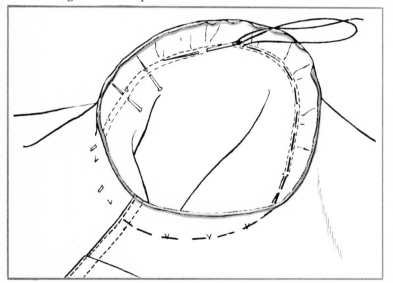

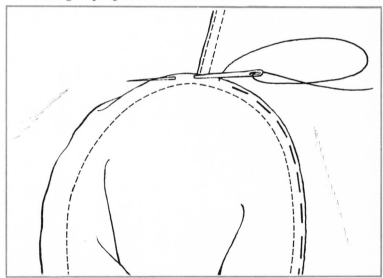

▼ **6.** *Stitching the sleeve in place*

▼ **9.** *Stitching the flat-fell seam around the armhole*

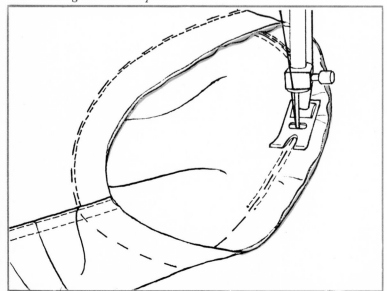

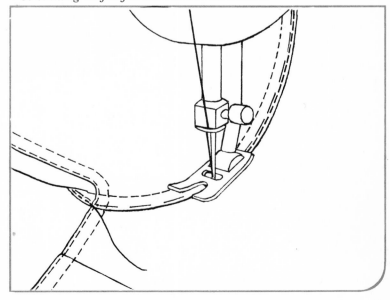

Making the cuffs
Green basic blouse

There are two ways of making the pointed cuff. You can make it deep as in the picture, using the outer solid line as the stitching line and the dash stitching line as the fold, or roll, line where the cuff rolls over the edge of the sleeve. Or, if you prefer a neat narrower cuff, the dash line becomes the stitching line.

For the narrower cuff, cut off the $\frac{3}{4}$in seam allowance along the length. You will also have to shorten the cuff slightly. Measure the difference between the dash stitching line and parallel solid stitching line, halve it and trim each pointed edge by this amount. Make a new roll line $\frac{3}{4}$in up from the dash stitching line and transfer the balance mark to the new stitching line. This balance mark meets the underarm seam.

After you have trimmed the cuff, the sewing instructions are identical.

Fold the cuff lengthwise, right sides together, and stitch the ends, beginning at the dash roll line and working toward the points. Fasten off the threads securely. Trim off the seam allowance across the points and turn the cuff to the right side. Baste along the stitched edge and press it flat.

Remove all basting stitches. Turn under the seam allowance on one edge of each cuff and baste.

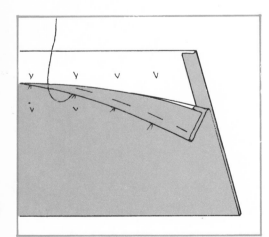

10. *Turning under one raw edge of the cuff*

To stitch the cuff to the sleeve, place the raw edges together with the right side of the cuff to the wrong side of the sleeve so the cuff meets at the roll line but is a little apart at the seamline.

Pin and baste. Press the seam toward the cuff edge.

Lay the basted cuff edge over the seam-line and baste in place.

Machine stitch along the basted folded edge.

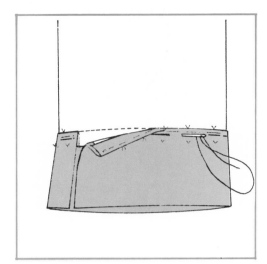

11. *Basting the folded cuff edge over the seamline*

Remove all basting stitches and turn the cuff up on the roll line.

To hold the cuff in position and stop the points from falling down, make a small bar $\frac{1}{2}$in above the roll line.

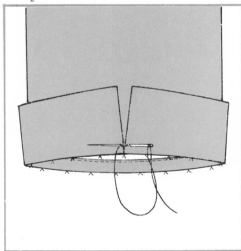

12. *Making a small bar $\frac{1}{2}$in above the roll line*

Floral, roll-up sleeve variation

To make the deep hem, turn under the lower edge along the line marked "upper edge of rolled cuff" (see pattern diagram in Blousemaking chapter 25) and pin. Turn under the seam allowance on the raw edge. Baste and stitch in place. Press. To form the rolled cuff, turn the hem up and over the sleeve so that the upper edge of the rolled cuff covers the stitching line.

Finishing touches

The blouse is finished except for the pleats, the hem, the buttonholes and buttons.

Pleats

Pin and baste the depth of the pleats on the inside of the blouse and stitch them. Press the pleats toward the center on back and front.

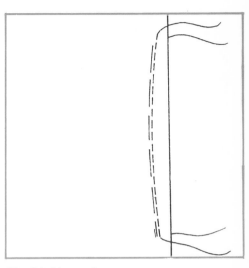

13. *Stitching a pleat*

Hem

Turn back the facings to the right side of the blouse and baste. Stitch the facings along the hemline, then turn them again to the inside.

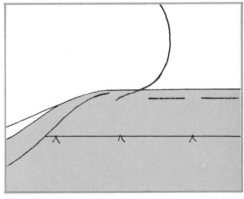

14. *Turning up the hem edge*

Turn up the rest of the hem. Turn under the raw edge so that the hem is $\frac{1}{2}$in wide and baste. Machine stitch close to turned-under edge and through the facings.

15. *Stitching the hem edge*

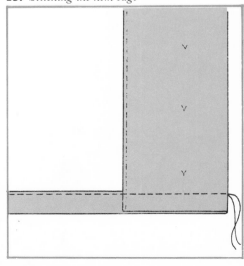

Topstitching

Topstitch the floral blouse down the fronts and around the collar.

Buttonholes

There are several types of hand-made buttonhole and each one is designed to do a certain job. For the blouse, use the buttonhole with a rounded end (this type is ideal for a button with a shank). At the rounded end the stitches are fanned out, leaving a close cluster on the edge which protects the fabric against the friction of the button movement.

Baste the facing to the blouse along the inner edge so that it cannot move as you make the buttonholes. If you have made the blouse in a fine fabric, you will need to underlay each buttonhole with a piece of thin cotton fabric. Test first, however, since if these pieces show through the blouse fabric, you will need to insert an interfacing strip down the front.

After making the buttonholes as shown, trim the underlaid pieces as close as you dare to the buttonholes. This will prevent ridges when you press the front edge.

Position the buttonholes as indicated on the pattern, making sure that they extend $\frac{1}{8}$in over the center front line.

Sew on the buttons in corresponding positions on the opposite center front line. When you have removed all basting thread, give the blouse a final pressing.

The completed buttonhole

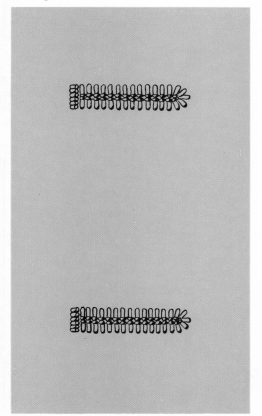

Hand-made buttonhole

The buttonhole described here has one bar and one rounded end.

Buttonhole length

For flat buttons, the buttonhole length should be the diameter of the button plus $\frac{1}{8}$in. For thick or domed buttons, add $1\frac{1}{2}$ times the thickness of the button to the button diameter.

Choosing the thread

For very close weaves work the buttonholes with ordinary sewing thread. Before you work on the garment, make a sample buttonhole to test the stitch on the fabric. If the fabric frays and the grain is coarse, use a heavier sewing thread or buttonhole twist.

Making the buttonhole

Mark the length of the buttonhole. Using sharp scissors, cut along the buttonhole length. The grain of the fabric will help you to cut a straight line. Overcast cut edges with shallow stitches. Starting with a piece of thread long enough to complete the buttonhole, work buttonhole stitches from left to right along the slit. Insert the needle into the back of the work and, before pulling it through, bring the thread from the needle under the point to form a loop. Pull forward into a small knot, placing it on the cut edge. Do not pull the loops too tightly or the edge will roll and the buttonhole will not meet properly. The spacing of the stitches is important. If the stitches are worked too close together, the edge will pucker. Judge the distance of the stitch by the thickness of the thread you are using and the grain of the fabric.

The depth of the stitch depends on how easily the fabric frays. A firm fabric can be worked with a very shallow stitch ($\frac{1}{16}$in). If the fabric frays easily take a deeper stitch. Use your thumb nail as a guide to help you regulate the depth.

Form a fan of stitches at the rounded end of the buttonhole (i.e. the end nearest the front edge), keeping the center stitch in line with the slit. Turn the work and continue along the top edge.

At the end make a small bar across both rows of stitches.

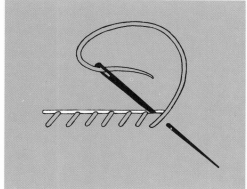

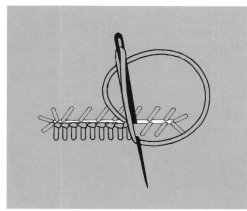

▲ *Overcasting the cut edges*
▼ *Working buttonhole stitch*

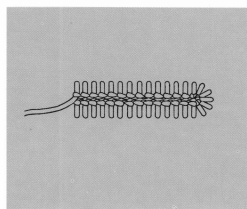

▲ *Buttonhole without bar end*
▼ *Detail of bar and fanned end*

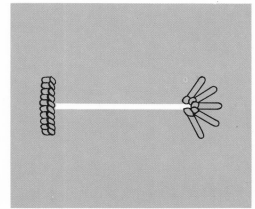

Accessories Graph Pattern

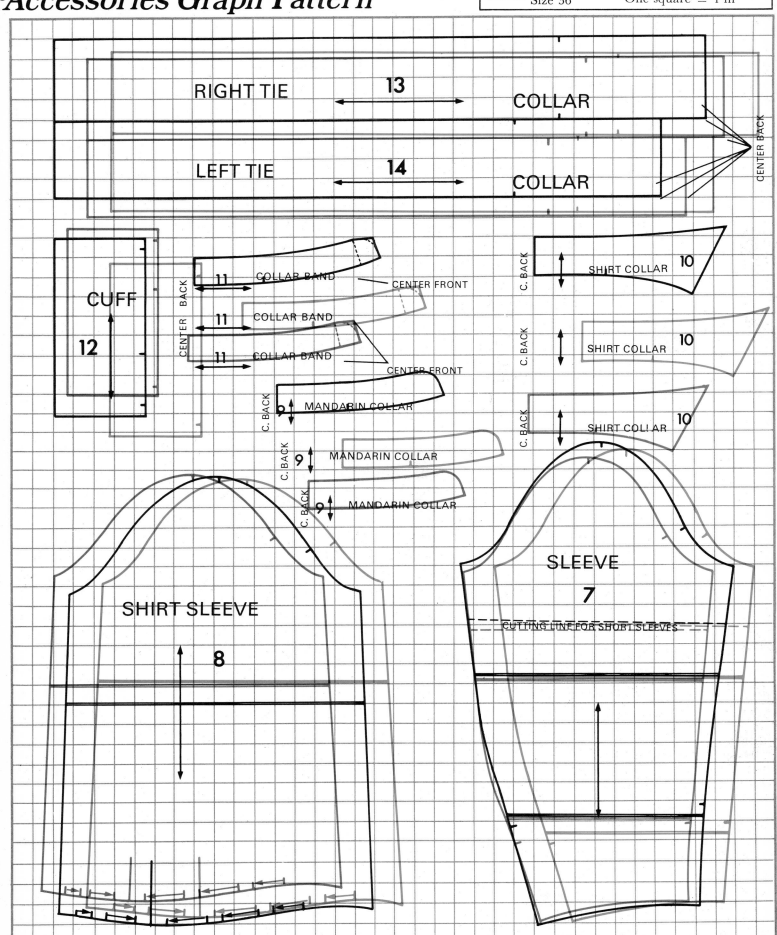

KEY

Size 32½
Size 34
Size 36

Lengthen or shorten here
Straight of grain
One square = 1 in

RIGHT TIE   13   COLLAR

LEFT TIE   14   COLLAR

CENTER BACK

CUFF

12

11   COLLAR BAND   CENTER FRONT

11   COLLAR BAND

11   COLLAR BAND   CENTER FRONT

CENTER BACK

MANDARIN COLLAR

9   MANDARIN COLLAR

9   MANDARIN COLLAR

C. BACK   SHIRT COLLAR   10

C. BACK   SHIRT COLLAR   10

C. BACK   SHIRT COLLAR   10

SHIRT SLEEVE

8

SLEEVE

7

CUTTING LINE FOR SHORT SLEEVES

The outlines given are the stitching lines. Refer to page 139 for seam allowances and check with the following chapters for any variations.

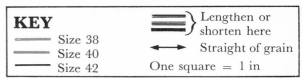

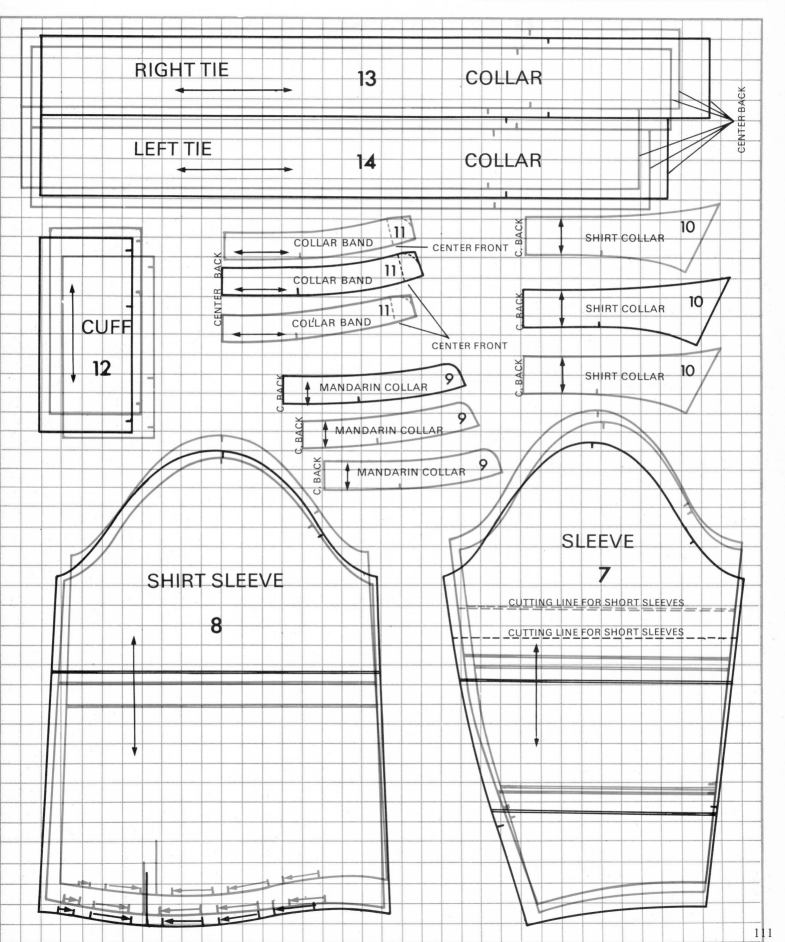

RIGHT TIE

13 COLLAR

LEFT TIE

14 COLLAR

CENTER BACK

CUFF

12

COLLAR BAND 11 — CENTER FRONT

CENTER BACK

COLLAR BAND 11

COLLAR BAND 11

CENTER FRONT

C. BACK SHIRT COLLAR 10

C. BACK SHIRT COLLAR 10

C. BACK SHIRT COLLAR 10

C. BACK MANDARIN COLLAR 9

C. BACK MANDARIN COLLAR 9

C. BACK MANDARIN COLLAR 9

SHIRT SLEEVE

8

SLEEVE

7

CUTTING LINE FOR SHORT SLEEVES

CUTTING LINE FOR SHORT SLEEVES

111

Chapter 27

Basic blouse into shirt

Here is the first of the blouse conversions from the Golden Hands Blouse Graph, which was introduced on pages 98 and 99. It is a traditional fitted shirt with tailored lines and classic good looks.

A special feature of this shirt is the seaming. It is stitched with French seams, a method which gives the seams a neat and durable finish—useful for garments like shirts that have to stand up to frequent laundering.

Another feature of the conversion is the way the cuffs are treated. With this blouse, the sleeves may be finished with single or double cuffs which fasten with link buttoning. Instructions for making the cuffs are in the next chapter.

The fitted shirt

Suitable fabrics
Plain and printed silk, cotton, linen or light woolen fabrics.

Fabric requirements and notions
- [ ] 36in wide fabric: for sizes 32½ and 34in, 2⅞ yards; for size 36in, 3 yards; for sizes 38 to 42in, 3⅛ yards.
- [ ] Interfacing: for all sizes, ⅜ yard. For silk fabric this should be preshrunk lawn; for other fabrics, a fine poplin.
- [ ] Buttons: 8 for single front buttoning, 12 for buttoning in groups of three. Allow 2 extra for linked button cuffs in both cases.
- [ ] Matching thread.

The shirt pattern
From the basic blouse pattern you will need pattern pieces 1 and 2, which are the front and back.

From the Accessories Graph you will need pattern pieces 8, 10, 11 and 12, which are the shirt sleeve, shirt collar, collarband and cuff patterns.

The shirt also needs a front facing, which you make as follows: Lay the front pattern section on a piece of paper and draw around the shoulder, neck edge, front edge and lower edge. Remove the pattern and make the facing as shown in figure 3. It should be 1½ inches wide at the shoulders and 3 inches wide at the lower edge. Unlike the basic blouse, this shirt is fitted and has back and front body darts. So, if you have made the muslin in Muslin-making chapter 23, copy the darts onto the pattern pieces; otherwise the body darts will be fitted later using the pleat lines as a guide.

Cutting out the shirt
Select the correct layout on page 115, according to your size. Remember that the patterns have no seam allowance, so add ⅝ inch seam and hem allowances all around. The seam allowance is not ¾ inch as for most of the other garments given so far, because less seam allowance is required for French seams.

For classic good looks the fitted shirt has few rivals

The following points should be considered.

Decide what sort of cuffs you want. If you want them single (i.e. cuffs half the depth of the cuff pattern, as figure 1), you will only need two cuff pieces. But if you want double cuffs (i.e. cuffs cut to the depth of the cuff pattern, folded over and closed with link buttons, as figure 2), you will need four cuff pieces.

If you have chosen a striped fabric and wish to make a feature of the stripes, copy the other half of the collar pattern and join the two at the center back. When laying out the collar pattern, place the lengthwise grain line on the pattern along the crosswise grain on the fabric.

Cut out the fabric and keep the remnants, as you will need them later.

Mark the pattern details. Pay special attention to the collar and collarband details, the balance marks and the center markings. The collar ends should meet on the center front line, with the ends of the collarband meeting the edges of the shirt front.

To hold in the fullness around the lower edge of the sleeves, you have a choice. If the fabric is soft, disregard the pleat markings,

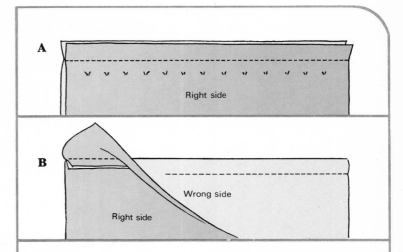

1. ▲ *The single cuff with topstitching detail*

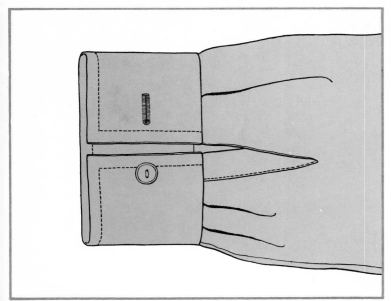

2. ▲ *The double cuff for link buttoning*

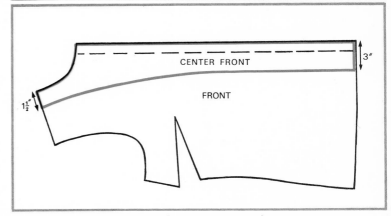

The French seam

The French seam is a double seam with the raw edges encased.

A. With wrong sides facing, first pin and stitch the seam $\frac{3}{8}$ inch from the seamline inside the seam allowance.
Trim and lightly press the stitched seam toward the front. Turn the garment inside out.

B. Working on the wrong side, pin, baste and stitch along the original seamline, encasing the raw edges in the seam.

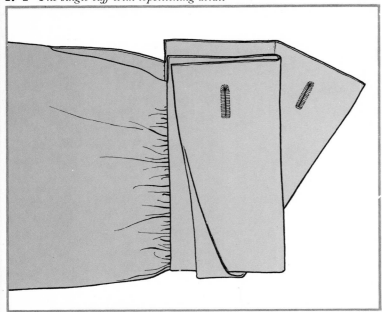

3. ▲ *Marking out the front facing for the fitted shirt*

as you can simply gather the lower edge to fit the cuff. For crisper and bulkier fabrics, mark the pleat details.
Remove the pattern pieces.

Interfacing

To give the collar and cuffs that extra crispness which is required for a shirt, they should be interfaced.
Cut one collar piece and one collarband from the interfacing with the center back on the fold, as indicated on the layout. If you are making double cuffs, cut two cuff pieces from the interfacing. If the cuffs are to be single, cut two pieces half the depth of the cuffs, as the interfacing needs to go only to the point where the cuffs are folded over.
Pin and baste each interfacing piece to the wrong side of a corresponding shirt piece. The interfacing should go on that piece which will be uppermost.

Fitting

Baste the darts, side and shoulder seams and try on the shirt,

pinning it together along the center front line. If you have not already marked the body darts on the pattern, extend the pleat lines into darts, running them out smoothly at each end.
Make any alterations necessary, following the fitting instructions for the muslin in chapter 23.
Try the sleeves for length with the cuffs basted in position.

Making the shirt

With right sides together pin, baste and stitch the facings to the front edges. Do not stitch them along the neck and hem edges. Turn the facings to the inside, edge-baste and press.
Stitch all the darts. Press the side bust darts flat and the underbust and all the back darts toward the center line.
Make French seams, as shown, on the side and shoulder seams. Before making the second row of stitches which encase the raw seam edges, press the edges lightly toward the front and then stitch along the seamline.
Press the finished French seams toward the front.
Turn up the hem as shown in Blousemaking chapter 26.

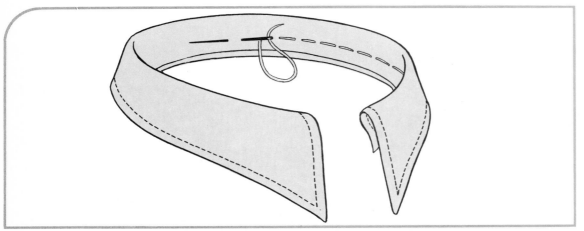

4. ▲ *Rolling the collar and basting along the lower edge*   **5.** ▼ *Stitching the collar between the collarbands*

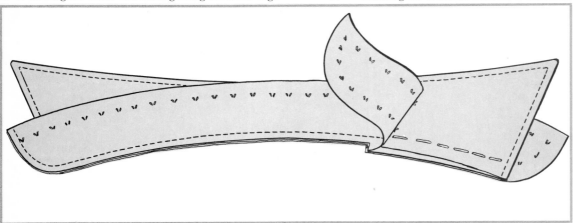

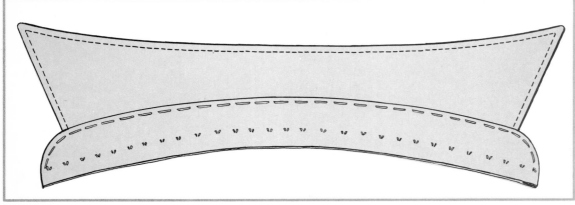

6. ▲ *Basting along the stitched edges of the collarband*   **7.** ▼ *Basting the outer collarband over the stitching line*

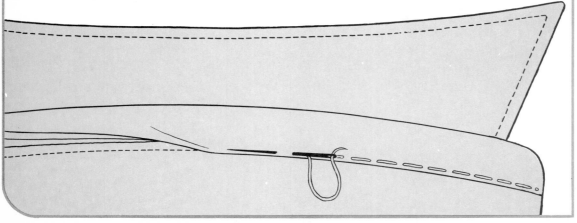

Making the collar

Working on a flat surface, place the top (interfaced) and under collar pieces together, right sides facing. Pin, baste and stitch along the front edges and the upper curved seam.

Trim the seam allowance to $\frac{1}{4}$ inch, trim across the corners and turn to the right side. Baste along the stitched edges and press.

If you want to topstitch the collar do so now, stitching $\frac{1}{4}$ inch from the edge.

Roll the collar in the position you would wear it, as shown in figure 4. You will see that the lower edge of the top collar rises above the edge of the under collar. Baste it firmly in this position along the seamline of the under collar.

To complete the collar, stitch it to the collarband. Matching all markings, place the collar between the inner and outer collarband pieces, as shown in figure 5, and stitch, leaving the lower edge open.

Trim the seam allowance on the stitched edges of the collarband to $\frac{1}{4}$ inch and turn to the right side. Baste along the stitched edges, as shown in figure 6, and press.

The ends of the collarband have now become the tabs for the button and buttonhole. Should you find that the tabs are too bulky, notch the seam allowance, as this will help to flatten them.

Stitching on the collar

Baste the front facing to the shirt along the neckline.

Pin the inner collarband along the inside of the neckline with the raw edges even, carefully matching the balance marks.

Baste, stitch and trim the seam allowance.

Turn under the seam allowance on the outer collarband, lay it over the stitching line to cover the machine stitches, as shown in figure 7. Carefully slip stitch in place.

Be very careful when you hand-sew along the tab, because this part will show when the collar is buttoned.

Layouts for the fitted shirt

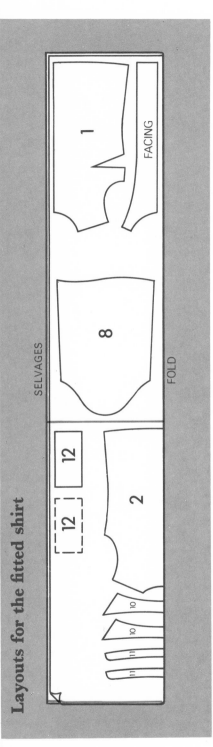

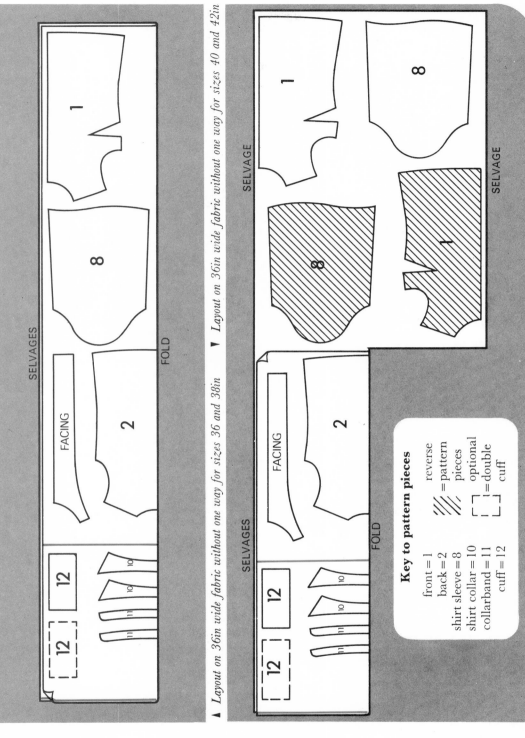

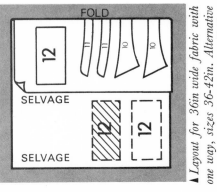

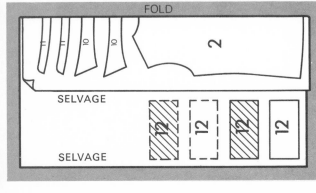

▲ Layout on 36in wide fabric without one way for sizes 32½ and 34in

▲ Layout on 36in wide fabric without one way for sizes 32½–34in. Alternative layout for section between red lines without one way, sizes 32½–34in.

▲ Layout on 36in wide fabric without one way for sizes 36 and 38in

▲ Layout on 36in wide fabric with one way, sizes 36-42in. Alternative layout for section between red lines without one way, sizes 36-42in.

▼ Layout on 36in wide fabric without one way for sizes 40 and 42in

▼ Interfacing layout for all sizes.

Key to pattern pieces

front = 1
back = 2
shirt sleeve = 8
shirt collar = 10
collarband = 11
cuff = 12

reverse
= pattern
pieces
optional
= double
cuff

Chapter 28

Tail of a shirt

Blouse — making

This chapter continues with blouse conversions from the Golden Hands Blouse Graph. The fitted shirt is completed and is followed by instructions for making the shirt with tails, pictured on page 119. The shirt with tails is made in a lightweight striped wool. It has flat-fell seams, single cuffs with link buttons, and the body darts are omitted.

The shirt sleeve openings

Before you stitch the sleeve seams, make the openings.
Here are two simple ways to do this.

A. The faced opening. This opening is suitable for both single and link buttoning.
To make a facing, cut a straight piece of fabric from remnants, 2 inches wide and 1 inch longer than the opening indicated on the wrist edge of the sleeve pattern piece. Do not cut the opening yet.
Lay the facing centrally over the opening line on the outside of the sleeve, right sides facing, and baste.
Stitch the facing to the sleeve (figure 1), tapering into a point at the end of the opening.
Cut through the center to within 1 grain of the stitches at the point.
Turn the facing to the inside (figure 2), edge-baste or topstitch close to the edge and press.
Turn in the raw edge of the facing, baste and hem to the sleeve.
B. Opening with wrap extension. This opening is not suitable for link buttoning.
From remnants cut a straight strip of fabric 1½ inches wide and twice the length of the opening.
Cut the sleeve along the opening line (figure 3). Pin and baste the

▼**1.** *Cutting through faced opening*

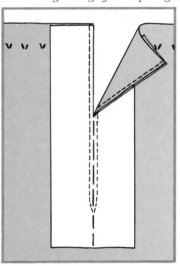

▼**2.** *Basting the faced opening*

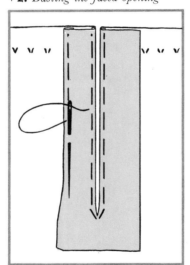

▼ *The fitted shirt*

▼**3.** *Cutting the sleeve opening*

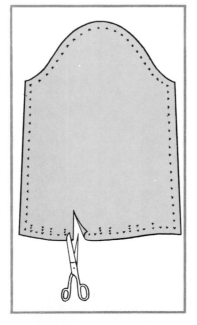

▼**4.** *The facing for the wrap extension stitched to the sleeve opening*

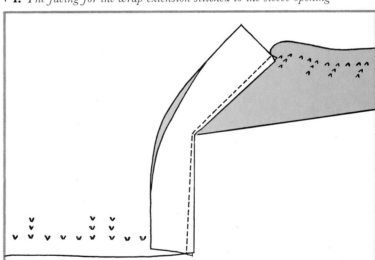

▼**5.** *Pinning the wrap extension strip to the right side of the sleeve*

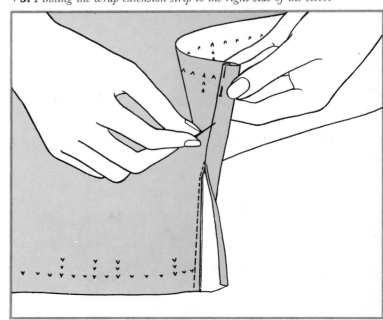

strip of fabric along the opening with the right side of the strip to the wrong side of the sleeve.

Stitch along the opening, taking $\frac{1}{4}$ inch seam allowance on the facing but tapering toward the point (figure 4).

When you have reached the point, pivot the work on the needle, ease the fold to the back of the needle and stitch along the other side. Press the seam toward the strip.

Fold in the long raw edge of the strip, pin and baste it over the seam on the outside of the sleeve and topstitch (figures 5 and 6). Press the wrap to the inside of the sleeve as shown.

After finishing the opening, stitch sleeve seams with French seam.

Making the cuffs

A. Single cuffs. Fold the interfaced cuffs lengthwise, right sides facing, and stitch each side up to the seam allowance at the top edge. Trim the seam allowance and turn to the right side. Edge-baste and press.

If you want to make single cuffs with link buttoning, stitch the upper edge as far as the two outer balance marks before turning to the right side, as for the double cuff in figure 7. Snip the seam allowance at the balance marks and turn out.

B. Double cuffs. Pin the interfaced and plain sections together, right sides facing.

Stitch around the edges as shown in figure 7. Trim the seam allowance and across the corners. Snip into the seam allowance at the top edge as shown.

Turn the cuffs to the right side, edge-baste and press.

Attaching the cuffs

Gather or pleat the lower edge of the sleeves. The pleats should be folded in the direction of the arrows on the sleeve pattern.

Pin, baste and stitch the cuffs to the right side of the sleeves as shown in figure 8. (Make sure the interfaced section will be uppermost on the finished cuff.)

Turn under the remaining raw edge on each cuff, pin and hand sew it over the seam on the inside (figure 9).

If you wish to topstitch the cuffs $\frac{1}{4}$ inch from the edge to match the collar stitching, do so now.

Stitching in the sleeves

Stitch the sleeves to the shirt with a French seam.
Press the seam toward the sleeve.

▼**6.** *The topstitched wrap extension with wrap pressed to the inside*

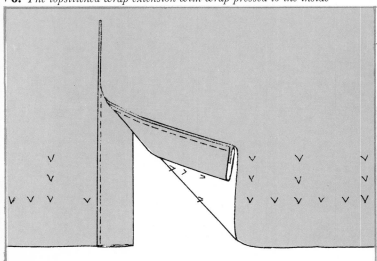

▼**8.** *Pinning the cuff to the right side of the sleeve*

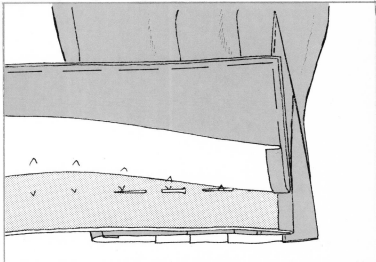

▼**7.** *Stitched and trimmed double cuff before turning to the right side*

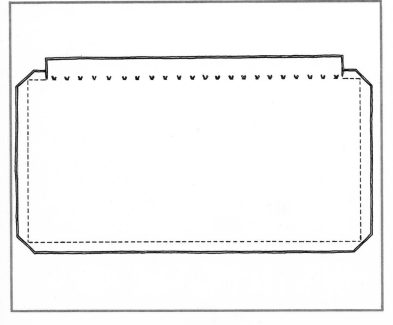

▼**9.** *Hand sewing the inside cuff edge over the seamline*

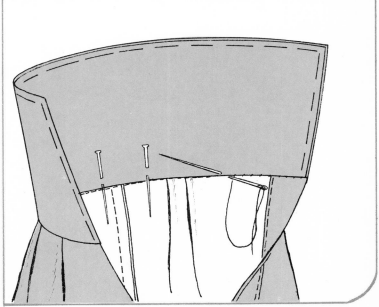

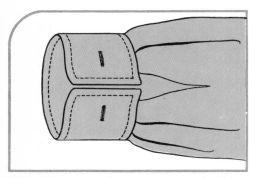

▲ 10. *The single cuff with buttonholes for links*

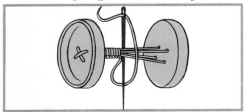

▲ 11. *Making the button link*

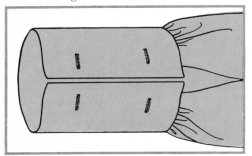

▲ 12. *The double cuff with buttonhole positions*

Buttons and buttonholes

Fitted shirt front. Follow the buttoning for the shirt with tails (figure 13) or, for a more unusual effect, arrange the buttons in groups of three, as shown in the sketch on page 116. Because the shirt is worn tucked in, it is best not to place buttons below the waist as these would bulge underneath a skirt.

Make the buttonholes as shown in Blouse-making chapter 26 and sew on buttons to correspond.

Single, unlinked cuffs. Make a buttonhole on each cuff on the edge furthest from the sleeve seam (see figure 1 in the previous chapter) and sew on a button to correspond.

Single, linked cuffs (figure 10). Make two buttonholes on each cuff. Make the button links as in figure 11, working the link as for the bar shown in Shirtmaking chapter 14.

Double, linked cuffs (figure 12). These need four buttonholes on each cuff. The thickness of the layers of fabric may cause the under cuff to pucker, so make the buttonholes which go to the top of the cuff $\frac{1}{8}$ inch closer to the edge than those on the underside of the cuff.

Make the button links as in figure 11.

118

Shirt with tails

Fabric requirements and notions

- [ ] 36in wide fabric: for sizes $32\frac{1}{2}$ and 34in, $3\frac{1}{8}$ yards; for size 36in, $3\frac{1}{4}$ yards; for sizes 38 to 42in, $3\frac{3}{8}$ yards.
- [ ] Interfacing: for all sizes, $\frac{3}{8}$ yard. Pre-shrunk lawn for silk fabric and fine poplin for other fabric.
- [ ] 9 buttons, or 11 for link buttoned cuffs.
- [ ] Matching thread.

The pattern

Use all the pattern pieces for the fitted shirt.

To make the tails, place the front and back bodice patterns on a sheet of paper at least 3 inches longer than the pattern. Draw around the pattern, then extend the side seams for 3 inches and draw in the new hemline on both pattern pieces, as shown in figure 13.

Draw curves for the tails which taper into the side seams, as shown. To make sure the curve is the same on the back and front, make a paper template, lay it on the extension of the back and front pattern pieces and draw in the new lines.

Then, at the top of the curve on the back, add $\frac{1}{2}$ inch to the side seam and taper into the curve, as shown in figure 14.

▼ 13. *Front pattern with extension and curve*

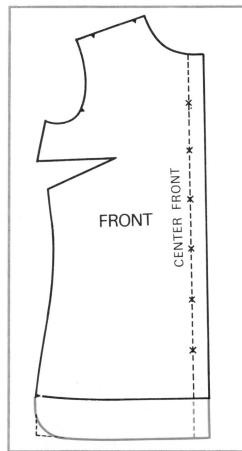

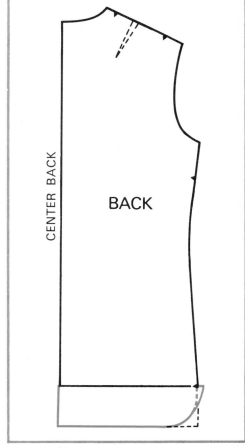

▲ 14. *Back pattern with seam allowance extension*

Make a balance mark on the side seams where the original pattern lengths end; this is the end of the side seam stitching line.

Cut out the new patterns.

Cutting out

Use the cutting instructions and layouts for the fitted shirt in the previous chapter as a guide, making the necessary adjustments to take in the new pattern lengths. The shirt is sewn with flat-fell seams which, like the French seam, require $\frac{5}{8}$ inch seam allowances.

Fitting

Follow the fitting instructions for the shirt in the previous chapter, but omit the back and front body darts.

Making the shirt

Follow the instructions for making the fitted shirt, but note the following points.
1. Stitch flat-fell seams instead of French seams. The flat-fell seams are stitched as those in Blousemaking chapter 25, but this time they are stitched with wrong sides facing and are folded on the outside of the garment, with the folded edge toward the front.

2. Stitch the shoulder and side bust darts only.

3. Position the buttons and buttonholes as shown in figure 13.

4. The hem edge is finished at the side seams as follows.

Hemming the tails. Stitch the side seams to the balance marks, wrong sides facing. Then snip into the front side seam allowance at the bottom of the seams and trim the front seam allowance for flat-fell seaming, as shown in figure 15.

Fold the back seam allowance over the trimmed front seam. Pin and baste.

Pin and baste the hem on the front to the wrong side. Machine stitch and continue the stitching into the folded flat-fell seam edge so that you stitch the hem and flat-fell side seam in one operation, as shown in figure 16.

Pin under the hem on the back. When you reach the point where the side seam and front hem merge, pin the folded edge of the back hem in line with the side seam, as shown in figure 16. Like this, it will lie flat over the top of the front curve and give a neat strong finish. Baste and machine stitch in place.

Stitch across the top of the hem as shown to hold it firmly in place and to strengthen this point.

▼ **15.** *Snipping into the front seam allowance*

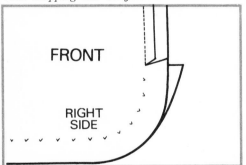

FRONT

RIGHT SIDE

▼ **16.** *The stitched tails at the side seam*

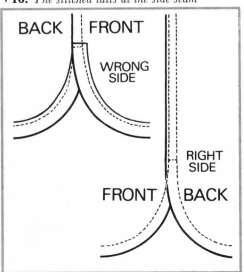

BACK | FRONT

WRONG SIDE

RIGHT SIDE

FRONT | BACK

Chapter 29

Three blouse conversions

The tie-neck blouse, shown here in a luxurious printed silk, is a soft and feminine variation of the Golden Hands basic blouse. In making it you will be taken several steps further in your dressmaking know-how. You will learn to apply couture finishes to a simple garment to turn it into something special, such as the finish on the sleeve openings which is especially suited to fine fabrics. This chapter, which includes layouts, goes to the fitting stage.

Suitable fabrics
You can use most of the fabrics mentioned for blouses in Blouse-making chapters 25 and 27, but for the gentle style of this tie-neck blouse the texture should be a little finer and the fabric quite soft. For instance, if you want to use a poplin, as for the basic blouse, make sure it is the fine type.

Yardages and notions
For yardages see layouts and note on tie collar on pages 122 and 123
- ☐ Interfacing, 36in width—the length of the blouse from the highest point on the shoulder to the hem plus $1\frac{1}{2}$ inches for seams (see notes below)
- ☐ 8 buttons (you will need 2 more for link-buttoned cuffs)
- ☐ 1 small snap fastener
- ☐ Matching thread

A note on interfacing
The texture of the interfacing is dictated by the top fabric, i.e. soft fabric, soft interfacing.

To see if the texture of the interfacing is correct, make the following test. Place an edge of the interfacing into the folded edge of the top fabric—if the fabric rolls over the interfacing in a gentle, soft roll it is the right type to use. If, however, sharp points and a hard edge are formed, you have chosen the wrong texture of interfacing.

To help you in your choice, select from the following:
- ☐ For soft, natural fiber fabrics, choose a soft lawn or a finely textured pre-shrunk cotton, sold specifically for interfacing
- ☐ For soft fabrics in man-made fibers, pure silk organza is often the only choice, because an interfacing in a man-made fiber of the same type as the blouse fabric can result in edges· which will not lie flat

The pattern pieces
For the tie-neck blouse you will need the following pattern pieces from the Golden Hands Graph Pages: from the Basic Blouse Graph Pattern the Front and Back pattern pieces, numbers 1 and 2; from the Accessories Graph the skirt sleeve, cuff and tie-collar pattern pieces, numbers 8, 12, 13 and 14.

The facing pattern
When making a garment in a soft fabric, it is advisable to avoid unnecessary seams—the finished garment will look smoother. So, when making the tie-neck blouse, the Front and front facing are cut out as one.

First make a facing pattern as shown in Blousemaking chapter 27, figure **3**.

Then join the Front pattern piece to the facing pattern along the front edges by pinning them alongside each other over a strip of paper (figure **1** below). The line along the join becomes the fold line of the facing.

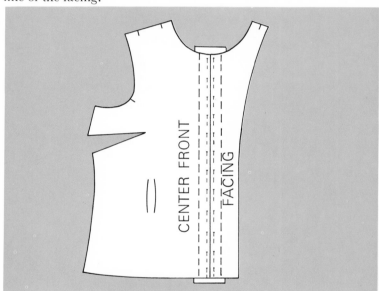

▲ **1.** *Joining the Front and front facing patterns along the front edges*

Cutting out
Blouse fabric. Select the correct layout for your size from those given on pages 122 and 123. Decide whether you want single or double cuffs (Blousemaking chapter 27) and a single or double-width tie.

Pin the pattern pieces onto the fabric, mark out $\frac{3}{4}$ inch seam and hem allowances and cut out.

Mark all details on the fabric with tailor's tacks, using the methods shown so far.

After you have marked the blouse Front, unpin and remove the facing pattern, then mark along the front edge of the Front pattern piece for the fold line. Remove all pattern pieces.

Interfacing. First cut or tear off the selvages of interfacing fabric. Fold in half and pin the cuff and front facing patterns onto the double interfacing fabric. Cut a full cuff section or a half section only, depending on your choice of cuff.

Mark out $\frac{3}{4}$ inch seam allowances along the Front, hem, neck and shoulder edges of the facing and along the cuff edges.

You will not need seam allowances along the inner edge of the facing or along the fold edge of the single cuff.

Cut out and mark the pattern details on the interfacing.

Remove the pattern pieces.

Choose pure silk for the soft, gentle lines of the tie-neck blouse ▶

Interfacing the Fronts for fitting

Pin and baste the interfacing to the wrong side of each blouse Front as shown (figure **2**), allowing the seam allowance on the interfacing to go over the fold line onto the facing. Note that it is basted both along the Center Front and the fold line. Attach the interfacing to the blouse with prick stitches (Generally Speaking chapter 9). Work the prick stitches in the seam allowance of the interfacing, just outside the fold line, so that they will not show on the top of the garment when the facing is turned under.

Turn the facing to the inside and baste along the fold line ready for fitting.

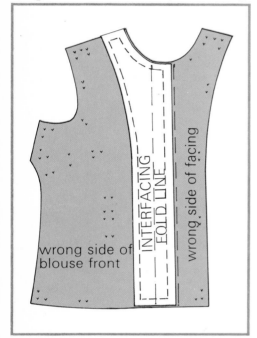

▲ **2.** *The interfacing basted to the blouse Front*

Fitting the blouse

Carefully pin and baste the blouse darts and seams and baste in the sleeves ready for fitting.

Make any corrections necessary (Muslin-making chapter 23).

Fitting the collar

It is also necessary to fit the tie-neck collar before completing it. The balance marks on the ties are only an approximate indication of where the ties begin when the collar is attached to the neckline, and they will fall about 1 inch in from the Center Front at each side.

It is always best to determine how far a tie collar should be attached to the neckline by fitting. A given length may be right for one fabric but may leave an unsightly gap in another.

Two ways to finish the ties are given here. They can be folded in half lengthwise to achieve the effect in the picture, or made

double width and left unfolded with rolled hem edges. The latter is particularly attractive in transparent fabrics.

For both versions, first stitch the collar sections together along the Center Back line and press the seam open.

Folded collar version. To prepare this for fitting, fold the collar and ties in half lengthwise, right sides facing. Pin and baste the seams of the ties as far as the balance marks.

With the collar still inside out, pin and baste it to the blouse neckline, matching Center Backs, and with the balance marks falling on the Front neck edge 1 inch in from the Center Front at each side.

The wider collar. To prepare this for fitting, fold the collar lengthwise at the neck only. Pin and baste it to the blouse neckline, matching Center Backs, and with the balance marks falling on the Front neck edge 1 inch in from the Center Front at each side (figure **3**).

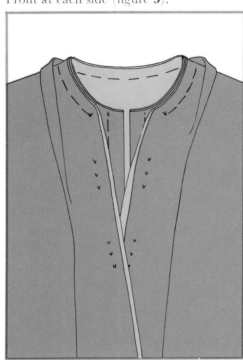

▲ **3.** *Basting on the wider collar for fitting*

Both versions. Try on the blouse again and tie a bow to see how far you need the collar stitched to the blouse at the neck edge.

The bow should lie comfortably in the opening and not be pushed forward through lack of space. If it is, the size of the space must be increased equally on each side.

If, however, the space is too large, just reduce the distance equally on each side between the collar ends and the Center Front of the blouse.

Carefully mark the position of the collar ends on both the blouse and the collar.

Yardages

36in width, without one way—sizes 32½ and 34, 2¾ yards; sizes 36 and 38, 3¼ yards; sizes 40 and 42, 3⅞ yards.

36in width, with one way—sizes 32½ and 34, 3 yards; size 36, 3⅜ yards; size 38, 3½ yards; sizes 40 and 42, 3¾ yards.

N.B. For transparent fabrics such as voile and chiffon, buy extra fabric and double the width of the tie collar to make a really full bow.

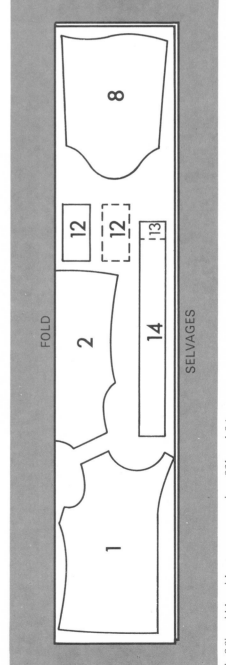

▲ *36in width, without one way—sizes 32½ and 34*

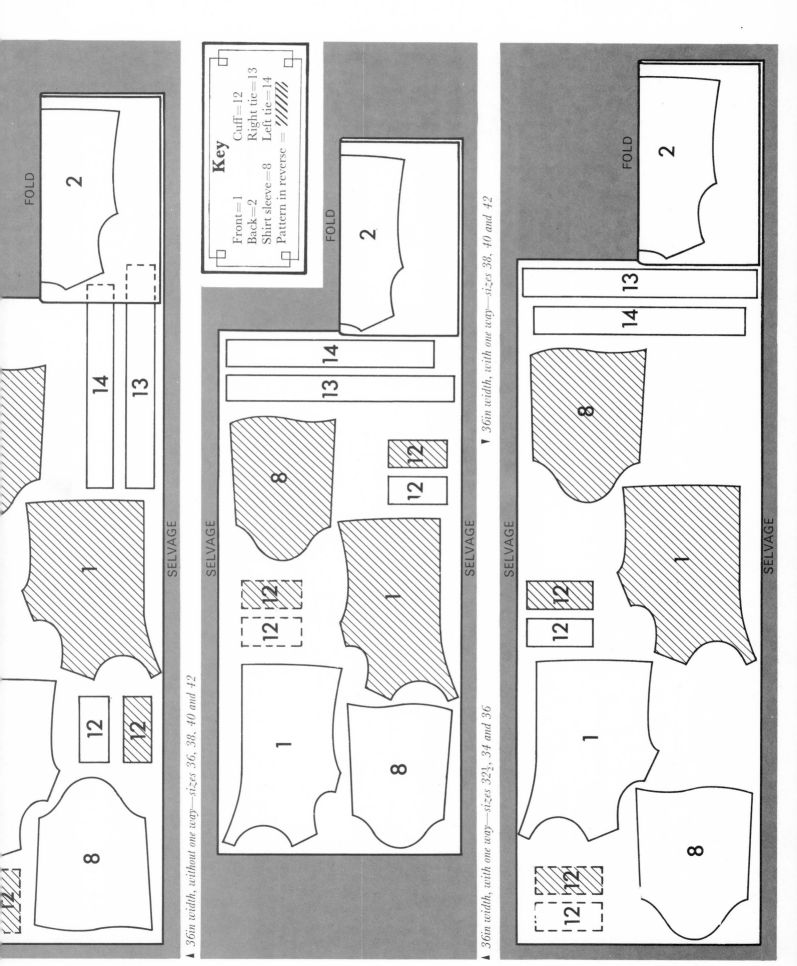

Key

Front=1   Cuff=12
Back=2   Right tie=13
Shirt sleeve=8   Left tie=14
Pattern in reverse = ///////

▲ *36in width, without one way—sizes 36, 38, 40 and 42*

▼ *36in width, with one way—sizes 38, 40 and 42*

▲ *36in width, with one way—sizes 32½, 34 and 36*

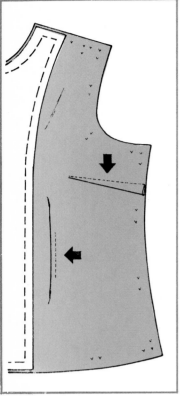

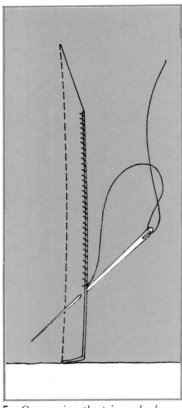

4. *Pressing the front darts*

5. *Oversewing the trimmed edges*

Making the blouse

Stitch all the darts and press. The body and shoulder darts (if you are using them) are pressed toward the center, and the side bust darts are pressed downward. If you pressed the darts open in a soft fabric, they would fold over or wrinkle because the fabric does not have sufficient body to hold them in place during wear.

If you are using a transparent fabric, cut the depth of the darts to $\frac{3}{8}$ inch and overcast the raw edges very finely together.

Stitch the side and shoulder seams and press them open.

Trim the seam allowances evenly. To finish the raw edges, fold them under $\frac{1}{8}$ inch and whip along the folded edge (Skirtmaking chapter 20).

If the fabric is transparent, press the seam allowance together toward the Front of the garment. Trim to $\frac{3}{8}$ inch and overcast as for the darts.

Finishing the Front edges

Fold each facing along the fold line to the right side of the garment, ripping the basting along the fold line.

Pin, baste and stitch along the neck edge from the marking for the collar end to the fold line.

Snip the seam allowance to allow it to follow the neckline curve (figure **6**) and at the end of the stitching line where it meets the collar mark.

Turn the facing to the wrong side, baste along the stitched neck edge and press.

Pin and baste the facing firmly to the inside of the blouse along the rest of the neck edge and along the inner edge and fold line.

Fold under the seam allowance on the shoulder of the facing and trim to the width of the shoulder seam on the blouse. Hand-sew to the seamline with small slip stitches.

Stitching the folded collar

Stitch the tie ends of the collar as far as the balance marks or the new marks made at the collar fitting (figure **7**). If you want the

ends to be pointed, as in the photograph, taper the stitching as shown (figure **8**).

Trim seams, snip off the seam allowance across the corners. Turn the tie ends to the right side, edge-baste and press.

Pin and baste the outside of the collar to the outside of the blouse, matching the Center Backs and the collar end markings on the neckline. Stitch.

Trim the seam allowance to eliminate bulk and press the seam into the collar.

Fold in the raw edge of the inside of the collar along the seamline. Hand-sew it to the stitching line to cover the seam allowance.

Pay special attention to the ends of the collar-seam, making a small bar at each end for extra strength.

Stitching on the wider collar

For the wider single tie, trim the seam allowance to $\frac{1}{4}$ inch, except where the collar is attached to the neck, on both sides of the tie. Roll the trimmed edges.

To do this, roll under the raw edges $\frac{1}{8}$ inch, then turn under again for $\frac{1}{8}$ inch and sew in place with fine slip stitches (figure **9**).

Stitch on the collar as for the folded version.

The rolled sleeve opening

On finer fabrics it is not advisable to make the usual sleeve openings as shown for the fitted shirt (Blousemaking chapter 28). They look heavy and the very narrow seam allowance inside the facings

▼**6.** *Snipped neck edge of facing*

▼**7.** *Stitching the double tie*

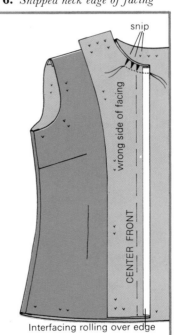

Interfacing rolling over edge

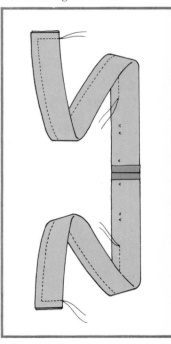

▼**8.** *Stitching the double tie for tapered ends*

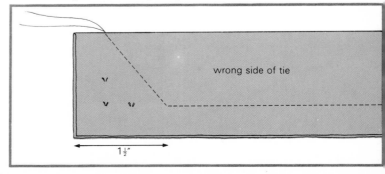

wrong side of tie

$1\frac{1}{2}$"

frays during wear because it cannot be double stitched. So for this soft blouse a special rolled opening is made.

First trim the seam allowance along the cuff edge of the sleeve to $\frac{1}{2}$ inch.

Then measure out the opening for the roll along the cuff seamline 1 inch to each side of the opening marking.

Starting at the center of this 2 inch opening, roll the seam allowance under for $\frac{1}{4}$ inch and turn it under again by the same amount. Let it taper out into the raw edges just beyond the mark on each side.

Hand-sew the small hem firmly in position (figure **10**).

On very fine fabrics this roll should not be more than $\frac{1}{8}$ inch deep, but do not forget to trim the whole length of the seam allowance accordingly or the ends of the cuffs will slant downward.

Finishing the sleeves

Stitch the sleeve seams, press and finish the seams.

Make the cuffs (single or double depending on your choice) as for the fitted shirt (Blousemaking chapter 28) with the extensions for link buttoning, or without if you are buttoning over.

When attaching the cuffs, work across the rolled edge as shown (figure **11**).

Stitch the finished sleeves into the blouse and finish the armhole-seam edges.

If the fabric is transparent, trim the armhole seam allowance and finish as for the blouse.

The hem

A beautifully finished garment deserves a beautifully finished hem, so hand roll it.

Turn up the hem edge for $\frac{1}{8}$ inch and then another $\frac{1}{8}$ inch. Then, with small slip stitches, sew it to the blouse along the folded edge. Take the hem right over the front facings and do not fold them back as for the other blouses.

Stitch the ends of the hem securely and press.

Finishing

Hand-work the buttonholes (Blousemaking chapter 26) and stitch on the buttons. Sew on a small covered snap fastener to the top corner of the wrap so that the point will not fall back during wear.

Covering a snap fastener

To cover a snap fastener, cut two circles of fabric as shown (figure **A**) and work a gathering stitch around the outer edge of each.

Cover each half of the snap fastener by drawing up the fabric to the wrong side of it and, in the case of the ball section, piercing the ball through the center of the fabric (figure **B**). Finish off the fabric at the back and stitch on the snap fastener (figure **C**).

A.   **B.**   **C.**

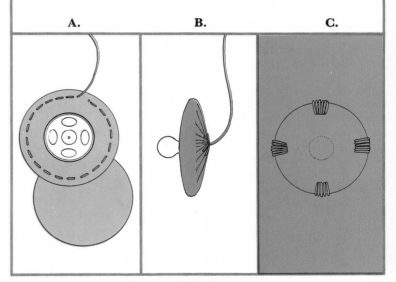

▼ **9.** *Rolling the edges of the wider tie*

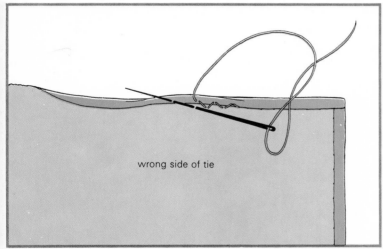

wrong side of tie

▼ **10.** *The hand-sewn rolled sleeve opening*

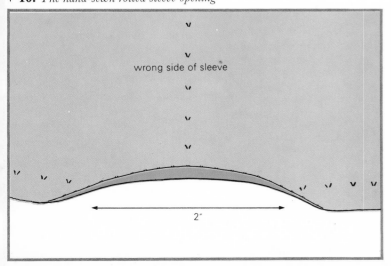

wrong side of sleeve

2″

▼ **11.** *Attaching the cuffs at the rolled edge*

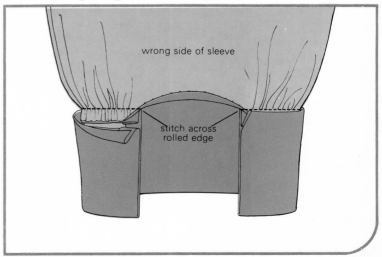

wrong side of sleeve

stitch across rolled edge

125

Blouse with Mandarin collar

The pattern
Back and Front. You will need the following pattern pieces from the Golden Hands Graph Pages: from the Basic Blouse Graph Pattern, the Front and Back pattern pieces, numbers 1 and 2; from the Accessories Graph, the short version of the straight sleeve and the Mandarin collar pattern pieces, numbers 7 and 9.

Facing. Make a front facing pattern and join it to the Front as for the tie-neck blouse (Blousemaking chapter 29, figure **1**).

Also make a back neck facing the same width on the shoulder edge as the front facing as shown in figure **1**.

Suitable fabrics
This blouse needs a firm, but not stiff, fabric. Soft woolen fabrics or soft silks are not suitable as the collar would not sit well.
Choose from the following:
- ☐ **Cotton:** soft poplin; shirtings
- ☐ **Linen:** blouse weight linen
- ☐ **Wool:** fine worsted; double knit
- ☐ **Man-mades:** Courtelle etc.

Layouts and yardages
Make a layout as shown in Know-How chapter 46 to work out the minimum yardage requirement. Place the Center Back of the Back, back neck facing and collar pattern pieces on the fold of the fabric. Do not forget to add seam and hem allowances all around.

Notions and other requirements
You will also need:
- ☐ Interfacing for collar and facings
- ☐ Small piece of sheeting
- ☐ 6 small buttons
- ☐ Hook size No. 0
- ☐ Matching thread

Cutting out
Before cutting the collar from the main fabric make a mock collar from sheeting as it may need adjusting. Cut out the collar with seam allowance along the neck seam only, and for extra support cut two layers of the sheeting.

Following your layout cut out the rest of the blouse, not forgetting the hem and seam allowances.
Mark the pattern detail carefully, especially along the neck edge.

Preparing for fitting
Pin and baste the front interfacing to the Center Fronts (Blousemaking chapter 29, figure **2**), then pin and baste the front facing to the inside of the blouse.
Pin and baste the darts and seams, and also baste the sleeves.
Pin and baste the layers of the mock collar together and use as one. Then pin and baste it to the neckline of the blouse, approximately ¼ inch inside the marked neckline (figure **2**). This will become the new stitching line for the stand-away Mandarin collar.
If you have altered the neckline of the blouse pattern in a previous fitting, this measurement may not be right for you. In this case, baste the collar to the neckline, matching centers and shoulder balance marks first, so there is no fullness on either collar or blouse neckline.
If you have made certain adjustments to the blouse for special back fitting problems, you may also find that the balance marks and the shoulder seams no longer line up.
To correct this move the balance marks forward, making sure that the distance is the same from the shoulder seams on both sides of the neck.

Fitting
Fit the blouse and check the sleeve fitting.
Check the fit of the Mandarin collar as follows:
Stand sideways in front of a mirror with your head held up. The collar should mold in a curve around the neckline, remaining upright and with no drag in any place.
The tilt of the collar should be at a good angle to the blouse and not jut out suddenly in any place. It should not touch the neck and should be at an equal distance from it all around.

▼ **1.** *The front and back facings*

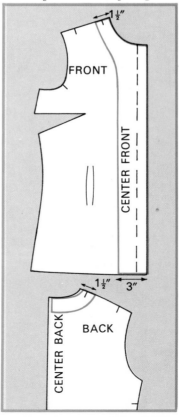

▼ **2.** *Mock collar basted in place*

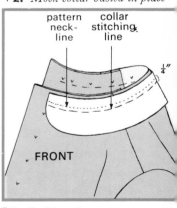

▼ **3.** *Problem A*

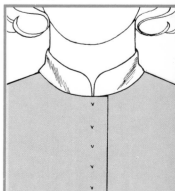

Fitting problems

Problem A. Pulling into the neck at the sides and dragging (figure **3**). The collar needs more length in the upper edge.

Problem B. The collar juts out at the Center Back (figure **4**). The shape of the neckline of the collar must be more rounded toward the Center Back to shorten the length of the upper edge at this point.

Problem C. Small neck and the collar stands away too far (figure **5**). The length of the upper edge of the collar must be decreased and the collar must be cut with more curve.

Problem D. Collar standing away at the sides of the neck (figure **6**). This can happen for two reasons:
i. Narrow front view of neck
ii. Collar too large.

Problem E. Collar is too small (figure **7**). The collar needs to be made larger.

Correcting the faults

When fitting for problems B, C and D pinch and pin the fullness into small pleats till the collar stands nicely out of the neckline of the blouse.

All five problems will then require the making of a new pattern.

Making a new collar pattern

Problem A. Pin the Center Back of the pattern to the straight edge of a sheet of paper and snip the pattern from the upper edge toward the balance mark on the lower edge (figure **8**). Spread the cut until the lower edge is almost straight and curves only a little at the Center Front. Pin the pattern down securely and draw around the new shape.

Problem B. Make a small tapering pleat copied from the mock collar on the upper edge of the collar pattern between Center Back and shoulder seam balance mark, and pin the Center Back of the pattern to the straight edge of a sheet of paper (figure **9**).

Draw around the new shape rounding the curve where it dips into the pleat on the pattern as shown.

Problem C. Copy the small pinned and tapering pleats on the mock collar onto the pattern and pin the Center Back to the straight edge of a sheet of paper (figure **10**).

Draw around the new shape, curving the lines gently where they dip into the pleats as shown.

Problem D. i. Copy the small pinned and tapering pleats on the mock collar onto the pattern and pin the Center Back of the pattern to the straight edge of a sheet of paper (figure **11**).

Draw around the new shape, curving the lines gently where they dip into the pleats as shown.

ii. Make a pleat in the collar pattern the same depth on both edges and then make a new pattern as above (figure **12**).

Problem E. Cut the pattern to enable you to spread and lengthen it to the required amount. Pin the Center Back of the pattern to the straight edge of a sheet of paper. Spread it and draw around the new shape as shown (figure **13**).

A closer fit

Finally, if you want the Mandarin collar to fit closely to the neck, fold off the extra length in the original pattern, making small pleats between Center Back and balance mark and balance mark and Center Front, until the neck edge of the collar equals the size of the original neck edge on the blouse, and make a new pattern. Use the new pattern to cut the collar for your blouse.

Making the blouse

Working on the Center Fronts first, sew the interfacing in position with small prick stitches as shown earlier in this chapter.
Next, stitch and press the darts.
Stitch, press and finish the side seams and shoulder seams.
Stitch the back neck facing to the front facing at the shoulder seams. Trim the seam allowances and press the seams open.

▼**4.** *Problem B*

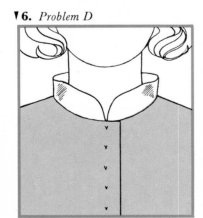

▼**6.** *Problem D*

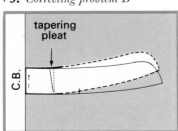

▼**5.** *Problem C*

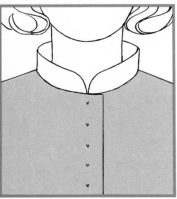

▼**7.** *Problem E*

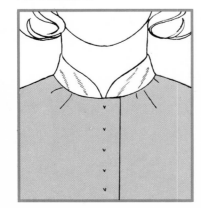

▼**8.** *Correcting problem A*

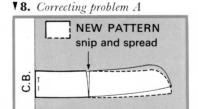

▼**11.** *Correcting problem D.i*

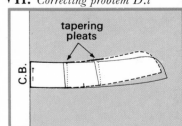

▼**9.** *Correcting problem B*

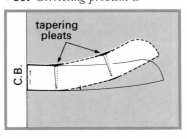

▼**12.** *Correcting Problem D.ii*

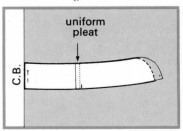

▼**10.** *Correcting problem C*

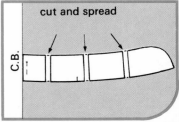

▼**13.** *Correcting problem E*

127

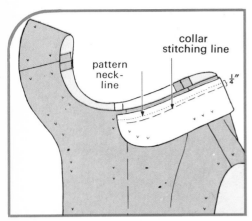

▲ 14. *Basting the interfaced collar in place*

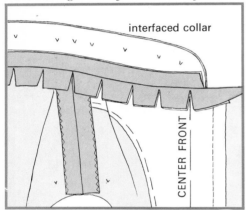

▲ 15. *The neck seam snipped and pressed open*

Attaching the collar

In the following text read "collar" for the outer section and "collar facing" for the inner section of the collar.

To check that all balance and center marks are lined up on the neck facing and the blouse, pin the facing to the neck edge. Unpin the facing and work on each layer as follows.

Pin and baste the interfacing to the inside of the collar.

The neckline of the blouse and facing for the mandarin collar falls $\frac{1}{4}$ inch inside the original pattern neckline.

Pin and baste the interfaced collar to the blouse neck edge with right sides together and all balance marks matching (figure **14**). Baste and then stitch.

Starting at the Center Front, snip the full length of the seam allowance on the blouse neckline (figure **15**). Press the seam open.

Pin and baste the collar facing to the neckline of the blouse facing, working just inside the seamline on the collar facing and allowing the Center Front edge of the collar facing to go a fraction over the Center Front on the blouse facing (figure **16**). This will make the collar facing fit slightly tighter when finished and allow the collar to roll over it to hide all seam edges.

Stitch the collar facing to the facing.
Snip the seam allowance on the neckline of the facing as you did on the blouse neckline and press the seam open.

Pin the collar to the collar facing, with right sides facing, using the seamlines as marked on the upper edge of both. But allow the seamline on the Center Front edge of the collar facing to fall outside the seamline of the collar by meeting the Center Front markings on the neckline of the blouse and the neck facing.

Baste the collar and collar facing together carefully along the collar stitching line. Then stitch, working with the facing uppermost but stitching along the basted line; stitch from the end of the wrap on one side to the Center Front, pivot the work on the needle, and work along the basted seamline of the mandarin collar, pivoting the work as you reach the Center Front on the opposite side.
Continue working along the wrap toward the end (figure **17**).

Trim the seam allowances and layer them as for the interfaced edges of the shirt dress in Dressmaking chapter 36.

After layering, make small notches into the seam allowance on the curved edges of the collar and turn the collar to the right side, thus turning the facings to the inside of the blouse.
The seamline along the collar edge will

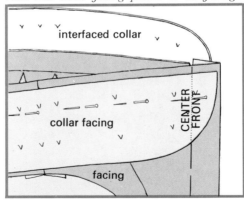

▼ 16. *The collar facing pinned to the facing*

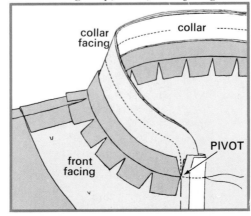

▼ 17. *Stitching wrap, collar, collar facing*

already be rolling toward the collar facing. The fullness in the collar will make it roll smoothly around the neck edge.
Edge-baste along the seamline, making sure that it is not pushed to the edge of the collar.
Baste the facing in position along the front edges and press lightly.

Finishing

To prevent the seam allowances along the neckline of the blouse and the facing from wrinkling up during wash and wear, it is necessary to secure them.
To do this, meet both seamlines along the neck edge and pin them together carefully. Place the shoulder seam of the blouse to the shoulder seam of the facing and Center Back to Center Back to insure that the collar does not wring.
Baste the seamlines together on the outside of the facing.
Then, working under the facing on the seam allowances, sew the seam allowances together by hand, using small running stitches. Leave the stitches a little loose, and make a small backstitch now and again to stop the seamline from moving. Hand sew the facing edge to the shoulder seams.
Stitch the sleeve seams.
Pin, baste and stitch the sleeves into the blouse. Finish and press the seams.
Finish the blouse hemline as shown for the basic blouse in Blousemaking chapter 26.
Mark out the buttonholes, starting 1 inch from the Center Front neck edge. Make the buttonholes and sew on buttons to correspond.
To keep the corner of the wrap in place when the blouse is buttoned, hand-work a bar and sew a small hook to the underside of the top corner.

Blouse with Back fastening

You will need the Front and Back patterns for the basic blouse, pattern pieces 1 and 2 on the Graph Pages.

The New Front pattern

The New Front is cut on a fold, so copy the original Front pattern up to the Center Front only (figure **18**) to exclude the wrap.

The New Back pattern

Copy the Back pattern, extending it for 1 inch along the Center Back (figure **19**) to make a wrap for the Center Back opening.

The Front and Back facings

If you are not going to make a rouleau type bound neck edge, copy the New Front

▲ *The sleeveless blouse with back buttoning*

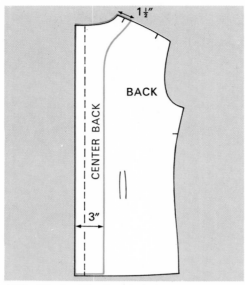

▲ **20.** *The back/back neck facing*

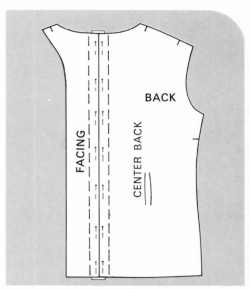

▲ **22.** *Attaching the back/back neck facing*

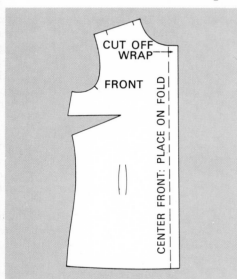

▲ **18.** *The Front pattern for cutting on fold*
▼ **19.** *The Back pattern for back buttoning*

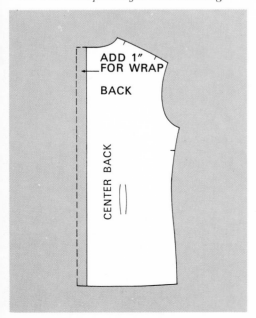

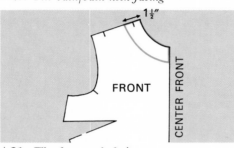

▲ **21.** *The front neck facing*

and New Back pattern pieces where necessary to make the front neck and back facings as shown (figures **20** and **21**). Attach the back facing to the Back (figure **22**).

If you are binding the neck edge with a rouleau type finish you will not need neck facings, so make a back facing as in figure **20** but excluding the neck section. Then attach it to the Back as shown (figure **23**).

The pattern outline is now complete.

Buttons and buttonholes

More ease is needed across the Back for back buttoning or else too much strain will be placed on the buttons and they will pop off.

To add this ease mark the positions of the buttons and buttonholes $\frac{1}{4}$ inch outside the Center Back line. No extra ease is needed at the neck edge, so this button position needs to be $\frac{1}{4}$ inch inside the Center Back line at the neck edge to compensate for the buttonhole which has been moved over, and then the other buttons are positioned as shown (figure **24**).

Making the blouse

Once you've converted the pattern simply follow the usual sewing procedure.

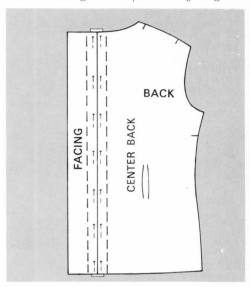

▲ **23.** *Attaching a back facing only to the Back*
▼ **24.** *Positioning the buttons and buttonholes*

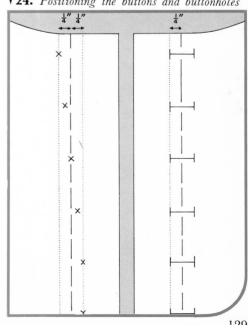

Chapter 30

Variations on bishop sleeves

This chapter is all about the bishop sleeve which is full, soft and glamorous. It is shown here with deep, tapered cuffs and rouleau loop fastening.

The bishop sleeve is an adaptation of the shirt sleeve on the Golden Hands Graph Pages. The variations sketched here show how it can be combined with Golden Hands blouse and dress patterns to give you a variety of looks. You'll also see from this chapter how to adapt the bishop sleeve pattern itself in some very exciting ways.

The chapter starts off with full instructions for making the bishop sleeve with rouleau fastening for the shirt dress conversion D, for which yardages and details are given overleaf. For this conversion choose a soft type of fabric to do justice to the lovely, full sleeve shape, but do make sure that the fabric is crease resistant or the sleeves will not look their best at all times. For a special occasion choose a printed chiffon, mount the Front and Back, collar and cuffs onto taffeta and use the chiffon on its own for the sleeves. Most printed chiffons have a little more texture than the plains and are quite easy to make up.

The bishop sleeve

The sleeve pattern

First make sure you have some large sheets of paper for making new patterns.

You will need the shirt sleeve pattern piece number 8 from the Accessories Graph on pages 110 and 111.

Copy the sleeve pattern and all its markings.

Slash the pattern as shown (figure 1). First slash along the centre then make three slashes equally spaced to each side of the first one. Make them all to within a fraction of the sleeve head, or crown, which must remain intact.

To spread the pattern you need a sheet of paper 36 inches wide and the length of the sleeve pattern. Draw the lengthways straight of grain centrally on the paper.

Place the slashed pattern on the paper, spread the centre slash 1 inch to each side of the grain line and spread each side slash 2 inches apart.

Pin all sections of the pattern securely in place then extend the sleeve-seams 3 inches on each side, at the wrist edge, as shown. This gives a lovely full sleeve which is ideal for fine fabrics. If you are using a heavier fabric you may prefer less fullness, in which case simply spread the pattern less and omit the extension on the side-seams.

Draw the new pattern carefully, shaping the wrist edge and tapering the sleeves-seams correctly. Mark the opening. Also transfer the markings on the sleeve head.

Cut out the new pattern.

From left to right—bishop sleeve with: tie-neck blouse and pinafore; tie-neck tunic; shirt with collar band finish; basic, open-neck blouse; rouleau loop fastened dress

▼ **1.** *Spreading the shirt sleeve pattern for the full bishop sleeve*

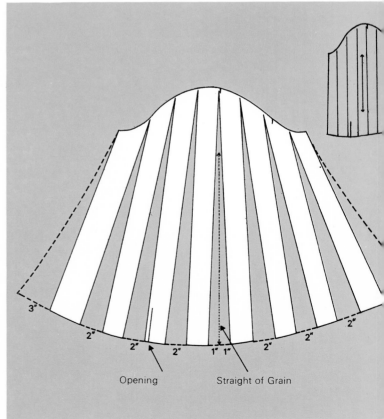

Opening   Straight of Grain

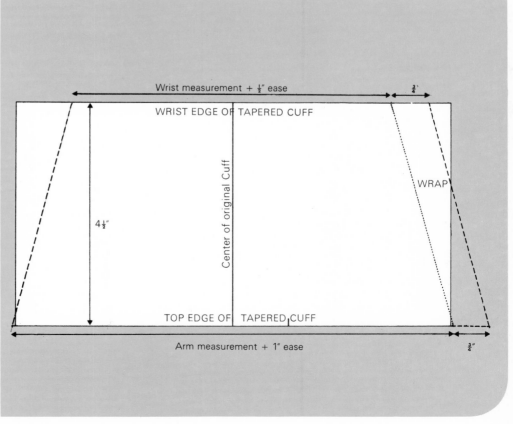

The cuff pattern

To make the new deep, shaped cuff, first copy the shirt cuff (pattern piece number 12 from the accessory sheet) onto paper.

Mark the center of the cuff as shown in figure **2**, then measure your wrist. Allow $\frac{1}{2}$ inch for ease and mark this measurement centrally on one cuff edge as shown. The depth of the cuff pattern is $4\frac{1}{2}$ inches, so measure your arm $4\frac{1}{2}$ inches above the wrist, add 1 inch for ease, and mark off on the opposite, top edge of the cuff. Taper the sides of the cuff toward the wrist, add $\frac{3}{4}$ inch on one end for the wrap.

Helpful hints

Make the bishop sleeve with a rolled opening (see Blousemaking chapter 29). Cut two fabric sections for each cuff and interface the top section.

It is essential that you buy the buttons before you start making the cuffs. This is because the cuffs are fastened with rouleau loops and buttons and the size of the loops is determined by the size of the buttons. For loop fastening high-domed, covered buttons are the most attractive (many stores provide a button-covering service). Alternatively, the ball type, such as pearl buttons, may also be used.

▼ **2.** *Making the tapered cuff pattern for the full bishop sleeve*

Wrist measurement + $\frac{1}{2}$" ease

$\frac{3}{4}$"

WRIST EDGE OF TAPERED CUFF

Center of original Cuff

$4\frac{1}{2}$"

WRAP

TOP EDGE OF TAPERED CUFF

Arm measurement + 1" ease

$\frac{3}{4}$"

Making the rouleau loops

For the loops, first make a $\frac{1}{8}$ inch wide rouleau.

Cut a bias strip four times the width of the finished rouleau (that is, $\frac{1}{2}$ inch wide). The length of the bias strip depends on the size and number of buttons you are using. For a quick, and safe, calculation measure over the dome of the button, add $1\frac{1}{2}$ inches to this measurement and multiply by the number of buttons to be used.

Make the rouleau as shown.

Attaching the loops

To find the length of each rouleau loop, take the dome measurement of one button, add $\frac{1}{2}$ inch at each end for seam allowance, and cut the loops to that size.

To find the correct spacing for the loops on the cuff edge, pin one loop to the top, interfaced, section (right side) and button it. If it is correct, measure out equal spacings along the cuff edge, allowing for the thickness of the rouleau on both sides of each loop (figure **3**).

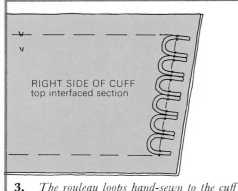

3. *The rouleau loops hand-sewn to the cuff*

Sew the loops in place by hand first, as shown.

Place the top, interfaced, and lower cuff sections together, right sides facing, then baste and stitch along the sides and wrist edge, leaving the top edge open.

Trim the seam allowance and snip across the corners, then turn the cuff to the right side, edge-baste and press (figure **4**). Do not press the loops.

If you find that the fabric you are using is not suitable for rouleau loops, use rat tail braid, applied as above, or hand-

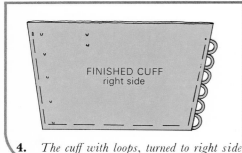

4. *The cuff with loops, turned to right side*

made loops. Work handmade loops (Skirt-making chapter 20) to fit the button size along the finished edge.

Finishing the cuff

With right sides facing, baste and stitch the open edge of the top, interfaced, cuff piece to the wrist edge of the sleeve. Make sure that the loops go to the top of the sleeve—that is, to the end of the opening furthest from the sleeve seam

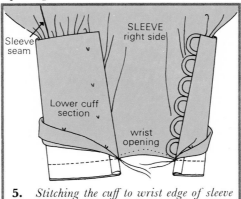

5. *Stitching the cuff to wrist edge of sleeve*

(figure **5**).

Trim the seam allowance and press the seam into the cuff.

Fold under the seam allowance of the remaining raw edge and slip stitch it in place over the stitching line on the inside of the sleeve. Press the sewn inside edge. Sew on the buttons opposite the loops, spacing them evenly.

Stitching on ball buttons

For loop fastening sew on ball buttons firmly, but for buttonholes sew on ball buttons loosely (but without a shank) to allow them to settle into the round ends. If they are sewed on too tightly, they will slip out of the buttonholes.

D. Shirt dress with bishop sleeves

Make this shirt dress like the shirt dress version A in Dressmaking chapter 36 but with the full, bishop sleeve.

Layouts for this dress are in Dressmaking chapter 37.

Yardages

54in width. Without one way—size $32\frac{1}{2}$, $3\frac{1}{8}$ yards; sizes 34 and 36, $3\frac{1}{4}$ yards; sizes 38 and 40, $3\frac{3}{8}$ yards; size 42, $3\frac{1}{2}$ yards.

54in width. With one way—size $32\frac{1}{2}$, $3\frac{1}{4}$ yards; size 34, $3\frac{3}{8}$ yards; sizes 36, 38 and 40, $3\frac{7}{8}$ yards; size 42, 4 yards.

36in width. With and without one way—sizes $32\frac{1}{2}$ and 34, $4\frac{5}{8}$ yards; size 36, $4\frac{3}{4}$ yards; size 38, $4\frac{7}{8}$ yards; size 40, 5 yards; size 42, $5\frac{1}{4}$ yards.

Making a rouleau

Tips. Before cutting the bias strip for a rouleau, experiment to find the correct width for the type of fabric you are using. You should have enough seam allowance to fill the tubing, and the heavier the fabric, the narrower the seam allowance.

Avoid using fabrics which fray easily.

Technique. Cut the bias strip to the length and width required and fold lengthwise, right sides facing.

Machine stitch twice leaving threads 10 inches long. Thread these through a darning needle and knot securely (figure A).

Insert the eye of the needle into the fabric tube as shown and gently start to push the rouleau back over the needle so that, by careful pushing and pulling of the thread, the rouleau is turned to the right side (figure B). Roll the finished rouleau between your fingers, gently stretching it and making sure that the seam goes along one side.

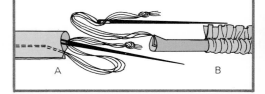

Bishop sleeve variations

A. Full sleeve without cuff

The fullness in this sleeve is held in with an elastic casing or a bound rouleau finish.

The pattern. Use the bishop sleeve in figure **1**, but lengthen it to compensate for the cuff.

To do this cut across the pattern horizontally, halfway between underarm and wrist. Spread the pattern and draw in the new lines as shown (figure **6**).

Elastic casing. Make an elastic casing on the wrist edge as for the child's dress version B in chapter 65.

Bound rouleau finish. Prepare a rolled opening at the wrist as for the bishop sleeve and gather the wrist edge similarly. Cut a bias strip to your wrist measurement plus 2 inches, and four times the required width of the finished rouleau.

Bind the gathered edge leaving the 2 inch extension on the top of the sleeve. Fold the extension and slip stitch the edges together to give a neat finish.

Form a loop with the extension and sew a

button on the opposite end of the opening to complete the fastening.

B. Gathered sleeve crown

The pattern. Slash the bishop sleeve pattern as shown (figure **7**) and draw in the new lines.

The armhole line for this sleeve is set higher on the shoulder, so work out how much you will move it in, then raise the crown by this amount plus ½ inch for ease. When setting in the sleeve, start the gathers about 4½ inches on each side of the balance mark which falls on the shoulder seam, drawing up the gathers as close as possible.

C. The full sleeve with fitted top

The top of this sleeve is the same width as the basic shirt sleeve but extra width is added to the lower part.

The pattern. Copy the sleeve pattern piece, number 8 on the Accessories Graph. Following the diagram (figure **8**), slash the pattern horizontally halfway between the underarm and elbow and a third of the way into the sleeve on both sides of the sleeve seam.

Next, slash the lower section vertically, in line with the inner ends of the horizontal slashes.

Make one or two more vertical slashes on each side of the sleeve between the first slash and the sleeve seam, depending on how full you want the sleeve. Spread the vertical slashes. The sides will rise above the horizontal cuts, so add the amount by which they overlap to the wrist edge of the sleeve seam. Draw in the new lines.

D. Sleeve with frilled wrist

This can be gathered with elastic and a self-casing on the inside of the sleeve, or it can be drawn up with cord or ribbon slotted into a casing on the outside of the sleeve. You can use self fabric or contrasting lace or braid.

The pattern. Use the bishop sleeve pattern in figure **1**, but without the extra extension on the sleeve seams.

To compensate for the cuff, extend the pattern downward by the amount required and use the original wrist edge as a guideline to stitch on the casing (figure **9**).

Inside casing. Make a bias strip casing on the inside of the sleeve as for the child's dress version B in chapter 64, and slot with elastic. Finish hem.

Outside casing. Make a casing on the outside of the sleeve with lace, braid or self fabric.

Leave the opening in the casing on the top of the sleeve for the ribbon ties. Or, if you prefer, you can make small buttonholes on each side of the opening to slot the ribbon through. Finish hem.

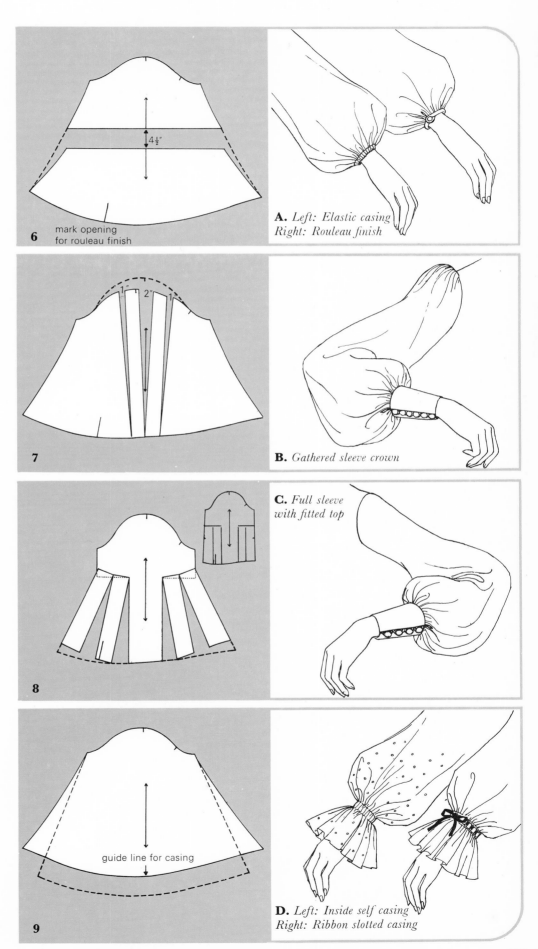

6 mark opening for rouleau finish

A. *Left: Elastic casing*
Right: Rouleau finish

7

B. *Gathered sleeve crown*

8

C. *Full sleeve with fitted top*

9 guide line for casing

D. *Left: Inside self casing*
Right: Ribbon slotted casing

Basic Dress Graph Pattern

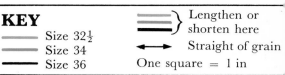

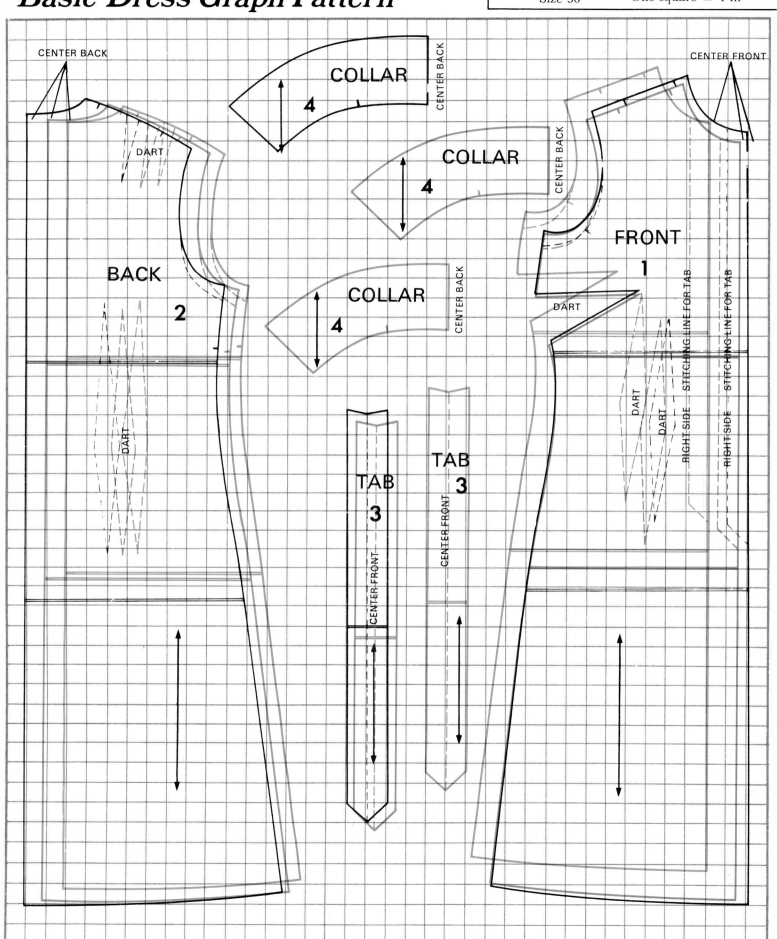

CENTER BACK

COLLAR
4

CENTER BACK

COLLAR
4

CENTER BACK

COLLAR
4

CENTER FRONT

DART

BACK
2

DART

FRONT
1

DART

DART

DART

RIGHT SIDE · STITCHING LINE FOR TAB

RIGHT SIDE · STITCHING LINE FOR TAB

TAB
3

TAB
3

CENTER FRONT

CENTER FRONT

The outlines given are the stitching lines.
Refer to page 139 for seam allowances
and check with the following chapters for
any variations.

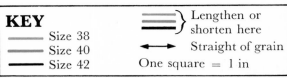

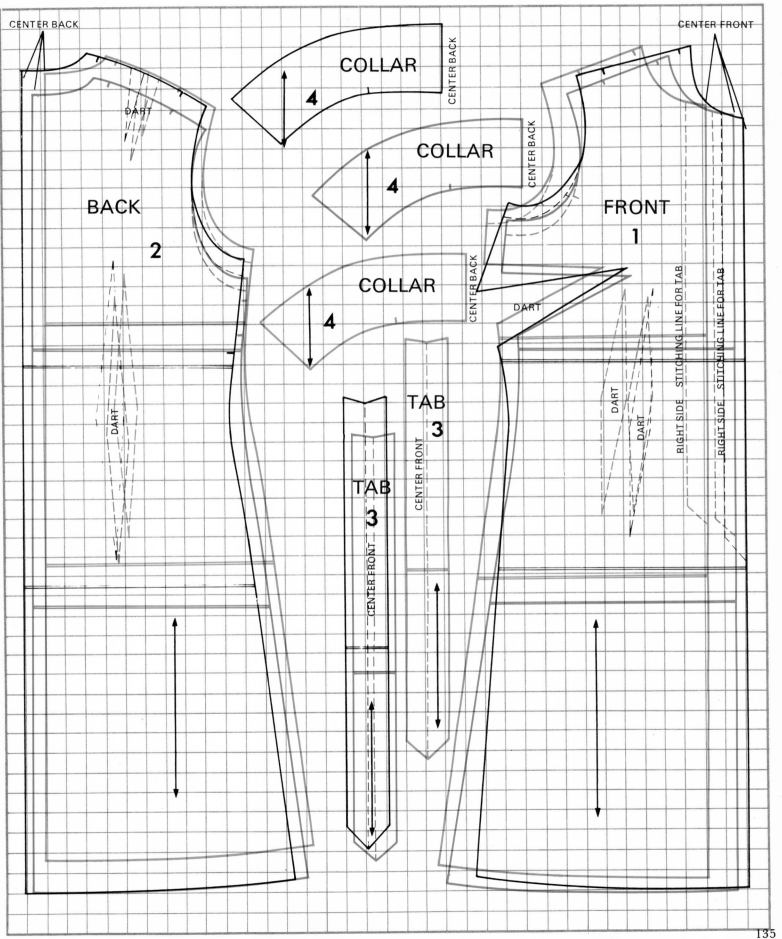

135

Chapter 31

Begin with the basic dress

It is every would-be dressmaker's ambition to make a dress successfully, but many give up in despair. They buy a paper pattern, cut out the fabric and plunge in and stitch it together without marking the pattern detail, basting the seams, or trying on the garment for fitting.

Halfway through they find that the garment does not fit, and since they haven't transferred the pattern detail to the fabric, there are no guidelines for altering the dress. Often the result is that the garment is thrown into the back of a drawer and forgotten. With more careful initial preparation, there would be no cause for discouragement and it would be a relatively simple matter to put things right.

The dress (r.), which was made from the Basic Dress Graph, was designed with both the beginner and the accomplished dressmaker in mind. If you are a beginner, you will find that all the stages of making a dress and detailed fitting instructions are given and also that the pattern pieces are kept to the minimum needed to assemble a dress. Every piece is clearly marked and easy to identify. And, to prevent confusion at the cutting out stages, only the main pattern pieces are cut at first; the facings are cut as you need them.

Watch out for tips for the experienced dressmaker, too. The method used for finishing the inside of the basic dress, the neckline, armholes and center front fastening is the one used by experts to limit bulk on these edges, especially when thick and weighty fabrics are being used. Other finishes are covered in later chapters.

Since assembling the basic dress is clearly explained step by step, when you come to other dresses you will be able to refer to the techniques for putting on tab front fastenings, finishing and fitting contained in these chapters.

The basic dress

The basic dress with collar and tab front, shown here in soft blue wool, is cut from the graph on pp. 134-135.

The pattern is so versatile that you can make a whole wardrobe of dresses based on this one pattern. Being a semi-tailored dress, the style lends itself to a wide variety of fabrics, the mood of the dress depending on the fabric and trimming used to make it.

Here are a few suggestions: For a sporty version, use a crisp fabric and top stitch the collar and tab details; for parties use voile or silk; for more formal occasions extend the pattern to full length and make an evening dress in a glamorous printed silk.

Later chapters explain in detail how to use the basic dress to make various attractive styles, which are only a few from the complete Golden Hands wardrobe of styles to make. However, for those of you who are advanced dressmakers, using the graph enables you to make any one of these versions of the basic dress right away.

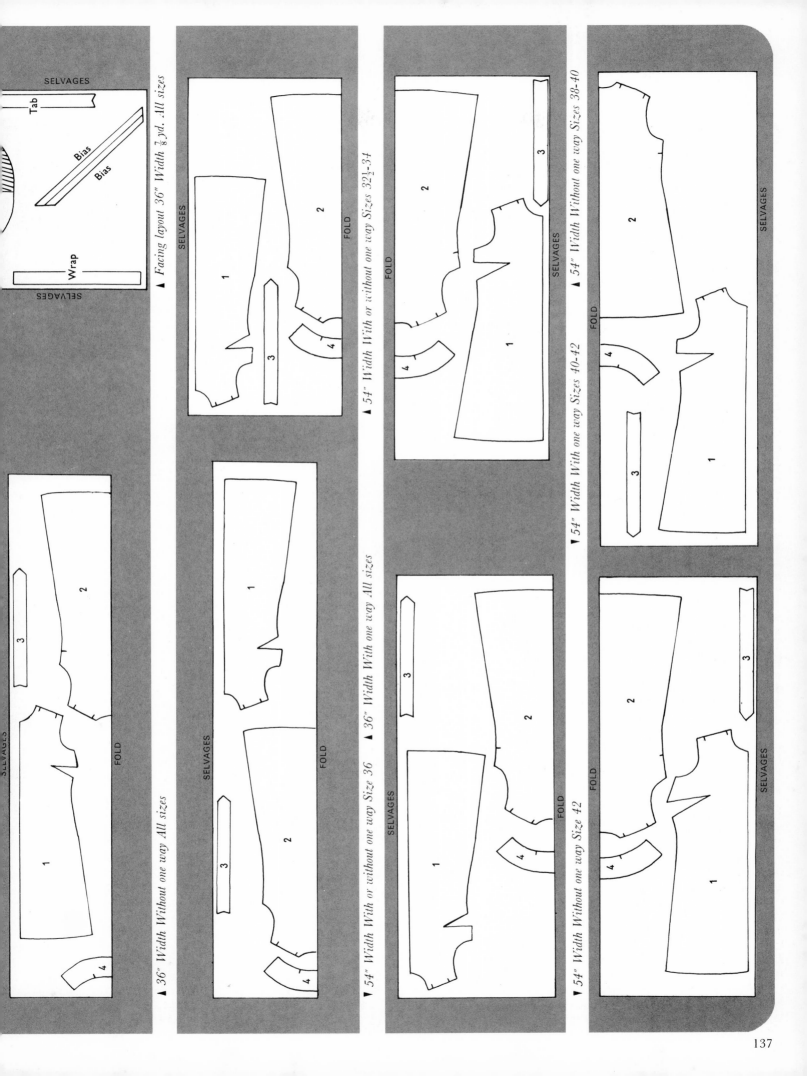

SELVAGES

Tab

Bias

Bias

Wrap

SELVAGES

▲ *Facing layout 36" Width ⅞ yd. All sizes*

SELVAGES

▲ *36" Width Without one way All sizes*

▲ *36" Width Without one way All sizes*

FOLD

SELVAGES

FOLD

▲ *36" Width With or without one way Size 36*   ▲ *36" Width With one way All sizes*

▼ *54" Width With or without one way Size 42*

FOLD

FOLD

▼ *54" Width With one way Size 42*   ▼ *54" Width With one way Sizes 40-42*

SELVAGES

FOLD

▲ *54" Width With or without one way Sizes 32½-34*

SELVAGES

FOLD

▼ *54" Width Without one way Size 42*

SELVAGES

▲ *54" Width Without one way Sizes 38-40*

137

Choosing your fabric

If you're a beginner, use a firmly woven fabric which does not fray easily, such as wool flannel, fine tweed or a worsted woolen fabric. All these are easy to handle, retain their shape and will not slip around during making.

Here is a list of other fabrics which are also suitable for the basic dress.

☐ **Firmly woven cottons:** Sailcloth, dress-weight poplin, lightweight denim and piqué.
☐ **Linens:** Dress-weight, plain or embroidered.
☐ **Man-made fabrics:** Cloth made from, or containing, acrylic or polyester fiber, such as Acrilan or Dacron.
☐ **Wool or wool mixtures:** Viyella, wool crepe and many traditional woolen dress-weight fabrics.

And here are some more fabrics which require a little more dressmaking know-how.

☐ **Silks, pure and synthetic:** Shantung, Honan and Thai silk, foulard and brocade.
☐ **Cotton:** Organdy and voile.

The basic dress can also be made from knit fabric, with the exception of the silk or silk-type knits. Before buying knit, test it by holding it up over your wrist. If there is a downward drag to the fabric—almost as though it is weighted—it is more suitable for softly draped styles and not for the semi-tailored style of the basic dress.

Fabric requirements and notions

Before buying the dress and facing fabric, look at the yardages given on the pattern sheet. To face the woolen and silk fabrics, use pure silk or rayon taffeta. Avoid triacetates or nylon, because they will not stand as much pressing as is necessary on wool. For cotton and linen use poplin for facing. Man-made fiber fabrics should be finished with fabric of equal weight, strength and texture. If your dress is washable, remember to buy washable facing fabric. You will also need the following notions: 8 buttons; 9 sew-on snaps size 0; matching thread.

Sewing psychology

Dressmaking needs careful planning. In order to be successful, each job must follow the preceding one in natural and logical succession. Never let each step of the work become an end in itself, but let it be a means to an end.

Making a basic skirt is a simple task, but with a dress the detail increases. It takes more time to make and real planning is essential. It can be a great temptation to rush ahead and do things out of order because you are impatient to see the finished result, but unless you are methodical you can easily ruin the garment.

When you've pinned the paper pattern onto the fabric, and cut the dress, tailor's tack all the details, bearing in mind that this will help you with the next step. The next three stages are the most important ones: basting the seams together, fitting the dress, and making the fitting alterations before sewing up the seams. If you neglect these preliminaries, you can find yourself with an ill-fitting garment when it's too late to alter it.

So, plan your dressmaking. Always remember to concentrate on doing the job in hand so that you can do the next one properly.

In this way you will enjoy your work and the results will be good. It is also worth the extra time to read through the whole of each chapter before taking action, because this will help your planning and avoid possible disaster later on.

Reading the Golden Hands pattern pieces

Make your paper pattern from graph, transferring all the markings. Before cutting out the pattern, take time to study it carefully so that you can identify the pattern pieces and get to know what the markings mean. You may find it easier to study the pattern pieces on the opposite page.

The four pattern pieces needed for the basic dress are the back, front, tab and collar patterns. Note the seamlines: The pattern does not give seam allowances, so the solid lines are also stitching lines. Look at the balance marks, which will have to be matched. For instance, the balance mark on the side seam of the dress back meets the end of the side bust dart on the dress front. The shoulder balance marks on back and front will have to meet when stitching the shoulder seams.

Next, look at the dotted lines, which indicate stitching lines and optional darts. The dart shown on the shoulder of the dress back is optional, as some fabrics will ease in between the balance marks; but if you need more fullness across the back shoulder line, or if your fabric is too stiff to ease in, then you will need this dart for a smooth fitting shoulder line.

The long body darts are also optional and largely a matter of style and fashion, except in the case of larger bust sizes, when they become a must.

The long, pointed dotted line parallel to the center front is the stitching line for the tab on the right front and the meeting line for the tab on the left front, when the tab is wrapped over for fastening.

The two solid horizontal lines across the back and front are for lengthening or shortening the pattern. The dotted line on the tab pattern is the center front, and the dotted lines below the solid line of the lower armhole are stitching lines used when making the dress with sleeves.

Cutting out the paper pattern

Cut out the back, collar and tab paper pattern pieces along the solid outlines. Then cut out the front, leaving a ½in margin along the shoulder and side seams, outside the solid pattern outline. Do not cut out the side bust dart, however (see the upper diagram on page 179).

Correcting the pattern length

As the pattern has been made with neither seam nor hem allowances, it is easy to check the final length as follows:

Pleat the pattern at the side bust dart by placing the lower seamline at the upper seamline, and securing it with pins.

Lap the back shoulder seam over the margin on the front shoulder seam to meet the solid seamlines, and pin. Join the side seam in the same way.

Slip the pattern over your shoulder and stand sideways in front of a long mirror so that you can see the final length of your dress. If you need more or less length, measure the amount you need, take off the dress and unpin it. Then make the length adjustments along the two solid horizontal lines.

The dress length given comes to just below the knee for a 5ft 5in height. If you are taller or shorter and want to alter the dress to obtain this length, use the two solid lines as described below. If, however, you simply want the dress to be longer, you can add up to 5in by using the two solid lines across the skirt of the dress. If this is not enough and you need still more length, just add that to the hemline.

To lengthen the pattern, cut the pattern along the solid horizontal lines and fix strips of paper between the pattern sections to make up the required length.

To shorten the pattern, simply make a pleat along each horizontal line, to the depth of the required amount.

Re-pin the darts and the shoulder and side seams and slip the pattern on once again for a final check to see that you have made the right adjustments.

Take out all the pins and cut off the margins on the dress front. Also cut into the underarm bust darts.

Preparing the fabric for cutting

Prepare the fabric in the same way as for the basic skirt in Skirt-making chapter 11. Smooth out any creases with a warm iron and a damp or dry cloth, according to the fabric type.

When working on longer lengths of fabric, it becomes difficult to find a surface large enough to accommodate the full length, so use a chair back to support the rest of the fabric. This prevents any pull on the fabric on which you are working.

Check that the selvages of the fabric are not tight and making the fabric pucker. If they are, make small snips through the selvages only, about 2in apart. If this doesn't make the fabric lie flat, cut off the selvages altogether.

Select the appropriate layout from the special sheet and follow it carefully.

Leave enough room between pattern pieces for ¾in seam and 2½in hem allowances. Pin down your pattern pieces securely.

Beware—before you cut

Having studied the various figure types and problems in chapter 4, you may have discovered that you need to make certain adjustments to your pattern before cutting out. Later chapters deal fully with pattern adjustments, but because of the soft fit of the basic dress, figure problems are quite easily overcome, provided you take the following precautions.

Straight shoulders. For very straight shoulders, add ½in to the normal seam allowance toward the outer edge of the shoulder seam, as you may have to let it out.

Rounded back and sloping shoulders. For a slightly rounded back and sloping shoulders, leave an extra deep seam allowance along the back armhole edge, about 1½in at shoulder level, tapering into normal seam allowance toward the underarm.

Thick-set neck. If you have a thick-set neck, measure your neck around the base, then measure the neck edge of the center back to center front of the pattern. This measurement should be 1in larger than your own. If it is not, do not cut the collar until you have fitted the dress.

Large proportions. It is always a good idea to leave an extra seam allowance where you know your measurements are slightly larger than standard proportions. You can then make the necessary adjustments when you are fitting the garment.

Pinning the hem and seam allowances

Mark the hem and seam allowances with pins or tailor's chalk. Pin ¾in seam and 2½in hem allowances all around, and if you need to make any of the alterations mentioned above, add the additional allowances now.

Add the extra seam allowance at the darts as shown in the top right-hand diagram.

You will notice the layouts given earlier in this chapter show extra width on the center front seams. This is a double seam allowance of 1½in and you will see how to use this later. Leave on this double seam allowance when you cut out.

You are now ready to cut out the fabric. The pattern details will be marked after cutting.

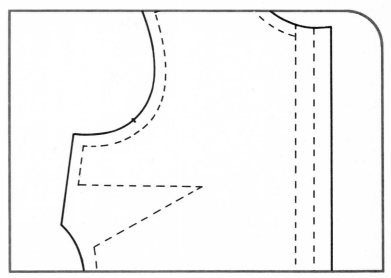

▲ *Add seam allowance at the darts*　　▼ *Basic dress pattern pieces*

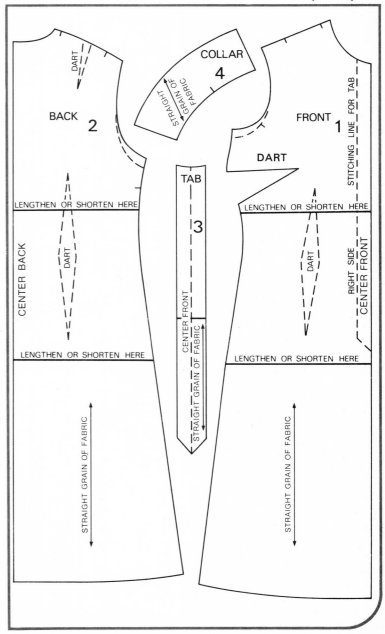

Chapter 32

The next step

The next stage of making the dress is to mark the pattern details on the fabric. For the skirt in Skirtmaking 11, these were marked before cutting to prevent the beginner from being confused. In this case, however, it is easier to mark the pattern details once the pieces have been cut out.

Marking the pattern details on the fabric

First mark the details on the dress back. Lay it on a flat surface and mark around the pattern edges with continuous tailor's tacks. Make single tailor's tacks at right angles to the seam edges to indicate the balance marks.
Next, the dash lines. Those on the back indicate optional shoulder and waist darts, and need to be marked only if you are using them. To do so make short slits about 3in apart through the pattern with a needle, along the dash lines. Make single tailor's tacks through each slit, being careful not to stitch into the pattern.
Mark the center back fold line with a row of long basting stitches, as you will need this line to check the hang of the dress.
The dress fronts are marked in two stages. First the general pattern details are marked and then the fastening details.
Mark the center front line from hem to neck.
Make slits through the dash line of the tab stitching line and mark with single tailor's tacks. Mark the corner and point especially carefully, because they have to match the shape of the tab. Similarly mark the waist darts if you are using them.
Tailor's tack around the rest of the pattern and into the darts. Mark the balance marks.
For the second stage the layers must be separated as described for the skirt in Skirtmaking chapter 11, so cut through the tailor's tacks. Lay the right front, right side up, on a flat surface in front of you. Mark the $\frac{3}{4}$in seam allowance along the center front, from the hem upward to where it meets the stitching line of the tab. Then mark a seam allowance along the tab stitching line and cut off the surplus as shown in the diagram.
With the left dress front in front of you, right side up, look at the diagram carefully. You have already marked the center front line and the meeting line for the tab.
Halve the double seam allowance along the center front and mark the line with long basting stitches. Following the red line on the sketch, cut off the extra seam allowance from the lower edge on the center front, where you don't need it. The extra seam allowance along the upper edge will provide you with enough wrap to fasten the dress.

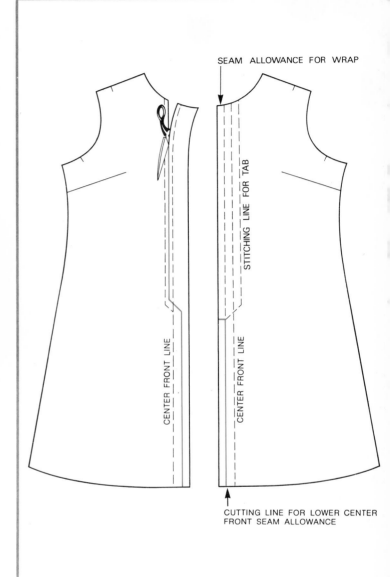

▲ *Preparing the right front*   ▲ *Preparing the left front*

A wrap is usually half the width of the tab (in this pattern, 1 inch) and meets the tab stitching line when closed. But to simplify the cutting of your first dress, only a seam allowance width ($\frac{3}{4}$in) has been given, and this is really plenty. Instructions for cutting a conventional wrap are given later.
On the tab make long basting stitches around the outline and mark the center front line.
Tailor's tack around the collar.
Remove the pattern pieces and separate the layers in the usual way.

Preparing for fitting

The dress is now ready to be pinned and basted to prepare it for fitting.
Pin and baste the darts.
Pin and baste the center front seams from the pointed end of the tab stitching line to the hem.
Pin and baste shoulder and side seams, carefully matching the balance marks.
Press the seams open lightly and turn up the hem.
The fastening detail is not put together at this stage.

Fitting the dress

Before you start fitting, put on the undergarments you will wear with the dress when it is finished. Make sure your bra shoulder straps are adjusted correctly, because if you alter them later your side bust darts will not fit properly.

Slip on the dress and pin the center front opening closed by lapping the raw edge of the seam allowance on the right over the seam allowance for the wrap on the left front.

Now look at the dress in a full length mirror. This is the time when most people wish they'd never started; your dress looks raw and bulky, but don't despair—even experienced dressmakers have to remain very objective at this stage.

When fitting, start from the top and work downward. Here is a list of fitting stages in order:

1. The neck   5. The body darts
2. The shoulders   6. The side seams
3. The armholes   7. The hang
4. The bust   8. The length

1. The neck

Make sure that the row of tailor's tacks around the neck, indicating the stitch line for the collar, lies flat around the base of the neck. If it is strained, or rises on the neck, carefully snip into the seam allowance until you have the required fitting. Do not snip too deeply, because the seam allowance will have to be trimmed and snipped again after you have stitched on the collar. Mark a new stitching line with pins.

2. The shoulders

If the dress lifts at the inner shoulder or feels tight over the top of the arm, it means that your shoulders are straighter than the standard slope of the pattern. Let out a little from the seam allowance on the outer edge of the shoulder line and taper into the original seam allowance toward the neck.

If sloping shoulders make the dress rise at the outer shoulder edges, you will need to lift the seams. Start at the armhole edges and taper into the original seams toward the neck, until the shoulder line lies flat. This may tighten the armholes of the dress. If so, snip the seam allowance carefully where it is tight, until the armholes feel comfortable, and pin new armhole lines.

3. The armholes

If the armholes feel tight and the dress shoulders are caught over the upper arms, your problem is large upper arms.

If the armholes are merely too tight, pin new armhole lines. But if the dress is held away from the neck through tightness around the armholes you must fit this in two stages.

First cut off the seam allowance from the armhole edges around the underarm and slip the dress on again. Then pin new armhole seams. If you have more than the normal seam allowance left outside the new pin lines, take the dress off and pin the armholes together. Mark the pinned armhole line through both layers of fabric and trim to the normal seam allowance. Try on the dress once more to make sure everything is all right.

Finally look at the armhole seamlines over the shoulders and make sure these are in the correct position.

4. The bust

The well-made look of a dress does not depend on your figure, but on the way the dress is fitted to it. So always take the trouble to fit your dress really well, especially over the bustline. The dress should fit smoothly and not strain, even when you are moving. Look at the dart points; these should be in line with the highest point of the bust. If not, pin them higher or lower as required.

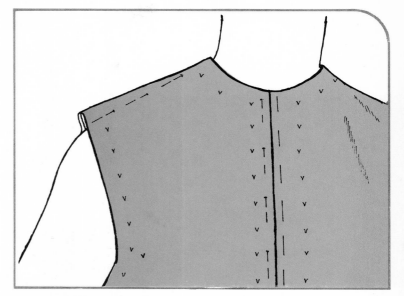

Cutting through the tailor's tacks

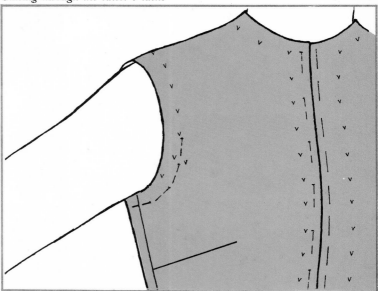

Pinning the bust dart
Pinning the side seams

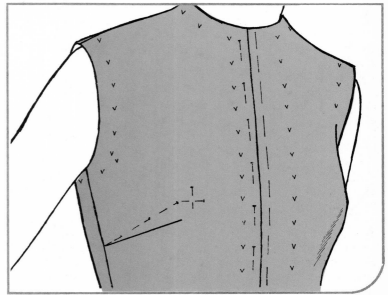

Small adjustments can be made by altering the angle of the darts, but if you have to alter them by more than ½in, it is best to move the whole dart by that amount.

When you have made the necessary adjustments, move around and swing your arms to see how much room you require for movement. Also sit down, as this can tighten the bustline of the dress if you have a large bust.

5. The body darts

If you have used the body darts to make your dress fit more closely, make sure the front darts run toward the bustline and finish just under the highest point of the bust.

The body darts in the back should finish about 2in above the seat. The deepest curve must go through the waistline and not above or below it, as this would leave strain lines.

6. The side seams

Stand sideways in front of a mirror and look at the way the side seams hang. They should run in a straight line all the way down, fitting close to the body at bust level, bypassing the waist and gently flaring toward the hem.

A swing toward the front may be caused by a large bust, which will be dealt with under point 7. If this is not the case and they swing toward the front or back of the dress, it may be that when basting the side seams you eased one side into the other. If so, undo

the side seams and baste them again, making sure that both sides are smooth and flat.

If the dress is too loose, adjust it by pinning the fullness into the side seams.

If your dress is too tight, let out the side seams.

7. The hang

Look at the back of the dress with the help of a hand mirror. The line of basting stitches along the center back line should hang straight. If it is dragged sideways because of tightness, let out the dress at the side seams.

If the basting line hangs toward the right or left, and this is not caused by tightness, you will have to lift the corresponding side seam until the basting line hangs straight. To do this, undo the side seam and lift the dress back into the armhole till the hang is straight. This may leave your armhole too large. If so pin the surplus into the shoulder seam.

The hang of the dress can affect the side seams. A large bust, for instance, will pull the dress up in front, making it jut forward at the hem and pull the side seams toward the front. Undo the side seams and lift more fabric into the underside of the side bust darts. If this gives you too much width in the side seams over the hips, pin extra width into the seam.

A rounded back can cause the same trouble at the back of the dress. To counteract this, undo the side seams and lift the dress

Fitting the dress

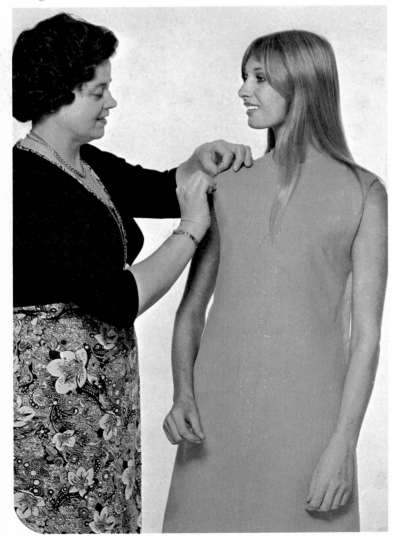

Stitching the dart

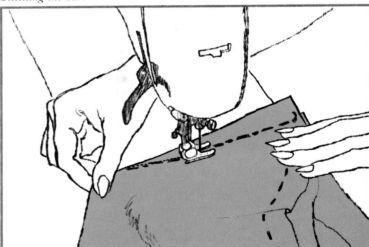

Pressing the dart

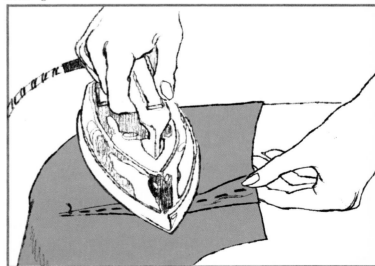

back into the armholes, making sure that you lift it evenly on both sides. Use the balance marks as a guide.

It is difficult to guess the amount to lift, so start by lifting the back by one inch, re-pin the side seams and slip the dress on again. You will then see if the drag toward the underarm has been corrected; if not, lift the dress back a little more.

This adjustment gives you surplus width around the armholes at the back. Lift this surplus into the shoulder seams by first deepening the darts and then making the back shoulder seams slope down a little more, otherwise it will poke out at the armhole points of the shoulder seams.

Line up the armhole seams on the back to the armhole seams on the front, which you will be able to do because you added extra seam allowance when cutting out the fabric.

3. The length

Adjusting the hem is the final stage in the fitting.

If in making your fitting alterations you have adjusted the hang of the dress on one side, level the hemline on that part of the dress with the hemline on the other side.

Marking the corrections

Trace the pin lines, which indicate the new fitting, with basting thread, tracing on each side of the new seamline where the fabric

Pinning the tab to the tab facing

Basting the tab along the stitched edge

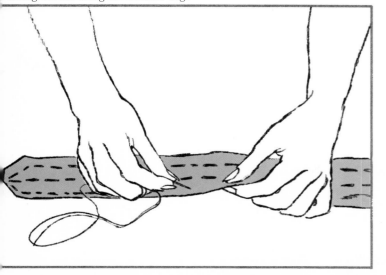

is double, being careful not to catch in both layers at once.

Then remove the pins and basting stitches from these seams. Make sure the fitting corrections are the same on both sides of the dress as shown for the skirt alterations in Skirtmaking chapter 12, unless of course your figure is uneven, when you must fit each side to the shape of your body. Mark the paper pattern pieces too for future reference.

When all the corrections are done, baste the dress together again and make a final fitting.

Stitching

You will be cutting out the under collar and the facings for the center front, tab and armholes as you need them, so have your facing fabric and paper pattern pieces ready.

Test the machine stitches on a scrap of dress material.

To help you plan your work and show you how the stitching and finishing progress, here is a list of the steps involved:

Step 1. The dress front: Darts; center front seam; front fastening, tab and wrap.

Step 2. The dress back: Darts.

Step 3. Joining the dress sections: Shoulder seams; side seams.

Step 4. Finishing the dress: Armholes; collar; hem; finishing the fastening; sew-on snaps; buttons.

Step 1

The dress front. Whenever you have details on a dress such as the center front fastening, it is better to tackle this task before the section you're working on is joined to the remaining sections. This makes for easier handling without the bulk of the dress getting in your way. Undo the basted shoulder and side seams.

Darts. Stitch the side bust darts first. Note that both slanted underarm darts must be sewed in one direction, or else they will twist. This means that one dart will be sewed toward the point and the other toward the base. See in the illustration how the fabric is guided through the machine in the seamline of the dart. Do not pull darts while stitching; they may stretch. After stitching the darts remove the basting and press them flat as you did for the skirt. Pay special attention to the pointed ends. Lay them over the rounded end of the ironing board so that you can mold them into the roundness of the body shape. They must not rise sharply into a point. Molding and shaping the fabric are secrets of good dressmaking. Stitch the waist darts if you are using them. Press them toward the center.

The center front seam. Stitch the center front seam from the pointed end of the tab stitching line to the hem. Remove the basting and press the seam open to within 2in of the upper end.

Front fastening, tab. The first stage is the preparation of the tab. Using the tab pattern, cut out the tab facing from lining fabric with $\frac{3}{4}$in seam allowance all around. Mark the tab pattern details onto the fabric with long basting stitches and make single tailor's tacks through the slits along the dash line.

Pin and baste the tab to the facing with right sides together and with the facing uppermost. Starting at the center front, stitch along the top, down the right side, turn and stitch to the point. Fasten off the stitches securely at both ends so that as you work on the tab the seamlines remain secure.

Trim the seam allowance and clip into the seam at the beginning of the stitching line (center front). Turn the tab to the right side and baste firmly along the sewed edge with small stitches, rolling the facing slightly under to prevent it from showing.

Press this edge carefully on the wrong side of the tab, making sure that the basting stitches do not leave impressions on the fabric, as they will be very difficult to remove.

Chapter 33

The basic dress continued

In this chapter the pieces are assembled and the finishing touches are put to the dress.

Step 1

Front fastening, tab (continued). Before you stitch the tab to the dress, prepare the corner on the dress front as shown in the diagram below, to prevent it from fraying.

Machine stitch a row of stay stitches just outside the marked-out stitching line, then cut into the corner without cutting the stay stitches.

Pin, baste and stitch the raw edge of the tab to the right dress front on the tab stitching line, but avoid catching the facing fabric into the seam. Spread the corner on the dress so that you can stitch comfortably toward the pointed end of the tab. Make sure that the corner stays in position and does not drag inward, by pivoting the machine needle just inside the stay stitching at the corner. The point of the tab must be in line with the

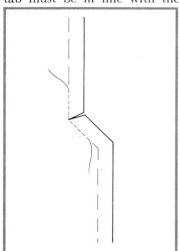

The stay-stitched corner

center front seam.

If the fabric is thick and the seam allowance on the tab at the corner does not lie flat after pressing, trim it carefully across the corner.

Fold under the seam allowance on the facing and pin it over the seamline to cover the raw edges. Slip stitch in place by hand. Remove all remaining basting on the tab.

To press the tab, lay it full length, wrong side up, on the ironing board with the sides of the dress front fully supported. Fold the left front double to keep it out of the way of the iron, but without dragging the center front seam, and press.

The wrap. To complete the center front fastening, make the wrap on the left front edge. Cut out the facing from the lining fabric, leaving a $\frac{3}{4}$in seam allowance, using the tab pattern as your guide, but without the pointed end. Instead, extend both sides of the

tab pattern to the length of the point and cut straight across the lower edge, not forgetting the seam allowance. It is not necessary to mark the seam-line of the facing strip, as you can use the marking on the dress front for your stitching lines.

Pin and baste the facing to the left front edge of the dress, with right sides facing. Stitch the facing and fabric together, starting at the center front, along the top edge and down the front, leaving the lower edge unstitched.

Trim the seam allowance, clip into the seam at the beginning of the stitching line (center front), and turn the facing into the dress. Baste firmly along the sewed edges and press carefully.

Turn under the long raw edge on the facing until it is even with the meeting line for the tab, and sew it with a slip stitch. Working on the inside, lay the wrap over the tab and you will see that the center front seam folds over too. To make the seam lie flat and open, cut into the seam allowance as shown below, press the seam

open and press the wrap over the tab.

Oversew the raw lower edge of the wrap facing by hand, catching in the center front seam allowance.

To hold the wrap in position, make several small stitches at the lower edge, catching it to the stitching line of the tab.

The fastening detail is now complete, so give it a final pressing.

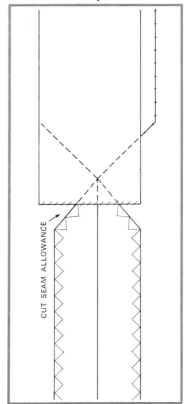

Detail of the stitched wrap

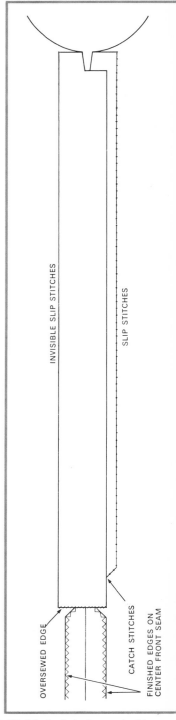

Finished stitched wrap inside

Step 2

The dress back: Darts. First stitch the darts at the shoulder if you are using them.

Slash the darts along the center to within 1½in from the point and press them open as for a seam. This way they will lie flat when the shoulder seam is stitched and not leave a bump showing above the seam. Overcast the raw edges to finish them off.

If you are darting the waist, stitch the darts and then press them toward the center.

Step 3

Joining the dress sections: Shoulder seams. Pin, baste and stitch the shoulder seams, matching balance marks and seamlines. Overcast the raw seam edges. Remove the basting. Press seams open.

Side seams. Working on a flat surface, lay the side seams together. Match the side seam balance marks on the back to the ends of the side bust darts on the front. Pin, baste and stitch the side seams, making sure that both layers of fabric are perfectly smooth, otherwise the side seams will not hang straight.

Overcast the raw seam edges and remove the basting. Press the seams open. Take out any impressions the seam may have made on the fabric by running your iron under the seam allowance.

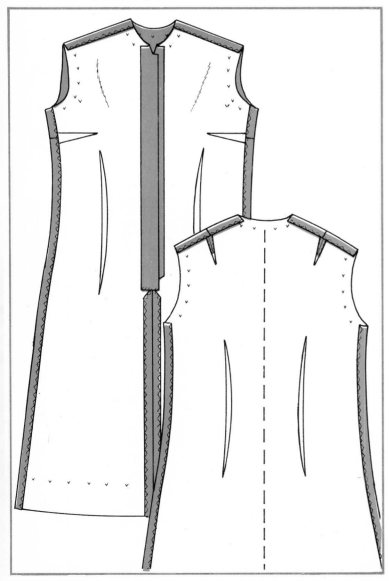

Step 4

Finishing the dress. When you make a garment with sleeves, it is important to finish the neckline first, as it is essential to see if the firm fit of the collar affects the armhole line over the shoulders. When you make a sleeveless dress, it does not matter if you finish the armhole edge first.

The armhole edge is finished here, so that you can see the technique more clearly.

The armholes. First measure the size of the armholes along the seamline.

Find the true bias of the facing fabric by laying one side of a 45° set square to the selvage of the fabric, and mark the diagonal of the fabric with pins or tailor's chalk (see layout of facing fabric on page 137.

Cut 1½in wide bias strips of facing fabric and join them as shown on the diagram to make up the length required for the armholes plus 2in for ease and 1in for seam allowance.

The bias strips will have to be curved to follow the line of the armholes. To do this, place one bias strip on the ironing board and press around the outer edge, gently stretching this into a curve as you press; then press in the fullness along the inner edge of the curve so that the material is as flat as possible.

Turn under ½in seam allowance at one end of the bias strip.

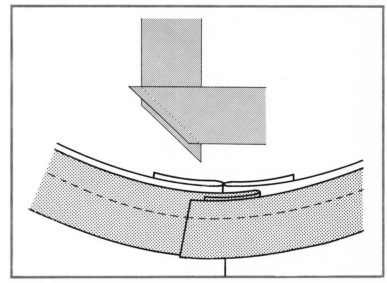

Top: Joining bias strips   Bottom: Bias strip basted around lower armhole

Starting at this end and working on the outside of the dress with right sides facing, pin the inner curved edge of the bias strip around the armhole seamline. Start at the top of the side seam and take only $\frac{3}{16}$in seam allowance. The inner curve on the bias will still be a little full and you will have to ease the fullness into the underarm curve of the armhole seam.

Let the end of the bias overlap the turned-under seam allowance, as this will make for a secure joining and also give a little extra stretch where you need it.

Because the curve of the armhole shape varies so much, it is not advisable to join the ends of the bias strip in the straight of the grain where they meet at the side seam, as is usual with a straight edge. So leave the strip untrimmed and unstitched until the facing is complete, then stitch it as it falls.

Leaving the overlap still unstitched, baste the bias firmly in position and machine stitch it in place around the armhole seamline.

Remove the basting stitches and trim the armhole seam allowance on the dress to the width of the seam allowance on the bias.

Clip into the seam allowance on the dress only to within a grain or two of the stitches, then turn the bias to the inside. Roll the seam

145

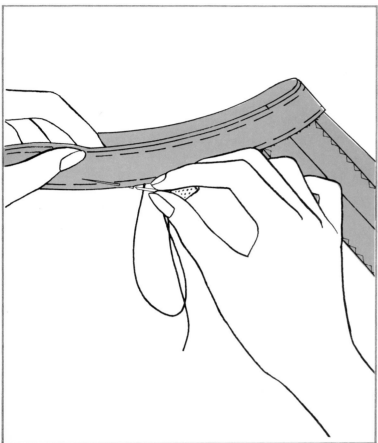

Hand sewing the armhole facing in position

edge slightly to the inside to prevent the bias from showing, and baste in place. Press the basted edge gently. Turn the raw edge of the bias under for about ½in and pin and baste it to the dress.

Now carefully hand sew the bias in place.

Slip stitch the lapped ends of the bias in place.

Remove all basting stitches and give one final pressing.

Face the other armhole in the same way.

The collar. The first consideration is whether you need to enlarge the collar. If you had to make the neckline larger, you will also need to cut a new collar pattern.

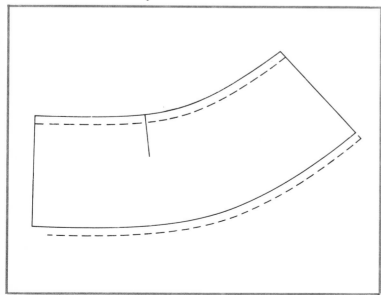

The dotted lines indicate where to enlarge the collar pattern

Measure the new stitching line around the neck edge of the dress. Halve this measurement and deduct ¼in.

To find this length on the collar pattern, measure into the collar from the neck edge and draw a new stitching line inside and parallel to the original neck stitching line of the pattern.

Mark the new position of the balance marks. Then cut the pattern along the new stitching line.

Place the cut pattern on a sheet of paper and pencil around it. Then add the amount you trimmed off the neck edge to the outer edge of the new collar pattern, so that the collar remains the same width as before.

Using the new pattern, cut the collar from the dress fabric. Remember to place the center back of the pattern on the fold of the fabric and to add and mark with tailor's tacks the ¾in seam allowance all around the outer edges.

Before you can put the collar together, you will need to cut out an under collar.

Fold the facing fabric in the position shown in the layout and cut out the under collar, allowing only ⅝in for seams. This will make

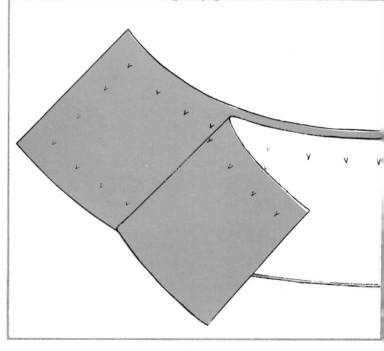

Smaller undercollar in place over collar

the under collar slightly smaller, and you will see why later.

Before removing the pattern, mark the balance marks. Remove pattern and mark the ordinary seam allowance ¾in on the neck edge of the under collar, but do not mark the seam allowance on the outer edge.

With the outer raw edges even, pin and baste the collar and under collar together around the outer, not neck, edge using the seamline on the top collar as your guide.

Working with the under collar uppermost, stitch around the collar leaving the neck edge open.

Remove the basting thread, cut off the seam allowance across the corners and trim it along the stitched edges.

Now turn the collar to the right side and you will see why the under collar is cut slightly smaller than the collar; this is to prevent the under collar from showing on the outside.

Baste along the stitched edges, rolling the upper collar edge under so that both pieces lie perfectly flat. Press lightly.

With the right side of the outer collar facing the wrong side of the dress, pin, baste and stitch them together along the neck edge, with

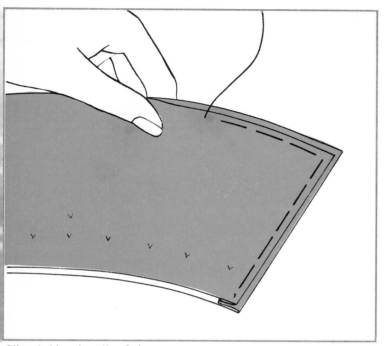

Slip stitching the collar facing

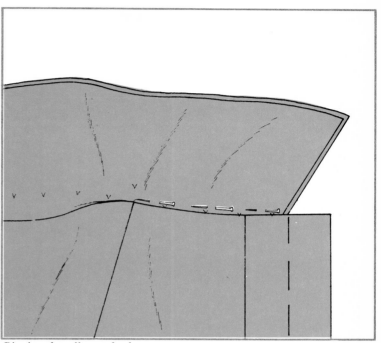

Pinning the collar to the dress

the ends of the collar meeting on the center front lines on the dress fronts.

Trim both seam allowances and snip into the allowance on the collar only. Press the seam into the collar.

Turn in the raw edge on the under collar for a full ¾in seam allowance and pin. To avoid strain at the center front you may have to adjust the depth of the seam allowance on your under collar. Snip into it as for the collar, then baste it to the stitching line so that the seam is just covered by the folded edge.

Slip stitch neatly in place.

Remove all basting and press.

The hem. After you have checked the hem, turn it up and finish it exactly as you did on the skirt in Skirtmaking chapter 13.

Finishing the fastening. All that remains to be done is to sew on the snap fasteners and buttons.

To find the correct position for the snap fasteners it is necessary to work out the button positions first.

Use 8 buttons to trim the tab. Mark the place for the first button 1in down from the neck edge. Measure the remaining length of the tab and work out equal distances for 7 more buttons, leaving half a button distance between the last button and the pointed end of the tab. Mark the button positions along the center front line with pins so that you can see them on both sides of the tab. Sew on the snap fasteners first, one under each button position. Sew the ball part of the fastener to the tab and the sockets to the wrap. To find the socket positions on the center front line of the wrap, fold the tab over and mark the corresponding positions with pins.

To hold the top corner of the tab under the collar when it is fastened, sew on a snap fastener as shown in the picture.

Finally, sew one button over each of the other snap fasteners on the outside of the tab.

Give the dress one more careful pressing and it is ready to wear!

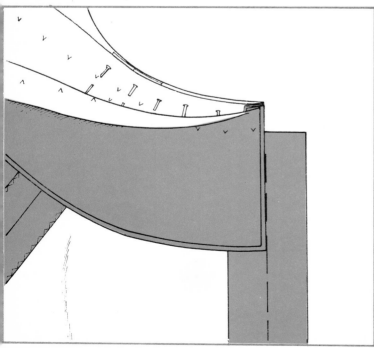

Turning under the lower edge of the collar facing

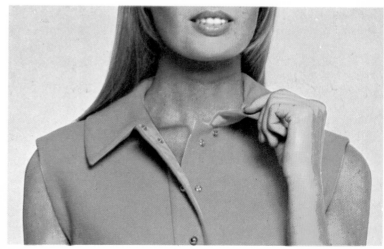

This shows the position of the snap fasteners

Chapter 34

The jumper conversion

In this chapter, the basic dress pattern, from the Golden Hands Graph Pages on pages 134 and 135, is converted into two jumper dresses—a day version, and one for the evening with a wide flared skirt. The day version has front body darts, while on the evening version the front shaping is achieved with slanting bust darts instead of the usual darts.

Full instructions are given for increasing the flare of a skirt to as much as a full circle. Suitable fabrics, the new patterns, and the layouts for both versions are given here so that you will be ready to start sewing by the next chapter.

The secrets of achieving perfect proportioning

Cutting the basic pattern to create new styles is fun and being able to do it shows real progress in dressmaking. At the same time, it is very important to know where to cut the pattern because misplaced seams can spoil a garment.

Decorative seaming, whether vertical, diagonal or horizontal, is very attractive, but all seams must be considered in relation to the length and width of the finished garment.

By careful seaming and proportioning you can create a definite line, such as a square, elongating or flowing line. But if you have a square build, or if you are tall and thin, a similar line will only tend to accentuate it and you will need to alter the proportions to suit you.

Proportioning does not mean that you must have equal lengths of bodice and skirt when the garment is finished. It means that all parts of the garment divided by seams remain in good proportion to each other when the garment is worn, and do not emphasize figure faults or make the garment look clumsy. Nor should the outline of a design be destroyed by bad positioning of seams—they should flatter a figure as well as enhance the style.

Finding the correct position for the horizontal seam

The position of the horizontal seam on the jumper is determined by your figure type, height and size. See Generally Speaking chapter 5 on figure types before you read the following:

To find the cutting line for the horizontal seam, first read the instructions for your figure type, then modify them according to your height and size.

Figure type

Standard: 5 inches below the waistline.

Large bust: First, consider the information in Generally Speaking chapter 5, relating to the particular problems of a large bust, before deciding to make the jumper. The cutting line must be determined very carefully but, unless the bust is very much larger than the hips, the cutting line should be around hip level. This gives emphasis to the widest part of the hips, thus helping to balance the large bust proportions.

Leave plenty of seam allowance on bodice and skirt horizontal seams to allow for adjustments when fitting.

If your bust is much larger than your hips, pin the front and back pattern pieces together along the side and shoulder seams over strips of paper. Slip the pattern over your shoulders and pin. Place a length of dark colored tape around your body over the pattern where you think the cutting line for the horizontal seam should go. Pin the tape down and look at the line from the front and the sides to see if the position is right for you.

Large hips: All figure types with larger hip proportions should cut the pattern around hipbone level, 3 to 4 inches below the waist. This puts the emphasis of width on a narrower part of the body.

Height

Short, 5ft 3in and under: There is no way to create the impression of length through horizontal seaming, but the jumper can look right for you as long as the sections are perfectly proportioned.

Mark the cutting line 3 to 4 inches below the waistline, but when you are cutting out the dress leave at least 2 inches for the horizontal seam on both bodice and skirt so that you can check and perhaps adjust the seam line on the basted garment. This way any adjustments made will not interfere with the length. Here is a guide to the proportioning for short figures.

For a day length jumper, the skirt should look a little shorter than the bodice. For a full length evening jumper, you may be able to drop the horizontal seam line if your hip proportions are good.

Medium to tall, 5ft 4in to 5ft 9in: See instructions under Figure Type where the cutting lines given were for average heights.

Very tall, 5ft 10in and over: Most tall people have to cope with the problem of a long waist or long legs, or both. Since the horizontal seaming divides these lengths, it presents no real problem. However, the following will help you to determine the right position for the seam.

Pin the front and back pattern pieces together along the side and shoulder seams over strips of paper. Slip the pattern over your shoulders and pin it.

Place a length of dark colored tape around your body over the pattern where you think the cutting line for the horizontal seam should go. Pin the tape down and look at the line from the front and the sides to see if the position is right for you.

Size

Small to average: See previous instructions under Figure Type and Height which were based on small to average sizes.

Larger sizes: This problem must be taken into consideration when making the jumper.

If your bust size is over 38 inches, you should use the darts on the pattern and fit the bodice. A loose look will only add to your size. On the other hand, the gentle flare of the skirt on a fitted bodice, combined with a carefully positioned horizontal seam, will create a very flattering line.

Suitable fabrics

Whether for day or evening wear, choose a fabric that is suitable for the style of the dress you are making. Fabrics with horizontal, vertical or diagonal design details are not suitable as the design would interfere with the cut of the jumper—especially the day dress with its topstitching detail.

Fabrics to suit the geometrical appearance of the day length jumper are:
- ☐ Firmly woven tweed and worsted woolens.
- ☐ Double knit wool, polyester and heavy cotton knits.

Fabrics to suit the soft look of the evening jumper are:
- ☐ Wool, silk and rayon crepes.
- ☐ Lightweight wool and polyester knits.
- ☐ Pure silk and rayon satins.

Yardages

Day length jumper: The following yardages are for the given pattern length. If you want to make the skirt longer, don't forget to add the extra skirt length required on each pattern section to the yardage.

54 inch width, without one way—sizes 32½ and 34, 1¾ yards; size 36, 1⅞ yards; size 38, 2 yards; sizes 40 and 42, 2¼ yards.

54 inch width, with one way—sizes 32½ and 34, 1¾ yards; size 36, 1⅞ yards; size 38, 2⅛ yards; sizes 40 and 42, 2¼ yards.

36 inch width, without one way—size 32½, 2⅞ yards; size 34, 3 yards; size 36, 3⅜ yards; sizes 38, 40 and 42, 3½ yards.

36 inch width, with one way—size 32½, 3⅛ yards; size 34, 3¼ yards; size 36, 3½ yards; size 38, 3⅝ yards; sizes 40 and 42, 3¾ yards.

Evening jumper: The following yardages are for a dress length of 58 inches. If you want to make the skirt longer, don't forget to add the extra skirt length on each pattern section to the yardage.

54 inch width, without one way—sizes 32½ and 34, 2⅞ yards; size 36, 3¼ yards; size 38, 3⅜ yards; size 40, 3⅝ yards; size 42, 3¾ yards.

54 inch width, with one way—size 32½, 3⅜ yards; sizes 34, 36 and 38, 3½ yards; sizes 40 and 42, 3¾ yards.

36 inch width, without one way—size 32½, 4¾ yards; size 34, 4⅞ yards; size 36, 5½ yards; size 38, 5⅝ yards; sizes 40 and 42, 6 yards.

36 inch width, with one way—size 32½, 6½ yards; size 34, 6⅝ yards; sizes 36 and 38, 6¾ yards; size 40, 6⅞ yards; size 42, 7 yards.

By careful proportioning and seaming, jumper-style dresses can suit all figure types ►

149

Making the new pattern

First, make sure you have plenty of paper handy for copying the pattern so that you will not have to cut up the original.

Copy and cut out the front and back pieces on the Dress Graph (pieces 1 and 2 on the Graph Pages).

Next, mark your waistline on the new pattern. To determine its position, use either the corrected bodice muslin pattern (see Muslin-making chapter 23) or use a measuring tape.

Front: Square neckline

Mark out the new neckline (figure **1**).

Measure 2 inches along the shoulder seam from the neck edge and mark. Measure 5 inches down, make another mark and connect to the center front edge by a straight line, using a tailor's square or set square. Measure back along this line $3\frac{1}{2}$ to 4 inches, depending on how wide you want the neckline to be, and mark. Connect this point to the original mark on the shoulder seam.

Cut out the new neckline as shown in red.

Back: Neckline

Mark off the same distance from the neck edge along the back shoulder seam as you did for the front. Then, measure $1\frac{1}{4}$ inches from the neck down the center back line and connect both marks with a curved line (figure **2**).

Cut out the new back neck curve.

Center back seam

If you want to make the jumper fitted, it is necessary to curve the center back seam slightly before you start dividing the pattern for the bodice and skirt.

Draw a gentle curve (figure **2**) through the waist from a point about 4 inches below the waistline to a point about halfway between the waistline and neck. Make sure that the curve tapers gradually back into the original line.

If you are also using the back darts, you must compensate for the center back curve by drawing the darts a little less deep, or the back will become too fitted.

Any further adjustments necessary to make the jumper more fitted should be left until the fitting stage.

Cut out the center back curve.

Horizontal seam

Measure your correct horizontal cutting line at equal distances below the waistline across both back and front pattern pieces and draw in the new lines.

Measure the side seams of the bodice to make sure that they are the same length on the back and the front. Also check that the skirt back side seam is the same length as the skirt front side seam.

Since the back and front skirt patterns are very much alike, mark the pieces clearly

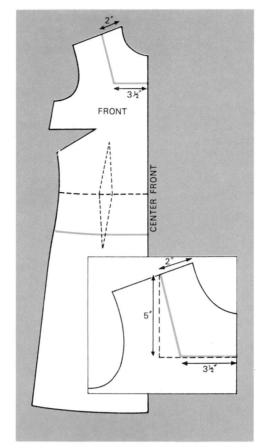

1. ▲ *Making the square neckline on the front*
2. ▼ *Making the new back neckline on the Back and curving the Center back seam*

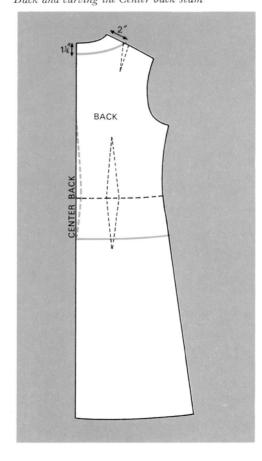

front and back and mark in the center front and center back before cutting along the horizontal lines.

Also mark the center front line on the bodice as "fold," since there is no seam in the bodice front.

Cut the pattern along the horizontal lines.

Back and front facings

Here is a new type of facing to finish the neck and armhole edges of the dress.

To avoid the bulky finish which two separately cut facings would make over the shoulders, the neck and armhole facings are cut in one piece.

Lay the center back and front of the bodice pattern pieces along the straight edge of a sheet of paper and draw around the top edges (figures **3** and **4**). Remove the patterns and draw in the inside lines of the facings as shown.

Reduce the width of the facings a little over the shoulders as shown by the red dash lines (figures **5** and **6**). This insures a perfect finish when the facings are stitched in place and avoids showing a roll along the edges. Cut out the facing patterns.

The skirt darts

If you are not fitting the dress with body darts, use the skirt pattern as it is, ignoring the darts. But if you are stitching body darts, you must deal with the darts in the skirt before cutting out the dress. Here are two ways to do this.

Method A. Leave the darts in the skirt in line with the body darts so that they look like one long dart after stitching.

Method B. Alter the shape of the skirt pattern (figure **7**). This method will also add a little more flare around the hem.

To achieve this, first fold the darts on the pattern pieces to meet along the stitching lines and hold them securely in position on both sides of the pattern with transparent tape. Lay the center of each skirt pattern piece along the straight edge of a piece of paper, wider than the pattern, and pin along the center line.

Slash each pattern from the hem upward to the end of the dart. Spread the slash until the pattern lies flat and pin down. Draw around the new pattern shape, remove the original and cut out the new skirt pattern. Transfer back and front markings.

Increasing the skirt fullness

The diagram (figure **8**) shows you how to add width to the skirt and obtain the lovely fullness shown in the evening version of the jumper. The short skirt can also be made with an increased flare.

Using this method you can even increase the skirt until it is a quarter circle, for a circular skirt, but you would need to increase the number of slashes to get a good waist curve.

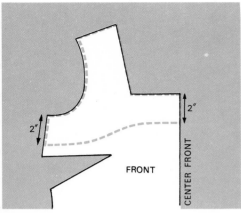

3. ▲ *Making the front neck and armhole facing*
4. ▼ *Fold off dart and then make back facing*

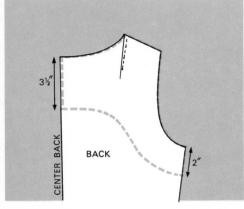

5. ▲ *Reducing the shoulder width of front facing*
6. ▼ *Reducing the shoulder width of back facing*

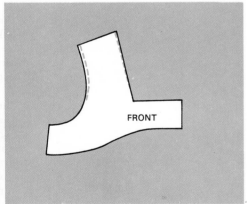

Step A. First prepare the back and front skirt patterns as shown in figure **7**, then make two more slashes evenly spaced between the slash for the darts and the side seam. Make all three slashes to within $\frac{1}{8}$ inch of the waistline, which means cutting through the darts.

Step B. Pin the center of each skirt pattern piece to the straight edge of a sheet of paper large enough to accommodate the extra width and length needed for the evening skirt.

Step C. Following figure **8**, add 24 inches to the width of the hem of the short skirt by spreading each slash 2 inches along the hem line. Pin the pattern down.

You will notice that the waistline starts to curve up and lift considerably toward the side seam. This is correct to retain the waist measurement.

Step D. Draw around the pattern edges with a pencil and extend the side seam. Plot out the new hemline, an equal distance from the original, using a yardstick, and draw in the new curve. Cut out the new skirt pattern.

**Making the pattern
for a slanted side bust dart**

For the soft molded look of the evening dress, the front body darts are dispensed with and the side bust darts are slanted.

The slanting of the side bust dart should be about 45 degrees. Although this may vary from person to person it should not be more than 45 degrees. If you alter the dart by that amount, you can always lessen the slant without much trouble if it is too steep for you. This will be done at the fitting.

To make the new pattern, pin the front bodice pattern to the straight edge of a sheet of paper wider than the pattern. Draw around the pattern and into the dart. Remove the pattern.

Extend the upper side seam (figure **9**) downward as shown. Then turn the end of the dart upper stitching line downward through 45 degrees, make a mark on the extended side seam and connect the point of the dart to it.

To find the lower stitching line, measure the distance between the original dart stitching lines at the side seam and mark off this distance between the new stitching line and the side seam. Draw in the dart lower stitching line from side seam to point.

Draw a straight line from the dart point through the center of the new dart to meet the new side seam and then connect it to the dart lower stitching line at the original side seam, as shown.

Cut out the new pattern but do not cut out the dart yet, as it may not be in the correct position.

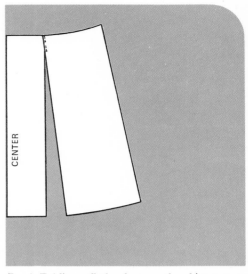

7. ▲ *Folding off the dart on the skirt pattern*

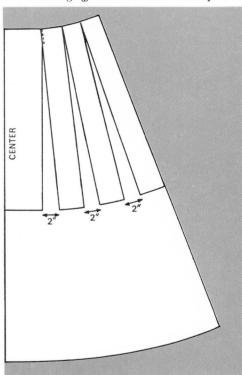

8. ▲ *Lengthening skirt and increasing the flare*
9. ▼ *Altering the slant of the side bust dart*

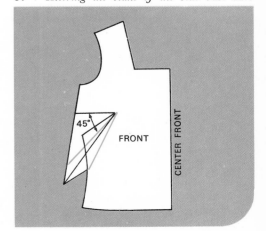

Day length jumper

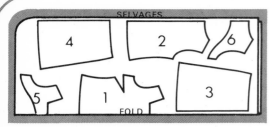

▲ *54 inch width, with & without one way, sizes 32½ & 34*

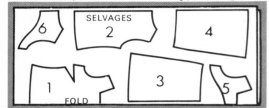

▲ *54 inch width, without one way, sizes 36 & 38*

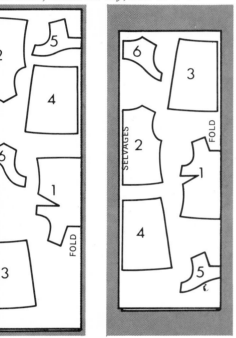

▲ *54 inch width, without one way, sizes 40 & 42*

▲ *54 inch width, with one way, sizes 36 & 38*

▼ *54 inch width, with one way, sizes 40 & 42*

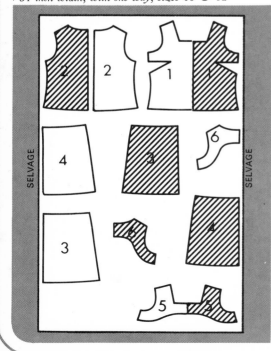

Layouts for the jumpers

The layouts given here are for the day length jumper without extra flare, and the evening jumper. If you increase the flare on the skirt, you may need extra yardage. Using these layouts as a guide, first make a trial layout on paper before buying the fabric to calculate how much extra you need.

Key to pattern pieces

Bodice front = 1
Bodice back = 2
Skirt front = 3
Skirt back = 4
Front neck facing = 5
Back neck facing = 6
reverse
pattern =
pieces

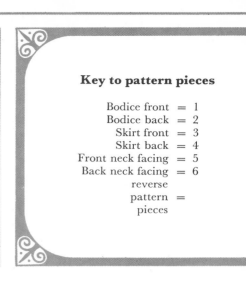

▼ *36 inch width, without one way, sizes 32½ & 34*

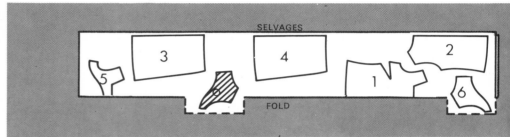

▼ *36 inch width, without one way, sizes 36 & 38*

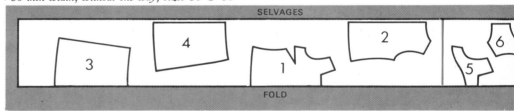

▼ *36 inch width, without one way, sizes 40 & 42*

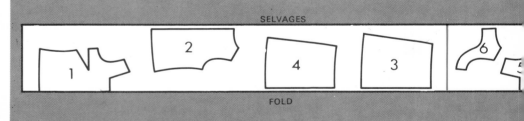

▼ *36 inch width, with one way, sizes 32½ & 34*

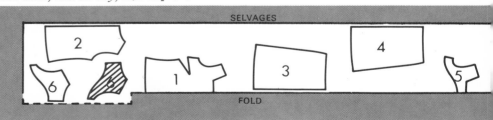

▼ *36 inch width, with one way, sizes 36 & 38. Alternative layout for section between red lines on layouts for fabrics without one way, sizes 36 & 38*

▼ *36 inch width, with one way, sizes 40 & Alternative layout for section between red lines on la for fabrics without one way, sizes 40 & 42*

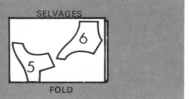

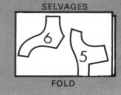

152

Evening jumper

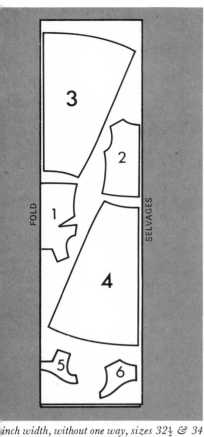

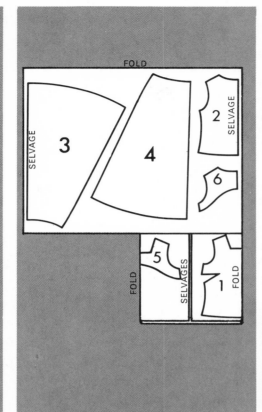

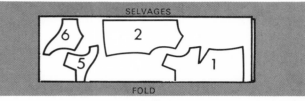

▲ *36 inch width, without one way, skirt layout for all sizes*

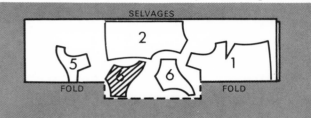

▲ *36 inch width, without one way, bodice layout sizes 32½ & 34*

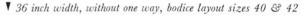

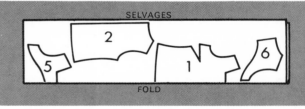

▲ *36 inch width, without one way, bodice layout sizes 36 & 38*

inch width, without one way, sizes 32½ & 34

▲ *54 inch width, without one way, sizes 36, 38, 40 & 42*

inch width, with one way, sizes 32½ & 34

▼ *54 inch width, with one way, sizes 36, 38, 40 & 42*

▼ *36 inch width, without one way, bodice layout sizes 40 & 42*

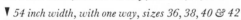

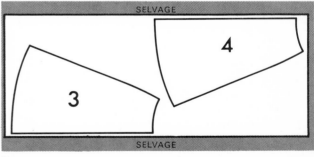

▼ *36 inch width, with one way, skirt layout for all sizes*

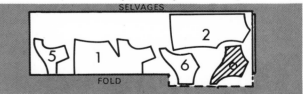

▼ *36 inch width, with one way, bodice layout sizes 32½ & 34*

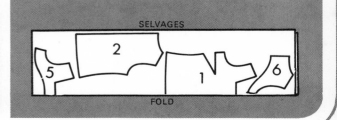

▼ *36 inch width, with one way, bodice layout sizes 36, 38, 40 & 42*

Chapter 35

Jumpers easy and elegant

The two elegant jumper dresses from the last chapter are cut out and completed here. Separate sets of instructions are given for the day length jumper—both with and without flare—and for the evening dress. Follow the construction steps in the order given for the quickest, most successful results when making these dresses.

Notions

First make sure you have all the notions necessary. For all the jumpers you will need:
- ☐ 24 inch zipper
- ☐ 1 or 2 spools of buttonhole twist and thicker machine needles for topstitching
- ☐ Hook fastener
- ☐ If you are lining the dress you will need suitable lining fabric $\frac{1}{4}$ yard less than the dress yardage for fabric without one way
- ☐ If you are increasing the flare on the skirt you will also need $\frac{1}{2}$ yard soft interfacing suitable for the fabric you are using

Day length jumper

These instructions are for the day length jumper without extra flare on the skirt.

Procedure

Here is an outline of the steps in making the jumper:
- ☐ Cutting out
- ☐ Marking
- ☐ Assembling and basting
- ☐ Fitting
- ☐ Stitching the bodice
- ☐ The lining
- ☐ The facings
- ☐ The pocket flaps
- ☐ Making the skirt
- ☐ Topstitching
- ☐ Finishing: zipper, lining, hem

Cutting out

Lay the patterns on the fabric using the appropriate layout for your size and fabric width from pages 152 and 153.

For topstitching the center front seam in the skirt and the horizontal seam, you will need extra-deep seam allowances. The topstitching can vary between $\frac{1}{4}$ and $\frac{1}{2}$ inch from the seam, so decide on the width and add an extra $\frac{1}{2}$ inch to give you the correct width for these seam allowances.

For all other seams allow $\frac{3}{4}$ inch, and $2\frac{1}{2}$ inches for the hem.

Marking the pattern detail

For those who now feel confident working with paper patterns, it may no longer be necessary to tailor's tack in a continuous line around all the pattern pieces. Select strategic points only, such as where seams meet, or important shapes, or special seam distances for detail (figure **1**) and make just enough continuous tailor's tacks to guide you, so that you can follow the continuation of the seams without difficulty.

Drawing lines with chalk is another quick way to mark details on fabric, but these lines can be lost very easily when handling the work. You would then have to refer back to the pattern, which could result in inaccurate copying, and you may even have to start ripping. A little extra work at the beginning is worth the effort.

Assembling and basting

Pin and baste the darts, side seams and shoulder seams of the bodice, leaving the center back open. Press lightly.

Pin and baste the skirt seams and press lightly.

Pin the bodice and skirt along the horizontal seamline, carefully matching centers and side seams. Pin and baste, then press this seam into the bodice.

Fitting

If you want to wear the jumper over blouses and sweaters, wear one during the fitting or you may fit the dress too tightly.

Pay special attention to the armholes, since a thick sweater will need extra room. If you have to increase the size of the armholes all around, remember that if you want to wear the jumper on its own, a large armhole can look very ugly. So try on the dress both ways and reach a compromise.

Make sure the horizontal seamline is straight and at the same level back and front.

If the seam is not level, adjust in the following way:

As long as the general hang of the dress is good, just lift or lower the seamline as required, remembering that you must let out from one side of the seam what you take in from the other, otherwise you will upset the hang of the dress.

If the hang of the dress is wrong, go through all the fitting stages of the basic dress in Dressmaking chapter 32. Finally, check the horizontal seam and adjust as above if necessary.

Correct all the faults, then baste the garment together again for a final fitting.

Stitching the bodice

Stitch all the darts. Then press the body and shoulder darts toward the center. The shoulder darts must lie flat, so if the fabric is thick, make an open dart by slashing along the center toward the point as far as the scissors will allow, and press open. If the fabric frays, just slash the dart past the shoulder seamline and press the rest of the dart flat.

Press the side bust darts flat or open.

Stitch the bodice side seams and press.

If you have fitted the dress closely to the body, you will notice that the curve of the side seam through the waistline has deepened. This makes it difficult for the seam allowance to lie flat after pressing and, as you turn the garment to the outside, you will see that the side seam is strained at the top and bottom.

To enable the seam allowance to follow the contours of the seam, snip into the deepest part of the curve to within $\frac{1}{4}$ inch of the stitching (figure **2**).

To stop the points of the snipped seam allowance from curling, round them off (figure **3**), then overcast them carefully to prevent fraying which would weaken the seam at this point.

Overcast all stitched seam edges.

Do not stitch the shoulder seams yet.

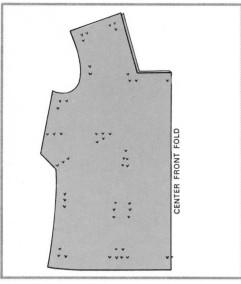

1. ▲ *Tailor's tacking strategic points only*
2. ▼ *Snipping the bodice side seam at the waist*

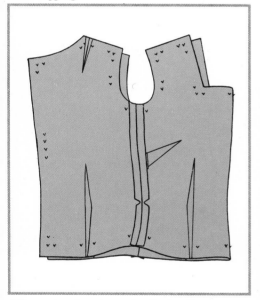

The evening dress has soft, clinging lines ▶
3. ▼ *The snip at the waist, curved and overcast*

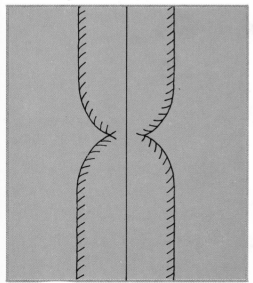

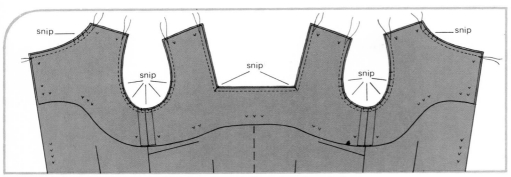

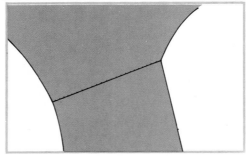

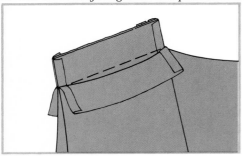

4. *The all-in-one facing stitched in place around the neck and armholes*

5. *The shoulder seam stitched with facing open*

6. *The hand-sewn shoulder seam on the facing*

The lining

If you are lining the dress, it is time to make the lining for the bodice.

Cut out the lining as for the dress, but without facings.

Stitch the darts and seams as for the dress, leaving the shoulder seams open. Press and finish the seams.

Pin and baste the lining to the bodice, with wrong sides facing. See that the raw neck and armhole edges are even and that centers and seams coincide.

The lining seams should face the wrong side of the dress, and dress and lining fabric are used as one when the facings are attached.

The facings

Stitch the facings together in the side seams, leaving the shoulder seams unstitched. Press the side seams open and overcast the lower raw edge.

With right sides facing, pin and baste the facing to the dress, matching seams and centers carefully.

Stitch the facing to the dress (figure **4**) around the neckline and armholes. At the shoulders, stop stitching at the point where the stitching line meets the shoulder seam, as shown. Fasten off the threads securely. Do not stitch the shoulder seams yet.

Trim and snip the seam allowance where shown and turn the facing to the inside. Baste along all stitched edges and press.

With right sides facing, pin and baste the shoulder seams of the dress only (figure **5**), paying special attention to the ends of each seam. These must coincide absolutely or you will have a step where one side

projects when the seams are finished.

Stitch and press the shoulder seams open and work the allowance under the facing. Trim the shoulder seam allowance on the facing to $\frac{3}{8}$ inch and fold it under, so that the edges almost meet over the dress shoulder seam (figure **6**).

Slip stitch them together by hand and press.

The pocket flaps

To break the length of the horizontal seam, you may like to make pocket flaps as shown in the day length version of the jumper. These are entirely optional and only serve to decorate, so you need not apply tailoring techniques.

To make a pocket flap, cut a strip of fabric from the remnants $5\frac{1}{2}$ inches long by 4 inches wide. Fold it lengthwise, right sides facing, and stitch $\frac{1}{4}$ inch seams across both ends (figure **7**).

Turn to the right side, edge baste and press. Topstitch around the outside edges to match the topstitching you will be making on the dress.

Pin and baste the flaps to the horizontal bodice seamline, $2\frac{3}{4}$ inches to each side of the center front line, taking only $\frac{1}{2}$ inch seam allowance on the flaps (figure **8**).

Making the skirt

Stitch the skirt seams, remembering to leave the opening for the zipper in the center back. Press seams open and finish them. Pin, baste and stitch the skirt to the bodice along the horizontal seamline, matching centers and side seams. If you are lining the dress don't catch the lining into the seam. Press the seam open.

Topstitching

Measure out the distance of the topstitching from the seamline along the horizontal and center front seams (figure **9**).

Then, using buttonhole twist, start topstitching the horizontal seam on the skirt from the right center back to the center front. Pivot the work on the needle when you have reached the corner of the "T" shape at the front, and continue stitching down the center front seam toward the hem.

Topstitch the left side of the skirt, but this time start stitching from the hem, to the left of the center front seam.

To topstitch the bodice, work from the left side of the center back toward the right side. Where the fabric is especially thick, such as over the seam allowance of the pocket flaps, pause before you stitch over the extra thickness and ease the pressure foot onto the work.

Finishing: zipper, lining and hem

The unlined dress. Insert the zipper into the center back opening, starting $\frac{1}{2}$ inch down from the neck edge and using the method that is given in Skirtmaking chapter 13.

To finish the neck edge, fold under the raw edge of the facing and place the fold over the zipper tape, but leave it clear of the teeth. Hand sew it firmly to the tape and press. Stitch a hook fastener and work a bar on the neck edge to hold it together. Finish all raw edges and make the hem.

7. *The pocket flap folded and stitched*

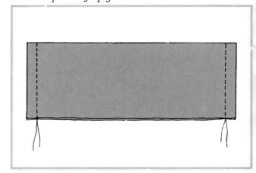

8. *The topstitched pocket flap in position*

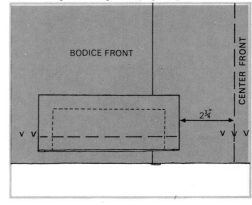

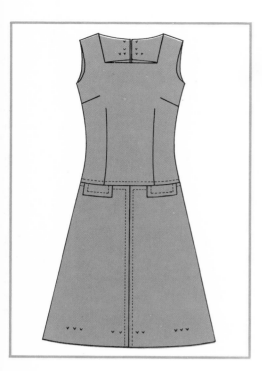

9. *The topstitching lines on skirt and bodice*

The lined dress. Before you insert the zipper, cut the lining along the neck edge just inside the stitching so that the seam allowance on the center back opening and facing can be folded back free of the lining. Insert the zipper, leaving the lining free. Start the zipper $\frac{1}{2}$ inch down from the neck edge and use the method given in Skirt-making chapter 13.

Make the skirt lining as for the top skirt, but without topstitching. Join it to the bodice lining along the horizontal seamline and press both seam allowances toward the bodice.

Finish the raw edges and make the hem on both dress and lining.

Fold the center back seam allowance on the lining over the zipper tape and sew it down by hand. Then fold under the raw edge of the facing and place the fold over the zipper tape, clear of the teeth. Hand sew it firmly to the tape and press. Stitch a hook fastener and work a bar on the neck edge to hold it together.

Both versions. Give the dress a final pressing and, when pressing the topstitching, lay it over a double blanket to preserve the roundness of the stitches made in buttonhole twist, taking care that the edge of the seam allowance does not leave an impression on the outside of the fabric.

Day length jumper with extra flare

This is worked like the jumper without extra flare except for the topstitching.

Because of the increased flare on the skirt the top edge is very curved and when the horizontal seam has been pressed open the skirt horizontal seam allowance falls short of the skirt width (figure **10**). To enable the seam to lie flat, the seam allowance will have to be snipped and therefore becomes unsuitable for topstitching. If you did topstitch it, the snips would show up as dents on the outside.

There are two ways to topstitch this seam. **Method A.** After stitching the horizontal seam, press the seam allowance on the skirt and bodice together toward the bodice. Trim the bodice seam allowance to $\frac{1}{8}$ inch less than the width of the topstitching. Baste the seam allowances together to the bodice and just work the topstitching on the bodice.

Method B. Topstitch the skirt before sewing the horizontal seam and underlay the topstitching with strips of soft interfacing cut on the bias.

Decide on the width of the topstitching and measure this distance from the horizontal seam on the skirt. Mark with pins on the right side.

Using the soft interfacing, cut two bias strips a little less than double the width of the topstitching, and the length of the topstitching along the horizontal seam from the center front to the center back. Do not join them.

Center the strips over the pin line on the inside of the skirt from the center back to center front and position the ends

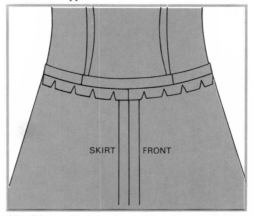

10. *The snipped horizontal seam on the skirt*

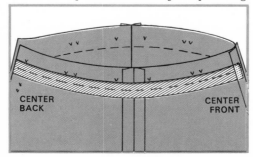

11. *Bias strip basted on skirt for topstitching*

just under the seam allowance on the center front to avoid a dent in the stitching line at this point (figure **11**). If the jumper fabric is thick, you should cut each bias strip at the side seams and slip the ends under the side seam allowances.

Baste each strip to the pin line. Then, using the buttonhole twist, topstitch the skirt over the basting line, starting from the right center back to the center front. Pivot the work on the needle when you have reached the corner of the "T" shape at the front, and continue the stitching down the center front seam toward the hem.

Topstitch the left side of the skirt, but this time start stitching from the hem to the left of the center front seam.

Join the skirt and top. Trim the horizontal seam allowance on the skirt to $\frac{1}{2}$ inch, snip into the seam allowance on the skirt until it lies flat and press (figure **10**).

Finish the raw seam edges and lightly stitch the seam allowance on the skirt to the underlay of the topstitching.

Topstitch on the bodice as for the day length jumper without extra flare.

The evening dress

The jumper is ideal for evening wear. With its clever cut and subtle fit, it will be a firm favorite and a very easy dress to wear.

To achieve the right look—which is soft, long, and molds to the figure—use one of the fabrics recommended in Dressmaking chapter 34.

When using soft fabrics, especially jersey, use as little darting as possible. Slant the side bust darts as shown in Dressmaking chapter 34, and take any surplus fabric into the side seams and the center back seam. This way you will avoid having to use body darts in the front and the back. Also flare the skirt as shown in the previous chapter.

When marking the pattern details, mark the stitching lines of the new dart on the fabric through small slits made through the pattern.

When fitting you can easily alter the slope of the dart if it is wrong—remember to mark any necessary changes to the dart on the pattern for future use.

Making and topstitching

Follow the same construction procedure as for the day length jumper without extra flare, remembering to press the slanting side bust darts open and to omit the body darts.

Also, if you wish to topstitch the skirt, follow the topstitching instructions for the skirt with extra flare.

Chapter 36

The shirt dress story

The shirt dress is a true fashion classic, remaining with us through all the style changes that fashion designers have created. Season after season, the shirt dress reappears in new shapes and forms. Fabric, color and detailing all combine to give the impression of variety although the basic style remains the same. Take the styles illustrated here—they are all simple variations of the shirt dress, but each has a completely different look—all made from the Golden Hands Basic Graph Pattern.

Instructions are given for four of these versions, starting in this chapter. They are: A. the button-down shirt dress with shirt collar and cuffs; B. the shirt dress with collar band finish; C. the evening shirt dress with tab fastening and D. the shirt dress with full bishop sleeves.

Although the instructions deal specifically with these versions, all the details are interchangeable and can be combined with garments from previous chapters to give you the full range of styles featured here. You can apply some of the techniques to commercial paper patterns as well.

So you see, all you need for a distinctive wardrobe is a basic set of patterns and a lively fashion sense.

Suitable fabrics

There simply isn't a fabric which has not been used to make the shirt dress. You can make it in a lightweight knit or a crisp cotton for summer, warmer and heavier fabrics for winter, and more sophisticated fabrics for cocktail or evening wear.

Here is a list to help you decide:

For summer wear: eyelet embroidery; gingham; cotton and man-made fiber mixtures; cotton knit.

For winter wear: most fine woolen dress-weight fabrics; cotton and wool mixtures such as Viyella; wool jersey; man-made fiber knits; fine tweeds.

For evening wear: all types of fine or medium-weight silks; voile; organdy; brocade and embroidered fabrics; some firm crêpes.

Ideas and variations

Four versions are given in detail. These have been selected because they entail a number of pattern adaptations, but you don't have to stop there.

Pockets. Go on by adding pockets to the button-down version. Topstitch the pockets in position and then topstitch the edges of the dress to match.

Sleeves. Another style could be created using the roll-up short sleeve pattern given in Blousemaking chapter 25:

Many women like a ¾ length sleeve and this can easily be made by shortening the long shirt sleeve. But don't forget to make the cuffs larger as they have to encircle a larger part of the arm. If you want to link button the cuffs for ¾ length sleeves, it is best to make the links with hat elastic so that they will not be too tight.

B.   A.

left to right:

n B.
dress with
band finish

n A.
a-down
ress with
ollar and

ht-cut shirt
with shirt
patch
s and
ching

-style dress
ab fastening
ll-up short
over basic

n D.
ress with
shop sleeves

g shirt
with bead
dered collar
ffs

less shirt
with bishop
and
loop
ng over

n C.
ess evening
ress with
stening, and
ching

D.

C.

The straight shirt dress. This is another version you can make. Just straighten the side seams from the hipline down and do away with the flare. Remember that the hemline will be tighter and the buttons on the button-down version will have to withstand a lot more strain.

Embroidery and beads. To decorate a plain silk shirt dress for evening wear, embroider the collar and cuffs with beads and paillettes. Choose the plastic variety which are lightweight and will not make the collar points flop.

Belts. Belts can also make a change, but avoid the stiff and tightly buckled ones. They are meant to be worn over fitted waists and a dress cut without a waist seam would gather up under them.

A. The button-down shirt dress

This version has a button-down front, a shirt collar and shirt sleeves.

The pattern

You will need the following pattern pieces from the Golden Hands Graph Pages: from the Dress Graph Pattern, the Front and Back pattern pieces, numbers 1 and 2; from the Accessories Graph Pattern, the shirt sleeve, shirt collar, collar band and cuff pattern pieces, numbers 8, 10, 11 and 12.

The Front. To adapt the pattern for the button-down dress, first make a new pattern.

Pin the Front pattern piece securely on a piece of paper with the Center Front 1 inch from the straight edge of the paper. Draw around the edges with a pencil and extend the hem and necklines to the edge of the paper.

The 1 inch margin between the pattern and paper edge on the new pattern is the Center Front wrap for the button fastening (figure **1**).

Cut out the new Front pattern.

Space out the positions for the eleven buttonholes on the Center Front line of the new Front pattern as shown in figure **1**.

You will have one buttonhole in the collar band, so allow equal spacing between the first buttonhole on the dress Front and that on the collar band.

Leave a complete buttonhole distance between the hemline and the last button and do not try to work a buttonhole through the turned up hem.

The front facing. Copy the neck, shoulder and front edges of the Front pattern and measure out the front facing as shown (figure **1**). The facing is 4 inches wide

along the Front and hem edge and 2 inches wide at the shoulderline.

Cut out the front facing pattern.

Yardages

54in width. Without one way—sizes $32\frac{1}{2}$, 34 and 36, $2\frac{5}{8}$ yards; size 38, $2\frac{7}{8}$ yards; sizes 40 and 42, $3\frac{1}{8}$ yards.

54in width. With one way—size $32\frac{1}{2}$, $2\frac{5}{8}$ yards; size 34, $2\frac{3}{4}$ yards; size 36, $3\frac{1}{8}$ yards; sizes 38, 40 and 42, $3\frac{1}{4}$ yards.

36in width. Without one way—size $32\frac{1}{2}$, 4 yards; size 34, $4\frac{1}{8}$ yards; size 36, $4\frac{3}{8}$ yards; sizes 38, 40 and 42, $4\frac{1}{2}$ yards.

36in width. With one way—size $32\frac{1}{2}$, 4 yards; size 34, $4\frac{1}{4}$ yards; size 36, $4\frac{3}{8}$ yards; size 38, $4\frac{1}{2}$ yards; sizes 40 and 42, 5 yards.

Notions

You will need:
- ☐ 14 small buttons (2 extra for link buttoned cuffs)
- ☐ Matching thread
- ☐ Interfacing (see below), the length of the shoulder to hem plus $\frac{3}{4}$ inch seam allowance

Hints on interfacing

Unlike the shirt blouse, the Center Front edge of the dress needs interfacing.

The best type to use is a soft pre-shrunk cotton lawn. It is available in different colors, so choose one to match the fabric you are using. This will stop the interfacing creating shading through the top fabric.

If you want to make the dress in a sheer fabric and have a good fabric store near you, you may be able to obtain pure silk organza for an interfacing. This is so colorless that it can be used for the sheerest fabrics. Otherwise, ask at the store for the right kind of interfacing for your particular fabric.

If you find that the interfacing shows through and changes the color of the fabric, it is best not to use it, as long as the fabric has enough substance to support itself. If not, don't use that particular fabric to make the shirt dress.

It is always best to buy and try fabric and interfacing at the same time. This way you will avoid being committed to an unsuitable fabric.

Lining the shirt dress

Lining the button-down shirt dress is not easy or advisable, even if the fabric is mounted straight onto the lining. In washable dresses, a lining makes ironing very difficult. You also lose the shirt-like feel of the fabric and it becomes bulky.

Cutting and marking

Choose the appropriate layout for your style, size and fabric width from the layouts

included in this chapter.

Fold the fabric as shown on the layout. If you are working on a large area of a lightweight fabric, pin the selvages and fold lightly. This will prevent the fabric from rolling out of the correct fold, which could result in your cutting the sides unevenly without even noticing it.

Note: The collar and collar band are cut in the same grain of the fabric.

Remember, the pattern has no hem or seam allowance, so add $\frac{3}{4}$ inch for seams all around and $2\frac{1}{2}$ inches for the hem.

Cut out the dress, mark the pattern details and remove the pattern pieces.

Cut out the Front, collar, collar band and cuff interfacings as you need them.

Fitting

Baste the dress, including sleeves and cuffs, together for fitting and make any necessary alterations.

For the fitting it is best to baste the Center Front seam from hip level to hem.

Making the Center Fronts

Having ascertained the correct length of the dress when fitting, cut out two front interfacing pieces using the front facing pattern. You will not need seam allowances along the inner edge or a hem allowance.

Pin the interfacing to the inside of both dress Fronts.

Baste in position with two rows of basting stitches, the first just outside the seam lines, and the second about $\frac{3}{4}$ inch in from the inner edge so that you can work on it later.

Pin and baste the facings to the right side of the dress.

Stitch in place along the seamlines of the Front wrap—that is, from the neck edge down to the hem.

Layer the seam allowance by trimming as follows: Trim the interfacing to $\frac{1}{8}$ inch, the facing to $\frac{1}{4}$ inch and the dress Front to $\frac{1}{2}$ inch.

Turn the facings to the wrong side. Edge-baste and press lightly.

Lay out the dress Fronts wrong side up. Pin and baste the loose inner edges of the facings to the dress about 1 inch from the edge, so that the interfacing edge is accessible.

Baste the facing to the dress along the neckline.

Overcast the inner raw edge of the facing and stitch the interfacing to it with long running stitches. To do this, start the stitches about 10 inches above the hemline, work toward the shoulder seam and then across toward the neckline, so that the interfacing is firmly caught in position and so that it cannot roll or wrinkle during wear.

Darts and seams

Stitch the Front and Back darts and press them according to the fabric.

Pin, baste and stitch the shoulder and side seams. Finish the seam allowances and press seams open.

Turn under the seam allowance on the shoulderline of each Front facing and lightly hand sew it to the shoulder seam.

The collar

Following the collar instructions for the shirt in Blousemaking chapter 27, cut out the interfacings for the collar and collar band.

Then make the collar and band and stitch it to the dress.

The sleeves

Again following the shirt instructions in Blousemaking chapters 27 and 28, cut out the cuff interfacing, make the cuffs and make the sleeve openings. Or, if you are working on a fine fabric, make the sleeve openings as shown for the tie-neck blouse in Blousemaking chapter 29.

Pleat or gather the sleeve edge and attach the cuffs.

Make the buttonholes in the cuffs now, because the weight of the garments after the sleeves have been set in can be very irritating when making small buttonholes, even though the weight is supported.

Pin, baste and stitch the finished sleeves into the armholes. Trim and finish the armhole seams, then press them into the sleeves.

Hem, Front buttonholes and finishing

Pin and baste the hem, leaving the interfacing inside the hem. Fold in the ends of the facing over the hem and sew it down by hand (figure **3**). Sew the hem, making very sure that the seam allowance on the Front edge is turned toward the facing in the hem (figure **2**), otherwise you will have a thick ridge on the outside which will force the seam to roll outward when it is supposed to remain hidden just behind the edge of the wrap.

Check the button positions if you had to alter the length of the dress; then make the buttonholes by hand or machine. Sew on the buttons and give the dress a final pressing.

Make a tie belt to match from the remnants, following the instructions for tie belts in Know-How chapter 58.

B. Shirt dress with collar band finish

The neckline is the main feature of this version where the collar band has been

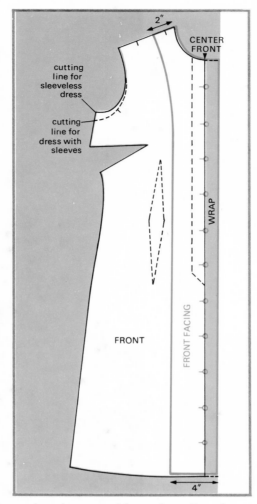

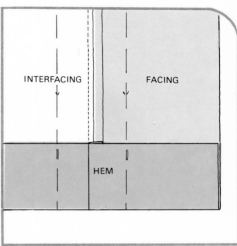

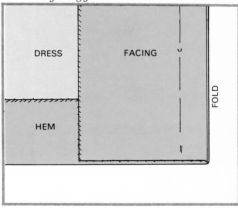

▲ 2. *Seam allowance turned toward facing in hem*
◄ 1. *Adapting the pattern for the shirt dress*
▼ 3. *Front facing folded and sewed over the hem*

used on its own without the collar. Apart from this detail, the dress is made with a button-down front and shirt sleeves as for version A.

The dress will look particularly attractive if the collar band and cuffs are made in a contrasting color to the rest of the dress.

The fabric

The fabric used should be firm as a soft fabric would roll and the shape of the collar band would be lost.

The pattern

You will need all the pattern pieces for version A except the shirt collar, number 10. Also adapt the pattern as for A.

Collar band. You can make the ends square or rounded. But remember that the square ends need two small buttons for fastening to stop the corner falling down.

Yardages

54in width. Without one way—sizes $32\frac{1}{2}$, 34 and 36, $2\frac{5}{8}$ yards; size 38, $2\frac{7}{8}$ yards; sizes 40 and 42, 3 yards.

54in width. With one way—size $32\frac{1}{2}$, $2\frac{5}{8}$ yards; size 34, $2\frac{3}{4}$ yards; size 36, $3\frac{1}{8}$ yards; sizes 38, 40 and 42, $3\frac{1}{4}$ yards.

36in width. Without one way—sizes $32\frac{1}{2}$

and 34, $3\frac{5}{8}$ yards; sizes 36 and 38, $3\frac{3}{4}$ yards; sizes 40 and 42, $4\frac{3}{8}$ yards.

36in width. With one way—sizes $32\frac{1}{2}$ and 34, $3\frac{5}{8}$ yards; sizes 36 and 38, $3\frac{3}{4}$ yards; sizes 40 and 42, $4\frac{1}{2}$ yards.

Notions

As for version A.

Cutting out, marking and fitting

Choose the correct layout for your style, size and fabric width from the layouts in this chapter.

Cut out, mark the details and fit the dress as for version A.

How to make the collar band

For this finish the collar band is worked in reverse to the one which you attach to a collar (see Blousemaking chapter 27).

Here you interface the outer, not inner, section of the collar band, and, with right sides facing, stitch the outer collar band to the neckline and then hand sew the inner section, or collar facing, to the seamline inside.

Making and finishing

Apart from the neck finish, the dress is made exactly as version A.

Layouts for the shirt dress: Version A

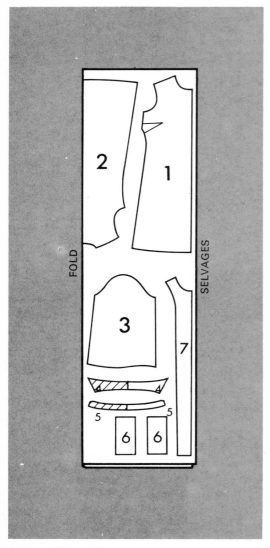

▲ *54in width, without one way, sizes 32½, 34, 36 & 38*

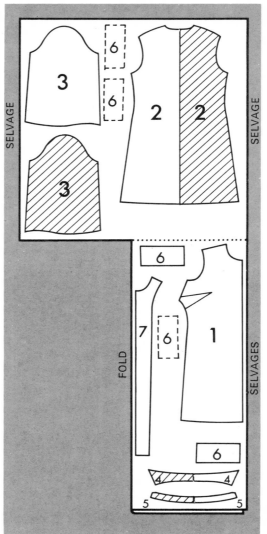

▲ *54in width, with and without one way, sizes 40 & 42*

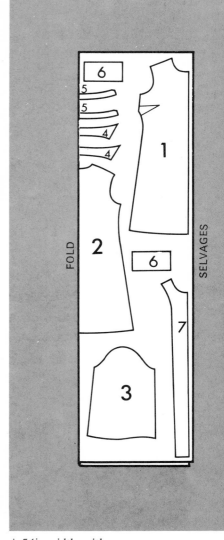

▲ *54in width, with one way, sizes 32½, 34, 36 & 38*

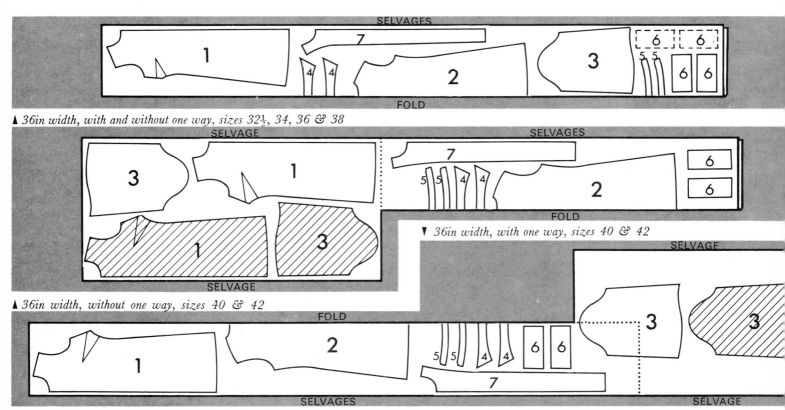

▲ *36in width, with and without one way, sizes 32½, 34, 36 & 38*

▲ *36in width, without one way, sizes 40 & 42*

▼ *36in width, with one way, sizes 40 & 42*

Version B

Key to pattern pieces

Front = 1   Back = 2   Sleeve = 3
Collar = 4   Collar band = 5   Cuff = 6
Front facing = 7

– – –   alternative for without one-way
/////   reverse pattern pieces

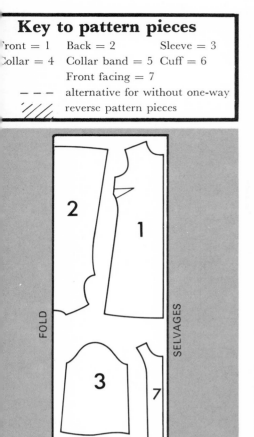

54in width, without one way,
sizes 32½, 34, 36 & 38

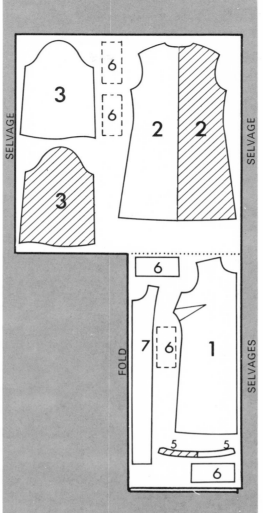

▲ 54in width, with and without one way,
sizes 40 & 42

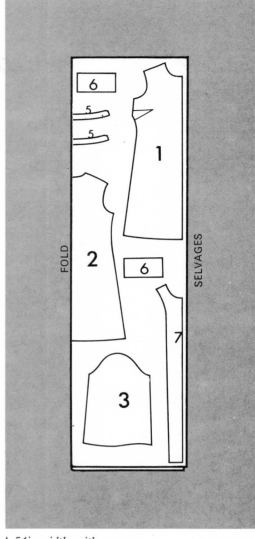

▲ 54in width, with one way,
sizes 32½, 34, 36 & 38

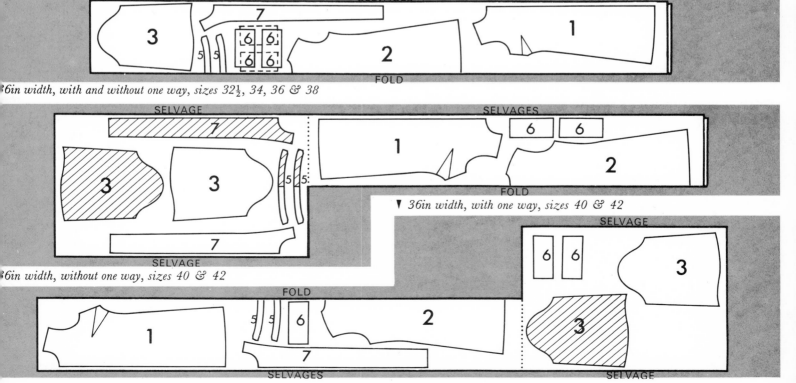

36in width, with and without one way, sizes 32½, 34, 36 & 38

36in width, without one way, sizes 40 & 42

▼ 36in width, with one way, sizes 40 & 42

163

Chapter 37

Shirt dress conversion

The shirt dress story, which began in chapter 36 with instructions for version A and B, continues here with this glamorous evening shirt dress, version C.

This style is flattering to all age groups and it is easy and comfortable to wear. It can be dressed up for really formal occasions or left plain and elegant to make the perfect dinner gown. It travels well, too. Made in a light, printed silk you have something ideal for holiday wear—a gown in which you can feel both well-dressed and relaxed. This chapter includes the instructions for making this dress with the layouts on pages 166 and 167. Also included are layouts for version D, the shirt dress with full, bishop sleeves. The instructions for adapting the pattern and making this sleeve follow in the concluding chapter of this ingenious tale!

C. The evening shirt dress

Suitable fabrics

The fabric used will dictate the mood of this shirt dress. While all those mentioned in Dressmaking chapter 36 are suitable, this style lends itself particularly well to evening wear fabrics.

Made sleeveless, in heavy brocade, it becomes an elegant gown for formal occasions, but made in a lovely printed hand-woven Indian silk, like the one in the photograph, it becomes the type of garment which can be worn on many occasions. A characteristic of these silks is their slightly creased appearance which complements the casual look of the dress.

The pattern

You will need the following pattern pieces from the Golden Hands Graph Pages.

From the Basic Dress Graph, the Front, Back and tab pattern pieces, number 1, 2 and 3.

From the Accessories Graph, the shirt collar and collar band pattern pieces, numbers 10 and 11.

The right Front pattern. For this dress you need a right Front pattern piece and one for the left Front.

First copy the Front pattern using a sheet of paper which is long enough to include the extra length needed for the evening dress. Place the Center Front of the pattern along one edge of the paper as shown (figure **1**) and draw around the pattern.

Copy the stitching line for the tab.

Measure the extra length you need for the evening dress. Starting at the side seam, measure off this amount from the hem edge with a yardstick. Continue doing this along the full width of the hem, so that you retain the original shape of the hem, and draw in the new lines as shown.

Remove the original pattern and cut out the new one along the solid line in figure **1**.

The left Front pattern. In Dressmaking chapter 32 it was mentioned that a conventional wrap would be cut later, and now is the time to do this.

Place the original Front pattern on a large sheet of paper as before, but reversing it and with the Center Front of the pattern 1 inch from the straight edge (figure **2**).

Draw around the shape of the pattern and extend the length as for the right Front.

Draw in the tab stitching line and connect the pointed end to the straight edge of the paper, drawing a straight line across. Cut out the new pattern along the solid cutting line. The 1 inch extension above the pointed end of the tab stitching line is the wrap for the front opening.

The Back pattern. Copy the Back pattern piece on a sheet of paper long enough to include the extra length needed for the

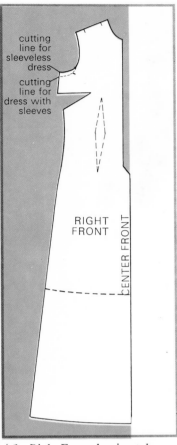

cutting line for sleeveless dress

cutting line for dress with sleeves

RIGHT FRONT

CENTER FRONT

▲ **1.** *Right Front showing tab stitching line and length extended*

▼ **3.** *Wrap and tab facing*

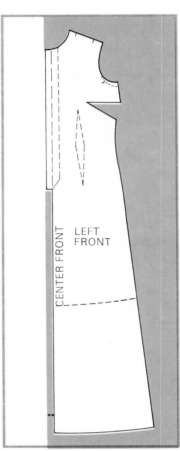

CENTER FRONT

LEFT FRONT

CENTER FRONT

▲ **2.** *Left Front showing wrap extension and length extended*

▼ **4.** *Interfacing inside of wrap*

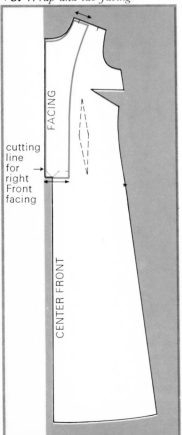

FACING

cutting line for right Front facing

CENTER FRONT

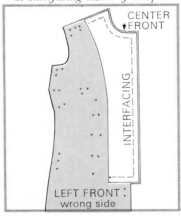

CENTER FRONT

INTERFACING

LEFT FRONT
wrong side

▲ **5.** *Topstitching collar and band*

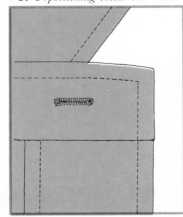

evening dress, then draw in the new hemline as for the Front pattern pieces.

Facing patterns. To make the facing patterns for the tab and wrap, pin the Center Front of the left pattern piece along the straight edge of a sheet of paper. Draw around the shape of the neck and shoulderlines and mark the lower end of the wrap. Remove the pattern, measure out the width of the facing and complete as shown (figure **3**). Cut out the facing pattern.

This outline is for the wrap facing.

For the tab facing outline, pin the tab pattern piece to the front edge of the facing pattern and draw the shape of the pointed end, extending it straight to the inner edge as shown (see dotted line, figure **3**). Use this line when cutting the facing for the tab, but do not cut out along this line yet.

Yardages

48in width. Without one way—size $32\frac{1}{2}$, $2\frac{7}{8}$ yards; size 34, 3 yards; size 36, $3\frac{1}{8}$ yards; size 38, $3\frac{3}{8}$ yards; size 40, $3\frac{5}{8}$ yards; size 42, $3\frac{3}{4}$ yards.

48in width. With one way — sizes $32\frac{1}{2}$, 34 and 36, $3\frac{5}{8}$ yards; sizes 38, 40 and 42, $3\frac{7}{8}$ yards.

36in width. Without one way — sizes $32\frac{1}{2}$ and 34, 4 yards; size 36, $4\frac{1}{4}$ yards; sizes 38 and 40, $4\frac{1}{2}$ yards; size 42, $4\frac{3}{4}$ yards.

36in width. With one way—sizes $32\frac{1}{2}$ and 34, 4 yards; size 36, $4\frac{1}{2}$ yards; size 38, $4\frac{5}{8}$ yards; size 40, $4\frac{3}{4}$ yards; size 42, $4\frac{7}{8}$ yards.

Notions

You will need:
- ☐ 6 small buttons
- ☐ Matching thread
- ☐ Interfacing, the length of the front facing plus $1\frac{1}{2}$ inches for seam allowance, or interlining (see below)

Interlinings and interfacings

If you want to line this dress, use a fully mounted interlining chosen to complement the fabric of the dress, such as a Japanese silk lining for pure silks and fine rayon taffeta for brocades. The interlining is cut out the same way as the dress fabric, using the layout and yardage for the 36in width without one way. It is then basted to the fabric and used as one. This way you will not need an interfacing. If you decide not to interline the dress, you will need interfacing for the tab, wrap, collar and collar band. See Dressmaking chapter 36 for suitable interfacings.

Cutting and marking

To cut out the evening shirt dress you will need a very large area to work on since the full length of the dress is cut in one.

Choose the correct layout for your style, size and fabric width from the layouts, pages 166 and 167. Lay out the fabric carefully, pinning the selvages and folds to make sure that they cannot move.

The pattern has no seam or hem allowances, so mark $\frac{3}{4}$ inch for seams and $2\frac{1}{2}$ inches for hems all around.

Cut both tab and wrap facings together, using the wrap facing pattern piece. The tab facing will be trimmed to shape later.

Note that the shirt collar and collar band are cut on the same grain of the fabric.

Cut two bias strips $1\frac{1}{2}$ inches wide for the armhole facings, joining the strips to make the desired length if necessary.

Trim the wrap facing pattern piece along the dotted line for the tab facing, then trim one of the facings for the tab, similarly—don't forget to add the seam allowance.

Mounting the fabric

If you are mounting the dress, cut out the interlining as for the dress and baste it to the wrong side of each dress piece.

Interfacing

If you are not lining the dress, cut one collar, one collar band, one tab and one wrap facing piece from interfacing, adding seam allowance on all edges except the inner edge of the wrap facing.

Baste the corresponding interfacing pieces to the wrong side of the top collar and outer collar band sections, and the tab. Also baste the wrap interfacing to the inside of the wrap (see figure **4** on previous page) on the left Front.

Stitching the Front fastening

Since it is not possible to pin the Center Front at the top of the dress for fitting, it is best to make the Front fastening detail before you try and fit the dress. It is possible to do so as there will be no alteration to this particular area.

Make the tab as you did for the basic dress in Dressmaking chapters 32 and 33, using the front facing with the shaped end to face the tab. Do not stitch the tab and facing together along the neck edge—this remains open to take the collar band.

To avoid thick seam edges on the tab if you are using it, trim the seam allowance of the interfacing to $\frac{1}{8}$ inch.

Stitch the Center Front of the dress from the pointed end of the tab stitching line to the hem. Finish the seam and press open.

Stitch on the tab and finish the pointed end inside as for the basic dress, but do not fold, and sew the inner facing edge to the stitching line.

Topstitch the tab $\frac{1}{4}$ inch from the edges.

Face the left Front of the dress with the straight ended facing. Do not stitch along the neck edge. It is not necessary to stitch across the lower end of the wrap; this often creates an unwanted thickness and it is best to leave it open.

Trim the interfacing seam allowance to $\frac{1}{8}$ inch if you are using it. Finish the wrap end inside as for the basic dress, but do not fold, and sew the wrap facing down on the inner edge.

If you have used interfacing on the wrap, attach the inner edges to the facing with loose catch stitches.

Overcast the inner edges to finish off.

Fitting and finishing the dress

Baste and fit the evening dress making any necessary adjustments. Stitch the darts and seams, and finish the armhole and hem edges as for the basic dress, Dressmaking chapters 32 and 33.

Interface collar and band (if necessary), stitch together, then attach to dress as instructed in Blousemaking chapter 27.

Topstitch collar and band to match the tab (figure **5** on previous page). Make buttonholes and sew on buttons to finish.

Finishes with mounted interlinings

After stitching and pressing the seams open, carefully trim the seam allowance and overcast by hand to finish. Avoid machine finishes in any way since they tend to curl the two layers of fabric creating a thick and hard seam edge; this in turn makes an impression through the fabric, often showing up noticeably on the outside of the dress.

Facings should be lightly caught to seamlines and not be firmly sewn in place. So work under the facing edge and hand sew loosely. To prevent the interlining from folding up inside the hem, it is necessary to prick stitch fabric and lining together just below the hemline before the hem is turned up and finished. (For prick stitch see Generally Speaking chapter 9.)

When sewing the inner edge of hems and bias facings to the mounted dress, make sure that you do not sew through to the outside fabric, but only catch the interlining fabric to give the outside a smooth finish.

If you follow all the instructions given for making bias facings and sewing hems, they will be secure and will not roll out.

Layouts for the shirt dress: Version C

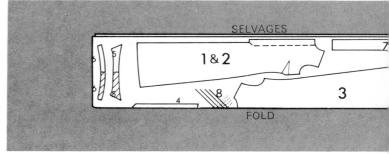

▲ *48in width, without one way, sizes 32½, 34, 36, 38, 40 & 42*
▼ *48in width, with one way, sizes 32½, 34, 36, 38, 40 & 42*

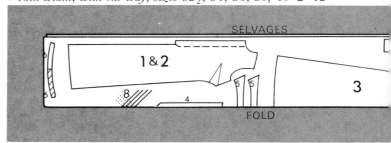

▼ *36in width, with and without one way, sizes 32½ & 34*

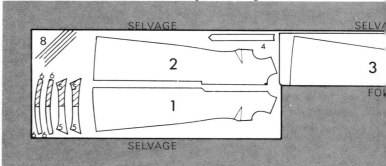

▼ *36in width, without one way, sizes 36, 38, 40 & 42*

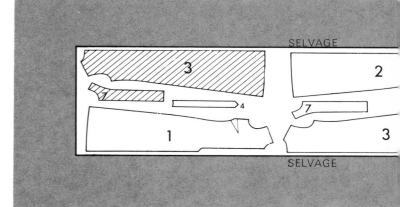

▼ *36in width, with one way, sizes 36, 38, 40 & 42*

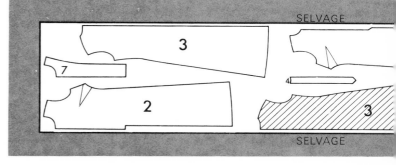

Version D

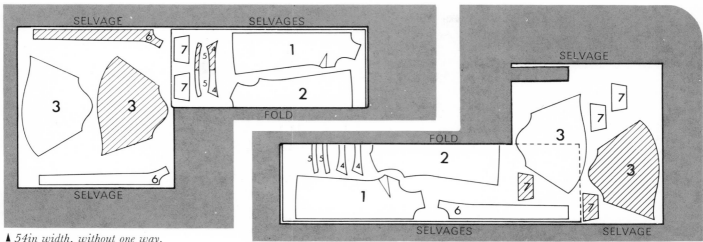

▲ *54in width, without one way,*
sizes 32½, 34, 36 & 38

▲ *54in width, without one way, sizes 40 & 42*
▼ *54in width, with one way, sizes 32½ & 34*

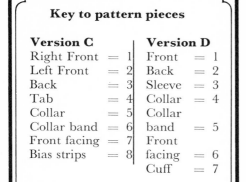

Key to pattern pieces

Version C		**Version D**	
Right Front	= 1	Front	= 1
Left Front	= 2	Back	= 2
Back	= 3	Sleeve	= 3
Tab	= 4	Collar	= 4
Collar	= 5	Collar	
Collar band	= 6	band	= 5
Front facing	= 7	Front	
Bias strips	= 8	facing	= 6
		Cuff	= 7

Reverse pattern pieces

▼ *54in width, with one way, sizes 36, 38, 40 & 42*

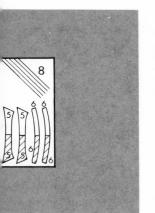

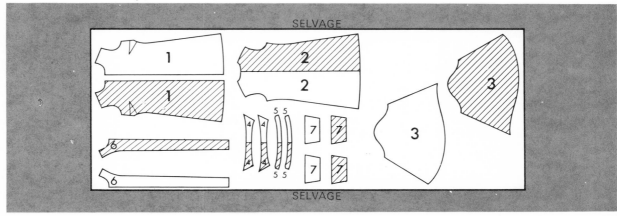

▼ *36in width, with and without one way, sizes 32½, 34, 36, 38, 40 & 42*

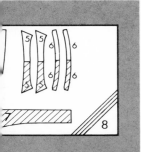

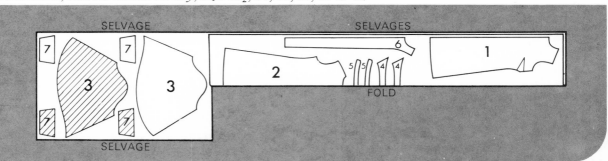

167

Chapter 38
The tailored knit look

Dresses made in knits are very comfortable, easy to wear, allow complete freedom of movement and, if made from a man-made fiber knit, are also extremely practical because they wash well—in fact, many of the man-made knits do not even need an iron to smooth them out after washing. In addition, some of the double knits, such as polyester, are so hard wearing that they are almost indestructible and still look like new after many, many washings.

This chapter gives hints on sewing knits and how to fit garments made in this fabric. Because knit has natural stretch, the fitting is a most important feature.

The dress illustrated here, with its smooth lines and long fitted sleeves, is an ideal style for knits, which in this particular case is a double knit pure wool jersey with a fine, stockinette stitch surface. This knit handles very well in all stages of making the pattern.

The dress is an adaptation of the basic dress pattern from the Basic Dress Graph Pattern and you can make it from the instructions given in this chapter. These are special instructions for fitting and making garments made in knit, and you will find them invaluable for other styles too.

Details of the dress include a loose lining which is stitched into the neckline with the facing and into the armhole seams. Since there is a natural give in knit the long, fitted sleeves can be closely fitted and then finished with a zipper opening at each wrist edge.

About knits

Types of knits

Knit fabrics are made in a variety of textures. Starting with the plain, printed or jacquard knits, there is the honeycomb finish and the stockinette stitch finish. Generally the honeycomb surface is found on the heavier and coarser knits and the stockinette stitch surface on the finer ones. But both finishes come in double or single knits.

Then there are knits with a raised surface pattern resembling a cloque. These are usually in man-made fabrics where the resilience of the fiber helps to retain the pattern shape on the surface. These are found mostly in double knits.

Added to the difference in texture is the fact that knits are now made in many different fibers, both natural and man-made. You will find that each knit has different characteristics, so that when shopping for a knit fabric you will have to keep the style of the garment you are making in mind. Once it could be assumed that knits only lent themselves to a particular style; this is no longer true and knits can be used for tailored designs as well as for the more molded, draped or figure-hugging ones. Be sure to choose the correct texture for the style you want to make.

Don't forget to find out whether the fabric should be washed or dry cleaned when you buy it.

The tailored knit look

Although all knits will mold well to the figure, the heavier ones are most successfully used for really tailored and sculptured styles. They give you freedom of movement and a crisp looking garment without bulk, and contrary to what you may expect, it does not take a clever dressmaker to combine all these qualities in one garment.

Stitching knits

Since knit fabric spreads when under pressure, reduce the pressure on the presser foot of the machine.

Use the finest needle size possible on the machine and a thickness of thread to suit the needle size.

To stitch the seams, engage the smallest zigzag stitch setting plus a stitch length setting of 12 to 14 stitches per inch. Then, as you are stitching, stretch the seams very gently to give the maximum elasticity to the zigzag stitches.

Seams which have to withstand a lot of strain, such as the Center Back and armhole seams, should be stitched over twice.

If the machine is missing stitches as you stitch the seams, and this often happens when stitching knits, it usually means that the combination of needle and thread is wrong. However, if your machine is very light, it may mean that the fabric is too heavy for the machine to cope with.

Curved seams in knits

The curved seams in knits do not usually need snipping if the seam allowance is narrow, that is $\frac{1}{2}$ to $\frac{3}{4}$ inch. But if you have found a fabric which rolls and does not mold easily, then snip the seam allowance to not less than $\frac{1}{4}$ inch from the stitching line.

Finishing raw edges in knits

Although the inside of a dress looks better when the raw edges of the seam allowances are finished, it is not necessary to finish knit because it does not fray. But if you want to apply a seam edge finish, make sure it is very flat and does not create a thick ridge which would make an impression through the fabric to the outside of the garment.

Zippers in knits

When inserting a zipper into the Center Back of a knit dress, make the opening 1 inch longer than the zipper to allow for the $\frac{1}{2}$ inch distance from neck stitching line and $\frac{1}{2}$ inch for ease. If you find that the opening has dropped when you begin to insert the zipper, it will be safe to ease in the surplus.

With some knits you may have to pin in the zipper and hold the dress up to see if the fabric drops away in folds. If it does, keep repinning until the folds have disappeared. It does not help to tape the opening as you will still have the same problem.

Fortunately, most double knits will take a zipper without any problems at all.

Fitting

Knit fabrics need special and careful fitting, and it is well worthwhile reading the fitting instructions for the knit garment even if you don't intend to make this particular version.

The dress pattern, yardage and notions

The pattern pieces

For this dress you need five pattern pieces: the Front, Back, long fitted sleeve, front neck facing and back neck facing.

Front and Back patterns. Copy the Front and Back pattern pieces from the Basic Dress Graph Pattern on pages 134 and 135, numbers 1 and 2, incorporating any corrections you may have made previously for figure faults. Do not cut them out yet.

The dress is made with a Center Back opening and a Center Front seam, so mark both for seaming.

As with all knit fabrics, avoid darts as much as possible and do not use the body darts. Although the dress is semi-fitted, the ease is taken into the seams and the side bust darts instead.

The Center Front and Center Back seams are slightly curved through the waistline (figures **1** and **2**). So first mark in your waistline on the Front and Back pattern pieces and then curve the center seams as follows.

For the Front, measure $\frac{3}{8}$ inch from the Center Front at the waistline and taper into the original Center Front top and bottom (figure **1**). Curve the Center Back in the same way, but measure in $\frac{3}{4}$ inch at the waistline (figure **2**).

Slant the side bust dart on the dress Front downward by $1\frac{1}{2}$ inches at the outer end, leaving the point of the dart where it is (figure **1**). This will help to take in some of the fullness at the waistline of the dress.

When you have moved the dart, make sure that you compensate on the side seams as shown, so that the seamlines of the upper and lower stitching lines are the same length.

Do not deepen the dart or curve the waistline at the side seams yet. This is done more accurately at the fitting stage.

Front and back facing patterns. Using the Front and Back pattern pieces copy the relevant top sections of each (figures **1** and **2**) and make the front and back neck facings as shown. They are 2 inches wide and should be trimmed shorter at the shoulder by $\frac{1}{8}$ inch (figure **3**). Mark the Center Front on the front facing pattern to be cut on the fold.

Sleeve pattern. Use the sleeve pattern piece number 7 from the Accessories Graph on pages 110 and 111.

Cut out all the pattern pieces.

Layouts and yardages

Know-How chapter 46 explains the process of making layouts and finding the minimum yardage requirements. As knit fabrics are available in 36 inch to 72 inch widths, it is helpful to know the width you intend to buy to save yourself making trial layouts for 36, 48, 54, 60 and 72 inch widths to work out the required yardage!

Before you start making a trial layout here are a few points to note: The facings are very small and can be cut from the scraps.

The seam and hem allowances are not included in the Golden Hands Graph Patterns so you will need to add $\frac{3}{4}$ inch for seams and $2\frac{1}{2}$ inches for hems.

The hem allowance on the long fitted sleeve should be $2\frac{1}{2}$ inches so that you can adjust the length at the fitting.

If you are using knit with a heavy drop, such as a rayon jersey, allow plenty of margin between the pattern pieces on the layout since it is advisable to cut slightly wider seam allowances. Garments in these fabrics often require a little more ease because they fall so close to the body.

To start you off on your layout, here is a guide for the yardage requirements for 36, 54 and 72 inch widths. Measure out the amounts and work from there.

36 inch width. For standard sizes, start with twice the dress length plus one sleeve length plus hem and seam allowances.

Large sizes may have to be cut on an open layout when it becomes necessary to add one more dress length for safety.

54 inch width. For standard sizes start with one dress length plus

The long sleeved dress version made in a double knit wool jersey ▶

one sleeve length plus hem and seam allowances.

For large sizes the pattern pieces may have to be staggered and may require up to half a dress length extra.

72 inch width. One dress length plus hem and seam allowances should be sufficient for all sizes.

Lining. Only the Back and Front of the dress are cut from lining fabric. The sleeves are not lined, nor are the facings.

Notions

☐ One 24 inch zipper for the Center Back
☐ Two 5 inch zippers for the sleeves (optional)
☐ One hook, size no. 1
☐ Fine machine needles
☐ Matching thread

Cutting out and marking pattern details

Cut out the knit fabric adding hem and seam allowances.

Mark the pattern detail with a fine soft thread, such as a number 50 basting thread sold for this purpose. A sharp thread can cut the knit stitches, resulting in nasty runs.

Fitting knit fabrics

When making a knit dress fitting stages are very important. There are three fitting stages. The first is with the body of the dress semi-basted. The second fitting stage is with the body of the dress completely basted to include corrections made in the first stage.

The third stage is the final check with zipper, lining and sleeves basted in position. If you make any alterations at this stage, then try it on finally to see that all is well.

Preparing for the first fitting

Pin and baste the shoulder darts if used.

Pin the side bust darts but do not baste them.

Pin and baste the Center Front seam, and the Center Back seam from the end of the opening to the hem.

Pin and baste the shoulder seams.

Pin the side seams and baste them from underarm to dart and from waist to hem.

Do not press at this stage, as for other fabrics.

Before you slip on the dress, remove the pins from the darts and that section of each side seam which has not been basted.

The first fitting

It is best to do this fitting with the help of two mirrors so that you can see the back as well as the front.

Fit the side bust darts first, by taking the lower dart stitching line and folding it toward the upper dart stitching line. You will then see how much more fabric you can take into the dart to get rid of the fullness above the waistline. Roll the surplus fabric into the dart by rolling the lower dart stitching line under until the front looks smooth (figure **4**).

Deepening the darts does not mean that you take any more depth into the ends of the darts where they go into the side seams (see figure **4**). You only do this when you have to pin off a lot of surplus fabric into the side seams—and this is the next stage.

Now stand relaxed in front of the mirror with both arms beside the body. The area above the waistline should look perfectly smooth without fitting too snugly to the body. There should be no upward drag lines toward the darts. If there are, it means that you have taken in the darts too far down the stitching line and they must be let out.

The remaining fullness in the dress must now be pinned off at the

side seams by deepening the curve through the waistline and over the hips.

Now fit the back of the dress.

If pinning fullness into the side seams causes the dress to pull into the waistline and toward the sides at the back, unpin some fullness from the side seams on the dress Back only and deepen the Center Back seam curve until the back hangs smoothly.

The Center Back and Center Front should not, however, be fitted too closely to the figure, but should fall into a softly molding line.

The second fitting

Correct all the fitting faults from the first fitting and mark them on the pattern ready to cut the lining for the third fitting. Then baste the dress as corrected and try it on, making any small alterations that may be necessary.

Preparing for the third fitting

Stitch and press all darts and seams in the dress. The darts should be slashed along the centers and pressed open and the seam allowances reduced to $\frac{5}{8}$ inch, or less in the case of the shoulder darts. To obtain a perfect molding at the points of the side bust darts, press them carefully over the rounded end of a pressing ham.

If you wish to overcast the seam edges, do so now but omit the shoulder seam edges.

Press the Center Back opening seam allowances as fitted and pin and baste in the zipper.

Make the lining as for the dress. The darts are stitched on the outside of the fabric, that is, the side of the lining which goes to the body. This will prevent the thickness of the darts from making an impression on the knit fabric. The seams are stitched on the inside of the lining as usual.

Finish the seams of the lining as flat as possible so that they will not show through. Trim the shoulder seams to $\frac{1}{2}$ inch but do not overcast them.

Pin and baste the lining to the dress around the neckline and armhole seams (figure **5**). The lining will be caught into the armhole seams when the sleeves are stitched in. This secures the shoulderline as in some knits fitted sleeves can cause the shoulder seams to drop.

Pin and baste the sleeve seams, leaving 5 inches open at each wrist end for the zipper opening if you intend to make the sleeves really fitted.

Pin and baste the sleeves into the armholes.

The third fitting

Slip on the dress and close the zipper.

Check the sleeve fitting around the armholes and over the shoulders, then fit the sleeves as follows.

Pin the sleeve openings together and fit the sleeves close to the forearm as far as the elbow. If you want to dispense with the zippers, make each wrist edge just wide enough to enable you to push your hand through.

The upper arm area of the sleeves should be close fitting but not tight, so move your arms up and down to make sure that the seams will not break. All long fitted sleeves restrain your movement somewhat, even in knits, but you must sacrifice some freedom for style. Long fitted sleeves must always be made a little longer than other sleeves as they have a tendency to ride up on the arms and look too short if made the usual length. The extra length is only needed if you are fitting the sleeves closely.

Check the length of the dress, and trim the excess hem allowance on the sleeves to make a 1 to $\frac{3}{4}$ inch hem.

Finally check the back fitting of the dress once more, especially around the zipper area. The zipper should lie flat and the fabric around it should not bulge, nor should it be held in too tightly.

Finishing the dress

Zipper and facing. Stitch in the zipper.

Stitch the front neck facing to the back neck facing at the shoulder seams. Trim the seam allowance, then pin and baste the facing to the neck edge of the dress, right sides together, pinning the ends of the zipper tape out of the way.

Stitch the facing to the dress around the neck edge and trim the seam allowance.

Snip into the seam allowance of the lining at short intervals. The seam allowance of the knit fabric may also have to be snipped if it does not lie easily. But before deciding to snip the knit fabric, first turn the facing to the inside and edge-baste and press it to see how much resistance there is on the seam edge.

Turn in the raw edges of the lining clear of the zipper teeth down the Center Back opening and hand sew to the zipper tape. Then fold in the ends of the back neck facing to clear the zipper teeth and sew to the tape.

Sew the facing to the lining with long slip stitches.

Press the top edge of the opening and close with a hand-worked bar and a small hook.

Sleeves. Finish the sleeve openings before stitching the sleeves into the armholes. If you are not putting zippers in the openings, finish the sleeve hems in the usual way. Otherwise stitch in the zippers and make the hems as shown (figure **6**), mitering the ends of each hem over the ends of the zipper tape.

Finally stitch the sleeves, trim the seam allowance of the armholes and overcast to finish (see Pantsmaking chapter 42, figure **7**).

Hem. When finishing the hem, use the invisible catch stitch as shown in Skirtmaking chapter 15. This gives extra strength and allows the stitches to give with the fabric.

Turn up the lining hem 1 inch shorter than the dress and machine stitch or hem in place.

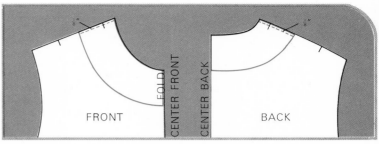

▲ **3.** *The trimmed front and back neck facings*
▼ **4.** *Deepening the side bust dart*

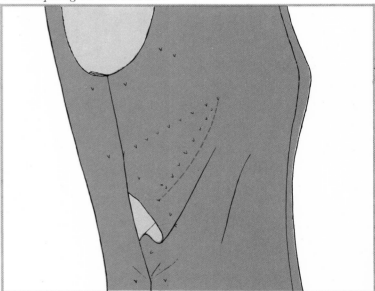

▼ **1.** *The dress Front pattern*   ▼ **2.** *The dress Back pattern*

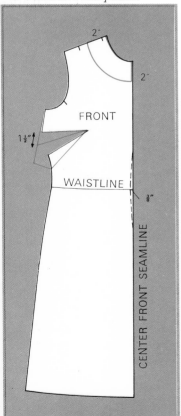
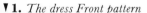
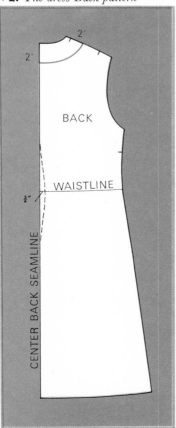

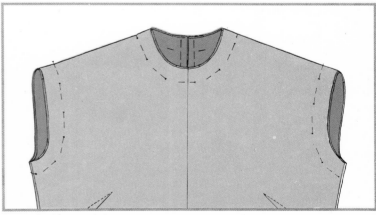

▲ **5.** *Pinning the lining around neck and armholes*
▼ **6.** *The sleeve hem with zipper fastening*

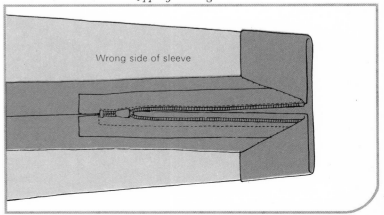

171

Chapter 39

Dress-making

Making a fitted slip

Nothing is nicer for a party than a dress made in a floaty, sheer fabric. Often these dresses are unlined and then the problem arises of what to wear underneath. The obvious answer is a simple, well fitting slip that molds to your body. Sometimes, even a well fitting slip in a neutral color can be hard to come by, so if you have a dress which really needs well shaped undergarments and where an attached lining would add too much bulk in the seams, a fitted slip pattern provides an ideal and easy answer. Another good reason for substituting a fitted slip for a lining is that some dress fabrics require special treatment for cleaning which could ruin the fabric of an attached lining.

The slip featured in this chapter is a version of the basic **dress pattern from the Golden Hands Graph Pages.** It has body darts and attractive contour darting added to the Center Front so that it fits properly over the bustline giving a smooth finish.

Full instructions are given here for making the basic slip, but there is no reason why you should not make it longer or shorter, shaped at the top or trimmed in any way you wish. In addition, if you already have a commercial paper pattern for a simple dress style, you can use the same methods for converting it to a slip.

Choosing the right fabric

You should use the same care when choosing fabric for a slip as you would for dress linings. In the following paragraphs suitable and unsuitable fabrics are featured to help you avoid making mistakes.

Suitable fabrics

The suitable fabrics are the ones which have some weight and firmness. For these choose from the wide range of washable lingerie taffetas made in nylon, rayon and other synthetics.

You may choose a stiff quality if the outer garment is made in a heavy fabric, but for more versatile use choose one of the softer taffetas in the above mentioned fibers. These will tailor better and mold to the body and can therefore be worn under a variety of dress fabrics without making impressions on the outside, and yet they are strong enough for hard wear.

Other suitable fabrics are the traditional, old fashioned lingerie crêpes made from pure or artificial silks, but these can be difficult to find.

Nylon and Dacron satins are ideal, and a cheap but good quality satin de Lys and crêpe de Lys is available which is a mixture of nylon, polyester and silk fibers.

Nylon and other synthetic jerseys, which are not too fine and have a feeling of some weight, can be used very successfully, especially if you have an automatic or zigzag sewing machine.

If you are making a slip to wear under a see-through voile dress, choose a plain lightweight dress fabric.

Unsuitable fabrics

The most unsuitable fabrics are those which hold static electricity. Not only does this distort the fit of the slip, but it also interferes with the hang of the garment worn over it.

These fabrics are mostly in the finer weaves and are usually man-made, although some silks will also cling. Here is a reliable test to see if the fabric is suitable.

Static electricity test. Lay a length of fabric on the store counter and stroke it with your hand several times. Most fabrics will develop some electricity with this treatment, but avoid the ones which do not lie flat and which form air pockets and folds as you try to straighten them out. These are the fabrics which can not be made successfully into a slip as they will always cling.

Suitable for sheers

You must also test for static electricity when you are making a slip to go under sheer fabrics, especially chiffon. Some taffetas will make chiffon cling to them although the taffeta itself shows no sign of static electricity. Be sure to test the combination of the fabrics before you start.

Longer slips

You may find that in spite of all your precautions static electricity occurs with longer slips because of the area involved. To give the garment a little more weight to counteract this, insert a fine roll of covered lead pellet weights into the fold of the hemline. Lead pellets are easily obtainable in the curtain or notion departments of stores.

Finding the correct finish

A fitted slip must fit smoothly and must not have bulky seams which would cause impressions on the outside of a garment. But although the finish must be kept as flat as possible, it must be strong enough to withstand really hard wear. In addition, this type of garment fits close to the body and is subject to body moisture, which weakens the structure of the fabric and the seams.

In the old tradition lingerie was finished by hand, but it is best to finish modern fabrics by machine. French seaming may be used in soft fabrics, but the seams in the stronger or heavier fabrics must be kept flat like dress seams and finished inside in the same way.

The upper edge of the slip can be finished in many ways. The one featured in this chapter lends itself to a plain or trimmed finish. For hem finishes other than the one used here, turn to Skirtmaking chapter 20, where you will find a number of suitable alternatives are shown.

The slip pattern

Copy the Front and Back dress pattern pieces (numbers 1 and 2) from the Basic Dress Graph Pattern.

Before cutting out the pattern pieces, add 1 inch to the side seam of the Front between the armhole and the darts as shown (figure **1**).

Next, reduce the ease on both the Front and Back as the slip has to fit closer to the body than the dress. To do this, deduct $\frac{1}{8}$ inch from the Center Front and Center Back and $\frac{1}{4}$ inch from each side seam, including the bit added to the side Front.

Cut out both pattern pieces.

Bust darts

For a perfect fit it is very important that all horizontal darts

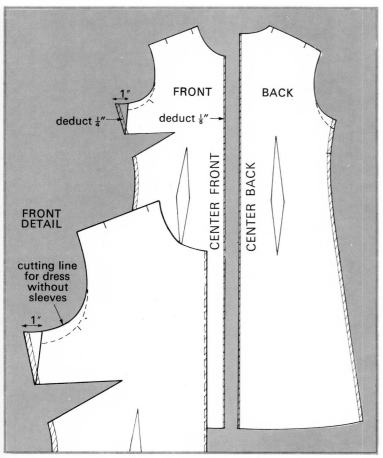

FRONT   BACK

deduct ¼″

1″

deduct ¼″

deduct ⅛″

CENTER FRONT

CENTER BACK

FRONT DETAIL

cutting line for dress without sleeves

1″

▲ **1.** *Adding to the Front side seam and reducing the ease on Front and Back*
The fitted slip is adaptable to any dress length, style or color ►

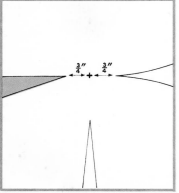

¾″   ¾″

▲ **2.** *Detail of the front darting*

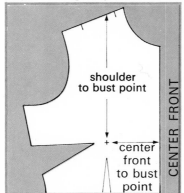

shoulder to bust point

CENTER FRONT

center front to bust point

▲ **3.** *Marking the bust point*

(see figure **2**) run toward the point of the bust but never actually onto the point as this would create a ridge. So all darts should end ¾ inch from the bust point.

Marking the bust point. You can use the bodice muslin to find the correct position of the bust point, if you have made one, otherwise just measure on your body.

Measure the distance from bust point to bust point. Then, starting on the Center Front line, mark off half this measurement on the Front pattern.

Measure the depth from shoulder to bust point and mark the pattern where both points coincide (figure **3**).

Using a 45° set square on the Center Front, draw a line straight across the pattern through the bust mark. If your basic dress pattern was adjusted accurately on a previous occasion this line should touch the pointed end of the dart.

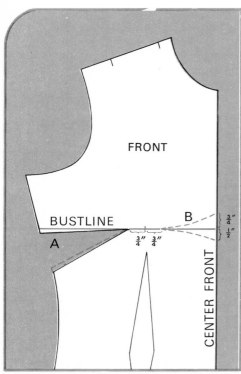

▲ 4. *Marking out the horizontal darts A and B*

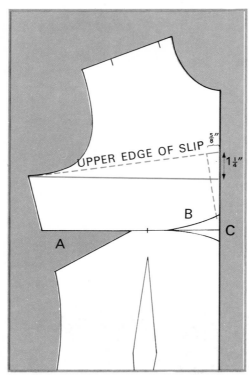

▲ 5. *Marking the upper edge and vertical dart*

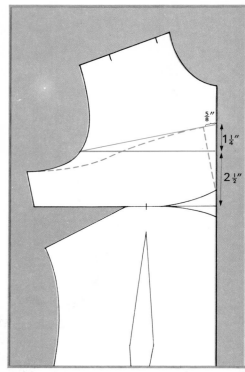

▲ 6. *Marking the upper edge for a high bust*

The side bust dart (**A**). Raise the slant of the side bust dart, using the bustline for the upper stitching line. Raise the lower stitching line by the same amount (figure **4**).

If necessary, adjust the dart point ¾ inches from the bust point marking.

The Center Front horizontal dart (**B**). Mark the dart point ¾ inches from the bust mark toward the Center Front (figure **4**).

The depth of the dart is 1¼ inches. Mark ½ inch below the bustline and ¾ inch above on the Center Front. Draw in the dart, curving it as shown.

Finding the upper edge of the slip. Except in the case of a very high bustline, draw a straight line across the Front pattern from underarm to Center Front, parallel to the bustline.

To keep the upper edge of the slip looking straight, you must compensate for the depth of the horizontal dart by raising it 1¼ inches at the Center Front and tapering to nothing as shown (figure **5**).

If you have a very high bustline, work exactly as above but draw the upper line 2½ inches above the bustline and curve it out of the underarm line (figure **6**).

Vertical dart (**C**). To fit the cleavage, make a dart as shown in figure **5**, measuring ⅝ inch in from the Center Front along the upper edge, tapering to nothing on dart B.

Finishing the pattern

Mark the upper edge on the Back in line with the upper edge on the Front in the

side seam and curve it slightly down at the Center Back as shown (figure **7**).

Mark a 14 inch opening in the side seams on both Front and Back pattern pieces, starting at the upper edge of the slip. Adjust the pattern length as required, then cut out along the new lines.

A final word

As the slip has to be so closely and carefully fitted to the body, the depth and positions of the darts serve only as a guide at this stage—they may well have to be adjusted later.

If you should suspect that you may have to deepen the darts, it is wise to add a little more than the usual seam allowance.

Yardages, notions, cutting out

Layout and fabric requirements

Make a layout as shown in Know-How Chapter 46, placing the Center Back and Center Front on the fold of the fabric. Add seam allowances and 2 inches for the hem. Also include an extra ⅜ yard in the yardage to be used for a bias facing to finish the top edge.

Notions

You will also need
- ☐ 14 inch fine nylon zipper
- ☐ Matching satin or taffeta ribbon for shoulder straps
- ☐ Small hook
- ☐ Matching thread

Cutting

Using the layout, cut out the fabric.

Carefully mark the pattern details on the fabric including the shape of the side seams. This is necessary so that you can check the adjustments to each side at the fitting stage.

Fitting

Pin and baste the darts and the side seams, leaving an opening in the left side for the zipper.

Use tape or ribbon to stand in for the shoulder straps at the fitting. Pin them to the basted garment, so that they are in line with the darts in the Back and ¾ inch to the outside of the center of the bust in Front. Leave some extra length on the tape or ribbon to make adjustments.

The first fitting

Fitting the slip is done in two stages. The first stage should always be done with the garment inside out, except if you know you have uneven sides. Then it is safer to fit the slip with the right side out. (For the first fitting for uneven sides see the following instructions.)

Put on the slip and pin the opening together in the side seams. This is now on the right side of your body.

Check that the bustline of the slip is perfectly in line with your own and that all the dart points run toward it; if not, raise or lower it with shoulder straps. Start fitting the bustline first and take out

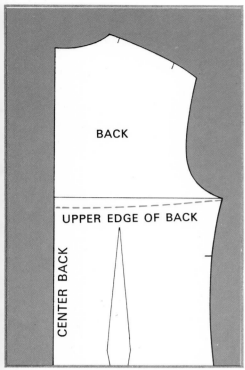

▲ **7.** *Marking the upper edge on the Back*

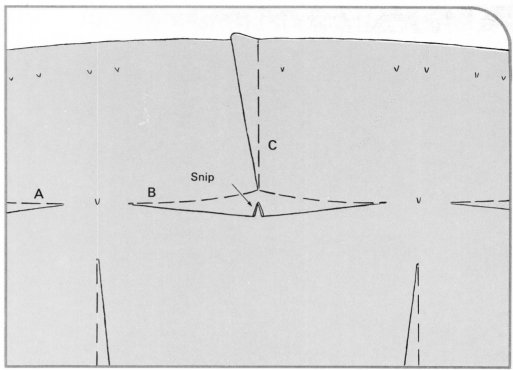

▲ **8.** *Snipping the horizontal dart for the second fitting*

any fullness by pinning it into the side seams at this point.

Next fit the Center Front darts so that they curve into the bust contour and run out flat onto the bust.

If you have a very large bust, you may need to take the horizontal darting in more deeply. It then becomes necessary to make a second horizontal dart ½ inch below the original one to stop the dragging from under the bustline which would occur if all the fullness was lifted into one dart. Do not deepen the original dart, but try and take all the extra depth into the second dart, which is parallel to the first but will be slightly shorter because it does not run toward the bust point.

If you make any alterations to the horizontal dart, you will find that the vertical dart also needs adjusting.

Taking in the vertical dart may result in tightness at the upper edge, and you will have to compensate for this by letting out from the side seams.

Adjust the side bust darts if necessary.

Any surplus fabric around the midriff and the waistline should first be pinned off into the Front and Back body darts. Here too, the fitting will vary with each figure shape and the fullness may have to be distributed between the darts and the side seams. If you find, when making the body darts deeper, that drag lines show toward the side seams, stop and pin the rest into the side seams.

The shoulder straps should now feel comfortable and not drag the garment.

First fitting for uneven sides

If you have the problem of uneven sides, especially differences in the bust height, it is necessary to fit the slip right side out. You will have to pin and baste the Center Front horizontal dart on the outside of the garment because the depth of the dart on the inside would make the line stretch across the front and prevent your checking if it is correct. The dart is turned to the inside of the garment after the fitting. Fit the rest of the slip, using the same sequence as above.

The second fitting

Correct all the fitting faults and prepare the garment for a second basted fitting. Snip carefully into the depth of the horizontal dart in the Center Front halfway as shown (figure **8**). This way you will be able to check if the ends of the dart run out smoothly.

Baste in the zipper fastener. Put on the slip right side out, and stand before a mirror with your arms beside your body.

At this stage the slip should fit closely, but not tightly, over the bust and the waistline. All the darts should run out flat toward the bust and not create any folds or creases.

If there is lift in the ends of the darts, it means that you have slightly overfitted them and you will have to let them out a little.

Do not try to pin off any fullness at the dart points; this only makes the problem worse and you would have to make one

dart end run into the other to get rid of this fullness.

Move around, stoop and bend and then sit down. It must be a close fit, but it must not strain in the seams.

Check the strap positions. If the slip is to be worn under sheer garments, they should be directly in line with the straps of your bra.

Make sure at this stage that the upper edge of the slip has remained straight. Pin the seam allowance under along the front edge and see where adjustments are necessary. Finally, try a dress over the slip to make sure that you have the correct length adjustments, and your slip will be ready for stitching.

Making the slip

Before removing the tailor's tacking and the basting stitches, transfer all the fitting corrections of the slip to your paper pattern. This will allow you to work more quickly when you want to make up the pattern again.

The darts

First stitch the horizontal dart (B). Trim the inside fold to ⅛ inch and snip it at the Center Front to within a few grains of the stitching line (figure **9**). Carefully finish the raw edges together, taking special care with the snipped edge, and press the dart downward.

Next, stitch the vertical dart (C). Slash it along the center to within ¾ inch of the end, trim the seam allowance to ⅜ inch

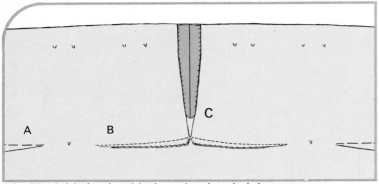

▲ 9. *The finished, snipped horizontal and vertical darts*

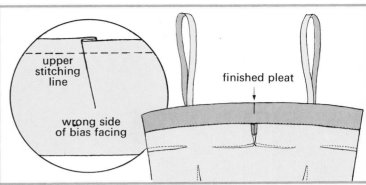

▲ 11. *The inverted miter on the bias facing at the Center Front*

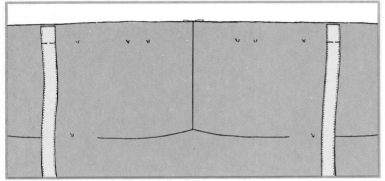

▲ 10. *Basting the straps to the upper edge of the slip on the right side*

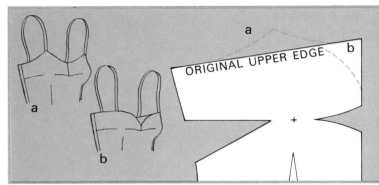

▲ 12. *Alternative shapes for the upper edge of the slip*

and press the dart open (figure **9**). Finish the raw edges.

To stitch the side bust darts (A), rip the right side seam sufficiently to enable you to work on the dart.

Stitch the darts and trim the depth of the dart fold to $\frac{3}{8}$ inch, finish the raw edges together and press the darts down.

Stitch the body darts on the Front and Back and press them toward the center. To relieve any strain in the dart fold, make a small snip.

Side seams
Stitch the side seams, using the method suitable for the type of fabric.

For French seams, prepare the zipper opening as follows:

Start 1 inch below the balance mark for the end of the opening and, with wrong sides together, stitch the seam as for the first row of stitches for a French seam.

Trim the seam allowance along the stitched section only from 1 inch below the balance mark to the hem. Turn the seam to the inside in the usual way and make the second row of stitches, starting at the balance mark, to cover the raw edges of the first row of stitches.

Fasten off the ends of the thread carefully at the balance mark.

Next, pin and baste the seam allowance on the opening to the inside of the garment and insert the zipper in the normal way. If you find that the seam allowance strains where it folds into the French

seam, rip the first row of stitches a fraction until the seam allowance rolls into the French seam without strain.

Press the French seams toward the front and finish the raw edges of the seam allowance on the opening. Do not be tempted to snip the seam allowance, since this would weaken the seam here.

The shoulder straps
For the shoulder straps, use a matching satin ribbon, which is nice and strong, or taffeta ribbon. You can also make a narrow tube of self fabric $\frac{1}{2}$ inch wide, which is cut on the straight of the grain. Pin and baste the seam allowance of the right side of the straps to the seam allowance of the right side of the upper edge of the garment, raw edges even, so that the seam allowance of the straps can be caught in with the bias facing (figure **10**).

The facing
To make a bias facing, cut a strip of bias fabric from the rest of the fabric $1\frac{1}{4}$ inches wide, long enough to fit the length of the upper edge of the slip. If you must join the bias strip, make the seams so that they correspond with the garment.

To avoid straining the lower edge of the strip when it is turned to the inside of the garment at the Center Front, add $\frac{1}{2}$ inch to the length measurement and make an inverted miter in line with the seamline of the vertical dart. To do this, make a small pleat in the bias along the

upper stitching line as shown (figure **11**). This means you can then stitch the lower edge of the facing to the slip without it straining over the dart seam. Stitch on the bias facing as given in Dressmaking chapter 33, but do not curve it.

Sew on a hook and hand-work a bar at the top of the side opening.

The hem
The hem finishes featured in Skirtmaking chapter 20 are suitable for the fitted slip. Do not hand sew the hem in place. The constant friction of nylon stockings on the hem when walking will actually fray the sewing thread and the hem will need constant repair.

Make firm small machine stitches along the folded edge of the hem allowance—they will be more durable.

Alternative shapes for the upper edge
When fitting the slip it is easy to alter the shape of the upper straight edge into a center front dip, or raise it to follow the line of your bra (figure **12**).

This can be done without fear that the basic fitting structure will be affected. Face the shaped edge with a bias facing which must be carefully mitered in dips and points so that it corresponds with the top of the garment. It is best to fit the strip and pin the miters as necessary as you work. Take off the bias strip and then stitch the miters by machine and press the seams open. This will give you a good flat finish.

Chapter 40

Matching tops for pants

Adapted from the Basic Dress Graph Pattern, these soft-line tops, with rouleau loop or tie fastening, are designed to be worn with the pants in Pantsmaking chapters 43 and 44, making a stunning complete pants outfit that is suitable for practically any occasion.

Suitable fabrics

Most soft blouse fabrics are suitable for these tops, as well as the more substantial fabrics like the knit and crêpe used here. If you buy a knit fabric for a garment fastened with rouleau loops, make sure that the knit is close and firm. Loops tend to stretch and gradually become too large for the buttons if they are made in a loose-knit jersey. Also the seams of the rouleau break and the loops become useless and untidy.

The patterns

A. The day tunic

The pattern pieces you will need are: Front, Back, sleeve, front facing and back neck facing, which should be made as follows:

Front and Back. Copy the Front and Back dress pattern pieces from the Basic Dress Graph Pattern.

This is a slip-on garment which has no zipper opening. The Center Front seam is opened from the neckline down to a point of your own choosing, so mark the Center Front edge of the pattern where you want the opening to end, but make it long enough to get the garment over your head.

If you have made the basic dress and fitted it more than the original, and have altered the pattern accordingly, it is necessary to return the gentle curve of the orginal through the waistline in the side seams or the top will be too narrow to slip over your shoulders. Measure the length you want the tunic top to be and cut both Back and Front pattern pieces to that measurement. If you are going to wear the tunic belted, remember to make the pattern longer to allow for the fabric riding up under the belt.

Facings. To make the front facing pattern, lay the Front pattern piece along the edge of a sheet of paper and copy the Center Front from the opening mark to the neck edge and along the neckline and shoulder seam. Draw in the facing 2 inches wide at the shoulder-line and 2 inches wide at the lower edge as shown (figure **1**). Also make a back neck facing (figure **2**).

Cut out the facing patterns, then pin the front facing to the Front of the new tunic pattern along the Center Front, with the edges meeting over a strip of paper so that the Front and front facing can be cut as one (figure **1**).

Sleeves. For the sleeve pattern, make the bishop sleeve version A (the full sleeve without cuff from Blousemaking chapter 30). If you are using a heavy fabric such as the double knit shown here, do not make the pattern quite as full.

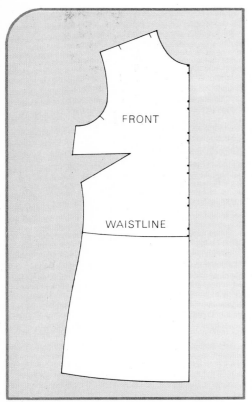

▲ **3.** *Right Front version B: the loop positions*

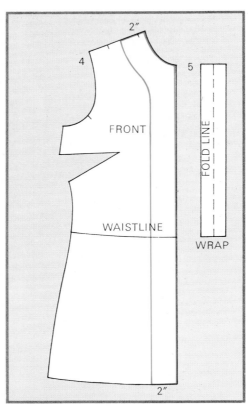

▲ *Version B:* **4.** *front facing:* **5.** *wrap pattern*

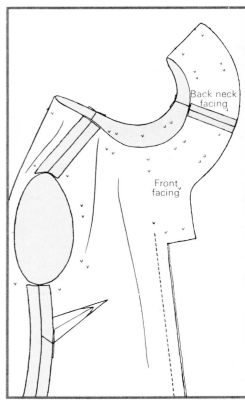

▲ **6.** *Version A: the stitched neck facings*

B. The evening overblouse

The pattern pieces you will need are: Front, Back, sleeve, cuff, front facing, back neck facing and wrap, which should be made as follows:

Front and Back. Copy the Front and Back dress pattern pieces from the Basic Dress Graph Pattern.

This top has a front opening and can therefore be cut to the shape of a fitted pattern if you have altered the basic pattern accordingly.

The Center Front on the finished garment meets edge to edge and fastens down the front from neck to waist with rouleau loops and buttons.

To mark the Front pattern for buttoning, first take your front neck to waist measurement and mark this measurement on the Center Front of the pattern.

Then mark the positions for the loops which go on the right Front, $2\frac{1}{2}$ to 3 inches apart, between the neck and waistline (figure **3**).

Measure the length you want the overblouse to be and cut both Back and Front pattern pieces to that measurement.

Facings. To make the full length front facing pattern, lay the Front pattern piece on the edge of a sheet of paper, copy the neckline and the shoulder seam and make a facing as shown (figure **4**) which is 2 inches wide at both hem and shoulder edge. Also make a back neck facing as for the day version (see figure **2**).

Wrap. For the wrap on the left Front, cut a strip of paper 2 inches wide to the length of your front neck to waist measurement and mark the lengthwise center fold line (figure **5**).

If you prefer to leave the top two buttons undone, do not take the wrap to the neck edge, but from the waist to the last button that you are going to wear done up. This way the wrap will not show.

Sleeves and cuffs. For the sleeve and cuff pattern pieces, make the bishop sleeve or bishop sleeve version C (the full sleeve with fitted top and tapered cuff shown in Blousemaking chapter 30).

If you are using a heavier crêpe type fabric as shown in the picture, do not spread the pattern too full. Some of these fabrics are made only to resemble crêpe with the finishing treatment, while the basic weave—which in real crêpe consists of highly twisted crêpe yarns—is often plain and flat. The folding and draping qualities of the simulated crêpe fabric are therefore not the same as in real crêpe. If you cut the sleeves too full, the fullness will stand out not only around the wrist, where it looks beautiful, but also along the full length of the sleeve and will therefore look very bulky around the upper arm. So use the bishop sleeve version C, but cut the sleeve a little longer, especially at the curve in the wrist. This is a professional's trick used to give the impression of greater fullness.

Yardages and layouts

Make your own layout and calculate your yardage requirements as shown in Know-How chapter 46.

Start your yardage calculation for 36 inch wide fabric as follows: twice the length of the blouse, plus twice the length of the sleeve, plus $\frac{1}{2}$ yard for cutting a rouleau. Do not forget to add seam and hem allowances to the lengths.

Interfacing. The evening overblouse B, made in a fabric such as crêpe, will need the support of interfacing on the neck edge and the Center Front edge to the waistline.

You can use the back and front facing patterns for the interfacing. The cuffs also need interfacing, so make a small layout to work out the amount of interfacing you will need.

Making the tunics

A. The day tunic

This version can be made in two ways. You can stitch the side seams from underarm to hem or you can leave them open from the waist down in true cossack style. Pin, baste and fit the tunic. If you are going to wear it with a belt, try on the belt when deciding the length as soft fabric gathers up considerably when it is belted. Stitch the Center Front seam from the end of the opening to the hem, overcast, press.

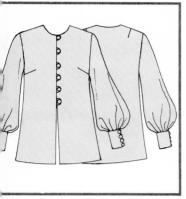

...ening overblouse, B, shown on page ...worn with flared pants in crepe

...y tunic, A, shown right in jac-...d knit with cossacks in plain knit

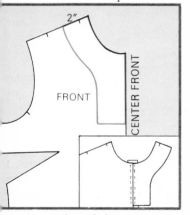

Version A: front facing
Versions A and B: back neck facing

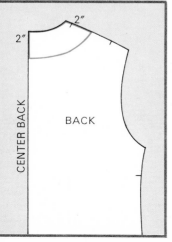

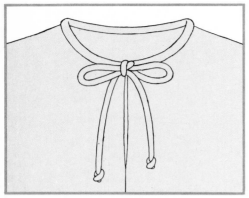

▲ 7. *Version A: the tied and knotted rouleau*

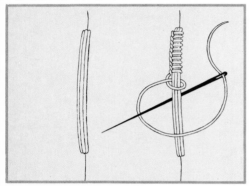

▲ 8. *The bar carrier for a belted style*

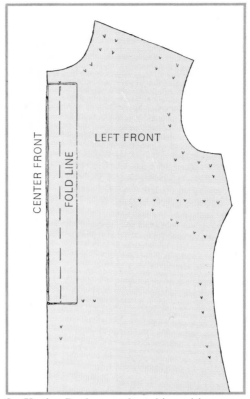

CENTER FRONT

FOLD LINE

LEFT FRONT

9. *Version B: the wrap basted in position*

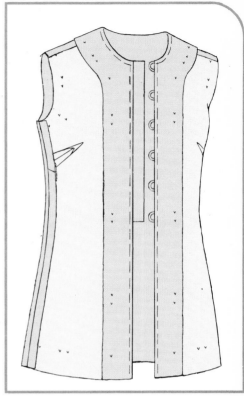

▲ 10. *Version B: the stitched and turned facing*

Stitch the side bust darts and press.

Stitch the shoulder and side seams, finish seams and press. Make the hem.

If you have left the side seams open from the waist down, finish the hem at the seams as for the slit in the shorts (Pantsmaking chapter 44, figure 4) and slip stitch the side seam allowances in place from waist to hem.

To finish the neck edge, stitch the back neck facing to the front facings at the shoulder seams (figure 6). Trim the seams to ½ inch and press open.

Pin and baste the joined facing to the inside of the neckline, raw edges even, with wrong sides facing and seamlines corresponding.

Trim the seam allowance on the neck edge to within a fraction of the seamline and finish the raw edge with a bias strip turned over the edge as for a rouleau type binding (see chapter 63).

Fasten the Center Front of the neck edge with a handmade loop and small button.

Cut a bias strip about 24 inches long to the width required for a ¼ inch wide rouleau.

Make a rouleau as shown in Blousemaking chapter 30.

Tuck in the ends of the finished, turned rouleau and handsew them together. Then tie a knot in the rouleau on each end. Finally, tie the rouleau into a bow and sew it to the neck edge to cover the button and loop fastening (figure 7).

180

Make the sleeves as shown in Blousemaking chapter 30 and stitch them in. If you want to wear a belt with the tunic, make a handworked carrier on each side seam at waist level (figure 8).

B. Evening overblouse

Pin, baste and fit the overblouse. After fitting, rip the side and shoulder seams and work the Center Front first.

Make a rouleau for the loops following all the steps given in Blousemaking chapter 30 and prepare the loops for the chosen button size as shown in the same chapter. On the right Front, place a loop over each mark and hand sew to the seam allowance as for the loops on the tapered cuff.

Fold the strip for the wrap lengthwise on the fold line, wrong sides facing, folding in the seam allowance at each end. Pin and baste the whole strip and press lightly. With raw edges even, pin and baste the wrap to the outside of the left Front along the Center Front seamline (figure 9).

Stitch the side bust darts, and the body darts if you are using them. Press.

Stitch the side and shoulder seams, finish seams and press.

For interfacing the neck and front edges, lap the seam allowance of the back neck interfacing over the seam allowance of the front interfacing at the shoulder seams and stitch as shown in figure 4, Pantsmaking

chapter 42. Trim the seam allowances and pin and baste the interfacing to the inside of the overblouse.

Join the back neck and front facings at the shoulder seams. Trim the seam allowances to ½ inch and press open.

With right sides facing, pin and baste the facing to the outside of the overblouse (the loops on the right side and the wrap on the left are hidden between overblouse and facing).

Stitch the facing in place along the Center Fronts and neck edge, trim and snip the seam allowances and turn the facing to the inside of the overblouse. Edge-baste and press (figure 10).

Anchor the facing to the overblouse with small catch stitches at the waistline and around the back neck.

Make the hem.

Make the bishop sleeves as shown in Blousemaking chapter 30 and stitch them into the armholes of the overblouse.

Pin the edges of the Center Front so that they meet on the wrap, mark the positions for the buttons and sew on the buttons. At the waistline, stitch on a hook and bar to support the loop and button at the waist edge. Large buttons and loops are more decorative than functional, and if they are subjected to any strain it is best to support them with a small hook and bar. Or if, as with this overblouse, you have a wrap, you can use small snap fasteners instead of hooks.

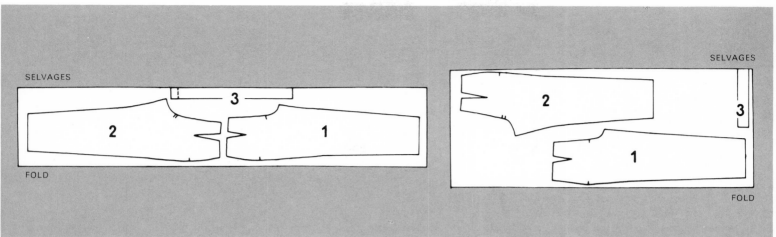

36" Width Without one way All sizes ▲

54" Width With one way Sizes 32½-34 ▲

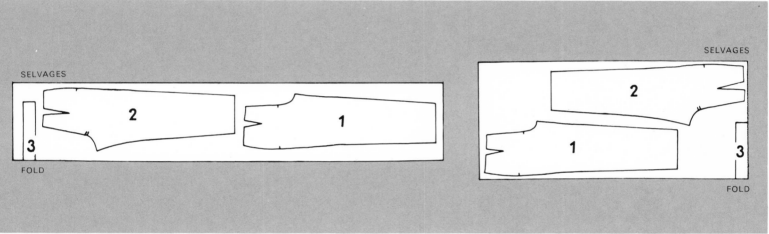

36" Width With one way All sizes ▲

54" Width Without one way Sizes 32½-34

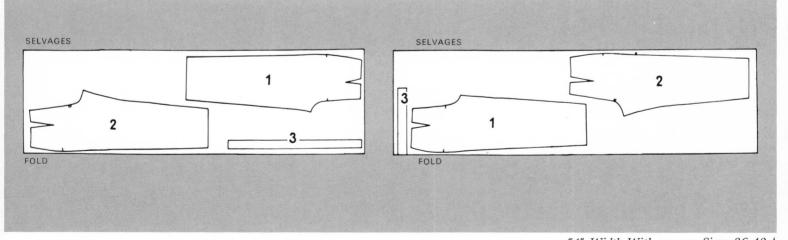

54" Width Without one way Sizes 40-42 ▲

54" Width With one way Sizes 36-42 ▲

▼ *54" Width Without one way Sizes 36-38*

Pants Yardages

Sizes	32½	34	36	38	40	42
36" Without one way ..	2¾	2¾	3	3	3	3⅛
With one way ..	2⅝	2⅝	3	3	3	3⅛
54" Without one way ..	1¾	1⅞	2⅜	2⅜	2½	2⅝
With one way ..	1⅞	2	2⅜	2½	2⅝	2⅞

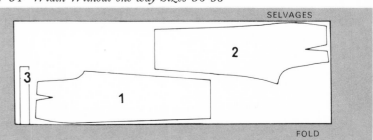

181

Basic Pants Graph Pattern

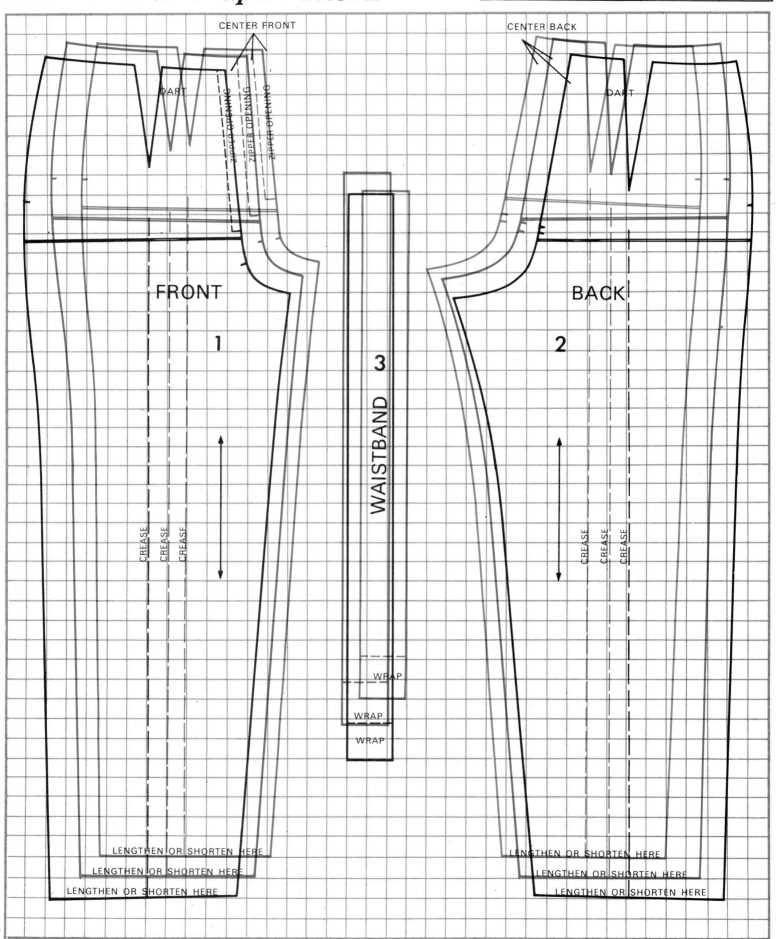

The outlines given are the stitching lines.
Refer to page 139 for seam allowances
and check with the following chapters for
any variations.

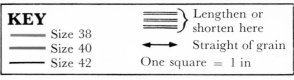

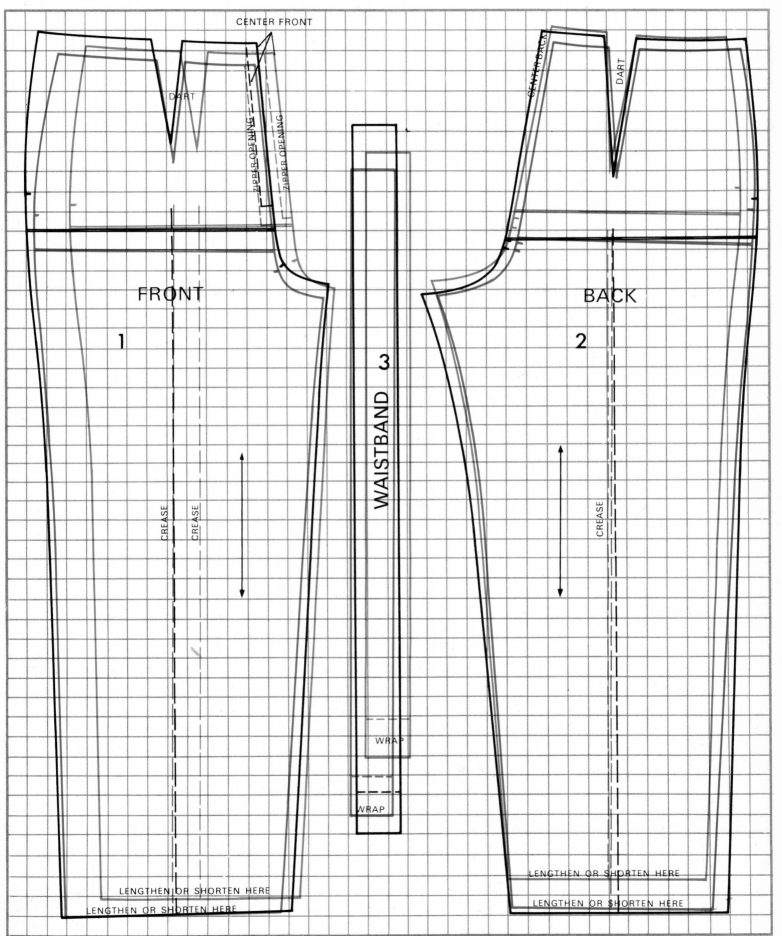

CENTER FRONT

DART

ZIPPER OPENING

ZIPPER OPENING

FRONT

1

CREASE

CREASE

LENGTHEN OR SHORTEN HERE

LENGTHEN OR SHORTEN HERE

WAISTBAND

3

WRAP

WRAP

CENTER BACK

DART

BACK

2

CREASE

LENGTHEN OR SHORTEN HERE

LENGTHEN OR SHORTEN HERE

Chapter 41

Pants-making

Pants from the graph

There was a time, not so long ago, when pants were reserved for casual wear only and women who wore them in public were considered anti-social. Designers took the situation in hand and caused a revolution in the fashion world—they transformed this once ungraceful garment into something truly feminine, so that now pants have become acceptable wear for many occasions. Also, such is the inventiveness of fashion that variations in style, fabric and cut can add up to an all-purpose wardrobe when coordinated with coats, jackets and tunics, for both day and evening wear.

Another, less noticeable revolution, has been a radical change in attitude—you no longer need a model's figure to wear them. The truth is that if pants are well fitted it doesn't matter what shape or size you are. The basic pants from the Golden Hands Graph Pages, shown here, are straight cut fitted pants which are easy to make, easy to wear, and which will suit most figure types. This chapter sets out to prove this point and takes you through the early, most vital stages of pattern alteration, cutting and fitting.

A perfect fit

Before you start making pants for yourself, study your figure carefully from all sides and be honest with yourself. Pants need to be carefully fitted, especially if you have a figure problem. Don't think that if you wear a tunic long enough to cover the poorly fitting areas that you are out of trouble; badly fitted pants are very uncomfortable, and everyone knows what it feels like to be constantly reminded that one is wearing an ill fitting garment. Also, if pants fit poorly at the top the hang will be affected and the pants legs will pull and look strange as you walk or sit. Badly fitted garments always show off figure faults. But if you take a few simple precautions before the cutting stage, you will find a pair of pants one of the easiest and most rewarding garments to make.

Checking the pattern

First check the pattern for size. Check the length from waist to crotch and the leg length. Figure faults must also be dealt with on the pattern because it is almost impossible to correct these at the fitting stage.

Checking the length

For the waist to crotch measurement, sit on a chair and measure yourself along the side of your body from the waist to the chair. Add ½ inch for ease, or more if you are working with heavier fabrics. Draw a line across the pattern from the crotch to the side seam as shown (figure **1**) and compare your measurement to that of the pattern. If it is necessary to adjust, use the lengthening or shortening lines on the back and front pattern pieces.

Measure your inner leg length from the crotch to below the ankle-bone and, if necessary, adjust the pattern on the given line.

184

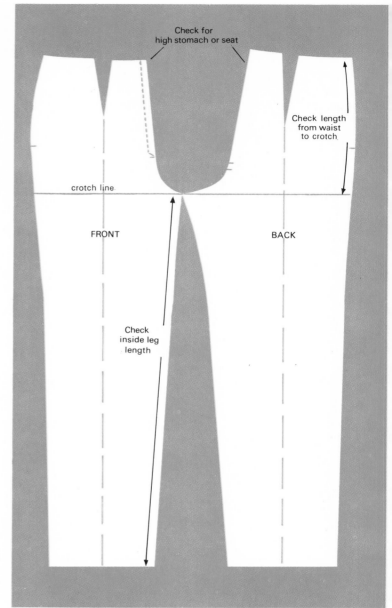

▲ **1.** *Preparing back and front patterns for waist to crotch measurement*
Firmly woven wool gabardine makes slim work of the basic pants ▶

Adjusting the pattern for figure problems

The following figure problems will need pattern alterations: larger hip measurements caused by a high seat or wide hips; larger waist measurements caused by a high stomach, and heavy thighs.

High seat. This problem can also occur on standard figure proportions if your figure is narrow and the measurement is taken up around the back.

Adding to the size of the pattern along the side seams will not solve this problem. You will have to make a new pattern to give you the extra fabric where it is needed.

Pin a tape around your waist and measure yourself from the center front of the tape through the crotch to the center back of the tape.

Place the pattern pieces together as shown (figure **1**) and compare your measurement with that of the pattern. If the pattern is short, you will need to correct the back section only.

To make a new pattern, pin the back pattern piece on a sheet of paper and draw around it, excluding the darts. Then draw a line parallel to the crotch line 2½ inches above it.

Unpin the top of the pattern from crotch to waistline and cut along the new line to within $\frac{1}{4}$ inch of the side seam (figure **2**). Divide the extra amount needed by two, spread the pattern upward by this amount and pin it in position.

Draw around the shifted pattern edges, this time including the dart. Add the remaining half of the extra amount to the end of the crotch as shown. Remove the pattern. Extend the center back line upward and connect the new waistline shape to it as shown.

Add the difference between the original center back line and the center back line after the pattern shift to the depth of the dart as shown to preserve the original waist measurement. Or, if you prefer, you can halve the amount of the new dart and make two.

Reshape the side seam and the inner leg seam as shown.

Wide hips. If your figure is flat in the back and front, and the extra hip measurement is taken up by wide hips, add the width required to the side seams on the back and front pattern pieces.

High stomach. Follow the instructions for a high seat, measuring and adjusting the pattern in the same way, but this time all the alterations are made to the front pattern piece only (figure **3**) and the front dart will need to be made smaller for the larger waist measurement.

Heavy thighs and inner thigh bulge. Heavy thighs and bulges at the inside of the upper thigh require extra width across the legs of the pants.

Measure your thighs about 2 inches down from the crotch and add 2 to 3 inches to this measurement for ease. The actual amount of ease depends on the thickness of the fabric you are using—add 2 inches for thin fabrics and more for heavy ones. Lay the pattern front and back together along the side seam and measure across, the same distance down from the crotch. Any difference between your measurement and that of the pattern must be divided into four, and a quarter added to each side and inner leg seam (figures **4** and **5**).

Outer thigh bulge. Bulges at the outside of the upper thigh, which often occur after wearing tight-fitting undergarments, need an adjustment to the side seam only. It is best to deal with this by cutting an extra seam allowance and adjusting it when fitting.

Pants muslin

If you have figure problems and you want to make several pairs of pants for yourself, it might be cheaper in the long run to test the pattern on a muslin first. This way you can also test the amount of ease you need for comfort.

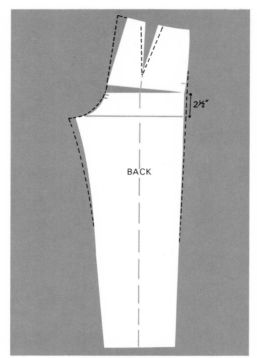

2. *Altering back pattern for a high seat*

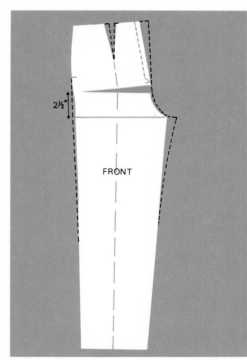

3. *Altering front pattern for a high stomach*

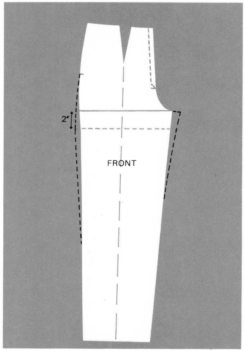

4. *Altering front pattern for heavy thighs*

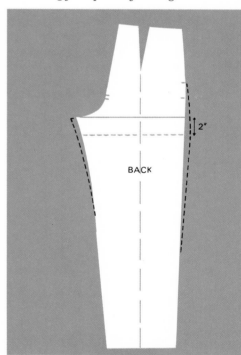

5. *Altering back pattern for heavy thighs*

Choosing the correct fabric

Although pants are made from many different fabrics—not always suitable either—when making the straight, fitted pants from the Basic Pants Graph Pattern it is best to choose one of the fabrics listed below to assist you with your first attempt at pants making and to achieve the right look for the style.

Large sizes should avoid jerseys and tweeds, because these fabrics will appear bulky and give a rounded effect, and choose a firmly woven fabric which has an elongating effect.

No matter what your size, it is important to consider whether the pants will be worn mainly for walking or for sitting before deciding on the fabric. If you are sitting a lot, and this includes driving, avoid softly woven fabrics such as tweed and camel hair; they will bulge and begin to look very untidy after a few hours' wear. Also, when you get up and try to straighten your clothes, pants in these fabrics tend to hold the sitting position. Even for walking, pants made in soft fabric should be lined. Here is a list of fabrics:

☐ Worsted suitings—barathea, flannel, gabardine, men's suiting
☐ Tweeds—Donegal and Harris tweeds
☐ All suit-weight double-knits (most have a crease-resistant finish).

Here are some fabric suggestions for summer-weight pants:

☐ Pure linen and linen mixtures
☐ Cotton twill
☐ Cotton gabardine
☐ Heavy cotton jerseys
☐ Denim

Fabric yardages and notions

On page 181, listed in the panel, you will find the correct yardage for your size and fabric width. If you have added to the length of the pants, don't forget to add this amount to the yardage.

You will also need:

☐ 7 inch skirt zipper
☐ Waistband stiffening
☐ Hooks and eyes size No.3, or pants hook and bar
☐ ¾ inch diameter button with 4 holes (if you want to button the waistband)
☐ Matching thread
☐ Suitable lining fabric the same yardage as the pants fabric (optional)

Cutting out

Select the layout for your size and fabric width from the series of layouts on page 181.

Pin on the pattern. Remember the pattern has no seam allowance, so add ¾ inch for seams and allow at least 3 inches for hems. You need a deep hem for adjustments later; even shoes can make a difference to the length of the pants.

Cut out the front and the back of the pants, but do not cut out the waistband at this point.

Marking

Mark all around the pattern pieces with continuous tailor's tacks. (You can mark strategic points only as shown in Dressmaking chapter 35).

The long dash lines along the center of each pattern piece are the crease lines. These should be marked at intervals with single tailor's tacks through slits made in the paper.

Mark the end of the zipper stitching line only. After you have removed the pattern pieces, measure the length of the zipper and the stitching line from the front edge of the pants and mark on the right front of the pants only with a row of basting stitches. The finished width of this line may vary according to the type of zipper used.

Preparing the pants for fitting

Remove the pattern and put it away safely; it will be used for making conversions later.

Working on a flat table, first pin and baste the side seams. Then pin and baste each inner leg seam. You now have the two halves of your pants basted.

Pin and baste the darts.

Slip the left pant leg into the right leg with right sides facing. Join the sections along the center back seam, through the crotch and as far as the end of the zipper marking in the center front seam.

Pull the pant leg out and press all the seams lightly.

When making pants, special attention must be paid to the width of the waistband. It should not fit as tightly as a skirt waistband or it will be pulled into the stomach as you sit down. It is difficult to know how much ease each individual person needs and therefore it is best if the correct length is decided at the fitting stage. So cut the waistband stiffening only, and cut it 3 inches longer than your waist measurement to allow room for adjustment.

What to wear under the pants

Any type of girdle should be dispensed with for those who can do without one. Pants look their best if they are worn over the soft contours of the body.

But there are some women who never feel properly dressed without a girdle and always like to wear some form of foundation garment, even under pants. The answer to this is a pantie girdle.

Try to wear one which is not too firm—it won't do anything for the fit and line of the pants. Try the pants on over the girdle and look at yourself from the back. If the girdle is too firm, it will create a solid line across the seat which never looks well with pants. So choose a very light girdle with no, or only very short legs; this will follow the shape of the body better. It will never look absolutely natural, but it will give the softer look which is so necessary for this type of garment to hang properly.

Fitting

Try on the pants over your choice of undergarment and pin the center front seam opening together.

Pin the waistband stiffening around your waist and pin it to the pants as you did for the skirt in Skirtmaking chapter 12. If the pants are wide in the waist, make the adjustment at the side seams and also in the darts if necessary. The center front and center back seams should not be altered unless you have altered

the pattern for a high seat or stomach, when a small adjustment may be necessary. If you made pattern alterations for a high seat or high stomach, you will see that there is some fullness below the area for which you have made the alteration.

Do not be tempted to pin this fullness into the seams. You are making straight pants, and the fullness will help to disguise your figure problem by allowing the crease to hang straight from hip to hem. If you want the pants to fit closer to your legs, start tapering them in well below the hip line.

The pants should fit well if you have prepared the pattern properly. Sit, bend and stoop to make sure you have enough room for easy movement.

Look at yourself in a mirror; the pants should hang straight from the hips without dragging or pulling.

Put on the shoes you will be wearing with the pants and pin up the hem of each pant leg.

Check the length again after all the seams have been stitched.

Making the pants

Clearly mark any corrections you have made; mark the waistline and take off the waistband.

Rip the crotch seam so that the pants are in two halves again. Then rip the inner leg seams.

You are now ready to start stitching.

Stitch the darts and press them open flat or toward the center, depending on the type of fabric you are working with.

Stitch each side seam, finish the raw edges, then lay the seam over the center of an ironing board and press it open.

Pressing pants can be very difficult, so it is best to give pants a complete pressing now because you will not have another opportunity to get at the width of the fabric so easily.

After pressing the side seams pin, baste and stitch each inner leg seam and finish the seam edges.

To press these seams open, you will have to pull each leg over a sleeveboard.

Since few sleeveboards are long enough to take the full length of a pant leg, you must be prepared to press the seam in stages. This can result in impressions left by the iron, so as you move the seam along the sleeveboard, always leave a little of the section already pressed on the board so that you can smooth out any impressions as you work along the seam.

Start pressing this seam at the crotch end where it is shaped, and carefully place the fabric on each side of the seam out of the way of the iron to avoid sharp creases under the seam after pressing.

Chapter 42

Suit yourself in pants and tunic

In this week's chapter, the basic pants are completed. Although correcting the pattern and fitting (fully explained in the last chapter) are vitally important stages, no less important are the skill and know-how you put into the stitching, pressing and all the finishing details. Here you will find all the information you need to achieve perfect results with a truly professional look. The pants are followed by instructions for making a matching tunic which is adapted from the Golden Hands basic dress. It has topstitching detail, short sleeves and a front zipper fastening. When combined with the pants, it makes a stunning couture outfit, suitable for many different occasions.

Finishing the pants

How to stitch the crotch seam

Slip the left pant leg into the right, with right sides facing as when preparing for fitting. Pin and baste along the center back seam, through the crotch and as far as the end of the zipper marking in the center front seam.

The seam at the crotch has to bear a great deal of strain during wear, so for stitching use a No.40 mercerized cotton, or a pure silk thread of equal strength to withstand the strain.

▼ 1. *Inserting the zipper in the center front pants opening*

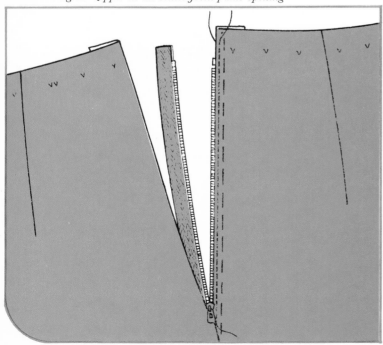

In addition, the lower end of the seam is cut very much on the bias of the fabric and therefore the stitches should have a certain amount of elasticity. If you have a zigzag machine, engage the shallowest zigzag stitch on the machine and stitch along the seamline, stretching the seam a little as you stitch along it.

Press the seam open. Do not snip the seam allowance at the curve where it will not lie flat, but carefully press with the point of the iron on the seamline only.

Then stitch along the seamline once again, using the same shallow zigzag.

Fasten off the threads securely at the end of the zipper opening, trim the seam allowance to $\frac{1}{2}$ inch and finish edges.

If you have no zigzag on your machine, make the same two rows of stitches but use an ordinary straight stitch.

These methods should give you a hard-wearing seam.

Inserting the zipper

Insert the zipper in the center front opening, using the lap-over method (figure **1**) described in Skirtmaking chapter 13.

If you want to finish the front placket as a decorative feature of the pants use buttonhole twist, as for topstitching, when you stitch in the right side of the zipper.

Lining

If you have decided to line the pants, now is the time to do it. Cut out the back and front pattern pieces in lining fabric as for the pants. Make them in the same way, but without the zipper. Slip the lining into the pants, wrong sides facing, and baste them together along the waist seam.

At the zipper, turn in the raw edges of the lining and slip stitch to the zipper tape, clear of the teeth.

Work the pants and lining as one fabric when you put on the waistband.

The waistband

Having worked out the length required for the waistband at the fitting, you can now cut it out. Don't forget to add seam allowances and a wrap.

Any of the waistbands shown for skirts in Skirtmaking chapters 13 and 14 are suitable for the pants.

Since the pants fasten at the center front, you may like to fasten the waistband with a button and buttonhole.

For button fastening, divide the length of the wrap in two and add half the wrap to each end of the waistband. Shape the right end, which goes on the top, into a point with the help of a template, as shown for the buckled belt in Know-How chapter 58.

Stitch on the waistband and make a buttonhole (Blousemaking chapter 26) at the pointed end. The front of the buttonhole should be in line with the center front line of the pants. Sew on the button to correspond.

To take some of the strain off the button, fasten the waistband on the inside with a No.3 hook and eye, or use a pants hook and bar.

Making the pants hems

Turn up the hems, then pin and baste as for the skirt hem in Skirtmaking chapter 13. The finished pants hem should not be more than 2 inches deep, so trim if necessary.

As you baste the hems you will notice that the width at the top is slightly narrower than the outside of the pants. This is correct, and you will find when you press in the creases that the tightness will disappear.

Finish the raw edges of each hem allowance, then hand sew in place with catch stitches. Make the stitches small, but not tight, to avoid catching the hems as you put on the pants.

If you are lining the pants, turn up the lining hems separately,

1 inch shorter than the pants.

To make pants with a long, long look, taper the hems down at the back with the lowest point at the center back on each pant leg.

Tapering the back hems

Let down the center back of each pant leg hem about $\frac{1}{2}$ inch, depending on the resistance of the fabric, and graduate back into the hemline toward the front. If this pulls the hemline, rip the seams in the hem allowance as far as the hemline and let out enough from the seam to allow the hemline to lie flat.

Pressing in the creases

With the inside of the pant leg uppermost, lay each leg in turn on an ironing board to press in the creases.

Lay the pants legs seam on seam. This should bring the crease line markings to the edge of each fold.

The markings may vary a little over or under the folded edge because movement of the fabric when marking, and particular figure corrections made on the pattern, may have displaced the lines a little.

If this is so, follow the fold made by meeting the seamlines from the hem to just above the knee, then pick up the crease line markings from this point up to the lower end of the waist dart.

As you reach the upper part of the pant leg, you will notice that you have more fabric on the inside leg, and if you were to follow the seam-to-seam method all the way up the crease would come out crookedly.

Gently press the creases, using either a damp or dry cloth according to the fabric being pressed.

As you finish pressing one section, stop for a moment to allow the steam to evaporate and the fabric to cool down before you move on. Finally, lay both pants legs together on a flat surface and allow the creases to set.

The tunic

Fabric yardages

These fabric yardages are for a tunic length of 32 inches, so if you add to the length of the tunic, don't forget to increase the yardage accordingly.

54in width, without one way—sizes $32\frac{1}{2}$, 34, 36 and 38, $1\frac{7}{8}$ yards; sizes 40 and 42, 2 yards.

54in width, with one way—sizes $32\frac{1}{2}$ and 34, 2 yards; sizes 36 and 38, $2\frac{1}{8}$ yards; sizes 40 and 42, $2\frac{1}{2}$ yards.

36in width, without one way—sizes $32\frac{1}{2}$ and 34, $2\frac{3}{8}$ yards; sizes 36 and 38, $2\frac{5}{8}$ yards; sizes 40 and 42, $2\frac{3}{4}$ yards.

36in width, with one way—sizes $32\frac{1}{2}$, 34 and 36, $2\frac{5}{8}$ yards; sizes 38, 40 and 42, $2\frac{3}{4}$ yards.

Notions

☐ Lining fabric twice the tunic length measured from the inner shoulder to hem plus seam and hem allowance

☐ $\frac{1}{4}$ yard soft cotton interfacing, suitable for the fabric you are using

☐ Dress zipper, the length of which is determined by measuring $\frac{3}{4}$ inches down from the neck seam to the end of the tab stitching line indicated on the basic pattern

☐ Paper to make new patterns

☐ 2 spools buttonhole twist for topstitching and a larger machine needle

☐ Matching thread

The pants and tunic are made to match in worsted woolen gabardine ▶

189

Making the pattern

The pattern pieces used are the back and front of the Basic Dress Graph and the sleeve pattern piece number 7 on the Accessories Graph.

It is best to make a new pattern, otherwise you will spoil the originals.

For the back and front, copy the basic dress pattern pieces by drawing around them and then adjust to the necessary length for the tunic. To retain the curve of the hemline, measure off the amount by which the pattern has to be altered from the hem and then draw in the new hemline parallel to the old one.

Make two facings, a back neck facing and an all-in-one front opening and neck facing as shown (figures **2** and **3**) using the back and front pattern pieces as your guide.

To make the short sleeves, copy the sleeve pattern as far as the short sleeve cutting line. Transfer the balance marks on the sleeve crown and the front of the sleeve cap.

Cut out the new patterns.

Cutting out

Select the appropriate layout for your size and fabric width from the layouts in this chapter.

You will need extra seam allowance to underlay the topstitching. The topstitching should be $\frac{3}{8}$ inch wider than the zipper on each side of it. To calculate the seam allowance needed for the center front, first measure the width across the zipper tape and divide it in half, then add $\frac{3}{8}$ inch to this measurement and another $\frac{1}{4}$ inch. The seam allowance around the neck edge is not affected because the facing will act as an underlay.

Allow $1\frac{1}{2}$ inches for the sleeve hems and $2\frac{1}{2}$ inches for the tunic hem; these allowances will underlay the topstitching when the hems have been turned up.

Cut the front facing $1\frac{1}{2}$ inches longer than the front opening. For a $\frac{7}{8}$ inch wide zipper, allow 1 inch seam allowance along the center front. But if your zipper is wider, you must add the extra width to the seam allowance.

Allow $\frac{3}{4}$ inch seam allowance on the other edges.

Allow $\frac{3}{4}$ inches for the other seams.

Cut out the fabric.

Mark all details on the fabric and remove the patterns.

Lining the tunic

To enable the tunic to sit well it should be lined, especially if you are using a woolen fabric.

Cut the lining back and front as for the tunic, but do not add any seam allowance

190

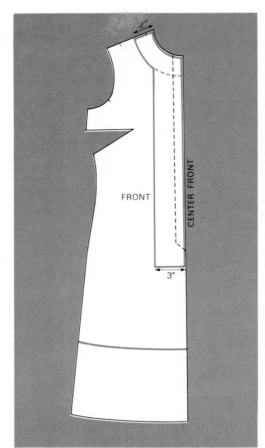

▲ **2.** *Front : hem and facing cutting lines*
▼ **3.** *Back : hem and facing cutting lines*

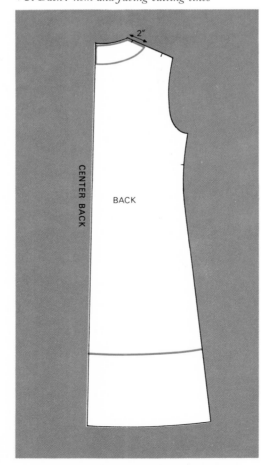

to the neck edge or along the center front from the neck to the end of the zipper opening.

You will not need any lining facings, and it is not necessary to line the sleeves.

Interfacing

The neck edge of the tunic needs the support of a soft cotton interfacing.

For the back neck interfacing pattern use the back facing pattern. To make the front neck interfacing pattern, cut the front facing pattern piece along the red dotted line shown in figure **2** and just use the neck section.

Fold the interfacing fabric and place the back and front interfacing pattern pieces on the double fabric with the center back on the fold.

Add $\frac{3}{4}$ inch seam allowance all around and cut out.

Fitting

Pin and baste all darts, shoulder and side seams and press lightly.

Pin and baste the center front seam from the end of the opening to the hem and press lightly.

Fold under the seam allowance along the opening and pin and baste in the zipper.

Pin and baste the sleeve seams and then pin and baste the sleeves to the bodice.

Turn up the sleeve and tunic hems.

Fit the tunic over the pants since the thickness of the pants fabric will affect the tunic fitting at the hipline.

If you are going to wear a belt with the tunic, it is essential to put one on at the fitting because the hemline may be affected. Look at the hem and proportioning again when the belt is on.

If any alterations to the tunic are necessary, read the alteration instructions for the basic dress in Dressmaking chapter 32 and make the necessary corrections.

After you have checked and corrected all fitting faults, remove the sleeves and the zipper, and rip the shoulder and side seams.

You are now ready for stitching.

Making the tunic

Before you start to work, here is an outline of the steps:

- ☐ Making the front
- ☐ Inserting the zipper
- ☐ Joining the back and front ready for facing
- ☐ Stitching on the interfacing and facing
- ☐ Topstitching the center front and neckline
- ☐ Stitching side seams, sleeves and making hems
- ☐ Finishing
- ☐ Lining the tunic

Making the front

Stitch and press the side bust darts flat or open. Also stitch the body darts, if you are using them, and press them toward the center.

Stitch the center front seam from the zipper opening to the hem.

Pin and baste the seamline for the zipper opening. Finish the raw edges of the seam allowance along the center front and remove all traces of the tailor's tacks.

Press the seam.

Leave the opening basted together.

Inserting the zipper

First, a word about the zipper. A heavy zipper may be used but it is not necessary. The Golden Hands tunic has an ordinary dress zipper which gives a neat, flat finish with the decorative seaming. Very heavy brass zippers are not suitable for this type of opening as they have to be inserted in such a way that the zipper teeth remain showing and are not hidden under the seam edges.

The zipper is stitched in a special way so that you can quickly and easily replace it if it should break.

Pin the closed zipper carefully over the seamline with the center of the teeth in line with the basted opening, starting about ¾ inch down from the neck seamline. Baste the zipper in place working very close to the zipper teeth.

Hand sew the zipper to the seam allowance only, working along the center of the zipper tape. Use a small, firm backstitch and make sure that you do not sew through to the outside of the garment.

To insure that the zipper stays in position, sew the outer edge of the zipper tape to the seam allowance with felling stitches.

Trim the loose ends of the tape at the top of the zipper to ½ inch. Turn them back and hand sew down.

Press the zipper lightly, covering it with a cloth to protect it from too much heat.

Joining the back and front ready for facing

Stitch and press the back darts.

Pin, baste and stitch the shoulder seams, finish the edges and press open.

Stitching on interfacing and facing

The interfacing. To join the back and front neck interfacing pieces at the shoulder seams, lay one front interfacing piece over the corresponding end of the back interfacing so that the shoulder seams coincide (figure **4**).

Pin and stitch with two rows of stitching. Join the other front interfacing piece similarly.

This method insures a minimum of bulk.

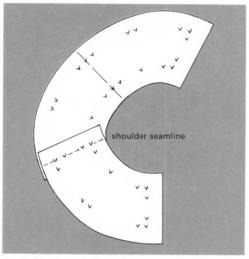

▲ **4.** *The interfacing joined at the shoulder seam*

Pin and baste the interfacing to the wrong side of the tunic along the neck seamline, matching center backs and shoulder seams.

Trim off the interfacing seam allowance at the center front edge and push the front ends under the center front seam allowance of the tunic so that it meets the folded seamline. Rip as much of the basting at the center front opening as is necessary.

To hold the center front edge of the interfacing in place, it is best to hand sew it lightly to the seamline with loose catch stitches.

The facing. Stitch the back and front facings together in the shoulder seams and press the seams open.

If you are not lining the tunic, finish the inner raw edge of the facing.

The facing is stitched to the neck edge only at this stage.

Pin and baste the facing to the neck edge of the tunic, with right sides facing, center backs and shoulder seams matching. Unfold the seam allowance on the center front of the tunic so that you can attach the ends of the facing.

Stitch on the facing along the neckline.

To allow the neck edge to lie flat after the facing has been turned into the tunic, the seam allowance along the stitched neck edge needs layering.

First, cut back the seam allowance on the interfacing to ⅛ inch, then the seam allowance on the facing to ¼ inch, and the seam allowance on the tunic to ½ inch.

Snip into the neck seam allowance at the curves.

Turn under the center front seam allowance of the tunic again, then turn under the seam allowance of the neck facing and turn the facing to the inside of the tunic. Edge-baste along the neckline and press lightly.

Trim the interfacing ½ inch shorter than the facing and attach it to the underside of the facing with long catch stitches. This will prevent it from gathering up during wear and cleaning.

Fold in the seam allowance along the center front of the facing ⅛ inch inside the stitching line, tapering into the original stitching line at the neck edge to avoid the seam pulling away from the zipper when it it closed. Pin, baste and press lightly.

Lay the facing over the zipper so that the folded edges are ⅛ inch apart (except at the neck edge where they meet) and do not fully cover the zipper teeth. Pin and baste in place through all layers of fabric.

Topstitching the center front and neckline

Topstitching the tunic has to be done in two stages; the center front and neck edge are worked first while the dress is still open in the side seams and the area is easily accessible. The sleeve and hem topstitching is worked after the hems are sewn.

First, where you have ripped the basting at the center front opening, rebaste.

To find the starting point for the topstitching to the left of the center front seam, measure the stitching width up from the hemline and in from the center front. Mark this point with a pin.

Next mark the width of the topstitching at the top left of the center front to find the point where you pivot the work on the needle to stitch around the neckline. Mark the right side in the same way.

▼ **5.** *Detail of the topstitching on the tunic*

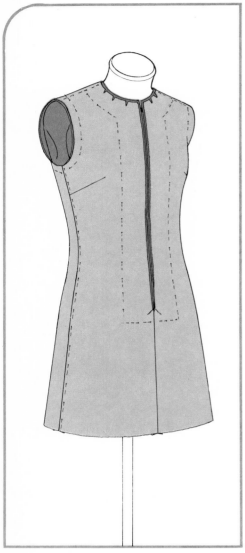

▲ **6.** *Pinning the lining before sewing to the facing*

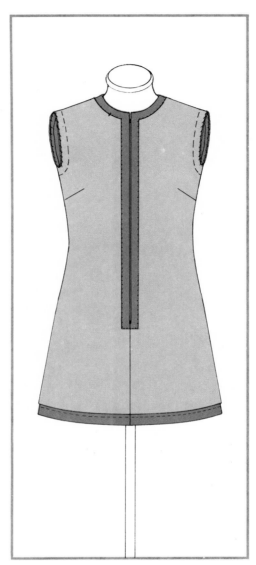

▲ **7.** *The finished lining in the tunic*

or if the neckline were closer fitting, you don't have to fasten the top of the front opening with a hook and bar. The corners are well supported by facing and interfacing and should not collapse.

With a few stitches, catch the loose edges of the facing to the seam allowance at the shoulder seams and the lower center front.

Lining the tunic

To make the lining, first stitch the darts. Press the side bust darts down, and the shoulder and body darts (if you are using them) towards the center.

Stitch the shoulder and side seams and the center front seam from the end of the front opening to the hem.

Finish the seam allowance on the side seams only. Press all the seams open.

The simplest way to attach the lining is to use a dress stand for which instructions are given here, but even if you do not have a stand, follow the same working procedure.

Turn the tunic inside out and slip it over the stand.

Slip the lining over the tunic, right side out, with the lining and tunic seams facing. Pin the lining to the tunic along the side, shoulder and armhole seams (figure **6**).

Feel the edge of the facing through the lining and pin the lining close to the edge as shown.

Make snips $\frac{5}{8}$ inch deep around the curve of the neck edge and turn this edge under by $\frac{3}{4}$ inch. Pin the folded edge to the facing. At the lower end of the lining center front opening, make a diagonal snip $\frac{3}{4}$ inch deep on each side of the center front seam as shown.

Turn under the raw edges for $\frac{3}{4}$ inch along the center front and across the lower end of the lining opening and pin. The lower end should now be neatly squared off around the zipper fastening.

Slip stitch the lining to the facing (figure **7**) and press flat with a warm iron.

Sew the lining to the armhole seam with long running stitches and finish the raw edges of tunic and lining as one.

Make the lining hem 1 inch shorter than the dress hem.

Since the lining in the tunic is short and some lining fabrics hold a lot of static electricity which makes them ride up, it is best to catch the lining to the tunic in places.

Make a 1 inch long French tack just above the hem of the lining on each side seam and fasten it to the tunic side seams.

To make a French tack. Work a bar as shown in Skirtmaking chapter 14, attaching one end to the lining and the other end to the tunic.

Work the center front and neck topstitching in one operation. Work from the starting point to the left of the center front, stitch up to and around the neck, then down the right side.

Draw the thread ends to the inside of the garment at the hemline and fasten them off securely. Remove the basting at the center front opening.

Stitching side seams, sleeves and making hems

Pin, baste and stitch the side seams. Finish the seam allowance and press the seams open.

Pin, baste and stitch the sleeve seams. Finish the seam allowance and press the seams open.

Turn up each sleeve hem and finish the raw edge. Sew the sleeve hems with an invisible hemming stitch.

Ease in the fullness around the sleeve crown with gathering stitches and set the sleeves into the armholes of the tunic. When you

stitch them in, don't forget to work with the sleeve uppermost.

Finish the seam allowance around the armholes if you are not lining the tunic.

Turn up the tunic hem and sew with an invisible hemming stitch.

Finishing

To topstitch around the hem of the tunic, start on the right of the center front seam, inserting the needle into the last stitch of the topstitching. Work your way around the hem to meet the topstitching to the left of the center front so that you have a continuous row of topstitching.

The sleeve hems are also topstitched. Measure the stitching width from the hemline, start at the sleeve seam and work around each hem.

Fasten off all threads securely on the inside. Figure **5** shows the completed topstitching in detail.

Since there is no strain on the neckline as there would be on a center back fastening,

Layouts for the tunic

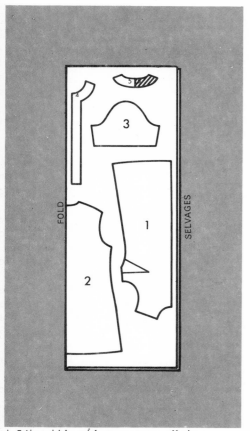

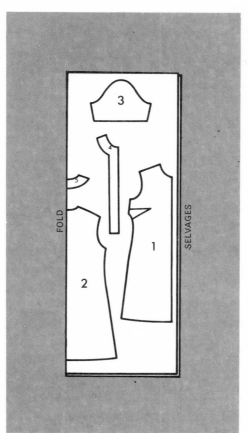

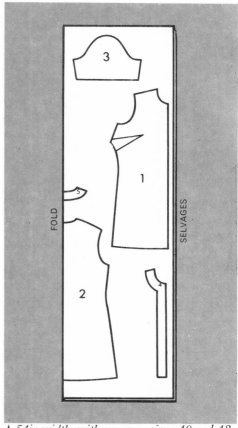

▲ *54in width, without one way, all sizes* ▲ *54in width, with one way, sizes 32½ to 38* ▲ *54in width, with one way, sizes 40 and 42*

▼ *36in width, without one way, sizes 32½ and 34*

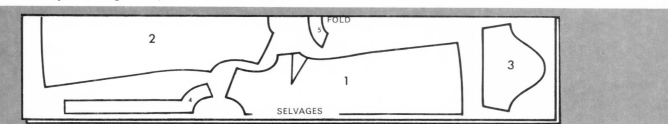

▼ *36in width, without one way, sizes 36, 38, 40 and 42*

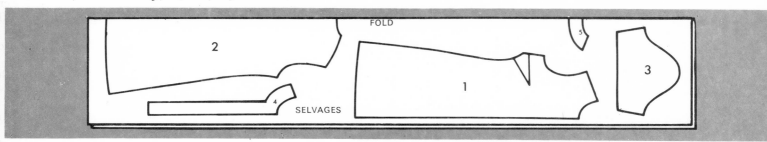

▼ *36in width, with one way, all sizes*

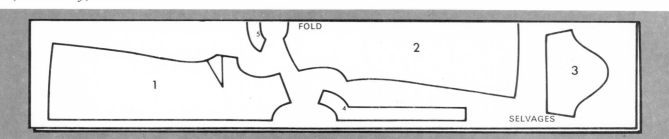

Chapter 43

Pants pattern variations

To keep you in step with the changing shapes in fashion, Golden Hands has set to work on the basic pants from the Graph Pages and shows you how simple it is to adapt the pattern to a variety of pants shapes. You can then add your own ideas to each style, such as pockets in the side seams or patch pockets for a more sporty look.

The fastening, too, can be changed from Center Front to side seam or Center Back and, if you choose a stretchy knit for your pants, you can dispense with an opening altogether. To do this, leave out the darts and add extra seam allowance at the waist edge to make a casing for a band of elastic. Nothing could be simpler!

This chapter gives all the patterns for the pants variations sketched on this page together with ideas for suitable fabrics for the individual styles. The instructions for making them follow in the next chapter.

Suitable fabrics

Pants can, of course, be made in just about every conceivable fabric, but the shape of the pants is a very important consideration when choosing the cloth. Here is a list of suitable fabrics, given for each version in turn, giving you a guide to the qualities to look out for rather than naming the fabric itself. This is done because these qualities are found in so many different types of fabric.

A. Pants with cuffs
Use any fabric which is suited to tailoring and will hold a crease, such as the fabrics suggested for the basic pants in Pantsmaking chapter 41.

B. Flared pants
These pants have no creases and therefore can be made in most soft fabrics. On the other hand they will also look stunning in stiff fabrics, like brocade, which will hold out the fullness.
If you use a very fine fabric make sure that you cut the pattern really wide to prevent strain on the seams.

C. Shorts
Since the seams in fitted shorts have to withstand a lot of strain, make sure that the fabric you choose is firmly woven, even if it is soft. For crisp tailored shorts use a fabric which will hold the creases, but if you make them very brief, knits and other soft fabrics are ideal.

D. Bermudas
True Bermuda shorts are for sunshine wear and should therefore be made in firmly woven printed cottons. But for an eye-catching

▲ *The pants versions from left to right:* **C.** *shorts;* **D.** *Bermudas*

effect, make Bermuda shorts to go with a long button-down skir in a firmly woven silk for evening wear.

E. Cossacks and knickers
The most suitable fabrics are soft tweeds, knitted or jersey fabrics These give you a soft fullness and most of them are sufficiently crease resistant to avoid collapse.

F. Gaucho pants
This is a type of pants-skirt, and your fabric choice depends on the look you want to achieve.
If you want to retain the true gaucho peasant look and the original ity of the garment, use a coarse-weave fabric. However, if you wan a more skirt-like or tailored appearance, they can be made in othe fabrics, such as the tailoring fabrics mentioned for the cuffe pants, version A.
A word of caution when buying fabrics for gaucho pants—the look very ugly when they lose their shape, so make very sure that the fabric you choose is crease resistant.

The pattern

It is best to make a separate pattern for each version. So if you want to make a pants wardrobe, have plenty of paper available for pattern making.
For each version you are going to make, first copy the basic pants pattern shape including any necessary alterations as show in Pantsmaking chapter 41.
Copy the pattern full length for the long pants and up to the

E. knickers; **A.** *pants with cuffs;* **F.** *gaucho pants and* **B.** *flared pants showing the full flare version*

knee if you intend to make one of the short styles.

A. Pants with cuffs

Straighten the pants legs from just below the knee to the hem (figure **1**).

Calculate the depth of the cuff. This depends on the thickness of the fabric you are using; make it 1½ inches for a fine fabric and 2 inches for a heavy or bulky fabric as heavy fabric tends to create a roll rather than a fold if the cuff is too narrow.

Mark out the roll lines for the cuffs as follows: one cuff depth between hemline and first roll line, one depth plus ¼ inch between first and second roll line, and then add the hem allowance, which should be just slightly less than the depth of the cuffs. Mark the roll lines on both Back and Front pattern pieces and continue the crease lines to the bottom.

Write "hem allowance" on the pattern to avoid confusion when cutting.

B. Flared pants

The pattern can be made for a hem flare, full flare, and a very full flare. With all versions, make sure that you add enough length because flared pants look best when they are very long.

Hem flare. For a hemline flare, start the flare at knee level (figure **2**).

Full flare. First decide on how wide you want the pants legs to be. Then straighten the inside leg seams by drawing a straight line from the end of the Back and Front crotch seams to the hem (figure **3**). This line should run parallel to the straight of the grain or crease line.

Add the rest of the required width to the outside leg seams, starting

to extend them from hip level down as shown.

Very full flare. If you want the pants to be exceptionally full, you can also add more width to the inside leg seam. But for very full pants it is also necessary to add a little more ease to the crotch seams (see detail figure **3**), because a tightly fitting crotch causes the full pants legs to flap and not move easily with the movement of the body.

C. Shorts

Draw a straight line across the pattern 2 inches below the crotch seam (figure **4**). Then decide on the shape of the shorts, whether you want them straight across the legs or tapered up toward the outside leg seams.

If you like them tapered, raise the straight line at the side seam about 1½ inches and connect this to the point 2 inches below the crotch seam as shown by the dash line on the diagram.

Because the hem allowance for both versions has to be shaped (figure **5**), you will need to include it on the pattern. So add 1½ inches hem allowance below the line on both pattern pieces. To shape the hem allowance correctly, turn the hem allowance under the pattern, folding along the hemline, and pin it firmly in position. Then cut out the shorts pattern, cutting through the turned under hem allowance at the side seams. Unpin the hemline and you will have cut the correct shape of the seamline through the hem.

Mark this area "hem allowance" on the pattern to avoid confusion when cutting.

D. Bermudas

To determine the correct length for Bermuda shorts measure the length of your thighs from just above the knee where the leg bends. Also measure the circumference of the leg at this point.

Draw a straight line across the pattern to the measurement of the leg (figure 6), and to make the shorts fit your legs closely taper the inside and outside leg-seams equally into the hem line on both Back and Front pattern pieces as shown so that they add up to your leg width measurement plus 2 inches for ease.

Here, as for the shorts C, the hem allowance needs to be added to the pattern and shaped at the seams, so follow the previous instructions for doing so.

E. Cossacks and knickers

To be really smart these pants should fit quite close around the hips and upper thighs, with the fullness starting halfway between hip line and knee and caught in at a length of your own choosing. Draw a straight line across the pattern about 3 to 4 inches below the crotch (figure 7).

Measure the length you want the pants to be and draw a straight line across the pattern to this measurement. Then straighten each leg-seam between these straight lines, starting at the top and continuing the width all the way down as shown.

The fullness at the bottom can be caught in with elastic, for the cossacks, or with buttoned cuffs for the knickers.

For the elastic casing pattern draw a rectangle $\frac{3}{4}$ inches wide to the length of the pants hem edge. On the pattern mark the length to be cut on the cross of the fabric.

If you want cuffs make a pattern for them as shown (figure 8). First measure round your leg where you want the pants to end. Then make the pattern 2 inches wide to this length plus 2 inches for ease and 2 inches for a wrap. 1 inch of the wrap goes to each end. This will give you a cuff 1 inch wide.

On the top half of the cuff pattern mark the buttonhole position 1 inch in from the end and $\frac{1}{2}$ inch down from upper edge. Mark the pattern to be cut on the straight of grain of the fabric.

Here's a good tip if you intend to wear short boots. Dispense with the cuffs, buy a pair of stretch socks and sew the ends of the pants legs to the tops of the socks, which will keep them firmly in place.

F. Gaucho pants

Gaucho pants are really only short flared pants, but they should not be so wide that they hang in folds.

So straighten the inside leg-seam and add flare only to the outside leg seam so that the finished pants hang in a nice round flare. Make them about 35 to 40 inches around each leg (figure 9). The length is something of a personal choice, so decide on the length you want them and shorten the pattern accordingly.

Yardage and cutting out

You can follow the basic layout guide for most of the pants versions, with the exception of the flared styles. For those and to work out the yardage for all styles, follow the tips given in Know-How chapter 46 for making your own layouts.

The Golden Hands pants pattern has no seam allowance so remember to add $\frac{3}{4}$ inch seam allowance all around. Also remember to add hem allowance of at least 3 inches unless allowance has been included on the pattern as in versions A, C and D.

Before cutting your pants remember that the pattern has ease built in to suit ordinary thicknesses of fabric. If you use extra thick fabric it becomes essential with pants cutting that the ease be slightly increased. This is done by simply cutting slightly more seam allowance then, when you mark around the pattern on the fabric, remember to add on the additional ease. This can then be adjusted at the fitting.

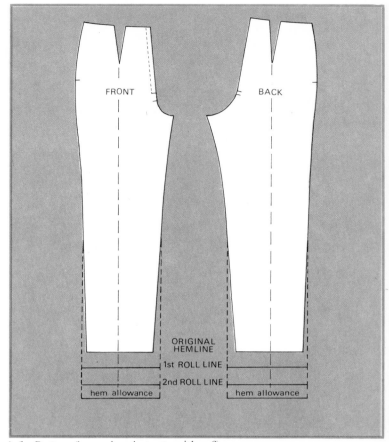

▲ **1.** *Pattern for version A. pants with cuffs*
▼ *Patterns for version B. flared pants* **2.** *Hem flare* **3.** *Full flare and very full flare showing detail of the crotch-seams extended*

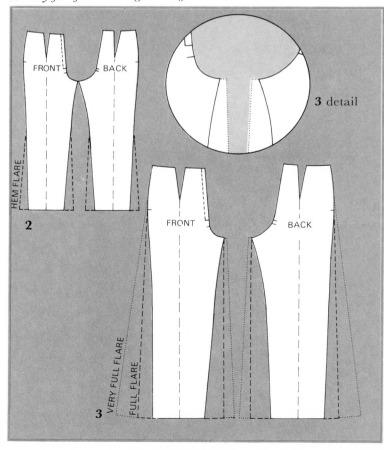

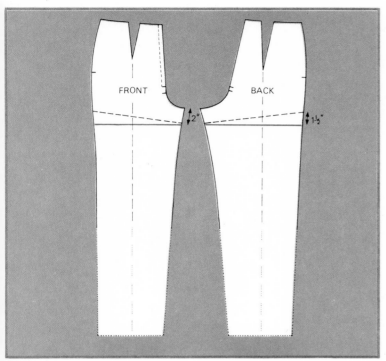

▲ **4.** *Making the pattern for version C. shorts*
▼ **5.** *Finished pattern for the shorts showing the shaped hem allowance*

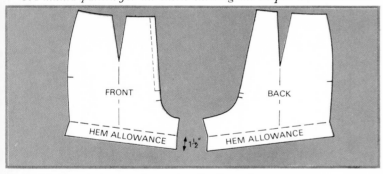

▼ **6.** *Making the pattern for version D. Bermudas*

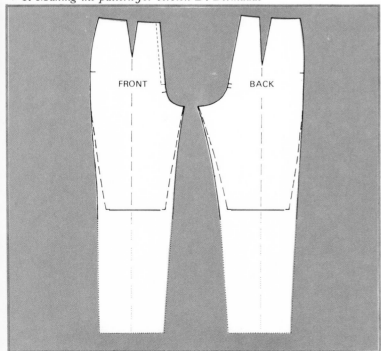

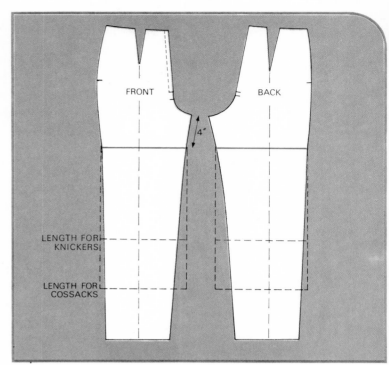

▲ **7.** *Pattern for version E. cossack pants or knickers*
▼ **8.** *The cuff pattern for the cossack pants or knickers*

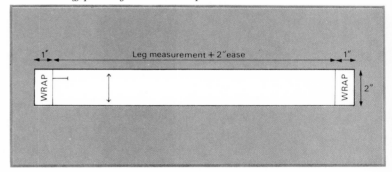

▼ **9.** *Pattern for version F. gaucho pants*

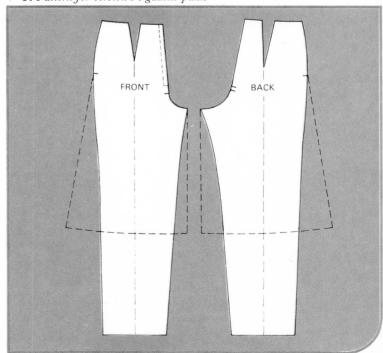

Chapter 44

Making the pants

In this chapter the pants versions are made. Before cutting, make sure that all necessary personal figure adjustments have been incorporated in the adapted pattern pieces. Fitting and instructions for making are the same as those for the basic pants in Pantsmaking chapters 41 and 42, except where the style requires special techniques for perfect results.

A. Pants with cuffs

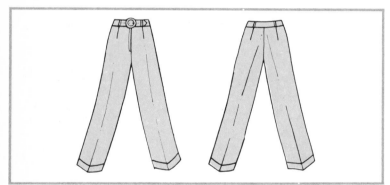

When you come to these hems, make each cuff as follows: Fold under the fabric for the cuff on the first roll line (figure **1**, a and b) and baste in position.

Turn the pants inside out and press the edge of the cuff carefully on the outside fabric using a pressing cloth to avoid marking the fabric (figure **2**). Do not put the pant leg over a sleeveboard. This would stretch the outside fabric which folds to the inside of the cuff when it is finished and cause it to pucker.

Remove the basting stitches and carefully press again.

Pin the edge to prevent it from moving. Turn the pants to the right side and turn the folded edge over the outside of the pants legs, folding along the original hemline (figure **1**, c). Hold in place with long basting stitches.

Then use the second roll line and turn under the hem allowance (figure **1**, d). Pin and baste firmly in place.

Press the folded edge lightly from the inside and finish the raw edge.

Hand sew the hem to the pants with small firm felling or catch stitches.

Finishing the hems in this way will inevitably make an impression on the outside of the fabric, but pants with cuffs need to be stitched very securely at the hems. However, the stitches will not show because the hem allowances were cut slightly narrower than the cuffs, so the hem edges are below the top edges of the cuffs and are therefore hidden.

To hold the cuffs in position, make a small bar tack at each side seam.

198

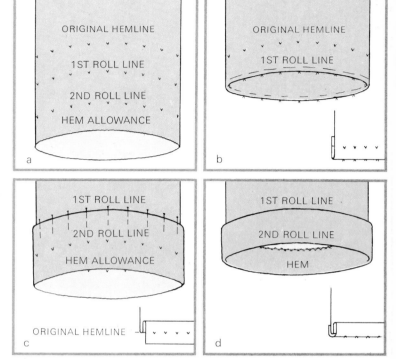

▲ **1.** *Stages in folding the hem edge for the pants with cuffs*

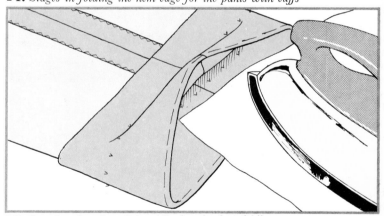

▲ **2.** *Pressing the edge of the cuff after the first folding*

Remove all basting stitches.

Press the cuffs, then press in the pants creases which are continued over the cuffs. Use a double thickness of the pressing cloth to avoid shiny pressing marks.

B. Flared pants

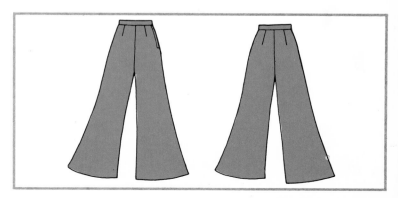

The hemline needs to be checked with care and it is best to do it with the help of a friend so that you can stand straight.

As the length of flared pants is a very important factor, make sure you wear shoes with the right height of heel for the fitting. You should not press creases into flared pants.

C. Shorts

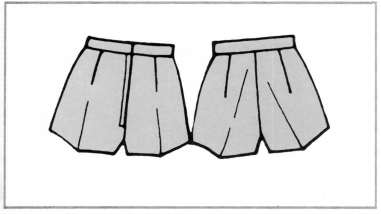

If you like your shorts to fit tightly, make sure that you move when fitting them. If the basting stitches split, take that as an indication of too much strain and allow a little more ease, or the stitched seams will first distort and then eventually split.

Tight fitting shorts are often uncomfortable to sit in. A 1½ inch slit in both side seams at the hemline will ease that and also look attractive.

To make each slit, stitch the side seam to within 3 inches of the hem edge and fasten off the thread securely. Leave the remainder of the seam basted.

Finish off the seam allowance and press the seam open. Do not snip into the seam allowance at the hem where it was cut to follow the shape of the side seam, but press into the corners, ironing from both directions to avoid pressing through the strained part, and thereby causing creases on the outside (figure **3**).

Turn up the hem and hand sew in place.

Rip the basting stitches at the end of the side seam and invisibly hand sew the folded edges of the seam allowance in place on each side of the seam to leave a slit opening (figure **4**).

Work a bar across the top of the slit to strengthen the seam at this point. You can work the bar on either the outside or the inside.

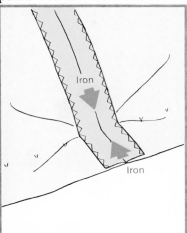

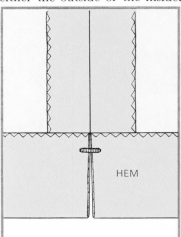

▲**3.** *Pressing the seam allowance on the hem edge of the shorts*

▲**4.** *The finished slit on the side seam of the shorts*

The hem flare version of the flared pants made in smooth crepe ▶

199

Shorts can be very rough in the crotch since here there are not only seams crossing, but also the seam allowances in each hem, creating extra thickness.

To protect the body from being chafed at this point, cover the seam allowances with a piece of soft fabric. Cut an elongated diamond about 3 inches long and 2½ inches wide, with the center of the diamond in the straight of the grain. Finish the raw edges and place the center of the diamond over the seams where they cross as shown (figure 5), with the shallow points of the diamond into each leg. Hand sew the diamond to all seam and hem allowances where it touches them. The shorts are pressed with or without creases, depending on your choice of fabric.

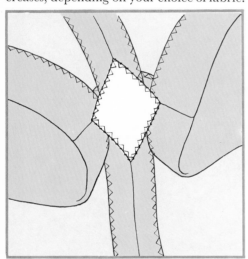

▲ 5. *The diamond sewn into the crotch on the shorts*

D. Bermudas

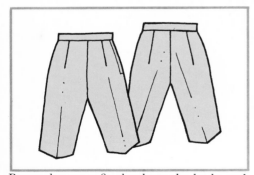

Bermudas must fit closely to the body and the legs. But, as with the shorts, you must be careful that the close fitting does not restrict your movement.

When you are turning up the hems, you may find that some fabrics will not roll sufficiently to avoid a kink where the seams go through the hemline. If so, straighten the seams a little.

Creases are not usually pressed into Bermudas except on occasions when they are cut straight.

200

E. Cossacks & knickers

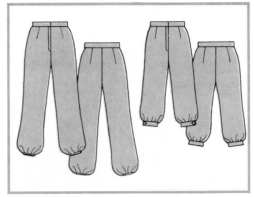

Here's a style pointer. Knickers finish just below the knee and often have a cuff—cossacks are mid-calf to ankle length with an elasticized hem edge.

At the fitting, draw up the hemline of each pant leg into gathers (or pleats if the fabric is difficult to gather) to check if the length is correct. After checking the length, cut back the hem allowance to ¾ inch.

Elasticized hemline. If you are finishing the hem edges with elastic, and the fabric you are using to make the pants is thick, cut the casings from a length of matching cotton sateen. This is a much neglected fabric, but its usefulness in dressmaking and tailoring is unlimited. Since most tailoring fabrics need heat when pressing, which ordinary lining fabrics will not take, the ability of cotton sateen to withstand heat is ideal. In addition, it is crisp but it has a smooth surface at the same time. On the casing strips, trim the seam allowance to ½ inch, turn in and baste.

Pin under the allowance on the hemline of each pant leg and baste. On each pant leg, pin one folded edge of the casing to the wrong side of the pant leg ⅛ inch above the folded hemline edge, with the ends of the casing meeting over the inside leg seam.

Baste in place, then edge-stitch to the folded edge of the hemline.

Carefully trim the seam allowance on the pants under the casing so that it is slightly less than the casing seam allowance. Pin and baste the upper edge of the casing to the pants and edge-stitch in place. Slot elastic through the opening, overlap the ends of the elastic and sew them together. Slip stitch the opening to close it.

Cuffed hem edge. Rip each outside leg seam at the hem edge for 2½ inches to make an opening. Work a small, strong hand-made bar across the top of the opening on the outside or the inside, then sew the seam allowance on the inside of the opening to the pants (figure 6). Gather in the fullness at the hem edge or

make small pleats of equal depth if the fabric is difficult to gather. Make a row of machine stitches in the seam allowance over the pleats to hold them in place. Press them in the seam allowance only. You will need only one cuff piece for each cuff. Fold each cuff piece lengthwise and stitch as shown (figure 7). Then stitch the cuffs to the hemline of the

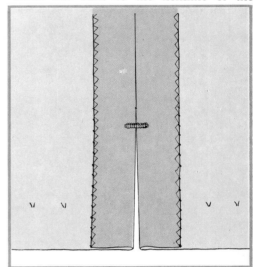

▲ 6. *The bar worked at the top of the leg opening*

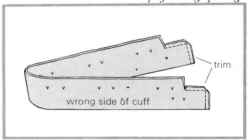

▲ 7. *The stitched cuff for knickers*

pants as for the shirt cuffs in Blousemaking chapter 28, except that you leave a wrap on each end of the pants cuffs. Then make the buttonholes. These must be in line with the back edge of the opening. Sew a button on each cuff.

F. Gaucho pants

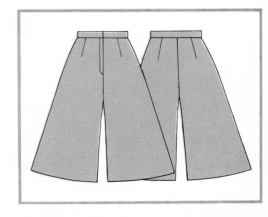

Fit the pants carefully, trying them on in front of a long mirror.

The pants legs should hang softly and without any strain toward the center of the crotch. Take a few steps toward the mirror. The pants legs should move in an easy movement with the legs and not show any drag. If there is drag, let out the crotch seam back and front, which means that you must also let out the inside leg seams.

Gaucho pants are worn without creases and the hem should create a rounded effect. You may have to help the fabric a little to retain this shape by interlining the hems. This trick can also be applied to skirt and dress hems.

For each hem, cut a bias strip of soft cotton interlining 2½ inches wide and the length of the hem edge, plus seam allowance. Press under ½ inch along one long edge of the strip to give a sharp fold line. Pin and baste the fold to the hemline as shown (figure **8**) with the ends overlapping slightly on the inside leg seam.

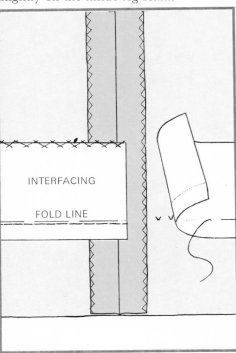

INTERFACING

FOLD LINE

▲ **8.** *The interlined hem edge of the gaucho pants*

Prick stitch the interlining to the pants, catching one or two threads from the outside fabric into each stitch, working just outside the hemline and the fold line of the interlining as shown.

Attach the upper, raw edge of the interlining to the pants fabric with loosely worked catch stitches.

Pin and baste the hem allowance over the interlining and finish as you would a skirt hem.

Cossack pants made in double knit ►

Chapter 45

Making hipster pants

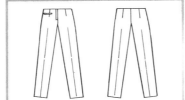

These hipster pants are a Graph Pattern adaptation. They are made in exactly the same way as the basic pants, except for the waist edge which is finished with a facing, and the addition of a bound pocket.

Suitable fabrics
Hipsters should be made in a firmly woven fabric which holds its shape well since they have to fit really close to the body.

Making the pattern
How low you wear the hipsters depends on the shape of your figure. The greater the difference between waist and hip measurement the more daring you can afford to be, but the pants will be most comfortable if they rest on the hipbone. These instructions are for the average figure shape and the pants are made to sit 3 inches below the waistline.

Use your favorite pants pattern, flared or straight, and find the position for the new waistline. Following the waistline curve on the pattern carefully, draw in the new waistline 3 inches below the original (figure 1) and cut off the surplus.

To check that the new waist measurement is correct, measure yourself 3 inches below your natural waistline, add 1 inch to the measurement for ease and compare it to the new pattern waistline. Take any surplus into the darts and the side seams.

Taper each alteration line into the original line of the darts and seams at hip level. Do not alter the shape of the Center Front and the Center Back except for reasons of fitting.

You will also need facing patterns but these are left till the garment has been fitted and all adjustments made.

Make and fit the pants, except for the waist edge, as for the basic pants in Pantsmaking chapters 41 and 42.

Making a bound pocket
This bound pocket is a simplified version of a tailored pocket and can be made very quickly. The pocket is set right through the dart and should be made before you finish the waist edge.

Mark the pocket position on one pant Front, 1½ inches below the waistline, 3 inches from Center Front and 3½ inches long (figure 2).

Underlaying the pocket. First, underlay the pocket opening with a strip of soft interfacing 1½ inches wide and 4½ inches long, cut on the straight of grain.

Pin and baste the strip to the inside of the Front over the pocket position and mark the pocket position on the underlay (figure 3).

Binding the pocket. The pocket binding and the front lining of the pocket are cut in one. For this you will need a piece of pants

fabric 5½ inches wide by 6¾ inches long, cut on the crosswise grain of the fabric.

Mark the position of the pocket on the binding 1½ inches from the upper edge, then pin the binding to the pants, right sides facing, as shown (figure 4). Baste in place.

Working on the pocket underlay, make two rows of stitches the length of the opening and ¼ inch to each side of it (figure 5).

Following figure 6, cut the pocket opening between the stitching lines through all the layers of fabric as shown. Pull the binding through the opening and press the seam allowances away from the opening.

Roll the top of the binding down and the bottom up so that the binding meets at the center of the opening to form the bound edge (figure 7). Baste in position as shown, then make small prick stitches along both seamlines, working from the front and stitching through all layers of fabric. Press and then remove the basting.

Lift the pocket lining so that you can get at the seam allowance at the lower edge of the pocket opening, then stitch the seam allowance to the pocket lining close to the seamline.

Carefully baste the bound edges of the pocket together on the right side (figure 8), first pushing the unstitched ends under with the point of the needle to form a neat corner at each end.

Turn the work to the wrong side and stitch the loose triangular end at each side of the opening to the rolled edges (figure 9).

Use a one-sided zipper foot so that you can work very close to the fold line at the sides of the pockets to secure the corners firmly.

Completing the pocket lining. The pocket back lining is taken into the waist seam for extra support, so cut a piece of pants fabric 5½ inches wide by 7¼ inches long, on the straight grain of the fabric.

Pin it to the pocket front lining, to cover the bound edges and to reach the seam allowances at the waist edge (figure 10).

Stitch the seam allowance of the upper bound edge to the binding and pocket back lining close to the seam.

Stitch the pocket linings together around the edges (figure 11).

On the outside of the pocket hand-work a small bar at each end of the opening to avoid strain on the corners of the pocket.

Making the facings for the waist edge
If you have made any alterations to the waistline during fitting, transfer these to the pattern.

Pin the darts on the pattern. Lay the upper section of the Center Front and Back to the straight edge of a sheet of paper and pin. Draw around the waist and side seam edges of the pattern to obtain the facings, then make them 2 inches deep as shown (figure 12).

Cut out the facings from double fabric, placing the Center Back on the fold and cutting the Center Fronts with seam allowance.

The waist edge also needs the support of an interfacing and stiff canvas is recommended for this. Cut out the interfacings as for the facings but without seam allowance along the lower edges. Overlap and stitch the side seams of the interfacing. Then, after the zipper is stitched in place, pin and baste the interfacing to the inside edge of the waistline of the pants.

Trim the Center Front edges of the interfacing so that they can be pushed under the seam allowance of the pants. Hand-sew the interfacing to the darts and seam allowances of the pants.

Stitch and press the side seams of the facing.

With right sides together, pin and baste the facing to the waist edge of the pants and stitch in position.

Trim the seam allowance, turn the facing to the inside, edge baste and press. Sew the facing to the zipper tape in the usual way.

For extra strength, and to stop the facing from rolling out during wear, topstitch the pants ¼ inch from the waist edge.

Finish lower facing edge and hand-sew lightly to seams and darts. Fasten the opening at the top with a strong hook and eye (figure 13).

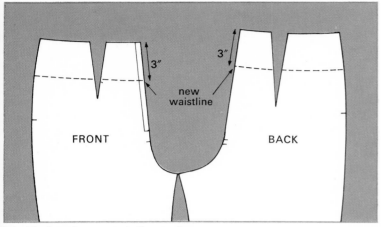

▲ **1.** *Finding the new waistline on the pattern*

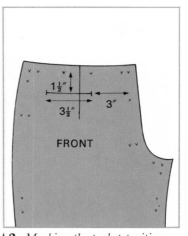

▲ **2.** *Marking the pocket position*

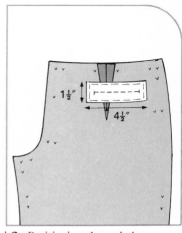

▲ **3.** *Positioning the underlay*

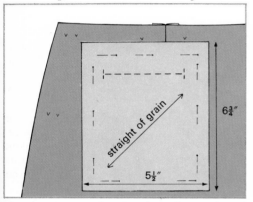

▲ **4.** *The binding pinned to the pocket opening*

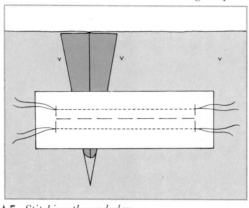

▲ **5.** *Stitching the underlay*

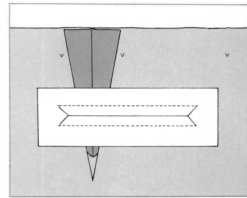

▲ **6.** *Cutting the pocket opening*

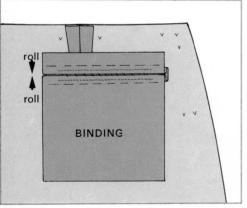

▲ **7.** *Meeting the binding at the opening center*

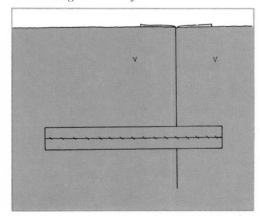

▲ **8.** *The basted, bound edges, corners neatened*

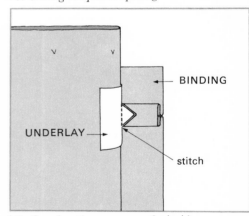

▲ **9.** *Securing the corners on the inside*

▼ **10.** *Pocket back lining pinned on*

▼ **11.** *Stitching the pocket linings*

▼ **12.** *Making the facings*

▼ **13.** *The finished front opening*

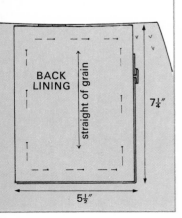

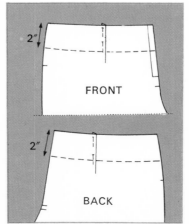

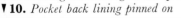

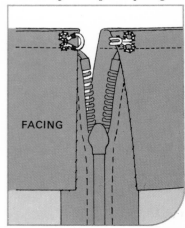

Chapter 46

Making your own layouts

Know-How

Many dressmakers approach pattern layouts with apprehension, thinking that specialized knowledge is required to do them. But good layouts are only the result of using common sense to make the maximum use of the minimum of fabric.

Commercial paper patterns always come with layouts which are based on the yardages quoted on the envelope. These layouts are only a guide and do not take into consideration any individual alterations that might be necessary, such as the length or other special allowances. Usually, commercial paper patterns allow extra yardage as a built-in safety margin, so you may find that in many cases you may save a little money by working out your own yardage requirements. This chapter gives you a very easy formula for doing this, and explains the various kinds of layouts.

Quick yardage calculations

The most important things to know when calculating yardage are the width of each pattern piece at its widest part and the folded width of the fabric.

Back and Front. The width of these pattern pieces will tell you if you can cut both front halves and/or both back halves from one width ór if you will need more fabric to cut them out separately.

Sleeve. You must also take into consideration the type of sleeve you have to cut. On the narrower fabrics, most sleeves will take up the full folded width even if they are fitted. So check to see if the pattern is wider at the hem than the half fabric width, as you will then have to cut the sleeves separately.

Facings. These fall into three groups: A. small neck and armhole facings; B. the all-in-one neck and armhole facings; C. the button-down front dress and blouse facings.

Group A facings can usually be accommodated between the main pattern pieces on a layout and do not require extra yardage except, perhaps, in large sizes.

Facings in group B definitely require extra yardage because they are in fact the same width as the main pattern pieces.

With group C, much depends on the size of the facing pattern, as smaller sizes can often be cut out of the spare fabric alongside the main pattern pieces. But most sizes, from medium upward, require extra yardage for cutting out these long facings.

To sum up

To work out a yardage quickly for a simple garment consisting of Back, Front, sleeves and facings without collar and cuffs, you will need one or two lengths for each main pattern piece plus seam and hem allowance, depending on the width of fabric and pattern piece, plus extra allowance for the facings if necessary.

Making layouts

If you are not sure of the yardage, or if you are buying an expensive fabric, it is worth the time to work out the minimum fabric requirements first by making a mock layout on paper.

When you have made the layout on paper, draw around the pattern pieces or make a rough sketch of the layout so that you can copy it when you get to cutting out. Sometimes a layout can take hours to recall.

The following information will guide you when making paper layouts.

Without one way folded layouts

36in width. Take a piece of paper 36 inches wide—newspaper will do—measure your pattern width first and if no part is wider than 18 inches, including seam allowances, fold the paper to an 18 inch width, which is the folded width of 36 inch wide fabric.

If some pattern pieces are wider than 18 inches, an open layout is necessary for which notes are given later.

Starting with the largest pattern piece, see if it has to be cut on a fold or selvage. Lay it on the paper at one end with the widest part nearest the edge (figure **1**), placing on fold or selvage as necessary and making sure that each end of the straight of grain marking is equidistant from the paper edges.

Take the next widest pattern piece, again observing any directive for fold or selvage, and lay it as close to the other as the fabric width allows (figure **1**). The main pattern pieces are followed by the sleeve and the facing pieces.

If your pattern is without seam and hem allowances, like the **Golden Hands Graphs**, add these to the mock layout to arrive at the correct yardage.

If you have collars, cuffs, pockets or other trimmings, see the note below before finalizing the yardage.

54in width. Here you have more width of folded fabric to work on and you will find that layout making is quite simple.

If you are making a dress in a small size with small facings and short sleeves, the dress length plus the sleeve length will be enough to make your layout and cut out the dress.

For larger sizes and full sleeves, you will obviously need more fabric to spread the layout enough to accommodate the width of the pattern pieces (figure **2**).

Collars, cuffs, pockets and other trimmings

These items vary considerably in size from garment to garment, and the necessity of including them in your layout depends on their size. Cuffs and pockets can often be cut from the scraps.

If your layout is very compact and close, it is best to make a separate small layout for these accessories rather than open up the original layout—you may save fabric this way.

One way layouts

Here all the pattern pieces must run in the same direction (compare figure **1** and **3**). You may also need more fabric, as you may not be able to squeeze in one pattern next to the previous one.

However, you may be able to save fabric by using the smaller pattern pieces to start the layout and fit the larger ones in between them. It is wise to experiment with your pattern pieces until you have found the minimum yardage.

Open layouts

An open layout is used when the pattern pieces are too wide to be accommodated by the folded fabric width, and so the pattern has to be laid down twice, once in reverse, for the left and right sides. Make a copy of each half pattern, joining it to the original if placed on a fold.

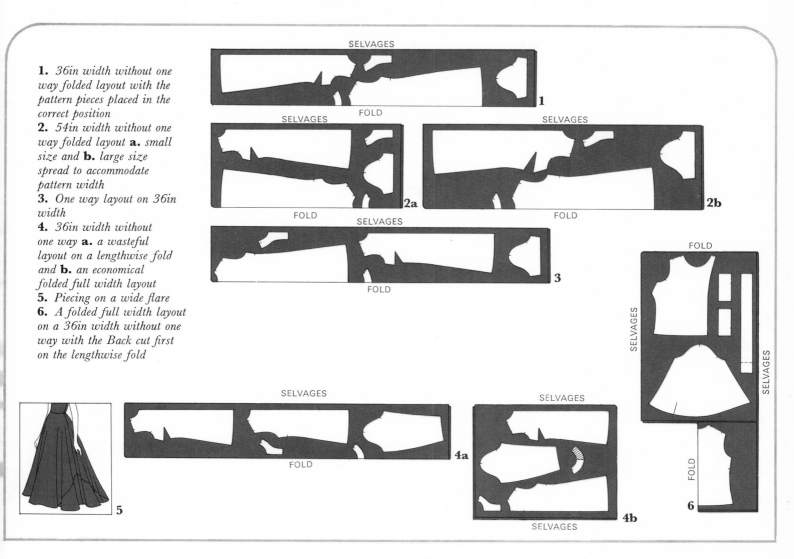

1. *36in width without one way folded layout with the pattern pieces placed in the correct position*

2. *54in width without one way folded layout* **a.** *small size and* **b.** *large size spread to accommodate pattern width*

3. *One way layout on 36in width*

4. *36in width without one way* **a.** *a wasteful layout on a lengthwise fold and* **b.** *an economical folded full width layout*

5. *Piecing on a wide flare*

6. *A folded full width layout on a 36in width without one way with the Back cut first on the lengthwise fold*

You need a large area to work on and a sheet of paper the full width of the fabric. To help you, mark the straight of grain through the center of the paper, then lay all the pattern pieces on the paper to make the best use of the area.

You cannot compromise on an open layout if the fabric is not wide enough to accommodate the full width of the pattern. Don't think that adding pieces to the side seams (piecing) is the answer to your difficulty—the only time piecing is permissible is when you are cutting on the bias, or a very wide flare (figure **5**). The only answer is to cut that section of the garment with a center seam. If a half pattern is still too wide for the fabric width, you must give in and choose another style.

Folded full width layouts

If you find that the layout on the folded width is wasting a lot of fabric between the pattern pieces, you may find a folded full width layout is the answer to your problem. Open the width of the fabric and double it by folding it across the width (figure **4**), as long as there is no pattern piece to be cut on a fold. Make sure that the fabric is without one way. If you are using a one way fabric you will have to cut the fabric along the halfway fold first and turn one piece around so that both sides of the design, or nap, run in the same direction and have the right sides of the fabric facing each other. This way, you will not cut out two right sides or two left sides.

If you have one pattern piece which must be cut on a fold, you can use a combination layout as shown in figure **6**.

A word on pants layouts

Pants layouts are the easiest to make, because with most sizes you have enough room on the layout to place the pattern pieces close together. They are also very economical.

If you use a one way fabric, you may find that you require twice the amount of fabric unless you are small and can cut from one width.

There is one special point about pants layouts to keep in mind. The upper hip and waist area requires less space on the layout width than the lower hip or pant leg, even the narrow section, and it is necessary to start your calculations by laying the pattern together first, lower hip section to lower hip section, in order to find out if it can be cut from one fabric width.

To be sure of having the correct yardage, it is advisable to make a mock layout.

Using your layout

As you make the layout on paper, you will also find out if the fabric width is right for the style of garment you want to make from it. Some layouts on narrow width fabrics are very wasteful, and since you are working on paper you may decide to change the style to one which makes better use of the fabric width.

Once you have made a basic layout for a particular garment, it is worthwhile keeping it, because the next time you are laying out fabric all you may have to do is juggle the pattern pieces around on the new length of fabric using the first layout you made as your guide.

Chapter 47

For the fuller figure

Rather unjustly, "outsize" covers all sizes with hips over 42 inches. But most women with fuller figures do not think of themselves as being outsize with its suggestion of being "out of the ordinary"—simply larger than the sizes usually covered in ready-made clothes and patterns.

If a large figure is your problem, let Golden Hands help you dressmake your way out of it. You can dress just as fashionably as those with slimmer proportions if you take extra care with design, fabric and fitting. So start by finding out which of the groups below describes you best.

Group 1

This is the girl who has grown up with the "I am different" complex—as long as she can remember, people have said, "Isn't she a big girl."
She is usually tall, has good proportions, and moves well. Her bust and hip measurements vary between 42 and 48 inches.
Because of her good proportions, clothes look well on her and most styles designed for smaller sizes can be adapted to suit her. She can wear frills or flowing garments and look stunning in them.
If this is your figure type, you should avoid plain dresses with unbroken seams since they only emphasize a large area by their monotony. The exception is the "little black dress," but even that needs to be dressed up so that there is a focal point to break up the area of the dress.

The garments which you need to look at with caution are separates —skirts and blouses, or skirts and jackets. If wrongly proportioned, they can look square and boxy, especially in the case of blouses and skirts of contrasting colors. If you wear your blouses tucked in, make sure that the skirt waistband doesn't sit above the normal waistline, creating the impression of a short waist. Instead, choose the hidden waistband which sits just on the waist. Belts, too, can create a short-waisted look, so if you want to wear a belt, choose a shaped one which sits lower down than a straight belt. Another point to watch is the fitting of sleeves over the shoulders. Look at yourself in a mirror and make sure that the shoulders do not look wider than the widest point across your hip line. They may, of course, have to be as wide to allow for your shoulder width, but to allow them to look wider will create an impression of largeness.

Group 2

This is the plump child who has grown up into a well-rounded adult, or what is quite often called a motherly type.
She is small, has good proportions and quick movements. Her bust and hip measurements are between 42 and 50 inches.
If this is your figure type, the most important point to watch is the line of any garment—it should look narrow. This does not mean that you have to resign yourself to a perpetual straight jacket, but the garments you choose should be made of soft fabrics and any

Group 1: Junoesque type—big but well-proportioned

fullness in them should hang toward the body. Avoid stiff and bulky fabrics and fit your dresses with special care, always aiming toward a straight look.

Plain colors are suitable for you, but your dresses should be broken with interesting details. Some gathers in the right places can do a lot for your figure type, as can soft body drapes or good seaming. Simulated fastenings, which avoid the thickness of wraps, can give particular interest and be very flattering.

Choose blouses and skirts in matching colors to give an impression of length. Skirts and jackets need careful proportioning and should be made in the fine woolen fabrics which can be tailored and molded to the shape of the body.

Never try to hide your figure inside a bulky garment since this will not help to disguise your shape—it will only make you feel self-conscious.

Because your figure is inclined to be short, paper patterns invariably need adjusting, so it is especially helpful to follow the **muslin making instructions in Muslin-making chapter 23. By** making a perfectly fitted bodice muslin, you will know exactly where to adjust your paper pattern.

Your figure type needs a well fitted shoulder line. Since you are more rounded than the group 1 figure, you may have to allow the shoulder line to be wider than the hips. But you can fit the sleeve carefully to take as much of the fullness as possible out of the sleeve crown so that it fits smoothly into the armhole without restricting the sleeve for easy movement.

You should also watch the length of your clothes. Unless fashion dictates a very long look, make sure that the amount of leg showing is in proportion to your height.

Group 2: Motherly type—well-developed bust and hips

Group 3: Big throughout

Group 3

This group consists of the really outsize figures with bust and hip measurements that are anything up to 60 inches.

Usually this figure type starts as a normal size, even skinny, during childhood but throughout adult life steadily puts on weight. Her movements are slow and large because the bone structure was not made to cope with the extra circumference and weight.

This group is much more difficult to dress because, apart from the outline of the figure, there are problem areas such as bust, stomach and hips.

Plenty of room is needed in garments because freedom of movement is an essential factor for this figure type. Movements such as stooping, bending and even walking often take garments up, so that, if not carefully chosen, they can look very ungainly.

If this is your figure type, then garments which allow the style to run into fullness, such as paneled skirts, are a must for you; however, all fullness built into the garments should be carefully planned. Otherwise the result will be a voluminous outfit which would only make you appear larger.

Pleats are not for you because they need to be firmly anchored to the figure to hang properly and in your case, tight fitting garments should be avoided.

Concentrate on contour seaming over the bust, which allows for good fitting and takes the bulk of fabric out of the bodice, combined with lower necklines and flat collars to break the width.

One of the main fitting problems is the armholes which have a tendency to be cut too large. This point should always be checked on paper patterns. There is a mistaken idea that the deeper the cut of the armhole, the more freedom of movement there

is. Actually, there is no extra freedom of movement to be gained from cutting extra deep armholes; they should only be large enough to allow the arm to pass into the sleeve and then sit comfortably around arm and shoulder.

In your figure type there is a tendency for the arms to tilt outward and not hang straight beside the body. But unless you have wide and square shoulders, this outward curve of the arms means that the distance between the top of the sleeve crown and the underarm is actually shortened. So, although you need extra width in your sleeves for the extra circumference of your arms, you do not need extra large armholes. Later in this chapter you will be shown how to increase the sleeve size without increasing the size of the sleeve head.

Pay particular attention to the length of your dresses and skirts. Walk around and move your arms when fitting to see if the garment hitches up at the back. Unless this is caused by tightness, the only way to deal with the problem is to make the back of the skirt longer than the front, enough for the garment to settle where it wants and look even during wear.

Here are a few do's and don'ts. Avoid bulky or stiff fabrics or fabrics with small all-over prints. Choose medium sized prints with all-over designs instead, or better still, those with up or down directional interest.

Choose plain dark colors with care, since they emphasize a large area. A possible exception is silk with a good finish which will create subtle shading to help minimize size.

When you look at fabrics with dull finishes, choose slightly lighter colors which show a color variation through shading. These help you to look slimmer because the color will look slightly darker on the sides of the body.

The Golden Hands basic skirt pattern

The basic skirt pattern in Skirtmaking chapter 10 is suitable for larger sizes; in fact, you can make it as large as you like. There are, of course, certain figure problems that are detailed below which should be taken into account when making the pattern.

Making the skirt pattern

First make a basic skirt pattern in your hip size from the Golden Hands graph pattern in Skirtmaking chapter 10. Ignore your own waist measurement and draw in the corresponding standard waist measurement of the pattern, which is 12 inches less than the hip measurement.
Cut out the pattern.

Altering the pattern

For a large stomach. You will need to add to the waist measurement and the center front of the front pattern piece.
First move the dart position on the front to halfway between the side seam and the original dart, reduce the width of the dart to $\frac{3}{4}$in and repin the length of the dart as required (figure **1**).
Then lay the pattern piece on a sheet of paper and pin the center front to the straight edge.
Measure the length from your waistline, at the side, to the widest part of your hips or to the top of your thighs—whichever is the wider—and mark off this distance on the pattern side seam. From this point draw a straight line across the pattern.
Starting at the center front, slash the pattern along this line to within $\frac{1}{4}$ inch of the side seam.
Unpin the top half of the cut pattern and make sure the lower half is pinned down securely.
Measure the difference between your waistline and that of the pattern. Then raise the center front of the top part of the pattern until the space between the straight edge of the paper and the original center front measures half the difference of the waist measurements. Pin the top of the pattern down securely.
This may result in a kink in the side seam. If so, place a yardstick from the upper edge of the pattern side seam to the outer point of the hem and draw a connecting line.
Draw in the new waistline and draw around the rest of the pattern. Cut out the new front pattern.
For a high seat. Alter the back pattern piece. Measure the depth from your waist to the highest point of the seat and mark off this distance along the side seam of the pattern piece.

208

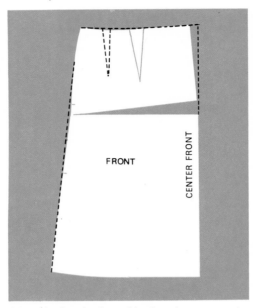

▲ **1.** *Altering the front skirt for a large stomach*
▼ **2.** *Altering the back skirt for a high seat*

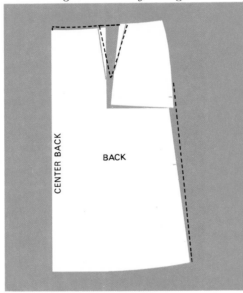

Draw a straight line through the center of the dart toward the hem (figure **2**). Then draw a straight line across the pattern from the mark on the side seam to meet the line through the dart.
Cut out the upper side section, cutting along the lines as shown in the diagram.

▼ **3.** *Altering sleeve pattern for large upper arm*

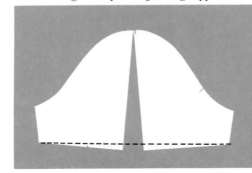

Pin the rest of the pattern securely to sheet of paper with the center back alon the straight edge.
Since the pattern already includes stan dard ease or tolerance, you only have t add extra ease over the seat, so take mor depth into the dart and lengthen th center back a little.
To do this, move the cut-out section of th pattern outward for $\frac{1}{2}$ inch and then ti it up $\frac{1}{2}$ inch as shown in the diagram.
Still following the diagram, draw in th new waistline and side seam and the draw in the new dart.
Since any extra width at the waist goe into the depth of the new dart, the waist line will remain the same. As each wais fitting is different, especially on large sizes, it is necessary to fit the waist wit special care during the fitting stage.
Draw around the rest of the pattern an cut out the new back pattern.

The basic skirt conversions

You may like to try some of the ski conversions for a change. The six-gor version (Skirtmaking chapter 18) ca be very flattering to larger sizes. The fou gore and knife-pleated skirts in Skir making chapters 16 and 17 are al suitable.

The Golden Hands Graph Pattern and larger sizes

The Graph Pattern size range already i cludes a perfectly graded set of pattern for larger sizes, namely the 42 inch bu size. These patterns are designed to meet th requirements of the larger figure.
Experienced dressmakers will have alread realized that they can safely enlarge th pattern to the next size by adding to th center back and front, side seams an armholes. If you are not confident, make muslin first to get the extra size, that is, 4 inch bust and 46 inch hips, (Muslin making chapter 23.)

The basic dress

The basic dress featured here has bee made in the largest size, plus. The gentl flare and the classic detail make it favorite for larger sizes.
To make the dress, use all the patter pieces on the Dress Graph Pattern an the sleeve pattern piece number 7 o the Accessories Graph.
To make the short sleeve, first copy th sleeve pattern as far as the cutting line fo short sleeves and pin this to a sheet o paper. Straighten the slope of the unde arm seam and add the length for th turned back cuff as shown for the roll-u sleeve blouse in Blousemaking chapter 2

Altering the sleeve pattern for a large upper arm

To make the upper sleeve section larger without increasing the size of the sleeve cap, slash the sleeve pattern through the sleeve center to within $\frac{1}{4}$ inch of the sleeve crown. Spread the slash outward as shown and make a new pattern (figure 3). You can use this method for other sleeve patterns of your choice.

Making the dress

Make the dress as for the basic dress in Dressmaking chapters 31 to 33, then make and set in the sleeve as for the roll-up sleeve blouse. Make buttonholes in the tab so that it can be fastened down flat and use small decorative buttons which complement the color of the dress.

Making a muslin

It is an impossible task to cater to all figure types in each pattern size, so to deal with your personal fitting problems it is strongly recommended that you make a body muslin.

For the purpose, choose a paper pattern in a basic style such as Vogue 1002. Or, if your size is larger than the given sizes, choose a simple waisted style from any other commercial paper pattern.

When making this, follow the bodice muslin instructions for fitting and making pattern alterations in Muslin-making chapter 23 and the dress muslin described in Muslin-making chapter 24. Incorporate the sleeve adjustment shown here (figure 3) if necessary. Do not fit the muslin as closely as the bodice muslin, but fit it like a dress. This way, you can make a perfectly fitted garment for yourself, whatever your shape or size.

It will be well worth the effort, because once you have achieved a perfect fit you will be able to use the body muslin to adjust any pattern to your own personal requirements before you cut out the fabric.

Fitting on a stand

Larger sizes may find it easier to use a dressmaker's stand or dummy during the early stages of fitting.

Having identified yourself from the three groups of larger sizes featured in this chapter, remember these points when purchasing a stand. These come in many different figure types, with varying proportions, and must be chosen with great care. It is advisable to go to a speciality store where all types and sizes of stands are available.

They vary so much that you can even take specific points such as a rounded or straight

The Golden Hands basic dress pattern enlarged one size with simple sleeve conversion

back into consideration.

You may not be able to find a perfect fit, but if you can find a stand which corresponds to your basic measurements, you can make it fit you perfectly by padding where necessary.

Do not buy your stand as you buy patterns. Patterns should be bought to fit the bust measurement because this is the most difficult area on a pattern to alter.

When buying a stand, it is essential to know

that your hip measurement is not less than 2 inches larger than the bust; otherwise, you will not be able to get the garment over the shoulders of the stand. If you have difficult proportions, such as identical bust and hip measurements or a smaller hip measurement, buy the stand to fit your hips and increase the bust size by padding. If your hips are larger than normal proportions, buy the stand to fit your bust and pad the hip area.

209

Chapter 48 Quilting, shirring and couture embroidery

Know-How

This chapter on various techniques deals with decorating garment sections with quilting, shirring, soutache braiding and cord embroidery.

You can use these methods to decorate simple garments—turning them so simply into something special.

Quilting

Although quilting large areas requires some practice, smaller areas can be done very successfully by the home dressmaker. The traditionally favorite areas for quilting are lapels, collars, cuffs, pockets and hemlines. Shoulder yokes, too, can be quilted successfully.

Decoration apart, quilting can also have a practical use in adding warmth to a garment, hence its frequent use in dressing-gowns, bed-jackets and coat linings. A good idea for adding warmth to a medium-weight coat is to make a detachable quilted lining which can be popped in on cold days and attached to the coat with large snap fasteners stitched to the edge of the lining and the coat facing. Before deciding to quilt a garment a suitable fabric has to be chosen together with an appropriate underlay.

Choosing the top fabric

When choosing a fabric for quilting first look at the weave. The fabric must be firmly woven because it has to retain the underlay and prevent it from working through to the outside. In addition the stitches used for quilting are an essential and attractive part of it and should lie on the surface of the fabric and not disappear into it as they would into a soft weave.

Next, consider the surface. Fabrics with a soft sheen will give you the most satisfying results. The obvious choices are satins and sateens because they are firmly woven, supple, and have a surface which reflects light. Velvet is another very suitable choice.

The underlay

Choosing the right underlay is simple; it is chosen according to the function the quilting has to perform. Use waddings for warmth and tailor's lamb's wool or a double layer of loosely woven, light-weight, fleece filler (cotton or wool) for decorative quilting.

If you are using wadding it is important to buy one which is specially prepared for quilting. This usually comes with a gauze backing (figure **1**), but if not you will have to add your own.

Another important point to consider when choosing the underlay is how you propose to clean the garment. If you use wool or any other natural fiber underlay, the garment will need to be dry cleaned since these underlays hold moisture and are hard to dry out. Natural fiber waddings, too, should be avoided as some actually bleed during washing and stain the outside fabric.

So, if you want to wash the garment, confine yourself to man-made fiber waddings and make sure at the time of purchase that they are washable. Of these, Dacron wadding is the best for washable garments as rayon waddings will become lumpy after frequent washings. But special care must be taken in choosing the top fabric when quilting with Dacron wadding. The outside fabric must be very closely woven since the little fiber ends of this wadding have a tendency to work through the weave of the top fabric and cause pilling on the outside, dragging out more wadding in the process.

Lining

If you use wadding for the underlay it must be protected by a suitably firm lining, because the gauze backing is not strong enough

◄ *A simple Vogue coat pattern, ideal for all-over quilting.*

to stand up to wear.

If the quilting is worked in small sections on a woven backing such as fleece filler, lining is not necessary, but if a garment is quilted all over it should be lined.

Cutting out for quilting

Quilting will, of course, reduce the size of the fabric both lengthwise and widthwise: be prepared to lose anything up to 4 inches on a 36 inch width and length. This is approximately $\frac{5}{8}$ inch for every 6 inches. So, when cutting out allow for this over the amount you add for the seam allowance (figure **2**).

After cutting and quilting the fabric, lay on the pattern again and mark the pattern details.

Underlaying the fabric

If you are using fleece or other woven underlays, pin and baste it to the wrong side of the top fabric with long basting stitches. Fleece filler should be used double to be effective.

For the basting use a fine smooth silk thread to avoid dragging the underlay as you work.

Thin wadding, together with its gauze backing, can be similarly basted, but heavier wadding can only be pinned in position.

Stitching

The stitching is an important part of quilting and should be prominent. So choose a thread one or even two shades darker than the color of the fabric.

To obtain a lustrous appearance use embroidery thread, buttonhole twist or sewing silk, and carefully test the thread first to make sure that it is suitable for your particular fabric and underlay combination.

Adjusting the machine

Most modern machines have quilting attachments for straight line quilting, in addition to general quilting hints, so follow the manufacturers instructions to set up your machine. Do not be deterred, however, if yours is an old family heirloom—quilting can be done on almost any machine which has a good straight stitch action.

Prepare a scrap of fabric ready for quilting, make the correct tension adjustments and loosen the pressure on the presser foot until the fabric passes under it without pushing fullness in front of it as you go.

If you have an old sewing machine, the thread tension may no longer have enough spring to take differing thicknesses of sewing thread, so you may have to stick to the thread you usually use. In this case, make the stitches a little longer so that they will show up by lying on the surface of the fabric.

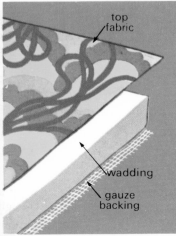

▲**1.** Quilting with wadding

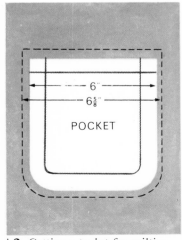

▲**2.** Cutting a pocket for quilting

▲ Ideas for decorating Golden Hands patterns: **a.** Long dirndl skirt with diamond section quilting; **b.** Flared hem pants with tunic decorated in simple cord embroidery; **c.** Dress with fitted sleeves extended to full length and decorated with soutache braid embroidery

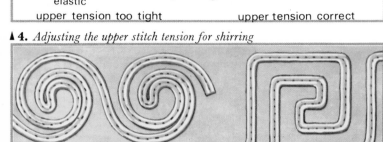

▲ **4.** *Adjusting the upper stitch tension for shirring*

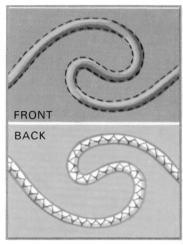

▲ **3.** *Ring quilting around a hem*　　▲ **5.** *Scroll and Greek key designs for soutache braid embroidery*　　▲ **6.** *Soft cord embroidery*

Quilting garment sections

Cuffs and collars, lapels, pockets and hemlines can be underlayed with double layers of fleece, basted firmly in position and stitched in the design of your choice. If you are quilting in straight lines, measure out the distance of the stitching lines and mark them with pins. If your machine has a quilting guide use that too. Hemlines look very attractive when stitched in ring quilting. This consists of parallel rows of straight stitching about 1 inch apart to the depth required (figure **3**). Instructions for design quilting are below.

All-over straight quilting

Cut out and underlay the fabric as given and quilt each section of the garment before making it. Stitch each row right up to the edge of the fabric.

Pin on the pattern and mark out the pattern details, then make the garment. Do not press the fabric after quilting but carefully press the seams only, laying the work on a soft blanket to avoid flattening the design.

Quilting velvet

Quilted velvet has a luxurious appearance and it is just as easy to quilt as a flat surface fabric.

Here you should avoid using wadding as an underlay. Use tailor's lamb's wool or a double layer of fleece, which will give enough bulk and does not draw up the velvet into puckers as you stitch.

Quilting a design

Apart from the straight quilting already described another form of quilting is to raise a design from the flat background of a fabric. This type of quilting is not often found in dressmaking as straight line quilting on a plain fabric is usually considered decorative enough.

You can apply design quilting to printed

fabric, underlaying the area as described before and stitching around the outlines of the design.

If you want to work a raised design on a plain fabric you will require a paper transfer which you can make as follows.

Copy the outlines of the chosen design on a sheet of thin writing paper or tracing paper. Then, using the largest stitch setting on your machine, and no thread in the machine, perforate the outline of the design. If you want to duplicate the design perforate two or more sheets of paper at the same time.

Having underlayed the area to be quilted, pin and baste the paper securely in place on the right side of the fabric.

Stitch over the perforated lines and tear away the paper after completion.

Shirring with elastic yarns

This is a practical application which becomes decorative by its use in certain places on a garment.

Shirring with elastic yarn gives an almost unrestricted gathering of fullness which is self adjusting to many sizes. Holding in fullness by shirring is softer than inserting elastic into a casing and is particularly suitable for children's garments for this reason.

Shirring is used on adult garments too. It can be applied to a depth of 3 or more inches to the wrist edges of long and full sleeves, to simulate cuffs, or around the waistline of an otherwise shapeless dress, where it becomes a pretty simulated belt. Shirring yarn has a fine elastic core around which is wound a cotton or rayon thread. It is widely available in several colors.

Setting up the machine

Once you have decided on the areas to be shirred all that remains is to set up the

machine and then, once the rows of shirring have been worked, to knot each thread end securely to prevent the threads from slipping back.

Shirring with a modern sewing machine. Most modern machines carry special instructions for using shirring yarns, so all you have to do is follow the manual.

Shirring with an old sewing machine. If yours is an old machine, or has no sewing manual, you will have to experiment to find the best way to use the elastic shirring yarn.

Wind the yarn on the bobbin and loosen the bobbin thumb screw sufficiently to allow the yarn to pass under the spring clip without undue stretch.

The elastic yarn in shirring lies on the underside of the work, so if the elastic yarn is wound around the bobbin, work on the right side of the garment to do the shirring.

Make sure that the upper stitch tension is sufficiently slack to allow the elastic yarn to go through the stitch loop without being drawn up into the fabric (figure **4**). This will also enable you to draw up the elastic thread to take away more fullness if necessary.

If you still cannot manage shirring satisfactorily enlist the help of your nearest sewing machine center. They may have a gadget which you can attach to the machine to make shirring easier.

Couture embroidery

Soutache braiding

Soutache braid is approximately $\frac{3}{16}$ inch wide and shapes and bends so well that it can be used for all kinds of designs, from an angular Greek key design to the most intricate scrolls (figure **5**). The design is applied to the work by means of transfers.

Working by hand. Copy the outlines of the required design onto a sheet of thin writing or tracing paper. Then, using the largest stitch setting on your machine, and no thread in the needle, perforate the design lines.

Pin the design over the required area and make pinhead pencil marks onto the fabric through the perforations on the transfer. Remove the paper then apply the braid over these markings and sew on by hand with small invisible prick stitches, working through the dip in the center of the braid.

Working by machine. Set up the machine with the necessary attachments for applying and stitching the braid. In most cases the braid is applied from underneath and you will have to work with the wrong side uppermost. If this is the case you can use a suitable ready-made iron-on transfer.

If, however, you want to use your own design or you are applying the braid from the top of the fabric, then make a transfer as for the hand application. If you want to duplicate the design, perforate two or more sheets of paper at the same time. Once the design is ironed on or pinned in place, feed the braid through the attachment and stitch it in position working over the lines of the design.

Finishing the ends. To make the ends of the embroidery neat, make a small hole between the threads of the weave of the fabric, draw through the ends of the braid and sew them by hand to the wrong side of the fabric.

Corded embroidery

This is another very elegant form of couture embroidery and it is very simple to achieve effective results. Here the design is outlined with two rows of silky stitches and is filled with soft cord underneath, which helps to raise it slightly from the background (figure **6**).

Corded embroidery is best worked on a smooth plain fabric such as doeskin cloth, and looks most effective when used in a number of parallel rows around the hemlines of skirts, pants and sleeves. Another idea is to embroider a criss-cross pattern on a section of a garment.

To work the cording you will need a zigzag or automatic mechanism on your machine together with twin needle attachments. Look in the machine manual for instructions on how to work it.

If you are working on a dress fabric make sure that you use a soft cord. To emphasize the stitches, use a silk thread and a slightly larger stitch setting.

Press the finished work over a soft blanket to bring out the design.

Making a quilted skirt

Make this skirt in either 54 inch wide dress cotton or 48 inch wide lightweight home furnishing fabric. Choose suitable underlay and lining fabric.

The diagram shows the details of the finished skirt. The Front and Back are the same, each piece having 4 waist darts and a 1 inch wide waistband with 2 long ties attached. There is a 7 inch zipper at the top of each side seam.

Use any simple flared skirt pattern and adapt it to the measurements given in the diagram.

Cut the skirt pieces with seam and hem allowances from top fabric, underlay and lining. Underlay the top fabric and quilt the pieces with all-over straight quilting in squares with 2 inch sides.

Stitch the side seams on the quilted sections, press and insert the zippers. Stitch the lining side seams leaving openings for the zippers. Press. With wrong sides facing, baste the lining to the skirt at the waist.

Cut 3 inch wide waistbands and ties from the remnants. Attach the waistbands to the skirt Back and Front, finish and press. Make the ties, make neat and press. Hand sew the ties firmly to the ends of each waistband.

Slip stitch the lining to the zipper tapes at the openings. Turn up the hems on both lining and skirt; press lining to finish.

213

Chapter 49

Frills, flounces, ruffles and scallops

Know-How

This is another chapter that deals with special trims and finishes. Here are ruffles, frills, flounces and scallops, all of which you can easily add to a garment yourself.

Single edged frills

Frills are usually caught into bound or faced seams. They may be used to trim necklines and sleeve edges on soft blouses and dresses. Children's garments, lingerie and nightwear are also favorites for the use of pretty frills.

When a frill is attached to a hem edge it becomes, strictly speaking, a flounce.

How to cut a frill

There are four basic ways to cut a frill. Which you choose depends mainly on the effect you wish to achieve.

On all single edged frills cut a full seam allowance on the edge which is joined to the garment. On the other edge the seam allowance is cut according to the finish you choose.

Cutting single width in the straight grain of the fabric (figure **1a**). This type of single layer frill is most suitable for crisp fabrics (figure **2**).

Cutting single width in the bias grain of the fabric (figure **1b**). Single layer bias cut frills are suitable for attaching to slanted edges such as cross-over dresses. They must be cut generously to look their best (figure **3**).

Cutting double width, in the straight or bias grain (figure **1c**). This method of cutting is for a double, or fluted, frill. The frill is cut on a double width which is then folded lengthwise to make the fluting. Full seam allowance is, of course, added to both edges (figure **4a** and **b**).

Whether you cut on the bias or the straight grain of the fabric depends on the width of the frill as well as on the fabric.

Circular cutting, single width (figure **1d**). The circular cut frill is the type used for a waterfall effect and is therefore sometimes called a waterfall frill. It looks best when cut from fine, soft fabric. This type of frill is rarely gathered as it is cut from a circle or spiral, the inside edge being the length of the garment edge to which the frill is attached (figure **5a** and **b**).

For long waterfall frills, two or more circles or spirals are joined together to the desired length.

How to measure for the frill length

Before cutting a frill always test for effect on a short length of the fabric, and at the same time check measurements for length. The length of the frill depends in the first instance on the type of fabric you are using.

Frills in heavy fabric should not be cut too long as the fullness would add a lot of weight and bulk to the seam.

214

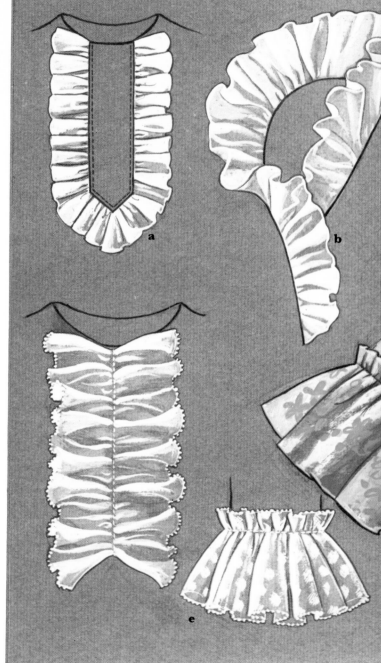

▲ **1.** *Various frills, flounces and ruffles:* **a.** *single edged frill in the straight grain;* **b.** *single edged frill in the bias grain;* **c.** *double width frill;* **d.** *circular or waterfall frill;* **e.** *double edged frill;* **f.** *fluted edged frill;* **g.** *lace ruffle*

▼ **2.** *Single frill cut in the straight grain*

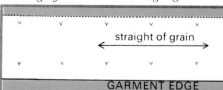

straight of grain

GARMENT EDGE

▼ **3.** *Single frill cut in the bias grain*

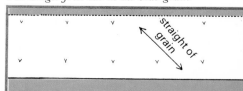

straight of grain

▲ *Shades of Victoriana for mother and child*
▼ *Two party dresses from Butterick patterns*

▼**4.** *Cutting a double frill:* **a.** *straight grain;* **b.** *bias grain*

▼**5.** *Cutting a circular frill;* **a.** *from a circle;* **b.** *from a spiral*

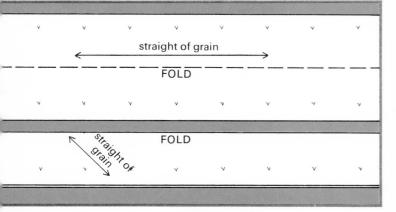

straight of grain

FOLD

FOLD

straight of grain

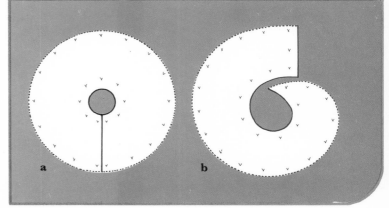

Frills in thin fabrics, however, need to have extra length otherwise they will look skimped and some fullness is always taken up into the fabric even before you start gathering it up. This applies to both straight or bias cut frills, but not to waterfall frills.

To obtain the correct length of frill for the type of fabric you are using, make this quick test.

Cut a sample length of frilling 15 inches long. Make two rows of gathering stitches along one edge and draw them up so that the fabric looks nicely gathered. Measure the length of the gathered up piece and divide the 15 inches by this measurement. Then use this proportion when cutting the frill.

For example, if the gathered length measures $7\frac{1}{2}$ inches, this goes twice into 15 inches. This means that for every 1 inch of the edge to be frilled you will have to cut 2 inches of frilling.

Finishing raw edges on frills

It is necessary to finish the outside edge of the frill before attaching it to the garment. It is often difficult to decide which type of finish to apply. Here are a few pointers to help you.

When dealing with single layer frills, the sewing machine can considerably reduce the work in hemming, or otherwise finishing the raw edges.

Machine hem finish. The edge can be finished with the hemming attachment on a machine, or it can simply be turned up into a narrow hem and straight stitched. For the latter, first try out the width of hem which looks best for the fabric. Roll under the edge for $\frac{1}{8}$ inch, then turn under again for $\frac{1}{8}$ inch and stitch in place. If this looks wrong try a slightly wider hem.

If you are making an ordinary machine hem on a frill, make sure that the fabric does not tighten up as you stitch. The effect may be all right to begin with, but after the garment is washed you will find that the edge tends to roll.

Hand rolled finish. There is one occasion when a machine hem is strictly taboo and that is on a beautifully hand finished garment. Here a fine hand roll should be applied (see Blousemaking chapter 29) or, of the machine finishes, a picot edge is suitable provided you are working on a fine fabric.

Picot finish. A picot edge, or picot type finish, can be applied to both bias and straight cut frills. Make sure you find out, either from your machine manual or local store, how much to allow on the edge of the frill so that the width of the frill will not be reduced after it is finished.

Zigzag finish. You can apply a zigzag finish to frills cut on the bias, which include waterfall frills. Work over the raw edge twice to avoid weakness and, for safety's sake, allow an extra $\frac{1}{4}$ inch seam allowance which will be taken up in the zigzagging.

Gathering the frill

This can be done by hand or machine. A frilling attachment on a machine will gather the frill as it is stitched in place, and dispenses with gathering stitches. Be very careful and follow the manual to the letter or you may find yourself running out of fabric before you have gathered enough for the hem edge.

Otherwise the frill must be gathered with two parallel lines of gathering stitches along the seamline.

Attaching frills

Single frills. Whether you are using a bound or faced finish, always catch the frill into the seam when you are stitching it.

If you are attaching a frill, or flounce, to a hem edge, just stitch it to the seam allowance, with right sides facing, overcast both hem and frill seam allowances together and turn into the garment. Facing is not necessary.

To prevent the seam allowance from tilting downward, you can topstitch through all the layers of fabric, close to the edge of the hem.

Double frill. The frill is folded lengthwise and pressed. Gather and attach as for single frills using the two layers of fabric as one.

Double edged frills

A double edged frill (figure **1e**) is an attractive variation of frilling and is applied to the surface or stitched onto an edge of a garment. The frill is cut on the bias and both edges are finished with a fine hem, sewn by hand or machine.

It is then gathered with two rows of stitches along the center or nearer the top edge as desired, and stitched to the garment between the rows of gathering. The gathering stitches are removed carefully after stitching.

Double edged frills can be made on the sewing machine with a frilling attachment, but the same precautions apply as for single frills.

Fluted upper edge (figure **1f**). A pretty variation of the double edged frill, which you can use when attaching it to the hemline of a skirt, is to make a narrow fluted frill of the upper edge.

To do this, cut an extra 3 inches onto the desired width and turn under the upper edge $1\frac{1}{2}$ inches. Make one row of gathering stitches on the right side of the fabric 1 inch down from the folded upper edge, then make a second row parallel to the first. Draw up the gathers to fit the hem edge, pin the gathering over the seamline and stitch in position. Carefully remove the gathering stitches.

Ruffles

Traditionally, frills of lace are described as ruffles. A ruffle (see figure **1g**) is made from wide lace edging or flouncing, gathered into a rouleau or bias strip binding, and attached to the neck or sleeve edge of a garment (figure **6**).

Ruffles are rarely taken into seams since the texture of the ruffle fabric, in most cases, varies from the texture of the garment fabric.

Scallops

Scalloping (figure **7**) is an easy way to decorate a garment. All that is required is some simple arithmetic and careful measuring. Scallops must be evenly spaced, as any miscalculations will be very noticeable in their shapes.

Scallops are most easily applied to a straight edge where the grain of the fabric will assist you when stitching.

When applying them to a rounded edge, the decreasing factor in the length of the base line of the scallops must be taken into account.

Whether you apply scallops to a straight or shaped edge, it is always done best with the aid of a template, shaped to the edge of the garment (figure **8a**).

The ideal measurement for the depth of the scallops is a third of the width. Measure out the scallops on the template first. Draw them on in pencil and you will then see if your calculations are right and that you have the correct number of scallops to fit along the edge.

If you are left with odd measurements, leave the depth of each scallop as it is but widen the base line to take up the extra length (figure **8b**). Conversely, if you have too little length, decrease the width of the base line on each scallop to accommodate all the scallops evenly (figure **8c**).

When applying scallops, cut a facing to the exact shape of the edge to be scalloped. Then carefully mark out the scallops with tailor's tacks on the facing fabric piece, using the shaped template as

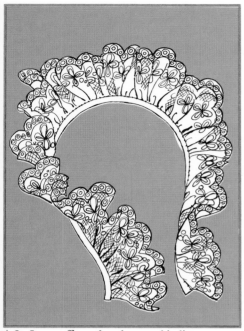

▲**6.** *Lace ruffle gathered onto a binding*

▲**7.** *Various applications of scallops*

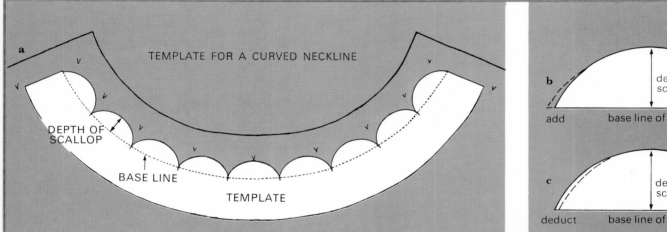

a

TEMPLATE FOR A CURVED NECKLINE

DEPTH OF
SCALLOP

BASE LINE

TEMPLATE

b

depth of
scallop

add   base line of scallop

c

depth of
scallop

deduct   base line of scallop

▲**8a.** *The template for the scallops on a curved neckline:* **b.** *widening the base line;* **c.** *reducing the base line*

▼**9a.** *Marking out the scallops on the facing;* **b.** *trimming and notching the scalloped edge for turning*

your guide (figure **9a**).

If the scalloped edge needs interfacing, such as around a neckline, baste the interfacing in place.

Then baste the facing in place, right sides together, and stitch the facing to the garment along the line of tailor's tacks. Trim the seam allowance around the scallops to about ⅜ inch; if the fabric is thick, layer the seams (figure **9b**).

Turn the facing to the inside, thus turning out the scallops, edge-baste and press. Remove the basting and the scalloped edge is complete.

Here is one final hint for making smooth looking scallops. If you find that after trimming and turning out the scallops they still don't lie flat, make small V-shaped notches in the seam allowance around the deepest section of each shape. This will prevent points and puckers on the shaped edges, even in firm fabrics.

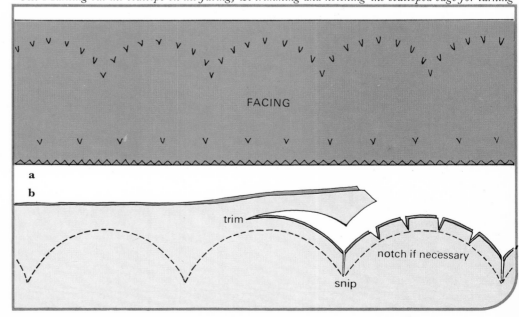

FACING

a

b

trim

snip

notch if necessary

Chapter 50

The velvet touch

If you think that velvet is a difficult fabric to work with, your fears should be dispelled after reading this chapter. It gives a description of the various types of velvet you will use for dressmaking, followed by useful tips on how to choose suitable styles, and work and handle the fabric for really successful results.

Armed with this basic velvet know-how, there is no reason why you cannot feel as relaxed handling this most romantic fabric as any other. You might start with a glamorous long evening skirt and coordinate it with a silk, satin or crepe blouse for the exclusive look of the outfit featured opposite, from a Vogue Pattern. The chapter ends with special hints for making a velvet dress using Vogue Pattern 2600, an obvious style choice since it lists velvet among the suitable fabrics to use. The instructions take you yet one step further in your dressmaking knowledge by telling you how to achieve a smooth finish for the beautiful contour seaming over the bust, a style feature of the pattern.

an alternative version
included in pattern

▲ *Back and front views of dress.*

Suitable fabrics and styles

Types of velvet

There are many types of velvet made from different fibers, as well as combinations of fibers, such as velvet with a cotton base and silk pile.

Their weight differs considerably too. Velvets are made as heavy as coating and as light as chiffon, and between these extremes are the easily worked dress velvets.

The most common and well known velvet is Lyons velvet, which is firm and usually made in pure silk. Rayon velvets are also common, they are made entirely from rayon and then treated for crease resist-

ance. Both Lyons and rayon velvet have short pile which makes them ideal for the beginner.

Panne velvets are also good for the beginner but are not always available as they are dependent on prevailing fashion. The nap or pile of panne velvet is brushed flat and in one direction. These velvets are often printed and the pile gives depth and texture to a printed design.

French street or coat velvets are quite light in weight, but the pile is somewhat deep and it becomes a little more difficult to work. Recently a velvet has appeared which is washable. This has a most luxurious surface but can be treated almost like an ordinary flat weave. This velvet is made from a man-made fiber, the appearance of which resembles ordinary artificial silk. Not only does it wash easily and wear well, but it is also quite inexpensive.

Since this velvet is suitable for washing it is the obvious choice for garments in light colors.

Cotton velveteen is a different type of fabric. Here the base and pile are both made of cotton. Velveteen is made to resemble velvet but the construction of the weave is different. There is really no problem in making a garment from this fabric.

Choosing the velvet

As the textures of velvet vary, consider the fit and hang you require for the style of garment and choose the velvet accordingly. If you are a beginner use a short nap velvet to get used to working on velvets before attempting the longer pile ones. So look for a good close pile which feels firm in the hand and will allow you to work with the fabric without too much slipping.

Choosing a suitable design

Avoid styles which rely on heavy darting for the fit as darts are difficult to press in velvet.

The beginner should also avoid styles which are cut in one with no dividing waist seam. It is best to learn to sew velvet on smaller sections of a garment as the seams are easier to control.

The Vogue Pattern 2600 featured in this chapter incorporates all the above qualities and is therefore a particularly suitable design for working with velvet.

General hints

Supporting fabrics

Interfacing. It is rare for velvet garments to need interfacing, especially when there is a loose lining attached to the neck and armhole lines.

Facings. Facings must be kept to a minimum to avoid heavy rolls on the edges of the garment. It is best to face velvet garments with matching silk bias facings which are neat and firm.

Interlinings. Few velvets benefit from inter or underlinings and the stitching of seams in underlined velvet can become a nightmare, since the whole seam appears to move.

To support full skirts in velvet, always construct a suitable under garment and do not use stiff linings or underlinings. Stiff fabrics will catch the pile on the inside of the fabric and slowly drag it out, resulting in bald patches all over the surface.

Hand-sewing

Hand-sewing should be practiced on a scrap of velvet. If the stitches are made too timidly they only catch the loops of the pile where it is anchored into the weave and gradually pull it out. So make sure you catch the weave but don't allow the stitches to mark the pile.

Background: Evening dress from a Vogue Pattern in rayon velvet
Foreground: Velvet skirt with crepe blouse also from a Vogue Pattern ►

Seam finishes

Seam finishes in velvet garments should be done by hand as a machine finish can cause a seam edge to tighten and roll, making it appear wrinkled on the outside. Do not be tempted to use pinking shears as this will only encourage fraying.

Zipper fasteners

It is often mistakenly thought that you require a fine zipper to fasten a velvet dress. Fine zippers usually come with a fine tape, and as you stitch the fine tape to the seamline through the folded thickness of the fabric, it is pulled with the stitches into the depth of the pile and there is no control or anchorage to hold the stitches in position. It does not matter how much you try, your zipper will always look wrinkled.

So always use a strong dress zipper with a cotton tape. This is slightly stiff and firm and will allow you to sew it in position without its puckering.

Tools for ironing velvet

For ironing velvet you should use a needleboard.

Needleboards are squares of wire pile anchored to a firm base. The fabric is then pressed with pile down on the needleboard. It is worthwhile buying an expensive one as a cheap needleboard can ruin the velvet.

You can of course draw your seams over an ordinary iron standing on its end and covered with a damp cloth. To do this, open the seam allowance and draw the seam section by section over the iron, patting the velvet gently on the outside with a soft brush.

Needleboards are obtainable in the notions departments of some stores. But if you cannot find what you are looking for, try one of the special stores selling dressmaker's equipment. They will also stock very narrow strips of needleboard which you lay over a sleeveboard to press the seams in fitted sleeves.

Stitching velvet

When stitching velvet the pressure of the upper presser foot on most sewing machines needs to be reduced unless the machine is self-adjusting. To test for this, place two scraps of velvet face to face and make a row of basting stitches as for a seamline. Stitch along the seamline. If the seam begins to twist, loosen the pressure and stitch again. Repeat until the fabric stops twisting and the seam remains flat.

For stitching velvet use a fine soft thread such as pure silk sewing thread. Carefully adjust the stitch tension on the machine, since the fabric is thick and a tightly set stitch tension will cause it to pucker.

Chapter 51

Successful dressmaking with checks and stripes

Know-How

A very important aspect of dressmaking is using a fabric to its best advantage, and making full use of checks and stripes is as exciting as creating a new design. Take a simple pattern, make it up cleverly in a checked or striped fabric, and the result is a garment with well projected detail.

Fixed fashion rules, such as lengthwise stripes for the large figure and checks for the small, have long been discarded. As long as the size of the design on the fabric is right for the proportions of the garment, and the proportions of the garment suit the wearer, there is no reason why large figures should not wear checks and small figures wear bold stripes.

This chapter gives advice on choosing the fabric and selecting the right style, and finishes with the all important aspects of cutting and fitting to help you achieve the best possible effect for your figure type.

▲ *Checks for a dashing pants suit*

Buying the fabric

Checks

With such a variety of checks available it is impossible to cover every aspect of making a purchase in one of these fabrics. However, there are some rules to observe which can be applied to most types of checks.

The main consideration must be matching the checks. So first look to see if the design is balanced (figure 1). Does the color repeat regularly, or are there colors in the lengthwise weave which are not repeated in the crosswise weave or vice versa? If so, you must treat the fabric as you would for one way.

Also look to see if there are the same amount of threads in the lengthwise pattern as there are in the crosswise pattern. If there aren't, the fabric must again be considered as one way. And even if the same amount of threads have been used in each direction, one

thread gauge may be greater than the other, thereby making the pattern irregular. A check may even look regular when in fact it isn't. Skirtmaking chapter 19 shows you how you can make a simple test to find out.

Stripes

The first consideration is the repeat of the design. This can create width if the pattern is bold and the colors show an obviously wide pattern repeat. For a slim look, the stripes should not be spaced too far apart.

Striped fabrics are made in two ways—horizontal and vertical. If you want to combine horizontal and vertical stripes in one garment, make sure they are designed well and make an interesting combination.

▲ **1.** *Left: balanced design; Right: unbalanced design*

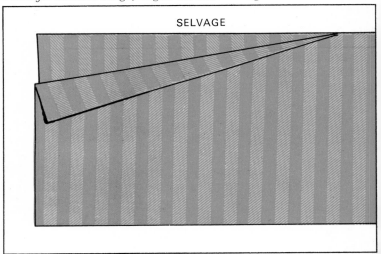
SELVAGE

▲ **2.** *Distortion on the selvages of a striped fabric*

Checking the fabric finish

As the fabric is unrolled on the shop counter, lift one selvage and see if the corresponding selvage meets it correctly. Look at the stripes and checks and see if the finish has distorted the pattern on the cloth so that they do not meet from side to side (figure **2**). Although some of these fabrics can be folded quite easily after the length has been cut off, others are very resistant to folding since they have been carelessly finished and dragged. Here one side is so much out of line it cannot be used with any success.

If you are in doubt, a good assistant who is familiar with the merchandise should be able to advise you. If, however, you cannot get assurance, buying the fabric could lead to disappointment.

Far right: wide stripes perfectly aligned. Top right: effective use of checks on a cape coat. Right: checks bias cut on a skirt. All five designs in this chapter from Vogue patterns ►

Choosing the right style

Checks and stripes have an all-over geometrical and predictable design. But the figure shapes they have to cover have rounded contours which are quite unpredictable. Since every figure is different, it is not possible to design an ideal checked or striped pattern for all figures. It is up to each dressmaker therefore to choose her style, at the same time observing the few golden rules given below.

○ Use large checks or wide stripes on large areas uncluttered by detail. Never distort the geometry of the design with unnecessary breaks, seams or darts. Only use them if they actually enhance the style and the design of the fabric. Figures **3** and **4** show a good and bad usage of large checks.

○ Avoid darts as much as possible. A wrongly placed dart will cut or distort the design. If darts are unavoidable, try to move them so that one side of the dart seamline remains in the straight or the crosswise grain of the fabric.

○ Rounded edges on collars, cuffs and pockets are not suitable for all types of checks or stripes. Confine them to small checks and fine stripes.

○ Closely fitted garments, such as dresses and tailored suits, look best in small to medium sized checks.

○ If the style has lots of detail such as pockets, yoke, collar, it is best to use small checks, otherwise the detail will be lost in the background of the fabric.

Designing for checks and stripes

A clever dressmaker can have fun designing for these fabrics. The illustrations in this chapter give ideas for styles which show checks and stripes to advantage.

A simple and most effective idea is to choose a fabric with light and dark alternating colors which are repeated regularly. Make a pleated skirt using the dark sections for the pleat distance and the light sections for the pleat depth. As the pleats spring open, the light color is revealed, creating a pretty striped effect.

Cutting notes

Be prepared; making a garment in checks and stripes takes longer than making a garment in other fabrics. Attention to detail starts on the cutting table where you must take great care to match the design. Be especially careful when cutting the long sections where a mistake could be disastrous.

Before cutting make the necessary adjustments to the length and width of the

222

▲ *Pants suit with band cross checked*

pattern and do not take a chance by adding or cutting off the pattern on the layout.

When pinning down the pattern, make sure that all corresponding pattern pieces are pinned in the same check or stripe. Start matching from the hem upward (figure **5**). If matched from the underarm section downward, any ease or side bust dart would throw the pattern out of line. If you are not sure what adjustments will be necessary to the side bust darts, add 2 inches to the hemline at the Back and add extra seam allowance to the armhole line. Then, should you have to lift fabric into the dart, you will have enough

▲ **3.** *A good choice of style for large checks*

▲ **4.** *An unsuitable style choice for large checks*

length to re-cut the Back line up the fabric pattern.

Matching checks and stripes for set-in sleeves is often difficult, especially if severe adjustments have been made to the armhole line at the fitting.

To allow you some play on the sleeve crown, cut the whole sleeve cap with at least 1 inch seam allowance (figure **6**). Be sure to mark out the seamline around the sleeve cap carefully so that if you should have to let out on the sleeve crown, you will be able to compensate on the underarm to avoid a large armhole.

Yokes, pocket flaps and collars must always be cut with special care (figure **7**).

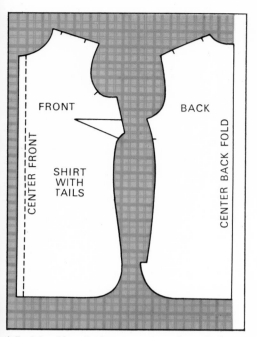

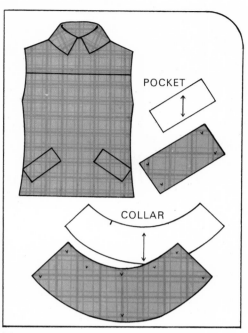

▲ 5. *Matching checks on a pattern from the hem*

▲ 7. *Matching checks on yoke, pockets and collar*

Center Back seam in a skirt. This can be made easier with slip-basting.

Slip-basting is a method of basting where one side of the seam edge is folded on the outside of the fabric along the straight of grain line and brought to meet the other seamline in the corresponding grain line. To baste the seam together, work through the folded edge into the flat fabric as shown, slip-basting along with small stitches (figure **8**).

Although slip-basting will help you match the lengthwise grain lines, do not rely on it to give you enough anchorage for matching the horizontal lines of the fabric pattern. You cannot control the tension of the basting stitches well enough, and after slip-basting it is always necessary to pin or rebaste from the inside, having laid the fabric flat.

Shaped seams

Pinning and basting shaped seams requires a great deal of care. Since the seam runs through the bias of the fabric it is so easy to accidentally drag the seam edge.

Use pins at right angles to the seamline to give you extra control over the edge and allow you to pin together matching pattern lines.

Fitting

The obvious lengthwise and crosswise grain lines and pattern lines are your fitting guide. Make sure they hang well and are not tilted or dragged to one side. Directional design will emphasize deviation, and figure faults are more obvious.

But if the fabric design is cleverly adjusted and incorporated into the fitting of the garment without affecting the straight and crosswise directional pattern, you will see that your dress allows you to forget your problems.

It is often said that the waist seam and hem must continue in the pattern line. This, of course, is wrong. If a figure fault makes the straight waist pucker, it is essential that the fullness is taken off into the waist seam. But always check that the crosswise grain continues around the figure perfectly horizontally.

Allow the waist seam to follow your natural waistline and to hide the adjustment make a belt wide enough to suit you. When making the hem, remember that the checks or stripes will only go straight around the hem if the garment is cut perfectly straight from hips to hemline. If the skirt is cut with a flare, however slight, your hemline will be rounded and not run in the line of the fabric pattern.

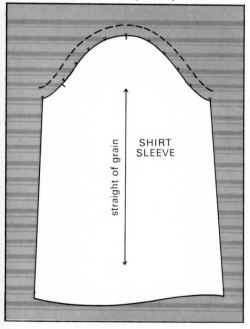

▲ 6. *Cutting 1 inch seams on a sleeve cap*

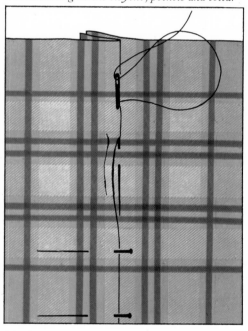

▲ 8. *Slip-basting a seam*

Make sure that the checked or striped pattern continues through the pocket or yoke. Tilted pockets must be adjusted precisely to the straight of the grain line on the pattern so that, although the pocket is cut on the cross, the pattern continues across the garment.

When cutting a collar from prominent colored checks or stripes, lay the complete collar pattern on the fabric to see that the colors repeat on both collar ends similarly. If not, it is best to cut the collar in two halves with a Center Back seam, making sure that the pattern lines coincide. Careful attention to detail is important.

Preparing for fitting

Mark out the pattern detail with care since fitting alterations on these fabrics are movements of consequence. Altering one section may make it out of line with a corresponding section which must then also be adjusted to realign the pattern.

Baste the sections together quite firmly and gently press the seam allowance to get as smooth a fit as possible for the first fitting.

Slip-basting

It is often difficult to match the straight of grain lines of vertical seams such as the

Chapter 52

Working with lace fabrics

Lace comes in so many different forms that here it would be impossible to describe every type in one chapter. Many countries have their own traditional laces, handmade by craftsmen over many generations, which are of a perfection no machine could ever achieve. But machines have taken over and today many manufacturers are producing laces of great variety and of a high standard and quality.

This chapter concentrates on the main types of machine-made dress laces you are likely to find in your local stores, and sets out to give you general advice on how to handle these delicate fabrics. There are useful tips on buying lace for garment making, and choosing the right style to make the most of the design of the fabric.

Making lace garments requires patience and a knowledge of the fabric in order to work with it in the correct way. For instance, many laces can only be worked by hand, and at the end of this chapter you will find some techniques that will help you to begin to acquire this particular skill.

The beautiful wedding dress on page 227 is from a Vogue Pattern and shows lace in its most romantic mood.

Types of lace

The difference in the construction of various machine-made laces divides them into three main groups.
Group 1. Knitted and crocheted lace.
Group 2. Woven lace.
Group 3. Embroidered lace.
Under these main groups you will find lace both for garment making and for trimming.

Group 1. Knitted and crocheted lace

Under this heading comes raschel knitted lace (figure **1**), which is the cheapest form of lace on the market today. It is cheap because the construction is simple and therefore fast.

This category includes crochet-type lace which comes in the form of curtain lace (figure **2**). Curtain lace, as its name suggests, is, strictly speaking, a home furnishing lace, but manufacturers are selling more and more today for dress wear in keeping with current fashion demand.

Group 2. Woven lace

Woven, or Leavers lace (figure **3**), is perhaps the most popular form of lace available today and is easy to obtain through most retail outlets. Here, the threads are twisted, rather than knitted

1. *Raschel knitted lace showing the edge finish for all-over lace;* **2.** *Crochet-type curtain lace;* **3.** *Woven, or Leavers, lace showing a flouncing edge finish;* **4.** *Re-embroidered ribbon lace;* **5.** *Guipure lace*►

together. The background of woven lace is usually net, which may be of even design or may form part of the intricate design of the lace itself.

A variety of designs are to be found in this category. Because weaving is so versatile manufacturers can achieve a greater variation in design than with any other form of lace construction.

Group 3. Embroidered lace

Embroidered lace ranges from eyelet embroidery on woven fabric to raschel or Leavers lace, which is re-embroidered with ribbon (figure **4**) or braid or cord over the original design to give a more bulky or textured appearance. Some re-embroidered laces have very heavy braid incorporated into the design, and this is done either in the process of manufacture, or the braid is applied afterwards. Guipure lace (figure **5**) is a special type of embroidered lace and may be placed under this heading, although this is the only lace not made on a lace machine. It is made on a Schiffli embroidery machine which originated in Germany. Here the lace is embroidered onto an acetate fabric which is dissolved in a special acid solution after the embroidery has been completed.

In spite of the open-work appearance of guipure lace, it is a heavy, chunky type of lace and falls in the more expensive price bracket.

Edge finishes

When you buy lace you will find that there is a choice of two edge finishes, and this may determine the yardage available to you.

All-over lace (see figure **1**). Here the design is extended from side to side and all-over lace is usually available in any yardage desired.

Flouncing (see figure **3**). This lace has one or both edges of the fabric length finished with scallops. In most cases flouncing is only obtainable in lengths of $4\frac{1}{2}$ to 5 yards, although many stores are willing to cut you a shorter length if desired. The only variation is raschel flouncing which is available in any yardage.

Lace widths

Raschel lace. This is usually available in 46 to 47 inch widths, both all-over lace and flouncing.

Crochet-type curtain lace. This usually comes in 43 to 44 inch widths.

Leavers lace. The all-over lace is usually in 34 to 46 inch widths. Flouncing varies from 34 to 36 inch, 47 to 48 inch and 70 to 72 inch widths, the latter being available in white only for bridal wear, usually with flouncing on both edges.

Guipure lace. Here the widths are usually 36 to 48 inches. Occasionally you might find both guipure and raschel laces in 54 inch widths, but these types are usually imported from Germany or Austria.

Fiber content

Raschel and Leavers laces are usually composed of a nylon and rayon mixture. Exceptions may be found in a raschel all nylon lace and Leavers nylon and cotton, or all cotton, laces.

Curtain laces are all cotton, as, on the whole, are guipures.

Taking care of lace

Although the fiber content of a lace may suggest that it can be washed, manufacturers recommend dry cleaning only because of the finishing processes involved which, with washing, can result in shrinkage and design distortion.

The only exception is an all nylon lace which can be washed with comparative safety, but even here be sure to check on the washability at the time of purchase. Also, you must take into consideration the lining fabric being used.

But, as a general rule, it is best not to risk washing lace because there are too many intervening factors.

▲ **6.** and **7.** *Left: simple evening dress in curtain lace. From Butterick Right: tunic top in guipure lace, plain pants. From a Vogue pattern*

Buying lace and choosing the style

Many dressmakers cherish the ambition to make a lace dress, and perhaps the most obvious opportunity arrives with a wedding or a special dinner or cocktail engagement. Wearing lace has long been associated with special occasions, but today there are many types of laces which are suitable for more casual styling, such as tunic pants suits and simple summer day and evening dresses. The Vogue and Butterick patterns in figures **6** and **7** are ideal styles.

It is therefore important when buying lace that you not only have an idea of the style of garment you wish to make but also the occasion for which it is to be worn.

If this is your very first attempt at dressmaking with lace, it is advisable to choose a raschel all-over lace where you are less likely to run into trouble with widths and yardage and construction of the garment itself.

Some lace designs require careful matching, so look at the design carefully when buying and, if there is a very large pattern repeat, make sure that you buy sufficient yardage.

How to use lace

○ All-over lace can usually be cut like any ordinary fabric with a surface design.

○ Flouncing, by its very nature, dictates the design of the garment. This type of lace is put to best use when the flouncing becomes part of the design. An illustration of this is given in figure **8** using a commercial pattern.

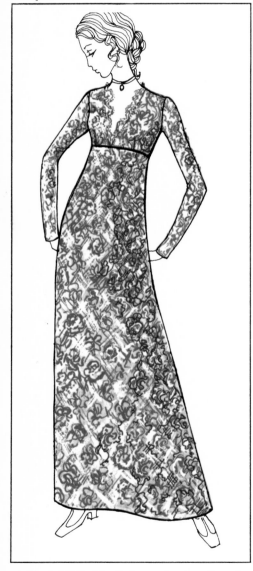

▲ **8.** *A Butterick Pattern showing flouncing used on the neckline as part of the design*

If you decide not to use the flouncing and cut it off, remember that the fabric width will be decreased quite considerably. It would also rob you of a lovely ready-made edge and design interest.

Lace very rarely has a direction for the grain line or fall woven in, and it can be turned when cutting to enable you to make the most of the finished edge. With flouncing you can therefore have the scallops in almost any place you wish.

On large areas, such as skirts, you can use the scallops around the hem if the skirt is cut straight. But skirts cut with flare would make the scalloped hemline uneven.

If you want to use the scallops on a rounded shape it is necessary to cut the scallops carefully away from the edge of the fabric and then appliqué them by hand. This delicate process is explained later in the chapter under hand-sewing techniques.

○ All lightweight laces should, whenever possible, be used as a single layer of fabric and not mounted. Mounting destroys the fine, see-through appearance and the full effect of the delicate fabric will be lost.

○ Heavy laces should not be used lavishly to create folds and drapes—simple designs are best. Too lavish use of a heavy lace will obliterate the design of the fabric. To reveal the design, mount the lace on a matching or contrasting fabric; this also helps to support the weight of the lace and avoids dragging. Garments made from a combination of mounting fabric and lace tend to be heavy, and the tailored or sculptured styles are the best.

Garments which are cut in small sections are ideal for heavy lace because there is plenty of anchorage in the seams.

Mounting and lining fabrics

For both mounting or lining lace fabrics choose a smooth surfaced fabric such as rayon taffeta, slipper satin or pure silk taffeta.

Sewing lace

Since there are many types of laces, there are also many ways in which to sew them. The method chosen often depends upon the type of garment it is made into and the kind of wear it will receive.

On some laces, hand-sewing is the only method possible, and this is covered later in the chapter. The methods below apply to machine stitching.

Seams. With many ordinary dress laces the seams can be stitched by machine, but heavy lace is rarely stitched on a machine. When stitching seams in unmounted lace, trim the seam allowances after stitching to not more than $\frac{1}{4}$ inch and whip stitch the raw edges together.

A machine zigzag finish on raw edges should be confined to the stronger nylon laces. Soft laces gather up under this treatment as the seam itself stretches, and although this can usually be pressed back into shape, the seam will distort again during hanging and wear.

Threads and stitches. If you are using fine or open-work lace, which may have large areas of net between the design, use fine sewing thread in the machine.

Uneven tension of the stitches can have a gathering effect on the lace and the seams will break, so first try the stitch tension on layers of lace scraps.

Also test the stitch length to find the most suitable for the lace you are using. The stitches should be small and neat but remember, if you have to rip the seams, stitches which are too small will only break the delicate fabric.

Edges and hems. On edges requiring facing, to avoid thickness and the confusion of double color and pattern use fine matching net and work this in the same way as a bias facing.

Hems in all-over lace can be turned up in the usual way. There is too much movement in a hem for a net finish.

What to wear under a lace dress

The fitted slip in Dressmaking chapter 39 gives a bare shouldered look and is an ideal garment to wear under lace.

If you don't want a separate undergarment, make the opening of the slip correspond with the opening of the lace dress and catch slip and dress together. A waisted style, too, can be attached to the waistline of the slip.

Mounting and lining lace

For lace garments without waist seams, the garment and the lining are made separately and then stitched together at the neckline and armholes only.

If the dress is waisted, make the bodice and skirt lining separately and stitch them into the waist seam of the dress as well as the neckline and armholes.

Sleeves are mostly left unlined, unless they are long and fitted, in which case the strain is supported by an underlining of matching net.

When mounting heavy lace make sure that the lace does not tighten and form pockets of surplus fabric in the mounting. This could be the result of undetectable stretch in the lace or shrinkage, through heat, of the lace when pressing. So, to minimize the latter, always press the lace first and mount it with care.

When pressing, avoid stretching the lace by moving the iron over it in a lifting and pressing motion and make sure that the lace is supported over the sides of the ironing board to prevent drag.

Openings

Never insert a zipper into lace unless it is mounted. Instead, make a separate placket-type fastening as shown in figure **9**, which is held together with tiny hooks and metal bars. Buttonhole stitch over the bars and hooks with matching thread so that they will not show. This type of fastening can be used with most laces.

If the fastening is not subject to any strain, it may come undone. To prevent this, alternate the hooks and bars with tiny snap fasteners.

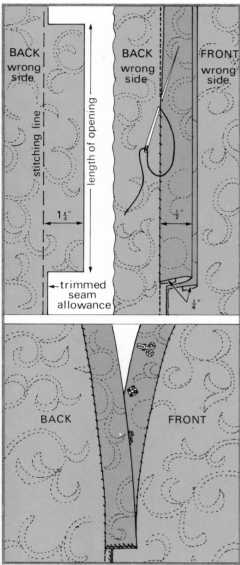

▲ **9.** *Steps in making a placket-type fastening*

Fitting a lace dress

Never fit lace too closely at the underarm, waist or hips because it wouldn't stand the strain. It is therefore especially important when fitting to try all those movements which are going to put strain on the seams.

With some laces, you may find that the ease in the seams of the pattern cannot be dealt with as in other fabrics, and "bounces". If this happens, fit these areas very carefully by taking out the ease as far as movement will allow.

You may have to leave the hem of the dress until the very last stages of sewing since gathers and weight can affect the evenness of the hemline.

A wedding dress made in Leavers lace ▶

▲ **10.** *Appliquéd scallops: cutting the scallops away from the edge of the lace*

edge of garment backed with organza

RIGHT SIDE

▲ **11.** *Working the scallops onto the shaped edge*

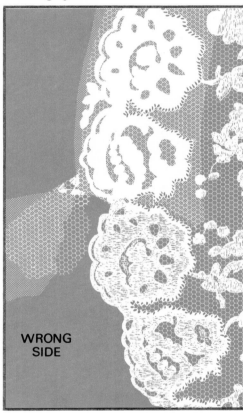

WRONG SIDE

▲ **12.** *Trimming the finished scalloped edge*

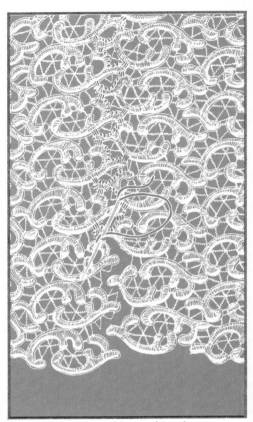

▲ **13.** *Joining the motifs on guipure lace*

▲ **14.** *Making a join on heavier Leavers lace*

Hand-sewing techniques

Of the numerous hand-sewing techniques which are applied to lace, two of the most useful are given here—how to appliqué flouncing scallops to a rounded edge, and how to join lace for a hand-sewn seam.

Appliquéd scallops

If you want to use scallops on a rounded shape, such as a neckline, flared skirt or sleeve hem, first make sure that the design of the lace can be worked in this way.

Flouncing varies so much that sometimes the scallops form just a simple edging to the lace design, and sometimes the design extends deep into the lace before a

borderline for cutting is reached.

So, having satisfied yourself that the lace is suitable, carefully cut the scallops away from the lace fabric (figure **10**).

Then cut the dress as you want and appliqué the lace scallops to the shaped edge after the dress has been assembled. Use a silk thread and work the appliqué over a piece of fine, pure silk organza to avoid distorting the pattern (figure **11**).

Carefully trim away the organza and lace after the appliqué is finished (figure **12**). If the scalloped edges are somewhat untidy and weak, secure them with a row of whip stitching, again using silk thread.

This will create a fine cord-like effect. You will find that a detailed, illustrated reference to whip stitching is given in Generally Speaking chapter 9.

Joining lace

Seams on some laces have to be avoided completely and any necessary joins worked by hand following the design of the lace. Use a suitable hand-sewing thread for the lace and work the join in an overcasting motion.

On guipure lace the edges of the lace design are drawn together to form the join in the continuous repeat of the design (figure **13**).

On heavier Leavers lace the outline of the lace is lapped and matched so that the top side of the join provides the final outline (figure **14**).

Joining lace by hand is delicate work and the join must be so fine that it cannot be detected from a reasonable distance. The final effect, however, is worthwhile.

228

Chapter 53

Working with suede and leather

With the vast advances made by the tanning industry in the last decade, a greater variety of skins is now available to the home dressmaker than ever before. This has resulted in a growing interest in the use of leather and suede which is being nurtured by the major pattern companies, who are including more and more patterns in their ranges for leather and suede skins.

Despite the growing interest, however, dressmakers still tend to shrink from the relatively simple task of making a garment in this medium. Certainly leather and suede requires care in handling, plus know-how, but the rewards of working with such rich and beautiful 'fabrics' are great.

This chapter gives information on buying skins, choosing styles, fitting and making up. There are also many ideas for decorative stitching and using leather for appliqué and patchwork. The chapter concludes with advice on the important aspects of care and cleaning.

Buying the leather and suede

Types of skin

Briefly, for the purposes of this chapter, skin can be split into two distinct groups: sheep and cow.

Sheep. This animal provides those soft, velvety suedes and fine leather skins which are so much in demand, and from which most of the better quality ready-to-wear coats and skirts are made. Because of their suppleness, sheep skins are suitable for coats, skirts, waistcoats, trousers and a variety of accessories.

Sheep skins are available in sizes between 5 and 8 square feet, in a wide range of colours.

Remember, area is length by breadth, and as all the skins are animal shaped, the approximate dimensions across the furthest points for say 7sq ft are 3ft by 2ft 4in(figure 1).

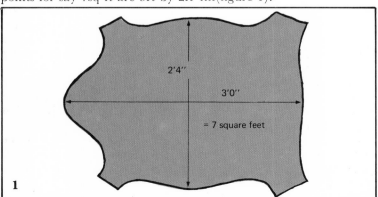

2'4"

3'0"

= 7 square feet

1

Sheep also provide chamois-type skins which are mostly oil dressed and undyed skins, similar to the wash leathers you can buy in the shops. New techniques, however, are making ranges of subtly dyed washable skins more easily available to the home dressmaker.

Cow. This animal supplies soft, fine calf leather in addition to a tough, long pile, double sided suede in the form of suede splits. Although suede split is used extensively in the boot and shoe industry, it is equally suitable for making skirts and jerkins.

Both calf leather and suede split are available in a good range of colours. In size, calf skins average 12sq ft and suede splits 17sq ft.

Choosing the right pattern

If you're new to suede and leather, choose as simple a pattern as possible, without sleeves and preferably panelled. A panelled style is less likely to lose its shape when worn and you can utilise more skin when cutting out. A skirt or waistcoat, where intricate seaming and cutting is not required, is an obvious choice.

If you want to be more ambitious in your choice of style just bear in mind that the size and shape of the suede and leather skins will impose certain, obvious limits. For instance, it is unlikely that you would be able to cut a full length coat piece from shoulder to hem from one suede skin, and so a dress or coat will have to have seams at waist or hip level and, for all practical purposes, set-in sleeves.

Also, as each section of a garment, such as a Front, or Back, or long sleeve, usually takes one skin, you may need to relate your style choice to your handbag!

An effective and also economical idea is to make only a part of the garment in leather or suede, such as the front bodice of a coat. But if you decide on this course of action be very careful to choose a woven fabric which 'works' satisfactorily with the skin.

How many skins will I need?

It's all a matter of square footage! As skins vary in size, the number you will need depends on the type of skin you are using. The supplier will be able to advise you when you buy the skins.

As a starting point for your calculations, here is a rough guide to the number of sheep skins (of 6 to 7sq ft) you will need for particular garments.

Short skirt, length 15in, hips 34in	Longer skirt, up to midi length	Bolero style waistcoat
1 skin	**2 skins**	**1 skin**

Long line waistcoat	Hip length jacket	$\frac{3}{4}$ to full length coat
2 skins	**4/5 skins**	**6/7 skins**

If you have selected a pattern which specifies leather or suede, it usually states the type of skin to use and the square footage required. So, if you work to the pattern, all you need to do is to go to the supplier, who will help you convert the square footage into number of skins.

If, however, you wish to use a different type of skin to that stated on the pattern, or you have selected a pattern which does not specify the use of skins at all, it will be necessary to convert the fabric yardage into square footage, or number of skins. Again, you will need to seek the advice of the supplier.

Here is another chart, also based on sheep skin (6 to 7sq ft), as a further guide to your calculations.

Yardage 36in wide fabric	yds $\frac{2}{3}$	yds $1\frac{1}{3}$	yds 2	yds $2\frac{2}{3}$	yds $3\frac{1}{3}$	yds 4	yds $4\frac{2}{3}$
Equivalent number of skins	**1**	**2**	**3**	**4**	**5**	**6**	**7**

Making the garment

Equipment

Although there are many fine and expensive gadgets on the market for leather work which you could use, the following is a list of the essentials.

- [ ] Sharp scissors
- [ ] Clear tape (to secure the pattern when cutting)
- [ ] Stapler (to secure seam allowances when stitching), and staple remover
- [ ] Adhesive, preferably rubber cement (for sticking down seams)
- [ ] Brown paper (for pressing)
- [ ] Tissue paper (for use when stitching seams)
- [ ] Medium/heavy sewing machine needles or special, triangular leather needles (size No. appropriate to the make of sewing machine)
- [ ] Glover's needles (as used for glove making) for hand sewing
- [ ] Pure silk thread or synthetic thread (the thread must have a certain amount of elasticity as skins stretch slightly)
- [ ] Ball point or felt tip pen (for marking out the pattern details)

Checking and preparing the pattern

Before you start cutting, make sure that you check the pattern for size and make any necessary alterations. If you are not sure whether the garment will need alteration, it is a good idea to make a mock garment in muslin first, as any adjustments made after stitching will be unsightly.

If you are using a commercial paper pattern, trim all seam allowances on the pattern tissue to $\frac{1}{4}$ inch.

If any pattern piece is larger than the skin, decide where it would be best to have a join in the garment and cut the pattern accordingly, adding a $\frac{1}{4}$ inch seam allowance to both pieces.

Where a left and right pattern piece is required, make a copy of that pattern piece and label it "left", label the other "right". This will help you to avoid the classic mistake of cutting two left sides and will also help you to juggle the pieces around on the skin. Likewise, you will have to make another half of any pattern piece where the layout calls for placing on a fold.

Cutting out

When you are placing the pattern pieces on the skin, make sure that the maximum area is utilized, at the same time making a note of any blemishes on the right side.

If you are working with suede, you will have to decide whether or not you can afford to be a purist and keep all the pattern pieces running in the same direction. On a good suede you can get away with ignoring the nap; the surface is very flexible and it will be difficult to detect the direction of the pile when the garment is being worn.

Once you are satisfied with the placing of the pattern pieces, secure them with clear tape on the wrong side of the skin. Mark all the cutting lines and darts using a ball point or felt pen. Cut from the neck edge of the skin using very sharp scissors. Place corresponding pieces together when cutting and staple the seam edges together within the seam allowance. This will prevent the pieces from sliding apart during machine stitching.

Fitting

Try on the stapled together garment for fit and adjust if necessary. This is a very crucial moment. Remember that you cannot erase the marks made by a line of stitching if alterations prove necessary at a later stage. The first row of stitches must be the final one. On suede it is just possible to make slight alterations after stitching as the pile acts as a disguise, but on leather it is impossible.

230

▲ *Long jerkin with thonging, in soft, supple suede from a Vogue pattern*

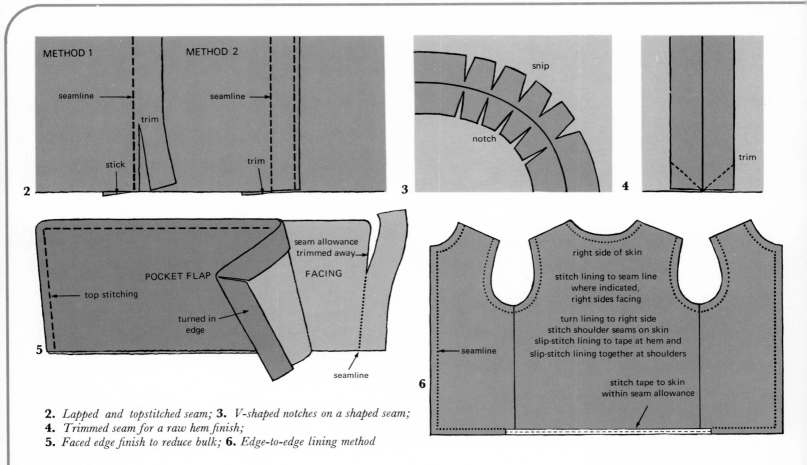

2. *Lapped and topstitched seam*; 3. *V-shaped notches on a shaped seam*;
4. *Trimmed seam for a raw hem finish*;
5. *Faced edge finish to reduce bulk*; 6. *Edge-to-edge lining method*

Stitching

○ Use tissue paper under the leather when stitching. This will prevent the feed teeth of the machine from damaging the skin, and the tissue can easily be torn away after stitching.

○ Reduce the pressure on the presser foot and do not force the leather under the needle. You will either break the needle or damage the skin.

○ Use a sewing machine needle of medium to heavy thickness or a special leather needle. Change the needle immediately if it shows signs of becoming blunt and punching holes in the leather.

○ Use longer stitches than for fabric, about 8 to 10 stitches to the inch, and stitch slowly without stretching.

○ Do not stitch sharp corners, but round them off very slightly. This will make it easier to turn the corners out.

○ Staple the seam allowances together when stitching. The staple remover will facilitate removal of the staples after stitching.

○ For topstitching you will find a roller foot a useful attachment (see Generally Speaking chapter 2).

○ For all hand-sewing, use glover's needles.

Finishing

Seams and darts. Make plain seams, and where seams are subject to strain or stretch, stitch narrow straight tape into those seams.

Cut darts open. To remove excess bulk on seams and darts, pare away (or skive) the under surface of the seam allowance, either with a razor blade or by using one of the scissor blades turned on its side.

An alternative way to finish a seam is to lap the seam allowances and topstitch them (figure 2). This reduces bulk and is particularly suitable for shaped sections. Press plain seams and darts open. If you are using a bulky skin it will help if you first pound the seams open with a heavy wooden object such as a rolling pin or a meat hammer; for fine skin, just finger press the seams open.

Then press using a warm iron (a hot iron will stretch the skin) over brown paper or a dry pressing cloth. Use no moisture. The seam allowance can then be topstitched or stuck down with adhesive.

Here's a good tip when applying the adhesive, but to make use of it the adhesive must be perfectly fresh. Pour the liquid into a clean, empty dish-washing liquid bottle and replace the top. The nozzle makes an excellent applicator.

Edges. Where an edge is curved, cut V-shaped notches into that edge to enable it to lie flat (figure 3).

Hems. Hems can be left raw as leather does not fray, or they can be glued down; this will give a firmer edge finish. If you decide to leave a hem raw, cut back the seam allowance as shown (figure 4).

Facings. On unlined garments, facings can be used to give a certain amount of body. To reduce bulk on the faced edge, trim the seam allowance on the facing to the seamline before stitching and turn back the seam allowance on the garment edge. Place the raw edge of the facing seamline to the folded garment edge and topstitch (figure 5).

This is also a useful tip for the edges of collars, lapels and pocket flaps.

You can, if you wish, omit the facings altogether, turn back the raw edges and either topstitch them or glue them down.

Sleeves. With most domestic skins it is possible to set in sleeves in the normal way, even to ease in the skin around the sleeve cap. Also, you should have no problem in stitching the sleeve seams. If, however, you do find there is too much bulk for stitching, sew in the sleeves by hand using a very firm backstitch.

Interfacings. Where the pattern calls for interfacing, use a non-woven type, such as Pellon, appropriate in weight to the skin you are using. In some cases, a preshrunk tailor's canvas may be suitable. But it is always best to ask about the right type of interfacing before buying.

Linings. Stitching a lining into a leather garment can be tricky as you cannot slip stitch successfully onto skin. The answer is to stitch tape to the seam or hem allowance, or facing, and slip stitch the lining to the tape. Or, make an edge-to-edge lining as shown in figure 6.

Use a strong, durable lining which is

231

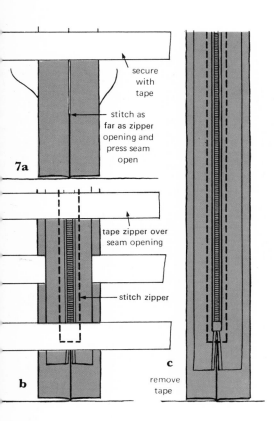

7a, b, c. *Steps in inserting a zipper: secure with tape before stitching*

washable, otherwise you will find that the skin outlasts the lining. Even so, you may have to replace the lining.

Make skirt linings fractionally narrower than the skirt to prevent seating. When finishing the waist on lined skirts, attach the lining to the waist seam before applying the waistband as described in Skirtmaking chapter 20. Then make a hidden belting waistband (see Skirtmaking chapter 14).

Zippers. Zippers can be inserted in the normal way either by machine or hand-sewing. To hold the zipper in place while stitching use clear tape on the wrong side of the garment (figure **7**). This can easily be torn away when the stitching is completed.

Buttonholes and eyelets. You can make bound buttonholes successfully in soft leather or suede, or the buttonhole edges can be zigzagged by machine.

Alternatively, if buttons are part of the finished effect, a useful ploy is to dispense with buttonholes altogether and use covered buttons with snap fasteners on the reverse side. These are generally easier than buttonholes for most dressmakers to cope with and look just as good.

Eyelets used in conjunction with thonging can make a very attractive fastening, especially suitable for casual garments such as the jerkin illustrated on the previous page. Making eyelets is a relatively simple job with an eyelet-making kit which you can buy in most large stores or craft shops.

Different ways with leather

Binding

To bring a new look to an old jacket or blazer, and to save you the expense of buying a new one, apply a leather binding to the frayed edges.

Using a stapler, secure the strip of leather over the garment edge and stitch in place (figure **8a**). Remove the staples and trim away the leather, together with the staple marks, leaving the edges raw (figure **8b**). When you want to join the binding, simply overlap the raw ends and complete the stitching (figure **8c**).

If you want to add a little interest to an otherwise plain coat, you can bind pocket flaps and collar with strips of leather using the method described above.

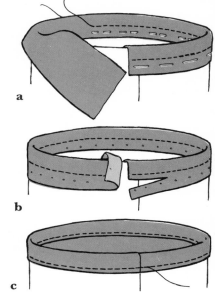

8 a, b, c. *Binding with leather*

Decorative stitching

Saddle stitching can be both decorative and useful (figure **9**). It is useful instead of topstitching for keeping seam allowances in place without the need for gluing. For added effect work light colored saddle stitches on a dark background, or vice versa.

For fine skin you can use embroidery thread for the stitches. For heavier skins, waxed thread is more suitable.

Zigzag stitching can be very effective for joining two pieces of skin without bulk (figure **10a**), or for decoration (figure **10b**). Thonging can be used as a surface decoration. Worked over stitched seams or raw pocket edges, it looks like giant overcasting stitches (figure **11**). Use an eyelet punch to make the holes for the thonging and be sure to select a small hole setting to prevent the thonging from slipping about too much.

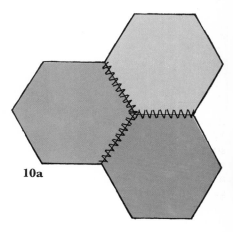

10a

10b

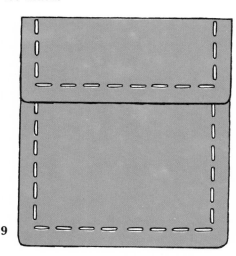

9

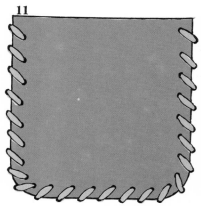

11

9. *Decorative saddle stitching on a pocket;* **10a.** *Zigzag stitch joining pieces of skin;* **b.** *Zigzag stitch used to decorate a pocket;* **11.** *Thonging used as surface decoration*

12-16. *Give all sorts of commercial paper patterns a personal touch with leather or suede appliqué (figures 12, 14). Or make up only certain portions of a garment in a contrasting skin (figures 13, 16). Leather or suede used in patchwork (figure 15) is another idea.*

Appliqué, patches and patchwork

With appliqué, you can achieve some striking effects by using simple shapes in various colors and applying them around a hem or sleeve edge, or on the bodice of a garment (figure **12**). Use an existing design or work out your own design on paper first. Apply the shapes by zigzagging or hand sewing over the raw edges; you can also straight stitch close to the raw edges. An interesting variation of appliqué is seen in figure **13**, where suede is applied to the pocket area and is then extended into a belt.

Patches of leather or suede can be used as pockets, to repair worn elbows in jackets or to make colorful belts and bags (figure **14**). Apply the patches as for appliqué.

Patchwork is definitely for the patient worker, but with clever color combinations the effect can be quite beautiful and well worthwhile.

For patchwork choose a simple skirt or vest pattern (figure **15**). Choose geometric shapes for the patches, such as squares, oblongs and hexagons (ready cut patches are available, or you can cut your own using a template), and make the areas of patchwork slightly larger than the size of the pattern pieces. When stitching the patches together, place them edge to edge and zigzag over the raw edges, or use plain seams. Then simply make the garment using the areas of patchwork

as if they were plain leather or suede.

Whether you are working with appliqué, patches or patchwork, you can use scraps of leather or suede, bought as such, or make use of the unworn parts of an old leather garment. Also, in addition to those featured here, you will be able to find many more commercial paper patterns which you can easily adapt to these ideas.

Sectional uses for leather and suede

An extension of the appliqué idea is seen where sections of leather and suede are built into a garment. For instance, suede yokes can be teamed with woven fabric for added interest, or a suede front added to a coat or a man's vest (figure **16**). Here again, there are many patterns which can be adapted for this purpose.

Care of leather and suede

If you've taken a lot of time in making a garment in leather or suede, it really is worthwhile having it professionally cleaned by experts. Take time to "shop around" as a lot of firms specialize in this sort of work and it's worth seeking them out even if you do have to send the garment by mail to have it cleaned.

Today, some suede is washable, and not only that which is guaranteed to be so. Before you plunge your new suede skirt into water, check with the supplier

that it is safe to do so. If you have a scrap of suede left over, try this piece first. If the result is satisfactory, and you decide to go ahead, be prepared for some dye loss and no guarantee from the supplier if anything goes wrong.

Wash with a liquid soap and rinse very thoroughly, adding a few drops of baby oil to the final rinse to keep the skin supple.

After rinsing, gently squeeze out as much water as possible without wringing—do not lift up the garment while it is still full of water. Place the garment on a thick towel and gently pat out any excess moisture.

Dry garments by pinning them up by their linings or by placing flat on a large wire tray away from direct heat. When doing so, do not stretch the garment but just smooth it out so that it will return to its original shape. When dry, the skin will feel a little stiff, so rub the sueded surfaces together and then press as already described.

For general grubbiness, use a proprietary cleaner. Oil or grease marks must be treated by a specialist dry cleaner—do not attempt to remove them yourself. If you get mud on the garment, let it dry before removing with a soft brush. Suede brushes, so called, are for shoes and shoes only—if you were to use one on a fine, soft suede skin you would be rewarded with a very ugly bald patch!

Chapter 54

Reversible and double-faced fabrics

Sewing with reversibles can be challenging and exciting, as these double-sided fabrics enable you to present two different faces to the world. Although some of the sewing techniques involved may be a little more complicated than with ordinary fabrics the end result is well worth the effort, and remember— you do get two garments for the price of one!

What is a reversible fabric?

Reversible or doubled-faced fabrics are those in which either or both sides of the material can be used as the top fabric. Although the weave of certain cloths can give this effect, a true reversible consists of two fabrics held together by a random thread and firmly woven together at the selvage. The two parts of a reversible fabric can be gently pulled apart revealing the threads which hold them together (figure **1**).

Some reversibles consist of two layers of fabric lightly bonded together. These should not be confused with laminated or bonded fabrics, where one cloth is purely a backing for the other.

There is a wide variety of reversible materials available: combinations of checked or plaid fabrics reversing to show one plain color; two contrasting plains; nubbly tweeds with plains—the variations are endless.

Choosing a pattern

To make a reversible garment, choose a simply styled pattern where all details can work on both sides of the garment. Avoid collars which have too marked a roll, details such as pockets slotted into seams which cannot be made reversible, and complicated fastenings. A pleat in the front or back of a garment may have to be taken out to make a garment reversible.

By their very nature, reversible fabrics are firm and often bulky, and are best suited to loose swinging styles rather than to anything too closely fitted. Avoid gathers, pleats or soft draping.

A poncho or a cape is an ideal garment for a first attempt at working with reversibles (figures **2a** and **b**).

Figure **2c** shows a wrap-around skirt pattern which can be very easily adapted to a reversible fabric, while figure **2d** shows a suitable vest. For a reversible coat or jacket choose a loose fitting wrap-around with raglan or kimono sleeves (figure **2e**).

Special techniques for reversibles

Seams and darts

There is, of course, no right or wrong side on a reversible fabric, and the following seams can be worked on either side of the garment, depending on the effect you want to achieve.

Flat-fell seam. This is the seam most commonly used.

Cut a $\frac{3}{4}$ inch seam allowance and stitch a plain seam. Press the seam open (to give a good crisp finish) and then to one side. Separate

▲ **2.** *Reversible fabrics at their best;* **a.** *a cape;* **b.** *a poncho;* **c.** *a skirt;*

the layers on each seam allowance and layer them as shown (figure **3a**), leaving the top layer $\frac{3}{4}$ inch wide and trimming the bottom one to $\frac{1}{4}$ inch.

Turn in the raw edge of the top layer, baste over the trimmed seam allowance and either slip stitch in place or machine close to the fold (figure **3b**).

Strap seam. Here the seams are stitched normally and pressed open. The layers are separated and trimmed to different widths, and then covered with a bias strip cut from one layer of the reversible fabric (figure **4**). Alternatively, you could use a bias strip of matching or contrasting lighter-weight fabric or a fancy braid. It is best to slip stitch the "strap" in place to leave the reverse side of the fabric unmarked.

Plain seam. Separate the layers to a depth of $1\frac{1}{2}$ inches at the edges to be seamed. With right sides facing stitch two layers together (figure **5a**) and press the seam open. Then turn in the seam allowances on the other two layers and slip stitch together (figure **5b**).

Darts. Pull the fabric apart to the point of the dart so that the dart is accessible. Stitch the dart on the inside of each fabric layer and press open (figure **6**).

Facings, interfacings and linings

A reversible garment will have none of these.

Collars and sleeves

Collars. To make a collar, separate the two layers around the outer

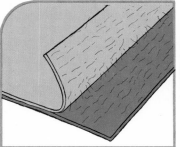

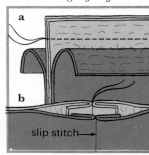

▲ **d.** *A vest;* **e.** *a coat;* **f.** *a jumper*

▲ **1.** *Separating reversible fabric*

▲ **3.** *Making a flat-fell seam*

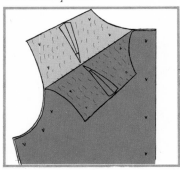

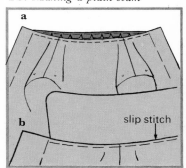

▲ **4.** *A strap seam*

▲ **5.** *Making a plain seam*

▲ **6.** *Stitching the darts*

▲ **7a.** *and* **b.** *Inserting a collar*

collar edges for $1\frac{1}{2}$ inches, then turn in the seam allowances and slip stitch together. Separate the neck edges of the garment and clip the curve of the neck on both layers to within $\frac{1}{8}$ inch of the stitching line. Turn the seam allowances to the inside, baste each edge separately and press so that you get a smooth edged pocket into which you can insert the collar (figure **7a**).

Clip the seam allowance along the neck edge of the collar and insert between the garment neck edges, matching centers and notches. Slip stitch each edge of the neck to the collar separately (figure **7b**).

Sleeves. Raglan or kimono sleeves can be stitched to the garment using any of the seaming methods above, but set-in sleeves should be attached in the same way as the collar.

Hems and edges

There are two ways of finishing the edges of reversible fabrics. One method is to trim the seam allowances to the seamline and bind the edges with braid (see Know-How chapter 59) or a bias strip cut from one layer of the fabric.

For the second method, trim the hem or seam allowances to $\frac{5}{8}$ inch. Separate the two edges to a depth of $1\frac{1}{2}$ inches, turn in the seam allowances and slip stitch the edges together. Additional top-stitching will give a really firm, crisp finish.

Pockets

Only patch pockets are possible. Separate the layers around the edge of the patch, turn in the seam allowances and slip stitch to-gether. Slip stitch the pocket to the garment.

Fastenings

Choosing fastenings for reversible garments can be a problem. Wrap-around styles are the simplest and often the most effective, and will look the same whichever side of the garment is worn out-side. A simple jumper with side slits or a blanket-type poncho present no difficulties either (figure **2f**).

For fastening a simple vest or coat try some of the novelty closures such as buckles, clips, frogs or toggles which can create an unusual effect.

Another idea is to make rouleau loops, inserting them into the edges before finishing, and close with lacing. Punched eyelet holes closed with lacing is another possibility.

Zippers. These are simple to insert but are not suitable if either layer of fabric is very thick. To insert the zipper separate the layers along the zipper opening to a depth of $1\frac{1}{2}$ inches. Turn in the edges of each layer along the seamline and press lightly. Sandwich the zipper between the folded edges and stitch in place in the usual way.

Buttons. You can fasten the garment with buttons. Either make two sets of buttonholes and fasten them with link buttoning or make one set of buttonholes and sew on two sets of buttons. It is best to make the buttonholes by hand, but they can be worked by machine. Bound buttonholes are also possible if carefully made. Separate the layers along the buttonhole edge, work the front of the bound buttonhole in the top layer of fabric and finish the bottom layer as you would for the facing (see Know-How chapter 56).

Chapter 55

Working with simulated fur fabrics

The wearing of fur has long been a sign of wealth and position which, until recently, nothing could emulate. But today simulated furs have done just that, and the home dressmaker can buy fur as simply as buying a yard of cloth.

This chapter deals with the techniques of handling fur fabrics, giving advice on choosing the fabric, the right style and making up.

The aversion to trapping wild animals for their skin is growing and this is where fur fabric really comes into its own. There is a wide variety of fabric weight and color to choose from and so long as the pattern you choose is simple and unfussy, a coat or jacket in this material will be as simple to make and as successful as in any other fabric.

Jacket by Vogue in Mongolian lamb fur fabric.

Simulated fur fabrics and how to handle them

The most exciting aspect of today's simulated furs is their wide range and variety. Some are exact replicas of real furs, while others are wild and colorfully imaginative fabrics bearing no relation to any animal's skin.

Close imitations are often hard to distinguish from real fur since their colorings and markings are carefully copied. The fabric can also be grooved to give the impression of real fur pelts sewn together. "Wild life" by the yard includes leopard, mink, seal, otter, Mongolian lamb and pony.

Some fur fabrics, with either smooth or curled hairs, are permanently brushed in a swirling pattern just like an animal's skin. Others have a distinct one-way nap and must be treated just as you would normal napped fabric.

The facts about simulated furs

Basically, simulated furs are pile fabrics with either woven or knitted backings. Those with knitted backings are normally more flexible than those with woven backings, which are stiffer and often more difficult to handle.

The backing can be of a different fiber to that of the surface pile. Backings are usually of cotton or man-made fiber, while the surface pile may be of man-made fiber, such as rayon, nylon, or polyester, or of a natural fiber such as mohair or wool. Sometimes the backing is printed or vinyl coated to be used as a reversible fabric, although here the layers cannot be separated as with ordinary reversibles.

Simulated furs are available mainly in 48 inch or 54 inch widths.

Cleaning. For woven backed simulated furs the manufacturers recommend fur cleaning, and it is important to realize that this process is quite different from ordinary dry cleaning. Most reliable dry cleaners today have a fur cleaning service.

Simulated furs with knitted backings are usually washable but they must always be hand-washed and with extreme care. After washing, the fabric will benefit from a good shaking which lifts the pile.

Choosing the pattern

Simulated fur is soft and luxurious and can never be crisply tailored. Look for a style which will make the most of your fabric rather than trying to chisel it into an unsuitable shape.

By its very nature this fabric is dramatic, so play up this quality by choosing simple uncluttered lines. Remember that seams will not show in fur fabric and that clever details will be lost.

Remember, too, your own figure shape; fur is bulky and will add extra inches, so use it to draw attention to your good points and minimize your larger features by combining the fur with plain fabric. For example, if you have heavy thighs in comparison with the rest of your figure, wear plain dark pants with a gay fur jacket.

Avoid patterns with gathers or pleats; besides creating an enlarging effect, your machine may not be able to stitch through too many thicknesses. For the same reason avoid intersecting seams wherever possible.

Do not limit yourself to those patterns which suggest fur fabric, as many others may be suitable, but for your first attempt it would be best to choose a simple shape.

Adapting the pattern for simulated fur

Having accepted the principle that when working with fur fabric excessive bulk is undesirable, you must now try to remove unnecessary thickness wherever possible in the pattern you have chosen. If the Center Back seam is parallel to the grain line, trim off the seam allowance and place the stitching line on a fold (figure **1**).

Similarly, to adapt the pattern you can dispense with the Center Front wrap seam by cutting the Front and front facing in one. Place the Center Front line of the facing over that of the Front and pin (figure **2**).

Alternatively, you can cut the facings in a plain firm fabric and so avoid having two layers of fur fabric down the front.

The garment could also be lined to the edge.

To add a realistic touch to a grooved mink fabric why not emulate the furrier; shorten the pattern to allow for a band of horizontal stripes at the hemline or a single band at the cuffs, such as you might find on a real mink (figure **3**).

Checking the pattern

Of course the first rule when making any garment is to check the pattern measurements. This is particularly important when working with fur fabric as it is not easy to alter seams in this fabric. For this reason it is a good idea to first make a mock garment in muslin.

Try the mock garment on, remembering that the fur fabric itself will look far bulkier. Make any necessary alterations and transfer them back to the pattern, or take the muslin garment apart and use it as your pattern.

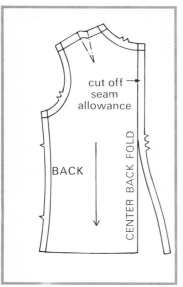

▲ **1.** *Trimming at the Center Back Butterick pattern in Dacron Sherpa pile* ►

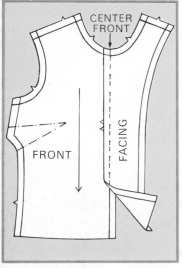

▲ **2.** *Joining Front and front facing*
▼ **3.** *Allowing for horizontal bands*

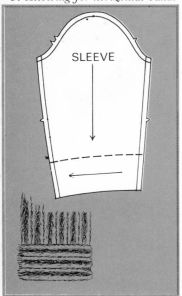

237

Choosing underlining, interfacing and lining

It is not usual to underline simulated fur fabrics since they have plenty of body. Interfacing, however, is usually very necessary to prevent the weight of the fabric from stretching out of shape at vital areas, such as neckline, armholes, hem and cuffs.

As fur fabrics vary so much in weight and texture it is safest to inquire when buying about the correct interfacing to use.

When choosing a lining for fur fabric bear in mind that the fixative with which many fur fabrics are treated makes their backings stiff, and this may wear away a lining which is too fragile. So choose a medium to heavy-weight durable lining such as synthetic taffeta or lining satin. Although a more expensive insulated lining, such as Milium, is often a good idea for a simulated fur which may not be as warm as it looks.

▼ **4.** *Using seam tape for stitching seams*

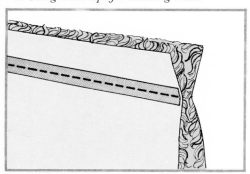

▼ **5a.** *Shaving the pile;* **b.** *teasing out the pile*

▼ **6.** *Pushing the long hairs out of the way*

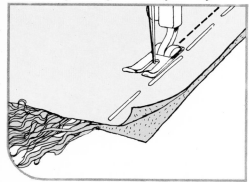

If you are using a washable fur fabric, make sure that the lining you choose is also washable.

Cutting out the pattern

Lay out simulated furs with a distinct one-way nap as for one-way fabrics. With long-haired fur fabrics, always make sure the nap runs downward.

However, furs with a curled, swirling pile have no nap to consider.

Remember that prominent fur markings must be matched as carefully as a patterned fabric.

Open out the fabric, place it with the pile side down and lay out the pattern pieces on the backing. If you are using the muslin pattern you will already have two of each pattern piece, if not, remember to reverse pattern tissues to match.

You will be able to pin the pattern in place on short-haired furs, but when the pile is long and thick use transparent tape to secure the pieces.

Use very sharp scissors when cutting, and to avoid cutting the pile, lift the fabric with one hand and carefully cut through the backing only. For thick fur fabrics it may be necessary to use a single-edged razor blade instead of scissors.

Mark the pattern details with tailor's chalk or a soft pencil. Since fur fabric tends to fray very easily notches should be marked and not cut out. All markings can safely be chalked or penciled on the back of the fur fabric since the pile will prevent them showing through to the right side.

Stitching and finishing

First test the stitching on scraps of the fur fabric before you attempt any seams on the garment itself. The heavier the fabric, the thicker and stronger the needle and thread will have to be. A thread with elasticity, such as pure silk or one of the new synthetic threads, gives good results.

Use a stitch length of 8-10 stitches to the inch.

Simulated furs with flexible knitted backings should be stitched with a narrow zigzag stitch.

Fur fabrics with vinyl coated backings should be stitched with a roller foot on the machine.

A roller foot is also useful if you have to stitch directly onto the right side of the fur. Alternatively, you can cover the surface of the fabric with a strip of tissue paper.

Seams. Plain seams are the most suitable for fur fabrics. If the fur fabric has a slippery long piled surface, baste the seams carefully before stitching.

Simulated lamb's wool or similar fur fab-

rics lock together well and can be pinned. Seams in heavy fur fabric can be held together with paper clips.

When joining simulated fur to a flat fabric baste it securely in place to prevent it slipping and stitch in the direction of the nap with the flat fabric on top.

With seams subjected to strain, use seam tape in with the stitching (figure **4**).

After stitching, shave the pile from the seam allowance with a safety razor or scissors (figure **5a**). Then use a pin to tease out the pile from the seam (figure **5b**).

With long-haired fur fabrics it is easier to shave the pile from the seam allowance and push the remaining hairs toward the right side before you stitch the seam (figure **6**).

Trim enclosed seams (collar seams or faced seams) as close as possible, layering them to reduce bulk. Stitch these seams twice, reducing the stitch length at corners, to make them as strong as possible.

Pressing. Most seams can be finger pressed open and rubbed on the inside with a thimble to make them lie flat. Use an iron sparingly, testing first on fabric scraps. Dry press with a cool iron on the wrong side only, using a needle-board or toweling to protect the pile.

Finishing the seams. After stitching and pressing finish the seam edges carefully. They can be bound with bias binding, overcast by hand or finished with a wide machine zigzag stitch.

You can also slip stitch the seam allowance to the backing, thus finishing it and holding it flat at the same time.

On heavier fur fabrics seam allowances can be glued back in place with an adhesive or fabric glue.

Darts. Cut darts open and trim, then shave and finish seam allowances as you would on a plain seam.

Fastenings. Machine-made buttonholes work in some fur fabrics, but usually it is better not to use them. Instead, use soft leather or imitation leather and make bound buttonholes, using the method described in the following chapter. Imitate the fastenings used on real fur coats such as large hooks and eyes or frogs, or make a mock button opening with large covered snap fasteners underneath the buttons.

Zippers. It is best to sew zippers in place by hand. Shear the pile from the seam allowance to prevent it from catching in the teeth of the zipper.

Lining. Linings can be slip stitched in place in the normal way through the pile, but if you have difficulty shave the pile away on the edges of sleeve hems and facings.

Know-How

Chapter 56
Bound buttonholes, stitched yokes and piping

Nothing gives away the careless dressmaker quite so distinctly as haphazard finishes. To avoid such a situation, this chapter gives hints on the perfect buttonhole, as well as several methods of decorative seaming.

Bound buttonholes

There is one basic technique for making bound buttonholes which is varied according to the type of fabric used.

The fabric
The fabric on which the bound buttonholes are being made must have some depth into which the extra fabric used for binding the buttonhole can sink, otherwise the binding will create bulk and rise above the fabric surface.

Fabrics which fray easily must have the fraying arrested first. This is achieved by lining the binding for the buttonhole as well as the area for the buttonhole itself. Fabrics which fray even after these precautions are unsuitable.

The size
When using thick coating fabric make sure the buttonhole is not less than ¾ inch long. If shorter there will not be enough length to work it properly and the buttonhole will look lumpy.

Unlike hand-worked buttonholes, which have a solidly stitched edge, bound buttonholes are soft and give a little, so it is not necessary to make an extra allowance

The knit of this simple fitted coat is a suitable fabric for bound buttonholes.

when measuring out the length of the buttonhole—the buttonhole can be made to the exact diameter of the button. However, if the button is exceptionally thick add half the thickness of the button to the length for ease.

Stitch size
The stitching needs to be very firm and small as it comes very close to the buttonhole opening.

Engage the smallest stitch setting on your machine and stitch two layers of fabric together. The stitches should be about the size of a pinpoint.

Width

The buttonhole width depends on the type of fabric you are working on. If made in thick fabrics the buttonholes should be about $\frac{3}{8}$ inch wide, but in thin fabrics you can make them quite narrow—about $\frac{3}{16}$ to $\frac{1}{4}$ inch wide.

Making the buttonholes

Here are step by step instructions:

☐ Measure out the buttonhole positions and length and mark them as shown (figure 2).

☐ For each buttonhole cut a strip of fabric on the cross 2 inches wide and 1½ inches longer than the buttonhole length. Working on the outside of the garment, lay the strip centrally over the buttonhole position with right sides of the fabric facing (figure 3).

☐ Working on the wrong side of the fabric stitch the outline of the buttonhole, shaping it into a perfect rectangle and carefully pivoting the work on the needle at each corner (figure 4). Run the last stitches over the first stitches as shown, to prevent the buttonhole from splitting.

☐ Using sharp, pointed scissors, cut into the stitched area as shown (figure 5) taking care not to cut the stitches at the corners.

☐ Pull the binding fabric to the inside (figure 6). Then lay each buttonhole seam allowance over the edge of a sleeveboard and press the seam allowances away from the opening as shown.

☐ **Small buttonholes.** For small buttonholes turn the work to the outside and gently roll the folded edges of the binding so that they meet along the center of the buttonhole with equal width to each side (figure 7). Lightly baste along the opening as shown.

Turn the work to the inside and gently pull the horizontal edges of the binding fabric to make the rolls continue evenly beyond the opening of the buttonhole. Catch them together permanently with matching thread (figure 8).

☐ **Large buttonholes.** Large buttonholes are made as above but each rolled edge must be worked separately. As it is rolled it must be secured with small prick stitches along the fold of the seamline on the right side (figure 9). Do not pull the stitches tight into the fabric or they will make dents which will show in the finished work.

Baste along the opening (figure 10) then stitch the ends of the rolled edges together on the wrong side as shown in figure 8.

240

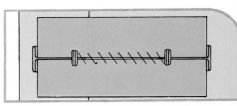

▲ 2. *The marked out buttonhole*

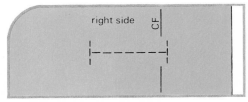

▲ 3. *The bias strip laid over the buttonhole*

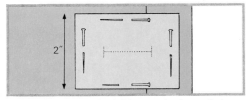

▲ 4. *The stitched rectangle for the buttonhole*

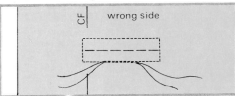

▲ 5. *Cutting the buttonhole*

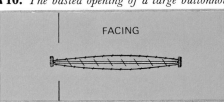

▲ 6. *The binding pulled through the opening*

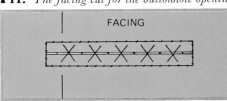

▲ 7. *The rolled edges on a small buttonhole*

☐ With the basting stitches still in place, carefully press each buttonhole. Then, while the work is still warm from the iron, gently pull the ends of the rolled edges of the bias strip to settle them into the fabric and fix the shape of the buttonhole. Remove any impressions made in the fabric by pressing under the binding fabric strip.

Turn the garment facing over the buttonholes and baste the front edge of the facing firmly in position.

Feel the buttonhole through the facing fabric and make a cut through the facing to the length of the buttonhole opening. Turn in the edges of the cut and hem them

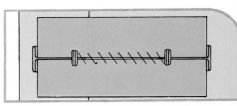

▲ 8. *The rolled edges sewn at the sides*

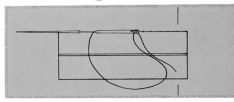

▲ 9. *Large buttonhole: the prick stitched edge*

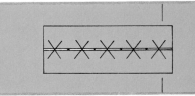

▲ 10. *The basted opening of a large buttonhole*

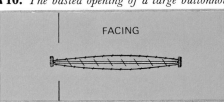

▲ 11. *The facing cut for the buttonhole opening*

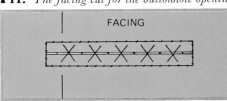

▲ 12. *The facing cut for a thick buttonhole*

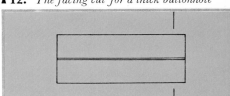

▲ 13. *The finished buttonhole*

to the buttonhole (figure 11).

If the ends of the cut are tight you must make the snip a little longer to take away the strain.

Make a small bar across each end as shown, to strengthen the opening.

On heavy fabric it may be necessary to cut the facing as for the buttonhole since the turning of the raw edges makes it necessary to make a cut very much longer than the opening of the buttonhole (figure 12).

☐ Lightly press over the hemmed edges, remove the basting thread from the rolled edges of the buttonhole and give a final pressing (figure 13).

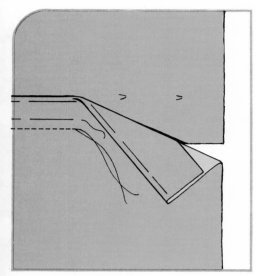

8. *A lapped seam*

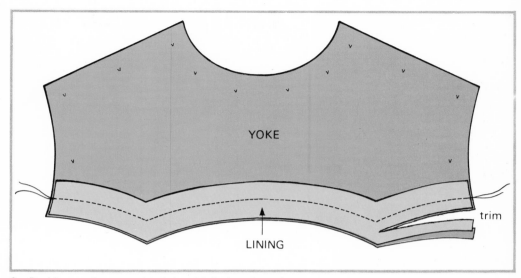

9. *Backing a yoke seam with lining fabric for a lapped seam*

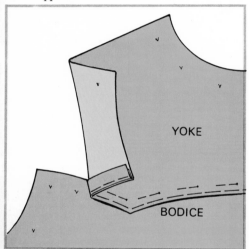

10. *The lined lapped seam pinned in place*

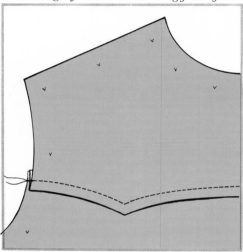

11. *The stitched lapped seam*

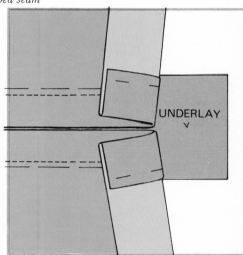

12. *A channel seam*

Stitching yoke seams

The way yoke seams are stitched usually determines the character of the garment. Lapped seaming (see below) is used for sporty versions and ordinary seams give a formal look. Topstitching creates a casual effect which softens the appearance and also brings out good detailing.

In addition to lap seaming two other seam types are dealt with here, the slot, channel or open seam and the piped seam, both of which add an interesting change of detail.

Lap seaming

In lap seaming the seam allowance along one seam edge is turned under, basted and pressed. It is then lapped over the corresponding seam allowance, with the fold meeting the stitching line, and stitched the required distance from the folded edge (figure **8**).

A lapped yoke seam on a bulky fabric can result in a rather thick seam, especially if the yoke seam is shaped. To avoid this, first back the yoke seam with strong matching lining fabric (figure **9**). To do this, cut a strip of lining fabric to the shape of the seam and twice the width of the seam allowance, in the same grain of the fabric. Pin it to the yoke, right sides facing.

Stitch the fabric and lining together along the yoke seamline, trim the seam allowance about $\frac{3}{8}$ inch and turn the lining to the inside. Edge-baste and press the stitched edge.

Pin and baste the lined edge to meet the seamline of the corresponding section (figure **10**) and topstitch in place (figure **11**).

Channel, slot or open seaming

The seamline in this kind of seam is not stitched together. Instead, the seam allowances are turned under, basted and pressed, and brought to meet over an underlay, then topstitched in position (figure **12**).

This type of seaming is easy to work and can be very effective on a yoke. Figure **13** shows how Belinda Belville has used V-shaped channel seaming as the main feature of a design.

There are two ways to work this type of seam.

i. Here each seam allowance is turned under, basted and pressed. The folded edges are then brought to meet along the center of the underlay and basted in place and stitched.

ii. First baste the seam together, right sides facing, and press open. Center the basted seam over the underlay, stitch to each side and then remove the basting. This method can only be used on straight seams.

Here are a few do's and dont's.

O Always cut the underlay so that the straight of grain runs in the same direction as the straight of grain through which the seam goes. If you ignore this precaution the underlay will twist during wear.

13. *Channel seaming in a Vogue Pattern*

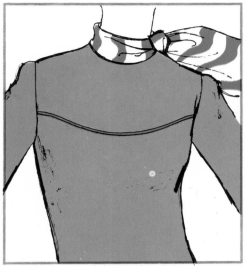

14. *A yoke seam finished with piping*

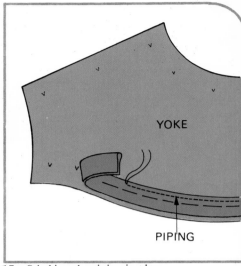

15. *Stitching the piping in place*

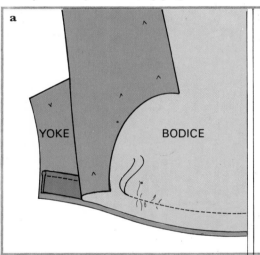

16a. *Method (i) for attaching the piped section*

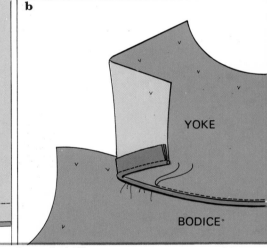

b. *method (ii)*

O Channel seaming should only be used in fabrics with a firm weave, since the strain on the single layer of fabric of the underlay can easily distort the seamline during wear.

O Never make a channel seam where one seamline of corresponding sections has ease built in for fitting purposes; that side of the open seam would always tilt or stand away since it has more length.

O If the seam is used on areas which are subject to strain when sitting, such as the bust or hips, allow more ease in the garment to avoid the seam edges gaping.

Piping

Apart from attractive stitching the seamline of a yoke can be finished with piping (figure **14**).

Piping can give increased importance to a seam in plain fabric or will bring a yoke out of the background of a patterned fabric.

242

How to pipe

For the piping, cut a bias strip twice the width of the seam allowance plus ¼ inch. Cut the strip long enough for the length of the seam to be piped and do not make any joins.

Fold the piping strip lengthwise and press. Pin and baste the folded edge ⅛ inch over the seamline, seam allowances even (figure **15**).

Stitch the piping to the seamline as shown.

To join the piped section to the corresponding section, work in one of the following two ways.

i. Pin and baste the piped section to the corresponding section as for ordinary seaming and stitch together, stitching over the first row of stitches as shown in figure **16a**.

ii. Fold under the seam allowance of the piping and the piped section, and pin and baste it to the seamline of the corresponding section ready for topstitching.

Work the topstitching close to the folded

piped edge as shown in figure **16b**.

Precautions

Before deciding to pipe a seam, here are a few practical considerations.

Piping introduces thickness into seams which creates a lot of bulk. This bulk produces problems when laundering a garment. While the main parts of the garment become too dry for ironing the piped section is still wet. So special attention is required when the garment is pressed.

In addition, piping often needs hard pressing, so make sure that the fabric of the garment can withstand this before pressing.

There are very few fabrics which can be used successfully for piping. One suitable fabric is cotton piqué. Here the back of the weave is constructed so that twisting is resisted when it is sewn into the seam. It is also quite rigid and will prevent buckling when inserted between two layers of fabric.

Chapter 57

Godets and gussets

This chapter deals with godets and gussets. Both are seam insertions which every dressmaker should know about. As the exact cut of these is decided by the design of a particular garment it is impossible to give general advice on cutting. But it is particularly important that these insets be perfectly applied, so here are some useful hints on the various techniques which can be used.

Godets

Godets (figure **1**) are cut to suit the design of a garment. Their function is both ornamental and practical, and the rest of the garment is cut so that the godet becomes a necessary addition to the design.

Cutting a godet
Godets come in varying degrees of a circle, depending on the effect the designer is trying to achieve. They are basically cut as follows:
Full godet. This is cut in a full 180 degree semicircle with the straight lengthwise grain through the center of the godet from point to hem, and with both seams in the crosswise grain (figure **2a**).
Medium full godet. Here the godet is cut in a 90 degree quarter circle with the center of the godet from the point to hem going through the lengthwise grain of the fabric and the seams through the bias of the fabric (figure **2b**).
Soft fall godet. For a really soft fall cut the center of the 90 degree godet on the bias of the fabric so that one seamline is on the crosswise grain and the other on the lengthwise grain (figure **2c**).
This cut is also suitable for sunray pleating.

Suitable fabrics
When choosing a fabric for a garment with godet insertions select a soft but firm weave. The fabric must not have the dead drop of a crêpe knit since this would make the godet look untidy, although some knits are suitable.

Inserting godets into seams
The method for inserting godets varies with each design. Here is the method most commonly used.
These instructions go a bit further than most pattern instructions in concentrating on the finish for the point of the godet, where a certain amount of skill comes into play.
First prepare and stitch the seam to where the godet starts. Fasten off the threads securely and press the seam open.
Stitch one side of the godet to the open end of the seamline and press the seam open or away from the godet according to the pattern instructions. Make sure that the godet seamline meets the end stitch of the upper seamline and fasten off the threads securely.

▲**1.** *The straight paneled six-gore skirt version with godets*

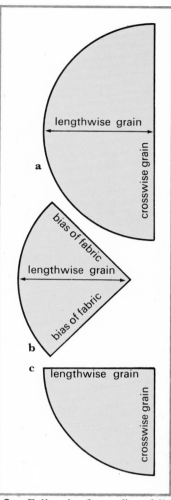

▲**2a.** *Full godet;* **b.** *medium full godet;* **c.** *soft fall godet*

Stitch the other seamline of the godet similarly.
The junction of the upper seamline and the godet point is usually very weak. This is how to strengthen it.
Unfold the seam allowance at the point of the godet and spread it over the end of the upper seam (figure **3a**).
Turn the work to the outside and make a tiny bar, catching in both sides of the upper seam and the underlying godet seam allowance (figure **3b**).
Turn the work to the inside again and gently press the seam allowance back into position.

Gussets

Gussets are cut according to the purpose they have to fulfil, and it is most important that the gusset is related exactly to the cut of the garment.
Although gussets are inserted to give freedom of movement, they should never be inserted just because something is too tight. Gussets are an integral feature of the design and the width they provide is no more than has been left out in the cut of the garment. As the exact shape of the gusset has been carefully determined by the cut of the rest of the garment, the cutting of gussets is a complicated process which requires much expertise. Because of this the instructions for gussets must be limited to their application.
First, it is most important that you follow the grain line in the pattern. You will have seen badly cut gussets inserted into the

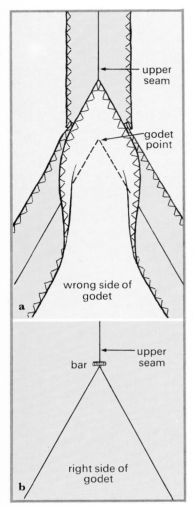

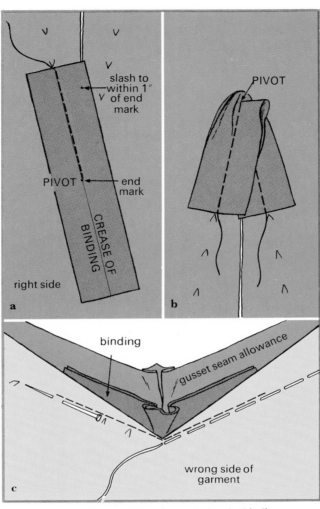

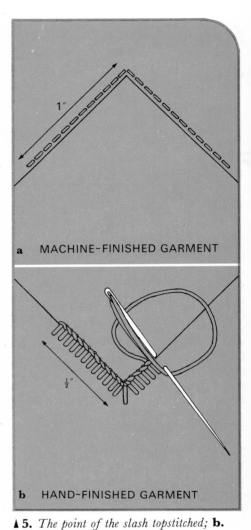

▲ **3a.** *The seam allowance spread over the upper seam;* **b.** *the bar*

▲ **4a.** *The binding laid along the slash;* **b.** *the binding stitched;* **c.** *the gusset pinned and basted in place*

▲ **5.** *The point of the slash topstitched;* **b.** *buttonhole stitches worked into the point*

underarm seams of a garment which droop and pull adversely with every arm movement, and look very ugly.

Hints on inserting gussets

The underarm gusset is the most commonly used in dressmaking. It is often inserted into a slash made in the fabric, which goes through the sleeve and into the side seamline at the underarm.

It is essential that the point of the slash is secured firmly to avoid tearing. The methods for this are given below and are chosen according to the fabric type and finish used.

Method 1. This method uses seam binding and is suitable for most fabrics. It requires practice as the application of the seam binding is done completely freehand; pinning and basting is impossible.

Working on the outside of the garment, first mark the end for the slash clearly and mark seamline. Slash to 1 inch of the end mark. Cut $2\frac{1}{2}$ inches of matching $\frac{5}{8}$ inch wide seam binding. Fold and press this lengthwise to obtain a center crease for stitching. Open the pressed seam binding and lay half of it to the left of the mark for the end of the slash, with the crease of the seam binding just outside the seamline (figure **4a**).

Stitch along the crease line to meet the mark for the end of the slash. Do not withdraw the needle, but pivot the work carefully so that you cannot lose your position.

Turn the seam binding around the needle ready to lay it over the other seamline then, with the help of a pin, maneuver the doubled up seam binding around the needle to one side and out of the way

244

of the downward row of stitches. Stitch along the crease line to the end of the seam binding as before (figure **4b**).

Carefully slash between the stitching to within one or two grains of the end. As you spread the slash the seam binding should lie flat across it.

When inserting the gusset, fold the seam binding over and toward the raw edges of the slash, leaving the seamline free. Pin and baste the gusset into position following seamline as marked (figure **4c**). Stitch and press as recommended in the pattern instructions.

For fabrics where seam binding is too heavy, cut a strip $\frac{5}{8}$ inch wide from the selvage of the fabric and fold, press and apply as for seam binding.

Method 2. This method makes use of top stitching to strengthen the points of the slash. It is suitable only for firmly woven fabrics —loosely woven fabrics must be mounted for extra strength.

Insert gusset into slash as above but without reinforcing the ends. After stitching, press the seam allowance toward the garment and away from the gusset.

On machine-finished garments topstitch around the point. Working on the right side, stitch close to the seam starting 1 inch down from the point, working around it and continuing 1 inch down the other side (figure **5a**).

On hand-finished garments, work fine buttonhole stitches into the point. Work the stitches on the right side using fine sewing thread. Start $\frac{1}{2}$ inch from the point, work into the point and along the other side, catching the edge of the seam and the seam allowance into the stitches (figure **5b**).

Chapter 58

Shaping up to belts

This chapter gives the basic method for making three types of belts — straight, shaped (there are graph patterns for two shapes) and crushed. With this know-how you can go on and make a whole collection of beautiful belts in different fabrics with a variety of fastenings. Junk stores are treasure troves for buckles and clasps.

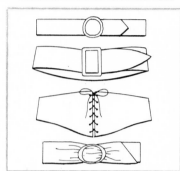

Materials for stiff belts

Top fabrics

Belts can be made from many materials. Any gay dress or home furnishing fabric will make an attractive belt. Leather, braids, velvet and suede are especially suitable as they are hard wearing, look attractive and provide a contrast to any garment.
Natural linen is a practical choice to tone in with all outfits. And for a really exclusive effect try making a belt from tapestry type fabric.

Stiffenings

☐ Back-a-belt kits
☐ Belting
☐ Non-woven interfacings such as heavy weight Pellon
☐ Tailor's canvas (this must be washed first as it shrinks in washing)
☐ Buckram
☐ Valance canvas which is obtainable in upholstery departments

Backings

Good quality taffeta, strong silk, skiver (thinly sliced leather) and soft leather are the most suitable. Felt is also used sometimes, but remember that it isn't washable.

Miscellaneous

☐ UHU glue for sticking belts
☐ Punch and eyelets
☐ Buckles for self-covering or decorative fastenings such as contrasting buckles, clasps, belt hooks and lacing

Straight belt

What you will need

Top fabric or braid, interfacing in the form of a back-a-belt kit, buckram or other interfacing. Your own choice of fastening.

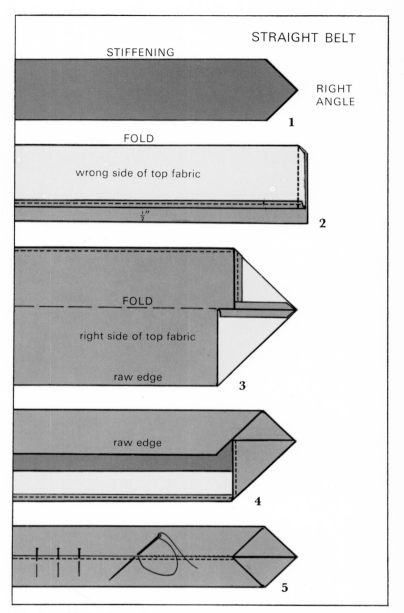

▲ **1.** *Cut stiffening into point* **2.** *Stitch one end of top fabric* **3.** *Fold seam into point* **4.** *Fold raw edge over stiffening* **5.** *Finishing back of belt*

Making the belt

Decide on the width you want the belt and cut the stiffening to the exact width, and to the length of your waist measurement plus 6 inches.
Cut one end of the stiffening into a right-angled point (figure **1**).
Cut a strip of top fabric twice the belt width plus $\frac{3}{4}$ inch and $\frac{3}{4}$ inch longer than the stiffening.
Turn in one long edge of the top fabric for $\frac{1}{4}$ inch and stitch.
Fold the top fabric lengthwise with the stitched edge $\frac{1}{2}$ inch in from the raw edge and right sides together (figure **2**). Pin and stitch the end securely with a $\frac{1}{4}$ inch seam as shown.
Trim the corner of the seam allowance and then, following figure **3**, fold into a point with the seam falling on the first fold and press the seam open.
Turn to the right side. Place the belt stiffening into the point and fold the raw edge over as shown (figure **4**). Press.
Fold and press the finished edge over the raw edge (figure **5**).
Pin the edge into position and hand-sew with very small hemming stitches.
Attach a buckle or clasp of your choice to finish.

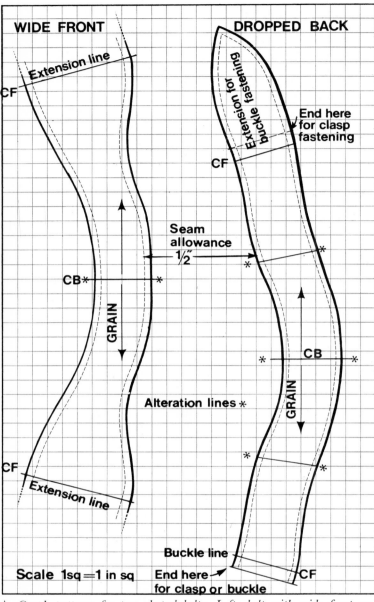

WIDE FRONT   **DROPPED BACK**

Extension line

CF

Extension for buckle fastening

End here for clasp fastening

CF

Seam allowance ½"

CB✶   ✶

GRAIN

✶

✶

CB

✶   ✶

GRAIN

Alteration lines ✶

✶

CF

✶

Extension line

✶

Buckle line

Scale 1sq = 1 in sq   End here for clasp or buckle   CF

▲ *Graph patterns for two shaped belts. Left: belt with wide front and narrow back. Right: belt of uniform width with lower back*

Shaped belt

Two patterns are given for shaped belts. One of these is for a belt which is wide at the front and narrower at the back. The other is a uniform width but slopes down at the back.

The patterns

Choose the belt shape from the patterns and draw the belt pattern on 1 inch squared graph paper. The patterns are for a 26 inch waist, so alter them to your measurement where indicated. The patterns include ½ inch seam allowance.

What you will need

Top fabric and interfacing (self-adhesive or otherwise) or tailor's canvas.

Felt, lining fabric or self fabric for the backing and your choice of fastening.

If you are using a felt backing you will need UHU glue.

A bunch of beautiful belts, laced, buckled and braid trimmed ▶

Making the belt

Cut out the top fabric and the interfacing the exact size of the pattern, placing the pattern straight of grain line on the lengthwise grain of the fabric.

Attach the interfacing to the wrong side of the fabric. Do this with a row of stitches within the seam allowance, or stick them together if a self-adhesive interfacing is being used. The two fabrics are now used as one.

Snip the long curved edges at $\frac{1}{4}$ inch intervals up to the seamline, which is $\frac{1}{2}$ inch from the edge (figure **6**). Press the edges to the wrong side as shown (figure **7**).

Felt backing. If you are using a felt backing cut the felt $\frac{1}{16}$ inch narrower than the desired belt width and stick to the inside.

Attach a buckle or clasp to finish.

Fabric backing. If you are using lining or self fabric backing use the pattern to cut two layers of the fabric. Stitch the two layers together with right sides facing just inside the seamline, leaving an opening for turning.

Turn to the right side and close the opening.

Pin the backing to the wrong side of the belt and topstitch in place or sew firmly with a very small hemming stitch.

Crushed belt

The fabric for this belt is cut straight and the belt is most effectively made in soft leather, velvet or satin materials.

What you will need

A fairly soft interfacing such as Pellon. Top fabric as above, and lining fabric for the backing.

Making the belt

Cut out the top fabric and interfacing 1 inch wider than the desired width of the belt and to your waist measurement plus 6 inches. Also cut the lining fabric to the same length but $\frac{1}{16}$ inch narrower. This is so that the lining will roll in nicely at the edges and not show on the outside.

Shape one end of all the layers as shown (figure **8**).

Baste the interfacing to the wrong side of the top fabric and use as one.

Place the lining and the top fabric together, right sides facing, and stitch all around taking $\frac{1}{2}$ inch seam allowance and leaving the straight end unstitched. The shaped end of the belt will have to be eased slightly onto the lining fabric, which was cut slightly narrower. Trim the seam allowance of the interfacing close to the stitches as shown (figure **9**). Then trim the other seams and the corners.

Turn to the right side.

Attach a buckle narrower than the belt to give a crushed effect as shown (figure **10**).

Paper ring fastening

The paper ring fastening used (figure **11**) has a 2 inch diameter. Make a straight belt as shown in the previous instructions, but make it only 4 inches longer than your waist measurement and narrow enough to fit through the ring.

Make both ends pointed.

Complete the fastening by turning each point back and stitching them securely in place (figure **12**).

6. *Shaped belt: snip seam allowance every $\frac{1}{4}$in* **7.** *Press snipped edges to inside* **8.** *Crushed belt: shape one end* **9.** *Trim seam allowances and corners* **10.** *Attach buckle* **11.** *Paper ring fastening* **12.** *Ring attached* ►

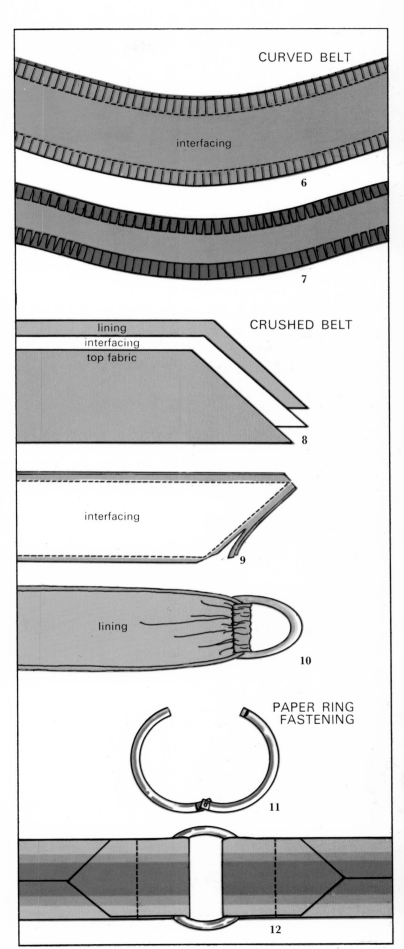

CURVED BELT

interfacing

6

7

CRUSHED BELT

lining
interfacing
top fabric

8

interfacing

9

lining

10

PAPER RING FASTENING

11

12

Soft belts, tied and buckled

With all the dressmaking you have done recently, you will probably have a little material left over, or you may even have a drawer full of remnants. So why not make a belt or two?

The simplest to make is a tie belt, which you can wear in a soft bow, loosely knotted or fastened like a tie.

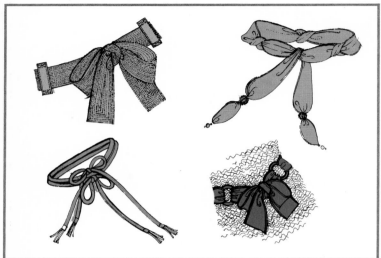

Make a collection of soft belts—here are some ideas to inspire you

How to make a tie belt

First make a pattern for the belt using the skirt waistband pattern with the wrap extension in Skirtmaking chapter 14 as your guide.

This will make a belt 1in wide, but if you want it wider just make a pattern twice the width you require.

Take the center of the waistband pattern, including the extension, as the center of the belt. You need to include the 2in wrap in the length, as the belt will be worn over other layers of fabric.

For the plain tie add 10 to 12in to each end of the pattern, but if you want to tie it in a bow add about 20in to each end, depending on the thickness of the fabric.

You can easily work out the length you need if you tie a tape measure around your waist and make a knot or bow. Mark the center of the waistband pattern by folding it in half. Then halve the length on the tape and measure this amount from the center of the pattern on each side.

Cut out the belt from single fabric along the straight of the grain, adding ¾in seam allowances all around.

Making a seam or joining the belt

If you have to cut the belt from two or more pieces of fabric, it is best to join it in line with the side seam(s) on the garment for which you are making the belt.

To find the position of the side seams on the belt pattern, mark off the length of the original waistband pattern centrally on the new pattern. Halve each section between the center mark and the end of the original pattern, then shift each mark 1in toward the center (the center back on the finished belt).

Cut out the belt pieces from single fabric along the straight of the grain, not forgetting to add ¾in seam allowances all around.

If you intend to tie the belt in a bow and want the ends to be even when tied, remember that one side of the bow takes up more fabric than the other. This amount is approximately 3in, depending on the thickness of the fabric. Therefore, if you are joining the fabric at the seams, shift the center back and side seam marks on the pattern about 3in toward one end.

How to complete the belt

First you must stitch the belt. Fold the material lengthwise, right sides facing. Pin, placing the pins at right angles to the fold to prevent the belt from twisting. Mark off the seam allowance with tailor's chalk and stitch the belt lengthwise, leaving the ends open and an opening about 3in long halfway along the stitching line; to turn the belt right side out.

Carefully press the seam open, because it must lie flat inside the belt and go to the center of the belt. If you leave the seam folded together in the crease of the belt, you will have a ridge on one edge with four layers of fabric inside it and a flat crease on the other edge with no seam at all. This will not only look ugly but will also make the belt roll.

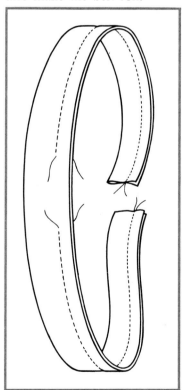

The tie belt stitched lengthwise

Be careful when pressing the seam open. Avoid pressing too hard and making sharp creases on the edges. You will only have to remove these creases when the belt is turned right side out, and this may be impossible with some fabrics.

After pressing, place the seam to the center of the belt and

trim the seam allowance to ½in. Pin in place, then stitch across the ends, fastening off the threads carefully.

Now turn the belt right side out by pushing the ends through the opening over the

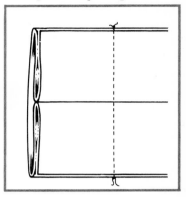

The stitched end of the tie belt

blunt end of a knitting needle or the unsharpened end of a pencil. Don't use anything with a sharp point—you will penetrate the fabric, push the weave apart and distort the ends of the belt, spoiling its shape.

When the belt is turned, fold in the edges of the opening along the seamline and slip stitch them together by hand. Pull out the corners gently with the point of a needle to make them square. Then edge baste the seams at both ends. Finally, press the belt from the back, making sure as much of the length as possible is lying on the ironing board. Again, do not use heavy pressure to get it flat or you'll leave a seam impression on the right side of the belt.

The buckled belt

For a soft belt with a buckle, again use the waistband pattern, including the wrap extension, as a guide for the belt pattern.

Mark the ends left and right; the left end is for the buckle and the right end slots through the buckle.

Remember, if you want the belt to be wider than the waistband pattern, just make the pattern twice the width you require.

Add 1½in to the left end and 4 or even 5in to the right end, depending on how much ease and movement you like. Before cutting the fabric, add $\frac{3}{4}$in seam allowances all around, except on the left end.

If you want the right end of belt pointed or slanted, prepare a cardboard template from the belt pattern to use after you have stitched the belt together lengthwise and pressed the seam open.

Place the seam in the center of the back of the belt and baste through all layers to hold the seam in place. Lay the template on the right end and carefully chalk around it. Remove the template, baste along the chalk line and stitch.

Trim off the seam allowance across the point to reduce the bulk and to allow the point to be clearly defined after

Buckled belt pattern and template

you have turned the belt right side out. Do not cut so close that the fabric will fray.

Turn the belt right side out, pull the point out with the sharp end of a needle, and edge baste the stitched end. If the belt is wide, you must also baste around the edges to make sure that the seam remains in the center of the back. Press the belt gently, remove the basting threads and press.

Buckles and how to attach them

In most cases, a belt is made to fit the buckle, but with a soft belt the reverse applies.

To prevent the belt from slipping back through the buckle, the buckle must fit tightly. So wait until you have made the belt before choosing the buckle, as you cannot judge before you have seen the number of layers that have to go through it.

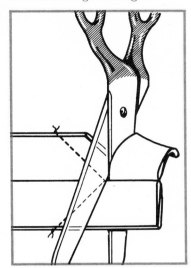

Trimming seam allowance at point

It is also possible for a soft belt to be gathered through the buckle, but you will have to be sure that the fabric is not so bunched that it will break the buckle bar.

To attach the buckle, fold the left end of the belt 1½in over the bar of the buckle. Turn the raw edge under about ½in and sew it to the back of the belt with firm hand stitches. Make a few stitches along the edges of the belt close to the buckle to prevent it from moving about in the turning.

To prevent the belt from loosening too much as you wear it, secure the end with a hook and bar to keep it in place.

Buckles with prongs

If the buckle has a prong, you will need to make eyelets.

These must be made by hand in a soft belt, because metal eyelets require stiffening as anchorage. Here is a simple way to make eyelets.

Use an eyelet punch, available from craft supply stores, to

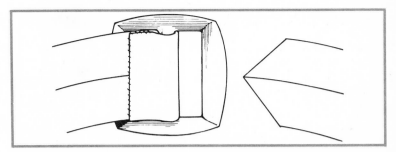

Buckle sewn in position and shaped belt end seen from the wrong side

make the hole. Select a hole setting slightly larger than the prong, because you will have to push the eyelet right down to the end of the prong to enable the buckle to sit well in the belt turning.

Make the eyelet 1½in from the left end, in the center of the belt. When you have punched the hole, overcast the raw edge very closely, working over it twice to make sure you have caught all the layers of the belt in the stitches.

For the eyelets on the right end, select a hole setting the same size as the prong, or very slightly larger if the fabric is tightly woven.

Use a tape measure to find the position for the first eyelet. Again make it in the center of the belt and then make two or three more eyelets so that you can adjust the belt as you please.

Clasp buckle

A clasp buckle like the one pictured here can be most attractive and unusual.

To make the belt for the clasp buckle, cut out the fabric as for the buckle belt above, but this time add 1½in to one end of the belt only.

Sew one end over the buckle bar as before and pin the opposite end in place. Try on the belt and adjust the pinned end before finally sewing in place.

Topstitching

You can give belts a more decorative appearance with topstitching. Either make one row of topstitches just around the edge or several rows down the length of the belt. If you topstitch the buckled belt, do so before attaching the buckle.

First, baste around the edges and then baste along the seamline through all layers of fabric so that you can keep the belt length under control.

If you decide to stitch several rows down the length, here is a tip to prevent the fabric from bubbling and the seams twisting. As soon as you see a bubble in the fabric in front of the presser foot, release the pressure on the fabric by lifting the presser foot, but leave the needle in the fabric. Replace the presser foot and continue stitching. If the seams twist despite this precaution, rip the seam and ease the pressure on the presser foot before starting again.

Turn a plain belt into something beautiful with a special clasp buckle

Chapter 59

Binding and trimming with braid

In this chapter and the one that follows, a selection of finishes and techniques are featured to help you add that perfect final touch to a garment which will turn it into something special.

This chapter is concerned with trimming and binding edges with braid. The technique can be applied to a new garment or to an old one to give it a new lease of life. Also included are ideas for combining and embellishing braids.

The most lavish use of braid was during the 17th and 18th centuries, when men's frock coats were braided according to the standing and position of the wearer, and many a tailor went out of business because his customer could not pay for all the gold and silver he had to use. But apart from its decorative effect, braiding in those days was a real necessity. Sewing machines had not been invented and facings had to be attached by hand, so braid was used as a quick method of finishing the raw edges. Today, of course, braid is used to add decorative fashion detail to a garment.

Braid and ribbon binding

Braids for binding

The braid used for binding is a kind of plaited ribbon which is sold in varying widths from $\frac{1}{2}$ inch upward. The $\frac{5}{8}$ inch and 1 inch widths are the most popular and are available in both wool and synthetics.

For edge binding a 1 inch width is the best to use. This gives a finish of slightly less than $\frac{1}{2}$ inch, depending on the thickness of the garment edge. Narrower braids are not really suitable for edge binding unless the fabric is especially fine.

Really wide braids of up to about 3 inches are also available. These should be reserved for the edges of single layer garments in firm fabrics, such as heavy velours or reversible fabrics, where no facings are needed. Here the braid forms a solid edge and serves both as trimming and facing at the same time.

Grosgrain and belting ribbon bindings

The ribbed grosgrain and belting ribbons are firmer than plaited braid and come in varying degrees of stiffness. For edge binding use the softer kind so that the ribbon will not stiffen the edge of the garment too much.

Grosgrain and belting ribbons used for binding are made from a combination of cotton and artificial silk, or from cotton only, and are available in a variety of widths.

Make sure at the time of purchase that the ribbon will not shrink, as this could spoil the whole garment and render it useless after washing or even dry cleaning.

These ribbons cannot be used to bind curved edges as they are not supple enough to turn the curve in a smooth line.

1. *Above: Simple braid or ribbon binding on a Vogue Pattern. Below: another Vogue Pattern shows a simple but effective use of binding*

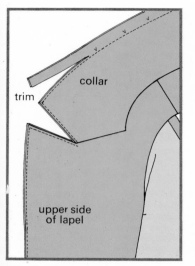

▲ 2. *Faced edge ready for binding*

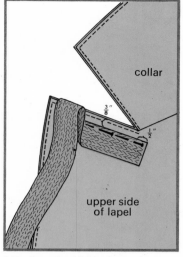

▲ 3. *Start braid binding on lapel*

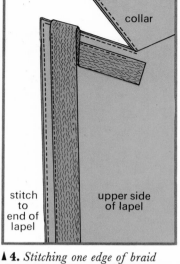

▲ 4. *Stitching one edge of braid*

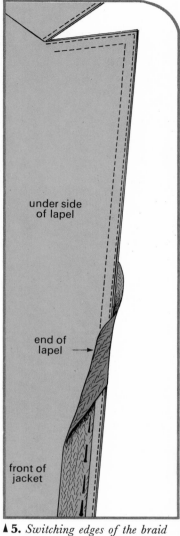

▲ 5. *Switching edges of the braid*

▲ 6. *Felling underside of braid*

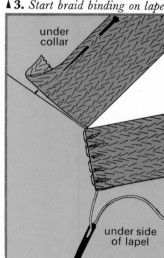

▲ 7. *Drawing up the folded ends*

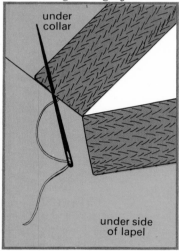

▲ 8. *The finished folded ends*

How to bind edges

The tailored blazer featured on the previous page (figure **1**) shows a typical example of simple braid or ribbon binding. The methods given below for binding edges can be applied to this pattern or to any other garment you might wish to bind.

First you need to prepare the edges of the garment. If you are using a commercial pattern prepare them as shown on the instruction sheet, then apply 1 inch braid as given below. For other garments, unless the edge is suitable for single layer binding, prepare as follows.

Baste the facings to the inside of the garment, with wrong sides facing, and raw edges even. Stitch together with a row of stitches $\frac{1}{8}$ inch inside the seamline. Then trim off the seam allowance completely (figure **2**). Turn up the hem before binding.

Two methods of binding the edges are given below, A for braid, and B for grosgrain or belting ribbon.

When binding it is important to remember that the side of the braid which will be uppermost should be stitched on first.

A. Braid

Start at the lapel corner and, working on the top side of the lapel (figure **3**), pin the braid $\frac{3}{8}$ inch from the raw edges as shown, leaving $\frac{1}{2}$ inch extending to turn in afterward. As you reach the corner of the lapel fold under enough fullness to make a fold miter. (For miters see the end of this chapter.)

When you have reached the point where the lapel ends, stop pinning and machine stitch the pinned edge of the braid to the lapel before continuing (figure **4**).

The folding over of the lapel causes the opposite edge of the braid to be uppermost so, to continue the braid down the front of the garment, turn it over the garment edge so that the opposite edge of the braid can be pinned to the outside of the garment, $\frac{3}{8}$ inch from the raw edge as before (figure **5**). You will need to leave a small gap between the end of the previous stitching line and the beginning of the pinning to enable you to do this.

Work around the whole garment edge until you reach the turning point of the lapel on the other side. Stitch the pinned braid in position first before going on to bind the other lapel. Switch edges again for the lapel, break between lapel and collar, and continue the braid around the collar to complete.

Turn the braid over the raw edge and cover the stitching line on the underside with the edge of the braid (figure **6**). Hand sew the edge of the braid to the garment with small, firm felling stitches.

Pay special attention to the ends of the braid where they are turned under for finishing off. If the folded ends spread make small running stitches through the fold and draw up the spread as shown in figure **7**.

Sew the folded ends to the garment with invisible stitches (figure **8**).

When pressing a braided edge, work very gently as squashed braid is not very attractive.

B. Grosgrain or belting ribbon

First fold the ribbon in half lengthwise and gently press in a fold. Do not make a sharp crease since the thickness of the garment fabric may start to roll the edge of the braid after the ribbon is sewn on.

Lay the raw edges into the fold of the braid, then pin and baste in position (figure **9**). Miter the corner into a fold or make a stitch miter, depending on the thickness of the braid (see mitering at the end of the chapter).

To sew the ribbon in place, make small prick stitches along the outside and inside edge of the ribbon. With each stitch catch in some of the fabric sandwiched between the ribbon, but never stitch through to the other side.

Braiding or binding ready-made garments

To give an old coat or jacket a new look you can braid the edges quite simply.

First baste ½ inch from the edges to be bound with small firm basting stitches, and working through all layers of fabric.

Where facings are stitched to the edge gently rip the seams, but only after they have been firmly basted in place. If the facings are cut in one with the garment and folded under you can work over the folded edges as for the hems.

Ease out the seam allowance and gently press out the creases of the seamlines. Make a row of machine stitches ⅛ inch inside the seamline and trim the seam allowance off completely (figure **10**). Apply the binding as shown before.

Attaching braid or binding to a single layer of fabric

Fabrics suitable for single layer binding are usually very bulky, and if you stitched on the braid by machine in the ordinary way you would find that a lot of the braid length disappeared into the depth of the fabric. This would result in either a tightening of the braid or, if you compensate, the braid looking too full.

So it is essential that you apply the braid by hand with a prick stitch, working first on the outside and then on the inside edge. Topstitching the braid or binding by machine may be done successfully if you have a braiding or binding foot on your machine which is capable of taking the thickness of braid and fabric. But even here it is wise to test on a fabric scrap first.

Flat braid

Flat braid applied to the surface of a garment such as in the commercial pattern

opposite (figure **11**) requires a little practice and patience.

First test the combination of braid and fabric on a scrap of fabric. Baste the braid firmly in place and find the best method of application: machine or hand.

Machine stitches should be made so close to the edge that they disappear into the weave of the braid edge. If you are sewing on the braid by hand work small prick stitches close to the edge.

When choosing flat braids, make sure that they are not stiffer or heavier than the surface to which they are applied as this would interfere with the fall of the fabric and the hang of the garment.

Making your own decorative braid

Ready-made garments often have expensive looking trimming which one cannot buy anywhere. This can be frustrating, but the answer is to make your own exclusive braids by embroidering or beading them or by combining braids.

Some of the most exciting fancy braids can be found in home furnishing trimming departments, and you can use your imagination to combine these types of braids for special effects and a very expensive looking trimming (figure **12a**).

Instead of paying a small fortune for bead embroidered braid, choose a metallic lampshade braid which is not too raised in the design and embroider or bead it yourself (figure **12b**).

This way, if you want to trim rounded shapes, you can choose the type of braid that will turn easily and then add the decoration yourself.

Combining braids

Buy a length of plain braid about 1 inch wide which has a pretty edge on both sides and match or contrast this with a length of fancy braid ½ inch wide.

Pin the narrow braid over the center of the wider braid and sew them together with medium sized running stitches along both edges of the narrow braid. Work in the fabric of the braid as much as possible to prevent the stitches from showing. Gently press the finished braid from the wrong side and stitch it to the garment as before.

Combining binding and braid

A plain braided or bound edge often gives a garment a severe appearance. To soften this effect on garments which are not strictly tailored, join the edging to a matching decorative braid (figure **13**), stitching it close to the edge of the functional bound edge. For the decorative braid, select one which has a straight edge on one side and a decorative edge on the

other.

For wide wool braid used on the edge of a single layer garment, the plain tailored appearance can be softened by applying a fancy braid over the width of the wool braid. There are many suitable chunky wool braids which are, at the same time, soft and light (figure **14**).

Miters

A miter is used in dressmaking when you want to turn a corner on a straight run of fabric or, in this case, a braid. Both stitched and folded miters are given below. A stitched miter should never be used on plaited braid as the construction of the braid would make it spread.

Folded miter

A folded miter is usually used on braids and bindings or other fancy weave edge finishes, and is always used on plaited braid. Here the fullness is simply folded to one side when turning the corner (figure **15**).

When mitering a corner which is sharper than 90°, it may be necessary to fold the fullness to both sides of the miter (figure **16**). This will also make the braid spread, but the angle of the corner will make the miter look longer anyway.

Try to contain the spread by pushing it very tightly under, sewing it in position as you do so (figure **17**).

Although folded miters can be used for bindings, if the binding is wide or heavy a stitched miter may become necessary.

Stitched miters

Simple stitched miter. A simple stitched miter (figure **18**) is used when you are applying a straight strip of fabric flat to a 90° corner. A 45° miter is made which goes through the bias of the grain line of the fabric. After stitching, the seam allowance is trimmed to approximately ¼ inch as shown and pressed open.

Stitched double miter. A 45° stitched double miter is used when you are binding a 90° corner with a straight strip of fabric, and both sides of the binding need to be mitered.

To do this, first fold the fabric in half lengthwise, find the center fold line and mark.

Then open the folded fabric and fold crosswise (figure **19**) at that point where the corner of the garment and the trim coincide.

Following the diagram, make a 45° miter on both sides, meeting on the lengthwise center fold line.

Trim the seam allowance on each miter

▲11. *Surface braiding makes an elegant dress and below: another idea for braiding by Vogue.*

toward the point, taking care not to snip too near to the stitching, or the point of the finished miter will fray. Then press the seam allowance open.

Fitted stitched miter. A fitted miter is needed when the corner is anything other than 90°. The miter has to be fitted or cut to a perfect pattern before applying (figure **20**).

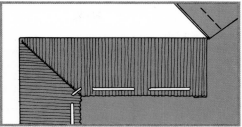

▲9. *Starting the ribbon binding*

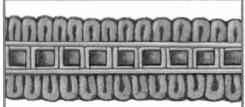

a home furnishing braids combined
b sequins on metallic braid

▲12a *and* **b.** *Combining braids for effect*
▼15. *A simple folded miter*

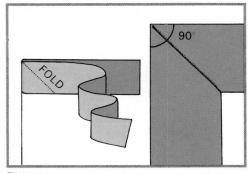

▼17. *The spread contained on a sharp fold*

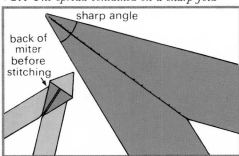

▼19. *A stitched double miter*

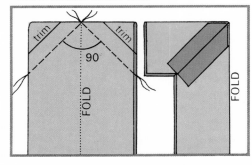

▲10. *Preparing ready-made edge for binding*

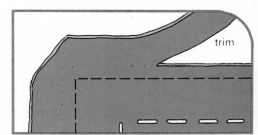

▲13. *Decorative braid on plain bound edge*

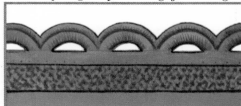

▲14. *Chunky wool braid on wool binding*
▼16. *Miter with fullness folded to each side*

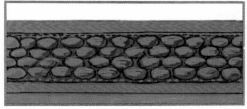

▼18. *A simple stitched miter*

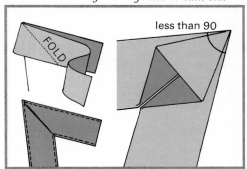

▼20. *A fitted stitched miter*

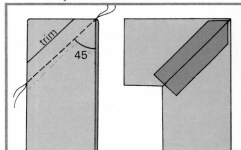

Chapter 60

All kinds of fastenings in dressmaking

The tone of a garment, casual or formal, is often set by the kind of fastening used on it, and in many cases a fastening may be the only fashion detail on a garment.

Fastenings can be functional, in which case they have to be very firmly and carefully constructed, or they can be purely decorative, as in the case of a simulated buttoned tab. Sometimes, however, a fastening can be both functional and decorative and a perfect example of this is a dress with a Center Front opening fastened from neck to hem with rouleau loops. A functional fastening in quite a different mood is the fly fastening, shown on the opposite page.

Previous chapters have dealt with some buttoned and tab Center Front fastenings, also rouleau loop and tie fastenings, and have shown the methods of constructing these so that you can apply them to any garment you wish. This chapter gives several more types of fastenings, including fly and rouleau loop cluster fastenings, to provide you with further ideas for completely changing the mood of your favorite styles.

Fabrics and fastenings

The fastening on a garment should be very carefully planned as it must not only suit the style of the garment but also the fabric it is made from. The basic construction must be correct if the fastening is to retain its shape for the lifetime of the garment, and also to insure that it does not break down and so make the garment look worn out before its time.

The weight of the fabric used is the deciding factor, and a lot of dressmaking experience is required to make the right decision.

On bulky fabrics the position of the fastening is also important, especially if you have certain figure problems.

Fastenings should always remain flat and not rise from the surface of the garment in a high ridge. If this happens it could be the result of faulty construction.

Fly fastenings

Fly fastenings are concealed fastenings used when it is necessary for the surface of a garment to retain an uncluttered look and when the cut of the garment is more important than the detail. They are mostly worked into a seamline, such as a Center Front seam or panel seam.

Although fly fastenings are often closed with a zipper, the traditional way to close them is with buttonholes set into a button bar attached to the underside of the right front.

For demonstrating the fly fastenings a dress with a Center Front seam and no waist seam has been used.

Buttoned fly fastening

The pattern. You will need pattern pieces for a right Front, left Front, right front facing, left front facing, back neck facing, Back. Use a right Front pattern without wrap (figure **1**).

Make a right front facing 2 inches wide at the shoulder edge and 3 inches wide down the front, the shape of the front and neck edges as shown (figure **1**).

For the left Front add 1½ inches to the Center Front edge for a wrap (figure **2**), then make a left front facing 2 inches wide at the shoulder edge and 3 inches wide down the front.

Make a back neck facing 2 inches wide (figure **3**).

Lining. Both right Front edge and right front facing need to be lined.

Make a lining pattern 2 inches wide, as in figure **4**, and use this pattern to cut the lining for both.

Cutting out. Cut facing and lining pieces with seam allowance all around.

Making up. To avoid showing seam edges at the neck edge of the fly fastening, start the buttoning 2½ inches down from the neckline. Line the right Front and right front facing as shown (figure **5**). To do this, place the lining and fabric together, right sides facing and Center Fronts coinciding, and stitch the Center Front starting 2½ inches down from the neck edge. Snip the seam allowance at the top of the stitching and turn the lining to the inside.

Working on the facing, baste and press the lining to the inside of the facing and make a row of vertical buttonholes ¾ inches from the Center Front edge to fit ⅝ inch diameter flat buttons.

Join the right and left front facings to the back neck facing at the shoulder seams.

Place the joined facing to the garment right sides together. Starting at the snipped seam allowance on the right Front, stitch the facing in place up to the neck edge, around the neck and down the left Front.

Turn the facing into the garment, pin in place and edge-baste.

Pin the buttonholed section of the facing to the garment a fraction inside the front edge so the facing will not show. Baste it firmly. Measure in 1½ inches from the edge of the right Front and topstitch as shown (figure **6**), catching in all layers of fabric.

Fasten the neck edge with a snap fastener or reversed button and buttonhole (figure **7**), and sew on the other buttons.

Zipper fly fastening

The pattern. You will need patterns for a Back, right Front, left Front, right front facing, left front neck facing, back neck facing. Make right Front, right front facing and back neck facing patterns as for the buttoned fly fastening (see figures **1** and **3**).

Make a left Front pattern as in figure **8**, adding ½ inch to the Center Front edge, also make a left front neck facing as shown.

Cutting out. Cut all edges with seam allowances.

Making up. Complete the garment first. Stitch the right front, back neck and left front neck facings at shoulders. Place on garment, right sides together. Starting at the bottom of the fastening on the right Front, stitch up to the neck and around the neck.

Fold under the seam allowance on the left Front along the zipper stitching line, then pin and baste the folded edge close to the zipper teeth. Stitch firmly in place (figure **9**).

Fold the faced right Front edge over the zipper so that the Center Front lines meet (figure **10a**) and baste down firmly.

Topstitch the zipper in place on the right Front working on the right side of the fabric, catching in all layers of fabric plus zipper tape. If the opening is in a seam which continues below the fastening, finish the lower end of the topstitching with a half miter.

Snip into the seam allowance on the left Front as shown (figure **10b**). Fold the neck facing on the left Front opening over the zipper tape and hand-sew in place. Fasten the top with a hook and eye.

▲ *A Vogue Pattern*

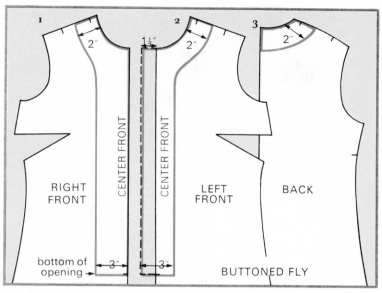

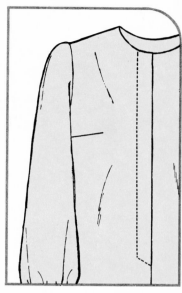

▲ *Buttoned fly:* **1.** and **2.** right and left Front patterns; **3.** back neck facing
▼ *Buttoned fly:* **4.** Lining pattern; **5.** The lined right Front and facing

▲**6.** *Topstitching the right Front*
▼**7.** *Reversed button and buttonhole*

I 2 3

2″ 1½″ 2″ 2″

CENTER FRONT   CENTER FRONT

RIGHT FRONT   LEFT FRONT   BACK

bottom of opening   3″   3″

BUTTONED FLY

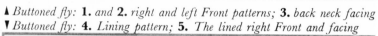

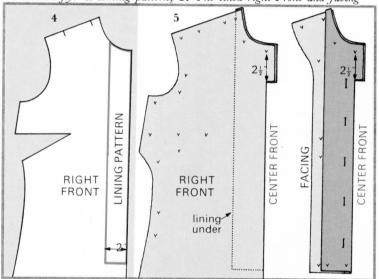

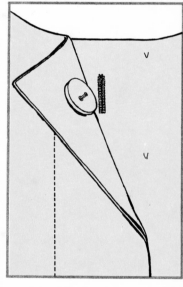

4 5

2½″ 2½″

RIGHT FRONT   LINING PATTERN

RIGHT FRONT

CENTER FRONT   FACING   CENTER FRONT

lining under

2″

▼**8.** *Zipper fly: left Front pattern*

▼**9.** *Zipper stitched to left Front*

▼**10.** *The completed fastening:* **a.** *from right side;* **b.** *from wrong side*

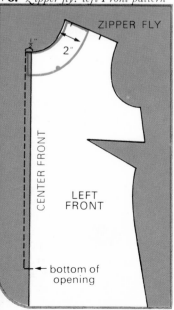

ZIPPER FLY

1½″ 2″

CENTER FRONT

LEFT FRONT

bottom of opening

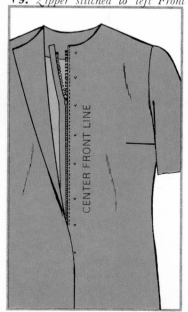

CENTER FRONT LINE

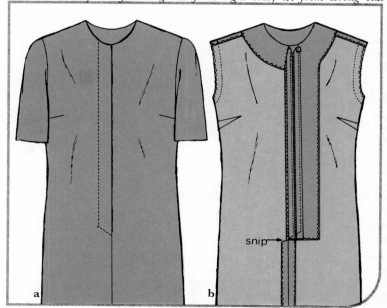

snip

a   b

255

Loops, buckles and bows

These are weak fastenings, so if they are likely to be submitted to occasional strain, such as at a waistline, always make a concealed hook and eye fastening at that point.

Looped fastening

Apart from the conventional placing of rouleau loops, an attractive couture idea is to make a cluster of loops and space them out evenly along a front bodice opening (figure **11a**).

Stitch two loops closely together then make a third forming the shape of a clover leaf (figure **11b**).

Since the center loop ends are longer, stitch the rouleaux together until there is only enough space left to allow the button to go through (figure **11c**).

Bow fastening

Where a fastening is closed with one button only it is often difficult to give it the right importance unless a single, really outstanding button can be found.

But all too often the search for a button in the right size, shape and color is fruitless. A bow of soft leather, or any other material, can make an attractive alternative (figure **12a**).

Following the illustrations, cut and make a pattern for a bow with splaying ends (figure **12b**). Make four vertical button-holes $\frac{3}{4}$ inch long, two on the right side and two on the left (figure **12c**). Slip the bow through the buttonholes and tie.

Buckled fastenings

An attractive alternative to a buttoned fastening, such as that illustrated here, can be achieved with a buckle (figure **13a**). To make the tab cut the right end of the yoke front 4 inches longer, splaying it out so that it is a little wider at the end. Attach a buckle, slightly smaller than the tab, to the left side and slot the end of the right yoke through it.

The diagonal seamline of a cross-over garment can be given detail by stitching tab ends into the seam and slotting the tabs through pretty matching buckles (figure **13b**).

Buckled fastenings need not have a sporty appearance. A silver or diamanté buckle can be used to good effect on a cocktail dress, adding an individual finishing touch.

Frogs

Frogs are a very easy method of decorating a garment.

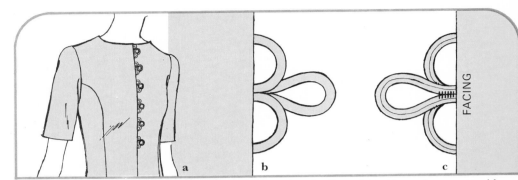

▲ **11a.** *The rouleau loop cluster along front bodice opening:* **b.** *from right side;* **c.** *from wrong side*

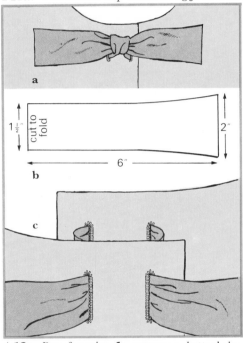

▲ **12a.** *Bow fastening;* **b.** *pattern;* **c.** *buttonholes*

▲ **13.** *Buckles on:* **a.** *yoke;* **b.** *diagonal seam*

Frogs can be made in rouleau, cord or braid.

When made from rouleau or cord the frogs are generally worked separately (figures **14a** and **b**) and then attached to the garment with small slip stitches. The button is also incorporated in the frog so that it can be used as an edge to edge fastening (figure **14c**).

When working with stitched rouleau make sure that the seam does not lie on top of the finished frog.

Using braid, the frog is usually worked straight onto the garment.

If you are matching opposites, make sure that the cord or rouleau goes over and under at the same places, but in reverse.

Tuck the ends of the cord carefully under the frog so that they can be stitched out of sight, and make sure they do not form a thickness which will lift the frog when it is stitched on the garment.

Simple frogs can be worked free hand by using the finger to gauge the size of the loops. More complicated designs, however, are usually worked over a drawn

up pattern, carefully pinned and then stitched together.

Buttons

All dressmakers know how the appearance of a dress changes when the buttons are sewn on. It is often just the buttons used which turn the fastening into something special.

The type of button you choose decides the number to use. If you want lots of buttons keep them plain so that the whole fastening shows up as cleverly planned detail. Important looking buttons should never be crowded even if they are small.

Thick buttons will always create a three dimensional effect and add to the impression of bulk, so use them sparingly. Choose either very large buttons or very small ones, and avoid in-between sizes.

Many buttons which do not look good on vertical fastenings can be used successfully on a diagonal fastening, which has a diminishing effect.

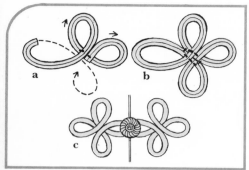

▲ 14. *Frogs:* **a.** *and* **b.** *making;* **c.** *with button*

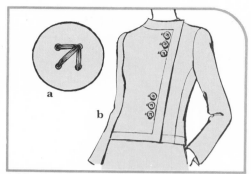

▲ 15a.*Button with arrowheads:* **b.** *attractive group*

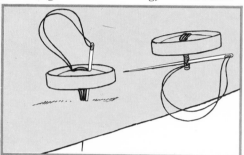

▲ 16. *Making a thread shank*

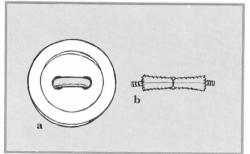

▲ 17a. *Rouleau shank;* **b.** *from wrong side*

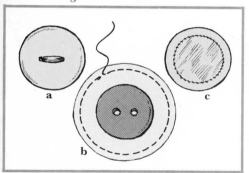

▲ 18a. *Covered button;* **b.** *covering;* **c.** *lining*

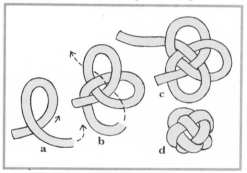

▲ 19. *Steps in making a Chinese ball button*

Ordinary fastenings are turned into something special when you stitch on a button attractively. Figure **15a** shows a four drill button stitched on in the shape of an arrowhead, which can be emphasized with shiny silk thread. Part of the attraction can be achieved by the arrangement of buttons in groups (figure **15b**).

The crossover method of stitching on buttons is only used on men's trouser buttons or on that type of button which has a sunken center. If a cross-stitch is used on a flat centered button the thread soon shows signs of wear and it often becomes shiny and discolored.

About button shanks

The length of a button shank should correspond to the thickness of the buttonhole.

Buttons with a built-in shank don't need the addition of a thread shank.

Buttons without a shank and with horizontal holes drilled into the underside are only intended for decoration, to be stitched on the surface of a garment. Making a

thread shank on this type of button will only result in sprawling and unsightly stitches.

To make a thread shank follow the steps in figure **16**.

The type of button to avoid altogether is one with a shank so wide that it makes the buttonhole gape when it fits around it. A thread shank here is not the answer either, as the shank and button will sit on top of the buttonhole and reveal the underside of the button.

When using buttons with small metal loop shanks for decorative purposes make an eyelet into the fabric and draw the shank to the inside of the garment. This will keep the button from tilting.

Rouleau button shank

Buttons with large drill holes can be stitched on with a fine rouleau (figure **17a**). Make a rouleau $\frac{1}{8}$ inch wide. Cut off a piece about $1\frac{1}{4}$ inches long and fill with buttonhole gimp (this is a cord-like thread mainly used by tailors). Then thread through the drill holes.

To attach the button, prize the weave of the garment open with a stiletto or the pointed end of a No.4 knitting needle, without breaking the threads of the fabric. Work the hole through the interfacing as well.

Push the ends of the rouleau through the hole to the underside. Leave enough rouleau between the button and the garment to make a shank and stitch the ends of the rouleau to the interfacing, spreading them quite flat and catching the ends of the gimp into the stitches so it cannot work out (figure **17b**). The gimp will keep the rouleau from stretching and making the button loose.

In hard weaves it may be necessary to make an eyelet through which to take the rouleau. It is then sewn on as before.

Fabric covered buttons

Fabric covered buttons should only be used with bound buttonholes, as the friction of a hand-made buttonhole will soon wear away the fabric of a covered button.

Just as there are wrong fabrics for bound buttonholes, there are wrong fabrics for covered buttons. Avoid stiff fabrics as they usually form points around the edges unless they are molded by machine.

A loose woven fabric used to cover buttons should first be lined.

Covering a button

Here is a quick way to cover buttons to match a garment (figure **18a**).

You can use odd buttons for this but make sure they are all the same shape on the underside first.

Cut a circle a little larger than the size of the button and sew a row of running stitches close to the edge. Place the button in the center and draw up the fullness (figure **18b**). Fasten off the stitches firmly underneath and line the underside with another circle of matching fabric (figure **18c**).

Stitch on the button with shiny matching silk using the drill holes.

Chinese ball button

This type of button is only used for decorative purposes as it will collapse if subjected to strain.

These buttons are made from cord, rouleau or braid, folded as shown (figure **19**).

To retain a good rounded shape when the button is sewn to the garment, make one knot from the ends, cut them off short and stitch them out of sight.

Chapter 61

Start with a pop-over pinafore

Every little girl needs a pop-over to keep her clothes clean, and if it's got a pretty pocket for her teddy bear or hanky it will be fun to wear. The next four pages include a tracing pattern complete with instructions for hand or machine sewing. Even if you're not very confident about your dressmaking, it's simple to make. Experienced dressmakers will enjoy thinking up other pocket designs based on similar shapes.

Fabric requirements

$\frac{5}{8}$yd of gingham, 36in wide. $\frac{3}{8}$yd of contrasting fabric for pocket, or piece 11in by 14in. 3yd of bias binding (for machine finish only). Two buttons. Sewing thread. Embroidery cotton and $\frac{1}{2}$yd of tape (for hand finish only).

Layout and cutting

Fold gingham selvage to selvage and lay out the pattern pieces as shown in the diagrams. Cut ONE pocket in gingham and ONE pocket and handle in contrasting fabric.
Mark out seam allowance on all pattern pieces and cut out.

Making up

Make line of basting down the center front on fold. Join side seams and shoulder seams. If you work by hand, use backstitch or running stitch. Overcast raw edges.

If you work by hand

Turn under, pin and baste seam allowance on neck, arm-holes and around hem up to the top of center back. Press lightly in position. Work around these edges with alternating blanket stitch. This not only looks attractive but ensures that you catch the folded edge every time.

Make stitches about $\frac{3}{16}$in apart. On both pocket pieces, turn under seam allowance all around, snipping corners. Wrong sides together, baste pockets together and work same blanket stitch all around.

If you work by machine

Take bias binding, open fold on one side and lay to seam allowance, right sides facing, around neck, armholes and hem. Ease into curves at neck and armholes, pin and stitch together. Turn bias binding to the inside and baste in position. Stitch to pop-over and press, taking care not to stretch edges.
For pocket lay gingham and contrasting fabric pieces together, right sides facing, and stitch around, leaving 2in opening. Snip corners and turn pocket right side out.

Slip stitch opening. Baste around edges and press lightly.

To make loop, by hand and machine

Fold fabric in half lengthwise and stitch. Pull through to outside with the aid of safety pin. Press flat.

To stitch pocket to pop-over and finish

Lay center of pocket on center front of pop-over, with wheels about 1½in from bottom edge. Tuck raw ends of loop for handle under end of baby carriage and stitch pocket, following dash line on pattern. If you stitch by hand, use firm backstitch. Do not sew over blanket stitches.
To fasten pop-over at back, attach two pieces of tape at neck and tie in a bow, or make two loops for buttons on right side of back and attach where shown on pattern. Sew on buttons opposite the loops.

Some pretty ideas for pockets

Of course there's no need to stick to the baby carriage if you have other ideas for pockets, or if you are making more than one pop-over. Use the basic pocket shape—but adapt it in different ways. You can make the shape, minus the wheels, into a boat, and appliqué a white or colored sail to the front of the pop-over. Or, make a basket, with a handle, and then appliqué bright flowers, or richly colored fruits on it.

▲ Pop-over seen from the back

▲ Pop-over front, with pocket

▼ Layout on 36in fabric, with pocket on contrast piece

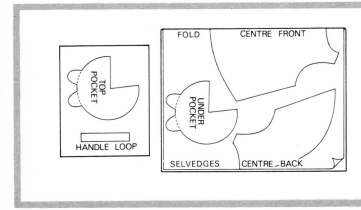

Pattern for pocket

Solid black line: stitching
line for carriage. Arrows
indicate corners for snipping.
Dash line: for stitching pocket
to pop-over.
Seam allowance to be added:
¼in all around carriage.

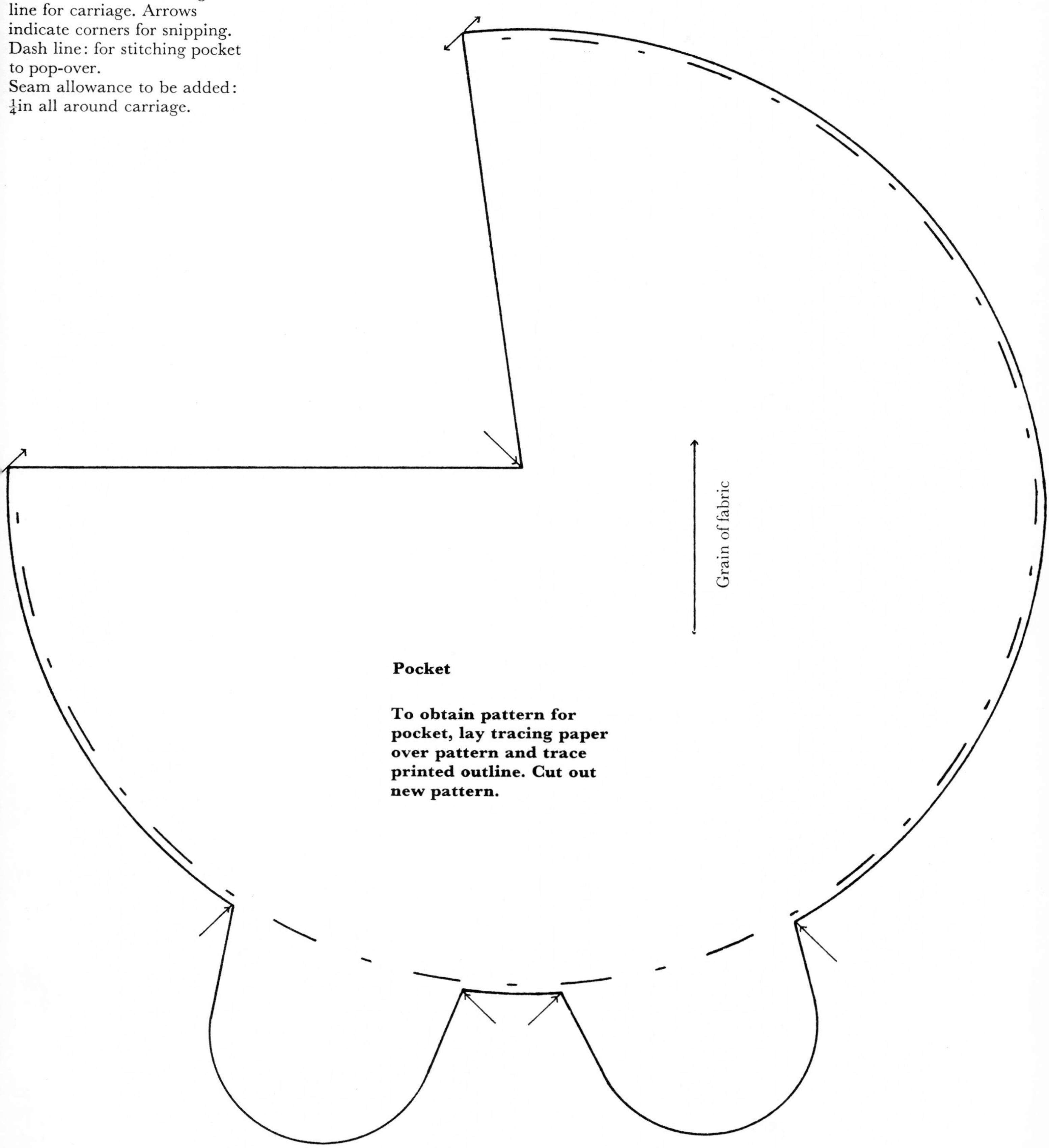

Grain of fabric

Pocket

**To obtain pattern for
pocket, lay tracing paper
over pattern and trace
printed outline. Cut out
new pattern.**

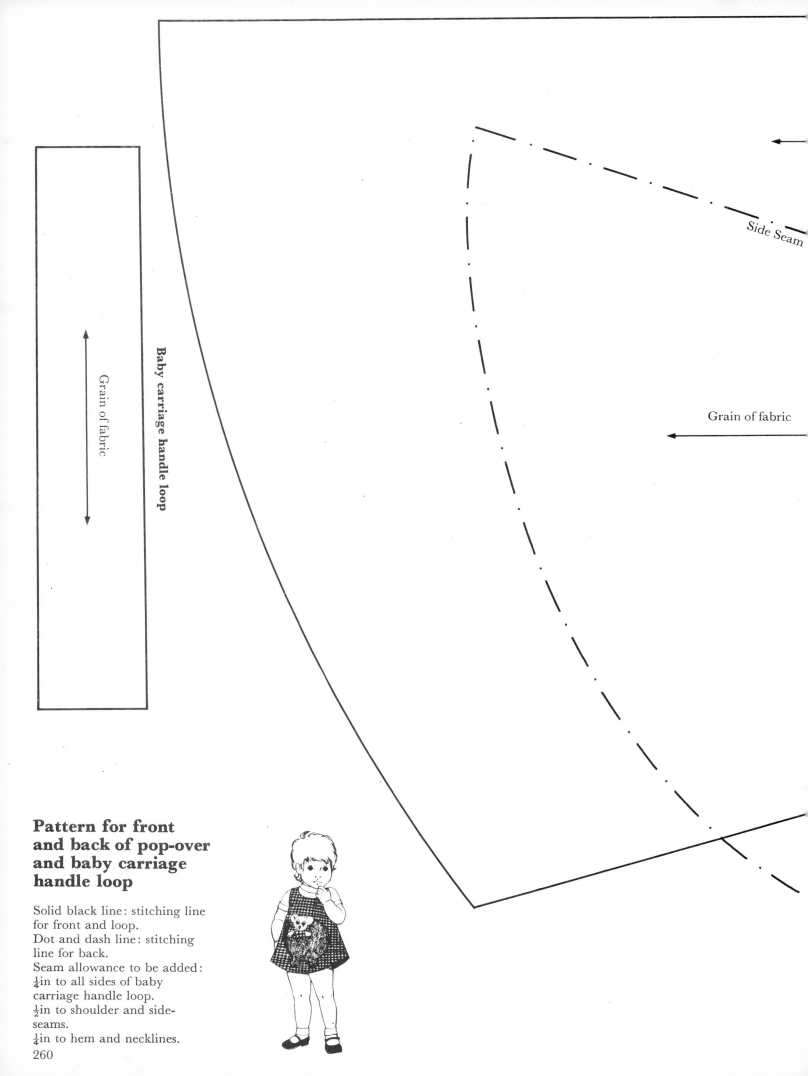

Grain of fabric

Baby carriage handle loop

Grain of fabric

Side Seam

Grain of fabric

Pattern for front and back of pop-over and baby carriage handle loop

Solid black line: stitching line
for front and loop.
Dot and dash line: stitching
line for back.
Seam allowance to be added:
$\frac{1}{4}$in to all sides of baby
carriage handle loop.
$\frac{1}{2}$in to shoulder and side-
seams.
$\frac{1}{4}$in to hem and necklines.

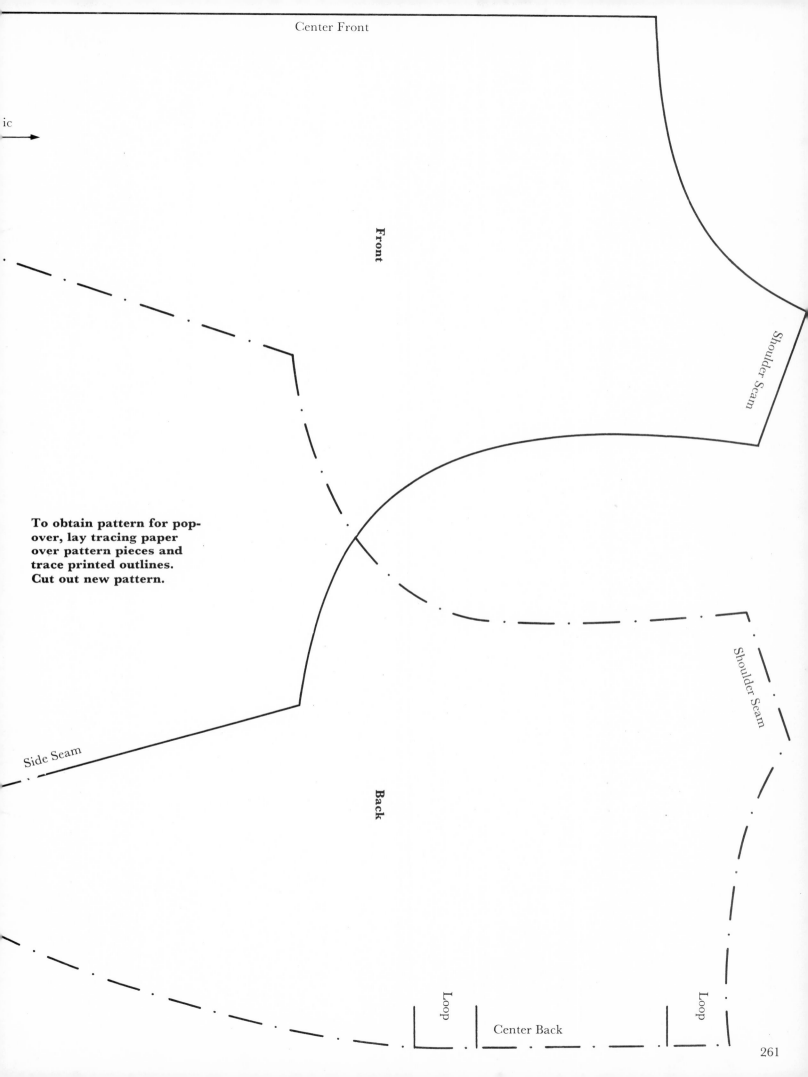

Center Front

Front

Shoulder Seam

To obtain pattern for pop-
over, lay tracing paper
over pattern pieces and
trace printed outlines.
Cut out new pattern.

Side Seam

Back

Shoulder Seam

Loop

Loop

Center Back

261

Chapter 62

Sewing for Children

Angel smock

Angel smocks are the most useful garments in a toddler's wardrobe. Made in a light fabric, with matching knickers, an angel smock becomes a pretty summer dress—or in soft wool, in a color matched to tights, a warm winter play outfit. Angel smocks in wipe-clean fabrics provide a protective cover-up for messy mealtimes and, at the other extreme, they can be the prettiest of party dresses made in eyelet embroidery.

You will need:
☐ 1⅝yd 36in wide fabric ☐ 1yd ¼in wide elastic ☐ Matching thread ☐ Graph paper for the pattern (or ordinary brown paper will do). If you are making the angel smock in eyelet embroidery edging, to find the amount you need add together the width across the widest point of both sleeves and the width across the hem line on the Back and Front, plus an extra 6 inches for seam allowances. If you have difficulty in finding an edging which is as deep as the length of the garment, overlap and stitch two rows together.

The pattern
The angel smock fits sizes 1 and 2 and is in 16 and 18 inch lengths. There are four pattern pieces, Back, Front, sleeve and facing. Make the pattern first from the instruction on pages 264, 265

The layout
Fold fabric to take in Back and Front. Place pattern on double fabric as shown with Center Back and Front on fold. Fold remaining fabric selvage to selvage, place center front of facing on fold.
The pattern has no seam or hem allowance so add ¾ inch to all seams (except on the outer edge of the facing) and 2 inch hems at the lower edge of the sleeves and hem edge.
Cut out the fabric and mark the pattern outline, stitching lines and balance marks.

Making in six easy stages

1. Sewing sleeves to Back and Front
With right sides facing, match the balance marks on the front armhole edge of the left sleeve to those of the corresponding Front armhole. Pin, baste, and stitch the seams. Then match the balance marks of the back armhole edge of the sleeve to those of the corresponding Back armhole. Pin, baste and stitch as before. Repeat for right sleeve. Oversew raw seam edges to neaten and press seams towards sleeve.

2. Joining the facing
Align the two Center Back edges of the facing, with right sides of fabric together, and stitch a short seam from neck edge to the balance mark, leaving the lower end open. Press seam open. The unfinished end of the seam provides the casing opening.

3. Stitching on the facing and making the casing
With right sides of fabric together, place facing round neck line, with raw neck edges level, balance marks and Center Backs and Fronts matching. Pin, baste and stitch along neck edge.
Trim the seam allowance and then clip into it close to the stitches. Turn facing to inside of garment, baste along edge and press. If the edge is inclined to roll, as on a springy fabric, top stitch through dress and facings close to the edge. Turn in the raw edge of the facing ¼ inch and baste.
Pin the facing flat into position round the inside of the neck edge. The folded edge should just cover the lower stitching line and the balance marks on the facing should meet the armhole seam.
Baste in place and stitch close to the edge, along lower stitching line.
Turn the garment to right side, make another row of machine stitches along the upper stitching line and the casing is finished.

4. Sewing the sleeve and side-seams
With right sides facing, pin, baste and stitch the left underarm sleeve and side-seams in one operation; starting at the wrist edge stitch to the underarm and then down the side seam to the hem edge. Repeat on right side.
Oversew raw seam edges and press seams open.

5. Making the sleeve casing
Turn in the lower edge of sleeves ¼ inch and baste. Turn up the hem allowance so that the folded edge falls just over the upper stitching line. Make the casing as before but leave a small opening in the upper stitching line for the elastic.

6. Finishing
Cut three pieces of elastic, one to fit the child's neck, the other two to fit the wrists. Thread the elastic through the casings and sew the ends firmly together. Slip stitch openings in casings to close. Turn up the hem to the required length and give all seams and edges a final pressing.

Alternative finishes

Since this garment is so quick and easy to make, you'll want more than one. Try ringing the changes with a different finish on the neck and sleeves.

Angel smock with bound edges
Cut off the pattern midway between the stitching lines for the casing around the neck, and do not allow for sleeve hems.
Lay out the pattern pieces as before, but place the Back pattern parallel to the selvages and ¾ inch in from the edge, to allow for a Centre Back seam.
Sew a Center Back seam leaving 4 inches open at the top.
Loosely measure the child's neck and wrists and gather the neck line and lower sleeve edges to these measurements.
Cut bias strips to the length of the measurements, adding 1 inch for neatening the ends, and bind the gathered edges.
Use loop and button fastenings to close the back neck opening.

Angel smock with back buttoning
To make a quick slip-over for playtimes or mealtimes, fasten the angel smock all the way down the Center Back with buttons.
When laying out the pattern for this version, place the Center Back parallel to the selvages, 3 inches from the edge of the fabric. This will give you a 1 inch wrap on each side and 2 inches for the self facing.
Make the buttonholes along the Center Back line.

▲ *Playtime, party time or anytime, angel smocks are tops for babies and toddlers*

Layout for the angel smock on 36in wide fabric for sizes 1 and 2 ▼

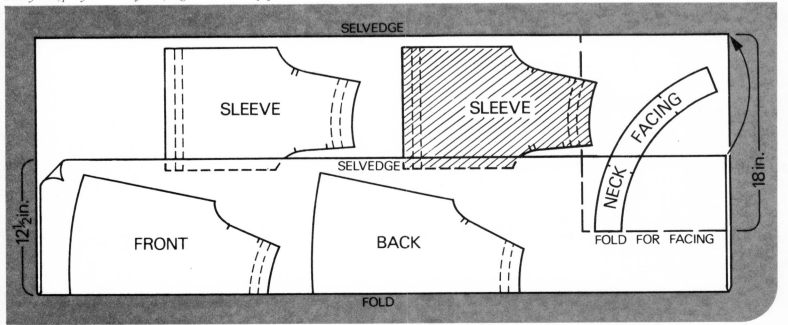

SELVEDGE

SLEEVE

SLEEVE

NECK FACING

SELVEDGE

FOLD FOR FACING

12½ in.

18 in.

FRONT

BACK

FOLD

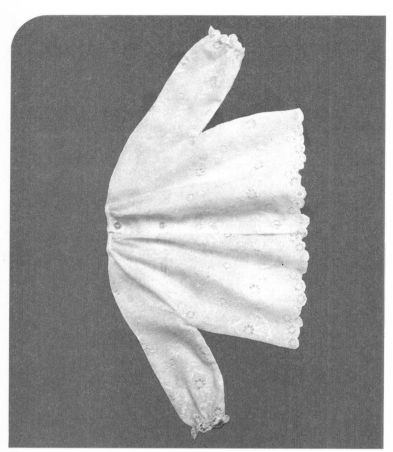

Two ways with an angel smock— ▲ *pretty in white or* ▼ *gay in a color print*

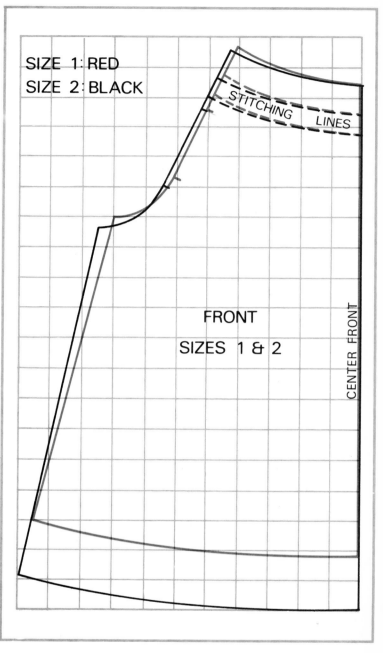

SIZE 1: RED
SIZE 2: BLACK

STITCHING LINES

FRONT

SIZES 1 & 2

CENTER FRONT

The pattern

Each square on the graph represents a 1in square.

All the pattern pieces are without seam or hem allowance.

To make the patterns, cut the following pieces of graph paper (or brown paper if you cannot buy graph paper):

    For the front cut a piece 19in by 11in.

    For the back cut a piece 19in by 11in.

    For the sleeve cut a piece 17in by 11in.

    For the facing cut a piece 13in by 10in.

If you are using brown paper, you'll find it easier to plot the pattern if you draw up all the pieces into 1in squares. Do make sure, though, that you draw the lines very carefully and absolutely straight or the pattern will not be accurate.

To make the pattern for size 2, copy it to scale from the graphs, using the outer solid black lines.

To make the pattern for size 1, copy it to scale from the graphs, using the solid red lines, except where the black and red lines merge.

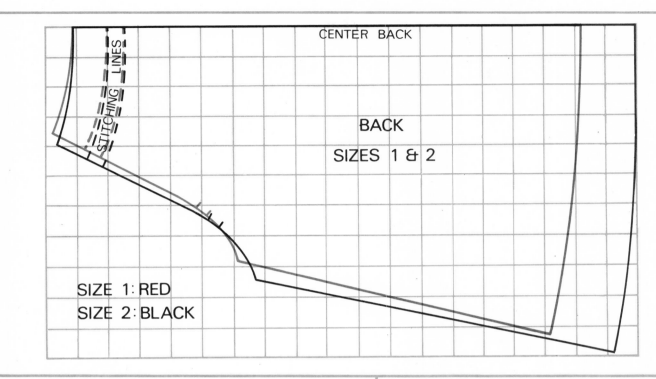

CENTER BACK

BACK

SIZES 1 & 2

STITCHING LINES

SIZE 1: RED
SIZE 2: BLACK

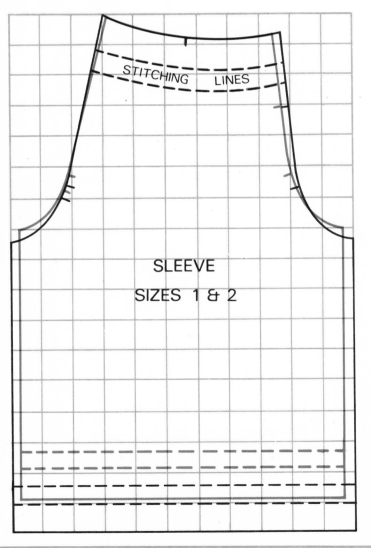

STITCHING LINES

SLEEVE

SIZES 1 & 2

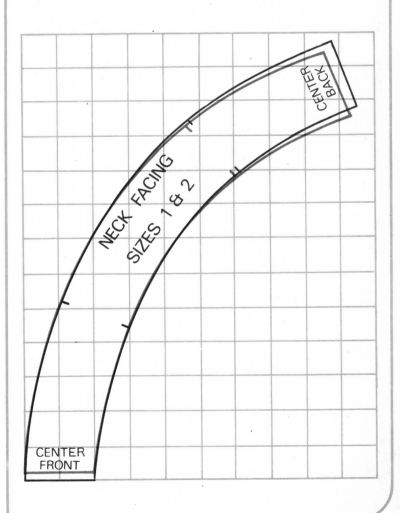

CENTER BACK

NECK FACING

SIZES 1 & 2

CENTER FRONT

Chapter 63

A great little dress

Sewing for Children

Key to graphs for the child's basic dress

The patterns are in three sizes
24in chest, length 22½in
26in chest, length 24in
28in chest, length 26½in
Each square on the graph represents a 1 inch square
The patterns do not include seam allowance

Color key to sizes
Size 24in chest = ─────
Size 26in chest = ─────
Size 28in chest = ─────

Here's a dress to delight a small member of the family. It's a basic pattern, shown here made up in hard-wearing cotton corduroy and trimmed with a sparkling white collar, which is detachable for easy cleaning. This little dress is given in three sizes, to fit a 24, 26, and 28 inch chest. The patterns are on graph and each dress consists of three pattern pieces only. It's quick and easy to do and yet it's versatile enough for you to be able to make a whole wardrobe of excitingly different little dresses for all sorts of occasions from this one pattern. Try it and see!

Dressmaking for children can be easy and fun

You can make this dress in different types of fabric with various trimmings, and here are some ideas to get you started.

For play, make it in hard-wearing cotton or corduroy and add big patch pockets. For parties, as a complete contrast, make it in something light and filmy. Choose plain or embroidered organdy, organza or voile for a top dress, then stitch it to an underdress in matching or contrasting cotton lawn or taffeta. For a really delicate look, trim it with lace or add frills.

For vacations and beach wear, make a sleeveless version in terry cloth and, to make it really practical, stitch a row of apron pockets across the front to hold all those pretty pebbles and shells gathered on the beach.

There are some excellent washable wools available for making cozy and practical winter dresses, and you can add detachable collars and cuffs to change the appearance of each dress quickly. You'll see how to make these in chapter 65.

The basic pattern

The patterns on the graph are in three sizes: 24in chest, length 22½in; 26in chest, length 24in; 28in chest, length 26½in. Each square represents a 1 inch square.

To copy the pattern, use graph paper or any firm paper drawn accurately into 1 inch squares. Before you begin, select the pattern size you want and cut the paper into pieces just large enough to accommodate each pattern graph. Then copy the outline of the pattern to scale.

It is easy to adjust the length of the pattern by adding to or deducting from the squares between the lower edge of the armhole and the hemline. Do not add or deduct at the hem, because the flare of the dress will be affected, as with the flared skirt pattern. If you need to cater to in-between sizes, select the larger of the two sizes and pin off the difference at the fitting stage.

Making fitting easier

Small children often get very fidgety if they have to stand still to be fitted, and sometimes a fitting session can end in tears and bad temper. You may only have an hour or two during the school

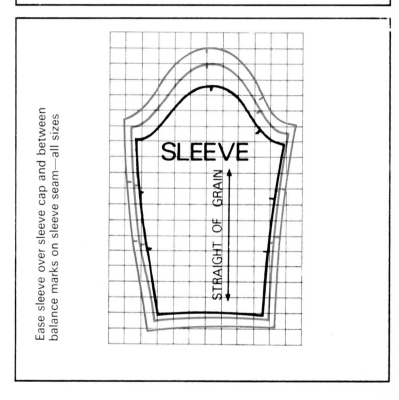

Ease sleeve over sleeve cap and between balance marks on sleeve seam—all sizes

SLEEVE

STRAIGHT OF GRAIN

day when you can get down to some dressmaking, and it may be difficult to get beyond the fitting stage.

One way to help you over these problems is to make a mock dress for the child (this is not quite the same as a muslin—it's not necessary to make a muslin for a child—but to be successful, children's dresses do need careful fitting).

Make it from sheeting or muslin as for the blouse bodice muslin. (It's a good idea to cut out a miniature dress for the child's doll at the same time. The child can copy all the fitting stages and it will keep her busy too while you do your work.)

Cut out the mock dress as if it were the real one with ¾ inch seam and 2½ to 3 inch hem allowance. Pin and baste the front and back together along the side and shoulder seams. Leave the center back seam open so that it is easy to slip on and off. Put the mock dress on the child and pin it together down the center back.

The first fitting

With most children, there are four special fitting points—dropped shoulders, chubby neck, chubby arms and a high tummy. All these points affect the fitting of a dress.

Ease front into back between side seam balance mark and armhole—sizes 24 and 26in chest

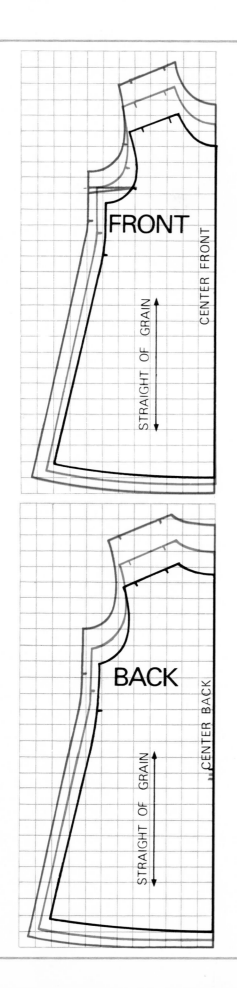

FRONT

STRAIGHT OF GRAIN

CENTER FRONT

Ease back into front between shoulder balance marks—all sizes

BACK

STRAIGHT OF GRAIN

CENTER BACK

Dropped shoulders. Pin off the required amount from the outer edge of the shoulder seam. Snip the seam allowance around the lower armhole until the creases running toward the underarm have disappeared, both back and front. Mark a new underarm seamline with pins or pencil if necessary.

Chubby neck and arms. Snip the seam allowance around the neck and armholes until the dress lies flat. Mark the new seamlines.

A high tummy. If the dress juts out in front, make a side bust dart as shown on the pattern for size 28 inch chest. If you are using this size already, lift a little more fabric into the dart. In either case, the amount you take into the dart must be added to the hemline at the side of the dress, otherwise the hem allowance will be reduced.

The child with a high tummy often stands very erect, a posture which will make the dress appear rather tight across the chest and full across the back. If you can avoid it, do not alter the width across the back because this is needed for movement—add width across the front instead. This means making a new front pattern, but this is not difficult.

To make a new front pattern, lay the pattern piece on a large sheet of paper, pinning the center front to one straight edge. Measure 4 inches from the edge and slash the pattern from the hem to within $\frac{1}{8}$ inch of the shoulder. Spread the left half of the pattern piece until the opening at chest level is about $\frac{1}{2}$ inch wide. If this results in too much flare at the lower side seam, trim the flare as shown in diagram 1. Straighten the shoulder line and cut out the new pattern.

The second fitting

Make the mock dress just as if it were the real one, except for the neckline. Trim off the seam allowance along the seamline to fit perfectly around the neck. Put in the sleeves to give you the correct setting for them and turn up all hems.

Try the dress on the child again. When you are satisfied that it fits, cut the dress into sections along the stitching lines. Place the sections flat, over the pattern pieces, and transfer all the alterations. Having done this, your problems are solved because you can use the pattern again and again with only a brief check on the fitting now and then.

Hems

Little dresses are often made with hems up to 6 inches deep, but it is a mistake to think that a child's dress will last longer if it is made with a really deep hem. The truth is that this adds a great deal of weight to the garment and can make it look quite shapeless. Bear in mind, too, that when a dress becomes too short for a growing child, it affects not only the hem but also the length between shoulder and underarm and this, in turn, makes the sleeves too tight. Of course it may be possible to alter the dress, but it is rather a waste of time to go to this trouble if the dress is only going to be worn once or twice before the seams split. Making a dress "on the big side" is not the answer either, because the sad result would be a new dress which is shapeless turning into a dress which fits only when it is worn out! The answer is to make a dress which fits well right from the start, then the child can enjoy wearing it and you can be proud of having made it. A hem of 3 to 4 inches, if you want to allow extra, is adequate and will give the dress a good life of two or three seasons.

Neckline finishes

Another important point to watch when making children's dresses is the neckline finish. This section is rubbed a great deal during washing and it has to withstand a lot of wear, so a good, firm finish is necessary.

To hold the neckline in shape, make a rouleau-type bound

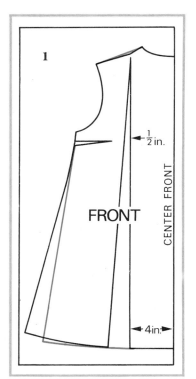
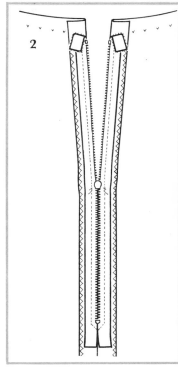

1. *Making a new front pattern* **2.** *Zipper tape ends sewn in place*

▼ *Detail of the finished neckline, bound with a bias strip*

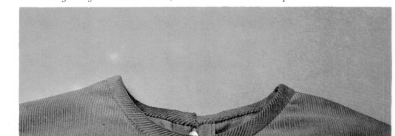

finish (described on the opposite page, item 4). Apart from being very hard-wearing, it looks neat and will also withstand the repeated stitching which is necessary when changing detachable collars for washing.

A flat bias facing is an alternate finish but does not give such a strong neck edge. This is because the seam allowance inside the bias must be snipped close to the seam to lie flat.

It is not advisable to use conventional fabric facings for children's dresses, because they become worn and very untidy after frequent washing.

Fabric requirements for the child's dress

36in wide fabric. Twice the dress length plus the sleeve length and hem and seam allowances.

54in wide fabric. The dress length plus the sleeve length and hem and seam allowances.

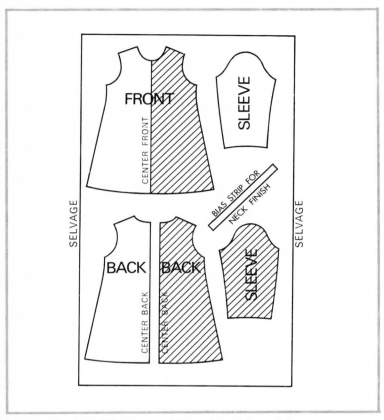

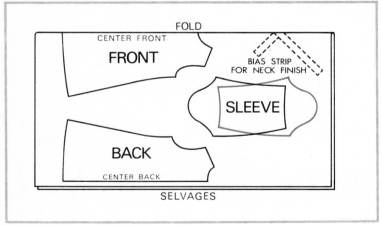

▲ *Layout for the child's dress on 36in width, with or without one way*
▼ *Layout for a child's dress on 54in width, with or without one way*

You will also need a zipper (12in for size 24in chest, 14in to 16in for sizes 26in and 28in chest, depending on the dress length), and one size 1 hook for the neck fastening.

If you want to be really economical when calculating the fabric length, make a trial layout on paper first, using the same methods as those given in some detail in Know-How chapter 46, P. 204. You can then measure the yardage from your own layout and buy the exact amount of fabric.

If you decide to add pockets or frills, don't forget to take this into account when working out the yardage.

The layout

Copy one of the layouts illustrated or use the layout you made on paper to calculate the yardage.

On your own layout, place the center front of the pattern on the fold and the center back on the selvages, allowing for a center

back seam. Make sure that the grain line marked on the sleeve pattern piece lines up perfectly with the grain of the fabric.

Pin all pattern pieces down securely and mark around them. Mark all pattern details, not forgetting the end of the zipper opening. Cut out the dress, adding seam and hem allowances.

Making the dress

This basic dress is so simple that you can make it in six easy stages. It's easier still if you have made and fitted a mock dress first.

1. Seams and darts

Pin, baste and stitch the small side bust darts (if you need to use them) and press them toward the hem.

Pin, baste and stitch the side and shoulder seams and the center back seam below the zipper opening. Finish all seam edges neatly and press the seams open.

2. The zipper

Stitch in the zipper as for a straight seam, leaving 1 inch between the zipper teeth and the raw edge of the neckline. Turn back the ends of the zipper tape at an angle so they will not show and hand-sew them down, as shown in diagram 2.

3. The sleeves

Pin, baste and stitch the sleeve seams, finish the seam edges neatly and press the seams open. Gather in the ease around the sleeve caps and pin the sleeves into the armholes, matching balance marks and seams. Stitch, remembering to work with the sleeve uppermost. Finish seam edges and press the seams into the sleeves.

4. Binding the neckline

First, to hold the shape of the neck edge and to prevent it from stretching, machine a row of stay stitches along the seamline. Trim off the seam allowance $\frac{1}{8}$ inch from the stay stitches.

To bind the neck, cut a bias strip from the dress fabric (or an equally strong contrasting fabric) $1\frac{1}{8}$ inches wide and $\frac{1}{2}$ inch longer than the neck edge measurement.

Pin and baste the bias strip to the neckline on the outside of the dress, right sides facing and raw edges even, leaving $\frac{1}{4}$ inch at each end for turning. Stitch in position, taking $\frac{1}{4}$ inch seam allowance to bring the stitching line for the binding $\frac{1}{8}$ inch below the stay stitching. Do not trim any more fabric off the seam allowance as this is now your guide for the width of the binding.

Turn in the $\frac{1}{4}$ inch seam allowance at each end of the bias strip and turn under the raw edge. The amount you turn under depends on the thickness of the fabric you are using, but the folded edge should meet the stitching line when turned to the inside of the dress.

Never force the bias strip over the neck edge or it will pucker. If the bias strip is tight, let out the folded edge a little until the bias strip can be turned over the raw edge without strain. Slip stitch the folded edge to the stitching line and close the ends of the binding. Finish with a hand-made bar and hook.

5. Making the hems

Turn up the hem allowance on the dress and the sleeves. Make the hem in the usual way on the dress, but on the sleeves use a firmer hemming stitch. Sleeve hems are easily caught by little fingers in a hurry to get dressed.

6. The finishing touches

Press the dress and all seams and hems on the inside, being as careful as you are with your own dresses. This final touch is not only necessary but also justifies all your dressmaking efforts.

Chapter 64

Converting the child's basic dress

This chapter shows you how to use the child's basic dress pattern in the previous chapter to create two new styles— A: the dress with a straight waist seam and straight sleeves, either long or short, and B: the dress with a shaped waist seam and full, three-quarter length sleeves. For both styles the bodice is fitted and the skirt fully gathered.

The size range is the same as for the basic dress, that is, to fit a 24, 26, and 28 inch chest.

A special feature of these dresses is the high waist. A dress with a fitted waist for a growing girl has a very short life span because the waist seam is never in the right place for long, and even if there is enough fabric to let the waist down, it is a very difficult task. But these dresses are designed with a high waist in the first place, so they will not look out of place even after two or three seasons' wear. If any adjustment to the length is necessary, it is simply a matter of letting down the hem.

Choosing the right version

It is important to take the child's figure shape into consideration when deciding which version to make.

A. Dress with straight waist seam The seam goes almost straight across the body and is only suitable for really slim children. This style is not suitable for larger children because the shape of the seam would need to be severely adapted and would never hide the problem of a high stomach.

B. Dress with shaped waist seam This shape is more flattering to sturdily built children. It is not so rigid and allows for more freedom of movement.

Making the bodice patterns

The basic pattern For both versions, make the basic dress pattern from the graph in the previous chapter and incorporate any necessary pattern alterations.

Marking the natural waistline For both versions, first find the natural waistline before marking and cutting the high waistline.

Pin a tape firmly around the child's natural waistline and take the following measurements on both back and front pattern pieces: i) center neck to tape, ii) inner shoulder to tape, iii) outer shoulder to tape.

Mark each measurement on the pattern pieces as you take it (figures **1** and **2**) and draw a line across the patterns connecting the points. This gives you the natural waistline.

A. Dress with straight waist seam

To find the high waist seam on both back and front pattern pieces, draw a line parallel to the natural waistline, 1½ inches above it (figure **3**). Cut the pattern along this line.

Mark the position for a waist dart on the front pattern piece, 3 inches from the center front line and 2 inches long (figure **4**). Draw in the dart ¾ inch wide (figure **5**).

Make a dart in the same way on the back bodice pattern, but make it 3 inches long and 1 inch wide.

Now check the high waistline for size. Measure the waist less the darts on the front and back bodice pattern pieces and note. Measure the child 1½ inches above the waistline tape and add 2 inches to this measurement for ease. The child's measurement plus ease should equal twice the pattern measurement.

If the bodice width needs adjusting, adjust the side seams.

Pass the ease in the upper front side seam (or the dart in the largest pattern) into the waist seam (figure **5**) so that the length of the side seams on back and front are equal. Ignore the side seam balance marks on the new pattern.

B. Dress with shaped waist seam

On both back and front pieces, draw a line parallel to the natural waistline and 1 inch up from it.

On the front pattern piece, make a pencil mark on the center front line, 2 inches above the natural waistline. Starting 3 inches in from the center front on the new waistline, make a curve to this point (figures **6** and **7**).

Cut out the front bodice pattern along this line and cut the back bodice along the high waistline.

Mark the position for a waist dart on the front pattern piece 3 inches from the center front line and 2½ inches long (figure **7**). Draw in the dart ¾ inch wide (figure **8**).

Make a dart in the same way on the back bodice pattern piece which is 3½ inches long and 1 inch deep.

To check that the high waist measurement is correct, measure the waist less the darts 1 inch above the cutting line on the front and back bodice pattern pieces and note. Measure the child 2 inches above the waistline tape and add 2 inches to this measurement for ease. The child's measurement plus ease should equal twice the pattern measurement.

If the bodice width needs altering, adjust the side seams.

Pass the ease in the upper front side seam (or the dart in the largest pattern) into the waist seam (figure **8**) so that the length of the side seams on back and front are equal. Ignore the side seam balance marks on the new pattern.

▼**1.** *Front: marking natural waist* ▼**2.** *Back: marking natural waist*

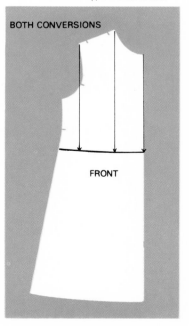
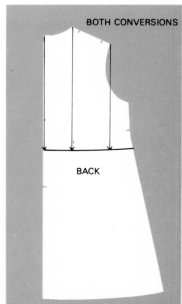

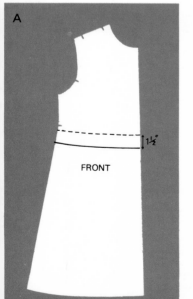

▲ *The dress with straight waist seam and short sleeves in a pretty print*

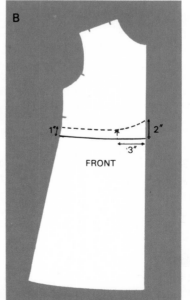

▲ *The dress with shaped waist seam and full, ¾ sleeves in white cotton*

▼ **3.** *Finding the high waistline*   ▼ **4.** *Measuring for front dart*

▼ **6.** *Curving the front waistline*   ▼ **7.** *Measuring for front dart*

A

FRONT

1½″

A

BODICE
FRONT

2″   3″

B

FRONT

1″   2″

3″

B

BODICE
FRONT

2½″   3″

▼ **5.** *Drawing dart, passing ease*

A

BODICE
FRONT

ease
or
dart

¾

▼ **8.** *Drawing dart, passing ease*

B

BODICE
FRONT

ease
or
dart

¾

▲ Details of the back view of dress A

Making the skirt patterns

A. Dress with straight waist seam
To make the gathered skirt, square off the back and front skirt sections as you did for the dirndl in Skirtmaking chapter 16 and cut out the new pattern

B. Dress with shaped waist seam
The skirt for this version is cut fuller at the hem than version A.

Slash back and front skirt pattern pieces in two places, the first 3 inches from the center lines, the second 2 inches from the side seams (figures **9** and **10**).

Use the center sections of the back and front pattern pieces for the straight of the grain.

Place all sections on a sheet of paper and spread each skirt pattern piece as shown,

allowing 2 inch spacings at the waist and $3\frac{1}{2}$ to 4 inches at the hem.

Draw around the new outlines. Mark in the center lines and straight of the grain before removing the original patterns to avoid mistakes.

Cut out the new pattern.

Making the sleeve patterns

For all sizes, make the sleeve pattern from the graph for the girl's basic dress in Sewing for Children chapter 63, incorporating any necessary alterations.

The long, straight sleeve
This is the same as the sleeve pattern for the girl's basic dress.

The short sleeve
Mark off the required length of the sleeve on the sleeve seams and cut across the pattern.

The full, $\frac{3}{4}$ length sleeve
The full, $\frac{3}{4}$ length sleeve is the most practical for children. It is long enough to be warm and full enough to be unrestricting during play. It is also a very pretty sleeve with its fullness gathered into elastic around the lower edge.

Using the basic sleeve pattern, measure the length of both sleeve seams and pin the amount allowed for ease in the back of the sleeve into a dart (figure **11**). Then make three equally spaced, lengthwise slashes from the wrist edge to within $\frac{1}{4}$ inch of the top as shown.

Lay the pattern on a sheet of paper and spread each section 2 inches apart at the wrist.

Add a little more width at the seams by extending them outward for 1 inch at the lower end and tapering into the original side seam between elbow and armhole. Draw each line in a gentle curve so that there is no kink where it joins the original seam again.

As the pattern is spread, the lower edge of the sleeve between the center and the sleeve seam will curve downward on the sleeve back. This is correct and necessary so that the sleeve will remain in place around the wrist when the arm is moved. Draw in the new sleeve outline, copy the balance marks on the sleeve cap and cut out the new pattern.

Take the child's measurement for the $\frac{3}{4}$ sleeve length and reduce the length of the pattern as required, allowing $\frac{3}{4}$ inch for the drop of the fullness.

Or, if you like, you can leave this sleeve long, gather it into a cuff and make an opening as you did for the shirt sleeve in Blousemaking chapter 29.

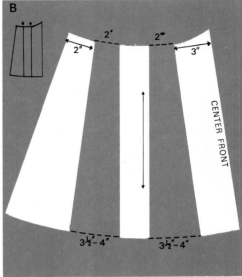

▲ **9.** *Widening the front skirt pattern*
▼ **10.** *Widening the back skirt pattern*

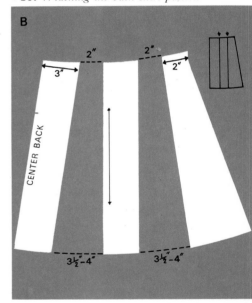

▼ **11.** *Altering the pattern for the full sleeve*

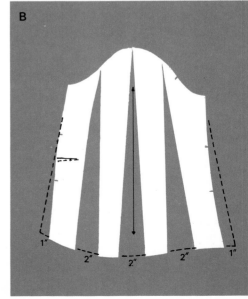

Fabrics, layouts, yardages and notions

Fabrics

There are many kinds of fabric you can use to make these little dresses. The style is suited to patterned or plain, soft or crisp fabrics.

The dresses can be made from remnants left over from other garments you have made because the individual sections of the pattern are quite small.

You could cut the skirt, sleeves and neck trimming from one fabric and use a contrasting fabric for the bodice, or perhaps a matching dotted print in contrasting colors.

Checks can be used effectively by cutting the bodice on the cross. Stripes can also be cut for effect and look very attractive.

You could try mixing textures on skirt and bodice, such as a jersey knit bodice and woven skirt, to make a pretty winter dress.

Layouts

Using the layouts in the previous chapter as a guide, lay the pattern pieces on paper to the width of the fabric you will be using.

Bodice For both versions, place the bodice center front along the fabric fold and cut the center back for an opening. Allow $\frac{3}{4}$ inch for seams.

Skirt Place the center front for version A along the fabric fold. The center front of version B and the center backs for both versions are cut for seaming. Allow $\frac{3}{4}$ inch for seams and $2\frac{1}{2}$ inches for hems.

Sleeves Allow $\frac{3}{4}$ inch for seams. Allow $1\frac{1}{2}$ inch hems on the short sleeve and the long, straight sleeve. But for the hem of the full, $\frac{3}{4}$ length sleeve allow only $\frac{3}{4}$ inch as it is finished off with a bias strip.

Binding Mark out a $1\frac{1}{8}$ inch wide bias strip for binding the neck edge as on the basic dress layout.

If you are making the $\frac{3}{4}$ length sleeve, mark out two bias strips $1\frac{1}{4}$ inches wide, and the length of the lower edge of the sleeve, plus $\frac{1}{2}$ inch seam allowance at each end.

Notions

- ☐ Zipper (12 inches for size 24 inch chest, 14 inches for size 26 inch chest, and 16 inches for size 28 inch chest)
- ☐ One hook fastener, size No.1, for the neck fastening
- ☐ Matching thread
- ☐ $\frac{1}{4}$ inch wide elastic for the full, $\frac{3}{4}$ length sleeve

Yardages

Measure the overall length of the paper to find the yardage required and mark around each pattern piece so that you can use it for a layout when the patterns are removed.

Cutting out

Cut out the fabric using the paper layout as a guide.

Tailor's tack around the pattern edges, taking special care with the curved seams, and mark all other pattern details.

A. Dress with straight waist seam

Preparing for fitting

Pin and baste the waist darts.

Pin and baste the bodice front to the bodice back.

Baste the skirt together at the side and center back seams. Do not forget to leave an opening for the zipper.

Run a row of basting stitches around the top of the skirt. Then pin and baste the skirt to the bodice in the waist seam, gathering the skirt to fit the bodice.

Pin and baste the sleeve seams. Baste the sleeves into the armholes.

Fitting

Check the sleeves for length.

Make sure that the fitted bodice sits well and is not strained by a tight seam allowance around the neck and armholes. If either one is tight, carefully snip the seam allowance until it lies flat.

Although the bodice is fitted, it should not be too close to the body. There must be enough room for energetic movements during play.

The gathered skirt on the flat bodice will give the impression of a close fit but is, in fact, very roomy.

A special fitting point—children with high shoulder blades usually have a hollow back and the center back seam on the bodice may need to be taken in at the waist.

To do this, rip the waist seam a little to each side of the center back. Pin off the amount along the center back seam by which the bodice must be taken in. Draw up the gathers on the skirt so that the seam allowance on the center back seam of the skirt remains the same. Repin, baste and check fitting.

Rip the waist seam and take out the sleeves ready for stitching.

Making the bodice

Stitch the darts. Press them open or flat if the fabric is heavy, and toward the centers if the fabric is light.

Stitch the side and shoulder seams, finish raw edges and press.

▲ *Details of the back view of dress B*

Making the skirt

Stitch the center back seam as far as the zipper opening and stitch the side seams. Finish the raw seam edges and press them open.

Make two rows of gathering stitches along the full length of the waist seam.

Joining the skirt to the bodice

Pin the skirt and bodice waist seams together on the side seams and center markings.

Draw up the gathers on the skirt between the pins and distribute them evenly until the skirt fits the bodice waist seam. Pin, baste and stitch.

If you are using a jersey knit fabric, reinforce the seam with a length of $\frac{1}{4}$ inch seam tape to stop the stitches from breaking. To do this, pin and baste the tape over the stitching line and make another row of machine stitches along the waist seam, catching in the tape.

Press the waist seam into the bodice and finish the raw edges together.

The sleeves

The straight sleeve Make the sleeves and set them in the bodice as for the girl's basic dress in chapter 63.

The short sleeve Make the sleeves and set in as for the straight sleeve.

Inserting the zipper

Pin under and baste the seam allowance along both center back edges and press. If the seam has remained on the straight grain of the fabric, insert the zipper using the straight seam method (Skirtmaking chapter 14). If, however, the seam has been curved for a better fit, use the lap over method shown in Skirtmaking chapter 13.

Finishing

Finish the neck edge and the skirt hem as for the girl's basic dress.

B. Dress with shaped waist seam

Basting and fitting

Baste the bodice as for version A.

Baste the skirt center and side seams.

The gathers on the skirt do not extend into the high point on the center front, but start even with the waist darts on the bodice. To find the right place, measure across the skirt pattern from the center front, 1 inch below the point. If you have followed the instructions for making the dart, this measurement will be $2\frac{5}{8}$ inches. Mark the measurement on each side of the center front of the skirt. Gather the top of the skirt to fit the waist seam.

Baste the shaped bodice waist seam flat over the skirt waist seam, but do not snip the seam allowance yet.

Baste the sleeve seams, then baste in the sleeves, gathering the lower edge so that they can be checked for length.

Fit as for version A, then rip the waist seam and remove the sleeves for stitching.

Making the bodice

Stitch the bodice as for version A.

Making the skirt

Stitch the center front seam, finish and press open.

Stitch the side seams, and the center back seam as far as the opening for the zipper. Finish seams and press open.

Gather the skirt. Make two rows of gathering stitches on each side of the center front, as marked for fitting,

274

working towards the center back.

Joining the skirt to the bodice

Snip the seam allowance of the center front on the bodice point as shown (figure **12**). Then fold the seam allowance along the stitching line of the waist seam into the bodice. Pin and baste into position.

As you work on the curved edge, place the pins at right angles to the edge and make sure that the seam does not pucker.

Lay the folded edge of the bodice over the seam allowance on the skirt to meet the seamline as marked, and pin together at the side seams and center markings. Draw up the gathers until the skirt fits the bodice.

Baste the bodice waist seam firmly to the skirt waist seam, and topstitch along the folded edge, making a perfect pivot at the point on the center front (figure **13**). Press the seams and finish the raw edges together.

The full, $\frac{3}{4}$ length sleeve

Stitch the sleeve seams, finish and press. If the seam allowances are a little tight, carefully snip them until they lie flat. Finish the raw edges where the seam allowance has been snipped.

To finish the wrist edge on each sleeve, make a casing for elastic to hold in the fullness.

To do this, fold under the seam allowance at each end of the bias strip and baste. Lay the strip along the sleeve edge, right sides facing. Pin and baste to the hemline so that the folded ends meet at the sleeve seam, taking no more than $\frac{3}{8}$ inch seam allowance on the bias strip (figure **14**).

Stitch the strip to the sleeve and trim the sleeve hem allowance to $\frac{3}{8}$ inch.

Turn the bias strip to the inside of the sleeve, edge baste and press.

Fold under the raw edge on the bias strip so that the casing is $\frac{5}{8}$ inch wide. Pin, baste and stitch the folded edge to the sleeve, topstitching close to the edge.

Remove the basting and press the casing. Cut a length of $\frac{1}{4}$ inch wide elastic to fit comfortably around the child's arm and slot into the casing. Stitch the ends firmly together. Sew the opening in the casing together by hand.

It may be possible to use the hem allowance on the sleeve edge to make the casing if you are using a fine fabric.

To do this, pin and baste the hem allowance to the wrong side and turn the raw edge under so that the channel is wide enough to take the elastic.

Topstitch to the sleeve along the inner folded edge, leaving a $\frac{1}{2}$ inch opening in the seam through which the elastic can be threaded.

▲ **12.** *Snipping center front bodice waist seam*

▼ **13.** *Topstitching the bodice waist seam*

▼ **14.** *Finishing the wrist edge with a casing*

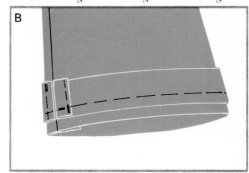

Insert the elastic as before and hand sew the opening closed.

Set the sleeves in the bodice as for the girl's basic dress.

Inserting the zipper and finishing

Insert the zipper as for version A.

Finish the neck edge and the skirt hem as for the girl's basic dress.

Pretty undies for little girls

Children's undergarments must be designed and made for practical wear. Children are not easy on their clothes, and pretty laces and fine fabrics have to withstand hard wear and frequent washing, usually in a machine. Fabric manufacturers realize this, so there is a wide choice in apparently delicate fabrics and trimming which meet the clothing standard set by a child's active life.

When you are selecting the fabric and trimming, make sure that they are of the same type of fiber, such as cotton trimming for cotton fabric. This is essential, as the wrong combination can lead to disappointing results when you wash and press the finished garments.

About finishes

Although lace and similar trimmings are very pretty, they are often very expensive. But if you make undergarments frequently, you should watch the trimmings counter of your local store. At sale times they generally sell batches of narrow lace in varying yardages which are much cheaper than when cut from a complete length. For everyday undergarments you may like to use less costly methods for the trimming, so here are some suggestions for doing this.

Frills. If you want to make fabric frills for slips, there are several economical ways to finish them.

You can stitch the hem of the frill with a pretty shell stitch, as in Generally Speaking chapter 2, or a machine scalloped border is an attractive alternative. If you are working a shell finish, this can be repeated around the neck and armholes. You can attach the frill to the garment with a narrow lace insertion, and narrow lace trimming can be applied to the hem of the fabric frill for a very attractive finish.

Neck and armhole edges. These edges, which come into close contact with the body, must be given particular attention because they can chafe and irritate a child's skin.

So, if you know that your child's skin is very sensitive, avoid a self rouleau finish for neck and armholes and buy a length of ready-folded soft cotton bias binding and make a bias bound edge finish. The leg edges of panties must also be kept soft so that they do not chafe or irritate. This will be discussed in the instructions which follow.

Slip

The pattern

The child's basic dress pattern in Sewing for Children chapter 63 is altered to make the pattern for the slip.

First copy the Front and Back pattern pieces and then adapt them as follows. Since children tend to get very hot when undergarments hang around them in folds, some of the ease should be taken from the pattern. To do this, take $\frac{1}{8}$ inch from the Center Front and Center Back and $\frac{1}{8}$ inch from each side seam. This will reduce ease by 1 inch all around (figure **1**). Increase the size of the armholes by drawing in a new armhole line $\frac{1}{2}$ inch inside the pattern edge as shown. Also cut the neckline wider by drawing in a new line $\frac{5}{8}$ inch from the previous one.

Measure the length desired for the slip and shorten the pattern.

If you are using a wide trim, make sure you reduce the length accordingly, as shown in Skirtmaking chapter 20, as for the adult slips trimmed with lace.

Before you cut the pattern consider whether or not you will want to lengthen the slip later.

As a frilled hemline has no hem allowance, make two narrow rows of tucks parallel to the hemline, the folded depth of each being $\frac{3}{8}$ inch. To allow for this on the pattern, add $1\frac{1}{2}$ inches to the length. Cut out the new pattern and mark the following allowances on the pattern edges: $\frac{1}{2}$ inch on the side seams and shoulder seams; $\frac{1}{8}$ inch on the neckline and armhole edges (except for a shell stitched finish, when you will need $\frac{1}{4}$ inch); $\frac{1}{4}$ inch on the hemline; and $\frac{1}{2}$ inch on the Center Back seam.

Cutting out

Make a layout as shown in Generally Speaking chapter 4 and calculate your yardage requirements.

The Center Front is placed on the fabric fold and the Center Back is cut for seaming. Also allow for rouleau binding and frills if you are cutting them from the fabric. Frills can be cut on the straight or the bias of the fabric, and should be $2\frac{1}{2}$ times the length around the hem to allow for a fully gathered frill.

Remember to add the seam and hem allowances given. Cut out the fabric.

You will also need

- [ ] Hem trimming, $2\frac{1}{2}$ times the length around the hemline
- [ ] One small button for fastening the Center Back
- [ ] Soft cotton bias binding (optional)
- [ ] Matching thread

Fitting and making the slip

Remove the pattern after cutting. It is not necessary to tailor's tack except for marking the position of the ease in the side seam.

Keep the pattern beside you and refer to it for the seam and hem allowances as you pin and baste ready for fitting.

Apart from the general hang, the most important fitting point is to make sure that the fabric clears the tender folds of skin around the underarm.

Make sure that the Center Back opening is long enough for the slip to go over the head without causing tears over a damaged hair style!

You are now ready to stitch.

Make French seams (see Blousemaking chapter 27) for the shoulder and side seams and press them toward the Front of the garment.

Stitch the Center Back seam as for ordinary seaming, as far as the end of the opening, and finish off the stitching securely.

To finish the opening, turn in the seam allowance and make a row of topstitching $\frac{1}{4}$ inch from the edges of the opening. If the Center Back has not been cut on the selvage, turn in the raw edge before topstitching to give a neat finish.

Finish the neck and armhole edges with a rouleau or bias binding.

Stitch on a button and work a hand-made loop at the top of the back opening to close it.

If you are making tucks, pin, baste and stitch them on the outside of the garment then press them down (figure **2**).

Finishing the hemline

If you use a hem finish of ribbon slotted eyelet embroidery as shown here, work as follows.

Pin and baste the hem allowance to the outside of the slip and pin the ribbon slotting section over the raw edge so that the fold of the hemline meets the frill (figure **3**).

Baste in place.

Pin and baste the upper edge of the ribbon slotting to the garment.

Working on the ribbon slotting section only, topstitch the trimming in place. To do this, work one row of stitches along the lower edge of the slotting catching in the folded edge of the hemline. Then work another row of stitches along the upper edge of the slotting just inside the edge (figure **4**).

The ends of the trimming should be stitched together by making a French seam through the frilled section only and snipping the seam allowance in the ribbon slotting so that the ends can be turned in flat to avoid bulk (figure **4**).

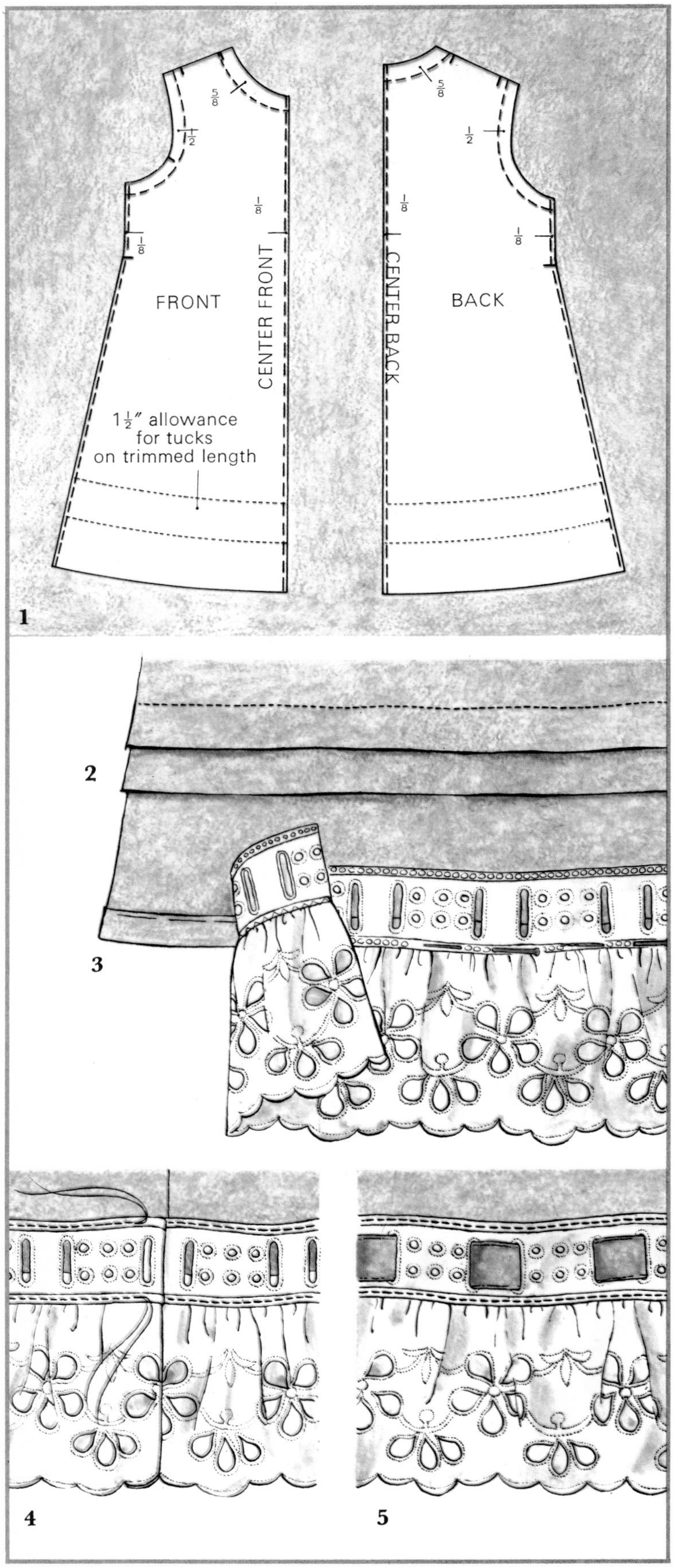
FRONT
CENTER FRONT
CENTER BACK
BACK
1½″ allowance
for tucks
on trimmed length
1
2
3
4
5

▲ **1.** *Altering the Front and Back patterns* **2.** *Tucking the hem edge* **3.** *Pinning eyelet lace to hem* **4.** *Stitching eyelet lace to hem* **5.** *Ribbon slotted frill*

The slip and panties ►

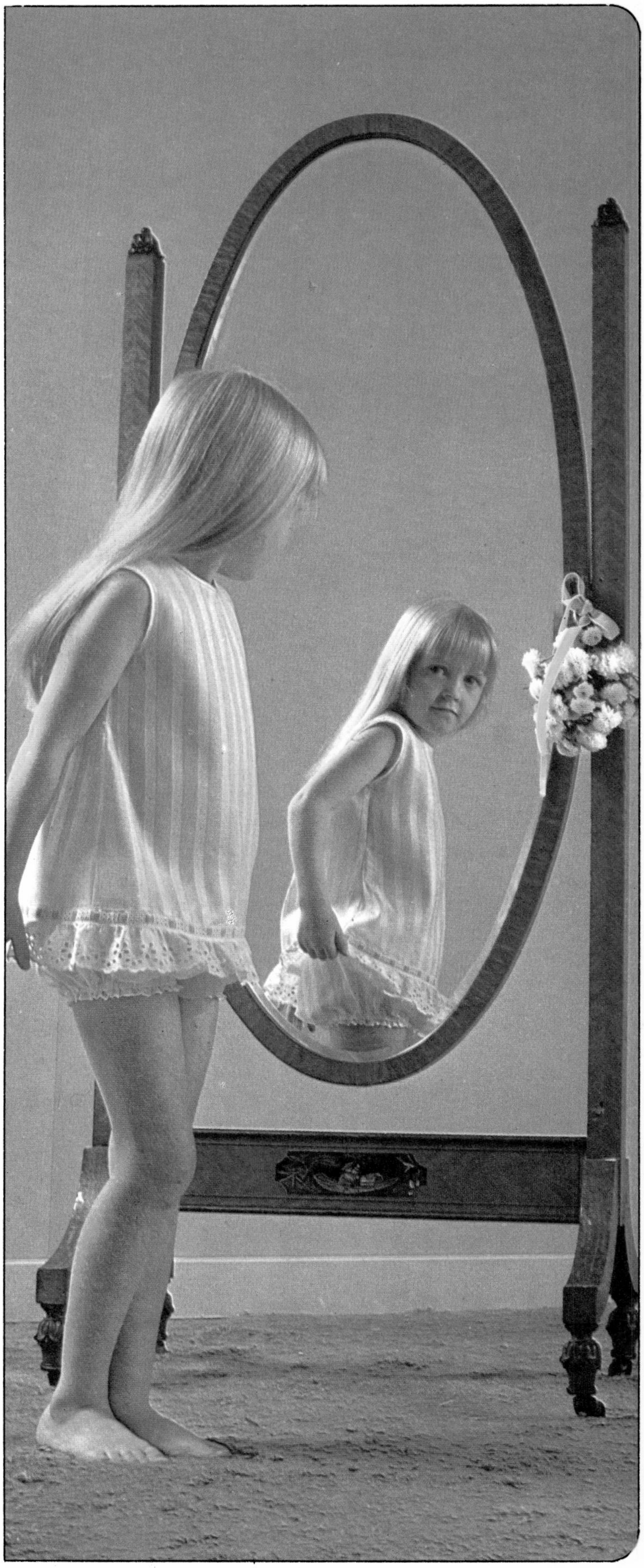

Slotting in the ribbon

Use a brightly colored narrow ribbon to slot into the trimming (figure **5**).

Slot it in and out of the eyelets, overlap the ends, and hand sew them together. Alternatively, you can start the slotting at the Center Front leaving enough ribbon at each end to make a pretty bow. This way, if you are not quite sure if the ribbon will withstand the same washing treatment as the garment, it can easily be removed for washing.

Alternative frilled edge

If you are making a fabric frill, pin and baste the gathered edge of the frill to the hem allowance of the slip, right sides facing, raw edges even, and stitch as for an ordinary seam.

Trim the seam allowance and finish carefully. Press the seam allowance upward and then topstitch along the hemline on the outside for extra strength. If you are attaching the frill with lace insertion, make the frill less full and stitch one edge of the insertion over the raw gathered edge of the frill. Finish the seam allowance on the frill carefully, then stitch the other edge of the lace insertion to the hemline of the slip as shown for lace insertion in Skirtmaking chapter 20.

Panties

The pattern

Copy the panties pattern from the graph, chapter 66, pages 284-285. Mark seam allowances on the pattern edges as follows: side seams, $\frac{1}{2}$ inch; crotch seam, $\frac{5}{8}$ inch for flat-fell seaming (Blousemaking chapter 25); leg edge, $\frac{1}{4}$ inch; waist seam, $\frac{3}{4}$ inch.

Cutting out

Make a layout as shown in Know-How chapter 46 and calculate your yardage requirements, remembering that the panties are cut from single layers of fabric on the crosswise grain.

Remember to add the allowances as given. Cut out the fabric.

You will also need

☐ Eyelet embroidery edging, with a deep plain edge, to trim the leg edges (figure **6**). For each leg you will need the length of the leg hem measurement plus 3 inches for ease (for other trimming get twice the length of each leg measurement)

☐ Soft $\frac{1}{4}$in elastic for the legs and waist

☐ Matching thread

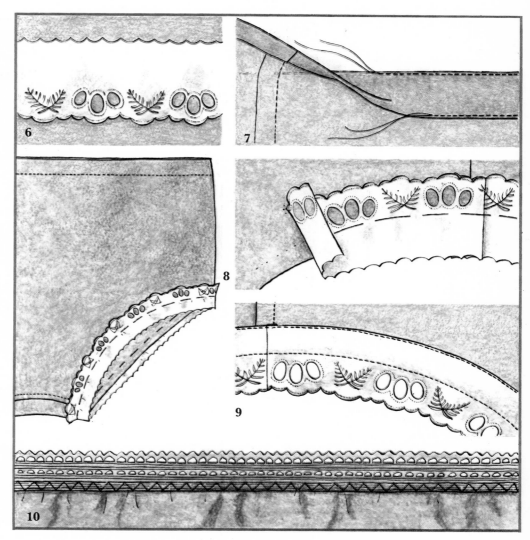

▲ **6.** *Eyelet embroidery trimming for panties* **7.** *Casing at waist of panties* **8.** *Eyelet embroidery basted to leg edge* **9.** *Leg trimming stitched in place* **10.** *Soft wide elastic stitched to waist*

Fitting and making the panties

As for the slip, it is not necessary to tailor's tack the pattern detail, but keep the pattern next to you to check on the seam allowances as you baste them. Make a flat-fell seam for the crotch seam. Then stitch the side seams with a French seam (Blousemaking chapter 27). Press the seams toward the Front.

To make a casing at the waist edge, turn under the raw edge $\frac{1}{4}$ inch, then the rest of the seam allowance, and stitch the lower fold in place (figure **7**). Also stitch the upper fold to prevent it from rolling over.

Finish the leg edge with the eyelet embroidery edging. With right sides facing, pin and baste the seamline of the leg edge close to the embroidery (figure **8**). Overlap the ends at the side seams, and ease the trimming onto the seamline so that when the leg edge is turned up the eyelet embroidery will follow the curve and not pull in the fabric.

To make the casing for the elastic, turn under the raw edge of the eyelet embroidery and topstitch the folded edge to the panties (figure **9**).

Leave a small opening in which to insert the elastic.

Plain leg finish. For a plain finish, use soft bias binding and make a casing as for the sleeve hems in chapter 64, figure 14, page 274.

Alternative waist finish. If you want to avoid the thickness of an elastic casing around the waistline, use the soft type of elastic which can be stitched to a raw edge (figure **10**). This is available in varying widths from $\frac{1}{2}$ inch upward. When cutting the panties for this finish, take off the depth of the elastic from the waist edge and allow about $\frac{1}{4}$ inch seam allowance.

Finish the seam allowance carefully since the elastic is stitched to the open seam allowance.

Pin the elastic over the seam allowance and topstitch in place with a machine zigzag stitch.

Chapter 65

Collars and cuffs

Sewing for Children

This chapter includes tracing patterns for Peter Pan, puritan and yoke collars, and also a simple cuff. They are designed for the girl's basic dress in Sewing for Children chapter 63, but the patterns can be adjusted for use on any simple dress.

Collars

Suitable fabrics for making collars

Cotton pique is a traditional fabric for making trimmings such as collars, and it is the most useful. It is very hard wearing, and collars made in this fabric will always look crisp and retain their shape even after frequent washing.

For really pretty collars you can use organdy or lace, but collars made in these fabrics will naturally be quite delicate and require more careful handling.

Collar making does not end with plain collar shapes—there are many ways you can trim them using braid, lace edgings or embroidery. A very pretty idea is to embroider a realistic little butterfly on one side of the collar to look as though it has just settled there.

Fabrics requirements and notions

You will need:
- ☐ ¼yd 36in wide fabric for the Peter Pan collar
- ☐ ⅜yd 36in wide fabric for each of the puritan and yoke collars
- ☐ One package of soft cotton bias binding

The collar pattern sizes

These patterns will fit a dress neck opening of 15¼ inches.

Trace the collar patterns, using the instructions given on page 518. Cut out the patterns.

To make any of the patterns larger, cut along the two dash lines and lay the sections on a sheet of paper. Divide the extra collar length required by four and spread each cut section by this amount. Pencil around the new outline and cut out the new pattern. To make a pattern smaller, divide the amount by which the collar is to be shortened by four and fold off this amount along both dash lines. Lay the altered pattern on a sheet of paper, pencil around the new outline and cut out the new pattern.

Cutting out the collars

You will need four collar pieces to make the Peter Pan and puritan collars and two pieces for the yoke collar.

Fold the fabric, following the layouts given on page 280. Be very careful to lay the patterns on the correct grain of the fabric; otherwise, when the collar is stitched in place, it will not lie well around the neck of the dress. The center front of the yoke pattern is placed on the fold as shown. Cut out, allowing ⅜ inch seam allowance on all edges.

Making the collars

All the collars are made in the same way, except that the Peter Pan and puritan collars are made in two sections and the yoke collar in one.

Lay two corresponding collar pieces together, right sides facing. Pin, baste and stitch around the outer edges, leaving the neck edge open.

Trim the seam allowance to ¼ inch and trim across the corners to remove the bulk. If necessary, make "V" notches around the front curves on the Peter Pan collar so that the seam allowance inside the collar will lie flat when the collar has been turned. Do not notch the seam allowance on the puritan or yoke collars because the notches will show as dents from the outside.

Turn the collar sections to the right side, baste the stitched edges and press.

On the Peter Pan and puritan collars overlap the seam allowance at the center front and hold together with a catch stitch as shown in the diagram opposite.

Stitch the collar along the neck edge, snip into the seam allowance, and finish the raw edge with bias binding.

Press the collar. Then press the bound edge to the underside of the collar, ready to sew in position on the dress. As you press the binding under the neck edge, stretch it so that it follows the shape of the collar.

Attach it to the dress with long slip stitches.

Using organdy and lace

Organdy. If you use this fabric, make the collars as described in the previous paragraphs, but trim the seam allowance to 3/16 inch, or, if the organdy is particularly firmly woven, to ⅛ inch. This is because the seam allowance will be visible through the fabric.

Lace. Some patterned lace is constructed in such a way that you can use the pattern to form a pretty edge simply by cutting around the outline. If the outline of the lace pattern is corded, as with guipure lace, and you can avoid cutting through this outline when cutting out the collar, you need not finish the outer edge any further. But if the lace is liable to fray, use a fine whip stitch (see Skirtmaking chapter 20) over the pattern outline to secure the edge and finish the raw neck edge with bias binding as before.

If the lace you are using does not allow you to cut in this manner, cut the shape for a top collar from the lace and an under collar from organdy or organza. This will highlight the pattern of the lace and you can stitch the collar as if you were using plain fabric.

Trimming the collars

A little lace edging can turn an ordinary collar into a party-goer. For washable collars use cotton lace which will stand up to handling and ironing.

Most fine cotton lace edgings can be gathered or pleated without being bulky. Just be sure to ease in sufficient fullness to allow the outer edge of the lace to remain nice and full too. Nothing looks worse than lace gathered on the inside of the curve and flat on the outer edge.

To make sure that you buy enough trimming, measure along the edge of the collar and buy at least twice this amount. If the lace is very fine, much of it will disappear in the gathers, so you'll need two-and-a-half times the length of the edge of the collar.

Guipure daisy and fine ball fringe edging are especially pretty. These cannot be gathered, so you simply stitch them to the outer edge, on top of the collar. Just remember to ease the trimming to follow the roundness of the edge, otherwise it will turn up and over during wear.

You can give a really decorative look to an organdy collar for a rich velvet dress by using either double-edged lace, which is drawn up through the center to make a double frill, or a fine slotted lace

1. *Peter Pan* **2.** *Puritan* **3.** *Yoke*

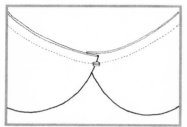

Overlapping the seam allowance

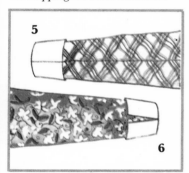

5. *Tube-shaped cuff* **6.** *Pointed cuff*

▲ *The child's basic dress trimmed with lace cuffs and Peter Pan collar*

with ribbon slotted through the center. Buy extra ribbon and you can make tiny bows to sew along the lace at intervals.

The lace collar, too, will look even more lacy if you trim the edge with matching lace edging.

Cuffs

Cuffs are another pretty form of trimming, either used on their own or made to match a collar. They can also be put to good practical use to lengthen sleeves which have become too short.

A point to remember when using cuffs as a trimming: Sleeves should be shortened $\frac{1}{2}$ inch because the roll of the cuffs will add to the sleeve length.

Cuffs are easy to make and just as interchangeable as collars. You can use the same list of suitable fabrics, too.

Fabric required: For the cuff pattern given here, you will need $\frac{1}{8}$ yard of 36 inch wide fabric.

The pattern: Trace the pattern from the outline on page 280. Lengthen or shorten as necessary, using the instructions given for the collars, but dividing by two instead of four.

Cutting: Lay the pattern on the correct grain and cut four pieces (two for each cuff), allowing $\frac{3}{8}$ inch seam allowance all around.

Two ways to stitch the cuffs

Tube-shaped cuffs. Stitch the ends of each of the four sections to make four tubes. Then, with right sides facing, pin, baste and stitch two matching sections together along the upper, wider, edge. Trim the seam allowance, turn to the right side, edge-baste and press. Stitch along the lower raw edges of each cuff and finish with bias binding.

Pointed cuffs. With right sides facing, pin, baste and stitch two matching sections along the sides and upper, wider, edges. Trim the seam allowance, turn to the right side, edge-baste and press. Stitch the lower raw edges together and finish with bias binding. You can trim the cuffs using the methods given for collars.

Attaching the cuffs

For both types of cuff, attach the narrower edge of the cuff to the sleeve. Using long slip stitches, sew the cuff to the inside of the sleeve, $\frac{1}{2}$ inch from the hem.

Position the tube-shaped cuff with the cuff seam corresponding with the sleeve seam, and the pointed cuff with the open end opposite the sleeve seam.

Roll up the cuff over the edge of the sleeve and make small catch stitches under each one where it meets the sleeve seam. With pointed cuffs, sew each point down invisibly. This will prevent the cuffs from rolling down.

Self cuffs

You can also use the cuff pattern to make cuffs from self fabric and attach them to the sleeves permanently.

Simply stitch the lower raw edge of each cuff to the seam allowance of the sleeve, turn both edges under and face with a bias strip.

279

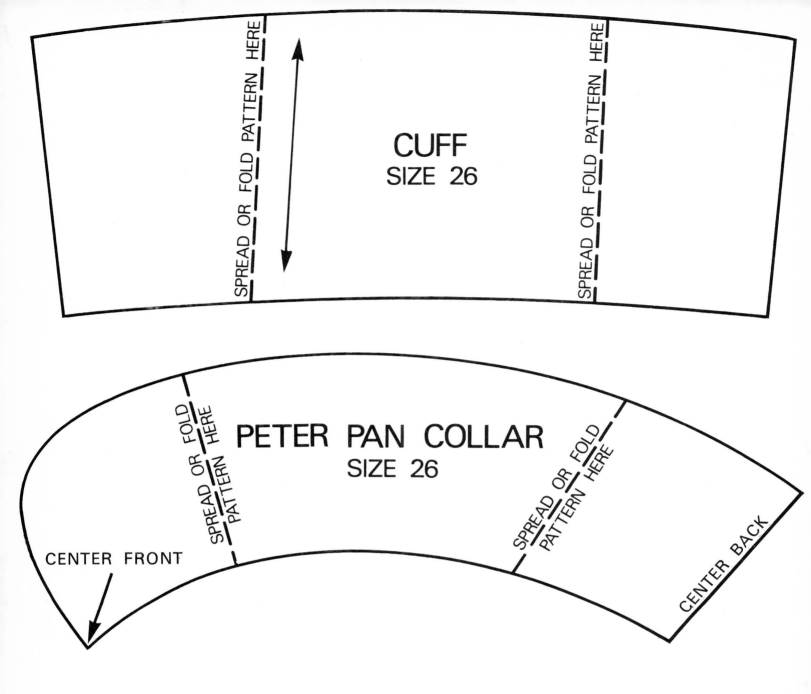

CUFF
SIZE 26

SPREAD OR FOLD PATTERN HERE

SPREAD OR FOLD PATTERN HERE

PETER PAN COLLAR
SIZE 26

SPREAD OR FOLD PATTERN HERE

SPREAD OR FOLD PATTERN HERE

CENTER FRONT

CENTER BACK

The patterns

The tracing patterns given here are for three collar shapes and one cuff shape, designed for the child's dress in Sewing for Children chapter 63. All the patterns fit the dress size 26in chest with a neck opening of 15¼ inches. No seam allowances are given.

The dash lines on the patterns indicate where to lengthen or shorten them.

The straight of grain for the Peter Pan and puritan collars is the straight edge along the center back. The straight of grain for the yoke collar is the fold edge of the center front. The straight of grain for the cuff is indicated on the pattern.

Layout for the Peter Pan collar on 36in wide fabric without one way

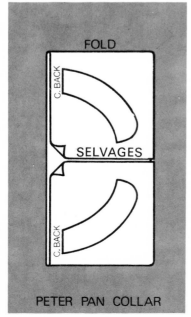

FOLD

C. BACK

SELVAGES

C. BACK

PETER PAN COLLAR

Layout for the puritan collar on 36in wide fabric without one way

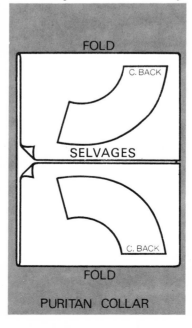

FOLD

C. BACK

SELVAGES

C. BACK

FOLD

PURITAN COLLAR

Layout for the yoke collar on 36in wide fabric without one way

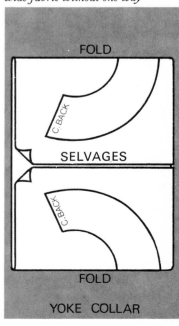

FOLD

C. BACK

SELVAGES

C. BACK

FOLD

YOKE COLLAR

280

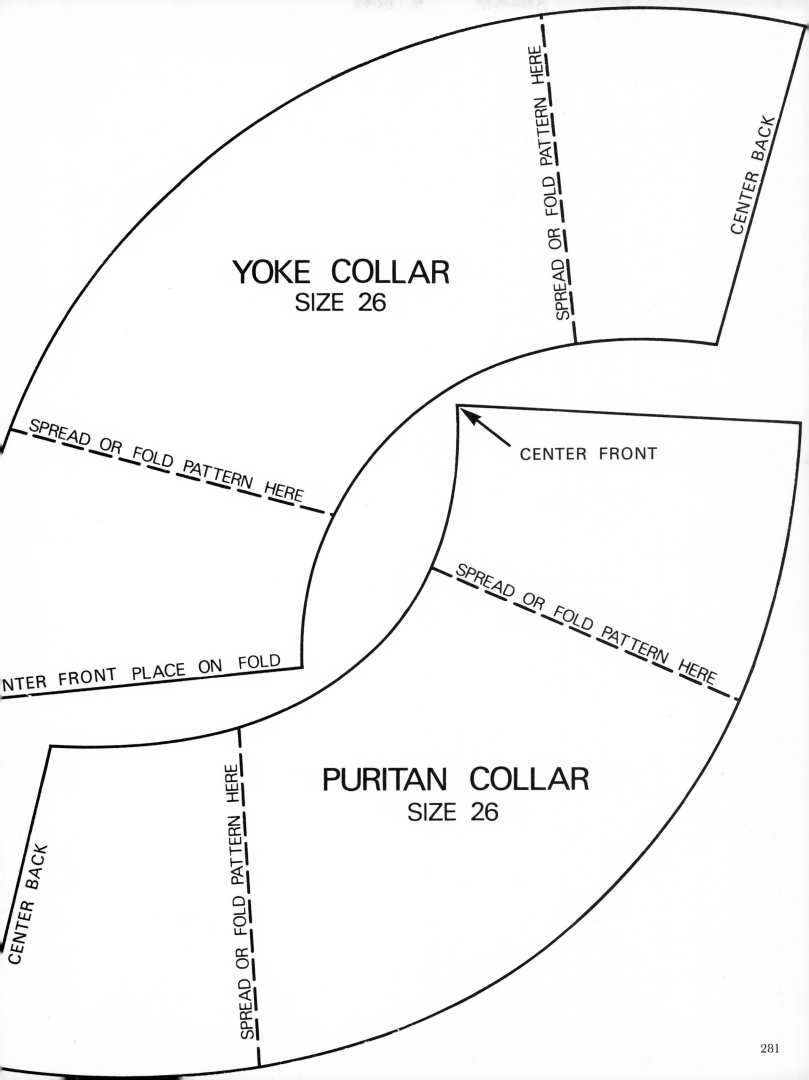

YOKE COLLAR
SIZE 26

SPREAD OR FOLD PATTERN HERE

CENTER BACK

SPREAD OR FOLD PATTERN HERE

CENTER FRONT

SPREAD OR FOLD PATTERN HERE

NTER FRONT PLACE ON FOLD

CENTER BACK

SPREAD OR FOLD PATTERN HERE

PURITAN COLLAR
SIZE 26

Chapter 66
Terry cloth playsuit for a girl

Terry cloth tips

Types of terry
There are four main types of terry cloth and they are mostly available in 36 inch to 45 inch widths.

Double-sided terry. This has loops on both sides of the fabric and most plain colors are reversible.

It is warm and cozy, but the depth of the loops makes it difficult to fasten with buttons and zippers.

Single-sided terry. Here the loops appear only on the top surface of the fabric. Garments made up in this fabric can be finished with conventional fastenings.

Stretch terry. This usually has loops on one side of the fabric.

It is particularly suitable for swimwear since it dries quickly and can be molded to the body.

Velours terry. This type has the loops on one side, sheared to form a velvety pile. The velours side is not particularly absorbent.

Cutting out
When pinning patterns on terry, do not use too many pins as pinning through thick fabric reduces the size of the pattern.

Seams in terry
The seams in terry don't present any problem. Make ordinary seams on single terry and flat-fell seams, $\frac{1}{2}$ to $\frac{3}{4}$ inch wide, for double-sided terry, depending on the thickness of the fabric (for flatfell seams see Blousemaking chapter 25).

Facings in terry
Neck and armhole facings cut in this fabric should be avoided. Instead, bind the

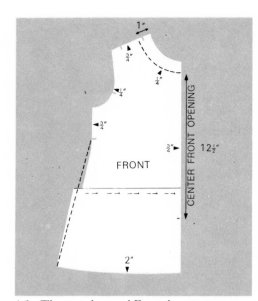

▲ **1.** *The new shortened Front dress pattern*
▼ **2.** *The new shortened Back dress pattern*

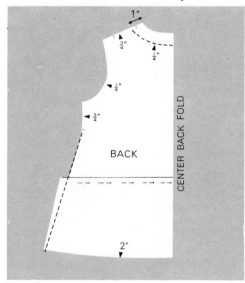

▼ **3.** *Pocket hem folded outside and stitched*

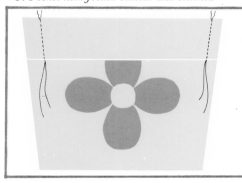

edges or use bias strip facings for a neat finish without bulk.

Pressing terry
When pressing terry cloth you will get a slight flattening of the loops, but if you brush over the loops with the flat of your hand while they are still warm, they will again quickly rise.

Girl's terry cloth dress

The dress pattern
This is made from the child's basic dress pattern in chapter 63, which was presented for sizes 24, 26 and 28 inch chest. Make the Front and Back pattern pieces from the graph, altering for size as necessary.

The length. Since the beach dress is worn short with the panties showing, the basic pattern needs to be shortened.

Do not shorten it at the hemline; terry is a lot more bulky than most fabrics and it would make a very narrow garment if you did. Instead, shorten both pattern pieces by making a fold about 7 inches above the hemline to the depth desired and pin.

Then pin the Front and Back to a piece of paper, draw around the pattern pieces and straighten the side seams as shown (figures **1** and **2**). Remove the original pattern and cut out the new one.

The neckline. Lower the neckline on both the Back and Front of the new pattern by 1 inch as shown (figures **1** and **2**).

The seam allowances. The garment has a front zipper opening, so mark the Center Front to be cut with seam allowance.

Mark the Center Back to be cut on the fabric fold.

The seam allowances on the pattern vary because of the finishes used for terry, so mark them too. Mark $\frac{1}{4}$ inch seam allowance at neckline and armhole edges and $\frac{3}{4}$ inch for other seams. Also mark a 2 inch hem allowance. This will act as a reminder when making the garment, as it is difficult to tailor's tack terry fabrics.

The pocket and daisy patterns
The bucket-shaped pocket is another type of patch pocket.

Trace the pocket on page 284 and cut out. Trace and cut out separate patterns for the daisy petals and center.

To find the position for the pocket on the dress, place the pocket pattern on the Front pattern piece $\frac{1}{4}$ inch up from the hem and with the upper edge $1\frac{1}{2}$ inches from the Center Front. Draw around it.

If the hem is slightly curved, tilt the pattern so that it is even with the hemline and check the position at the fitting stage.

Yardages and notions
To find the amount of fabric needed, make a layout on paper the same width as the terry, using the Back, Front and daisy petal pieces. The pockets and daisy centers are cut from contrasting fabric.

Allow for seam and hem allowances. Also allow for three bias strips to finish the neck and armhole edges. These should be

282

4 times the width of the finished rouleau, plus $\frac{1}{8}$ inch.

If the fabric you choose has a one way design, make allowance for this when calculating the yardage.

Draw around the pattern shapes so that you can use the paper as a layout at the cutting stage.

You will also need a 12 inch zipper and matching thread.

Cutting out

Lay out the pattern using your paper layout as a guide. Do not forget to place the Back on a fold and cut the Center Front with seam allowance.

Mark all the seam and hem allowances with pin lines except for the daisy, which has no seam allowance. Cut out. Also cut out the three bias strips.

Cut out 2 pocket shapes and 2 daisy centers from the contrast fabric.

Marking the pattern details

Tailor's tack only where it is absolutely necessary, such as at balance marks, darts (if you are using them), and seam ends. Also mark the pocket positions with single tailor's tacks through slits made in the dress pattern.

Mark the end of the opening for the zipper in the Center Front $12\frac{1}{2}$ inches from the neck edge.

Don't mark the seamlines, but keep the pattern at hand and measure them out as you stitch the garment.

Fitting

Pin and baste the dress for fitting and make any necessary corrections.

Inserting the zipper

Stitch the Center Front seam below the opening mark, then baste the opening together. Finish the seam allowance and press the seam open.

Insert the zipper using the straight seam method (Skirtmaking chapter 14), but sew it by hand with small firm backstitches. Stitching by machine will make the surface loops tilt in opposite directions.

Sew the zipper to the seam allowance with felling stitches.

Making the pockets

Pin and baste the daisy petals onto each pocket piece, working very close to the edges and using a matching sewing thread. If you have a zigzag on your machine, follow the instructions for appliqué in the machine manual, but engage a slightly larger stitch width to appliqué the daisy. For hand appliqué use a closely worked overcasting stitch in matching sewing or embroidery thread, catching through all

Girl's beach playsuit made in colorful terry cloth with daisy petal pockets

layers of fabric.

Appliqué the daisy centers the same way. Press the appliqué, then finish the pockets.

Fold the $1\frac{1}{2}$ inch hem allowance at the top to the outside of each pocket and stitch at the sides as shown (figure **3**).

Overcast the raw edge, turn the hem to the inside and sew by hand.

Fold under the remaining seam allowance and baste.

Position the pockets on the dress. Pin, baste and topstitch close to the edge. Press.

Finishing the dress

Pin, baste and stitch the side and shoulder seams, overcast the raw edges and press the seams. Also stitch the darts if used.

Using the bias strips, bind the neck and armholes as for the basic dress.

Finish the hem in the usual way and give the garment a final pressing.

Girl's terry panties

The pattern

The pattern on the next two pages will fit a 30 inch hip and corresponds to the largest dress size. Instructions for making the pattern smaller follow.

Trace the Front and Back pattern pieces. The tracing will only give you half a Front and Back, so you will need to complete the pattern pieces for an open layout.

Making the pattern smaller

To shorten. Measure the child through the crotch from Center Front to Center Back and compare the measurement on the pattern.

Divide the difference by 4 and deduct this amount equally from the waist and the depth of the crotch on both Back and Front pattern pieces.

283

To make narrower. If the child's hips are less than 30 inches, deduct the difference in equal amounts from the centers and side seams of both Back and Front pattern pieces until you have the correct width.

Yardages and notions

To find out the amount of toweling needed, make a layout on paper as for the dress. If you are making the dress as well, include the pocket and daisy center patterns in this layout.

As you can see by the straight of grain marking, the panties are cut in the cross of the fabric to give maximum comfort during wear.

You will also need 1 package of bias binding, $\frac{1}{4}$in elastic to fit the waist and legs, and matching thread.

Cutting out and marking

Using your paper layout, cut out the fabric and mark the pattern details as for the dress.

Making the panties

The seams. Because the panties are cut on the cross, ordinary seams will tend to curl, so an open flat-fell seam is used with zigzag stitching.

With right sides facing, stitch the side and crotch seams, using a shallow zigzag. Press the seam allowance to one side.

Trim the inside seam allowance as for flat-fell seaming (Blousemaking chapter 25) and trim the top seam for a flat-fell, but without the allowance for the turning.

Generally these seams should be as narrow as possible, but to make allowance for towelings which fray, leave $\frac{1}{4}$ inch on the inside and $\frac{3}{8}$ inch on the top.

Then, using a small zigzag setting, work over the raw edge of the double seam allowance to make the open flat-fell. If you don't have a zigzag on your machine, make ordinary flat-fell seams.

The waist and leg casings. Finish the raw edge of the seam allowance at the waist.

Turn the waist seam allowance to the inside and stitch in place with the same zigzag setting, or, if you are using a straight stitch, turn under the edge first. Don't forget to leave an opening in the seam to insert the elastic.

To make the casings at the leg edges, finish them with bias binding.

With right sides facing, raw edges even, stitch one edge of the binding around the leg edges. Turn the binding completely to the inside and machine stitch the other edge in place, finishing the ends.

Slot elastic into the waist and leg casings to finish.

284

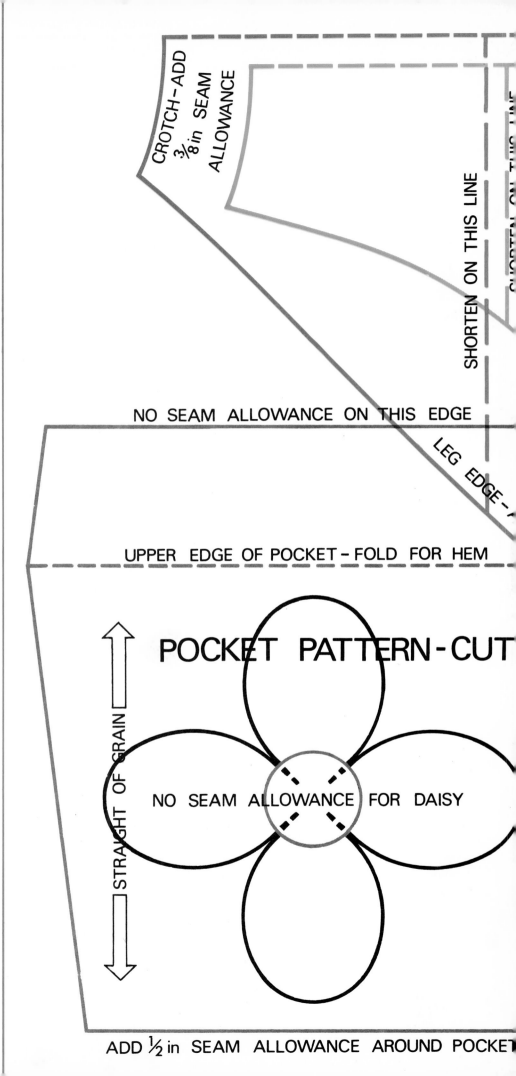

CROTCH–ADD $\frac{3}{8}$in SEAM ALLOWANCE

SHORTEN ON THIS LINE

NO SEAM ALLOWANCE ON THIS EDGE

LEG EDGE

UPPER EDGE OF POCKET – FOLD FOR HEM

POCKET PATTERN–CUT

STRAIGHT OF GRAIN

NO SEAM ALLOWANCE FOR DAISY

ADD $\frac{1}{2}$in SEAM ALLOWANCE AROUND POCKET

PANTIES PATTERN
FRONT —— CUT 1
BACK —— CUT 1
SIZE : 30in HIP

STRAIGHT OF GRAIN

EDGE - ADD ¼in SEAM ALLOWANCE

M ALLOWANCE

WAISTLINE – SHORTEN HERE – ADD ¾in SEAM ALLOWANCE

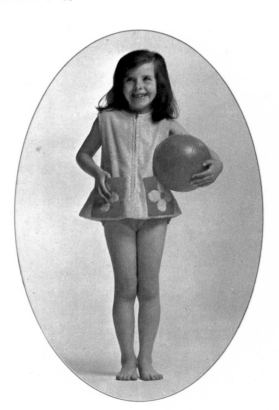

SIDESEAM—ADD ⅜in SEAM ALLOWANCE

Chapter 67

Playsuits in stretch terry cloth

Designed for active 1 to 7 year olds, tracing patterns for these s-t-r-e-t-c-h terry outfits are on pages 288 and 289.

General hints

The patterns all include $\frac{1}{4}$ inch seam allowances. The hem allowances are also included in the patterns but they vary with each garment and are given in the instructions.

The seams on stretch terry should be sewed on a swing needle machine with the stitch width set on the shallowest zigzag, but with the stitch length set for an ordinary straight stitch. After stitching, zigzag or overlock the raw seam edges together to finish unless otherwise stated.

Use a synthetic thread. This has a certain amount of stretch in it and is recommended for stretch terry.

When cutting out, place the patterns on the wrong side of the fabric, but be sure to follow the direction of the pile, which is indicated by arrows on the cutting diagrams, and to match up stripes if you are using a striped terry.

If you have to press, do so with a warm iron on the wrong side of the fabric.

A. T-shirt and crawler

Measurements

For a baby about 1 year old, weighing 19 to 27 lbs and measuring 15 inches from neck to crotch over diaper. Instructions for altering the size are given below. See figure **1** for details of the garment.

286

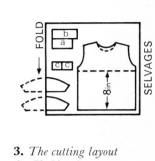

Sewing for Children

Fabrics and notions

For the T-shirt you will need:
- ☐ $\frac{1}{2}$ yard 36in wide plain stretch terry cloth
- ☐ $\frac{1}{8}$ yard $\frac{1}{2}$in wide snap fastener tape

For the crawler you will need:
- ☐ $\frac{7}{8}$ yard 36in wide printed stretch terry cloth
- ☐ $\frac{5}{8}$ yard $\frac{1}{2}$in wide snap fastener tape
- ☐ 4 inches $\frac{1}{2}$in wide tape

1. *T-shirt and front and back views of the crawler*

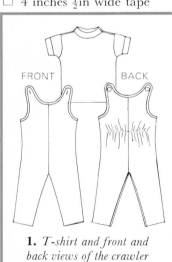

2. *Front, Back and sleeve patterns for the T-shirt A*

- ☐ $\frac{1}{4}$ yard soft $\frac{1}{4}$in wide elastic
- ☐ Two $\frac{1}{2}$in diameter buttons

For both:
- ☐ Tracing paper and pencil for the pattern
- ☐ Matching thread

The T-shirt

The pattern. Identify the T-shirt pattern in red from the tracing patterns. Trace the top of the body pattern with both Back and Front necklines and extend the body by 8 inches (figure **2**).

Also trace the sleeve pattern as shown.

Cutting out. Following the layout (figure **3**) fold the fabric, place the pattern pieces on the double fabric, and cut one Back, one Front and two sleeves. Also cut two sleeve bands (a), each 5in by 2in, two neck bands (b), one 6in by 2in for the Front and one $5\frac{1}{2}$in by 2in for the Back, and four shoulder facing strips (c) each $1\frac{1}{2}$in by 3in.

Making the T-shirt. Fold the sleeve bands in half lengthwise, wrong sides facing. Stretching them to fit, stitch the sleeve bands to the right side of the sleeves taking $\frac{1}{4}$ inch seams (figure **4**). Then zigzag the raw edges together as shown.

Similarly fold and stitch a shoulder facing strip to each shoulder seam. Then fold the front shoulder facings under (figure **5**) and trim to fit at the neck edge. Leave the back shoulder facings extending.

Lap each Front over the corresponding back facing. Baste and stitch them together at the armhole edge (figure **6**). Insert each sleeve with the notch to the shoulder seam and stitch.

Then stitch the sleeve seams and side seams in one operation. Zigzag the hem edge to finish. Turn up $\frac{3}{4}$ inch and sew by hand or zigzag in place.

Fold each neck band in half, right sides facing and stitch the short ends. Turn to the right side, then stitch to the neck as for the sleeve bands. Using a zipper foot on the machine, stitch snap fastener tape to the shoulders as shown (figure **7**).

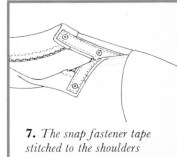

3. *The cutting layout for T-shirt A*

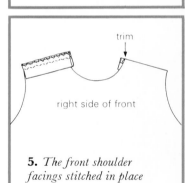

4. *The sleeve band stitched to the right side*

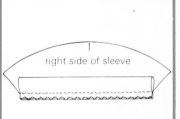

5. *The front shoulder facings stitched in place*

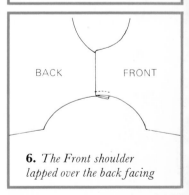

6. *The Front shoulder lapped over the back facing*

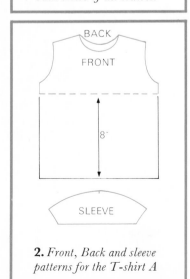

7. *The snap fastener tape stitched to the shoulders*

Playsuits in stretch terry. Left: for a 1
year old, crawler in a pretty print with plain
T-shirt. Above and below: for a 2-3 year
old, jumpsuit in plain terry with contrast
trim and for a 4-5 year old, striped T-shirt
with plain shorts. Right: for a 6-7 year old,
short legged jumpsuit with sleeves in stripes.

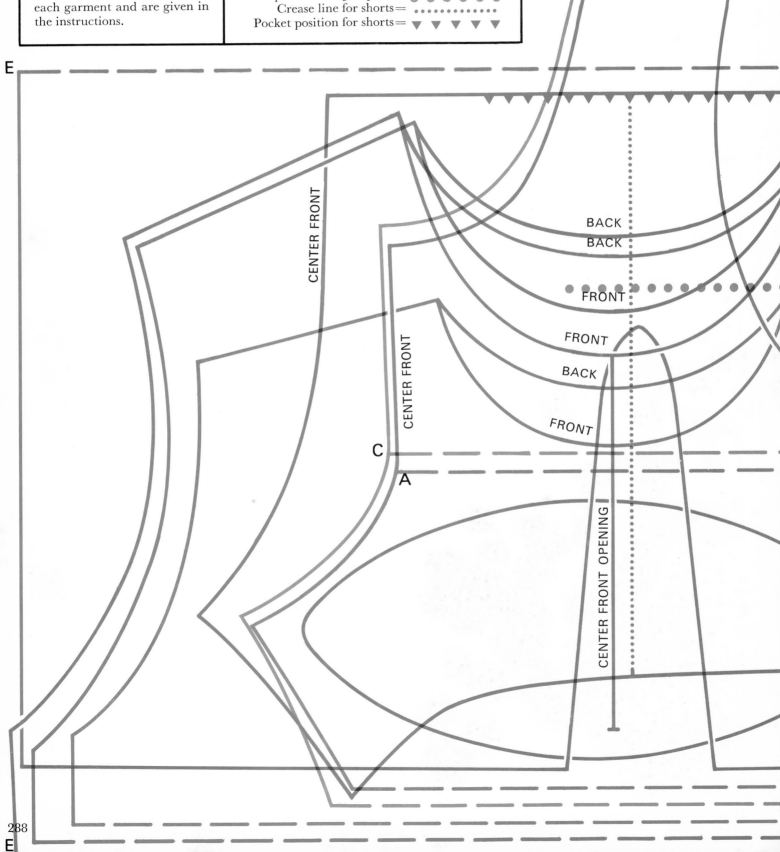

Tracing patterns for children's terry cloth playsuits

All patterns include $\frac{1}{4}$ inch seam allowance unless otherwise stated in the instructions. Hem allowances are also included but these vary with each garment and are given in the instructions.

Key to tracing patterns

T-shirt and crawler	Jumpsuit	T-shirt and shorts	Short legged jumpsuit

Pocket position for jumpsuit = ● ● ● ● ●
Crease line for shorts = ● ● ● ● ● ● ● ● ●
Pocket position for shorts = ▼ ▼ ▼ ▼ ▼ ▼

E

CENTER FRONT

BACK
BACK

FRONT

FRONT

BACK

FRONT

CENTER FRONT

C

A

CENTER FRONT OPENING

E

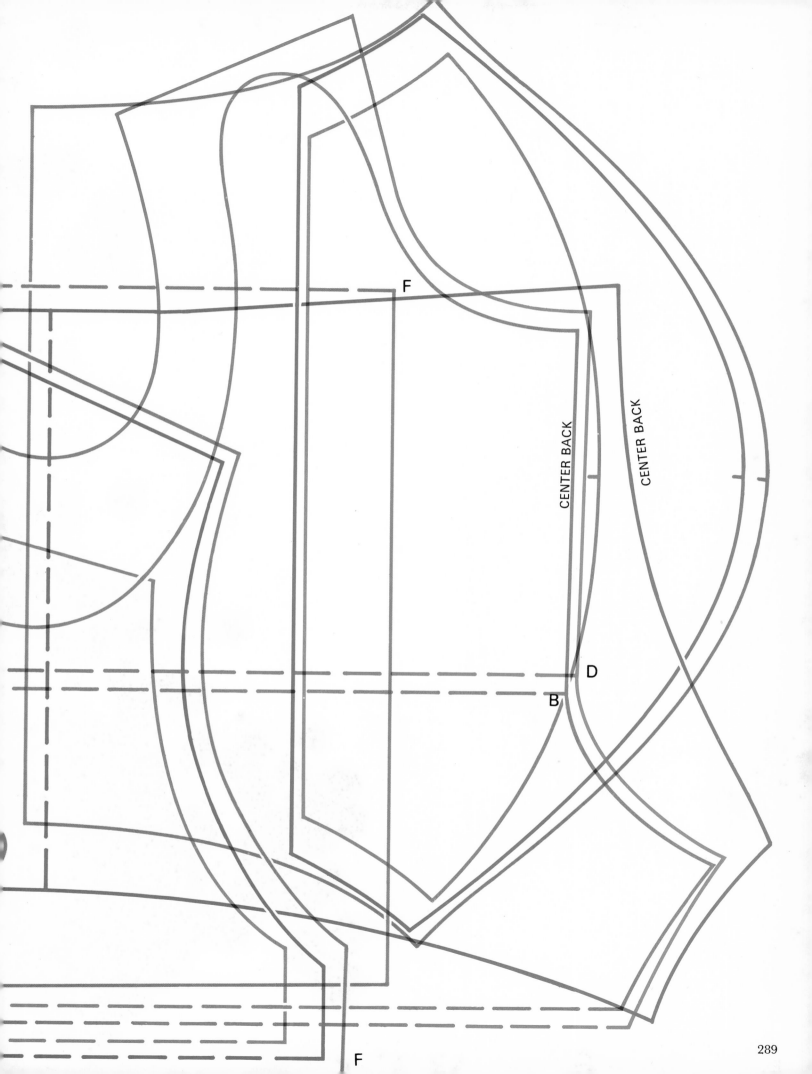

CENTER BACK

CENTER BACK

F

D

B

F

289

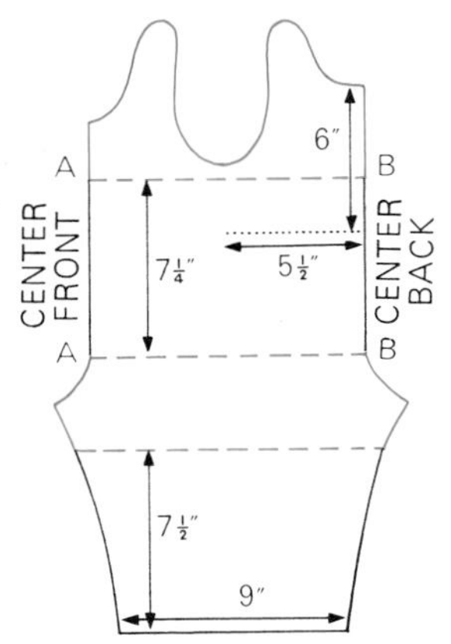

8. *The crawler pattern combining Back and Front*

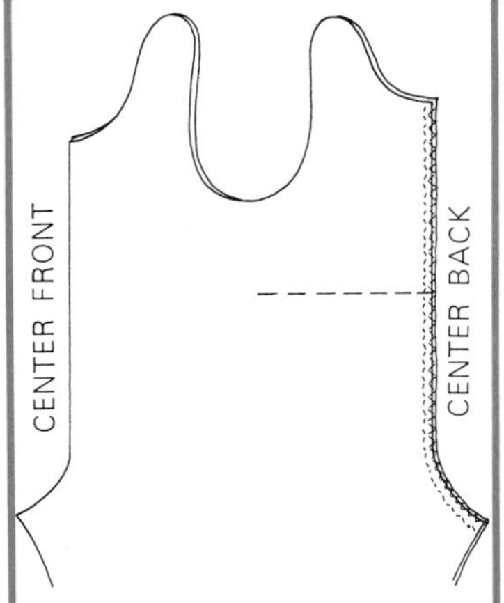

10. *The stitched Center Back seam of the crawler*

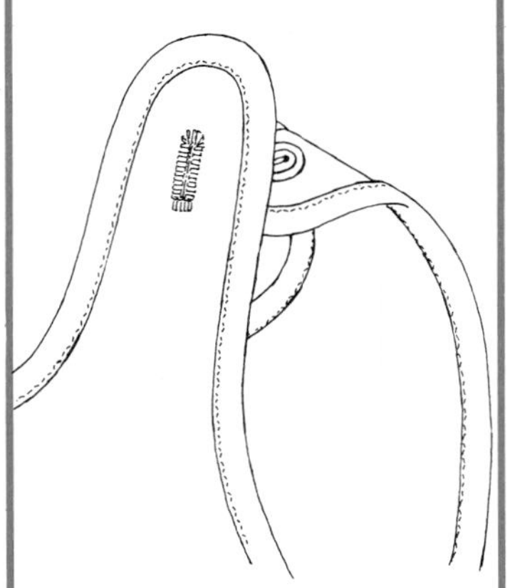

13. *The buttonholes on the Front straps of the crawler*

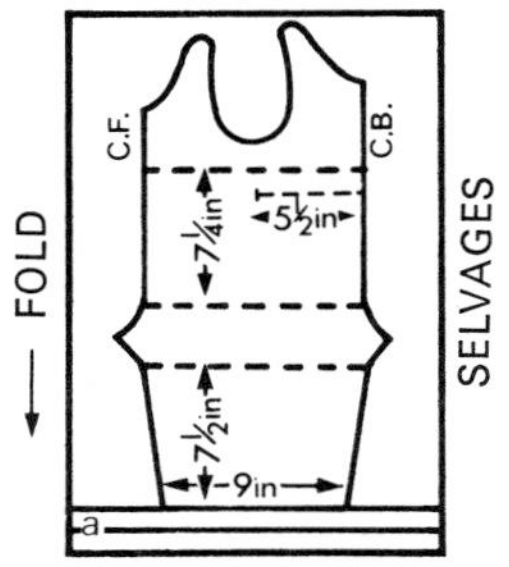

9. *The cutting layout for the crawler*

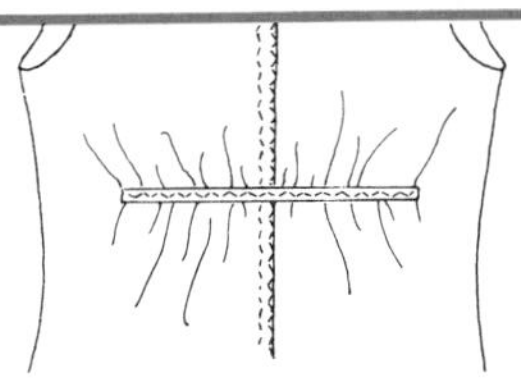

11. *The elastic stitched to the Back of the crawler*

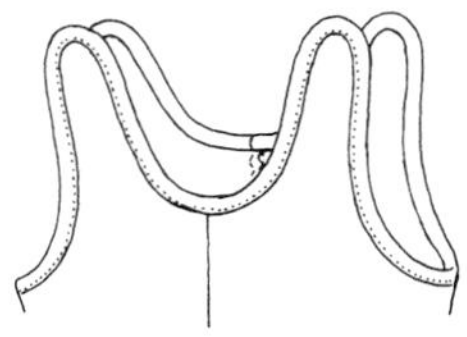

12. *The continuous bound top edge of the crawler*

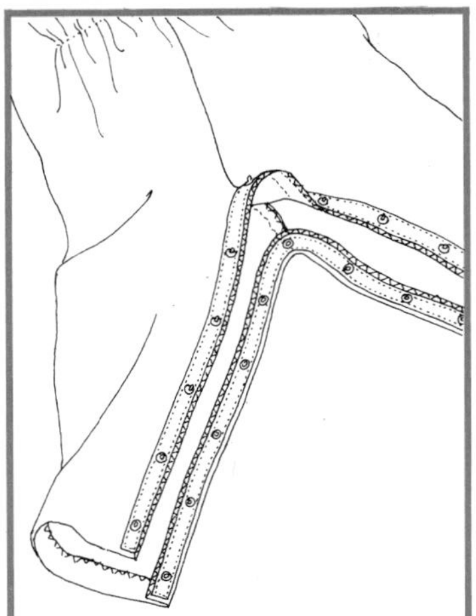

14. *The snap fastener tape stitched to the crawler*

The crawler

The pattern. Trace the crawler pattern letting in 7¼ inches at the AB dash line and extending the leg end for 7½ inches (figure **8**). Taper each leg seam toward the ankle to make 9 inches as shown.

Mark the position for the elastic on the Back, 6 inches down from the neck edge on the Center Back seam and 5½ inches across.

To alter the size of the pattern, lengthen or shorten the body and legs as required at the horizontal dash lines.

Cutting out. Following the layout (figure **9**) fold the fabric, place the pattern on the double fabric and cut out. Also cut two strips (a) each 36in by 1in from one end as shown, for the neck and armhole binding.

Making the crawler. Stitch Center Back seam (figure **10**). Cut a piece of elastic 6 inches long. Stitch it to the Back with a zigzag stitch, stretching it to fit the marking on each side of the Back (figure **11**).

Stitch the Center Front seam. Join two narrow ends of the binding strips to make a continuous strip. Starting at the Center Back, place the right side of the binding strip to the wrong side of the garment, raw edges even. Baste and sew around the neck and armhole edges. Cut off the excess binding.

Fold to the right side, turn in the seam allowance and topstitch in place (figure **12**), making the ends neat.

To close the shoulders, make buttonholes on the Front straps (figure **13**). Cut two pieces of tape 1 inch long and place on the wrong side of the Front shoulder straps to underlay the buttonholes. Work ¾ inch buttonholes ¾ inch from the ends as shown.

Sew buttons on the back shoulder straps to correspond, again underlaying with tape on the wrong side for reinforcement.

Zigzag the leg seam and hem edges to finish. Turn up the leg hems ¾ inch and stitch firmly.

Using a zipper foot, stitch the ball half of the snap fastener tape along the back leg section to the right side, ⅛ inch in from the edge (figure **14**).

Turn the Front leg edge under ½ inch and stitch the matching socket half of the snap fastener tape to the wrong side over the turned edge.

B. Jumpsuit

Measurements

For a 2 year old boy or girl; chest 21 inches, inside leg 11 inches, shoulder to crotch 18 inches. Instructions for altering the size are given below. See figure **15** for garment details.

Fabric and notions

- ☐ 1 yard 36in wide stretch terry in main color and ¼ yard in contrasting color
- ☐ 1 inch plastic buckle without prong
- ☐ Tracing paper and pencil for the pattern
- ☐ Matching thread

The pattern

Trace the jumpsuit pattern, letting in 7¼ inches at the CD dash line and extending the leg end for 10¼ inches (figure **16**). Taper each leg seam toward the ankle to make 10½ inches as shown.

To alter the size of the pattern, lengthen or shorten the body and legs as required at the horizontal dash lines.

Mark the top of the pocket position as shown on the tracing pattern. Mark the belt loops, one on the Center Back 7½ inches down from the neckline and a second one, in line with the first, 2½ inches in from the Center Front.

Cutting out

Following the larger layout (figure **17**) fold the main fabric, place the pattern on the double fabric and cut out. Also cut out three belt carriers (a) each 2in by 1in.

Following the smaller layout (figure **17**) cut from contrasting fabric one belt (b) 24in by 3in, one neck binding (c) 18½in by 2in, two armhole bindings (d) 8in by 2in and 1 pocket (e) 4in by 2¾in.

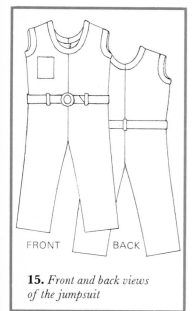

15. *Front and back views of the jumpsuit*

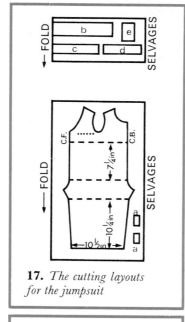

17. *The cutting layouts for the jumpsuit*

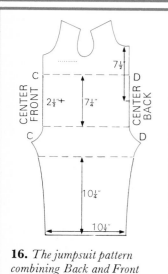

16. *The jumpsuit pattern combining Back and Front*

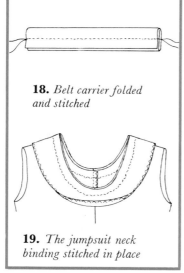

18. *Belt carrier folded and stitched*

19. *The jumpsuit neck binding stitched in place*

Making the jumpsuit

Zigzag the top $2\frac{3}{4}$ inch raw edge of the pocket, fold in $\frac{1}{2}$ inch and baste. Turn under the remaining pocket edges for $\frac{1}{4}$ inch and topstitch the pocket to the jumpsuit at the position marked.

Stitch the Center Back seam (as for the crawler, figure **10**). To make the belt carriers, fold them in thirds lengthwise and stitch through the center (figure **18**). Then fold each end under $\frac{1}{4}$ inch and topstitch the carriers to the jumpsuit where marked. Stitch the Center Front, leg and shoulder seams.

Zigzag the leg hems to make them neat. Turn up for $1\frac{1}{4}$ inches and firmly hand sew or zigzag in place.

To bind the neck edge, stitch the narrow ends of the neck binding together to form a circle. Zigzag along one edge of the binding.

With right sides facing place the remaining raw edge of the binding around the neck, raw edges even (figure **19**). Stitch, taking $\frac{1}{2}$ inch seam allowance. Turn the binding to the inside and topstitch in place over the first seamline.

Similarly form circles of the armhole binding and attach as for the neck binding.

Stitch the long edges of the belt, right sides facing, and stitch one narrow end, tapering it to a point. Turn the belt to the right side through the open end.

Fold this end over the bar of the buckle and stitch firmly with two rows of stitching.

C. T-shirt and shorts

Measurements

For a 4 year old boy or girl; chest 22 inches, waist 22 inches, hip 24 inches. Instructions for altering the size are given below. See figure **20** for details of the garment.

Fabric and notions

- ☐ $\frac{1}{2}$ yard 36in wide striped terry and $\frac{1}{2}$ yard plain terry.
- ☐ Four $\frac{1}{2}$in diameter buttons
- ☐ $\frac{3}{4}$ yard soft 1in wide elastic
- ☐ Tracing paper and pencil for the pattern
- ☐ Matching thread

The patterns

Identify the T-shirt in green from the tracing patterns. Trace the top of the body pattern with both Back and Front necklines and extend the body by $9\frac{1}{2}$ inches (figure **21**).

Also trace the sleeve pattern.

Trace the shorts pattern as shown and mark the crease line and pocket flap position. To alter the size of the T-shirt pattern, add or take off $\frac{1}{4}$ inch at the side seams and $\frac{1}{8}$ inch on the shoulder seams. Alter the sleeve seams and sleeve crown to correspond.

To alter the shorts pattern, add or take off $\frac{1}{2}$ inch at the vertical dash line and $\frac{1}{4}$ inch at the waist edge.

Cutting out

Following the layout (figure **22**) and using the T-shirt pattern, fold the striped fabric and cut out one Back, one Front and two sleeves. Also cut out two strips (a) each 3in by 2in for facing the left shoulder opening.

Fold the plain toweling and cut out the shorts as shown (figure **22**). Also cut one pocket flap (b) $3\frac{1}{2}$ inches square and one waistband (c) 3in by $23\frac{1}{2}$in for the shorts, and one neckband (d) $2\frac{1}{2}$in by 14in and two sleeve bands (e) $2\frac{1}{2}$in by $7\frac{1}{2}$in for the T-shirt.

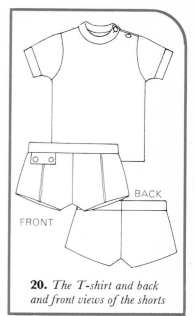

20. *The T-shirt and back and front views of the shorts*

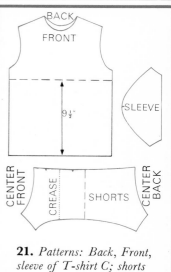

21. *Patterns: Back, Front, sleeve of T-shirt C; shorts*

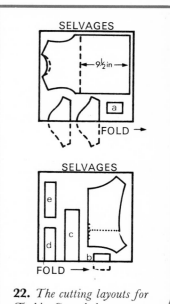

22. *The cutting layouts for T-shirt C, and shorts*

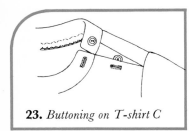

23. *Buttoning on T-shirt C*

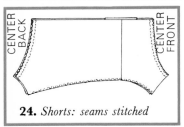

24. *Shorts: seams stitched*

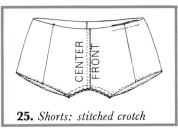

25. *Shorts: stitched crotch*

Making the T-shirt

Fold the shoulder facing strips in half lengthwise, wrong sides facing, and stitch one to each left shoulder seam on the right side (see figure **4**).

Stitch the right shoulder seam. Fold under the front left shoulder strip and baste in place, leaving the back one extending. Then lap the Front shoulder over the Back extension and stitch them together at the armhole edge (see figure **6**).

Apart from the shoulder seams, this T-shirt is made exactly like the version A T-shirt.

To finish, make two $\frac{1}{2}$ inch buttonholes on the Front left shoulder edge (figure **23**) and sew buttons to the Back.

Making the shorts

Fold along the crease lines and stitch in the creases, $\frac{1}{8}$ inch from the edge using a straight stitch, stretching the fabric as you stitch.

Fold the pocket flap in half, right sides facing, making sure that the pile runs in the same direction as the shorts. Stitch at the sides, turn to the right side and position on the right side of the shorts with the raw edges even. Stitch on the pocket flap.

292

Zigzag the leg edges to finish (figure **24**).

Stitch the Center Front and Center Back seams (figure **24**). Stitch the crotch seam. To do this, fold the shorts, right sides facing, so that the Back and Front crotch edges are even and Center Front and Center Back seams coincide (figure **25**). Join the narrow edges of the waistband to form a circle. Fit and cut the 1 inch wide elastic and sew the narrow ends together. Fold the waistband in half, wrong sides facing, and place the elastic in the fold. With the seam of the waistband at the Center Back, place the waistband to the waist seam on the right side, raw edges even, and stitch (see figure **4**). Zigzag the edges together to finish.

Turn up the leg hems for $\frac{1}{2}$ inch and sew firmly in place. Sew the two buttons onto the pocket flap, stitching through to the wrong side.

D. Short legged jumpsuit

Measurements

For a 6 year old boy or girl; chest 24 inches, waist 22 inches, hips 25 inches, shoulder to

26. *Short legged jumpsuit, front view only*

crotch 21 inches. Instructions for altering the size are given below. See figure **26** for details of the garment.

Fabric and notions

☐ $1\frac{1}{8}$ yards 36in wide striped stretch terry
☐ 3 small buttons
☐ Tracing paper and pencil for pattern
☐ Matching thread

The pattern

Trace the short legged jumpsuit pattern with both Front and Back necklines (figure **27**), adding 10 inches between the dash lines EF and tapering the side seams to make the waist measurement $11\frac{1}{2}$ inches. Also trace the gusset and sleeve pattern pieces as shown. To alter the size of the pattern, add or take off $\frac{1}{4}$ inch at the side seams and $\frac{1}{8}$ inch on the shoulder seams. Alter the sleeve seams and sleeve crown to correspond. Alter the length of the pattern at the waistline.

Cutting out

Following the layout (figure **28**) fold the fabric, place the pattern pieces on the double fabric and cut one Back, one Front, two sleeves and one gusset. Also cut out a strip (a) 7in by

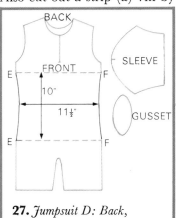

27. *Jumpsuit D: Back, Front, sleeve, gusset patterns*

$\frac{3}{4}$in to face the Front opening.

Making the jumpsuit

Stitch the shoulder seams.

Zigzag raw sleeve and leg hem edges to make neat.

Insert each sleeve with the notch at the shoulder seam and stitch.

Then stitch the sleeve seams and side seams in one operation. Baste the gusset between the legs of the Back and Front body pieces with the center of the long curve of the gusset at the crotch point as shown (figure **29**). Stitch.

Stitch the leg seams.

Turn up the leg hems $\frac{1}{2}$ inch and hand sew firmly in place. Zigzag one long edge of the front facing strip. Then place the opposite edge along the front opening, with right sides facing, raw edges even (figure **30**), $\frac{1}{2}$ inch from the neck edges. Stitch.

Turn the strip to the inside and topstitch close to the edge of the opening.

Zigzag the raw neck edge to make neat. Then, stretching the neck edge, turn it in for $\frac{1}{2}$ inch and hand sew firmly in place. Sew on the three buttons on the right of the opening and make three loops on the left edge to correspond (see figure **26**).

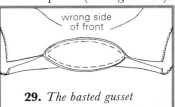

29. *The basted gusset*

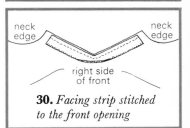

30. *Facing strip stitched to the front opening*

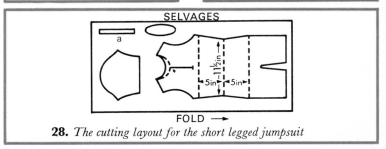

28. *The cutting layout for the short legged jumpsuit*

Chapter 68

Adaptable patterns for children's clothes

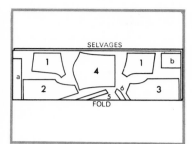

This chapter has adaptable graph patterns for day and night clothes for boys and girls from 3 to 7 years. Make the nightgown with short sleeves or turn the pajamas into long pants by making them as the shorts.

Boy's top and shorts

Sizing

For a boy aged 4 with 23in chest and 21in waist; aged 5 to 6 with 24in chest and 22in waist; aged 7 with 25in chest and 23in waist.

Suggested fabrics

Denim or sailcloth.

You will need:

☐ 1¾yd 36in wide fabric
☐ ¾yd ¾in wide elastic
☐ Two 1½in diameter metal rings for the belt or one 1in buckle
☐ Matching and contrasting thread
☐ Graph paper for patterns

The pattern

Copy pattern pieces numbers 1, 2, 3, 4, 5 and 6.

For the shorts copy the shorter length as shown on pattern piece number 1 and also draw in the side seam and cut the pattern along this line. Draw in the pocket position on the shorts Front.

Cutting out

Following figure **1**, lay out the pattern pieces on the fabric as shown.

The pattern has no seam or hem allowance, so add the amounts given with the graph.

Cut out the fabric and also cut a belt (a) 30in by 3½in and two pockets (b) 6½in by 5½in.

Making the outfit

Shorts. Overcast one short edge of each pocket and then turn under for 1½ inches. Using contrasting thread make two rows of topstitching along this edge 1 inch and 1¼ inches from the fold. This edge becomes the top of the pocket.

On each pocket turn under the lower edge and the edge which goes nearest the Center Front for ⅜ inch. Baste the pockets in position on the front of the shorts, with the remaining raw edge of each pocket even with the raw edge of the side seam. Using contrasting thread top-stitch the pocket along the front and lower edge with two rows of stitches ¼ inch apart. Stitch the side seams, leg seams and crotch seams, in that order, using contrasting thread and flat-fell seaming on the outside of the garment.

Make ¾ inch hems on the leg edges and stitch with matching thread.

Cut a length of elastic to fit the boy's waist and join the narrow ends to form a circle. Turn in the waist edge ⅛ inch,

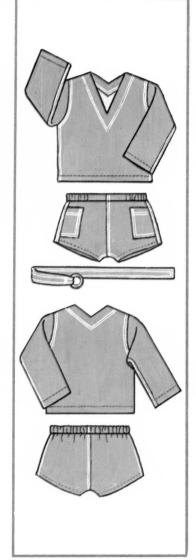

▲ 1. *Layout: boy's top and shorts*

▲ *Details of boy's top and shorts*

then turn in again 1⅛ inch and place the elastic in the fold. Stitch the waist casing with matching thread; be careful not to stitch over the elastic. Smooth any fullness away at Center Front, then stitch through the casing and elastic 3 inches to each side of the Center Front seam to give a flat effect at the front (see front view of shorts).

Top. Using contrasting thread and flat-fell seaming stitch the shoulder seams, armhole seams (pressing the seams toward the sleeves), and the side seams and sleeve seams in one operation starting at the hem.

Using matching thread stitch ¾ inch hems on sleeves and top.

Join neck facings at shoulder seams and Center Front seam. Sew to neck edge with right sides facing, taking ¼ inch seams.

Snip seam allowance, then turn and topstitch (or understitch) the facing to the seam allowance.

Finish the raw edge of the facing then, using contrasting thread, topstitch to the top with two rows of stitches 1 inch and 1¼ inches from the neck edge working on the right side.

Belt. Fold in half lengthwise, right sides facing. Stitch, taking a ¼ inch seam and leaving an opening for turning. Turn to the right side and close the opening.

Press, then topstitch all around with contrasting thread making two rows of stitches ¼ inch apart.

Firmly stitch two rings or a buckle at one end.

Boy's pajamas

Sizing

As for top and shorts with the following outer leg lengths: 24in, 26in and 28in respectively.

Suggested fabrics

Soft cotton fabrics like flannelette; plissé.

You will need

☐ 1¼yd 36in wide fabric for top and 1½yd 36in wide for pants and trimmings
☐ ¾yd ¾in wide elastic
☐ Matching thread
☐ Graph paper for patterns

The pattern

Copy pattern pieces numbers 1, 2, 3, 4, 5, 6 and 7. The pants pattern piece 1 is drawn full length and without side seams.

Cutting out

Following figure **2**, lay out the pattern pieces on the fabric as shown.

The pattern has no seam or hem allowances, so add the amounts given with the graph. Cut out the fabric.

Making the pajamas

Pants. Stitch the leg seams and crotch seams with flat-fell seaming on the outside of the fabric.

Stitch ¾ inch hems on the legs. Cut a length of elastic to fit the child's waist and join the narrow ends to form a circle.

▼ **2.** *Layout: boy's pajamas*

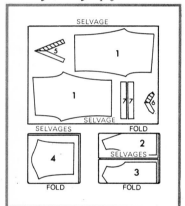

▼ *Details of boy's pajamas*

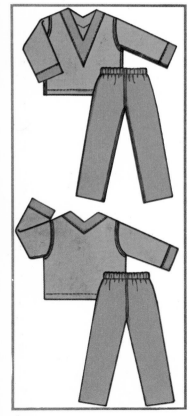

▲ *For the girl's smock, checked gingham with plain poplin—tough denim for the boy's top and shorts*

Turn in the waist edge ⅛ inch, then turn in again for 1⅛ inch and place elastic in the fold. Stitch the waist casing being careful not to stitch over the elastic.

Top. Stitch seams in sleevebands and neckband.

Stitch the shoulder, armhole, side and sleeve seams with flat-fell seaming. Press armhole seams toward the sleeves.

Stitch a sleeveband to each sleeve edge. To do this, place the right side of the band to the wrong side of the sleeve, with seams matching and raw edges even. Stitch with ¼ inch seam.

Press the seam allowances toward the sleeve and stitch to the sleeve very close to the hem edge. Do not stitch through the band at the same time.

Turn the sleeveband to the right side of the sleeve, turn under the raw edge to make the band 1¾ inches wide and topstitch close to the upper fold edge.

Stitch the neckband to the neck edge in the same way. But before topstitching in place, baste the neckband down making sure that the point is on the Center Front.

Girl's smock

Sizing

For a girl aged 3 with 22in chest; aged 4 to 5 with 23in chest; aged 6 with 24in chest.

Suggested fabrics

Gingham, poplin, denim or shirting.

You will need

- ☐ 1¼yd 36in wide main fabric and ½yd 36in wide contrasting fabric
- ☐ ½yd ¼in wide elastic
- ☐ Matching thread and contrasting topstitch thread for pocket detail
- ☐ Graph paper for patterns

The pattern

Copy pattern pieces numbers 1, 2, 3, 4 and 5 from the graph.

▼ **3.** *Layout: girl's smock*

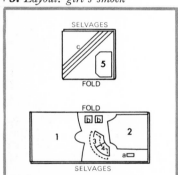

▼ *Details of girl's smock*

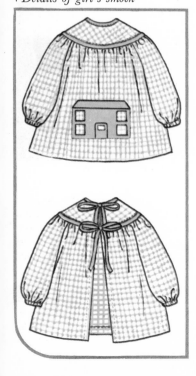

Cutting out

Following figure **3**, lay out the pattern pieces on the fabric as shown.

Make the other half of the Front yoke pattern and join them at the Center Front. Cut the yokes from single fabric as shown, with the Center Front and Center Backs on the crosswise grain of the fabric.

The pattern has no seam or hem allowances, so add the amounts given with the graph. Cut out the fabric and also cut the following: from main fabric, one pocket window (a) 2½in by 1½in, and four pocket windows (b) 2½in square; from contrasting fabric cut 3 yards of 1¼in wide bias strips (c) as shown.

Making the smock

Pocket. Place the pocket pieces together, right sides facing, and stitch around, leaving one side of the roof open. Turn to the right side.

Using contrasting thread and a large stitch, topstitch the top and bottom of the roof and the door.

Turn in the raw edges of each window for ¼ inch all around and stitch them to the pocket. Topstitch the pocket to the Front of the smock along the sides and lower edge. Backstitch the opening corners securely.

Sleeves. Stitch the sleeve seams with a French seam.

Stitch ½ inch hems leaving openings for inserting elastic. Thread a 7½ inch length elastic in each sleeve hem. Stitch ends of elastic firmly together and close the opening.

Stitch sleeves to skirt at underarm with a French seam and press seams toward sleeves.

Yoke. French seam the shoulders.

Bind Center Back edges of yoke with contrasting bias strip.

To do this, place the right side of binding to wrong side of Center Back, raw edges even. Stitch with ¼ inch seam. Fold binding to right side, turn in raw edge for ¼ inch and topstitch in place over the first row of stitching.

To bind neck edge, join two

bias strips in the straight of grain to make up 1 yard. Stitch the binding to the wrong side of the neck edge as above, leaving 12 inches extending at each end to make ties.

Fold the binding to the right side. Turn in ¼ inch along all raw edges, including the ties, and topstitch the folded binding from end to end.

Join bias strips to length of lower yoke edge plus 1 inch. Fold in half lengthwise, wrong sides together, turning in ½ inch at each end to make neat. Place around lower edge of the yoke on right side, with the raw bias edge ¼ inch from yoke edge and bias fold upward. Stitch in place ½ inch from the lower yoke edge.

Skirt. Make two rows of gathering stitches ¼ inch and ½ inch from the top edge of the skirt and sleeves, finishing the stitches 1½ inches to each side of the Center Back.

Draw up to fit the yoke, matching notches to seams and leaving ½ inch of skirt extending to each side of the Center Back. Pin, then stitch, taking a ⅝ inch seam. Trim the seam allowance to ⅜ inch and zigzag or overlock the raw edges together. Press the seam into the yoke. Topstitch through yoke and seam allowance close to seam.

Make a 1 inch hem on the skirt. Fold in the Center Back edges ½ inch and stitch down.

Make two 12 inch ties from the bias strips as for the neck ties and sew to the lower yoke edge at the Center Back.

Girl's nightgown

Sizing

As for girl's smock.

Suggested fabrics

Flannelette, brushed nylon, or seersucker.

You will need:

- ☐ 1¾yd of 36in wide fabric
- ☐ 3½yd eyelet embroidery edging
- ☐ Shirring elastic
- ☐ 1 hook and eye, size No.1
- ☐ Matching thread
- ☐ Graph paper for patterns

The pattern

Copy pieces numbers 1, 2, 3 and 4.

Cutting out

Following figure **4**, lay out the pattern pieces on the fabric as shown.

The pattern has no seam or hem allowances, so add the amounts given with the graph. Cut out the fabric and also cut a Front opening facing (a) 4in by 2½in, two bias strips (b) 1¼in wide by 6in and two bias strips (c) 1¼in wide by 19in. Cut a slit in the Center Front of the skirt 3 inches long from the neck edge.

Making the nightgown

Sleeves. With right sides facing, raw edges even, place eyelet embroidery trim on sleeve hem edges. Stitch, taking ¼ inch seams.

Press seam allowance on each upward, turn in the raw edges and stitch a ⅛ inch hem. Stitch the sleeve seams with a French seam.

With shirring elastic in the bobbin and a large stitch length, work two rows of shirring on each sleeve, ¼ inch apart and starting 1 inch up from the top of the trim. Knot ends securely.

French seam the sleeves to the skirt at the underarm and press seam toward the sleeve.

Yoke. French seam the shoulders.

Cut three pieces of eyelet embroidery, one 31 inches long and two 7 inches long. Machine gather each piece ³⁄₁₆ inch from the raw edge.

Gather the short pieces to the depth of the yoke at the Center Front. Pin to the right side of each Front yoke piece, placing the raw edge of the trim ½ inch from the Center Front. Topstitch in place over the gathering line then zigzag raw edge of trim flat to the yoke.

Gather up the 31 inch length to fit around the neck and Center Front edges. Pin in place to the right side with raw edges of yoke and trim even. Baste.

Using the short bias strips (b), bind both Center Front edges, taking ¼ inch seams.

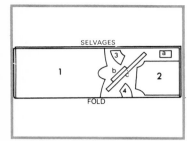

▲ 4. *Layout: girl's nightgown*

▲ *Details of girl's nightgown*

▲ *Pretty printed cotton is first choice for the nightgown—flannelette in contrasting colors for the pajamas*

Join the long bias strips in the straight of grain of the fabric. Place the strip centrally along the neck edge, with right sides facing, raw edges even. Stitch, taking a $\frac{1}{4}$ inch seam.

Stitch the strip extending at each end into a rouleau for the ties. Turn the rouleaux to the right side and complete the binding of neck edge.

Stay-stitch the yoke $\frac{1}{2}$ inch

from the lower edge.

Gather remaining eyelet embroidery to fit lower yoke edge with the ends extending at Center Front. Pin to right side of yoke $\frac{1}{4}$ inch from yoke edge. Machine stitch in place along the gathering line.

Skirt. Stitch $\frac{1}{2}$in Center Back seam.

Make two rows of gathering stitches $\frac{1}{4}$ inch and $\frac{1}{2}$ inch from

the top edge of the skirt and sleeves. Draw up to fit the yoke, matching notches to seams and leaving $\frac{1}{4}$ inch extending at both Front edges.

Stitch with $\frac{5}{8}$ inch seam. Trim seam allowance to $\frac{3}{8}$ inch and zigzag or overlock the edges together. Press seam upward. Make the raw edges of the facing neat, then pin the facing centrally over the Center Front

opening with right sides together. Stitch with $\frac{1}{4}$ inch seam graduating to nothing at the point to each side of the Center Front opening. Slash between the stitching. Understitch the seam allowance to the facing then turn to the inside.

Hand sew the top edges of facing to yoke seam and sew on a hook and eye at this point. Make a 1 inch hem on the skirt.

▼ Graph pattern: girl's smock and nightgown

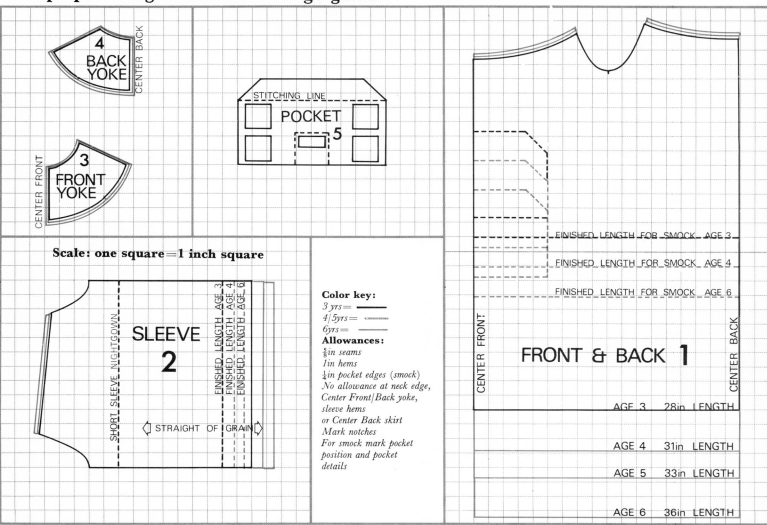

4 BACK YOKE — CENTER BACK

3 FRONT YOKE — CENTER FRONT

STITCHING LINE

POCKET 5

Scale: one square = 1 inch square

SHORT SLEEVE NIGHTGOWN

FINISHED LENGTH AGE 3
FINISHED LENGTH AGE 4
FINISHED LENGTH AGE 6

SLEEVE 2

STRAIGHT OF GRAIN

Color key:
3 yrs = ————
4/5yrs = ————
6yrs = ————

Allowances:
⅝in seams
1in hems
¼in pocket edges (smock)
No allowance at neck edge,
Center Front/Back yoke,
sleeve hems
or Center Back skirt
Mark notches
For smock mark pocket
position and pocket
details

FINISHED LENGTH FOR SMOCK AGE 3
FINISHED LENGTH FOR SMOCK AGE 4
FINISHED LENGTH FOR SMOCK AGE 6

CENTER FRONT

FRONT & BACK 1

CENTER BACK

AGE 3   28in LENGTH
AGE 4   31in LENGTH
AGE 5   33in LENGTH
AGE 6   36in LENGTH

▼ Graph pattern: boy's top and shorts, and pajamas

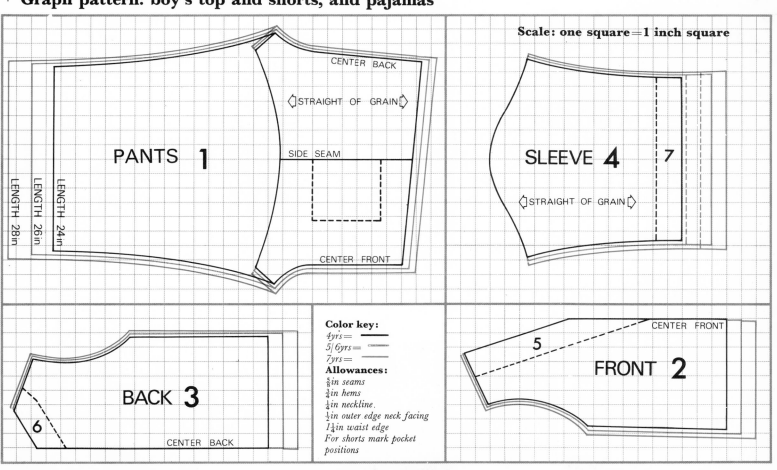

CENTER BACK

◁ STRAIGHT OF GRAIN ▷

PANTS 1

LENGTH 28in
LENGTH 26in
LENGTH 24in

SIDE SEAM

CENTER FRONT

Scale: one square = 1 inch square

SLEEVE 4   7

◁ STRAIGHT OF GRAIN ▷

BACK 3

6

CENTER BACK

Color key:
4yrs = ————
5/6yrs = ————
7yrs = ————

Allowances:
⅝in seams
¾in hems
¼in neckline.
½in outer edge neck facing
1¼in waist edge
For shorts mark pocket
positions

CENTER FRONT

5

FRONT 2

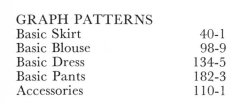

Sewing for Children

Generally Speaking

Know-How